RESERVED BOOKS

WITHDRAWN

THE
AMERICAN TRANSPORTATION
PROBLEM

THE BROOKINGS INSTITUTION

The Brookings Institution—Devoted to Public Service through Research and Training in the Humanistic Sciences—was incorporated on December 8, 1927. Broadly stated, the Institution has two primary purposes: The first is to aid constructively in the development of sound national policies; and the second is to offer training of a super-graduate character to students of the social sciences. The Institution will maintain a series of co-operating institutes, equipped to carry out comprehensive and inter-related research projects.

The responsibility for the final determination of the Institution's policies and its program of work and for the administration of its endowment is vested in a self-perpetuating Board of Trustees. The Trustees have, however, defined their position with reference to the investigations conducted by the Institution in a by-law provision reading as follows: "The primary function of the Trustees is not to express their views upon the scientific investigations conducted by any division of the Institution, but only to make it possible for such scientific work to be done under the most favorable auspices." Major responsibility for "formulating general policies and co-ordinating the activities of the various divisions of the Institution" is vested in the President. The by-laws provide also that "there shall be an Advisory Council selected by the President from among the scientific staff of the Institution and representing the different divisions of the Institution."

BOARD OF TRUSTEES

ROBERT S. BROOKINGS	DAVID F. HOUSTON
WHITEFOORD R. COLE	VERNON KELLOGG
NORMAN H. DAVIS	JOHN C. MERRIAM
FREDERIC A. DELANO	HAROLD G. MOULTON
CLARENCE PHELPS DODGE	JOHN BARTON PAYNE
JEROME D. GREENE	LEO S. ROWE

BOLTON SMITH

OFFICERS

ROBERT S. BROOKINGS, *Chairman*
LEO S. ROWE, *Vice-Chairman*
HENRY P. SEIDEMANN, *Treasurer*
HAROLD G. MOULTON, *President*
LEVERETT S. LYON, *Executive Vice-President*

ADVISORY COUNCIL (1932-33)

ARNOLD B. HALL	LEVERETT S. LYON
CHARLES O. HARDY	EDWIN G. NOURSE
LEWIS L. LORWIN	HENRY P. SEIDEMANN

THE
AMERICAN TRANSPORTATION
PROBLEM

PREPARED FOR

THE NATIONAL TRANSPORTATION
COMMITTEE

BY

HAROLD G. MOULTON

AND ASSOCIATES

PAUL T. DAVID
CHARLES L. DEARING
RALPH L. DEWEY
WILFRED ELDRED
CHARLES W. ELIOT, 2d
RALPH J. FOGG
CHARLES O. HARDY

LLOYD C. HOELTZEL
SUSUMU KOBE
ADAH L. LEE
ISADOR LUBIN
FRED W. POWELL
PORTER R. TAYLOR
BENJAMIN P. WHITAKER

CARL A. RUDISILL
LIBRARY
LENOIR RHYNE COLLEGE

WASHINGTON, D.C.
THE BROOKINGS INSTITUTION
1933

385
M86a

23061
May '47

COPYRIGHT, 1933, BY
THE BROOKINGS INSTITUTION

Set up and printed.
Published March, 1933

All rights reserved, including the right of reproduction
in whole or in part in any form.

CARL A. RUDISILL
LIBRARY
LENOIR RHYNE COLLEGE

Printed in the United States of America by
George Banta Publishing Company
Menasha, Wisconsin

PREFACE

In the analyses submitted herewith we have endeavored to marshal in a systematic manner the essential information with reference to the various subjects covered, and to relate the whole discussion to the issues involved in stabilizing and reorganizing American transportation. In the four months at our disposal we could not cover in detail every phase of the broad problem before us, nor have we been able to give adequate attention to literary form. Numerous topics pertaining to highly technical questions and of interest to particular groups have been omitted as falling outside the primary purpose of our inquiries.

In the conduct of the investigation I have had the collaboration of a number of the regular staff of the Brookings Institution and of several other specialists recruited for particular phases of the problem. Charles O. Hardy, Adah L. Lee, and Fred W. Powell have acted as a collaborating committee sharing responsibility in the preparation of the report as a whole. Dr. Hardy has contributed Part III and much of Chapters II and III; Dr. Powell is primarily responsible for Part IX and Chapter X; Miss Lee has collaborated with me in Part V. Dr. Isador Lubin is the author of Chapter IX; Dr. Benjamin P. Whitaker of Chapter XI; Charles L. Dearing of Chapters XXIV, XXV, and XXVI; and Paul T. David of Chapter XXXI. Dr. Frieda Baird, Sheldon B. Akers, Edwin A. Lamke, and Ralph P. Ward, of the Institution staff, served as statistical assistants.

Chapter VII was contributed by Dr. Ralph L. Dewey, of Ohio State University; Chapter VIII by Dr. Wilfred

Eldred, transportation specialist; Chapters XXXIV and XXXV by Charles W. Eliot, 2d, Director of Planning, National Capital Park and Planning Commission; Chapter XXIX and a part of Chapter XXXIII by Ralph J. Fogg, consulting engineer; Chapter XXX by Lloyd C. Hoeltzel, United States Department of Commerce; and Chapter XXVIII by Porter R. Taylor, formerly Director, Bureau of Markets, Pennsylvania Department of Agriculture. Dr. Susumu Kobe, of the University of Michigan, contributed Chapters IV, V, and VI, and assisted in connection with a number of other chapters.

The undersigned has contributed the chapters not otherwise designated and he accepts responsibility for the entire analysis.

We have received innumerable suggestions and a large number of special memoranda from persons and organizations interested in transportation, for all of which we are very grateful. We are especially indebted to the Interstate Commerce Commission for its generous aid in the assembling of statistical information.

HAROLD G. MOULTON

Washington, D.C.,
February, 1933.

CONTENTS

AMERICAN TRANSPORTATION PROBLEM

PART II. FACTORS AFFECTING RAILWAY NET INCOME

CONTENTS

CONTENTS

CONTENTS

REPORT OF THE NATIONAL
TRANSPORTATION COMMITTEE

Introductory

Herewith are presented:

A. The Conclusions of the National Transportation Committee.

B. The Report of the Committee.

C. Supplemental report by former Governor Alfred E. Smith who prefaces it, "While I am in substantial agreement with the greater part of the Committee Report, this supplementary memorandum states my conclusions in my own language, placing the emphasis where I think it belongs."

D. Special studies by the research staff to be published shortly by the Brookings Institution, Washington, D.C.

The Committee associated itself at the request of certain Business Associations, Savings Banks, Insurance Companies, and fiduciary and philanthropic institutions interested in railroad securities (see Appendix) in response to an invitation in essential part as follows:

"We, the undersigned organizations, representing many of the interests concerned, believe that there is no more important present task than a thorough and satisfactory solution of the railroad problem, as an integral but the most urgent part of the entire transportation problem. We beg that you examine all phases of the problem and recommend a solution which, with due regard for the public interest, will ensure an opportunity for the railroads of this country to be put on a business basis, so that neither now nor in the future will they constitute a present threat to the invested savings of our citizens, to loss of employment to our wage-earners, and to the stability of the insurance companies and savings banks; and so that the present burden on the Federal treasury and the American taxpayer may be in a fair measure removed."

The Committee met and organized on October 7, 1932. It was composed of Calvin Coolidge, Chairman, Bernard M. Baruch, Vice-Chairman, former Governor Alfred E. Smith, Alexander Legge and Clark Howell. John W. Power acted as secretary. The Committee selected Dr. Harold G. Moulton, of the Brookings Institution, to organize a research staff.

Just as the Committee's work was nearing a close, it lost the distinguished director of its deliberations who was giving his great talents unsparingly to this work. The report had not taken form at the time of his death, but the Committee has tried to carry on in the spirit of his leadership.

The Committee gathered its facts from three sources:

(1) Open hearings;

(2) Studies by other investigating bodies, memoranda, briefs and specific suggestions;

(3) The work of Dr. Moulton and the staff.

This mass of material is too voluminous and varied to publish in full, but the work undertaken by the research staff will be published shortly by the Brookings Institution. Dr. Moulton's conclusions are his own.

The transport problem has been with man since the first rude trails of pre-history. It has shaped the destiny of humanity. The closing of the caravan routes to the East Indies discovered America. History is full of similar consequences. Just now, largely due to the recent rapid development of new forms of transportation, the railroad problem is acute in nearly all important countries, including our own. Commissions more or less similar to this Committee have been at work in England, Canada and the Argentine Republic and we have considered their reports and analyses. There are railroad commissions in nearly every one of our forty-eight States and similar bodies in many other countries. These, the Interstate Commerce Commission and the very able Congressional Committees on these subjects have all been devoting themselves to the problems created by these rapid shifts. Much of this work and a great mass of other data have been assembled and given careful study by the Committee. The problem is very complex and while the Committee is in substantial agreement as to conclusions, it is too much to expect that four men of independent mental processes would all arrive at decisions by identical paths, or with equal emphasis on various factors.

A. Conclusions of the Committee

I. The railroad system must be preserved. Changed conditions require new policies but not abandonment of railroad regulation. The development of regulation and of new methods of transport make it unnecessary for Government further to create and foster competition with or among railroads as a defense against monopoly. That is an expensive and ineffective attempt to do indirectly what Government has shown its ability to do directly. Regulation is sufficient. Government policies should be freed of any purpose either to favor or to handicap any form of transportation with relation to any other form. We cannot solve the problem on the theory upon which horses are handicapped in a race. In a fair field and no favor competition should be permitted to decide the result. Regulation should not attempt to "run the business" of transportation. It should concentrate on protecting the public against discrimination and extortion and on requiring the most efficient service at the lowest competitive cost.

(1) Parallel lines and systems are wasteful and unnecessary. Regional consolidations should be hastened and, where necessary, enforced, looking eventually to a single National system with regional divisions and the elimination of all excess and obsolete lines and equipment. Neither holding companies nor any other device should be permitted to hinder consolidation or evade the letter or the spirit of regulatory law.

(2) Unprofitable railroad services should be replaced by cheaper alternative transport methods.

(3) Railroads should be permitted to own and operate competing services, including water lines, but regulatory jurisdiction should be extended to water rates and practices in coastal, intercoastal and lake shipping to relieve commerce of present chaotic conditions. Congress should

promptly clarify its intention on the long-and-short-haul clause of the Transportation Act.

(4) Government assumption of all or part of the costs of inefficient competing transport as a defense against monopoly is no longer warranted and should be abandoned. As a general principle inland waterways should bear all costs of amortization, interest, maintenance and operation of the facilities for their navigation. If they cannot bear such charges and compete with other forms of transport, they should be abandoned. The St. Lawrence Waterway should be tested by this rule of self-support and if it fails in that test the pending treaty with Canada should not be ratified. Governmental commercial operation of the actual facilities of transportation, such as barge-lines, should not be continued.

(5) Automotive transportation should be put under such regulation as is necessary for public protection. It should bear its fair burden of tax but only on a basis of compensation for public expenditure on its behalf, plus its share of the general tax load. Neither tax nor regulation should be applied for any purpose of handicapping the march of progress for the benefit of the railroads.

(6) Wages and working conditions of labor in transportation are determinable by established procedure in another forum and are not within the scope of this inquiry. There should be no heavier burdens on the railroads in employing labor to operate automobiles than on their competi-

tors. In the railroads (as in other industries) rates, capitalization, salaries and wages must all follow changing economic conditions, but none should be sacrificed for the benefit of others.

(7) Beacons, weather service and similar auxiliaries to air traffic should be maintained at public expense, and air transport should be encouraged during its development stage but we believe that every such service should ultimately pay its own way.

(8) The Committee has no recommendations to make on pipe lines.

II. The policy of trying to appraise railroad properties on some selected basis of valuation and then saying that they are entitled to earn a fair return on this appraisal should be reconsidered. Where competition with trucks and other methods exists, it will determine rates. In other cases rates must be regulated, but the basis of costs of operation under efficient management is a better general guide than any attempt to preserve capital structures regardless of economic trends. We see no reason why the rate-making rule should not say in plain English that railroads are entitled to make a reasonable profit based upon costs of efficient operation and that they are not entitled to earnings merely to preserve present structures if overcapitalized.

III. The railroads should do much that they have not done to improve their condition without any Government help at all. They should promptly be freed of all unnecessary restrictions on the doing of it. It has been estimated that less than a 20 per cent increase in traffic would put most of them on an earning basis. In view of the narrowness of this margin of loss and of the very great savings possible in railroad operation, we regard their outlook as far from hopeless.

(a) Railroads should adopt the competing methods of which they complain.

(b) Railroads should co-operate to reduce competitive expense.

    (1) Unnecessary services should be abandoned.

    (2) Metropolitan terminals should be consolidated and unnecessary facilities scrapped.

    (3) Circuitous haulage should be eliminated.

(c) Financial management should be improved.

(d) Transport methods and equipment should be brought up-to-date.

(e) In view of what could be done by better management, the general outlook seems far from hopeless.

IV. Regulatory jurisdiction should be extended to the whole National transportation system but applied only to the extent necessary for public protection. The existing regulatory mechanism of the Interstate Commerce Commission is inadequate and should be improved by reorganization without expansion or increased expense.

V. Emergency Recommendations.

    (1) Corporate reorganization can and should be facilitated by revision of the bankruptcy procedure.

(2) The recapture clause should be repealed retroactively.

(3) The statutory rule of rate-making should be revised.

(4) "Adequate security" does not necessarily mean "marketable collateral."

B. The Report

I. The railroad system must be preserved. Changed conditions require new policies but not abandonment of railroad regulation. The development of regulation and of new methods of transport make it unnecessary for Government further to create and foster competition with or among railroads as a defense against monopoly. That is an expensive and ineffective attempt to do indirectly what the Government has shown its ability to do directly. Regulation is sufficient. Government policies should be freed of any purpose either to favor or to handicap any form of transportation with relation to any other form. We cannot solve the problem on the theory upon which horses are handicapped in a race. In a fair field and no favor competition should be permitted to decide the result. Regulation should not attempt to "run the business" of transportation. It should concentrate on protecting the public against discrimination and extortion and on requiring the most efficient service at the lowest competitive cost.

At the foundation of our system of communication is the railroad web. It is the most important single element in our social and economic life. Its rapid extension enabled us to cover the greater habitable part of a continent with a cohesive form of liberal government of 125,000,000 people united in a common language, purpose and ideal and to maintain National solidarity through periods of stress. Both security and material welfare are involved in its continued efficient existence. The public interest is deeper than its investment or its need of good service. We are addressing a matter of National concern of the first magnitude. The railroad system must be continued and its efficiency preserved because of National necessity—economic, social and defensive.

> *(a) Governmental fostering of competition is no longer necessary as a defense against monopoly.*

Above all other enterprises, railroads are, therefore, "affected with a public interest" and, under an ancient doctrine of our law, peculiarly subject to Government regulation. In earlier development, the railroad franchise created an effective and complete monopoly against which industrial and social segments had no defense. Rigorous governmental control was inevitable. It took two forms: first, an effort to foster competition among different railroads and to create and maintain, by Federal financial aid, other forms of competing transportation such as waterways; second, an intense regulatory control of the railroads themselves. The latter has been practiced long enough and sufficiently extended to prove that it dominates competition or any other influence as the government law of railroad practice. To the extent that the monopoly inherent in the railroad franchise was a menace, it is of the utmost importance to recognize that current railroad regulation safely controls it. Other safeguards have appeared. With increasing effect, new methods of transport are invading customary fields of railroad patronage. On a basis of economic efficiency, independent of Government aid, pipe lines, motor transport and airways are all making bids for business which the railroads can retain only by offering equivalent service at competitive rates. In these areas of competition, there is no longer complete monopoly. These two developments—perfection of regulation and appearance of competing methods—have created a new principle, viz:

> *Insofar as government policies have been designed, by Federal intervention, to create and maintain competition with or among railroads as a defense against monopoly, they should be abandoned as wasteful and unnecessary. Regulation is sufficient.*

> *(b) Regulation should provide a fair field and no favor.*

The railroads complain that they are shackled by regulation while their competitors are free and unduly advantaged by various forms of discrimination in their favor. To the extent that this is true, it is unfair. But it must be equally clear that, notwithstanding the deep public interest in our railroads, the Government cannot stand in the way of progress. Certain regulation of competitive methods is necessary. They cannot be permitted to escape their just tax burdens. They ought not to be artificially advantaged by subsidy or otherwise. But regulation of them must arise from its own necessity, and burdens upon them must derive from justice. The Government cannot, for the sake of the railroads, invent and apply to their competitors either regulation or burden on the theory upon which horses are handicapped in a race. A similar principle applies to railroads, and to the extent that they are handicapped by burdens for which the reason is obsolete or non-existent, Government has a positive duty to remove them. The guiding rule of the whole matter seems to us quite clear:

> *With the danger of railroad monopoly going or gone and (whether going or gone) completely controlled by regulation, Government has a positive duty to see to it that neither the railroads nor their competitors are either unduly handicapped or unduly advantaged. Thereafter, in a fair field and no favor, economic competition must decide the question of survival under private ownership and operation.*

> *(c) Regulation should not be abandoned. It should be put on the simple basis of public protection.*

There is respectable opinion that the development of effective competitive methods argues for the abandonment of all railroad regulation. The Committee cannot concur. Competition of parallel methods is as yet limited and localized and, while it is a powerful and growing force against monopoly, it does not relieve the necessity for railroad regulation and, because of other aspects of public interest and dependence already mentioned, in our opinion, it never will. On the contrary, we regard regulation as necessary in the interest of both the railroads and the public and we think that it should be extended to other forms of transportation.

But, for reasons stated hereinafter, more care must be taken to maintain managerial initiative. Regulation, whether of railroads or other forms should not attempt to "run the business" of transportation. It should concentrate on protecting the public against discrimination, extortion and other abuses of monopoly and on insuring the most efficient service at the lowest competitive cost.

If these conclusions on general principles are correct, several changes in policy flow inevitably therefrom, viz:

(1) **Parallel lines and systems are wasteful and unnecessary. Regional consolidations should be hastened and, where necessary, enforced, looking eventually to a single National system with regional divisions and the elimination of all excess and obsolete lines and equipment. Neither holding companies nor any other device should be permitted to hinder consolidation or evade the letter or the spirit of regulatory law.**

The policy of maintaining parallel and competing lines or systems on the theory that thus extortionate rates and discrimination may be restrained is wasteful and, of course, untenable under a system which controls rates and practices to the ultimate.

Duplication and unnecessary overheads, facilities and services, inherent in the present multiplicity of railroads, are very expensive and consolidations should be hastened. In plans for this, consideration should be given to creating a single efficient system (rather than competing systems) for each natural trade area, even to the ultimate extent of a single National network with regional divisions. It has been estimated by good authority that several hundred million dollars, or enough to pay interest on a large part of the outstanding railroad bonds, can be saved. Consolidation is so vital to the public welfare that, unless it is voluntarily accomplished within a reasonable time, the Government should compel it. Neither holding companies nor any other device should be permitted to hinder consolidation or to evade the letter or spirit of regulatory laws.

(2) Unprofitable railroad services should be replaced by cheaper alternative transport methods.

In view of the rapid development of automotive and other transport, there is no justification for maintenance by railroads of losing services and lines, and there devolves upon regulatory bodies and controlling interests something more than a negative duty to hasten their replacement by alternative methods, such as motor transport, which can render adequate service on a profitable basis in cases where rail transportation can operate only at a loss.

(3) Railroads should be permitted to own and operate competing services, including water lines, but regulatory jurisdiction should be extended to water rates and practices in coastal, inter-coastal and lake shipping to relieve commerce of present chaotic conditions. Congress should promptly clarify its intention on the long-and-short-haul clause of the Transportation Act.

Restrictions on the ownership by railroads of waterborne, automotive or other competing services seems anomalous in a regime which has demonstrated its effective control of both rates and practices.

There are certain competitive situations where railroad rates between two ports are fixed by regulation and unregulated water rates are in chaos. This is disturbing to commerce and unfair to railroads. For this and other reasons, we believe that the jurisdiction of the regulating body should be extended to cover inter-coastal, coastal and lake commerce. We do not mean to recommend that water rates, based on actual lower costs, should be regulated upward to equalize traffic in favor of railroads. But we do believe that, in such a situation, some stabilizing influence should be applied in the interest of commerce generally as well as in fairness to railroads.

The law prohibits a railroad from charging less for a longer than for a shorter haul, over the same line, in the same direction, the shorter being included in the longer, but permits the Interstate Commerce Commission a discretion to relieve this restriction.

The law is not altogether clear and the Commission's interpretation and decisions have been the subject of long and persistent controversy. Grave consequences affecting wide economic areas are involved and the situation requires prompt clarification. Two pending suggestions by the Interstate Commerce Commission and one by the House Committee might contribute thereto. If jurisdiction of the Commission be extended to include inter-coastal commerce, or if a new rule of rate-making be adopted, the problem would be simplified. But if neither of these things is done, it is important that Congress act at once to declare its intention on this important application of the so-called "long-and-short-haul" controversy.

(4) Government assumption of all or part of the costs of inefficient competing transport as a defense against monopoly is no longer warranted and should be abandoned. As a general principle inland waterways should bear all costs of amortization, interest, maintenance and operation of the facilities for their navigation. If they cannot bear such charges and compete with other forms of transport, they should be abandoned. The St. Lawrence Waterway should be tested by this rule of self-

support and if it fails in that test the pending treaty with Canada should not be ratified. Governmental commercial operation of the actual facilities of transportation, such as barge-lines, should not be continued.

Creation and maintenance, by Government, of competing methods of transport, where the result is not (as in the Panama Canal) to provide more efficient service at lower cost, but only (as in some inland waterways) to maintain at the taxpayers' expense, more costly and less efficient service can no longer be justified as a defense against monopoly.

This Government has long been committed to the improvement and maintenance of shipways and of at least the outer harbors of ports accessible to great naturally navigable waterways. This involves expense, defrayed by taxation of the whole Nation, but applied at particular points, in the development of the instrumentalities of interstate and international commerce. To an extent, these waterways are the railroads' competitors and, as far as they go, these expenditures favor them. But in respect of accessories to naturally navigable waterways, such as ocean harbors and their approaches and the harbors and channels of the Great Lakes, this is a recognized function of government the world over, for naval as well as commercial purposes, and the railroads may be presumed to have been located, financed, and constructed with this in view. We have not heard it decried as an unjust handicap and with these remarks it passes from our consideration.

But, with inland waterways in general, the case is otherwise. For the sake of illustration, let us imagine a Federally constructed canal between, for example, Topeka and Oklahoma City—a stark ditch. If that canal fairly bore the burdens of its cost of construction and operation and yet could furnish transportation at an advantage over rails, nobody could cómplain, regardless of the extent to which it diverted railroad traffic. But if such was not the case and the canal could compete only if the public paid enough of these charges to undercut the cost of rails, it seems too obvious for argument that its creation and maintenance would be a direct impairment of the railroad system by public subsidy and distinctly inimical to the National interest.

Exactly the same principle of self-support seems applicable to any natural waterway upon which improvement and engineering devices are necessary to provide effective navigation. We think it is the very touchstone of the whole vexed problem and that every existing or projected improvement should be tested by its application. Any project which fails to answer that test should be abandoned, without hesitation, as an unwarranted waste of public money.

(a) The Great Lakes Waterway.

The connecting channels of the Great Lakes were not navigable in the modern sense in their natural state, but the Great Lakes Waterway now stands as a fully created, implemented and efficient system of navigation which, in many respects, falls under the considerations governing Federal improvement of ocean ports, harbors and shipways.

(b) The St. Lawrence Seaway.

There are obviously not at present any facilities for navigation, by ocean-going vessels, of the restricted waterways connecting the Great Lakes with each other and with the sea. The project to create such a shipway to the head of Lake Superior is a major engineering project of stupendous magnitude and very great cost. There is diversity of opinion as to whether the project is practicable. It is clear from our studies that the peculiar type of Lake bulk-carriers is far more efficient than any ocean freighter and from this fact that the area of economy is restricted practically to savings in cost of transshipment. But our studies also show that, in no reasonable probability, could this minor saving be enough to approximate even the carrying charges on this project.

In conformity with one of the general principles already announced, if this seaway could be shown to be the march of progress and if cheaper and more efficient transportation can thus be achieved, no barrier should be imposed against such a development. But we think that, before ratification of the pending seaway treaty with Canada bargaining away valuable American rights, this project should be fairly tested on the rule of self-support and, if it fails, the treaty should not be ratified.

(c) Government barge lines.

Argument for and against Government operation of barge lines was strongly pressed before us. In this case, not only is the waterway itself provided and maintained at public expense, but the actual business of transportation thereon is in part financed by Government. The claim is made, and in our judgment sustained, that, if the methods of accounting used by the Government in respect to the Panama Canal were applied, they would reveal operating losses which are charged to the taxpayer. We think that actual Government operation of the facilities of transportation, wholly or partly at public expense, is unjust to the vast majority of people, and unwarranted by any argument that has come to our attention.

(d) Inland waterways in general.

We recommend that the Congress give consideration to the formulation of a consistent policy on inland waterways. We think that the test of self-support should be applied to every existing or proposed inland waterway.

Unbearable tax burdens are generally recognized as a principal hindrance to economic recovery. Our waterway policy for the past few years has averaged a cost of about 100 million dollars annually and tremendous projects involving hundreds of millions are being considered. Our studies show no commensurate economic benefit resulting from much of this spending. In such circumstances, we think that a large part of this activity should be abandoned or at least suspended. It bears heavily on the taxpayer as a direct burden and even more heavily on the whole community in its contribution to the postponement of prosperity. At a time when the very stability of our system depends on the balancing of Federal expenditures with revenue and the sources of taxation seem almost dry, we find it difficult to justify this wasteful outpouring of hundreds of millions of dollars for results so barren of economic returns.

(5) Automotive transportation should be put under such regulation as is necessary for public protection. It should bear its fair burden of tax but only on a basis of compensation for public expenditure on its behalf, plus its share of the general tax load. Neither tax nor regulation should be applied for

any purpose of handicapping the march of progress for the benefit of the railroads.

The problem of the automobile is very difficult. Its roadbed is provided at public expense and it requires few, if any, terminal or similar facilities. It need not— as must railroads—load any part of its cost of operation with a charge for this construction and maintenance. It can make rates which do not involve charges for depreciation and amortization. It can pay whatever scale of wages and exact whatever hours of labor it can make effective. It can bargain closely and instantly and can walk away with business while the railroads are involved in a prescribed process before their regulating overseers. It is not attached to rails and can furnish swift door-to-door service which railroads as such cannot even approximate. It may be a common carrier, a contract carrier or a private operator. It moves intra-state and inter-state and may change its character in these matters instantly. It need not maintain continuous schedules and service. It can pick its business and is prone to take the cream of the traffic and leave the rest for the railroads, which must receive whatever is tendered. It can be permanently or sporadically in business and competition. With these advantages it has made inroads into railroad business and the difficulties are only partly suggested by this short recitation of complexities.

The problem thus presented has been regarded as serious in every important country and commissions similar to this Committee have been convened in several of them. The difficulty is not solely in the amount of tonnage diverted but resides also in the chaotic rate conditions presented to commerce in general and in many new necessities for public protection. It has been a matter of primary concern to our Interstate Commerce Commission, to State Commissions everywhere, to the Congress, to the highway users themselves, and to all who have given great study to the transport problem.

One thing is certain. Automotive transportation is an advance in the march of progress. It is here to stay. We cannot invent restrictions for the benefit of railroads. We can only apply such regulation and assess such taxes as would be necessary if there were no railroads, and let the effect be what it may.

On the question of whether public financing of roadbeds operates as a subsidy, there is a vast variety of circumstance. The automobile itself, its fuel, lubricants and operations are all heavily taxed. Does the total of these assessments bear its share of the general tax load and also sufficiently reimburse the public expenditure on the roads it uses? If it does, the circumstance that the charge is not comparable in amount to railroad costs of construction and maintenance of terminals and roadbeds is immaterial. The purpose is not to handicap automotive competition, but only to do justice.

These questions are of mixed State and Federal bearing and very difficult of determination. Both taxes and regulation on motor transport vary among the States and, while it has been strongly urged as the only solution, the Committee believes it impracticable to get uniformity by any plan for concert of State action. Our studies clearly indicate that in some States automotive vehicles do not bear their full burden of taxes. We think they should pay the carrying charges and cost of maintenance of the highways they use and also their share of the general tax load. The Interstate Commerce Commission recommends regulation of inter-state buses and extension of their jurisdiction to include inter-state trucks. The Committee believes that the situation requires general Federal jurisdiction of motor transport. It recognizes that no such intricacy of regulation as characterizes railroad supervision can ever be extended to this field, but it is convinced that a broad measure of Federal and uniform State control can and should be applied.

A valuable advance is registered in the recent report of the Joint Committee of Railroads and Highway Users on the regulation and taxation of highway transportation recommending principles governing the subject which have been agreed to by these diverse interests. This kind of public-spirited cooperation is one of the most hopeful aspects of this difficult problem.

(6) **Wages and working conditions of labor in transportation are determinable by established procedure in another forum and are not within the scope of this inquiry. There should be no heavier burdens on the railroads in employing labor to operate automobiles than on their competitors. In the railroads (as in other industries) rates, capitalization, salaries and wages must all follow changing economic conditions, but none should be sacrificed for the benefit of others.**

It is asserted in behalf of the railroads that certain restrictions imposed on them in the matter of hiring labor for truck and bus operation which automotive transport escapes, unfairly prejudice the railroads and that labor in this competing industry is not properly protected. The Committee thinks that the railroads should be under no greater restrictions in employing labor for automotive operation than are other automotive users but it would prefer to see equalization by improving conditions in automotive labor rather than by impairing conditions of employment in railroads.

The Committee regards the particular wages and conditions of labor generally as beyond the scope of its inquiry. It merely offers the suggestion that, while Governments cannot and should not attempt to regulate the use by owners of their own automotive property, they might, in assessing taxes or issuing licenses, impose conditions of employment on vehicles not operated by owners.

The Committee believes that a permanent and universal liquidation and downward adjustment of values and incomes of all kinds have occurred in this country and that railroad rates, capital structures, salaries and wages must all respond to this generally changed condition, but that none should be sacrificed for the benefit of others.

A considerable number of obsolete rules governing overtime, hours constituting days' work, and restrictions on service, survive in the railroad wage structure. The Committee does not wish to see labor lose any of its hard-won improvement in conditions, but it believes that the just substance of them can be retained without adherence to obsolete forms, and that labor is as eager as railroads to modernize and simplify the structure of wages and working schedules.

We regret that the labor organizations did not see fit to avail themselves of the Committee's invitation to submit their recommendations on the general subjects of our investigation. We had hoped to have the benefit of their wide knowledge concerning railroad labor conditions and also their views on the best methods of protecting labor in railroads from conditions in competing methods and of improving conditions in the latter field. It is only fair to call attention to the fact that our material does not include any presentation by the labor organizations of any facts that might have seemed pertinent from their point of view.

(7) Beacons, weather service and similar auxiliaries to air traffic should be maintained at public expense and air transport should be encouraged during its development stage but we believe that every such service should ultimately pay its own way.

Air service is diverting some traffic from railroads and threatens greater inroads. Here again the railroads are confronted with a development of human progress. It cannot be handicapped in their behalf. The most that they can ask is that it be not unfairly advantaged and, for reasons stated herein, we think that the real railroad remedy against this competition is to enter and help develop it.

Existing American airways are unquestionably subsidized at public expense. Various forms of flying-aids are maintained. Mail contracts, paying much more than receipts from air postage, are in effect with a deliberate purpose of subsidy and there is no doubt that lower rates on all air service are thus made possible at public expense.

The Committee believes that beacons and flying-aids are like lighthouses and navigation aids at sea and cannot be abandoned or charged for. The railroads were themselves subsidized in their development period. We cannot condemn Government aids to the inauguration of this valuable service. But, however much subsidy may be justified in a development period, we feel that every established transport service should ultimately be self-sustaining, that air service has a definite place, that it will inexorably take that place without the continuing necessity for the subsidy granted in the early stages of development and that the necessity for such aid is even now decreasing. It is of the utmost importance that such aid as is given should be fairly and economically distributed.

(8) **The Committee has no recommendation to make on pipe lines.**

There are projects for a wider use of pipe lines as a transportation agency but at present they do not constitute a problem. They are not subsidized and they are effectively regulated. The subject has been ably and exhaustively studied by the House Committee on Commerce in a forthcoming report. From our own studies we do not recommend further present affirmative action.

II. The policy of trying to appraise railroad properties on some selected basis of valuation and then saying that they are entitled to earn a fair return on this appraisal should be reconsidered. Where competition with trucks and other methods exists, it will determine rates. In other cases rates must be regulated but the basis of costs of operation under efficient management is a better general guide than any attempt to preserve capital structures regardless of economic trends. We see no reason why the rate-making rule should not say in plain English that railroads are entitled to make a reasonable profit based upon costs of efficient operation and that they are not entitled to earnings merely to preserve present structures if overcapitalized.

Notwithstanding social and economic dependence on railroads—right or wrong—we have, since the beginning, relied on private initiative for their development and financial support. Profit is the only incentive to private investment. Unless the railroads are permitted reasonable earnings on the cost of efficient operation, there is no alternative to Government ownership and complete socialization of our railroad system. But that does not mean that railroads, any more than other industries, are entitled to a guarantee of earnings on their investments in property. In early periods of railroad development and unregulated monopoly, the profit incentive was over-emphasized and resulted in unconscionable abuse. Extravagant profits, or the hope of them, contributed to the rapidity of the extension of the system, but they also got a sharp rebuke in certain instances of attempted confiscatory rate regulation. The courts intervened with an opinion that rate-making must be limited by the right to a "fair return" on the value devoted to public service. Though originally probably intended as a protection against confiscation in individual cases, this principle, by a process of evolution, became a rule governing the general level of rates.

We think this rule should be abandoned. Nobody ever thinks of saying that the costs of bricks and mortar in an industrial plant should determine what it shall charge for its products. If it can keep its costs low enough to earn a profit on what its product is worth to the public in competition with other products, then it is worth from ten to twenty times what it can earn. If it cannot do that, it is as apt to be a liability as an asset.

In this sense, the present railroad rule puts the cart before the horse. It tends to ununiformity of results, perpetuation of debt and of obsolete and exaggerated capital structure, insufficiency of allowance for obsolescence and depreciation, inadequacy of surplus and reserves, and maintenance of unnecessary properties and facilities. The results are unjustifiably high rates in some cases and low rates in others. It evolved on the theory that, if not so restricted, the railroad monopoly would earn inordinately. That theory is becoming obsolete. The day is not far distant, if, indeed, it has not already arrived, when, even if wholly unregulated, some of our railroads may have difficulty in earning a "fair return" on asset values, no matter by what rules such values are defined. These competitive developments are inexorable. The public is entitled to all benefits of the march of progress and nothing will prevent that consummation. We think that the right principle of rate-making is as follows:

> *Wherever there is fair economic competition it will decide the rate question and it should be permitted to do so freely. Where there is no such competition, the problem of rate regulation arises, but costs of service under efficient operation are a better general guide than some arbitrary determination of asset values.*

If, on that basis, a railroad cannot earn enough to support its capital structure, the remedy is not to raise rates. It is to revise the structure. And if on no reasonable revision can the capital structure be maintained, it is an economic misfit. Parts of it that cannot live should be abandoned and the rest either set up in a new system or consolidated with other groupings.

Fixed railroad indebtedness is not commonly retired. It is refunded. It is a universal rule of financing that any debt for purchase of productive facilities should be amortized during the lives of those facilities out of returns from their use. Railroads are not exempt from this well-established principle and rates should be subject to no restriction which contravenes it. A cause contributing to the present crisis is the unwieldy proportion of inter-est-bearing debt in railroad capitalization, much of it representing facilities long ago scrapped. We distinctly do not believe that past mistakes as represented by present unwieldy debt structures should be salvaged by increased rates. The present debt structure must be revised and losses written off. But, as to the future, we do think that rate-making should look to the retirement of new debt incurred for purchase of productive facilities during their lives and out of returns from their use.

The Interstate Commerce Commission petitions for "A simple rule which shall make it clear that, in regulating the general level of rates, we shall always keep in mind and be guided by the need for producing, so far as possible, revenues which are sufficient for the maintenance of an adequate National railway transportation system and also recognize the principle that the railroads may justly earn a surplus in time of prosperity to offset deficiencies in time of depression."

The Interstate and Foreign Commerce Committee of the House of Representatives recommends the following: "In the exercise of its power to prescribe just and reasonable rates the Commission shall give due consideration, among other factors, to the effect of rates on the movement of traffic, to the need, in the public interest, of adequate and efficient railway transportation service at the lowest cost consistent with the furnishing of such service; and to the need of revenues sufficient to enable the carriers, under honest, economical, and efficient management, to provide such service."

It will thus be seen that those who have given the subject of rate-making the closest attention have abandoned the theory of making rates on some basis of evaluation. It is said that the principles just discussed are implicit in both of these suggested rules. If so, we approve them, but the Committee sees no reason why a rule for rate-making should not say in plain English that railroads are entitled to make a reasonable profit on costs of efficient operation and that they are not entitled to preserve over-capitalized corporate structures.

III. The railroads should do much that they have not done to improve their condition without any Government help at all. They should promptly be freed of all unnecessary restrictions on the doing of it. It has been estimated that less than a 20 per cent increase in traffic would put most of them on an earning basis. In view of the narrowness of this margin of loss and of the very great savings possible in railroad operation, we regard their outlook as far from hopeless.

The effect of protracted depression is to reveal the underlying trends of an era. While part of our transport difficulties are, like other troubles, no more than reflections of depression, continued traffic stagnation has uncovered organic difficulties. It by no means follows, however, that this condition was either caused, or can be cured by Government. In this time of extreme stress on everybody, the public has a right to expect the railroads to do what they can for themselves before they call on the rest of us and we are convinced that there is a great deal which the railroads have left undone. It has been said by experienced and informed observers that—because of enforced reduction in expense—a 20 per cent or even a lesser increase in traffic volume would put most of the railroads on an earning basis and that less than a 50 per cent increase would restore them to net earning levels of 1929. Passing the question of strict accuracy in these broad assertions, the fact is that, here as elsewhere, there has been such liquidation of the general extravagance of the 1929 delusion, that a very moderate movement on the upward business spiral would dissipate much of the seeming cloud on the solvency of many railroads. The Committee is not proceeding on conjectures of unwarranted optimism, but it does seem that, if the margin of loss is as scant as this, it is narrow enough to invite some robust action in railroad administration to improve earning statements—not by increased traffic or Government intervention—but by economies and improvements in operation, and perhaps by a reduction in rates to attract more business. That has been the universal action in sister industries and that is the view of some of the leading authorities in railroad management.

Against this view it is urged that railroads have been prevented by statutes and regulations from acting freely or that, where they have been permitted to act, restrictions legally imposed upon them as railroads have been extended to them in new fields. While we believe that this argument is too much emphasized, we have found some substance in this complaint. The Committee believes that railroads should be permitted to act along the lines suggested herein subject to no more and no heavier restrictions than their competitors and that the Congress and regulatory bodies owe them a positive duty to relieve them promptly of any handicap whatever in this regard.

(a) Railroads should adopt the competing methods of which they complain.

Much of the difficulty which the railroads ascribe to automotive and potential air and pipe line competition should and could have been relieved by an alert and aggressive railroad policy. We believe that if the railroads had regarded themselves more accurately as purveyors of transportation rather than as guardians of a monopoly, they would have been more alert to take advantage of every development in their field and that a more progressive policy might have turned to their own distinct advantage the very things they now regard as a burden and a threat.

Resort to Government as an alternative to self-help is to be deplored. The early transport pioneers did not go to Washington to have their ferries and steamboats protected against rails. They developed the rail service and became controlling figures in the new field. We think it is quite clear that the railroads have been distinctly remiss in not getting the most out of the new methods. It seems to us that the truck, in local and terminal service, motor drawn equipment on rails and highways in many cases, and the airplane, where rapid transit is required, afford a way to a beneficent transport revolution, that the railroads themselves owed a duty to the public to have led, and that the quicker they do so now, the better it will be for all concerned. After they have taken this logical step, we wonder whether they will be so eager to restrict these other forms of transportation as they are now.

(b) Railroads should cooperate to reduce competitive expense.

(1) Unnecessary services should be abandoned.

We think that there has not been sufficient cooperation among the railroads. As an example, we quote from the Interstate Commerce Commission's 1932 report, P. 37:

> "The expenses so chargeable to passenger and allied services for the year 1931 before taxes, rentals and interest were 110.82 per cent of the revenues from those services. For the freight service the corresponding figure was only 68.62."

The public is familiar with the spectacle of "crack" passenger trains shuttling back and forth across the country empty or nearly so and perhaps, also, with the explanation that this "is necessary to retain the competitive reputation for service"—in other words, for sales promotion or advertising. The Committee believes that agreements in good faith and within the law could relieve this expense. We think empty trains should either be filled by reduced rates or taken out of service. With our whole economic structure at stress, sympathy with such extravagance is difficult.

(2) Metropolitan terminals should be consolidated and unnecessary facilities scrapped.

Terminal expenses constitute an astonishing proportion of railway costs. Great economies, and much improved service, are possible through the use of trucks in terminal areas and further large savings by unification of railway and other terminal facilities. Railroads have insisted on separate terminals in metropolitan areas for purely competitive advantage. The resulting multiplicity has imposed high costs, poor service, and great waste. This burden upon shippers is indefensible. Reform is as necessary to modern metropolitan convenience as to railroad economy. It is impossible to deal effectively with the manifold problem of a modern city without a unified plan of development for all forms of transportation. This problem differs in different cities and there are legal and other difficulties involved, but much could be accomplished at once by cooperation among railroads and a complete solution would be greatly facilitated if all forms of transportation were placed under a single regulatory agency and if railroad consolidation were worked out along regional lines.

These improvements would entail wholesale scrapping of some facilities. We cannot follow the argument against the writing-off of obsolete, non-earning, and unnecessary properties. We think that there are thousands of miles of trackage and many other facilities, both in terminals and elsewhere, which serve no necessary purpose and which do not now earn and never can. They are handicaps on efficient operation and burdens on the public. Their elimination would reduce capital assets but it would result in lower rates, better earnings and improved service.

(3) Circuitous haulage should be eliminated.

Circuity in haulage to keep traffic on the rails of a single system entails great waste for which the Committee can find no sufficient excuse. As in all attempts to apply general principles to the infinite variety of circumstance in a great nation, a flat rule requiring freight to be routed by the most direct route, letting the revenue fall where it may, would result in some hardship, but the present practice leads to grotesque results. It is not easy to reduce the effect to figures, but the unnecessary haulage of freight has been estimated at a large percentage of total ton-mileage. Until the railroads are willing, by cooperation, to eliminate this kind of waste, it is difficult to share their apprehension of competing methods.

(c) Financial management should be improved.

We have discussed our view of the contribution of existing rate-making rules to present financial distress, but we also question the policy of some railroads in applying too great a proportion of earnings to dividends and too little to the retirement of debt and the accumulation of surpluses and reserves—a practice which we regard as responsible, at least in part, for the existing unfortunate condition of some roads.

(d) Transport methods and equipment should be brought up-to-date.

We acknowledge the restrictions on railroad initiative through regulation of appliances and on railroad resources through rate regulation. We are also aware of the progress that has been made in speed, quality of service, and increase in the radius of use of material equipment. Nevertheless, it cannot be fairly said that railroad advance in applied science is abreast of that in other industrial fields. For example, the improvements in Germany with stream-lined Diesel and electric trains of very light tonnage maintaining schedules of 96 miles per hour to offset motor transport, has no counterpart here. The Committee has not found it practicable to make exhaustive studies on this subject, but offers the suggestion that the Interstate Commerce Commission authorize, and the railroads set up, one or more central research and engineering organizations to which all railroads in certain groups shall contribute—their products to be available to all contributors.

(e) **In view of what could be done by better management, the general outlook seems far from hopeless.**

Generally speaking, it must be recalled that, in railroads—almost alone among sister industries—rates remain at boom-time levels. Adjustment to new economic horizons lags. It is hard for us to believe that wholehearted cooperation and vigorous application of contemporary principles of industrial management and control, within the various railroad companies themselves, along lines just discussed, would not do more than can Government or any other outside force to rehabilitate this most important of American industries.

In depths of depression, as at peaks of prosperity, fundamental values become distorted by the fog of gloom, on the one hand, and the rosy haze of hope on the other. These opportunities for aggressive policy and management coupled with at least some of our suggestions in aid of the transportation situation as a whole seem to us to indicate a distinctly hopeful (rather than a despairing) prospect for the railroads and we think that both regulating agencies and others having interest and influence in the railroads should act promptly to overcome what seems to us a degree of inertia in this regard.

IV. Regulatory jurisdiction should be extended to the whole National transportation system but applied only to the extent necessary for public protection. The existing regulatory mechanism of the Interstate Commerce Com-

mission is inadequate and should be improved by reorganization without expansion or increased expense.

The work of the Interstate Commerce Commission is a contribution to the advancing science of political economy. One has only to read its most recent report to realize the sympathy and intelligence with which it addresses the problems confronting it. It has pioneered a complex subject and, if it has recently operated on principles which this Committee regards as in part obsolete, it is important to remember that they are statutory principles. We think that if critics would give more attention to the legal limitations upon the Commission and its own repeated recommendations thereon, they would find less ground for complaint.

The studies of the Committee clearly indicate the advisability of extension of regulatory jurisdiction to the whole transportation system. The Committee feels that a judicial type of organization, such as the Commission now has, is inappropriate to its present work and wholly inadequate to a wider jurisdiction. In extending its powers, it is not necessary to expand its personnel and expenditures. What is needed is to reorganize its functions, divide its work, and give it a form and method more appropriate to the tasks before it. At present they include rate-making, and that is at least a quasi-legislative function; decisions in conflicting causes, and that is distinctly judicial; and supervision of administration, and that is certainly executive. From another angle of analysis, we find it attempting to plan, and that is a staff duty, and to carry plans into execution, and that is purely operative. For all these inconsistent purposes, it must finally act in a body on many questions, with no sufficient latitude for delegation, and that is utterly inconsistent with any modern theory of operation except for legislative and judicial action of the very highest order.

The data before us indicate that (whatever may be the limits to which actual regulation or administration is extended) the necessity for planning and for comprehensive information on the whole transport problem is absolute. A cogent railroad argument is to the effect that the Government has regulated the initiative out of the railroads, and that by reason thereof, they are in their present plight. While there is a tendency to overemphasize this, three facts remain: first, that the Government, principally through the agency of the Commission, has for many years assumed to dominate railroad administration; second, that railroad policy and management are not abreast of sister industries; and third, that some railroads are in a perilous condition. Nobody can assume authority without accepting responsibility. The existing railroad condition speaks for itself to say that regulation by the Commission has left something to be desired.

The lack of incentive or authority in the Commission to plan and to act affirmatively is evident throughout its most recent report. It hopes that "efforts have been or will be made to bring the rival transportation agencies into some measure of agreement." It thinks that "no rival transportation agency should be given unfair advantage," but complains that "there is no adequate information . . . nor do we know of any comprehensive and definite plan for a cure . . ." It believes that the public "safety and convenience" should be protected by regulation of automotive agencies but asks for "a thorough investigation under authority of Congress." It says of regulation of port-to-port rates, "We have not in-

1

vestigated this subject, but are convinced that it merits serious consideration by Congress." Speaking of restrictions on railroad ownership of water-carrier lines, "If the railroads wish this prohibition removed, they should so request the Congress without further delay. Until the reasons for such a change have been fully presented, we have no opinion to express upon it." On the question of stifling of railroad initiative, there is the suggestion that the *railroads* "ask the appropriate authorities for definite relief." Without unduly extending these quotations, it is fair to say that the whole report is eloquent of a somewhat passive attitude toward acknowledged evils and also of grave difficulties that have arisen from drastic regulation verging on administration by an authority which sits and hears but has only a limited scope in which to inquire and plan and act.

If, as we think it should, the regulating body should pass on railroad corporate reorganization, there would be a new and expert function for which we think the Commission is not now equipped or organized. There should be a separate department and an appropriate expert personnel for this work. This is an emergency matter.

The organization should be reformed without expansion to act along wider and more affirmative lines with less attempt to run the business of transportation and with more concentration on protection of the public, and maintenance of a healthy national transport system. It should have inquisitorial powers and duties to keep constantly abreast of changing developments and should be required to report annually to Congress on the state of the nation's whole transport system with its recommendations for betterment.

Its activities should be reorganized with appropriate separate departments, with a chief at the head of each, for its legislative, executive and judicial functions, and for each major special function such as control of corporate reorganization. It should have also a planning department with a research staff and such other departments as experience indicates. Except in the exercise of its more important legislative and judicial functions, departmental hearings and decisions should be sufficient and action as a body should not be required. While all heads of departments should sit in council on basic policies and important problems, the body should have a vote only on the most important legislative and judicial decisions. Either one man, or at most an executive committee of three, should have exclusive responsibility and authority in all executive functions, and final decision in all but the more important legislative and judicial functions of the separate departments.

This form of organization and method divides, decentralizes and so speeds works, permits specialization yet assembles special views on general policies. It retains the advantage of the committee form for council but secures the advantage of a compact responsible group for action. All these attributes will be needed in the tasks inevitably confronting future transport regulation and only a few of them are available now.

V. Emergency Recommendations.

(1) Corporate reorganization can and should be facilitated by revision of the bankruptcy procedure.

Present railroad distress is sufficiently shown in the current report of the Interstate Commerce Commission, that 122 Class I railways failed to earn fixed charges in the first three quarters of 1932. The financial structures of many railroads carry too many inflexible charges and too few liquid surplus assets to survive protracted non-earning periods. This condition cannot be cured by increasing rates to salvage old mistakes or by lending Government money to preserve them. They require realistic reorganization in accordance with the facts. Some railroads can hope to survive only on drastic reorganization and scaling down of fixed obligations.

The Reconstruction Finance Corporation was created to tide over an emergency, in the hope of some recovery, but this use of Federal credit encountered a link between the emergent and the more permanent problems. The fixed charges of some roads are heavier than any fair prospect of restored traffic will bear. The corporation cannot pour public treasure into situations where, instead of temporarily supporting operations and loaning to maintain prudent interest payments, there is a wasteful delta of out-flowing streams of interest on unsupportable capital structures. That would postpone inevitable readjustments at public loss to no good purpose. There is need to reform these top-heavy structures to make them available for emergency aid before it is too late and the present legal mechanism is too slow and cumbersome to serve.

We recommend revision of bankruptcy procedure to permit prompt and realistic reorganization of overcapitalized corporate structures without destructive receiverships and judicial sales on depressed markets to the end that the railroads' justifiable borrowing requirements may be met with safety to the lender under adequate protection.

(2) The recapture clause should be repealed retroactively.

The so-called "Recapture Clause" of Section 15-a of the Transportation Act is based on an economic misconception and has proved to be an element of uncertainty in railroad financing. We join the recommendation of the Commission for its repeal "both for the future and retroactively."

(3) The statutory rule of rate-making should be revised.

Reasons and suggestion for amending the present rate-making rule are discussed beginning at page 21.[1] As was there stated, rate-making cannot be made to preserve unsound capital structures or to "attract capital" regardless of what the service is worth but if the rule is put on a common-sense and forthright basis, we can approach the railroads' financial problem with more intelligence. While this is a permanent as well as an emergency reform we think it is important to a prompt and sound solution of the railroad problem. We understand that both the Interstate Commerce Commission and the House Committee on Interstate and Foreign Commerce recommend a change and regard its necessity as emergent. Indeed the Committee found no opposition to change in any of the evidence or representations before it.

(4) "Adequate security" does not necessarily mean "marketable collateral."

The Reconstruction Finance Act requires "adequate security" for railroad loans. It should do so and we recommend no change in the law. As a matter of interpre-

---

[1] Page xxxviii in present volume.

tation, however, if, upon reorganization of overcapitalized structures or on sound existing structures, a particular loan is sufficiently protected by priority of lien and reasonable prospects of earnings available to its priority of payment, we do not regard marketable collateral as a determining factor. In fact we believe that, with prompt improvement of capital structures where necessary, private capital will be available for necessitous railroad loans.

BERNARD M. BARUCH,
Vice-Chairman
CLARK HOWELL
ALEXANDER LEGGE

New York, February 13, 1933

C. SUPPLEMENTAL REPORT OF ALFRED E. SMITH

While I am in substantial agreement with the greater part of the Committee's report, this supplementary memorandum states my conclusions in my own language, placing the emphasis where I think it belongs.

EMERGENCY ACTION

As to emergency action, I recommend the following:

1. The recapture clause of the Transportation Act should be repealed retroactively.

2. A debtor relief act with a special provision governing railroads, which will have for its object scaling down debts and composing differences without bankruptcy receiverships, should be passed, but its operation should be for the period of the emergency only, which for the purposes of this act should be declared to end on January 1, 1935.

After most careful consideration I cannot recommend

as an emergency measure that there is immediate need of action by Congress to make a new statutory rule of rate making, nor that the present powers of the Reconstruction Finance Corporation to make loans to railroads should be extended or materially changed. Specifically I believe no useful purpose will be served at this time by an extension of the powers of the Reconstruction Finance Corporation with regard to railroads so that they can make additional loans without full collateral, upon the assumption that railroad rates will be adjusted in such a way that these loans are bound to be repaid.

Coming now to the basic troubles which afflict the railroads I have considered carefully the diagnosis offered by numerous groups and individuals, and the corresponding cures. No purpose would be served by extended analysis and comment because this subject is fully covered in the report of the staff. My conclusions are stated herein in summary form.

THE RAILROAD'S COMPETITORS

As to the subject of competition by air, water, pipe and highway lines, I believe that the effect of competition of these lines upon the railroads has been exaggerated. Drastic regulation of competing services is not the solution of the railroad problem, and such regulation should be established only in the general public interest. Regulation is expensive. It is bureaucratic. Once established it expands, and it paralyzes private initiative without offering constructive leadership. I believe that the air lines should be left as they are at the present, with no more regulation than is now provided for. This is a new field, and the less private initiative is interfered with, the better it will be in the long run. The railroads had their day of freedom from restriction coupled with enormous government subsidies. That day is over and individual initiative in blazing trails and laying ties for railroad lines across the Rocky Mountains and the Sierras is no longer needed. Air lines are an infant industry and are entitled for the present to some government help without undue regulation.

The pipe lines are built. They serve a very limited purpose. They present no serious menace to the railroads. I see no advantage in extending regulatory control over them.

As to water transportation, with particular reference to inland waterways, I believe that government subsidies in this field should be curtailed, not primarily because they result in unfair competition with the railroads, but because these subsidies have not proved effective. Certainly the New York State Barge Canal cannot be said to compete with the existing railroads, because in spite of construction and maintenance by the State and free tolls, the barge canal carries so little freight that it presents no problem to the railroads. The New York State Barge Canal is an heirloom. Sentiment rather than common sense makes us keep it up. I am opposed at this time to the construction of the St. Lawrence Waterway, because it would be a waste of public funds. Present rail facilities are more than adequate to provide for everything which the proposed canal can accomplish. The cost of moving grain would not be lowered by this canal sufficiently to justify the enormous expenditures which it would involve; keeping in mind also, that this waterway would be open only for a part of the year, and that the railroads would have to be used anyway the rest of the year. I believe that a special investigation should be conducted into the Inland Waterways Corporation, to discover exactly what it costs the War Department to operate this corporation, and whether or not further expenditures for this purpose should cease.

As to competition by motor trucks and buses, the testimony given before us does not indicate to me that the competition is at this time as serious a menace to the railroads as they claim it to be. Interstate trucks and buses as yet carry only a comparatively small part of all freight and passengers. On the other hand, it is unquestionable that this form of transportation will soon be used more and more, because it is economical and efficient. In a number of cases, buses and trucks have actually relieved the railroads of burdens on short hauls, and have enabled them to cut down train service where these could not possibly pay.

Extravagant claims are made as to the penalizing of railroad as contrasted with highway transportation by taxes and by numerous regulations affecting service and labor. Trucks and buses are already substantially taxed through license, gasoline and oil taxes, and these are being steadily raised so that within a short time, in the course of normal events, the users of highways for commercial purposes will be paying their full share of the cost of construction, reconstruction and maintenance. The tendency in every state is to make them pay their way, and the Federal Government is already taxing them for gasoline. In fact, at the present time in many states of the Union, gasoline and license taxes are being diverted from highway maintenance and construction to other fields of government expenditure.

While there is much to be said for regulation of all common carriers on highways by the Interstate Commerce Commission or some other federal agency, and by the appropriate state regulatory agencies, it should be noted, however, that such regulation cannot reach the individual farmer, merchant, and owner who is not a contract or common carrier. I believe that such regulation should for the present, be for the purpose of insuring responsibility, and fixing the physical standards for vehicles and for similar purposes, rather than for the fixing of rates. This is practically what the railroad and bus representatives themselves have recently agreed on. The plan for a federal license tax with a return to the several states of their respective shares, suggested by various witnesses, seems to me to be impractical, undesirable and at present unjustified. I believe that the railroads should go into the bus and truck business on a larger scale, and that they should be encouraged to do so by appropriate legislation.

GRADE CROSSINGS

As to elimination of crossings at grade of highways and railroads, I believe that the railroads' share of the cost should be materially reduced. In many states the railroads' share is as high as 50%. This is unduly burdensome and unfair to the railroads, and it has naturally resulted in bitter opposition to elimination orders and the general slowing up of the crossing elimination program. This reduction cannot, however, be accomplished by federal legislation or fiat. It must be brought about by persuasion in the several states.

I cannot subscribe to the recommendation made to the Committee that Congress should fix a maximum rate of taxation on railroad property beyond which any state and local levies would be invalid.

VALUATION

Coming now to valuation, I have not been able to give this subject sufficient study even to attempt a solution. The questions involved are exceedingly intricate. Members of Congress and experts outside of the government have been studying them for years without coming to a satisfactory conclusion. From a superficial study, I am not entirely satisfied that the prudent investment theory is unworkable. The reproduction cost theory is obviously obsolete and must be discarded. I cannot subscribe to the idea of basing railroad rates on ability to attract new capital, on the present cost theory or on the theory of the natural rule of survival. I doubt whether the courts would sustain or the public tolerate the survival theory. The present cost theory would tend to put the seal of approval on existing chaotic and wasteful railroad organization. The theory of fixing rates to attract new capital begs the whole question. It starts with a conclusion and adjusts all the facts to meet it. Moreover, this theory would defeat itself because the public would not be able to pay the high rates which it would bring about. In the end there would be less traffic and less revenue than before. Moreover, even if the public were able to pay the bill, I believe that the adoption of this theory would perpetuate bad management, write up values of many railroad securities beyond their actual worth, and take away the incentive to consolidation and good management.

A new principle of valuation has recently been proposed by the Committee on Interstate and Foreign Commerce of the House of Representatives which seems to me to have considerable merit, but which is in such general language that it is difficult to see how it can be made the basis for the scientific determination of rates. It seems to me, however, that this is a subject which Congress should decide.

Whatever principle is adopted, I am satisfied that the general public will not tolerate writing up values or increasing rates merely upon the theory that a great many railroad securities are held by savings banks, trustees and insurance companies as security for widows, orphans or other beneficiaries of trust. It must be recognized that many railroad bonds are worth less than par in the light of conditions entirely separate from the depression, and that railroad stocks have declined even more in value. These assumptions are based upon any common sense theory of true valuation, whatever it may be. Similarly, I do not believe the public will approve the proposal that railroad rates should be high enough to retire a substantial part of outstanding bonds, because this will be regarded as just another way of attempting to give present bonds artificial values.

THE INTERSTATE COMMERCE COMMISSION

Taking up now the general question of federal regulation, we are all agreed that effective regulation is an indispensable feature of the solution of the transportation problem. I find, however, little in recent history to justify the continuance of the Interstate Commerce Commission as now organized. This implies no criticism of its members. They have attempted to function under an obsolete and unworkable law, and in the face of conditions which call for intelligent planning and leadership as distinguished from endless debate on details. Everyone admits that more and more of the work of the board must be delegated anyway, and if this is so, the question arises as to why a board is needed at all. I believe that too much emphasis has been placed on the judicial functions of the Interstate Commerce Commission, especially on valuation and rate making, and too little on planning and administration. The complete break-down of the present valuation formula has left the Commission in a condition which would be laughable if it were not so serious. The scrapping of the present formula opens up some very interesting questions for taxpayers. What, for instance, becomes of the tons of statistics and other data collected on the basis of the old formula? What of the payroll army of federal commissioners, counsel, experts and clerks? What of the wasted time of local officials, railroad representatives, farmers, business men and commercial organizations? Suppose that just a little common sense had been substituted for all this scientific hash, this maze of regulation and red tape? I favor the abolition of the Interstate Commerce Commission and the creation in its place of a new department of transportation headed by one man, or a one man bureau head in the Department of Commerce determining policies with the approval of the Secretary of Commerce. What we need is a new transportation system, not endless hearings on a system that does not work.

THE FUNDAMENTAL PROBLEM

I am convinced that the fundamental problem of the railroads is that of nation-wide consolidation and reorganization to reduce costs and rates, and to write off losses. The era of railroad pioneering and competition is over. The roads must reduce overhead and operating expenses. They must scrap unnecessary, competing and weak lines. They must get rid of obsolete equipment.

They must cut out unnecessary services. They must use trucks and buses, eventually air transportation and, if necessary, waterways and pipe lines as a supplement or substitute for rails wherever these new forms of transportation are more economical. The establishment of a limited number of strong regional railway systems would be a start in the right direction. Even this will leave a certain amount of wasteful and unnecessary competition.

Whatever may be the basis of valuation and rate-making, there must be a scaling down of many railroad securities. I believe that the banks, trust companies, insurance companies and other holders of railroad securities must be realistic about this phase of the problem. The public will not stand for making them a preferred class of investors, who must get a hundred cents on a dollar, irrespective of the true value and condition of the business they have invested in, when values in all other fields are being readjusted and cut down.

The question for the railroad executives, directors and security holders to decide is whether the steps taken in this direction should be compulsory or voluntary. To date voluntary regional consolidation under the auspices of the Interstate Commerce Commission has made little progress. The question has been raised whether compulsory consolidation is constitutional. As distinguished an authority as the late Senator Cummins thought it was, but there is no decision of the United States Supreme Court squarely on this subject. There is much to be said for the theory that we are moving inevitably toward one national railroad system. Upon this theory, the major railroad systems might well give serious consideration to the appointment of some sort of an impartial chairman, arbitrator or director-general to co-ordinate their present activities, and to prepare a plan of permanent consolidation.

If the railroads show no willingness to reorganize, re-organization can surely be brought about by some form of condemnation or eminent domain. I believe that the railroads will be unsuccessful in attempts to maintain their present physical, operating and financial structure at the expense of the general public by penalizing com-petitors and raising competing transportation costs, in-flating securities, raising rates, limiting taxation by states and municipalities through federal legislation, borrow-ing government money without adequate security and other like devices. Similarly, attempts to bring about economy largely at the expense of railroad labor will prove unsuccessful unless this is part of a logical gen-eral reorganization in the interest of the public. Un-doubtedly many wasteful and unjustifiable regulations have been made governing railroad wages, hours and conditions of labor, and others which, however admir-able in themselves, the country simply cannot afford to-day, but the railroads cannot expect public support in changing these regulations merely as a means of retain-ing and perpetuating other conditions which are equally wasteful. They cannot expect to make labor the only scapegoat.

Those who are responsible for present railroad man-agement need not complain of radical or drastic govern-mental action in the near future if they are unwilling even to attempt to meet their problems in a bold, forth-right way through their own initiative and cooperation. They have an unrivalled opportunity to do themselves and the country a great service. They should have the guidance and help of the national and state governments in this effort.

Alfred E. Smith

Appendix

LETTER OF INVITATION

Hon. Calvin Coolidge,
Hon. Alfred E. Smith,
Mr. Bernard M. Baruch,
Mr. Clark Howell,
Mr. Alexander Legge.

Gentlemen:

The present financial position of the railroads of the United States is a matter of grave concern. Collectively the greatest and most important industry of our country, the railroads have operated in this year at staggering deficits. Only wise and timely Federal aid has averted the financial breakdown of important systems.

This situation touches every citizen. It affects directly the security of wage and employment of the 1,500,000 railway workers. It affects equally the many and important industries supplying railway equipment and supplies. It touches the financial problem of local, State, and National government, to the support of which the railroads contribute over $300,000,000 annually in taxes. It has given rise to a severe decline in the value of the $19,500,000,000 of railroad obligations and shares, and has occasioned concern to institutions which hold such obligations among their assets, representing in part the savings of that thrifty portion of our population which is to be found among the policyholders of insurance companies and the depositors in savings banks. The relief that the present emergency has made it necessary to grant to the railroads is a drain on the Federal treasury, and any ultimate loss will constitute a burden on every taxpayer.

The present deplorable position of the railroads is not due wholly to the stagnation of traffic resulting from the long-continued depression. Many of the present ills are due to governmental, financial, labor, and management policies, some wrong in conception, some wrong in application, and others rendered obsolete by radically changed conditions. As a result, the railroads have not been in a position to adjust themselves, as well as have other industries, to present conditions.

There are many disagreements as to causes, many disagreements as to remedies, but unanimous agreement as to the urgent necessity of some thorough-going solution of the problem. No solution, however, will be effective unless the problem of the railroads is considered as an integral part of the entire transportation problem of the United States, whether by rail, highway, waterway, pipeline, or air.

Every industry in the country is entitled to fair treatment—the railroads no less than the others. The public interest must certainly be protected, but regulation should not place the railroads at a hopeless disadvantage with competing agencies and destroy flexibility of operation and management initiative. The railroad workers are entitled to a fair wage and the greatest possible security of employment. The holders of railroad securities are entitled to a fair and stable return on the true value of their investment.

But more important than the interests of any one group, the people of the United States are entitled to the most effective and economical form of transportation to meet their various needs, whether by land, water, or air. Each form of transportation should be unhampered to provide effectively at a reasonable cost and at a fair profit the service for which it is best fitted. No form of transportation should be favored either at the expense of another agency or at the ultimate expense of the people of the United States.

We, the undersigned organizations, representing many of the interests concerned, believe that there is no more important present task than a thorough and satisfactory solution of the railroad problem, as an integral but the most urgent part of the entire transportation problem. We beg that you examine all phases of the problem and recommend a solution which, with due regard for the public interest, will ensure an opportunity for the railroads of this country to operate on a business basis, to the end that there may be a stabilization in employment of wage-earners and in the values of investments made in behalf of insurance policyholders and savings bank depositors, and a general enhancement of the prosperity of the country which to so great a degree depends upon the prosperity of the railroads and of the many lines of business which in turn depend upon them.

UNDERSIGNED ORGANIZATIONS

Aetna Life Insurance Company
Connecticut General Life Insurance Company
The Connecticut Mutual Life Insurance Company
The Equitable Life Assurance Society of the United States
The Guardian Life Insurance Company of America
John Hancock Mutual Life Insurance Company
Home Life Insurance Company

The Lincoln National Life Insurance Company
Massachusetts Mutual Life Insurance Company
Metropolitan Life Insurance Company
The Mutual Benefit Life Insurance Company
The Mutual Life Insurance Company of New York
New England Mutual Life Insurance Company
New York Life Insurance Company
The Penn Mutual Life Insurance Company
Phoenix Mutual Life Insurance Company
Provident Mutual Life Insurance Company of Philadelphia
The Prudential Insurance Company of America
The Travelers Insurance Company
National Association of Mutual Savings Banks
Investment Bankers Association of America
Railway Business Association
American Central Insurance Company
Phoenix Insurance Company of Hartford
Connecticut Fire Insurance Company
Hartford Fire Insurance Company
Hartford Accident & Indemnity Company
National Fire Insurance Company of Hartford
Aetna Insurance Company
Caledonian Insurance Company of Scotland
Columbia Casualty Company
Commerce Insurance Company of Glens Falls
Glens Falls Insurance Company
The Continental Insurance Company
Fidelity-Phenix Fire Insurance Company
American Eagle Fire Insurance Company
Maryland Insurance Company of Delaware
Niagara Fire Insurance Company
First American Fire Insurance Company

The Fidelity and Casualty Company of New York
Eagle, Star & British Dominions Insurance Co. Ltd.
Lincoln Fire Insurance Company of New York
Fireman's Fund Insurance Company
Home Fire and Marine Insurance Company
Occidental Insurance Company
Fidelity and Guaranty Fire Corporation
Glens Falls Indemnity Company of Glens Falls
Great American Insurance Company
Insurance Company of North America
Norwich Union Fire Insurance Society Limited
The Eagle Fire Company of New York
Norwich Union Indemnity Company
Northern Assurance Company, Ltd. of London
London & Scottish Assurance Corp., Ltd.
Phoenix Assurance Company, Limited
Imperial Assurance Company
Columbia Insurance Company
United Firemen's Insurance Company
The Union Marine & General Insurance Company, Ltd.
The Pennsylvania Fire Insurance Company
Security Insurance Company of New Haven
Springfield Fire & Marine Insurance Company
Sentinel Fire Insurance Company
Michigan Fire & Marine Insurance Company
New England Fire Insurance Company
SVEA Fire and Life Insurance Company
Hudson Insurance Company
Skandia Insurance Company
Columbia University
Harvard College
The University of Chicago
Yale University

PART I
INTRODUCTION

CHAPTER I

INTRODUCTION

As background and basis for a discussion of the American transportation problem today it may be useful to review briefly the stages through which our transportation development has passed; to outline in general terms the situation as to regulation; and to indicate the relative importance of the various forms of transportation at the present time. We shall then set forth certain basic principles or considerations which should be borne in mind in determining the future transportation development of the United States and outline the major questions which it is the purpose of this investigation to answer.

I. SUMMARY OF AMERICAN TRANSPORTATION DEVELOPMENT

The first important inland canal in the United States —the Erie—was opened in 1825, and the first railroad—the Baltimore and Ohio—in 1829. Prior to that time transportation was confined to the highways, to inland rivers and lakes, and to coastal waters. In connection with the highways it was the common practice to charge tolls for the purpose of covering the costs of construction and maintenance charges.

The canal era, so-called, extended from 1825 to the decade of the seventies, when the railroads began to make heavy inroads upon water traffic. Some of these canals were constructed by state governments and some by private enterprise, usually with the aid of state or federal treasury subsidy. It was, however, the practice to charge tolls to cover capital outlays and annual maintenance costs. Indeed, it was usually assumed in the early days of canal building that the returns to the contributing state treasury "would support the government and educate every child in the commonwealth." Many of these early canals, however, came to grief along with railway and turnpike companies during and following the panic of 1837, and few of them proved successful from a financial standpoint. Nevertheless canal and river traffic continued to expand, as already indicated, until the decade of the seventies.

In the early eighties, as a means of arresting the decline in water transportation, tolls were abolished. On January 1, 1883 the State of New York abolished tolls on the Erie, thenceforth providing for maintenance and upkeep out of the public treasury; while on July 5, 1884 Congress passed an act which abolished all tolls on navigable waterways subject to federal jurisdiction. The pertinent clause reads as follows:

> No tolls or operating charges whatever shall be levied or collected from any vessel, dredge, or other water craft for passing through any lock, canal, canalized river, or other work for the use and benefit of navigation, now belonging to the United States or that may be hereafter acquired or constructed; . . . nothing herein contained shall be held to apply to the Panama Canal.

Notwithstanding the abolition of tolls the waterways continued to lose traffic, and by the end of the century both rivers and internal canals had come to play a relatively unimportant rôle in the carriage of freight and a negligible rôle in the movement of passenger traffic. "In Cincinnati and Pittsburgh hundreds of boats have given place to tens. Where once on the Missouri there were sixty, there now remains but one to remind us of the departed glories of our waterways. Along our wharves old gang-planks, anchors, and broken machinery are tangled in the grass growing in the crevices between the cobblestones." Railways ran in the very channels of abandoned canals or paralleled the banks of great rivers, deserted save for a few small boats of uncertain schedule.

A movement for the revival of water transportation began to bear fruit at the turn of the century when the federal government began to make substantial appropriations for the rehabilitation of various inland waterways, and the State of New York, in 1903, appropriated $101,000,000 for the remodelling of the Erie Canal. As we shall see in a later chapter, great sums have been expended upon waterway development in the ensuing years and there has been a considerable increase in water-borne commerce, particularly since 1920.

Railway development in the United States has also passed through several distinct stages. The period from 1830 to 1850 was one of experimentation both in technical matters and in methods of financing and management. It was assumed for a short time that anybody should be permitted to run vehicles on the public railroad tracks, and there was complete lack of standardization in the distance between the rails and in the character of railway construction and equipment. During the decade of the thirties it was an open question whether railroad construction should be under government or private auspices. Numerous state governments, and some city governments, did in fact engage in the actual construction of railroads, and they also rendered extensive financial aid in connection with private ventures. However, in consequence of the disastrous losses sustained during and following the panic of 1837, the state governments, and also the federal government, decided to leave the construction of railroads thenceforth to the field of private enterprise.

The second period, from 1850 to 1890, was one of rapid railway expansion, during which the great trunk line systems were in the main completed. By 1853 railroad systems had been extended over the mountains to Chicago, and by 1869 the first transcontinental railway line was completed and duly celebrated with the driving of a golden spike at the junction of the Union Pacific and Central Pacific Railroads at Promontory Point near Ogden, Utah.

The most rapid expansion occurred in the boom period preceding the crisis of 1873 and in the decade of the eighties, when a number of transcontinental lines were laid down. Between 1880 and 1890 the railway mileage increased by more than 70,000 miles, an amount greater than the total mileage of lines in operation in 1873. In the single year 1887, as many as 12,876 miles were constructed—the best year since then showing less than 7,000 miles.

During this period federal, state, and local governments, convinced that the railways were indispensable to the prosperity of the people, encouraged the expansion by means of extensive land grants and financial subsidies. Federal land grants ceased after 1871, but some financial aid was given by the federal government after this date, and state and local aid continued both in the form of land grants and financial contributions.[1]

The development of railroad transportation during the four decades preceding the beginning of federal regulation is often characterized as one of economic waste,

---

[1] For data as to the extent of these aids to railroads, see Chapter XXII.

financial chicanery, discriminatory rate practices, and destructive competition. There was cheap construction, unnecessary duplication of facilities, and extension of routes
into unproductive and unpromising areas. In the earlier
years numerous railways were built solely for the purpose of financial exploitation through blackmail of other
roads, and others for the purpose of procuring profits
through the manipulation of securities. The era of ruth-
less and criminal abuse of power and privilege culminated in the great financial scandals of 1869. There
were of course many railroad builders whose operations
were as constructive and legitimate as those of individuals
in other fields of enterprise. While profiting from the
development of the systems which they created, they
were at the same time providing a cheaper form of transportation than had ever existed before and consolidating
the nation politically.

In this period of development the evils of unregulated
competition manifested themselves in a striking way.
Because of the duplication of railway lines between competitive points, leading roads engaged for years in rate
wars which resulted disastrously for all concerned. In
order to procure traffic at any cost, both freight and passenger rates were at times cut so low that even the out-
of-pocket labor charges were not covered. To illustrate
how extreme were the reductions: round-trip excursions
between Philadelphia and Chicago were as low as one
dollar; and first-class freight rates from New York to
Chicago were reduced from $1.88 to 25 cents per hun-
dred pounds. Such ruinous competition eventually drove
the railroads into pooling arrangements and rate agreements, the legality of which, however, was later denied
by the courts.

The third stage, from 1890 to the World War, may

be described as essentially intensive in character. It involved in the main the construction of feeder and cross lines, of new branches, and the rounding out of the so-called railway net which we know today. The total mileage increased from 163,597 in 1890 to a peak of 254,251 in 1916. This was a period, moreover, in which the first great movement for the consolidation of parallel lines occurred, a movement which was arrested by a series of Supreme Court decisions beginning with the Northern Securities case in 1904.

Passing by the period of government operation during the war, a fourth period may be said to have begun after the war, when highway transportation entered upon a new era of change and development. As a result of highway competition, the revival of waterways, the extension of pipe-line transportation, and the coming of the airplane, not only have the railways been subjected to severe competition but many thousands of miles of railway lines have been rendered obsolete. The total mileage in operation in 1930 had been reduced to 249,052, while many thousands of miles were virtually obsolete. The factors responsible for this change are discussed in Chapter VIII. The railway mileage by decades from 1850 to 1930 is shown in the accompanying diagram.

The other significant forms of transportation at the present time are highways, airways, electric railways, and pipe lines. As is well known, we entered upon a new era of highway development with the coming of the automobile at the beginning of this century, and highway transportation is now a factor of tremendous importance in our national life. Air transportation as a practical factor may be said to date from the year 1926;

RAILWAY MILEAGE IN THE UNITED STATES, 1850-1930

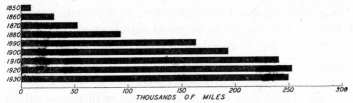

and it is still in the stage of infancy. The use of electric traction in street railways began in the eighties and showed a rapid expansion until very recent years. The electric interurban railway came just too late to realize its potentialities, being followed closely by the automobile, the competitive power of which was greatest precisely in the field of short-haul interurban transportation. Many of the interurban lines have been abandoned and most of those which remain are unremunerative.

The first important pipe lines for the transportation of oil were constructed in the seventies, by 1879 the producing areas of Western Pennsylvania being connected with the Atlantic seaboard. The growth of pipe lines has been very rapid during the post-war era because of the opening up of many new oil-producing areas. Gasoline pipe lines are almost entirely a development of the last ten years.

II. REGULATION AND REGULATORY AGENCIES

There has never been any general regulation of water transportation either on inland or coastal waterways. Individuals have been free to carry their own freight in their own vessels, and also to engage in common carrier service, and certificates of convenience and necessity are not required. The only regulation of rates is found in the requirement that intercoastal shipping companies must file maximum rates with the United States Shipping Board; but this regulation, as we shall see in a later chapter, is of no practical significance. There are, however, police regulations pertaining to navigation which are under the supervision of the Bureau of Navigation and Steamboat Inspection.

The regulation of railroads began with the so-called granger legislation of the seventies, confined to a number of Midwestern states. This accomplished two important results: First, the recognition of the right of a legislature or its agents to regulate rates of enterprises "affected with a public interest"; and second, the establishment of commissions with power to regulate railroad rates.

Federal regulation of railroads began with the Act to Regulate Commerce in 1887, which had two major objectives: (1) to insure a just and reasonable rate structure, and (2) to prevent discriminatory practices. The Interstate Commerce Commission was established for the purpose of carrying out these objectives. Owing to the open hostility of the railroads and a series of court decisions which left the Commission no power to fix rates and control long-and-short haul discriminations, federal regulation was relatively ineffective for two decades.

The Hepburn Act of 1906 greatly extended the powers of the Commission. One of the principal provisions was the extension of the Commission's jurisdiction to include express and sleeping car companies, pipe lines, and industrial railways. The power to fix maximum rates, after complaint and hearing, was granted. The control over accounts was extended to include powers of inspection and audit. Finally, the courts were directed to enforce the orders of the Commission, provided they were "regularly made and duly served."

A new phase of regulation began with the Transportation Act of 1920. Prior to this time regulation had been directed mainly toward securing just and reasonable individual commodity rates. Now it was seen that the railroad system of the country must be placed on a stable basis, and that rates as a whole must therefore be high enough to enable the railroads as a whole to perform their function in the economy of the country. To this end rates were to be established which would enable the carriers as a whole, or in groups, to earn a fair return upon the aggregate value of their properties.

This act also gave the railways permission, subject to the Commission's approval, to form pooling arrangements and combinations. It gave the Commission control of new construction, of abandonments of existing lines, and of other aspects of service; and it also gave the Commission supervision over security issues and provided for the establishment of new machinery for controlling labor disputes.

State regulation, following the short-lived granger legislation of the seventies, may be briefly summarized as follows. Many commissions were set up between 1885 and 1905 and they exerted considerable influence over railroad rates and discriminations until 1906, when the Hepburn Act restored to the Interstate Commerce Commission much of its lost power over railway rates. The powers of state commissions were gradually weakened through court decisions in 1913 and 1914, which upheld the Interstate Commerce Commission in its efforts to bring intrastate rates into harmony with interstate rates. This trend was confirmed by a clause in the Transportation Act of 1920 which provided that the jurisdiction of the Interstate Commerce Commission should include rates, regulations, and practices which, though purely intrastate in character, nevertheless created an undue preference as between persons engaged in intrastate and in interstate or foreign commerce. As a result, the state commissions have shifted their emphasis more and more to the regulation of other types of public utilities.

This brief summary of the history of railroad regulation in the United States indicates that the powers of the federal government over railroad transportation have been steadily expanded and intensified since the passage of the original Act of 1887. Since 1920 the Interstate Commerce Commission has had authority over all important aspects of the railroad industry except the regulation of holding companies, the determination of wages, and the supervision of detailed problems of management. The present body of law is the outgrowth of an effort extending over many years, representing the work of no single group of legislators, to control a great transportation agency in the interests of the public, without at the same time rendering it impossible for that agency to give adequate service.

Highway regulation is under state and local jurisdiction, the federal government's relation to the highway system being confined to such requirements as are incidental to the granting of aid for the construction of trunk-line systems. In most states truck and bus companies are now required to obtain certificates of convenience and necessity, and there are numerous, though far from uniform, regulations governing the weight and dimensions of vehicles, safety, etc.

The regulation of interstate pipe lines, with the exception of water and gas, was placed under the control of the Interstate Commerce Commission in 1906. The regulation of air transport is confined to police regulations governing safety and is under the jurisdiction of the United States Department of Commerce. There are also local regulations of minor importance. Local electric railways are under state and local jurisdiction; interstate electric railways are subject to the Interstate Commerce Commission.

The following tabular statement indicates the departments or agencies of the federal government which have more or less responsibility in connection with the regulation or development of the several types of transportation agencies:

Railways	Interstate Commerce Commission
Express service	Interstate Commerce Commission
Oil and gasoline pipe lines	Interstate Commerce Commission
Highways	Bureau of Public Roads: Department of Agriculture
Airways	Aeronautics Branch: Department of Commerce Post Office Department
Waterways and shipping:	
Inland waterways	Interstate Commerce Commission Corps of Engineers: War Department Bureau of Lighthouses: Department of Commerce Bureau of Navigation and Steamboat Inspection: Department of Commerce
Panama Canal	Responsible solely to President Reports to Secretary of War

Harbors
{ Corps of Engineers: War Department
Bureau of Lighthouses: Department of Commerce
Coast Guard: Treasury Department }

Inland, coastwise, and intercoastal shipping
{ Bureau of Navigation and Steamboat Inspection: Department of Commerce
Coast Guard: Treasury Department
Shipping Board }

Mississippi River barge system Inland Waterways Corporation: War Department

III. RELATIVE IMPORTANCE OF TRANSPORTATION AGENCIES

There are various possible means of indicating the relative importance of the different forms of transportation in the United States today, but no one of them is altogether satisfactory. The best single method perhaps would be to show the relative amounts of capital invested; but the data are unfortunately not precisely comparable. For example, the consolidated cost statement covering federal expenditures for waterways includes all expenditures back to the very beginning, relating in many cases to projects which no longer exist or which have been completely rehabilitated since the nineties. Thus the consolidated figure tends to exaggerate the amount of the investment at the present time. In the case of electric railways, which include both urban and suburban lines, available figures do not separate equipment from other physical properties. For the highways, we have precise data for the period since 1921 for construction of roads, but we have only estimates for garages, bus terminals, and other facilities. Finally, we have no data at all as to the investment in city streets. The diagram on page 16, however, presents a rough picture of the relative amounts of capital invested in our various forms of transportation. Air transportation is not included since the investment in physical properties, other than equipment, is negligible.

Another method is to compare the amount of passenger and freight traffic carried by the various forms of transportation. Difficulties also arise here, particularly in connection with freight traffic, because of the lack of data in some cases, and also because of variations in the character of traffic handled by the different agencies. Tonnage, for example, is negligible in the case of airplanes and relatively large in the case of waterways, which specialize in the carriage of bulky materials. Ton mileage is, of course, a better index than mere tonnage irrespective of the distance moved; but unfortunately in the case of truck transportation we have no very reliable data on ton mileage.

It will be seen from the charts on pages 17-18 that automobile traffic became more important than steam railway passenger traffic as early as 1918, and that the latter has decreased greatly since 1920. Traffic over electric railways, which includes urban lines, has also declined. With reference to ton mileage, data in some cases are available for only a few years, but the relative importance at the present time is clearly indicated. The ton mileage on the railways in 1929, for example, was roughly two and one-half times that on all the other forms combined.

Capital Invested in Various Forms of Transportation, 1930[a]

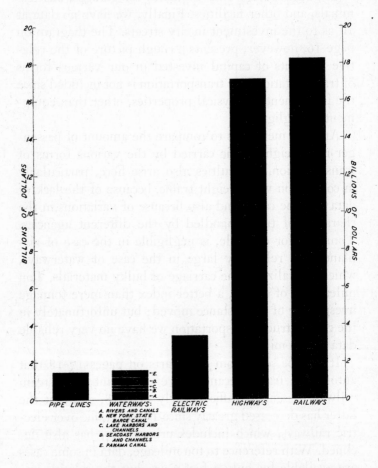

[a] The sources of the data used are as follows: Waterways: *Annual Report of the Chief of Engineers*, U. S. Army, 1931.

Panama Canal: D. H. Smith, *The Panama Canal*, pp. 331-35.

New York State Barge Canal: *Annual Report of the Department of Audit and Control*, 1931, p. 389.

Railways: *Statistics of Railways*, Interstate Commerce Commission, 1930, p. S-117. The figure there given has been reduced by 30 per cent to eliminate the value of equipment. *(Footnote continued, page 19.)*

Distribution of Passenger Traffic Among Transportation Agencies

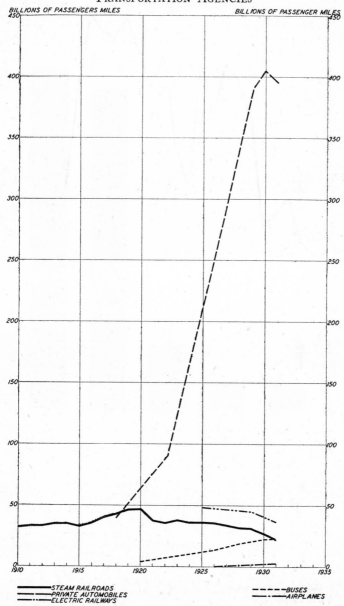

BILLIONS OF PASSENGERS MILES

BILLIONS OF PASSENGER MILES

STEAM RAILROADS
PRIVATE AUTOMOBILES
ELECTRIC RAILWAYS

BUSES
AIRPLANES

Ton Mileage of Various Transportation Agencies, 1910-31

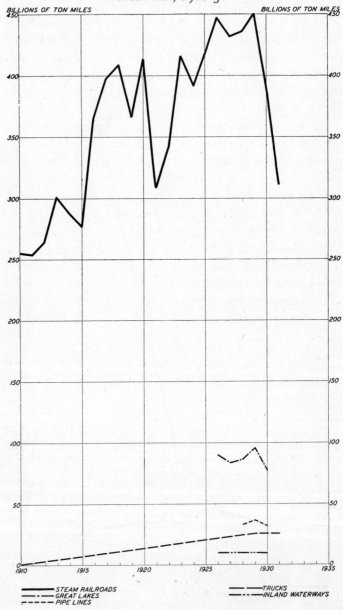

BILLIONS OF TON MILES

STEAM RAILROADS
GREAT LAKES
PIPE LINES

TRUCKS
INLAND WATERWAYS

IV. BASIC PRINCIPLES OF TRANSPORTATION

Since the purpose of this investigation is to lay the basis for a more efficient and satisfactory national transportation system than now exists it is essential that we give careful thought at the outset to certain fundamental economic issues underlying transportation policy. We suggest that the following general principles should be borne in mind:

1. The ultimate goal of all transportation policy is to furnish the people the transportation service which they require in the cheapest and most efficient manner possible.

This principle is of course derived from the elementary fact that in the long run the wealth of society depends upon the efficiency with which natural resources, labor, and capital are utilized, whether in the production of foodstuffs and raw materials, in manufacturing processes, or in the rendering of transportation services. This is true whether transportation be developed under government or private ownership.

Electric railways: *Census of Electric Industries,* 1927, p. 151. Data include only companies exclusively engaged in the operation of electric railways, but include equipment. The investment in interurban lines is now approximately a billion dollars.

Highways: Figure based on Federal Trade Commission estimate of value of highways for 1922 ($6,850,000,000) plus actual construction costs ($6,321,000,000) 1922-30 inclusive, plus Federal Trade Commission estimate of $4,000,000,000 for investment in bus terminals and public and private garages. The inclusion of private garages tends to exaggerate this figure for purposes of comparison.

Pipe lines: *Statistics of Railways in the United States,* 930, p. S-150.

The second chart is taken from H. E. Hale, Consulting Engineer, New York.

In the third chart pipe line data are from an estimate by Bureau of Railway Economics; truck estimate by Interstate Commerce Commission; and buses is an independent estimate.

2. Transportation rates should be just and reasonable and non-discriminatory in character as between persons, places, and commodities.

Inasmuch as transportation is in the nature of a public enterprise it has been established both in common and statute law that in the making of any particular rate a transportation company shall treat every person, community, or type of traffic fairly and without any undue preference in connection with essentially like services.

3. Government policy should not favor one form of transportation as against another, but should seek to place all as nearly as possible on the same competitive plane to the end that those agencies which demonstrate the greatest efficiency shall survive.

When any particular form of transportation is given preferential treatment, by means of subsidies or discriminatory regulation, the result is an allocation of traffic which is artificial in character, that is, which is not determined solely by considerations of economical and efficient transportation. In accordance with this principle, if one type of transportation pays taxes other types should pay taxes likewise.

4. No method of transportation and no part of a transportation system should be retained if it is not in the long run efficient and self-supporting.

Progress demands that whenever any particular transportation unit becomes obsolete it should be abandoned; otherwise society pays more for the cost of transportation than is necessary, and the burdens involved are borne either by other shippers or, as the case may be, by the tax-paying public. This means that if security owners have invested capital in a transportation agency which can no longer meet competition on even terms they should expect to pocket their losses. It means also that when it is demonstrated that a government-supported transportation agency cannot perform the service required as cheaply, with all elements of cost included, as it can be performed otherwise, that agency should be abandoned.

5. *Under regulated private ownership the minimum return allowed to investors in necessary transportation facilities should be sufficient to enable the industry to attract the volume of capital necessary to perform essential transportation services in the most efficient manner.*

So long as transportation companies must compete with other enterprises for capital in the investment market a return high enough to attract the necessary capital is a fundamental requirement. Otherwise the transportation companies will not be able to give the most efficient service possible.

6. *The wages of essential laborers engaged in the service of transportation should be as high as general economic conditions make possible.*

In stating that the wages of labor should be as high as is *economically possible* we call attention to the fact that wages in transportation cannot in the long run be higher than the industry can support, or widely at variance with rates in other lines of enterprise; but we emphasize that wages should be as high as possible rather than at the very minimum necessary to attract the labor supply required. This is not only because the livelihood of the workers is involved, but also because their capacity to contribute effectively to the life of the nation depends almost entirely upon what they obtain from the services which they render in this industry.

There are three major groups concerned with transportation—the shipper, the worker, and the investor of capital. At any given time the interests of these groups are to a considerable degree in conflict. It is the desire of the shippers to have low rates; it is the desire of the laborer to have high wages; and it is the desire of the investor to secure large returns on his investment. A reduction in rates, unaccompanied by an increase in efficiency, would mean either that the return to capital would be less or that wages would have to be reduced. Similarly, an increase in wages, efficiency remaining the same, would mean either that rates would have to be increased or that the return to capital would have to be reduced. Likewise, an increase in the return to investors, unless it is made possible by an increase in efficiency, would mean either that wages would have to be reduced or that rates to shippers would have to be raised. At times these conflicts of interest are very difficult to reconcile, and they present always a problem of more or less importance.

There is, however, in the long run and in a final sense, a mutuality of interest among these groups. It is not to the advantage of investors to have rates so high as to throttle the industries from which in the last analysis they draw their support. Similarly, the shipper will not in the long run benefit if rates are so low that the necessary capital will not be attracted to the transportation industry. In like manner it is to the long-run interest of labor that the necessary capital shall continue to be attracted and that the industrial development of the country shall not be handicapped by excessive rates.

In concluding this statement it will perhaps be useful to indicate the composition of these various groups. The shippers of freight are great industrial corporations, as well as small business men and farmers, and they comprise a substantial proportion of the total population. Moreover, since transportation costs find ultimate expression in the prices of commodities entering into consumption, the entire body politic, including the laboring population and investors, is concerned with cheap transportation.

The laborers directly employed in this field of enterprise in 1930 numbered about 1,500,000 in the railroad industry, approximately 200,000 in inland water transportation, some 2,500,000 in truck and bus transportation,[2] about 22,000 in pipe-line transportation, and some 8,000 in air transportation. The bulk, though by no means all, of the railroad workers are effectively organized, while in other divisions of the industry there is almost no organization.

The investors in the securities of transportation companies consist of individuals, business corporations, banks and insurance companies, and a wide variety of quasi-public institutions and agencies. Through savings deposits and insurance policies, if not by direct holding of securities, all classes of society, as is indicated in some detail in Chapter XII, are concerned, more or less, with the safety of and the return on transportation securities. Inasmuch as waterway and highway development is financed at public expense investments are mainly confined to railroad securities. Where transportation agencies are constructed by the government, it is of course taxpayers rather than investors who have an interest at stake.

The purpose of this investigation is to lay the foundations for a more economical and better functioning transportation system. It is therefore necessary to study the

[2] This does not include those working on highway construction.

several types of transportation agencies both independently and in their interrelations one with the other. It will also be necessary to reconsider our legislative policies and procedures with a view to promoting future transportation development along the soundest possible economic lines. Among the specific questions which the investigation will undertake to cover the following may be mentioned as of major importance:

1. What has been the trend of railway financial conditions over a period of years, and what is the relative importance of the primary factors responsible therefor?

2. What are the possibilities of increasing railway operating efficiency (a) through the initiative of individual lines, and (b) by means of consolidation?

3. What reorganization of railway financial practices and procedures and of capital structure may be required under present conditions?

4. In the light of changed agricultural and industrial conditions is a general reduction of railway rates necessary?

5. Are readjustments in railway wages essential to the stability of the industry?

6. What revisions are necessary in the Transportation Act of 1920 pertaining to the regulation of the level of railway rates?

7. What principles should be adopted in determining the feasibility of inland waterway development?

8. What modifications of policy are necessary in connection with coastal shipping?

9. What are the possibilities of effective co-ordination between rail and highway transportation?

10. What principles should be adopted in the regulation of highway transportation in general and in the

allocation of cost burdens as between commercial and private highway transportation?

11. What legislation is required to place the various forms of transportation on an even plane of competition?

12. What general considerations with reference to city planning should be borne in mind in the further development of transportation?

13. What reorganization in our regulatory system is necessary in order to carry out a constructive national transportation program?

CHAPTER II

THE TREND OF RAILWAY FINANCIAL CONDITION, 1890-1929

If we are to obtain a clear picture of the financial problem of American railways it is necessary to consider not only the immediate situation but also the trend over a considerable period of years. Only thus will we be able to ascertain whether, as is often contended, the machinery of government regulation combined with other factors has resulted in a more or less continuous deterioration of railway credit. For the purpose in hand we go back as far as 1890, virtually to the beginning of federal regulation, and far enough to reveal the effects upon railway finances of the great depression of the nineties. So far as this chapter is concerned we shall end our analysis with the year 1929, leaving the effects of the current depression for consideration in the following chapter.

I. FINANCIAL STATUS OF RAILWAYS AS A WHOLE

The first index of financial condition to which we call attention is the so-called "operating ratio," that is, the ratio of operating expenditure to operating revenue. Operating expenditure excludes taxes, bond interest, and other disbursements of a strictly financial character, and operating revenue does not include income derived from investments. The lower the operating ratio the more favorable is the situation from the standpoint of the railroads' finances. An operating ratio of 100 would indicate that the public is paying for railroad services an amount just equal to the direct cost of doing the work and keeping the carriers' property in repair, paying nothing for the use of the property. The table on page 28 shows the operating ratio for each year from 1890 to 1929.

It will be seen that from 1890 to 1910 the ratio was comparatively steady at 65 to 67 per cent. It was, however, noticeably higher in depression years than in periods of prosperity. From 1911 to 1927 the operating ratio fluctuated around a level 4 or 5 points higher than in the preceding period, except in 1916 when the extremely heavy traffic made possible a better showing. From 1918 to 1921 the ratio was extraordinarily unfavorable. This situation was due to the rapid rise in the price level, the inability of the roads to secure prompt rate readjustments, the special costs of war-time administration and, in 1921, the tremendous shrinkage of traffic. From 1922 there was a steady and substantial improvement through 1929, but the ratio of 71.8 which was achieved in the latter year was still higher than any figure recorded before 1914.

A second index of the railways' financial condition is the ratio of income to expense. In the table on page 29 we compare the operating revenue with the sum of the operating expenses, the taxes, and the interest on funded debt. This ratio gives an indication of the success of the railroads in retaining something for their stockholders out of the revenues which pass through their hands.[1]

---

[1] The ratio is not strictly a measure of the return received for conducting railway transportation, since (a) no account is taken of non-operating income and non-operating expense, and (b) the fixed charges include interest on obligations incurred for the purchase of securities which yield non-operating income. However, non-operating income and non-operating expense both consist chiefly of payments between railways and are therefore not significant for the purposes of this table. Computations for certain years made from consolidated income data which eliminate payments between railway companies indicate that only a negligible

RAILWAY OPERATING RATIOS, 1890–1929[a]

(Dollar items are in millions)

Year[b]	Freight Revenue	Passenger Revenue	Operating Revenue[c]	Operating Expenses	Operating Ratio
1890	$ 714	$ 261	$1,052	$ 692	65.8
1891	737	281	1,097	732	66.7
1892	799	287	1,171	781	66.7
1893	829	302	1,221	828	67.8
1894	699	285	1,073	731	68.1
1895	730	252	1,075	726	67.5
1896	787	267	1,150	773	67.2
1897	773	251	1,122	752	67.1
1898	877	267	1,247	818	65.6
1899	914	291	1,314	857	65.2
1900	1,049	324	1,487	961	64.6
1901	1,118	351	1,588	1,030	64.9
1902	1,207	393	1,726	1,116	64.7
1903	1,338	422	1,901	1,258	66.2
1904	1,379	444	1,975	1,339	67.8
1905	1,451	473	2,082	1,391	66.8
1906	1,640	510	2,326	1,537	66.1
1907	1,824	565	2,589	1,748	67.5
1908	1,655	567	2,441	1,710	70.1
1909	1,678	564	2,473	1,650	66.7
1910	1,926	629	2,812	1,882	66.9
1911	1,926	658	2,853	1,976	69.3
1912	1,969	660	2,906	2,035	70.0
1913[d]	2,199	696	3,193	2,236	70.0
1914	2,127	703	3,128	2,280	72.9
1915	2,038	646	2,956	2,089	70.6
1916	2,469	690	3,473	2,277	65.6
1916	2,631	722	3,691	2,426	65.7
1917	2,897	841	4,115	2,906	70.6
1918	3,522	1,046	4,985	4,072	81.7
1919	3,625	1,193	5,250	4,499	85.7
1920	4,421	1,305	6,310	5,954	94.4
1921	4,004	1,166	5,633	4,669	82.9
1922	4,086	1,088	5,674	4,510	79.5
1923	4,712	1,159	6,419	4,999	77.9
1924	4,437	1,086	6,045	4,609	76.2
1925	4,648	1,065	6,247	4,633	74.2
1926	4,906	1,049	6,509	4,766	73.2
1927	4,729	980	6,246	4,662	74.6
1928	4,772	905	6,212	4,509	72.6
1929	4,899	876	6,373	4,579	71.8

[a] Data are from the annual *Statistics of Railways in the United States*, Interstate Commerce Commission, 1922, p. LXXXVII; 1930, p. S.–118. Switching and terminal companies included 1890–1907; excluded thereafter.

[b] For 1890–1916 figures are for fiscal years ended June 30; for 1916–29 for calendar years.

[c] Operating revenue includes freight, passenger, mail, express, excess baggage, and other miscellaneous income.

[d] Class I and Class II railways only.

Year[b]	Operating Revenue	Operating Expenses	Taxes	Interest on Funded Debt	Operating Expense plus Taxes plus Interest	Ratio of Expenses plus Taxes and Interest to Operating Revenue
1890..	$1,052	$ 692	$ 30	$222	$ 944	89.7
1891..	1,097	732	32	220	984	89.7
1892..	1,171	781	33	240	1,054	90.0
1893..	1,221	828	35	250	1,113	91.2
1894..	1,073	731	37	253	1,021	95.1
1895..	1,075	726	38	252	1,016	94.5
1896..	1,150	773	38	250	1,061	92.2
1897..	1,122	752	41	248	1,041	92.8
1898..	1,247	818	42	246	1,106	88.7
1899..	1,314	857	44	251	1,152	87.7
1900..	1,487	961	44	253	1,258	84.6
1901..	1,588	1,030	47	262	1,339	84.3
1902..	1,726	1,116	50	274	1,441	83.5
1903..	1,901	1,258	53	284	1,595	83.5
1904..	1,975	1,339	57	298	1,694	85.7
1905..	2,082	1,391	59	311	1,761	84.5
1906..	2,326	1,537	69	323	1,929	82.9
1907..	2,589	1,749	74	344	2,167	83.7
1908..	2,441	1,710	79	368	2,157	88.4
1909..	2,473	1,650	85	383	2,118	85.6
1910..	2,812	1,882	98	400	2,380	84.6
1911..	2,853	1,976	103	410	2,489	87.3
1912..	2,906	2,035	114	429	2,578	88.7
1913..	3,193[c]	2,236[d]	122[d]	435[c]	2,793[e]	87.5
1914..	3,128	2,280	140	443	2,863	91.6
1915..	2,956	2,089	138	464	2,691	91.0
1916..	3,473	2,277	150	474	2,901	83.6
1916..	3,691	2,426	162	481	3,069	83.2
1917..	4,115	2,906	219	474	3,599	87.5
1918..	4,985	4,072	230	468	4,770	95.7
1919..	5,250	4,499	239	476	5,214	99.3
1920..	6,310	5,954	289	500	6,743	106.9
1921..	5,633	4,669	283	529	5,481	97.3
1922..	5,674	4,510	308	539	5,357	94.4
1923..	6,419	4,999	340	552	5,891	91.8
1924..	6,045	4,609	347	588	5,544	91.7
1925..	6,247	4,633	366	584	5,583	89.4
1926..	6,509	4,766	396	582	5,744	88.3
1927..	6,246	4,662	383	583	5,628	90.1
1928..	6,212	4,509	396	579	5,484	88.3
1929..	6,373	4,579	403	581	5,563	87.3

[a] Data are from the annual *Statistics of Railways in the United States*, Interstate Commerce Commission, 1922, p. LXXXVI; 1930, p. S–118. Switching and terminal companies included 1890–1907; excluded thereafter.
[b] For 1890–1916, figures are for years ended June 30.
[c] Class I and Class II railways and their non-operating subsidiaries only.
[d] Class I and Class II railways.   [e] Sum of three preceding items.

The table indicates that the proportion of the railways' receipts which was left for stockholders, to be used either for dividends or for reinvestment, increased steadily from the early nineties to 1906, then decreased steadily to 1920 when expenses surpassed the revenue.[2] After 1920 there was a steady improvement to 1929.

The trend of this ratio has been very similar to that of the operating ratio, as may be seen from the chart on page 32. However, the ratio shown in the table on page 29 shows a recovery since 1920 to a stronger position than was shown in any of the years before 1900, while the operating ratio has never since the war been as favorable as it was throughout the period before 1910. This difference is due to the fact that in the earlier years a much larger proportion of the total investment was in the form of bonded debt.[3]

Two other indices of financial condition are the relationship between income available for capital[4] and the investment, and that between net income and the equity of the stockholders in the property. In the table which follows we show the course of these two ratios during the period 1900-29:

---

error arises from the omission of non-operating income from sources outside the railways and the inclusion of the payment of fixed charges to other railways. Compare table on page 317.

[2] However, if account is taken of the payments made by the government to the railroads under the guarantee of earnings, the showing of these years is distinctly favorable.

[3] Interest on funded debt in 1890 amounted to 21.1 per cent of operating revenue, in 1900 to 17.0 per cent, in 1910 to 14.2 per cent, in 1920 to 7.9 per cent, and in 1929 to 9.1 per cent. Interest payments do not affect the operating ratio, but do reduce the balance for stockholders; hence they affect the ratio shown on p. 31.

[4] That is, net income plus interest on funded debt. The ratio of net income to the "physical valuation" of the carriers' property is discussed in Chapter XVII.

INCOME OF CARRIERS IN RELATION TO INVESTMENT IN ROAD AND EQUIP-
MENT AND TO STOCKHOLDERS' EQUITY THEREIN[a]
(Dollar items are in millions)

Year[b]	Invest-ment in Road and Equipment	Net In-come plus Interest on Funded Debt	Ratio of Net In-come plus Interest to Investment (Per cent)	Stock-holders' Equity[c]	Net Income	Ratio of Net In-come to Stockhold-ers' Equity (Per cent)
1900..	$10,263	$ 505.7	4.9	$ 4,618	$253	5.5
1901..	10,405	535.6	5.1	4,524	274	6.0
1902..	10,658	589.4	5.5	4,548	315	6.9
1903..	10,974	622.3	5.7	4,529	338	7.5
1904..	11,512	615.0	5.3	4,638	317	6.8
1905..	11,951	675.4	5.7	4,701	365	7.8
1906..	12,420	756.8	6.1	4,654	434	9.3
1907..	13,030	832.2	6.4	4,305	488	11.3
1908..	13,214	812.3	6.1	3,820	444	11.6
1909..	13,609	823.8	6.1	3,808	441	11.6
1910..	14,558	982.8	6.8	4,254	583	13.7
1911..	15,612	957.6	6.1	4,874	547	11.2
1912..	16,005	882.1	5.5	4,875	453	9.3
1913[d].	16,352	981.6	6.0	5,166	547	10.6
1914..	17,154	838.1	4.9	5,587	396	7.1
1915..	17,441	819.0	4.7	5,308	355	6.7
1916..	17,689	1,145.9	6.5	5,656	671	11.9
1916..	17,843	1,216.7	6.8	5,842	735	12.6
1917..	18,574	1,132.3	6.1	6,628	658	9.9
1918..	18,985	910.6	4.8	7,255	442	6.1
1919..	19,300	972.7	5.0	7,441	497	6.7
1920..	19,849	982.4	4.9	7,072	482	6.8
1921..	20,329	879.9	4.3	7,113	350	4.9
1922..	20,580	973.1	4.7	7,431	434	5.8
1923..	21,373	1,183.8	5.5	7,784	632	8.1
1924..	22,182	1,211.7	5.5	8,020	623	7.8
1925..	23,231	1,355.4	5.8	9,126	771	8.4
1926..	23,881	1,465.1	6.1	9,688	883	9.1
1927..	24,454	1,325.4	5.4	10,502	742	7.1
1928..	24,876	1,433.8	5.8	10,972	855	7.8
1929..	25,465	1,558.0	6.1	11,400	977	8.6

[a] Data are from the annual *Statistics of Railways in the United States.*
[b] For 1900–16, figures are for fiscal years ended June 30; for 1916–29 for calendar years.
[c] Investment in road and equipment minus funded debt.
[d] Class I and II roads and their non-operating subsidiaries only.

The investment figures for the earlier years, and hence also the figures for stockholders equity, are not strictly comparable with those for the later years, since the existence of serious overcapitalization in the earlier years

INDICES OF THE FINANCIAL CONDITION OF THE
RAILROADS, 1900-29

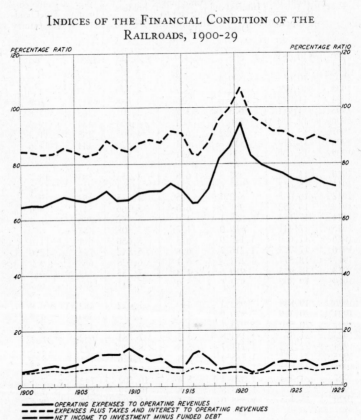

OPERATING EXPENSES TO OPERATING REVENUES
EXPENSES PLUS TAXES AND INTEREST TO OPERATING REVENUES
NET INCOME TO INVESTMENT MINUS FUNDED DEBT
NET INCOME PLUS INTEREST TO INVESTMENT

tended to inflate the book value of the investment in railways and equipment. For the years since 1906 the investment figures reported annually have been obtained by adding the net investment of the current year to the preceding valuations. As we come to the later years, therefore, the original inflated figure becomes progressively a smaller proportion of the total. Hence, the later the year the more closely the investment approximates original cost. This fact must be borne in mind in any comparison of the showings in recent years with those in the earlier years in the table.[5]

The chart on page 32 shows a comparison of the course of the four ratios which we have traced. In general the ratios of income to investment and of net income to that part of investment represented by the claims of common and preferred stockholders run courses which are similar to those of the ratios given in the tables on pages 28 and 29. From 1900 to 1910 there was a steady improvement, followed by a downward trend interrupted by the recoveries in 1912 and 1916, till the lows of 4.3 and 4.9 were reached in 1921. Since then there has been a substantial recovery until the beginning of the current depression. This recovery, though quite marked, did not place the railroads in the strong position they occupied between 1906 and 1913.[6]

It may be rejoined that the fact that the railroads applied for increased freight rates as early as 1909 and actually received a 5 per cent increase from the Interstate Commerce Commission in certain territories in 1914 is

[5] The figures involve an inaccuracy in that the funded debt includes railroad bonds held by other railroads and also non-negotiable debt of railroads to other railroads. To this extent the size of the stockholders' equity is understated. On the other hand, no deduction is made for holdings of railroad stocks by other railroads; this omission tends to inflate the figure for stockholders' equity.

[6] In view of the inflated valuation figures in the earlier years, it is doubtful in fact whether since 1921 the roads have earned as much on the actual investment of their stockholders as they did between 1900 and 1905.

evidence that the roads' financial condition in the late pre-war period was not as strong as is implied in our statement—particularly since the carriers in their application stressed the impairment of their credit as evidence of their need of increased revenues. In this connection the following points should be noted, however:

First, the Commission's decision, which was rendered in 1914,[7] was based on the fact that the net operating income of the roads was diminishing, rather than on evidence that it had been too low throughout the period of the controversy. Second, the finding applied only to carriers in official classification territory whereas our statement is based on data referring to the condition of all carriers in the country. Third, granting the impairment of the roads' credit, it does not necessarily follow that their revenues were inadequate.[8]

II. FINANCIAL STATUS OF REGIONAL GROUPS

It is not necessary for our purposes to analyze the showings made by individual railways. It is obvious that the results obtained by individual carriers must vary widely from those indicated by the combined experience of more than 200 companies. Under any system of regulation, or for that matter with unrestricted competition, it is to be expected that some companies will show results

[7] *Five Per Cent Case,* 31 I.C.C. 351.

[8] In this connection the Commission said: "The credit of our railroads has undoubtedly suffered in recent years, but largely from causes that were independent of their rates. Their borrowing power has suffered relatively because of the great competition for money by governments, states, municipalities, public service corporations, and industries. It has suffered actually because of the mismanagement of great railroad systems of international repute. The conspicuous decline in the securities of certain railroads and the circumstances leading up to the appointment of receivers for others have impaired the confidence of the public in the stability of railroad securities." The same, pp. 419-20.

far better than the average and that others will drop back or fail completely.

It is of interest, however, to compare the group results of the carriers in the various major geographical regions, especially since for rate regulation it is necessary to classify carriers according to the location of their lines rather than according to their individual financial needs. In the chart on page 36 we show for the eight regions recognized by the Interstate Commerce Commission, for the years 1922 to 1929 inclusive, the movement of the ratio of net income plus interest to total investment.[9]

It will be seen that the improvement in the financial position of the carriers was general throughout the country, though in the Great Lakes region and in the Central East the best results were shown in 1923, and in the South the peak was reached in 1925. The divergence of the movement in the Southern region from the general trend is presumably to be explained by the rise and passing of the Florida land boom.

In general, the chart shows clearly a tendency for the variations between the different parts of the country to disappear, the weaker regions gaining in relative strength, while the groups which include the roads of greatest financial strength suffered a relative decline. The scatter of results was smallest in 1928, when the percentage of net income and interest to investment for all but one of the regions fell within the range from 4.36 to 5.60. It was widest in 1923, when three regions were below 3.75 and two were as high as 5.85.[9]

---

[9] For the years 1926 to 1929 inclusive the data are those compiled by the Interstate Commerce Commission and published in the annual *Statistics of Railways in the United States.* We have carried the computations back to 1922 by adding up the data for individual lines.

RATIO OF NET INCOME PLUS INTEREST TO INVESTMENT, 1922-29

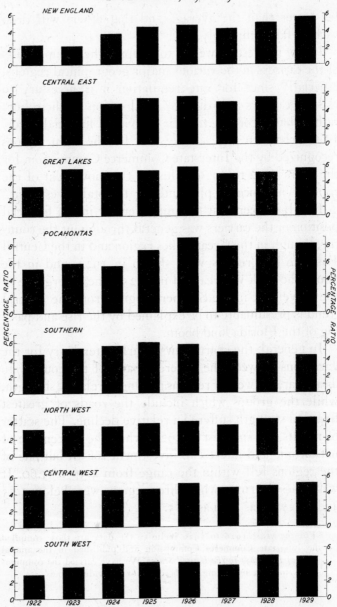

III. ABILITY TO RAISE CAPITAL

In this section we survey the record of railroad financing which occurred during the period between the crises of 1921 and 1930. Our purpose is to determine whether during those years the financial position of the railroads was strong enough to enable them to compete for new capital on reasonably fair terms with other industries, and to appraise the results of the financial policies which were either chosen by the roads or forced upon them by external circumstances.

In current discussions of railroad finances, certain points come up again and again. First, it is widely believed that the railroads have been so handicapped by rate regulation that they have not been able to earn a reasonable return on their investments. Second, it is alleged that because of this inability to earn a reasonable return they have been greatly handicapped in securing new capital. Third, it is occasionally stated that because of this handicap they have been compelled to pay for new capital an amount which is in excess of that which they could earn on the capital they already had, thereby giving the new security holder an advantage over the old investor. Fourth, it is argued that they have been compelled, because of inadequate earnings on their stocks, to do an excessive amount of financing by means of bond issues, thereby impairing their capital structures. We shall give attention in this chapter only to the first and second of these issues, reserving the others for consideration in Part III. We consider first the cost of capital obtained by bond issues.[10]

---

[10] It is impossible to make a worth while estimate of the cost of capital secured through stock issues.

1. Bond yields. The chart on page 39 shows the average annual yields of railroad, municipal, public utility, and industrial bonds from 1900 to 1929 inclusive. The 15 bonds selected in each group are all high-grade, and are issued by companies or municipalities which are ordinarily regarded as among the strongest in the group concerned.[11]

In the first section of the chart the yields are plotted on an inverted scale. These graphs show very plainly that the larger fluctuations in railroad bond yields have been due to conditions governing the long-term rates of interest in general. They also portray the stronger position of the railroad bonds as compared with the industrials and public utilities.

In the lower part of the chart the yields are plotted (without inversion) as percentages of the yield of municipal bonds. This part of the chart shows that railroad bonds have improved since 1920 in comparison with industrials, but have lost ground in comparison with public utilities.[12]

The course of these curves between 1910 and 1918 also substantiates the evidence of the three ratios which was presented in the preceding section. The chart also reflects the fact that the recovery of railroad credit after 1921 did not place the carriers' bonds in as strong a position, relatively to other bonds, as they had occupied in the period 1906-13.

---

[11] These bond yields are the ones compiled by the Standard Trade and Securities Service. For specific information on the bonds selected, see *Standard Statistical Bulletin*, 1930, pp. 103-04.

[12] This relationship between public utility and railroad credit is substantiated by data on the cost of financing in the two industries. See the *Journal of Land and Public Utility Economics*, February 1931, pp. 94-102.

RAILROAD AND OTHER BOND YIELDS, 1900-29
1. RATE OF YIELD

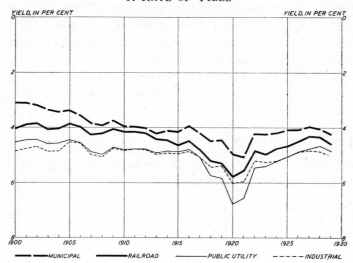

2. YIELDS OF CORPORATE BONDS AS PERCENTAGES
OF THE YIELD OF MUNICIPALS

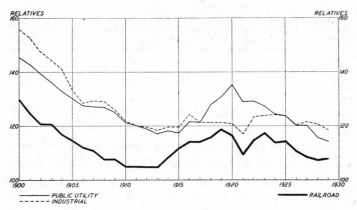

2. Cost of new capital. The chart on page 39 is based
on the yield of seasoned bonds already outstanding in the
hands of the public, and does not show the cost of new
capital. It is therefore chiefly significant as showing the
fluctuations from year to year in the absolute and relative
financial strength of the carriers.

The accompanying table shows by years the average
cost of new railroad capital obtained by long-term borrowing from 1920 through 1929.

YIELD OF NEW RAILROAD ISSUES, 1920–29[a]

Year	Bonds	Equipment Trust Certificates	All Issues[b]
1920	6.84	6.72	6.77
1921	6.73	6.68	6.74
1922	5.66	5.36	5.57
1923	5.22	5.34	5.29
1924	5.38	5.19	5.30
1925	5.44	4.75	5.21
1926	5.18	4.73	5.03
1927	5.00	4.51	4.90
1928	4.64	4.48	4.64
1929	4.89	5.08	4.97

[a] Computed from Roy L. Reierson and Ruth A. Foley, "Cost of Railway
Capital," *Journal of Land and Public Utility Economics*, November 1932,
Vol. VIII, pp. 435–38, by subtracting the cost of financing from the cost of
capital to get the yield to the investor. This procedure involves some small
inaccuracies because the data for cost of financing apparently do not apply
to all the issues which enter into the average cost of capital.

[b] Includes, in addition to bonds and equipment trust certificates, a number of smaller items such as notes, debentures, and receivers' certificates.

In the chart on page 41 we compare the yield on these
new issues with that of old high-grade railway securities.
The curve of yield of new issues is not as good a measure
of short period fluctuations as is the curve of high-grade
bond yields, since it is affected by year-to-year changes in
the make-up of the borrowing group and in the kinds of
securities issued. The fluctuations correspond with con-

siderable accuracy, however. As would be expected, the yield of new securities is always somewhat higher than that of the old ones.[13]

3. Amount of new capital. The capital investment of steam railways and their non-operating subsidiaries for

COMPARISON OF YIELDS OF NEWLY ISSUED RAILROAD BONDS
AND 15 OLD RAILROAD BONDS, 1920-29

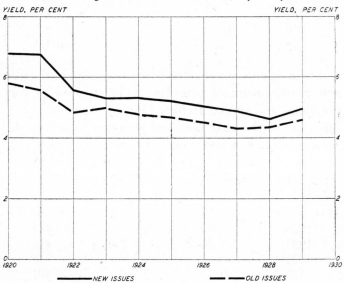

the years 1919-29 is shown at the top of page 42.[14] It will be noted that the investment has grown steadily at the rate of from 2 to 4 per cent a year.

[13] It may be worth noting that this difference does not prove that the new capital costs more than is paid to those who provide the capital already in the business. The curve of yields of old bonds is based on prior lien securities; it does not show the average yield of all funded claims against the railroads.

[14] Data are from *Statistics of Railways in the United States*, 1930, p. S-117.

December 31	Millions of Dollars
1919	19,300
1920	19,849
1921	20,329
1922	20,580
1923	21,373
1924	22,182
1925	23,231
1926	23,881
1927	24,454
1928	24,876
1929	25,465

These figures are affected by reorganization, the sale and abandonment of property, reclassification of corporations, and similar factors. Hence the increase from one year to the next does not measure accurately the amount of the new investment. The following data show the new investment in fixed property devoted to rail transportation purposes during the years 1920-29:[15]

December 31	Millions of Dollars
1920	544
1921	458
1922	342
1923	807
1924	724
1925	580
1926	666
1927	588
1928	468
1929	543
Total	5,720

[15] Data are from the same, p. S-111. They cover investments of Class I and Class II roads in new lines, extensions, additions, and betterments, less credits for retirements.

The tables which have been presented include capital which has been provided by reinvestment of railroad earnings as well as that invested from outside the industry. It is of interest also to examine the record of capital flotations to determine the success which railroads have had in securing a share of the national savings through public issues of securities.

For the years since 1919 the *Commercial and Financial Chronicle* has collected information concerning new security issues, which is classified in a fair amount of detail.[16] From these figures we have compiled the table on page 44. Some of the information is shown also in the chart on page 304.

This table shows that during the ten-year period 1920-29 the railroads obtained through the public money markets about 9 per cent of the total amount of capital which was raised through those markets—or 13 per cent of the amount which was raised by corporate industry. We may compare this figure with estimates of the proportion which the railroad industry bears to the total business enterprise of the country. According to Federal Trade Commission estimates, the steam railroads of the country owned, in 1922, about 17 per cent of the wealth used in corporate business in the United States[17] and produced about 12 per cent of that portion of the national income which is attributable to corporate business, or rather to those businesses which are usually organized in the corporate form (mining, manufacture, construction, trans-

---

[16] A similar compilation made by the Standard Trade and Securities Corporation shows railroad securities as a slightly higher percentage of the total volume of securities offered, but the fluctuations from year to year are very similar. The percentages are as follows: 1924, 17.8; 1925, 7.6; 1926, 5.6; 1927, 9.6; 1928, 9.1; and 1929, 8.6.

[17] *National Wealth and Income*, p. 133.

portation and communication, and banking). If mercantile business is included in the total used as the basis of computation, the percentage share of the railroads drops to 10.

While this comparison does not, of course, afford a precise measure of the amount of capital which the railroad industry ought to be able to secure, as compared with other industries, the figures indicate that the roads

RAILROAD FLOTATIONS AS PERCENTAGE OF ALL CAPITAL FLOTATIONS
1919–29[a]
(Dollar items are in millions)

Year	Railroad	Other Corporate	Non-Corporate[b]	Total	Railroad as Percentage of Total
1919	$208	$2,532	$1,621	$4,361	4.8
1920	378	2,588	1,044	4,010	9.4
1921	655	1,736	1,813	4,204	15.6
1922	652	2,421	2,172	5,245	12.4
1923	518	2,805	1,667	4,990	10.4
1924	940	2,899	2,488	6,327	14.9
1925	515	4,222	2,389	7,126	7.2
1926	423	4,877	2,130	7,430	5.7
1927	963	6,356	2,615	9,934	9.7
1928	728	7,090	2,174	9,992	7.3
1929	817	9,209	1,566	11,592	7.0

[a] Compiled from annual survey in the *Commercial and Financial Chronicle*. Includes foreign issues floated publicly in the United States.

[b] Chiefly borrowings of municipalities and foreign governments; includes also Federal Farm Loan bonds but does not include issues of the United States government or those of individual states.

have been able to get a share of the new capital which is not conspicuously out of line with the part which they play in the industrial life of the country. Considering that the railroad industry is an old one, whose capital needs arise from opportunities to reduce the cost of handling existing business and improving standards of safety and service, rather than from growth, the proportion seems to be rather higher than one would expect.

This brings us to the question whether the railroads' credit has not been too good; that is, whether they have not been able to attract funds in competition with other industries so easily that the country has been led to put into railway equipment savings which might better have been used elsewhere. Our data indicate that over six and one-half billion dollars of outside capital flowed to the railroads in the decade which ended in 1929. This includes refunding as well as new capital and foreign as well as United States issues. But the deduction necessary for these items is nearly offset by the reinvestment of surplus and the capital obtained from private sources. Thus the table on page 42 shows that the total increase of investment of Class I and II roads during these years, ran to 5.72 billion dollars, an increase of 28 per cent. During this period freight revenue ton mileage increased less than 10 per cent, and passenger mileage decreased over 30 per cent.

At first glance it might seem that these figures reflect misdirection of investment into a declining industry. But it must be remembered that the economic value of an investment of new capital cannot be tested merely by the gross volume of business transacted. Quite as important are the quality of service rendered to patrons, the safety of operation, and the costs. And on all these points there was much to show for the new capital. We comment elsewhere on the progress of the movement and on the startling improvement in the quality of freight service, as measured by car supply and car shortages.[18] This improvement was no doubt due in large measure to increased managerial efficiency,[19] but in no small degree

[18] See Chapter VI.
[19] It must be remembered that an improvement in efficiency of man-

it also resulted from the increase in capacity of cars and locomotives, the straightening of curves and reduction of grades, and the improvement of terminals. The most impressive result of the additional investment, however, is the reduction in direct cost of operation.

Coal consumption per passenger train mile fell from 18.8 tons in 1920 to 14.9 in 1929 in spite of a small increase in average length of trains; and in freight service it fell from 172 pounds per gross ton mile in 1920 to 125 pounds in 1929. Labor costs, measured in hours of service, have also declined. In 1922, 78 ton miles of freight service were performed for every employee hour; in 1929, 103.[20] These striking increases in the amount of service rendered per unit of labor and fuel can only be accounted for by the increased investment, which put the roads in possession of more powerful and economical locomotives, gave them better tracks to run on, and reduced the delays and inefficiencies which result from clumsy and congested terminal arrangements.[21]

The fall in the costs of operation of railways during the decade has been so great as to justify, from the economic viewpoint, a very substantial volume of new investment, in spite of the passing of the era of rapid traffic

---

agement nearly always involves some increase in investment. Longer trains, for instance, require longer sidings, heavier engines, and stronger bridges.

[20] The year 1922 is used as the basis of this comparison because operating conditions in 1920 and 1921 were somewhat abnormal. For those years the figures were 75 and 74 respectively. The figures, which are based on all employees, not merely those in freight service, are affected somewhat by the decline in the proportionate amount of passenger traffic, but this was probably not very significant, as the ratio of freight train miles to passenger train miles rose only from 0.98 to 1.05.

[21] This conclusion is confirmed by the fact that the great increase in investment was not accompanied by a significant increase in railway mileage. From the end of 1919 to the end of 1929 the increase in first track mileage was only 2,045 miles, or 0.8 of 1 per cent.

growth. It does not necessarily follow, of course, that the whole amount of the new investment was necessary in order to secure these economies. Some of the investment was unproductive, from the standpoint of the railways' finances, but was necessitated by public requirements. Some of it doubtless was productive from the standpoint of the individual railway but unproductive from the standpoint of the railway system as a whole because it merely made possible a diversion of traffic from one railway to another.[22]

IV. SUMMARY

1. The railroads were in a very strong financial position in the period roughly from 1906 to 1913, as is evidenced not only by the significant ratios of expenses, revenue, and investment, but by comparison of their bond yields with the average yield of bonds issued by other industries.

2. From 1910 to 1920 there was a progressive weakening which again is shown both in the ratio and in the comparative bond yields. The main explanation of the weakness from 1916 on lies in the failure of rates during the war period to follow the upward movement of prices and wages.

3. The recovery from 1921 to 1929 was substantial, though it did not quite restore to the carriers the financial strength they enjoyed in the period from 1906 to 1913.

4. Railroads in different sections of the country show widely differing degrees of financial strength, but during the years between the depressions of 1921 and 1930 there was a distinct tendency for these differences to disappear.

5. The railroads on the whole enjoyed a credit posi-

[22] Compare Chapters VI and XIV.

tion well above the average of corporate industries generally. Public utility bonds, however, gained in public favor as compared with railroad bonds during the post-war period.

6. Railroads were able to attract capital in a volume at least proportional to their importance in the national economy.

CHAPTER III

RAILROADS AND THE DEPRESSION

For the railroads, as for practically all other businesses, the world-wide depression of 1930-32 has been a major calamity. Some of its most important effects are so conspicuous as to require little more than mention; others are more readily overlooked. In this chapter we bring together a number of the most significant statistical measures of the extent and effects of the business depression on railway finances. The full analysis of their implications for railway policy must be deferred to later chapters.

In most cases we shall use 1928 as the base line from which to measure the effect of the depression, as the 1929 figures for traffic and revenue were in some respects abnormally high. The appropriateness of our choice of 1928 can readily be gauged by inspection of the tables in the preceding chapter. It will be noted that the net ton mileage for 1928 was almost the same as that for 1927 and was below the figures for 1926 and 1929.

I. TRAFFIC

By far the most important effect of the depression on the railways is its influence upon the volume of business handled. Net ton miles of revenue freight handled by Class I railroads dropped from 433 billion in 1928 to 383 billion in 1930 and to 309 billion in 1931. The latter figure was slightly below the low record of 1921 and far lower than that of any other year in the post-war period. For the first eleven months of 1932 there was a further drop of 73 million ton miles, or 25 per cent below the figures for corresponding months in 1931.

The decline in passenger service has been even more pronounced. Revenue passenger mileage of Class I roads (which was about the same in 1929 as in 1928) decreased in 1930 by 4 billion units, or about 13 per cent, and in 1931 by another 5 billion units, or 20 per cent of the

CHANGE IN THE PRODUCTIVE ACTIVITY OF VARIOUS INDUSTRIES, 1928–32[a]
(As percentages of 1928 figures)

Item	1929	1930	1931	1932
Railroads:				
Car loadings............	102.1	88.5	72.1	54.7
Revenue net ton miles[b]..	103.2	88.5	71.4	53.3
Passenger miles[b]........	98.4	84.8	69.3	53.0
Industrial production (index numbers)..........	106.8	85.8	68.7	51.9
Steel (ingot production)....	108.1	78.0	49.6	26.2
Automobiles and trucks (number produced).....	121.7	77.0	53.6	29.8
Road building (area)......	94.3	99.2	91.1	65.4
Gasoline (gallons)[c]........	116.6	116.9	116.2	100.5
Ship construction (tonnage)	127.0	259.9	160.6	130.6
Building contracts (area)...	81.8	52.7	37.8	16.0

[a] Data for railways are from annual *Statistics of Railways in the United States;* for other businesses from the statistical reports of the *Standard Trade and Securities Service.*

[b] Class I railroads only. 1932 estimated on basis of eleven months' data.

[c] 1932 estimated on basis of eleven months' data.

1930 figure. In the first eleven months of 1932 there was a further loss of 4.7 billion passenger miles, or 23.5 per cent.

How much of the decline from 1928 to 1931 in the aggregate tonnage originated is attributable to the fall in the general industrial activity during this period is a question of considerable importance from the standpoint of possible remedial action, but one which can not be answered with precision. One would expect in a severe de-

pression to find a decline in railway traffic roughly proportional to the general decline of productive activity,
and this is what we do find, as the table on page 50
shows.

On the other hand it is clear that to a certain extent
the shrinkage of traffic since the end of 1929 has been
merely an acceleration of forces which were already in
operation. Passenger service had been declining since
1926, chiefly because of the increased competition of
buses and automobiles. The volume of railway freight
traffic was still increasing up to the end of the prosperity
era, but the rate of increase was much lower than before
the war, and the railroads' percentage of the total volume
of traffic was falling.[1]

The chart on page 52 throws a considerable amount
of light on the question. In this chart the carload tonnage
of seven selected commodities originating on Class I
railroads is compared with the respective physical volume
of production or marketings of these commodities, both
series being expressed as percentages of the figures for
1928. These commodities account for about 40 per cent
of the total tonnage carried by the railroads.

It will be seen that the tonnage of cotton and of livestock originated in the depression years of 1930 and 1931
shows a much sharper decline than the decrease in the
quantity marketed. For the other five commodities the
decline in the freight tonnage from 1928 to 1931 was
on the whole no greater than the decrease in their respective volumes of production.

Clearly, the decline in railway traffic since 1929 reflects in part a decrease in the total amount of transportation work which is being done, in part a diversion to other

[1] Compare charts on pages 17-18.

CHANGES IN RAILWAY TONNAGE COMPARED WITH CHANGES
IN PRODUCTION OR MARKETING OF SELECTED
COMMODITIES, 1928-31[a]

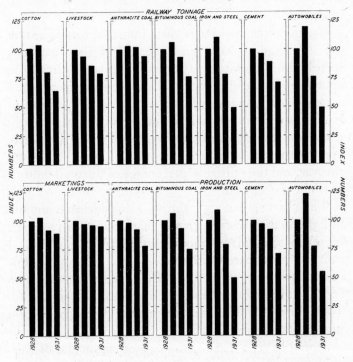

[a] All data are expressed as percentages of 1928. Railroad data are for Class I roads only and do not include less-than-carload freight.

Data for all commodities except anthracite coal were supplied by the Interstate Commerce Commission, Bureau of Statistics. The marketing index numbers used are those of the Department of Commerce; the production index numbers those of the Federal Reserve Board. Care was taken to include only those commodities for which the production or marketing index numbers and the Interstate Commerce Commission figures on the tonnage originating on the railroads were comparable. Wheat, petroleum and its products, lumber, and other important commodities were left out on account of the lack of production or marketing data comparable to the figures on tonnage originated.

agencies which would have taken place even under prosperity conditions, and in part the increased severity of
the competition of these other agencies under depression
conditions. So far as we can judge from the trend of
events up to 1929, however, the amount of freight traffic
the railways have lost because of the depression is not
far from the actual decrease in the freight ton mileage of
the depression years below the figures attained in 1928.
In the case of passenger service, however, it is probable
that somewhere from one-quarter to one-half of the
actual shrinkage would have occurred even under prosperity conditions.

II. RATES

We turn next to the effect of the depression on railway freight and passenger rates. Here we find comparatively little change. Railroad freight and passenger tariffs
constitute one of the most rigid elements of the general
price structure of the United States. Since the depression
started there has been no change in standard passenger
rates. There has been, however, a great increase in the
number of special concessions made in the form of week-
end and other excursion rates. Chiefly as a result of these
concessions, the average gross receipts of Class I railways
per passenger mile, exclusive of commutation service,
declined from 3.31 cents in 1928 to 3.06 in 1931. The
following table, which shows by years the receipts
from other than commutation service, indicates that the
drop after 1929 was chiefly a result of the depression,
though the figures had been trending slightly downward
ever since 1922.[2]

---

[2] The data for 1932 are for the first eight months of the year only.

Year	Cents per Mile
1922	3.43
1923	3.41
1924	3.38
1925	3.34
1926	3.35
1927	3.33
1928	3.31
1929	3.29
1930	3.25
1931	3.06
1932	2.71

Receipts for commutation service, when reduced to a mileage basis, have also declined since the depression started, as the following table shows:[3]

Year	Cents per Mile
1922	1.101
1923	1.093
1924	1.104
1925	1.107
1926	1.127
1927	1.114
1928	1.110
1929	1.105
1930	1.090
1931	1.064
1932	1.066

It is impossible to make a concise general statement with regard to the effect of the depression on freight rates. Some rates have been decreased in order to attract business; others have been increased in order to recoup the losses sustained in other directions. The average re-

[3] The data for 1932 cover the first eleven months of the year only.

ceipts per ton mile of Class I railroads since 1922 have been as follows:[4]

Year	Cents per Mile
1922	1.177
1923	1.116
1924	1.116
1925	1.097
1926	1.081
1927	1.080
1928	1.081
1929	1.076
1930	1.063
1931	1.051
1932	1.051

The decline in 1930 and 1931 is apparently not to be accounted for by any change in the length of haul or the character of the traffic. In fact, the average haul (that is, the number of revenue ton miles divided by the number of revenue tons originated) fell from 366.8 in 1928 to 346.3 in 1930 and to 317.1 in 1931. As the long-haul business typically takes a lower rate, this decline in the average length of the haul would lead us to expect slightly higher average revenues per ton mile, in the absence of rate changes. Moreover, the decline of business has been greatest in the products of mines and forests, products which typically are carried at less than average ton-mile rates. We conclude, therefore, that the decline in average revenue per ton mile in 1930 and 1931 was due chiefly to piecemeal reductions made as a result of the depression.

The rise in 1932 is also to be explained as a result of depression conditions, certain rates having been increased

[4] Only the first eleven months of the year 1932 are included.

early in that year in an effort to recoup the loss of income. In the summer of 1931 the railroads made application for a general increase of rates of 15 per cent. This was denied by the Interstate Commerce Commission, chiefly on the ground of doubt as to whether such an increase would really produce additional revenue for the carriers. In this connection the Commission emphasized the growth of waterway, truck, and pipe-line transportation, and the tendency of a relatively high level of freight rates to localize industry and impel the use of substitute products. The Commission noted also the danger that an increase of rates would "alienate or impair the friendly feeling toward the railroads on the part of the people of the country," and that it would "disturb business conditions and an already shell-shocked industry."[5]

In place of the general 15 per cent increase, the Commission suggested that the roads should propose changes in rates on particular movements or kinds of traffic. It also outlined a detailed plan for increasing rates, not on a percentage basis, but on the basis of a flat amount per car or per pound on all commodities except an enumerated list, chiefly farm products and livestock. The plan provided that all the revenue derived from the increased rates should be paid into a pool and redistributed to roads which were unable to meet their fixed charges. This plan was later so modified as to eliminate the pooling provision. It was understood that the roads would in fact pool the proceeds of the increase and loan them to distressed railroads. This has been done through an agency known as the Railroad Credit Corporation.[6]

[5] *Fifteen Per Cent Case*, 1931, 178 I.C.C. 575.
[6] It was estimated in 1931 that the new revenue created by this measure would amount to something over 100 million dollars, and would be sufficient to cover all deficiencies of interest on fixed obligations with

III. REVENUES AND EXPENDITURES

The combined effect of the large decline in the volume of traffic and the small changes in rates has been a drastic reduction of gross revenue. Total operating revenues of Class I roads declined as follows (in millions of dollars):

1928	6,112
1929	6,280
1930	5,281
1931	4,188
1932	3,127

The decline of 33 per cent in total operating revenues from 1928 to 1931 was a joint result of a 30 per cent drop in freight revenue, a 40 per cent drop in passenger revenue, a 45 per cent drop in express revenue, a 25 per cent drop in miscellaneous revenue, and a trifling increase in mail revenue. From 1931 to 1932 there was a further decline (according to preliminary reports from 165 Class I carriers) of 25 per cent in freight revenue, 32 per cent in passenger, 35 per cent in express, 8 per cent in mail, and 23 per cent in all other transportation.

Non-operating income and income from other than railway operations increased by over 10 per cent from 1928 to 1930 (being practically unchanged from 1929 to 1930), then fell in 1931 to a figure roughly 5 per cent below that for 1928. Preliminary reports indicate a shrinkage of about 25 per cent from 1931 to 1932.

To a considerable extent the decline in railway gross revenues has been offset by a decline in their operating expenditures. The most conspicuous of these savings are the direct reduction of cost of conducting transportation,

---

a substantial balance left over. This expectation has not been realized. Detailed figures of the Corporation's operations are given below, pp. 67-8.

and the reduction of expenditures for maintenance of way, structures, and equipment.

The reduction in the cost of conducting transportation is, of course, largely a direct result of the lessened volume of work to be done. The saving in maintenance is partly a result of decreased wear and tear, but it is also

VOLUME OF TRAFFIC COMPARED WITH MAINTENANCE AND TRANSPORTATION EXPENDITURES OF CLASS I RAILROADS, 1928–32[a]
(As percentages of 1928 figures)

	1929	1930	1931	1932
Volume of traffic[b].........	102.4	88.0	71.0	48.9[c]
Transportation expense....	100.5	89.3	74.6	54.8[d]
Maintenance of way and structures.............	102.1	84.2	63.3	42.2[d]
Maintenance of equipment.	103.1	87.4	70.0	53.0[d]

[a] Annual *Statistics of Railways in the United States.*
[b] Equated traffic units; one passenger mile considered equivalent to three revenue freight ton miles.
[c] Based on figures for first eleven months of the year.
[d] Based on preliminary figures.

in part a mere deferment of expenditures which must be made up later. The extent of the deferment may be gauged roughly by comparing the decline in maintenance with that in cost of conducting transportation. The table given above shows that, although in each year of the depression the cut in maintenance expenditures has been greater than that in the cost incurred directly in transportation service, the major part of the decrease in maintenance is a reflection of the decline in the volume of work done. Some saving has also resulted from an impairment in the quality of service rendered, such as the lowering of standards of cleanliness of stations and cars.

A third saving has been the fall in prices of goods which are bought by the railways. The most important item here is the cost of fuel. The average price of bitu-minous coal for locomotives fell from $2.53 a ton in 1928 to $2.40 in 1929, $2.30 in 1930, $2.20 in 1931, and $2.10 for the first eight months of 1932.[7] This, however, is part of a steady decrease which has been going on ever since the war. Fuel oil shows a sharper decrease, from 2.5 cents a gallon in 1928 to 1.78 cents in 1931 and 1.55 cents in the first eight months of 1932.

Lumber and ties declined in price much more than did most commodities. The West Coast Lumbermen's Asso-ciation composite price of 110 railroad items fell from 21.75 cents in 1929 to 12.23 cents in October 1931. Car lining which cost $25 in 1930 sold for $19 in 1931. Port-land cement, which sold for $1.87 a barrel in 1929, aver-aged $1.75 in 1930 and $1.44 in 1931. Copper, tin, zinc, and lead also declined sharply in price, and this change was reflected in prices paid for copper wire, brass castings, and other supplies made from non-ferrous metals.[8]

Steel, however, the most important railway material after fuel, was much less responsive to the downward trend of prices. The price of $43 for steel rails which was established in 1923 was not changed until November 1932. Miscellaneous maintenance-of-way materials, such as tie plates, bolts, spikes, and tools, were from 3 to 10 per cent cheaper in 1931 than in 1930, the 1930 prices having been but little lower than those of 1929. Car and locomotive materials also declined but little in price.[9]

By far the largest item of expense of the roads, how-ever, is wages, and wage rates of railway labor have

[7] 1932 figure for Class I roads only.
[8] *Railway Age.* Jan. 2, 1932, pp. 35-38.
[9] The same, p. 37.

shown even more resistance to the liquidating tendency than have the rates charged by the railroads. There was no general decrease in railway wage rates until 1932, though there were numerous reductions in rank and some cuts in the pay of unorganized employees. In February 1932 there was a general wage decrease of 10 per cent, limited to a one-year period.

Because of the decreasing number of employees, total compensation fell 12 per cent from 1929 to 1930 and 18 per cent more from 1930 to 1931. The average rate of compensation of employees, however, actually rose during 1930 and 1931, as the following table shows:

COMPENSATION OF EMPLOYEES OF CLASS I RAILWAYS, 1928–31[a]

Year	Average Rate		Total Compensation (Millions of Dollars)
	Hourly Basis (Cents)	Daily Basis[b] (Dollars)	
1928.............	62.5	8.26	2,826
1929.............	63.6	8.40	2,896
1930.............	64.4	8.53	2,551
1931.............	65.1	8.56	2,095

[a] Annual *Statistics of Railways in the United States*, 1930.
[b] Employment on "daily basis" includes executive and other salaried officials. About 15 per cent of the total is accounted for by compensation of employees who are paid on this basis.

The averages are affected by changes in the proportion of employees in the different pay groups as well as by changes in rates of compensation.

The current depression affords an illustration of the well-known tendency for revenues to shrink more rapidly than expenses in a period of declining business.[11] The operating ratio, which had fallen from 72.6 in 1928 to 71.8 in 1929 (the lowest figure since 1917), rose to

[11] Compare Chapter IV.

74.6 in 1930 and to 77.0 in 1931.[12] The striking thing about these figures, however, is that the increase is so small. The operating ratio for 1931 was actually lower than that for any year from 1920 through 1923, and was only a trifle higher than the ratio for 1924. The railroads have in fact succeeded in reducing their operating expenses almost as fast as their volume of business has fallen.[13]

IV. DISBURSEMENTS

The elasticity of the operating costs is in striking contrast to the rigidity of the taxes and fixed charges. Tax accruals of Class I roads fell only from 389 million dollars in 1929 to 348 million in 1930 and 304 million in 1931.[14] But the total "deductions from income" (chiefly interest and rentals) were 923 million dollars in 1928 and 925 million in 1931. The balance after fixed charges was as follows (in millions of dollars):

1928	787
1929	897
1930	524
1931	136

Thus, while the net income available for stockholders and creditors went down by only 40 per cent, the fixed charges rose by a fraction of 1 per cent, and the balance after interest and other fixed charges which was available for reserves, dividends, and additions to property shrank

[12] For the first half of 1932 the ratio was 79.97 (Class I roads only) as compared with 78.48 in the first half of 1931. The ratio is normally higher in the first half of the year than in the second.

[13] Operating revenues fell from 1928 to 1931 by 33 per cent, and total operating expenses by 28 per cent.

[14] The decline was almost entirely accounted for by federal income tax. State and local taxes were 301 million dollars in 1928 and 293 million in 1931.

by nearly 80 per cent. At this writing it appears certain that the 1932 earnings will fall far short of the fixed charges.

The shrinkage in the income available for the holders of railway securities as a group is greater than in some in-

NET PROFITS OF REPRESENTATIVE INDUSTRIES, 1928–1931[a]

Group	Number of Companies	Index Numbers			
		1928	1929	1930	1931
Tobacco...............	17	100.0	106.7	114.6	113.5
Telephone[b]...............	104	100.0	109.9	107.1	107.5
Other public utilities[c].......	63	100.0	108.7	103.3	89.5
Food products............	74	100.0	113.8	105.4	75.5
Chemicals and drugs........	26	100.0	120.2	100.9	75.2
Stores..................	37	100.0	102.5	62.1	50.9
Railroads[b]...............	171	100.0	106.8	74.1	44.5
Chemical equipment........	23	100.0	131.0	84.1	41.6
Mining and smelting........	23	100.0	47.8	48.7	19.5
Automobiles, parts, and accessories.................	67	100.0	90.9	38.9	15.0
Railroad equipment........	18	100.0	136.7	95.9	2.0
Clothing and textiles........	62	100.0	74.6	−7.5	1.5
Machinery...............	41	100.0	124.6	73.8	−6.6
Steel..................	27	100.0	162.6	72.1	−8.1
Oil....................	39	100.0	128.2	57.6	−16.8
Copper, coal and coke.......	30	100.0	1083.3	133.3	−250.0
Others..................	235	100.0	123.9	67.8	25.9
Total..................	719	100.0	118.3	67.0	26.2

[a] Computed from data in Federal Reserve Bank of New York, *Monthly Review of Credit and Business Conditions*, Apr. 1, 1932, p. 29. Negative items represent deficits.
[b] Net operating income.
[c] Net earnings.

dustries but much less than in others. Comparative data are given in the table above, which lists the industries in the order of their respective showings in 1931 as compared with 1928.

Though the showing of the railroads compares not unfavorably with that of other industries the fixed charges of the railroads are so heavy that the stockholders' share in the net income has almost disappeared. From 9.92 earned on the par value of railroad stock in 1929, the banner post-war year, the figure dropped to 5.77 in 1930 and 1.69 in 1931.

Railway finances were in so strong a condition at the beginning of the depression that the precipitate decline of income reflected itself only slowly in disbursements to security holders. Both dividend and interest payments held up to pre-depression figures through 1930, and it was not until late in 1931 that serious concern was felt as to the ability of most roads to take care of their fixed charges. During the last half of 1931 and in 1932, however, only extensive emergency relief, extended through the Railroad Credit Corporation and the Reconstruction Finance Corporation, prevented an epidemic of receiverships. Dividend declarations of all railways have ranged as follows (in millions of dollars):[15]

Year	From Current Income	From Surplus	Total
1928	300	219	519
1929	316	260	576
1930	225	392	617
1931	128	282	410

Data for 1932 have been compiled only for Class I roads, and for the first eleven months of the year. Dividends for this period amounted to 81 million dollars, as compared with 291 million for the same roads in 1931.

[15] These figures include Class I, II, and III railways, their non-operating subsidiaries and switching and terminal companies. Dividends received by one railway from another are included in these totals as well as stock dividends.

If inter-corporate payments are eliminated, dividends (in millions) are as follows: 1928, $402; 1929, $441; 1930, $492; 1931, $311.

V. INVESTMENT

The depression reflected itself in a pronounced shrinkage in the volume of new investment made by the railroads, both in roadbed and structures and in equipment. The investment in additions and betterments, to be sure, did not decline until 1931, the total for Class I and Class II railways being 543 million in 1929; 596 million in 1930; and 137 million in 1931. In part the high figure

RAILWAY EQUIPMENT BUILT AND ORDERED, 1928–31[a]

Equipment	1928	1929	1930	1931
Locomotives:				
Built................	636	926	972	181
Ordered..............	603	1,212	440	235
Passenger Cars:				
Built................	1,356	1,254	1,264	198
Ordered..............	1,930	2,303	667	11
Freight Cars:				
Built................	46,060	82,240	75,188	13,205
Ordered..............	51,200	111,218	46,360	10,880

[a] *Railway Age*, Jan. 2, 1932, pp. 42–43, 46, 48. Data for equipment cover only equipment for service in the United States; data on orders include foreign.

for 1930 is presumably due to the efforts of the railways to co-operate in the Administration's plan of deliberate maintenance of employment which was promulgated early in 1930. Chiefly, however, it is due to the continuance into 1930 of projects which were begun before the stock market crash and to the delivery of equipment materials ordered before that time. This is clear from a comparison of the installations of locomotives and cars with the new orders.

The following table indicates the extent of the shrinkage in the roads' use of rails and ties:

TIES AND RAILS LAID BY CLASS I RAILWAYS, 1928–31[a]

Year	Rails (In thousands of tons)		Ties (In thousands)
	New	Second-Hand	
1928............	2,147	2,029	84,585
1929............	2,037	1,982	81,964
1930............	1,592	1,410	69,325
1931............	1,030	849	54,449

[a] In replacement and in additional tracks in lines and extensions. From annual *Statistics of Railways in the United States.*

VI. PLACE OF THE RAILWAYS IN THE DEPRESSION

It is obvious that the present condition of the railways is at the same time a result of the depression and an important contributing cause of its continued severity. The present financial difficulties of the railroad industry are primarily a direct result of the shrinkage of traffic, as is clear from the abruptness with which the trend lines of traffic and of income turn down at the end of 1929. On the other hand, the railroads make up so large a fraction of the economic life of the country that their failure to maintain their customary rate of disbursements to their owners, their employees, and those from whom they buy, constitutes of itself a depressive factor of no small magnitude. True, the railroads employed (according to the Census of 1930) only 3.1 per cent of the persons gainfully employed in the country. But in 1929 they disbursed 11.6 per cent of the total interest and 5.3 per cent of the total dividends paid in the United States, and in the same year paid 7.2 per cent of the total federal corporate income tax.[16] They bought 18.4 per cent of the tonnage of finished steel produced, and used 20.3 per cent of the bituminous coal that was mined.

[16] Comparisons based upon data from Fifteenth Census, 1930; Statistics of Income 1929; and Census of Manufactures 1929.

The funded debt of the railroads is in very large part held by the financial and fiduciary institutions through which the savings of the mass of the population are invested. United States life insurance companies have more than three billion dollars invested in railroad bonds; mutual savings banks hold another billion; and other banks, insurance companies, and public service institutions have between two and three billion more.[17]

Thus the railroads' financial prosperity is intricately bound up with the prosperity of every element of the population. While it can not be said that the railroads have suffered a greater shrinkage of business than have other equally important lines of industry,[18] it is clear that the continuance of their present financial distress would be disastrous not only to their owners and employees, but also to the whole community.

Declining revenues since 1929 and the difficulties which railroads have experienced in obtaining funds either through short-term borrowing from commercial banks or the flotation of securities have made them dependent upon emergency credit institutions for their requirements in 1932. The Railroad Credit Corporation, which was organized at the close of 1931 to administer the proceeds obtained from the special freight rate increases authorized by the Interstate Commerce Commission, and the Reconstruction Finance Corporation, organized in January 1932, have assumed primary responsibility for financing railroad requirements. The scope of operations of these two institutions and the restrictions under which they operate are sufficiently different to necessitate a separate discussion of their activities.

[17] For details compare Chapter XII.
[18] Compare above, pages 50, 62.

1. Railroad Credit Corporation. Loans are made by the Railroad Credit Corporation solely for the purpose of preventing defaults by railroads in their fixed interest obligations. The loan resources of the Corporation are derived entirely from the pooled receipts arising from the increased tariffs on designated commodities which became effective in January 1932 and will lapse March 31, 1933, unless extended by later action of the Interstate Commerce Commission. The Credit Corporation is not authorized to make loans after May 31, 1933.

A participating carrier which is not in receivership or in default of its obligation, and which derives 50 per cent of its revenues from freight transportation is eligible for a loan to meet interest obligations, provided (a) such a loan will enable it to avoid default, and (b) its obligations cannot be met from other resources. The Railroad Credit Corporation is entitled to take the best available collateral to secure its advances, but cannot reject a loan merely on the ground of inadequate security. Consequently, participating carriers which cannot furnish security adequate to qualify them for loans from other sources may obtain loans from the Credit Corporation.

Loans from the Credit Corporation have been below the amounts which were anticipated because the revenues from the increased freight rates have fallen below the amount estimated. The report of operations up to December 31, 1932 shows that applications have been received from 57 railroads, aggregating $105,990,000. Loans amounting to $48,325,000 have been approved, while more than $55,000,000 were rejected because funds could be provided from other sources, or because the applicants were otherwise ineligible.

Loans from the Railroad Credit Corporation bear interest at a rate corresponding to the discount rate of the Federal Reserve Bank of New York. Until June 23, 1932 the rate was 3 per cent, but since that date it has been 2½ per cent. Since these rates are far below the charges on loans from other sources, participating carriers prefer to borrow from the Credit Corporation for their interest payments whenever possible.

2. *The Reconstruction Finance Corporation.* This agency is a much more important source of emergency funds. The Reconstruction Finance Corporation not only has larger resources but it can make advances for a larger variety of purposes, including the payment of taxes and the financing of repairs or construction projects. The Finance Corporation, however, can make advances only if the loans are "adequately secured." All the Corporation's loans to railroads must be approved by the Interstate Commerce Commission, but a loan approved by the Commission may be refused by the Corporation or approved for a reduced amount. The law does not define "adequate security," but the Corporation and the Commission have interpreted the term to mean that collateral must be available; potential earnings are not regarded as satisfactory security.

The railroads are second only to banks in the volume of borrowings from the Reconstruction Finance Corporation. Loans authorized under Section 5 of the Act[19] amounted to $1,554,500,000 on December 31, 1932, of which amount $337,200,000, or 21.7 per cent, was for railroads, while $897,000,000, or 57.7 per cent, went to

---

[19] Under Section 5 loans are authorized for banks and trust companies, insurance companies, building and loan associations, mortgage banks, federal and joint stock land banks, livestock and agricultural credit corporations, and credit unions. Loans under this section of the Act comprised 86.6 per cent of the total amount disbursed up to Dec. 31, 1932.

banks and trust companies. Of the total balances out-standing at the close of the year, railroads are responsible for 24.1 per cent and banks for 52.7 per cent. Re-payments of railroad loans have amounted to only $11,800,000. Most of these repayments resulted from loans obtained from the Railroad Credit Corporation, although in a few instances provision was made for re-payments from income from non-operating sources.

The amount of the advances to railroads authorized by the Reconstruction Finance Corporation up to December 31, 1932, and the purpose for which the proceeds have been used are shown in the following table:

Purpose	Amount Authorized (In thousands)	Percentage of Total
Maturing funded debt	$102,724.3	30.5
Loans from banks	37,793.9	11.2
Other loans	16,162.7	4.8
Interest on funded debt	73,960.4	21.9
Taxes	19,624.8	5.8
Construction and repairs	61,495.5	18.2
Past-due vouchers for wages, materials, etc.	20,188.0	6.0
Miscellaneous	5,485.5	1.6
Total	$337,435.1	100.0

Up to December 31, 1932, loans had been made to 62 railroads, but 12 roads accounted for 75.1 per cent of the total. Comparatively few of the small roads are able to qualify for loans from the Reconstruction Finance Cor-poration, most of their applications being denied on the ground that the security is inadequate.

It is difficult to state precisely the volume of loans re-jected because rejected applications are sometimes resubmitted and approved if additional collateral is offered or the amount reduced. To January 31, 1933, applications amounting to $11,000,000, affecting 31 roads, had been denied by the Interstate Commerce Commission,[20] and applications aggregating $16,000,000 had been withdrawn without formal action. With few exceptions the roads involved are small struggling roads whose difficulties are only in part the result of the present depression. Some of the larger roads whose earnings are normally satisfactory are also unable to secure loans as needed because of the lack of available *collateral* security.

Bond maturities for 1933 aggregate $199,000,000, of which $68,500,000 (to February 1) had already been provided for through loans from the Reconstruction Finance Corporation. The demands upon the emergency institutions in 1933 to finance construction work, to meet maturities, and to cover deficits will perhaps range from $300,000,000 to $350,000,000. Applications pending as of January 31, 1933 amounted to more than $65,000,000, a figure which exceeds the approvals in any month except May 1932. Until the volume of traffic increases and commercial banks are once more willing to finance the roads for their current requirements, and until the bond market improves, the railroads will continue to be almost entirely dependent upon emergency credit institutions.

[20] These data were obtained from the Commission and include denials that were made by letter, as well as those acted upon formally.

PART II
FACTORS AFFECTING RAILWAY
NET INCOME

INTRODUCTORY STATEMENT

In this division of our study we shall analyze the factors which are primarily responsible for the volume of fluctuations in the net operating income of railroads. If one is to have any accurate gauge of the relative importance of the various elements which enter into railroad operating costs on the one hand and railroad income on the other, he must have before him the facts as to the relative magnitude of various factors affecting income and as to the trends over a period of years. In general, our analysis in this division will begin with 1910, but detailed attention will be given to the trends in recent years. We shall not attempt in this section of the study to arrive at final recommendations as to policy. For the moment we are concerned only with revealing the facts.

CHAPTER IV

VOLUME OF TRAFFIC

Among the factors which cause the earnings and expenses of railroads to fluctuate the most obvious, and the most important, is the volume of traffic. We shall therefore undertake in this chapter an intensive study of the relation of both freight and passenger traffic to the net income of railroads. In the following chapter we give special consideration to the forces that have been responsible for the persistent decline in the volume of passenger traffic. The factors affecting the volume of freight traffic are discussed in other divisions of this study.

The railroads derive over three-quarters of their operating revenue from freight service. In 1928, for instance, this service contributed 76.8 per cent, and passenger service 14.6 per cent. The remaining 8.6 per cent was derived from various sources like the transportation of mail and milk, express service, switching service, storage, demurrage, etc. In the table on the opposite page freight and passenger earnings, expressed as percentages of total operating revenue, are shown for selected years. The diminishing importance of the passenger service is clearly brought out.

There is a close correlation between the volume of traffic and gross revenue. The factors affecting the gross receipts from freight service in any given year are the number of tons carried, the length of haul, the character of traffic, and the level of charges. Of these the volume of traffic is the most important, because it fluctuates more widely than the other factors. From 1900 to 1931, in no

FREIGHT AND PASSENGER EARNINGS AS PERCENTAGES OF
TOTAL OPERATING REVENUE[a]

Year	Freight Earnings[b]	Passenger Earnings[b]
1910	68.5	22.4
1915	68.9	21.9
1920	70.1	20.7
1921	71.1	20.7
1922	72.0	19.2
1923	73.4	18.1
1924	73.4	18.0
1925	74.4	17.0
1926	75.4	16.1
1927	75.7	15.7
1928	76.8	14.6
1929	76.9	13.7
1930	77.4	13.6
1931	77.8	13.0

[a] Computed from data in *Statistics of Railways in the United States*, Interstate Commerce Commission, 1931, p. S-99.

[b] Since a certain percentage of the total operating revenue is derived from services which are not included in either passenger or freight services, the two percentages for any year do not add to 100.

year did the average length of haul vary from the preceding year by more than 10 per cent. The changes in the character of traffic from year to year, too, have been relatively small.[1] Changes in the level of charges,[2] though more pronounced than changes in the character

[1] Over a period of 16 years (1916-31), the shipments of different groups of commodities, expressed as percentages of all tonnage originated, varied within the following limits:

	High	Low
Agriculture products	12.1	8.3
Animal products and by-products	3.2	1.9
Mine products	58.2	52.1
Forest products	9.1	4.8
Manufactures and miscellaneous	24.7	17.9
Less-than-carload traffic	4.7	2.5

[2] Charges, be it noted, are more inclusive than rates. They include not only rates on freight, but charges for lighterage, freight elevation, transportation of caretakers of freight shipments, and many other miscellaneous services.

of traffic, have always been less marked from one year to another than fluctuations in the volume of traffic. Between 1910 and 1931, in only two years (1918 and 1921) did average receipts per ton mile show a variation of over 20 per cent from the preceding year. Over a long range of years, the cumulative effect of gradual increases in charges may be very substantial, but so far as year-to-year fluctuations are concerned, all the factors except volume of traffic have remained relatively constant.

Volume of traffic as measured by the number of ton miles, on the other hand, shows consistently a very wide margin of fluctuation from year to year. From 1911 to 1931, in only seven years were changes less than 5 per cent over or under the preceding year. We may conclude, then, that within short periods the volume of traffic is vastly more important than the other factors in affecting gross freight revenues.

In the passenger service, gross revenue is affected by the number of passenger miles, the level of fares and other charges, and the proportion of different classes of passengers to the total. As in the case of freight service, the volume of traffic fluctuates more widely from year to year than the other factors affecting gross passenger revenue, and we find as a result that passenger earnings correlate closely with the volume of traffic and show no discernible correlation with the other factors.

How closely freight and passenger revenues fluctuate in sympathy with their respective volumes is shown in the chart on the opposite page.

Besides the freight and passenger services proper, the railroads perform various other services from which they derive revenues. Some of these revenues vary with the volume of freight traffic, some with passenger traffic, and some with neither freight nor passenger traffic. Revenues from switching services, as might be expected, move in sympathy with variations in ton mileage. On the other hand, revenues from special trains, water transpor-

RELATION OF VOLUME OF TRAFFIC TO FREIGHT
AND PASSENGER REVENUES, 1920-31
(CLASS I RAILROADS)

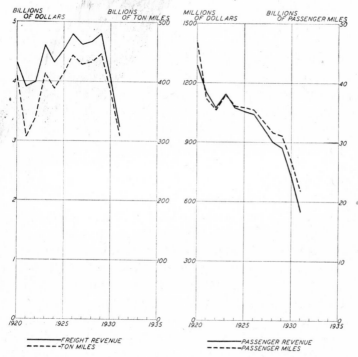

tation and water transfers, freight storage, grain elevators, stockyards, and demurrage show little or no relation to fluctuations in ton mileage. Among services connected with passenger transportation, revenues from sleeping cars, parlor and chair cars, hotel and restaurant service, and parcel room and baggage storage show a more or less consistent decline since 1923 in sympathy with the general shrinkage in the volume of passenger traffic. The decline in milk traffic, which is equally consistent, must be attributed to the effect of highway competition. Mail and express revenues show no downward trend.

Since all these sources of revenue which do not follow the course of the volume of either freight or passenger traffic constitute but a small portion of the operating revenues, it may be concluded that the aggregate operating revenues fluctuate in close sympathy with the variations in ton and passenger miles.

Having examined the relation between volume of traffic and earnings, we turn to a study of the effect of changes in the volume of traffic on operating expenses.

When volume of traffic decreases, operating expense per unit increases. The railroad industry is one which sells service. Unlike many classes of commodities, services cannot be produced in slack seasons and stored away to meet the demand in busy seasons. Railroads, in common with other industries which produce services, are built to accommodate demand at its peak. The same number of miles of roadway must be maintained in good condition whether ten or twenty trains are hauled over it every day. Again, rails and some equipment depreciate even though little used. Besides these physical factors inherent in railroad business, the carriers are hampered by conditions imposed upon them by the public. Branch-line services, for instance, must often be continued in spite of net operating loss. In the case of freight service, the inability of railroads to reduce the number of trains in accordance with the decline in traffic is clearly shown by the following table, in which the density of daily traffic (net ton miles per mile of road per day) and the net ton miles per train mile are shown for the first eight months of each year from 1927 to 1932:[3]

Year	Density of Daily Traffic	Net Tons per Train
1927	5,463	778
1928	5,243	778
1929	5,590	802
1930	4,889	786
1931	4,016	740
1932	2,857	649

In terms of operating expenses, the relation between the density of all traffic and unit cost is shown in a striking fashion in the chart on page 80. Operating expenses per equated traffic unit of 25 Class I carriers in the Eastern district are plotted against the density of traffic as measured by the number of equated traffic units per mile of road. The tendency, as the density of traffic increases, for the operating expenses per unit of equated traffic to fall until a certain minimum is reached is revealed in an unmistakable manner.

This tendency of unit cost to vary inversely with the volume of traffic is further illustrated by the fluctuations in the operating ratio during recent years. In the table on page 81, operating ratio and ton mileage on Class I roads for the first eight months of the year are given for the period from 1927 to 1932. It will be noted that every increase in volume of traffic was accompanied by a betterment in the ratio, and every fall by a rise in the ratio.[4]

[3] Data are from *Annual Report of the Interstate Commerce Commission*, 1932, p. 84.
[4] Compiled from the same, 1928, 1930, and 1932.

RELATIONSHIP BETWEEN TRAFFIC DENSITY AND UNIT
OPERATING COSTS, 1930[a]

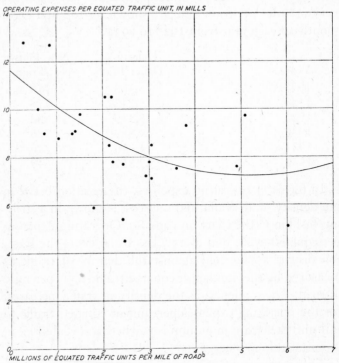

OPERATING EXPENSES PER EQUATED TRAFFIC UNIT, IN MILLS

MILLIONS OF EQUATED TRAFFIC UNITS PER MILE OF ROAD[b]

[a] Basic data are from *Statistics of Railways in the United States*, Interstate Commerce Commission, 1930. Data relate to 25 Class I carriers in the New England, Great Lakes, and Central Eastern regions. Roads with operating mileages of less than 100 or with average hauls of less than 50 miles have been eliminated to minimize the disturbing effect of terminal costs per mile of road. Roads whose traffic in products of mines was either less than 35 per cent or more than 90 per cent of their total traffic were eliminated to lessen the effect on cost arising from the different character of traffic. For the same reason, roads whose passenger revenue was more than 33 1/3 per cent of freight revenue, or whose passenger mileage was more than 10 per cent of ton mileage, were eliminated. The equation for the curve is $y = 11.6583 - 1.7074x + 0.1634x^2$.

[b] A combination of passenger miles and ton miles, with a weight of three given to passenger miles and of one to ton miles.

Year	Billions of Ton Miles	Operating Ratio (Per cent)
1927	314	75.48
1928	306	74.60
1929	325	72.02
1930	285	75.62
1931	234	77.40
1932	167	79.51

In view of the behavior of unit cost as shown in the chart on page 80, it is remarkable that the operating ratio has not risen more than it has in the depression period. The extent to which unit cost rises when traffic falls, as revealed in the chart, confirms the observation made in the preceding chapter that the ability displayed by carriers to keep down their operating ratios in the present depression must represent a considerable degree of deferment of maintenance expenses.

The inverse correlation between unit cost and density of traffic becomes more marked when fixed charges are included in cost. As the name indicates, these charges do not vary greatly from year to year. The chart on page 82 brings out clearly the relative constancy of such charges. Expenditures for the maintenance of way, structures, and equipment, and the total operating expenses on the whole vary closely with the operating revenues, but fixed charges remain substantially the same even in the face of marked decreases in the other items.

Since fixed charges remain relatively constant, it follows as an arithmetic truism that cost (including fixed charges) per unit falls when density of traffic increases, and rises when traffic decreases. This axiom is brought out in a striking manner in the chart on page 83, where equated units of traffic and cost (including fixed charges)

RELATIVE CONSTANCY OF FIXED COSTS IN COMPARISON
WITH OTHER COSTS, 1921-31[a]

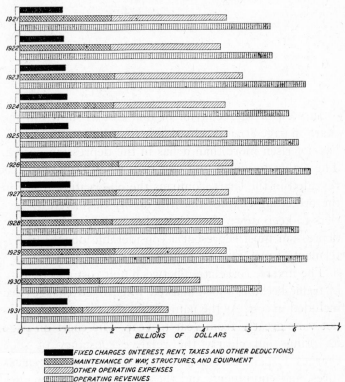

FIXED CHARGES (INTEREST, RENT, TAXES AND OTHER DEDUCTIONS)
MAINTENANCE OF WAY, STRUCTURES, AND EQUIPMENT
OTHER OPERATING EXPENSES
OPERATING REVENUES

[a] Data are from *Annual Report of the Interstate Commerce Commission*, 1932, p. 133.

per equated traffic unit on Class I roads are plotted for each of the years from 1921 to 1931. The inverse correlation is unmistakable: unit cost varies inversely with volume of traffic.

When unit cost (including fixed charges) varies inversely with density of traffic, it follows that the financial condition of the railroads must similarly vary with traf-

RELATION BETWEEN DENSITY OF TRAFFIC AND
UNIT COST, 1921-31
(CLASS I RAILROADS)

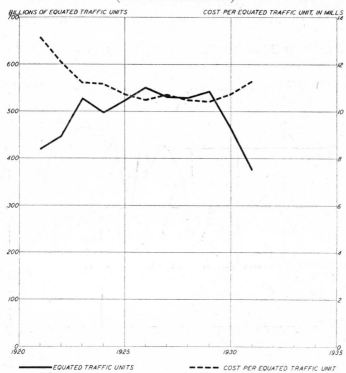

BILLIONS OF EQUATED TRAFFIC UNITS   COST PER EQUATED TRAFFIC UNIT, IN MILLS

——— EQUATED TRAFFIC UNITS   - - - - COST PER EQUATED TRAFFIC UNIT

fic. In a preceding chapter, we gave the ratio of net income plus interest to investment as indicating the relative
fluctuations from year to year in the financial condition
of the railroads.[5] This ratio for the years from 1900 to
1931 is reproduced in the chart on the following page,
where it can be compared with the volume of traffic. It is
evident that the secular or long-time trend in the growth

[5] See Chapter II.

of freight traffic does not affect the return on investment. The fact, for instance, that the number of ton miles in 1929 was about twice that in 1906 did not mean that returns on investment in 1929 were larger than in 1906.

RELATION BETWEEN VOLUME OF TRAFFIC AND RATIO OF NET INCOME PLUS INTEREST TO INVESTMENT, 1900-31[a]

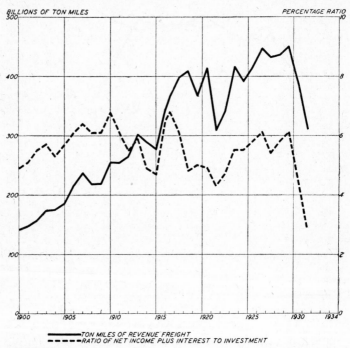

TON MILES OF REVENUE FREIGHT
RATIO OF NET INCOME PLUS INTEREST TO INVESTMENT

[a] Beginning with the year 1916 the data change from a fiscal to a calendar year basis.

Short-time fluctuations in ton mileage, however, are sharply reflected in the year-to-year variations in the return on investment.

While it is impossible to determine over a period of

years the precise extent to which the volume of traffic affects net income, it is evident from our analysis that it is much the most important factor in the fluctuations in income during short periods. In 1930, for example, the decline in net income is almost entirely attributable to the decrease in traffic, for other factors had remained practically unchanged. In 1931 deferred maintenance charges became important, and in 1932 changes in wages and in rates also affected the net income. The decline of traffic, however, continued to be the most important single factor affecting the income of the roads.

CHAPTER V

THE DECLINE OF PASSENGER BUSINESS

The passenger business on our railroads has been declining at a startling rate in recent years. Since some of the factors which affect the passenger traffic are not common to freight service, the passenger problem merits a separate study. This chapter undertakes to analyze the extent of the decline in the passenger business, and the reasons why the cost of conducting passenger service has not declined proportionally. The possibilities of improving passenger service and passenger income are not considered here.

I. THE INCREASING UNPROFITABLENESS OF PASSENGER SERVICE

The railroads of this country are primarily freight carriers. On many roads the passenger business has always been regarded as an unprofitable service. The contrast with other leading countries is striking. In 1928, for example, railways in the United States received about 14 per cent of their total revenue from passenger traffic as compared with 37 per cent in Great Britain; 28 per cent in Germany; and about 60 per cent in Japan. In Japan the entire population averaged 16 train rides in 1928, while in the United States the average was but six rides per capita. On 250,000 miles of railway in the United States, 798,476,114 passengers were carried in 1928, while in Japan on 12,198 miles 1,213,578,000 passengers were carried. In the same year Great Britain's 20,388 miles of railway carried 1,666,384,976 passengers. These figures in all cases include the commuting traffic of the great metropolitan centers.

86

Within the last decade, the passenger service in this country has become more and more unprofitable. In 1910, the passenger mileage amounted to 32,338,000,000 and till 1920 it steadily increased, a peak of over 47,000,000,000 being reached in that year. Since then, with the exception of a slight recovery in 1923, the volume of passenger traffic has been consistently declining. In terms of the number of trips per person, the passenger traffic has taken the same general trend, the peak coming in 1920. Since 1920, however, the number of trips per capita has shown a sharper decline than the number of passenger miles. The explanation of this discrepancy lies in the increase in the average length of journey, as is shown in the second table on page 91.

As the number of passenger miles has been declining since 1920, the analysis in the preceding chapter leads us to expect a steady rise since 1920 in the expenses per passenger mile. The extent to which this increase in unit cost has taken place is shown in the table on the next page, where operating expenses assignable to passenger service are reduced to a per passenger-mile basis, and compared with the volume of passenger traffic. In this and other tables data are given for Class I railways only.

The inverse correlation between the passenger mileage and unit expenses shown in the table is remarkable. In 1923 traffic increased, and expenses per unit declined. From then on, there was a steady decline in traffic and an equally consistent rise in the unit expenses. In other words, the passenger service has become progressively more costly.

The way in which the various items of operating expenses are apportioned to the passenger service is in some cases quite arbitrary. And what the effect of an apportionment of the fixed charges would be is problematical. It must be remembered also that the situation varies widely from road to road. In 1931, for example, the Virginian derived but 1 per cent of its operating revenues from passenger service, and the operating ratio of this service was 315.9, while on the New Haven, the passenger service contributed 34.3 per cent of the rev-

PASSENGER-MILEAGE, OPERATING EXPENSES, AND OPERATING RATIO
1922–1931

Year	Passenger-Miles (millions)	Operating Expenses per Passenger-Mile (cents)	Operating Ratio (Per Cent)
1922	35,470	3.341	83.8
1923	37,957	3.222	82.2
1924	36,091	3.294	83.2
1925	35,950	3.309	83.5
1926	35,478	3.403	85.1
1927	33,650	3.581	89.7
1928	31,601	3.696	91.7
1929	31,074	3.767	90.1
1930	26,815	4.022	101.2
1931	21,894	4.194	110.8

enues, and had an operating ratio of 73.3[1] But taking the country's railroads as a whole, there can be no doubt that the passenger service has become increasingly unprofitable.

II. ANALYSIS OF THE DECLINE IN THE VOLUME OF PASSENGER TRAFFIC

The discussion of the declining passenger traffic and the consequent decrease in the profits from such traffic leads to further inquiries. How far is the private automobile responsible for this decline, and have the decreases

[1] See Interstate Commerce Commission, *Comparative Statement of Operating Averages*, 1931.

been uniform in the different sections of the country and in the different classes of traffic?

It is obvious that the decline in railroad travel has not been the result of lessened desire on the part of the public to travel. And since aerial and water travel are negligible factors, there can be no doubt that the main cause of the decline in the rail traffic has been the automobile. It has been estimated that the private automobile is responsible for from 70 to 80 per cent of the traffic diverted to highways from the steam railroads. From 1926 to 1930 the number of passenger miles on motor buses operating between cities increased by 2.7 billions.[2] During the same period the railroads lost 8.6 billion passenger miles. Since a part of the increase in bus travel must represent a class of traffic which would not have moved on the railroads in the absence of the bus, not all of the 2.7 billion increase in bus travel can be regarded as diversion from railroads. As 2.7 is 31.4 per cent of 8.6, we come to the conclusion that, roughly speaking, the bus cannot account for more than 30 per cent of the loss suffered by railroads. The Interstate Commerce Commission comes to substantially the same conclusion.[3]

The degree to which the various classes of railroad passenger traffic have been affected by highway competition is shown in the tables on page 90.

It will be seen that in commutation traffic there was a steady though small increase from 1922 to 1929. Pullman travel shows a similar increase. In 1930 and 1931 both have decreased, as a result undoubtedly of the depression. Traffic other than commutation and Pullman

[2] *Facts and Figures of the Automobile Industry,* 1932, p. 62.
[3] *Co-ordination of Motor Transportation,* 182 I.C.C. 263, 313 (1932).

has shown a consistent decline, the rate of decrease becoming especially marked in 1930 and 1931. Eliminating the effect of the depression, it is at once evident that day-coach travel is the class which has suffered most from motor competition.

COMMUTATION, PULLMAN, AND OTHER PASSENGER TRAFFIC, 1922–1931
(In millions of passenger miles)

Year	Commutation[a]	Pullman[b]	All Other
1922	6,132	11,245	18,093
1923	6,401	12,982	18,574
1924	6,407	13,083	16,601
1925	6,592	14,017	15,341
1926	6,605	14,407	14,465
1927	6,650	14,097	12,903
1928	6,626	13,938	11,038
1929	6,898	14,059	10,117
1930	6,669	12,515	7,630
1931	6,018	9,892	5,989

[a] Interstate Commerce Commission, *Statistics of Railways in the United States*, 1931.
[b] Released by the Pullman Company.

The carriers in the West and South show greater decline in passenger traffic than do Eastern railroads. In the following table passenger mileages for 1931 in the various regions, exclusive of commutation traffic, are given as percentages of those for 1926:

Region	Per cent	Region	Per cent
Great Lakes	64.6	Northwestern	51.7
New England	62.8	Southwestern	46.0
Central Western	61.3	Pocahontas	44.8
Central Eastern	55.5	Southern	40.1

In 1931, the following roads among the Class I carriers had passenger-service operating ratios of less than 100. It is to be noted that most of the roads are those with large commutation traffic. Only two roads outside of the Eastern district are included in the list.

Railroad	Passenger-service Operating Ratio in 1931 Per cent
New York, Ontario, and Western	64.5
Long Island	69.0
New York, New Haven, and Hartford	73.3
Richmond, Fredericksburg, and Potomac	82.6
New York Central	82.9
Alton	93.7
Delaware, Lackawanna, and Western	93.9
Florida East Coast	95.2
New Jersey and New York	95.6
Staten Island Rapid Transit	97.0
Boston and Maine	97.2
Southern Pacific	97.3
Pennsylvania	97.4

Change in the average length of journey is also significant. As is shown in the accompanying table (in miles) the average journey, except in commutation traffic, has steadily increased. In other words, the proportion of long distance to short distance travel has increased.

Year	Commu- tation	Other Traffic	Year	Commu- tation	Other Traffic
1922	14.3	54.7	1927	14.9	70.3
1923	14.3	58.6	1928	15.0	71.9
1924	14.6	60.3	1929	15.1	75.2
1925	14.8	66.9	1930	15.2	76.0
1926	14.8	69.7	1931	15.6	76.0

Our analysis of traffic figures makes it clear that the falling off in the passenger business has been most pronounced in the case of short distance day-coach travel in the South, Southwest, and Northwest.

III. ANALYSIS OF THE OPERATION OF PASSENGER SERVICE

We have seen that the operating expenses assignable to passenger service reduced to a passenger-mile basis have shown a steady increase since 1923. Just where the carriers have been able to reduce expenses and where they have failed is shown by figures in the following table, where five major groups of operating expenses on Class I roads, allocated and apportioned to passenger service, are given for the period from 1923 to 1931:

OPERATING EXPENSES APPORTIONED TO PASSENGER AND ALLIED SERVICES
1923–1931
(In millions of dollars)

Year	Maintenance of Way and Structures	Maintenance of Equipment	Traffic	Rail Line Transportation	General
1923	214	323	36	570	37
1924	215	297	38	556	40
1925	220	292	42	548	42
1926	230	293	47	547	44
1927	231	287	48	546	45
1928	223	276	49	528	45
1929	226	276	51	521	45
1930	195	250	49	493	46
1931	151	210	42	434	45

It will be seen that all classes of expenses, with the single exception of those classed under "general" declined in the depression years 1930 and 1931. From 1923 to 1929, however, despite a decline in traffic, rail-line transportation and maintenance of equipment expenses are the only classes which showed decreases. The three other classes of expenses increased. The largest increase, that of $15,000,000, took place in "traffic" expenses. Most of this increase of $15,000,000 is accounted for by the increases in advertising and expenses for "outside agencies."[4] Advertising increased from $9,659,000 in 1923 to $17,720,000 in 1929, while the "outside agencies" account increased from $14,526,000 in 1923 to $19,767,000 in 1929, a combined increase of $13,302,000 from 1923 to 1929. How far such increased expenditures have been successful in preventing diversion to highways cannot be ascertained. To a very large extent, however, such expenses must have been competitive among the rail carriers themselves.

The railroads are often accused of operating excessively luxurious passenger trains in competition not with other modes of transportation but with other railroads. This criticism, while warranted in certain instances, is more plausible than it is true. It must be understood that the carriers are not in business to offer services with the benevolence of philanthropists. The expenses of operating seemingly luxurious trains are in most cases more than repaid by the revenues. In 1929, for instance, the New York Central collected 70 per cent, or about $2,500,000, of its extra-fare revenue, on the Twentieth Century Limited. And the operating cost in cents per dining car mile on Class I roads declined steadily from 1923 onward, as is shown below:

1923	26.49
1928	25.90
1929	25.96
1930	23.93
1931	21.82

[4] "Outside agencies," account No. 352 in Interstate Commerce Commission classification of accounts, include "the pay, and the office, traveling, and other expenses of general, commercial, city, and district agents and others soliciting traffic, the employees of their offices, and traveling agents and solicitors located on or off the line of the carrier's road." It also includes the rent, salary, and other expenses of city passenger ticket offices.

The cost of operating sleeping cars showed a more marked decline in spite of increases in Pullman car mileage, as follows:

1923	$1,033,000
1928	688,000
1929	646,000
1930	562,000
1931	387,000

While the figures above are operating costs and do not include capital expenditures, it is clear that the apparently luxurious services could not have been the main cause of the failure of the railroads to reduce expenses assigned to passenger service.[5]

Since the cost of operation varies more directly with the number of car miles than with the number of passenger miles,[6] to understand why the operating expenses assigned to passenger service have not been reduced in proportion to the decline in passenger mileage, we must turn to an examination of figures on car miles. In the table on page 95, the number of car miles for different classes of passenger cars are given for the years from 1923 to 1931. It will be seen that day-coach car mileage, given in the third column, is the only class that showed decline since 1923. The total car mileage increased from 1923 to 1929, dropping off only since the beginning of the depression in 1930. Leaving out traffic expenses,

[5] The figures on pp. 92-94 apply to Class I railroads only. The dining car mile costs are obtained by dividing the Interstate Commerce Commission account No. 441 by dining car miles. The cost of operating sleeping cars is account No. 403 in the Commission's classification.

[6] This is because it costs almost as much to haul a car with one passenger as it does to haul it with 50 passengers. Of course, if the traffic grows to very large proportions, new terminals, tracks, and other facilities become necessary, but within limits, cost does not vary with the number of passenger miles.

this increase in car mileage from 1923 to 1929 accounts for the failure of other expenses assigned to passenger service to come down in proportion to the decline in the number of passenger miles.

CAR MILEAGE OF DIFFERENT CLASSES OF CARS, 1923–1931[7]
(In millions)

Year	Sleeping, Parlor, and Observation Cars	Dining Cars	Passenger Cars	Other Passenger-Train Cars	Total
1923......	944	126	1,349	1,166	3,585
1924......	999	130	1,322	1,195	3,646
1925......	1,098	144	1,300	1,205	3,746
1926......	1,170	153	1,283	1,231	3,837
1927......	1,192	157	1,260	1,222	3,831
1928......	1,201	159	1,216	1,223	3,799
1929......	1,257	169	1,192	1,240	3,857
1930......	1,229	163	1,113	1,175	3,680
1931......	1,069	140	987	1,070	3,266

The increase in car mileage was due to the inability, or unwillingness for competitive reasons, of carriers to reduce the number of trains. In the table on page 96, the number of passengers per car and per train, and the number of cars per train are given for the years from 1923 to 1931.

While there was a slight increase in the *average* number of cars per train, this is of no great significance. It is explained not by a lengthening of trains but by the abandonment of many small local trains. The important fact is the decline of about one-third in the number of passengers per car and per train. A part of this decline is, however, attributable to an increase in the proportion of Pullman cars to coaches. During the period in question sleeping, parlor, and observation car miles increased from

[7] Interstate Commerce Commission, *Statistics of Railways in the United States*, 1931, p. S-46.

26.34 per cent of the total to 32.71 per cent, and dining cars from 3.52 per cent to 4.28. This also reflects the decline in local traffic.

Since it costs little more to haul several extra cars in a

PASSENGER TRAIN AND CAR PERFORMANCE IN PROPORTION TO TRAFFIC
1923–1931[8]

Year	Passengers per Car[a]	Cars per Train[b]	Passengers per Train[c]
1923	16.3	6.5	67
1924	15.3	6.6	63
1925	14.8	6.7	63
1926	14.3	6.9	61
1927	13.5	7.0	59
1928	12.9	6.8	56
1929	12.5	6.9	55
1930	11.3	6.8	49
1931	10.5	6.8	45

[a] Passenger miles per car mile.
[b] Passenger train car miles per train mile.
[c] Passenger miles per train mile.

train, the number of passengers per train is more important from the standpoint of economy than the numbers of cars per train. We must examine, then, into the reasons why the carriers have been unable to maintain the same number of passengers per train by reducing the number of trains.

Carriers are often criticized for operating an excessive number of trains between large cities in competition with one another. It is, however, often more profitable so far as individual carriers are concerned to operate a half-empty train than to lose all the traffic by running no trains at all. A large portion of the maintenance expenses assigned to passenger service, for example, must be incurred even if the passenger service is abandoned. And

[8] Same, p. S-41.

the mere fact that a number of trains operated by different carriers leave the same terminal and arrive at the
same destination at about the same time does not necessarily mean that the service is excessive. When, in the
Fifteen Per Cent Case, 1931, the Western carriers were
criticized on the score of maintaining excessive service between Chicago and other focal points, it was shown that
very few trains were in service exclusively between these
competitive points. Of the passenger trains of the Chicago, Burlington, and Quincy, for instance, 50 per cent
of the service between Chicago and St. Paul-Minne-
apolis was shown to consist of through trains to and
from the Pacific Northwest. On the Chicago and North
Western, 93 per cent of the trains between Chicago and
Omaha were through trains from and to points beyond
Denver. Similarly, it was shown that none of the trains
of the Santa Fe between Chicago and Kansas City were
exclusively for that service.[9] Many carriers are forced
by their charters to operate trains at certain intervals.
Statutory regulations of certain states, local opposition to
decreased frequency of service, the requirements of the
mail and express traffic, and many other factors have
prevented the discontinuance of services which do not pay
their way.[10] The failure of the carriers to reduce the

[9] See "Brief of Western Carriers Dealing with Passenger Train Service in Defined Territories," p. 5, submitted to the Interstate Commerce
Commission in the *Fifteen Per Cent Case, 1931, Ex Parte 103.*

[10] Compare *Co-ordination of Motor Transportation,* 182 I.C.C. 263,
322-32 (1932). Compare also *Western Trunk Line Class Rates,* 164
I.C.C. 1, 74 (1930); the Commission observed that "while there was a
material decrease in passenger revenues on the Northern Pacific, it was
not possible to make a corresponding reduction in passenger train mileage because the character of the service was such as to deny to the management the absolute control thereof. In some instances, however, gas
cars and gas-electric cars have been installed in an effort to accomplish
further economies."

number of trains in proportion to the decline in traffic is, thus, in most instances beyond the will of individual carriers. The competitive factor inherent in our system of individual railway companies, however, results in much duplication of service between important cities.

CHAPTER VI

OPERATING EFFICIENCY

In the two preceding chapters we have considered the bearing of changes in the volume of traffic upon the operating cost and the net income of railroads. The unit cost of moving goods is affected not only by the volume of traffic but by the efficiency with which a railroad is operated. Accordingly, we must now consider the relation of managerial efficiency to operating costs and net income. Since the purpose here is merely to ascertain the trend over recent years, we shall not, at this place, consider the question whether efficiency of operation on individual roads is as great as it might be, or whether substantial operating economies might not be effected through terminal and line consolidations. These issues will be considered in Part VIII.

I. THE MOVEMENT TOWARD GREATER EFFICIENCY

During the last decade the carriers have made a great effort to promote increased efficiency in operation. The World War and its immediate aftermath left railway finances generally in very bad condition, and there was urgent necessity for a reduction in operating cost. The Transportation Act of 1920 exerted pressure in the same direction, for it permitted a fair return only "under honest, efficient, and economical management." Until the end of 1922 the railroads failed to make any substantial gain; but since that time, as a result of persistent and co-operative efforts, very important results have been attained.

The American Railway Association has been an important factor in this movement for greater efficiency. In April 1923, as a part of its "program to provide adequate transportation service," the Association set for all Class I railroads of the country such standards of operating performance, slightly revised thereafter, as 30 tons per loaded car, 30 miles per car per day, 30 per cent empty mileage, and only 5 (later 7½) per cent of cars and 15 per cent of locomotives in unserviceable condition. In many other directions the Association has been instrumental in raising the level of efficiency. Individual roads, too, have not been behind in their efforts to show better operating performance. Many roads have set up standards of performance for their own use, competing against each other in the achievement of these standards.

At the same time there was a marked economy in capital tied up in materials and supplies, as the following table shows:

MATERIAL AND SUPPLIES ON HAND[a]

Year	Amount	Year	Amount
1920	$755,563,278	1925	$525,853,107
1921	665,147,099	1926	551,694,794
1922	546,284,853	1927	523,650,986
1923	682,725,812	1928	471,077,760
1924	560,048,899	1929	471,000,000

[a] Class I railways. Bureau of Railway Economics, "Railway Supplies and Expenditures," 1930, p. 7. Data for 1929 are approximate.

In this movement for greater operating efficiency, the railroads spent huge sums in improvements. During the five-year period beginning July 1, 1912 and ending June 30, 1916, the average annual investment in new lines, extensions, additions, and betterments less retirements, on Class I and Class II railroads and their non-operating subsidiaries, was $435,000,000. During the next five-year period from January 1, 1916 to December 31, 1920, the annual average was a slightly higher figure of $459,000,000. The annual net investment since 1920 was shown on page 42. It will be noted that in each of the years from 1923 to 1930, the annual net investment ran higher than the average for the period from 1916 to 1920. This increase took place despite the fact that the *rate* of traffic growth was declining.

Most of these capital expenditures were made not for new extensions of lines, but for additions and betterments on existing lines. This is clearly shown in the table below, where gross investments, that is, new investments without the deduction of retirements, are given for the years from 1920 to 1931:

ANNUAL GROSS INVESTMENT, 1920-1931[a]
(In thousands of dollars)

Year	In New Lines and Extensions	In Additions and Betterments
1920	18,950	628,904
1921	16,467	548,541
1922	20,853	484,511
1923	25,814	1,050,663
1924	25,378	912,465
1925	40,915	762,079
1926	37,217	847,931
1927	36,705	777,556
1928	51,369	676,733
1929	38,564	836,213
1930	37,826	806,082
1931	38,268	314,674

[a] Class I and Class II railroads and their non-operating subsidiaries, excluding terminal and switching companies. *Statistics of Railways in the United States,* 1920-1931.

CARL A. RUDISILL
LIBRARY
LENOIR RHYNE COLLEGE

The character of the expenditures on additions and betterments of existing lines from 1922 on is shown by the following table, which covers Class I roads only:

ALLOCATION OF CAPITAL EXPENDITURES, 1922–1931[a]
(In thousands of dollars)

| Year | Equipment | | | | |
	Locomotives	Freight Train Cars	Passenger Train Cars	Other	Total
1922	41,372	176,701	18,043	9,393	245,509
1923	208,966	409,665	40,105	22,988	681,724
1924	102,456	318,571	53,134	19,448	493,609
1925	59,778	222,476	41,207	14,653	338,114
1926	108,263	185,792	58,117	19,750	371,922
1927	76,975	136,490	53,770	21,466	288,701
1928	51,501	116,549	41,215	15,036	224,301
1929	70,660	191,917	38,670	20,059	321,306
1930	88,494	181,028	44,791	13,956	328,269
1931	25,821	29,548	13,850	3,886	73,105
Total	834,286	1,968,737	402,902	160,635	3,366,560

| Year | Roadway and Structures | | | | | | |
	Additional Track[b]	Heavier Rail	Additional Ballast	Shops and Engine Houses[c]	All Other Improvements	Total	Grand Total
1922	50,327	16,875	5,420	13,635	97,507	183,764	429,273
1923	108,745	27,866	9,471	51,214	180,129	377,425	1,059,149
1924	116,725	32,037	10,825	39,834	181,714	381,135	874,744
1925	145,757	32,952	11,665	31,345	188,358	410,077	748,191
1926	166,758	42,184	16,519	46,882	240,821	513,164	885,086
1927	139,175	43,742	16,230	35,236	248,468	482,851	771,552
1928	116,494	47,193	15,748	24,323	248,606	452,364	676,665
1929	129,148	46,862	17,049	36,561	302,795	532,415	853,721
1930	114,486	47,101	11,455	29,179	342,118	544,339	872,608
1931	64,535	29,341	5,319	9,041	180,571	288,807	361,912
Total	1,152,150	366,153	119,701	317,250	2,211,087	4,166,341	7,532,901

[a] Data compiled by the Bureau of Railway Economics.
[b] Including rail and tie fastenings and other track material.
[c] Including machinery and tools.

Besides increased capital expenditures the carriers in their movement for operating efficiency greatly increased

CARL A. RUDIS
LIBRARY
LENOIR RHYNE COLLEG

outlays for superintendence. As is shown in the table below, this item in the operating expenses has steadily increased from 1922 to 1929:

EXPENSES OF SUPERINTENDENCE, 1922-1931[a]
(In millions of dollars)

1922	196	1927	230
1923	212	1928	232
1924	213	1929	235
1925	219	1930	226
1926	226	1931	199

[a] The sum of Interstate Commerce Commission accounts 201, 301,
351, 371, and 451. Data relate to Class I roads only. From *Statistics of
Railways in the United States.*

We shall consider in a later chapter the extent to
which certain roads and divisions of roads have failed
to reached the standards obtained by the more progressive roads, and we shall also indicate the possibilities of
further improvement in efficiency.[1]

II. RESULTS OF THE EFFICIENCY MOVEMENT

Before attempting to measure the effects of these new
investments in railway properties, it will be useful to
indicate the character of the changes that occurred in
particular lines of equipment. The number of steam
locomotives on Class I railroads, for example, declined
from December 31, 1924 from 65,006 to 54,385 on
December 31, 1931, while the average tractive effort
increased from 39,891 pounds to 45,764 pounds.[2] This
increase in tractive power was attained without sacrifice
of speed. The modern locomotive is, moreover, capable of longer runs. On the Great Northern, the ex-

[1] See Chapter XXXIII.
[2] *Statistics of Railways in the United States,* 1931, p. S-9.

tension of runs made it possible to close 14 terminals and reduce the cost of locomotive operation by 10 per cent.

The number of freight cars decreased from 2,357,000 at the end of 1925 to 2,201,000 at the end of 1931. The average capacity meanwhile increased from 44.8 tons to 47 tons. There has been no net shortage of cars since the early months of 1923, and since the beginning of 1924 there have been only a few cases in which there was even a local shortage of cars to move traffic awaiting shipment. Since 1923 the maximum and minimum numbers of surplus freight cars for any date during the year were as follows:

MAXIMUM AND MINIMUM FREIGHT CAR DAILY SURPLUS
During Each Year[a]

Date	Maximum	Date	Minimum
Dec. 31, 1923	312,338	Apr. 22, 1923	11,062
June 14, 1924	362,961	Oct. 22, 1924	94,153
Mar. 31, 1925	344,959	Nov. 7, 1925	103,969
Jan. 7, 1926	310,155	Oct. 22, 1926	79,016
Dec. 31, 1927	464,005	Sept. 30, 1927	135,059
Jan. 7, 1928	461,669	Oct. 14, 1928	85,825
Dec. 31, 1929	447,141	Oct. 14, 1929	107,301
Dec. 31, 1930	706,538	Feb. 7, 1930	373,825
Dec. 31, 1931	750,696	Oct. 22, 1931	532,301
June 30, 1932[b]	772,565	Sept. 30, 1932	598,622

[a] Data compiled by the Bureau of Railway Economics.
[b] To October 1.

The result of the movement for operating efficiency is reflected in the averages of various operating performances. In the movement of cars, the three-year average of 24.6 car miles per car day in 1921-1923 was increased to 31.3 in 1927-1929. The average speed (including delays en route) increased from 10.3 miles per hour in 1920 to 14.8 in 1931. Coal consumption per 1,000 gross ton miles decreased from 162 pounds in 1921 to 119 in 1931. Gross ton miles per train hour increased steadily from 1920 to 1931, rising from 14,877 in 1920 to 26,702 in 1931. This unit is one of considerable use in the measurement of railroad operating perform- ance. It shows the results attained in moving freight and tare tonnage over the roadway in a given period of time, and hence represents the combined result of speed, length of train, and load per car and per train. The showing made by the carriers in this item of performance reflects the fact that they were able to move in 1929 a greater amount of traffic with a smaller number of cars and locomotives as compared with 1923. The various selected items of freight service operating performances for the period from 1920 to 1931 are brought together in the table on the following page. The figure which represents the best performance during the period is italicized in each column.[3]

It will be seen that the carriers have generally im- proved their operating performance during the period covered. But two items of operation which changed for the worse during the period need examination. Average net ton miles per loaded car mile as well as the percent- age of loaded car miles to total car miles steadily de- clined from 1920 to 1931.

So far as the decline in the ratio of loaded to empty car miles is concerned, one factor has been the increasing use of specialized cars for the transportation of particu- lar types of commodities, with a resulting increase in empty "back haul" movement. But a more important ex- planation of the decline in this ratio, as well as in the net tons per loaded car, grows out of the payment of high "per diem charges" for the use of cars belonging to other

[3] Some of the apparent improvement is unreal, since it is attributable to a greater movement of empty cars. (See discussion on following pages.)

SELECTED ITEMS OF OPERATING AVERAGES, 1920–1931[a]

Year	Gross Ton Miles Per Train Mile[b]	Net Ton Miles Per Train Mile	Gross Ton Miles Per Train Hour	Net Ton Miles Per Car Day[c]	Average Net Ton Miles Per Loaded Car Mile	Car Miles Per Car Day[c]	Per Cent Loaded of Total Car Miles	Car Miles Per Train Mile[d]	Pounds of Coal Per 1,000 Gross Ton Miles[e]
1920	1,443	708	14,877	498	29.3	25.1	67.9	36.6	...
1921	1,435	651	16,555	389	27.6	22.4	63.0	38.4	162
1922	1,464	676	16,188	424	26.9	23.5	67.2	38.4	163
1923	1,539	713	16,764	510	27.9	27.8	65.7	39.9	161
1924	1,588	715	18,257	471	27.0	26.8	65.1	41.7	149
1925	1,670	744	19,685	495	27.0	28.5	64.5	43.8	140
1926	1,736	772	20,692	531	27.4	30.4	63.7	45.2	137
1927	1,780	777	21,940	518	27.2	30.3	62.9	46.5	131
1928	1,836	792	23,600	526	26.7	31.2	62.9	48.1	127
1929	1,865	804	24,539	547	26.9	32.3	62.8	48.6	125
1930	1,870	784	25,837	469	26.7	28.7	61.4	48.9	121
1931	1,809	733	26,702	382	25.7	24.5	60.8	47.9	119

[a] Data relate to Class I railways only. Taken from *Statistics of Railways in the United States, 1931*, p. S-40.
[b] Excluding locomotives.
[c] Includes unserviceable cars.
[d] Including caboose.
[e] Includes locomotives; and includes equivalent coal tonnage for fuel oil consumed.

railroads. This means that every day a car belonging to the Baltimore and Ohio, for example, is moving over the Chesapeake and Ohio, whether loaded or empty, the charge must be paid to the Baltimore and Ohio. This practice has existed for many years. Between 1907 and 1916, the charge ranged from 25 to 50 cents. In 1917 it was increased to 75 cents. During the period of federal control, the charge was 60 cents for roads not in federal control, but it was abolished so far as roads in control were concerned. When the roads were returned to private owners, the charge was fixed at 90 cents, and in December 1920, it was raised to one dollar. It has since remained unchanged and is in force to-day. The reason for the successive increases was that it was cheaper to use cars of the other railroads than it was to buy new ones; and hence there was a tendency for a road to keep foreign cars as long as possible.

As a result of the increases in charges, however, it now pays to send a foreign car home as soon as possible; and there are cases in which foreign cars have been routed home empty at speeds greater than that maintained by passenger trains. In the absence of a high per diem charge these cars might have been retained and routed home with a near-capacity load. The desire to avoid payment of per diem charges has thus been an incentive to increase the empty car mileage and decrease the load per car.

It is difficult, so long as we have independent lines, to arrive at a per diem charge which would not be, on the one hand, an inducement to use the cars of other roads rather than build new ones, creating a shortage of cars for the country as a whole; or, on the other hand, an incentive to send cars home either empty or with light load. Yet the abolition of the per diem charge is not feasible so long as we have independent railroad systems. The problem might be handled by a pooling of all railroad cars or by the creation of an independent car company such as the Pullman Company, from which the roads would rent their cars; but neither of these devices appears feasible. A unified national transportation sys-

INVESTMENT AND OPERATING EXPENSES, CLASS I ROADS, 1920–1931

Year	Investment[a] (In Millions)	Capital Cost at 5.75[b] Per Cent (In Millions)	Capital Cost Per Ton Mile	Operating Expenses Per Ton Mile[c]
1920	$18,900	$1,087	$0.0024	$0.0098
1921	19,070	1,097	0.0032	0.0097
1922	19,381	1,114	0.0030	0.0087
1923	19,931	1,146	0.0025	0.0080
1924	20,710	1,191	0.0028	0.0078
1925	21,360	1,228	0.0027	0.0074
1926	21,978	1,264	0.0026	0.0071
1927	22,614	1,300	0.0028	0.0071
1928	23,149	1,331	0.0028	0.0069
1929	23,674	1,361	0.0028	0.0068
1930	24,266	1,395	0.0033	0.0068
1931	24,403	1,403	0.0041	0.0068

[a] Investment figure is the tentative final valuation of Interstate Commerce Commission (see 58 I.C.C. 220, 229, July 29, 1920), plus net additions and betterments as reported by Interstate Commerce Commission.

[b] The rate regarded as "fair" by Interstate Commerce Commission.

[c] Operating expenses related and apportioned to freight service divided by the number of ton miles. Figures relate to Class I roads only.

tem would, of course, promptly eliminate this element of unnecessary cost.

We have seen that with the exception of empty car mileage and the load per car, the improvements during the last decade in fixed structures, equipment, and in the operating methods, have brought about general increases in most items of operating performance. The final result in monetary terms of this movement for efficiency is shown in the table above.

It will be seen that the operating expenses per ton mile have steadily decreased since 1920, while investment costs per ton mile do not show any upward trend until the depression years 1930 and 1931. The capital expenditures and increased supervisory expenses during the period of traffic growth from 1920 to 1929 were thus justified by the reduction in the operating expenses per ton mile.

III. MANAGERIAL EFFICIENCY

Operating performance figures such as those given in the preceding section are often advanced as showing a remarkable increase in the efficiency of railroad management within the last decade. Before reaching such conclusion, one must consider the possible effects of factors other than management.

These factors are the increased investment, changes in the volume and character of traffic, in the average length of haul, and in operating conditions (climate and topography of the territory traversed) and, finally, the increased mechanical efficiency of machinery as a result of technological progress. During the period under consideration, the character of traffic and the average length of haul have not undergone a sufficient change to cause disturbance in the operating averages and may hence be ignored. Conditions of topography and climate may be similarly dismissed.[4]

There remain to be weighed, then, the following facts and considerations. During the last decade, investment and expenses of supervision increased. The mechanical efficiency of new equipments increased over that of the

[4] Class I carriers change slightly in identity from year to year and hence topography and other factors affecting operating conditions do change. The effect of this change is, however, negligible.

old ones. The volume of traffic increased until 1929, and the predominant importance of this factor is clearly seen when we recall our preceding analyses. In Chapter IV it was shown that expenses of operation varied inversely with the volume of traffic, and in Chapter V we saw how operating expenses per passenger mile increased in the face of declining traffic. If the decrease since 1920 in the operating expenses per ton mile bore no relation to the volume of traffic, and was imputable solely to managerial efficiency or to increased investment, then expenses per passenger mile should have similarly declined during the same period.

With these facts and considerations before us, we are now in a position to summarize the whole situation and reach a conclusion on managerial efficiency. The decline in operating expenses per ton mile in the period under consideration was brought about by improvements in operating performances, which, in turn, were made possible largely by increases in investment in newly invented or greatly improved equipment, machinery, and devices of all sorts. The huge investment in these things was justified, in fact made possible, by the increases in the volume of traffic. Without this traffic growth, the new investments would have been a detriment rather than an advantage.

The part played by management in this development was that it was alert to seize the opportunities presented on the one hand by the growing volume of traffic and on the other by technological progress. By judiciously installing or adopting newer and more efficient equipment, devices, and methods at places where they could be used to advantage as a result of the growth of traffic, and, by exercising stricter supervision, the managements undoubtedly promoted an effective use of the new capital that was attracted to the industry. As indicated at the beginning of the chapter the question whether further economies may not still be possible is reserved for discussion elsewhere.

CHAPTER VII

FREIGHT AND PASSENGER RATES

In this chapter attention will be directed to the trend of freight and passenger rates and to their relationship to railway earnings. Inasmuch as rates have been subject to effective federal control only since about 1910, our analysis is based upon the history of the period 1910-31. We shall consider the effects upon the rate level of decisions of the Interstate Commerce Commission under its mandate to prescribe reasonable and non-discriminatory rates. We shall also discuss the effect of the Hoch-Smith resolution, designed to give favorable rates to depressed industries. Finally, we shall consider the influence of competition, the tendency to adjust rates more nearly to costs, and the movement toward uniformity in the freight rate system.

I. THE TREND OF RAILWAY RATES AND EARNINGS, 1910-31

While no entirely satisfactory method of measuring rate levels has so far been constructed, the figures ordinarily given showing average revenue per ton mile for freight and per passenger mile for passengers are reasonably satisfactory.[1] The data, expressed as percentages of the figure for 1913, are shown in the accompanying chart covering the period 1910-31.

[1] The objection to this method, as it relates to freight traffic, is that it reflects not only actual rates but also the average length of haul and the character of traffic. However, during the period under survey the average length of haul has not increased rapidly enough to affect greatly the average revenue per ton mile. The average haul for all freight traffic was 249.7 miles in 1910; 303.5 in 1920; and 316.2 in 1930. The character of traffic has not undergone any significant change for many years. For example, the products of mines have fluctuated between 54.2 per cent and 56.7 per cent of total tonnage since 1910. So far as the

Freight rates, it will be seen, exhibited a general, though gentle, decline from 1910 to the end of 1916. Thereafter the direction of change was reversed for some years and rates rose rapidly to a peak in 1921. Be-

AVERAGE ANNUAL FREIGHT AND PASSENGER RATES OF RAILWAYS, 1910-31 (1913=100)

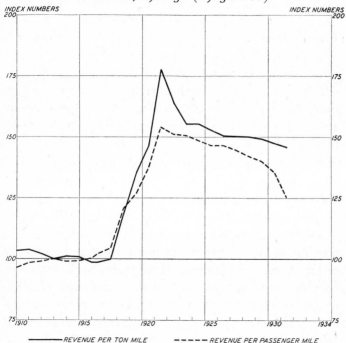

INDEX NUMBERS   INDEX NUMBERS

————— REVENUE PER TON MILE   – – – – – REVENUE PER PASSENGER MILE

tween 1921 and 1923 the level declined sharply as a result of general and piecemeal reductions established in 1921 and 1922. During the decade since 1922 the level

revenue per passenger mile is concerned the average length of haul has no bearing because passenger rates are set at so much per mile. There has, however, been a considerable change in the character of traffic, commutation having become relatively more important.

has gradually declined, standing in 1931 about 6 per cent under the average in 1923 but at the same time more than 45 per cent above the 1913 level.

Turning to the level of passenger rates we find the situation, between 1910 and 1931, not greatly different from that which has prevailed in connection with freight rates. Passenger fares remained practically unchanged from the end of 1910 to 1917 (see the chart on p. 113). For the next four years they rose rapidly although the relative advance did not equal the increase of freight rates. After 1921 passenger rates began a steady decline which has continued uninterruptedly to the present time. In 1931 the level of charges was approximately 17 per cent below the level in 1923 but 25 per cent above the level in 1913.

A comparison of railway rates (as shown by revenues) with earnings is presented in the accompanying chart. Two definite conclusions may be drawn from a study of the three curves. First, with the exception of the years 1918-21, the rate level has been more stable than railway earnings, neither rising nor falling as rapidly, or as far, as earnings. Second, there seems to be little correlation between high average rates and high earnings or between low average rates and low earnings. For example, although generally low railway charges prevailed from 1910 to 1917, earnings were on the whole satisfactory. In 1921 and 1922 earnings were unsatisfactory in spite of the highest rate levels in modern railway history. From 1923 to 1929 rates—particularly freight rates—declined but slightly, while earnings fluctuated widely. It appears to follow, therefore, that factors other than the rate level have contributed largely to the relative instability of railroad earnings of the past two decades.

COMPARISON OF RAILROAD RATES WITH NET RETURN ON
CAPITAL, 1910-31 (1913=100 for each series)

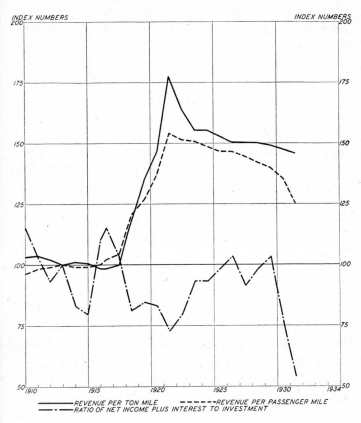

II. COMMISSION POLICIES AFFECTING RATES

The Interstate Commerce Act in its first three sections
stipulates that the Commission shall establish rates which
shall be just and reasonable, non-discriminatory, and
not unduly prejudicial or preferential as between persons, places, commodities, or classes of traffic. The Transportation Act of 1920 requires that the general level of

rates shall be such as will enable the railroads as a whole to earn a fair return upon the value of their properties. The Commission also has the power to prescribe maximum and minimum rates. In carrying out the intent of the law decisions of the Commission have naturally exerted a marked influence upon the railroad rate structure of the country.

The attempt of the Commission, under the Transportation Act of 1920, to adjust the general level of rates, is considered in Chapter XX. We need here therefore merely summarize the story. A few cases involving requests for advances in rates arose prior to and during the World War. No advances were allowed until 1914, and not until 1918 was there a general increase in rates throughout the country. The increase, amounting to approximately 25 per cent in freight rates, was inaugurated by Director General McAdoo on May 25, 1918. This was regarded as necessary because of the great advance in the costs of railway operation incident to the war.[2]

Since the war there have been only three cases involving nation-wide changes in the level of rates. The first was in 1920, when an increase in freight rates amounting to approximately 33 per cent was granted; the second was in 1922, involving a reduction of 10 per cent; and the third was in 1931, when a compromise adjustment was effected in lieu of a horizontal increase of 15 per cent. The net effect of the first two of these rate

[2] The principal cases were as follows: *Advanced Rate Cases of 1910*, 20 I.C.C. 243 (1911) and 20 I.C.C. 307 (1911); *Five Per Cent Case of 1914*, 31 I.C.C. 351 (1914) and 32 I.C.C. 325 (1914); *Western Rate Advance Case*, 35 I.C.C. 497 (1915) and 37 I.C.C. 144 (1915); *Western Passenger Fares*, 37 I.C.C. 1 (1915); *Rate Advances in Western Classification Territory*, 38 I.C.C. 94 (1916); *Fifteen Per Cent Case*, 45 I.C.C. 303 (1917).

adjustments was to produce from 1923 on a level approximately 20 per cent above that of 1918. The advances authorized in 1931 were not all put into effect and were in part offset by the reduction of other rates.

Turning now to changes in particular rates, there are three kinds of cases which come before the Commission: First, those brought by the shipper to complain of unreasonable or unjustly discriminatory rates. Second, those instituted by a railroad to propose changes in rates which require the Commission's approval (in the event of protest by either a shipper or another railroad, such cases may be suspended for a period of seven months). Third, those initiated by a railroad to request that action upon emergency changes may be taken in less than the statutory limit of 30 days.

A vast number of cases have come before the Commission in connection with each of these categories. During 1921 and 1922 numerous reductions were made, in part voluntarily by the railroads, and in part by the advice or order of the Commission. The most significant of these applied to hay, grain, grain products, and livestock.[3]

A careful study of the decisions of the Commission since 1922 indicates that cases in the first two categories produced no perceptible downward trend in rates. The fact is that numerically the increases exceeded the reductions.

The emergency cases almost always involve requests from railroads for reductions in rates in order to meet competition by other transportation agencies. In so far

[3] *Rates on Grain, Grain Products, and Hay,* 64 I.C.C. 85 (1921), *National Live Stock Shippers' League v. A. T. and S. F. Ry. Co.,* 63 I.C.C. 107 (1921).

as there have been reductions they have not been the result of actions initiated by the Commission. It has been contended by the carriers that the Commission has handicapped the roads by commonly refusing to allow them to change their rates to meet emergencies with less than the statutory requirement of 30-day notice. The charge is, however, not borne out by the facts. The accompanying table gives the number and disposition of carrier applications for special permission to establish such rates or fares, compiled for the period 1928-32 inclusive.

NUMBER AND DISPOSITION OF APPLICATIONS FOR PERMISSION TO ESTABLISH
RATES OR FARES ON LESS THAN THE STATUTORY 30-DAY NOTICE
1928–32[a]

Year Ending October 31	Applications Received	Applications Granted	Applications Denied	Applications Otherwise Disposed of
1928............	6,317	5,653	660	4
1929............	6,096	4,914	689	493
1930............	6,534	5,748	638	148
1931............	8,287	7,091	767	429
1932............	11,829	10,209	1,246	374
	39,063	33,615	4,000	1,448

[a] Compiled from the *Annual Reports of the Interstate Commerce Commission*, 1928, p. 53; 1929, p. 61; 1930, p. 56; 1931, p. 64; and 1932, p. 85.

During the five years under consideration, 39,063 of these applications were received. In 33,615 instances the railroads were permitted to establish the proposed rate changes in less than 30 days. Only 4,000 applications were denied. It is thus evident that in the vast majority of cases the carriers were allowed to have their changes and were not made subject to unwarranted delay by Commission action. The table also indicates that the carriers filed a much larger number of requests for emergency changes in 1931 and 1932 than in the three previous years. In 1932, for example, the railroads submitted nearly twice as many applications as in 1929. Apparently, the Commission was able to keep up with the expansion of work, because all but 374 of the 11,829 cases were definitely settled. More than 10,000, or 86.4 per cent, of all the applications were granted. On the average, about 40 applications are now being considered in each working day.

III. LOWER RATES FOR DEPRESSED INDUSTRIES: THE HOCH-SMITH RESOLUTION

Another significant factor in the rate-making picture is the Hoch-Smith resolution, adopted on January 30, 1925.[4] This joint resolution of Congress directed the Commission to make a comprehensive investigation of the railroad rate structure of the United States in order to remove maladjustments in relative rates and to afford relief to farmers and stockmen who had suffered from post-war depression in agriculture. The resolution declares that it is "the true policy in rate making to be pursued by the Interstate Commerce Commission in adjusting freight rates, that the conditions which at any given time prevail in our several industries should be considered in so far as it is legally possible to do so, to the end that commodities may freely move."

More specifically the Commission was ordered, in view of the then existing depression in agriculture,

"to effect with the least practicable delay such lawful changes in the rate structure of the country as will promote the freedom of movement by common carriers of the products of agriculture affected by that depression, including livestock, at the lowest

[4] 43 Stat. L. 801.

possible rates compatible with the maintenance of adequate transportation service."

For its guidance in carrying on a comprehensive investigation of freight rates, the Commission was required to consider, among other factors, "the general and comparative levels in market value of the various classes and kinds of commodities as indicated over a reasonable period of years."

The agitation for a lightening of the transportation burden on economically depressed industries is not new. In 1890, for example, the Senate passed a similar resolution in an attempt to have the Commission lower the rates on agricultural products.[5] Early in the present century, pig iron from Southern furnaces to Northern points of consumption was accorded low rates because of depressed conditions in the South.[6]

To what extent have the "true policy" of rate making and the collateral provisions of the Hoch-Smith resolution affected the policies of the Commission with respect to the establishment of rates? So far as consideration of the general and comparative levels in the market value of commodities is involved, no new principle was enunciated. The Commission had often and consistently recognized the value of commodities as one of the many factors in fixing rates. The other principle—the adjustment of rates according to the financial condition of an industry—seemed to represent a departure from traditional federal policy. The general practice of the Commission before 1925 is indicated in the following statement:

[5] *In Re Excessive Freight Rates on Food Products*, 4 I.C.C. 48, 66 (1890).
[6] *In the Matter of Proposed Advances in Freight Rates*, 9 I.C.C. 382, 386 (1903).

This Commission has often said that it cannot require of carriers the establishment of rates which will guarantee to a shipper the profitable conduct of his business. The railway may not impose an unreasonable transportation charge merely because the business of the shipper is so profitable that he can pay it; nor, conversely, can the shipper demand that an unreasonably low charge shall be accorded him simply because the profits of his business have shrunk to a point where they are no longer sufficient.[7]

The agricultural interests were not satisfied with this doctrine. When the prices of their products declined after 1920 to such a level that profits were small or nonexistent, the farmers sought lower freight rates as a means of increasing their earnings. The piecemeal reductions on grain and other products in 1921-22 and the horizontal reduction of 10 per cent in 1922 still left them dissatisfied with the level of rates. In a case in 1921, the claim was made that livestock rates should be reduced to a point below the standard basis prescribed by the Commission because the industry was not profitable. The Commission refused to accept the doctrine and observed, "If that be true, then the converse must be true, that at times when the industry prospers we may find justified rates higher than those which under accepted standards would be just and reasonable."[8]

---

[7] *Railroad Commissioners of Kansas* v. *A. T. and S. F. Ry. Co.*, 22 I.C.C. 407, 410 (1912). Even before 1925 the Commission began to give some consideration to the depressed condition of an industry as a factor in rate making. In *Rates and Charges on Grain and Grain Products*, 91 I.C.C. 105, 143 (1924), the Commission said: "In consideration of reasonableness of rates the economic condition of an industry may be relevant as it bears on the value of the service of the industry, and as it may permanently or for a long period of time affect the ability of that industry to pay the rates assessed, but taken by itself it cannot be accepted as controlling."

[8] *National Live Stock Shippers' League* v. *A. T. & S. F. Ry. Co.*, 63 I.C.C. 107, 116 (1921). See also *Rates on Grain, Grain Products, and Hay*, 64 I.C.C. 850 (1921).

The farmers were not alone, however, in their belief that rates were too high. The Joint Commission of Agricultural Inquiry in 1921 recommended policies which were later in large part incorporated into the Hoch-Smith resolution.[9] And President Coolidge in his message to Congress on December 6, 1923, said: "Competent authorities agree that a new reorganization structure for freight is necessary. This should be ordered at once by Congress."

While the agricultural interests and their sympathizers seemed to secure a new departure in public policy, the "true policy" of rate making was hedged about by several important restrictions which have tended to nullify its effectiveness. Conditions in particular industries were to be construed only "in so far as it was legally possible to do so," and the "lowest possible" rates on agricultural products were also to be "lawful" and "compatible with the maintenance of adequate transportation service." The Commission, as a consequence, while preventing rate advances on agricultural products in depressed areas and insisting upon rate reductions in some instances, has recognized that the resolution "sets no new standards of lawfulness but provides, in effect, that to the extent there are flexible limits to our discretion, we shall require the maintenance of lowest rates falling within these flexible limits."[10]

Even this qualified interpretation was not accepted by the Supreme Court in the "Ann Arbor case" of 1930.[11] The case grew out of an order by the Commission requiring the railroads to reduce their rates on deciduous

[9] See 67 Cong., *Report of the Joint Commission of Agricultural Inquiry*, H. rep. 408, 1922, Pt. 3, pp. 3 ff.

[10] *Grain and Grain Products*, 122 I.C.C. 235, 264 (1927).

[11] *Ann Arbor R. R. Co.* v. *U.S.*, 231 U.S. 658 (1930).

fruits shipped from California to areas east of the Rocky
Mountains.[12] The issue was whether the Hoch-Smith
resolution had changed the basic provisions of the Interstate Commerce Act relating to transportation rates and,
particularly, whether any lawful rate under the older
statutes would thereby be made unlawful. The Supreme
Court ruled that the Hoch-Smith resolution did not introduce any new "true policy" of rate making; that only
"lawful changes" in rates on agricultural products affected by the depression were permissible; and that the
resolution could not be construed as according "most
favored" consideration to the products of agriculture.
The decision led the Commission to remark that "the
effect to be given to the Hoch-Smith resolution . . .
has been profoundly influenced by the decision of the
Supreme Court."[13]

A word may now be said as to the character and extent of the general investigation undertaken in response
to the Hoch-Smith resolution.[14] The investigation was

[12] *California Growers' and Shippers' Protective League* v. *S. P. Co.*,
129 I.C.C. 25 (1927); 132 I.C.C. 582 (1927).

[13] *Annual Report of the Interstate Commerce Commission*, 1930, p. 61.

[14] The study was instituted under the title, *No. 17000, Rate Structure Investigation.* The parts and reported discussions are as follows:
Part 1, Revenues in Western District, 113 I.C.C. 3 (1926); *Part 2,
Western Trunk-Line Class Rates*, 164 I.C.C. 1 (1930), 173 I.C.C., 637
(1931), 178 I.C.C. 619 (1932), 181 I.C.C. 301 (1932); *Part 3, Cot-
ton*, 165 I.C.C. 595 (1930), 172 I.C.C. 53 (1931), 174 I.C.C. 9 (1931),
176 I.C.C. 249 (1931), 181 I.C.C. 474 (1932), 185 I.C.C. 769 (1932);
Part 4, Petroleum and Petroleum Products, 171 I.C.C. 286 (1931), 176
I.C.C. 637 (1931), 176 I.C.C. 707 (1931), 179 I.C.C. 19 (1932), 182
I.C.C. 470 (1932), 183 I.C.C. 24 (1932); *Part 4-A, Petroleum and Its
Products in the Southwest*, 171 I.C.C. 381 (1931), 174 I.C.C. 381
(1931); *Part 5, Furniture*, 177 I.C.C. 5 (1931); *Part 6, Iron and Steel
Articles*, 155 I.C.C. 517 (1929), 161 I.C.C. 386 (1930), 161 I.C.C. 608
(1930), 168 I.C.C. 107 (1930); *Part 7, Grain and Grain Products*, 164
I.C.C. 619 (1930), 173 I.C.C. 511 (1931); *Part 7-A, Grain and Grain
Products, Southern Territory Rate* (case not heard); *Part 8, Cottonseed*,

divided into 16 parts which included a survey of class and important commodity rates throughout a considerable portion of the country. At the present time reports have been issued on all parts except those dealing with non-ferrous metals, hay, and salt. In most cases the rates authorized by the Commission have become effective. In others it has been necessary to qualify certain adjustments or to postpone the effective date because of difficulties encountered in rate relations. Some cases have been reopened to take account of changed conditions in transportation and commerce. The amount of labor and money expended has been enormous. In the grain investigation alone approximately 55,000 pages of testimony and more than 2,000 exhibits were gathered during the 46 weeks of hearings.[15]

In its latest annual report the Commission expressed doubt concerning the wisdom of such an investigation:

Generally speaking, the Docket 17000 cases have developed into unwieldy proportions. Our experience with them has shown that the country is too big to make it generally practicable to deal with it as a whole or even with the major classification territories, except in proceedings especially adapted to large territorial treatment, such as the classifications themselves. Substantial benefits have resulted from the general surveys which have been made in the Hoch-Smith cases, but these have been offset by the disadvantages connected with unavoidable delay. . . .

---

188 I.C.C. 605 (1932); *Part 9, Livestock, Southern Territory Rates,* 171 I.C.C. 721 (1930), 176 I.C.C. 1 (1931), 182 I.C.C. 491 (1932); *Part 9, Livestock—Western District Rates,* 176 I.C.C. 1 (1931), 179 I.C.C. 104 (1932), 185 I.C.C. 457 (1932); *Part 10, Hay* (no decision); *Part 11, Sand and Gravel,* 155 I.C.C. 247 (1929), 157 I.C.C. 498 (1929), 177 I.C.C. 621 (1931); *Part 12, Non-ferrous metals* (no decision); *Part 13, Salt* (no decision). The principal developments are summarized in the annual reports of the Interstate Commerce Commission, 1925 to date.

[15] *Annual Report of the Interstate Commerce Commission,* 1930, p. 66.

Other benefits which its sponsors may have expected from the resolution were not realized because of the interpretation placed upon it by the Supreme Court of the United States in the so-called Ann Arbor case. . . .

Experience indicates that large proceedings like these should be initiated in the future only sparingly and in response to imperative needs which can be met to advantage only in that way.[16]

We may now summarize the effects on actual rates of the investigation inaugurated and carried out in accordance with the mandate of the Hoch-Smith resolution. This resolution involved, it will be recalled, both possible reductions of rates in the interest of depressed industry and readjustments of other rate schedules. Most of the cases did not affect the level of rates but were in the nature of readjustments in schedules. In some cases rates have been increased for certain distances and lowered for others. The only significant reductions to date have been made in the deciduous fruits case of 1927 and the grain and grain products case of 1930[17] In both cases the order of the Commission was disallowed by the Supreme Court and the higher level formerly in existence was restored.[18]

The most significant increases authorized by the Commission were in class rates in Western Trunk-Line territory[19] and on furniture[20] and cottonseed.[21] The rail-

---

[16] *Annual Report of the Interstate Commerce Commission*, 1932, p. 30.

[17] *California Growers' and Shippers' Protective League* v. *S. P. Co.* 129 I.C.C. 25 (1927). *Grain and Grain Products*, 164 I.C.C. 619 (1930).

[18] *Ann Arbor R. R. Co.* v. *U.S.*, 281 U.S. 658 (1930), reversing *California Growers' and Shippers' Protective League* v. *S. P. Co.*, 129 I.C.C. 25 (1927). The decision in *Grain and Grain Products*, 164 I.C.C. 619 (1930) was enjoined in *A. T. and S. F. Ry. Co.* v. *U.S.*, 284 U.S. 248 (1932).

[19] *Western Trunk-Line Class Rates*, 164 I.C.C. 1 (1930).

[20] *Furniture*, 177 I.C.C. 5 (1931).

[21] *Cottonseed*, 188 I.C.C. 605 (1932).

roads have not put the increases in furniture rates into effect and in some cases have even lowered their charges to meet truck competition. It seems likely that the advances in cottonseed rates will not be utilized for the same reason.

The conclusion is obvious, therefore, that the decisions rendered by the Commission as modified by the Supreme Court have not, as has been contended, materially reduced the rate level. The one significant change in rates, in fact, was the advance of *class* rates in Western Trunk-Line territory. Where substantial reductions have been lawfully put into effect, the carriers and not the Commission have taken the initiative; competition has had much greater influence in reducing rates than the Hoch-Smith resolution, particularly since 1929.

The most important effect of the Hoch-Smith resolution was perhaps the negative one of preventing increases in rates on agricultural products. The Commission blocked a number of proposed rate increases on such products and had it not been for the resolution and the investigations that were being conducted thereunder, other requests for advances would doubtless have been made. The principal advantage which agriculture has obtained from this resolution is, therefore, indirect in character.

The adjustment of railroad rates in the interest of depressed industries is not only difficult to administer but is unsound in principle. If low rates are to be established on the products of depressed industries several troublesome questions immediately arise. What are the earmarks of a depressed industry? How can we measure the degree of depression being experienced? How long will the depression last? When fundamental changes in industry are to be considered, what guide is there to probable future developments?

Of more significance is the principle involved. Why should we look to railroad rates for a solution of problems which have not been created by the railroads? The depression in agriculture, for example, had its roots in an over-expansion of production, stimulated by unusual war demands. It is apparent that the railroads were not responsible either for the war-time expansion in agricultural products or for the world-wide agricultural readjustments following the war which resulted in a decline of foreign demand for our products. While rates cannot in the long run be determined without reference to the ability of business and industry to bear such rates, it does not follow that it is a function of transportation to give an artificial protection in the form of especially low rates to industries or regions which are suffering from economic maladjustment or which, as a result of changing conditions, are unable to meet the competition of other producing areas. To do so would not only tend to keep labor and capital employed less productively than would otherwise be the case; but, under certain circumstances, might also result in depressing the railway industry itself. The principle enunciated by the Commission prior to the adoption of the Hoch-Smith resolution embodies a truer conception of the rate-making problem.[22]

IV. THE INFLUENCE OF COMPETITION ON RATE LEVELS

Having discussed the bearing of decisions of the Interstate Commerce Commission upon the level of railway rates, we shall now consider the effect of competition

[22] See the Commission's statement quoted above, p. 121.

upon rate making and the attitude of the Commission with respect to the proper role of competition in fixing rates.

The railways have always faced more or less competition either from competing routes or from competing markets. Historically, water competition was of the greatest significance. The railways paralleling the Great Lakes, the sea coast, and the navigable rivers found continuing and effective competition at the ports. As a result, cities situated on waterways came to enjoy extremely low railway rates. A classic example of the influence of water competition upon rates was in the South where the so-called "basing point" system was in vogue for many decades. Concurrently, the parallel building of railroads added to the severity of competition between railways for traffic to and from junction points. Competition between railways and between water and rail lines has resulted in many kinds of discrimination, as evidenced by higher charges for short than for long hauls over the same route in the same direction, the grouping or blanketing of rates, and, in general, the establishment of a system not based upon distance principles.

No less significant in many respects is the effect of market competition upon railway rates. The emphasis on the desirability of annihilating distance in industrial and commercial activities has led shippers to seek reduced rates to those markets where other producers or jobbers of like commodities possess certain advantages. The disadvantageously situated shippers prevail upon railroads to establish low rates because the carriers will gain by means of increased tonnage along with the shipper. All sorts of low rates have been and are now in existence as a result of market competition. Probably the best example of this development is the blanket rate system in transcontinental territory, whereby all localities lying east of the Rocky Mountains pay the same freight rates on most commodities to or from places on or near the Pacific coast. This equalization of rates can be explained on no terms other than the competition of producers for markets.

The troublesome character of railway competition may be illustrated by the further development of water-carrier, pipe-line, and truck competition since the war. The effect of water competition has been greatest in connection with intercoastal traffic made possible by the opening of the Panama Canal. There resulted an immediate reduction in water rates between Atlantic and Gulf cities and the Pacific coast. Moreover, the shipping situation that developed following the war served to intensify competition and to depress severely coastwise shipping rates. Two factors were involved in this situation. The first was the great surplus of shipping, and the second was the government's policy. Mail subsidies to boats going to the Canal Zone and points beyond were of aid in some cases; in other cases Shipping Board boats were sold at very low prices and on liberal payment terms; and loans were sometimes granted to private shipping companies at nominal rates of interest.

There is no effective regulation of rates in this intercoastal traffic. While *maximum* rates must be filed with the Shipping Board, they are so far above the actual rates as to be of no significance. In the absence of *minimum* prescribed rates partially subsidized or distressed shipping has made rates so low as to render the whole intercoastal shipping business highly precarious. This cutthroat competition has led a number of the inter-coastal lines to seek effective governmental regulation of all inter-coastal shipping.

The effect of this competition on the railways is felt for hundreds of miles inland. Indeed, in some instances traffic now moves from the Great Lakes region to the Pacific Coast *via* Atlantic and Gulf ports. This is sometimes a water and sometimes a rail movement. Similarly, east bound traffic entering at Gulf and Atlantic ports moves inland by rail or water for some hundreds of miles farther than was formerly the case. The steamship companies facilitate this movement by quoting "proportional rates."

One important result has been to weaken the competitive position of many Middle Western industries in connection with markets on the Pacific coast. In consequence, Middle Western industrial and shipping groups have sought in various ways to obtain a restoration of the former competitive relationships. Inasmuch as the Midwest is a thousand miles or more closer to the Pacific coast than is the Atlantic seaboard and from 500 to 800 miles closer than such cities as Pittsburgh and Buffalo, it is naturally felt that this section is entitled to at least an even chance in Pacific coast markets. This has been one of the primary forces back of the St. Lawrence waterway movement, for it was hoped that this route would place the Middle West on a parity with the East in foreign trade and at the same time make possible all-water shipment from Great Lakes ports to the Pacific coast. Similarly, it has led shipping interests of the Midwest to urge reductions of rail rates between the Midwest and the Atlantic coast and Gulf points, and also between the Midwest and Pacific coast ports.

The railroads connecting the Midwest with the Pacific

coast have naturally joined with the shippers in their request for lower rates to the Pacific coast. They wish to
have rates to coast cities reduced sufficiently to enable the
Midwest to compete in those markets. At the same time
they desire to maintain rates at such interior Western
cities as Spokane and Salt Lake City—the inter-mountain
territory—higher than those to the coast. Otherwise they
fear that they might lose more as a result of the lower
rates on the traffic to the inter-mountain territory than
they would gain as a result of enlarging their traffic to
coast cities. This request brings them into conflict with
the Fourth Section of the Interstate Commerce Act, the
so-called Long-and-Short-Haul Clause.[23]

The Commission has authorized reductions in the rates
on petroleum and its products in the Southwest to meet
both truck and pipeline competition,[24] and has recently
gone so far in its recognition of the force of truck competition as to sanction reduced rail rates in order to fore-
stall the development of such competition. On paper and
paper articles shipped in the Middle West, the Commission accepted rate reductions without requiring proof of
the actual existence of compelling truck competition.[25]
It may be inferred from this decision that *potential* truck
competition is now recognized as sufficient justification
for a reduction of rail rates.[26] Such a principle is not in accordance with the established practice of the Commission
in connection with other forms of competition.

[23] See page 139.
[24] *Refined Petroleum Products in the Southwest*, 174 I.C.C. 745 (1931).
[25] *Paper and Paper Articles between Western Trunk-Line Points*, 186
I.C.C. 536 (1932).
[26] The details of the character and extent of water-carrier, pipe-line,
and motor truck competition on rail rates since 1920 are set forth in the
Annual Report of the Interstate Commerce Commission, 1931, pp. 97-107.
See also, Parts V-VII.

In spite of the disturbed competitive conditions just noted, much has been done in the past two decades to bring some order out of the competitive chaos. The Commission has continued to recognize the compelling force of competition, but at the same time it has placed many limitations thereon. Greater consideration has been given to distance scales, particularly where competition is general and continuous throughout a given territory. Many large rate groups and blanket rates have been removed. The Commission says that each community is entitled to the benefits of its natural advantages and that the carriers have no duty to meet competition in every case or to equalize "fortunes, opportunities, or abilities." The carriers may not unduly prefer one port or locality to another, arbitrarily regulate the flow of commerce, establish competitive rates which tend to encourage wasteful transportation, or secure unnecessarily roundabout routing of goods between points served by direct lines, unless the existence of unused capacity or the overloading of the direct route justify a modification of general policy. Moreover, the railroads may not charge less than "reasonably compensatory" rates on long hauls, or violate the "equi-distant" principle, or employ indiscriminately "any quantity" rates, once so common in the South, as a means of meeting water competition and avoiding the use of minimum carload ratings.

V. RELATING FREIGHT RATES TO COSTS

It is difficult to determine with any degree of precision the cost of transporting particular units of traffic. In the first place, a very large proportion of railway expenses are fixed or do not vary in proportion to changes in traffic. In the second place, the railroad carries so many different kinds of traffic, under such varying conditions, that it is next to impossible to allocate the operating costs, taxes, and fixed charges to particular traffic. Hence rates have often borne no relation to cost or even to out-of-pocket expenses.

However, the shipping public and the regulatory agencies have attempted so far as possible to adjust rates in relation to the cost of service rendered. Under the leadership of the Interstate Commerce Commission the emphasis has gradually been shifted from the old policy of charging what the traffic would bear to an increase in the use of the cost-of-service principle. The Commission holds that all rates should more than cover the direct outlays and has evolved the rule that "rates that we may lawfully require must, in principle, be high enough to cover all the costs that may fairly be allocated to the service plus at least some margin of profit."[27] This may be termed a doctrine of minimum reasonable rates.

There is a distinction, however, between rates which the Commission may prescribe and those which the carriers may voluntarily establish.[28] The Commission, unlike the railroads, is restrained by the due process clause of the Fifth Amendment to the Constitution from proposing rates which are confiscatory. Though rates below a maximum reasonable level may be voluntarily established by the carriers, they must be more than sufficient to cover direct costs; otherwise the effect is to shift the burden of costs to other traffic. In the case of long-and-short-haul discrimination, the law provides that rates to

---

[27] *American National Live Stock Assn.* v. *A. T. & S. F. Ry. Co.,* 122 I.C.C. 609, 617 (1927). See also *Northern Pacific Ry. Co.* v. *North Dakota,* 236 U.S. 585, 596-97 (1915), where the Supreme Court upheld the same doctrine.

[28] *Cement from Linwood,* 140 I.C.C. 579, 582 (1928).

more distant points must be "reasonably compensatory."[29]

Where direct costs are not ascertainable other cost comparisons are often utilized. In general, the Commission holds the view that, other things being equal, a service which costs more ought to take a higher rate. Among the factors which are considered in these comparisons are risk, special services, loading characteristics, the quantity of shipment, volume, direction, and density of traffic, topography and climate, and distance hauled.

In the construction of tariffs, distance, though a very rough measure of cost, has received from the Commission a degree of recognition seldom given to any single cost factor. Although this is particularly true of class rates, the distance principle is being applied to commodity rates.

In the application of distance scales, certain compromises have been necessary. The Commission has allowed the formation of groups which are rather extensive where the hauls are long.[30] Use has also been made of "key rates" for long-haul and inter-territory traffic, whereby rates are quoted not by distance but by key-point stations which mark the boundaries of groups.[31]

---

[29] The Commission has defined a "reasonably compensatory" rate as one which "must (1) cover and more than cover the extra or additional expenses incurred in handling the traffic to which it applies; (2) be no lower than necessary to meet existing competition; (3) not be so low as to threaten the extinction of legitimate competition by water carriers; and (4) not impose an undue burden on other traffic or jeopardize the appropriate return on the value of the carrier property generally, as contemplated in section 15a of the act [of 1920]." *Transcontinental Cases of 1922*, 74 I.C.C. 48, 71 (1922).

[30] *Wool Rates Investigation, 1923*, 91 I.C.C. 235, 257 (1924).

[31] For an example, see *Western Trunk-Line Class Rates*, 164 I.C.C. 1, 252 (1930).

Furthermore, rates are typically quoted by the most direct line and subject to certain limitations. Roundabout railroads are generally allowed to meet these rates at junction points. Finally, there are "differential" rail and rail-and-water routes, which furnish a lower quality of service and which charge less than the standard groups.

Opinions differ as to the feasibility of constructing rates on the basis of distance. Generally speaking, any alternative means raising rates for shorter distances and lowering them for longer distances. The establishment of distance scales probably means the discouragement of relatively long hauls. Where such hauls involve competition with distant markets, the use of distance scales doubtless eliminates wasteful transportation.

The Commission has never allowed lower rates on train-load than on carload lots. They justify this policy, first, on the ground that it is impossible to determine the difference in the cost per ton in a train-load and in a carload lot, and second, by the contention that lower rates on train-load shipments would tend to be injurious to the small shipper. While it may be true that it is impossible to determine how much the cost is reduced when movement is in train-load lots, it does not follow that some use of the wholesale principle in this connection would not be justified. With reference to the second reason, the Commission has itself stated that it is not its function to equalize "fortunes, opportunities, or abilities" of shippers.

VI. THE LONG-AND-SHORT-HAUL PROBLEM

Of the various forms of discrimination none raises more controversy than the practice of charging higher rates for shorter than for longer hauls of traffic moving in the same direction over the same route, the shorter haul being included within the longer. This practice, which is known as long-and-short-haul discrimination, has from the outset been declared to be unlawful in the fourth section of the Interstate Commerce Act. The Commission may, however, permit a departure from this rule in special cases and after investigation.

The discretion of the Commission is limited by three other provisions incorporated in the fourth section of the Interstate Commerce Act (1) the rates to and from more distant points must be reasonably compensatory; (2) circuitous railroads when authorized to meet the charges of a more direct rail line or route at competitive points must not charge higher rates at those intermediate points to and from which the haul of the roundabout carrier is no longer than the distance over the direct line between the competitive points (this is known as the equi-distance principle); and (3) potential water competition may not be accepted as sufficient justification for relief from the long-and-short-haul provisions.

In its administration of the fourth section the Commission has had to consider two major questions: (1) whether a violation of the act is justified, and (2) the extent to which the railway may depart from the rule of the fourth section. On the first point the Commission has held that the presence of competition by other routes is the governing element. This competition must be the controlling force which places the railroad at a disadvantage as compared with rival rail, water, or motor carriers. It must also be sufficient to reduce the level of rates at competitive points below a reasonable level for intermediate localities.

In connection with the extent of relief the Commission has ruled that the long-haul rates should bear some relation to the value of the commodity carried and the value of the service rendered; that the intermediate rates must not exceed the maximum level of reasonableness which the Commission itself generally prescribes; that the rates to the intermediate stations shall not exceed the lowest combination based upon the local rate from the nearest competitive point plus the through rate to the competitive point.

By means of these rules the Commission has eliminated or reduced materially during the past 20 years the number and extent of so-called fourth section departures. Virtually all discriminations of this character have been eliminated in connection with direct lines between competitive points. In the South the old "basing point" system, by which rates to intermediate localities were for many years made on the basis of a combination of the local rate plus the through rate to the basing point, has been abolished.

The greatest controversies in connection with the long-and-short-haul problem have arisen in connection with the transcontinental rate structure which applies on all shipments between the East and the Pacific coast and Intermountain territories. In order to understand the nature of recent controversies it is essential to recall briefly the history of the transcontinental rate structure.

In the nineties there was established a so-called blanket rate structure under which virtually all points east of the Rocky Mountains had the same rates to and from the Pacific coast. There was no very effective water competition in connection with this transcontinental traffic, though the all-water route around the Horn, the combination water-rail route across the Isthmus of Tehauntepec, and the Sunset-Gulf route via Galveston and the Southern Pacific afforded potential competition—which might become actual if rail rates were raised beyond a certain level.

The primary explanation of this blanket rate structure was the desire of the transcontinental railways whose terminals were in the Middle West to encourage the development of industry in that section of the country. They were not primarily interested in moving traffic from the Atlantic seaboard to the West because that involved sharing joint rates with the Eastern railroads; nor were they desirous of decreasing rates between the Middle West and the Far West below the level of coast-to-coast rates because this would involve a reduction in revenue. Under the circumstances, the desirable rate structure was one which gave them a maximum return on traffic between the Middle West and the Pacific coast, and which at the same time placed Middle Western industry on a parity with that on the Eastern seaboard.

Rates from the East or Middle West to the Pacific coast, however, were not blanketed at the Western end, for the railroads saw no advantage in encouraging the development of industry in the intermountain states. Thus on shipments from anywhere east of the Rockies to the West the rates to cities in the intermountain territory were higher than those to the coast, where potential water competition governed.

This contradictory system, with blanket rates in the East and differential rates in the West, remained in force until 1918. In the meantime, however, decisions of the Interstate Commerce Commission had tended to reduce the extent to which rates to the Pacific coast were lower than those to the intermountain states.[32] In 1918 the Commission abolished the differentials altogether and established a blanket system for the intermountain and Pacific coast territories—on the ground that water competition no longer existed. While the Panama Canal had been opened in 1914, the development of traffic was arrested first by the slides which occurred in 1915 and then by the war, when ship tonnage was absorbed in trans-Atlantic traffic.

Since that time, notwithstanding the revival of water competition, the Commission has declined to restore the lower rates at Pacific coast ports. The reasons that have been assigned are (1) that the Transportation Act of 1920 requires it to maintain rail and water transportation in full vigor, (2) that lower rates to cities on the Western coast would be prejudicial to the intermountain territory, (3) that the roads had not demonstrated that such rates would be reasonably compensatory, and (4) that any gains which might possibly result to the western roads would be more than counterbalanced by losses of revenue to the eastern roads. Whatever may be the validity of these reasons, it may be pointed out that they are not in accord with the Commission's general policy with reference to alternative routes.[33]

With reference to rates between the Middle West and

[32] *Railroad Commission of Nevada* v. *S. P. Co.*, 21 I.C.C. 329 (1911); *City of Spokane* v. *N. P. Ry. Co.*, 21 I.C.C. 400 (1911); *Commodity Rates to Pacific Coast Terminals*, 32 I.C.C. 611 (1915), and 34 I.C.C. 13 (1915); *Reopening Fourth Section Applications*, 40 I.C.C. 35 (1916); 46 I.C.C. 236 (1917); 48 I.C.C. 79 (1918).

[33] *Transcontinental Cases of 1922*, 74 I.C.C. 48 (1922); *Commodity Rates to Pacific Coast Terminals*, 107 I.C.C. 421 (1926); *Southern Pacific Transcontinental Cases*, 182 I.C.C. 770 (1932); and *Transcontinental Eastbound Sugar, 1931*, 188 I.C.C. 523 (1932).

intermountain and Pacific coast points, the problem is somewhat different. The Commission has here refused to give Fourth Section relief, partly because it is believed the rates would not be "compensatory" but apparently also on the ground that it involves market competition rather than competition of alternative routes. Except in minor cases this mid-western traffic does not have the practical alternative of moving via the Atlantic or Gulf routes to the Pacific coast. This attitude is in accord with the general policy of the Commission with reference to *market* as distinguished from *alternative route* competition.

VII. THE FREIGHT RATE STRUCTURE AND THE MOVEMENT TOWARD UNIFORMITY

The freight charges of the railroads of the country taken as a whole constitute the so-called rate structure. This structure, which has always been and still is very complex, includes class rates applicable to broad classes of commodities and commodity rates applicable to particular commodities. The placing of commodities in classes reduces enormously the number of specific rates. Even so, railroad classifications are very complex affairs.

There are three classifications of importance in the United States—the Official, the Southern, and the Western. Official classification covers roughly the territory north of the Ohio River and east of the Mississippi: Southern classification includes the area south of the Ohio and east of the Mississippi; and Western classification covers that part of the country west of the Mississippi. In each of these classification districts we find a large number of commodity ratings.

A distinction is also made as to carload and less-than-carload rates. The class in which a given commodity will be placed depends upon whether it is to be moved in carload or less-than-carload lots. Similarly, packing and container rules affect the rate.

Rate territories in general follow the classification territories. The Eastern district, however, is divided into three sub-rate groups: New England, Eastern Trunk-Line, and Central territories. Southern territory is treated as a unit, with the exception of the Florida peninsula. The Western district is split up into Southwest, Western Trunk-Line, and Mountain-Pacific territories. In addition, there is the so-called Transcontinental rate structure which is applied to shipments between the Mountain-Pacific area and that portion of the United States lying east of the Rocky Mountains.

During the last two decades rates and classifications have become increasingly standardized. By 1918 there was enough uniformity in respect to rules and commodity descriptions to make possible a consolidation of the three major classifications, Official, Southern, and Western, into one. As a result the Consolidated Classification became effective December 30, 1919.[34] Uniformity was not achieved in this decision but rules, commodity descriptions, packing classifications, etc., were standardized.

Under the mandates of the Transportation Act (section 15a) and the Hoch-Smith resolution, the Commission has engaged in an exhaustive investigation of the class rates of the entire country.[35] No attempt is being

---

[34] *Consolidated Classification Case*, 54 I.C.C. 1 (1919). For a history of the efforts of the Commission and the carriers to bring about a uniform classification, see the various annual reports of the Commission. Consult also *Re Western Classification*, 25 I.C.C. 442, 453-64 (1912).

[35] *Southern Class Rate Investigation*, 100 I.C.C. 513 (1925); 109 I.C.C. 300 (1926); 113 I.C.C. 200 (1926); 128 I.C.C. 567 (1927).

Western Trunk-Line Class Rates, 164 I.C.C. 1 (1930); 173 I.C.C. 637 (1931); 178 I.C.C. 619 (1932); 181 I.C.C. 301 (1932).

made to bring about a complete uniformity of ratings, but a considerable advance has been made in the direction of uniformity in the number of classes and the percentage relationships. The number of classes has been increased to obviate the necessity of granting numerous exceptions and first class has been established as a standard to which all other classes are related by stated percentages.[36] The advantages of the new arrangement are two in number. First, it paves the way for greater uniformity of rates in the three classification territories.[37] Second, it renders unnecessary numerous exceptions in commodity rates.[38] In line with its policy of greater uniformity the Commission has made increasing use of the "tapering distance" principle, which grades rates according to distance but not at a uniform rate per ton mile.

Complete uniformity in class and commodity rates, as the Commission recognizes, is impossible if not undesirable. Operating and financial conditions are not uniform in the different regions of the country. For example, the factor of comparatively light traffic density

---

Eastern Class Rate Investigation, 164 I.C.C. 314 (1930); 171 I.C.C. 481 (1931); 177 I.C.C. 156 (1931).

Consolidated Southwestern Cases, 123 I.C.C. 203 (1927); 139 I.C.C. 535 (1928); 144 I.C.C. 630 (1928); 147 I.C.C. 165 (1928); 148 I.C.C. 282 (1928); 148 I.C.C. 613 (1929); 155 I.C.C. 504 (1929); 159 I.C.C. 93 (1927); 164 I.C.C. 565 (1930); 169 I.C.C. 789 (1930); 173 I.C.C. 263 (1931); 179 I.C.C. 17 (1932); 183 I.C.C. 405 (1932); 183 I.C.C. 665 (1932); 185 I.C.C. 357 (1932); 185 I.C.C. 799 (1932).

[36] In Official and Western territories, 23 classes were set up; in Southwestern, 22 classes; and in Southern, 12 classes. Second-class rates in Official and Western territories were 92.5 per cent of first-class, while rates in twenty-third class were 13 per cent of first class. In Southwestern territory the range was from 85 per cent on second class to 12 per cent on twenty-second class. In Southern territory the percentages were 85 on second class and 17.5 on twelfth class.

[37] *Eastern Class Rate Investigation,* 164 I.C.C. 314, 371 (1930).

[38] *Western Trunk-Line Class Rates,* 164 I.C.C. 1, 194 (1930).

has been held to justify higher rates for the upper half of the lower peninsula of Michigan and the upper portion of New England. Likewise, Western Trunk-Line territory has been divided into three zones, each having its own level of rates, as a means of handling varying transportation conditions. When a particular carrier needs greater revenue than is produced by the general level prescribed for the territory it serves, a number of devices are employed, including "arbitraries," or higher differential rates, and "constructive mileage," or a larger division of joint rates to the financially weak carrier than it would be entitled to receive on a mileage basis.[39]

Commodity rates by their very nature cannot be uniform throughout the country. They are explained by exceptional conditions, such as the volume and character of traffic, or the competitive conditions which may exist for a particular railroad in a given territory. The exceptional factors which often give rise to commodity rates may be illustrated by the action taken by the Delaware and Hudson Railroad in 1925. A commodity rate was established on electrical machinery moving from Schenectady to Brooklyn, a distance of 354 miles over the Delaware and Hudson route, to meet the class rate of the New York Central Railroad over whose line the distance

[39] In the *New England Divisions Case*, 66 I.C.C. 196 (1922), the Commission increased by 15 per cent the amounts received by the New England carriers on traffic to and from that territory in order to augment their revenues. The connecting railroads, affected by this ruling, asserted that the Commission did not possess the power of apportioning joint rates on the basis of revenue needs, and that, even if Congress had conferred such power, the division of rates on this basis was unconstitutional. On appeal, the Supreme Court upheld the Commission because "the provision concerning divisions was an integral part of the machinery for distributing the funds expected to be raised by the new rate-fixing sections." *New England Divisions Case*, 261 U.S. 184, 191 (1923).

was only 171 miles.[40] The expectation was that the low rate would move a larger volume of traffic, but it was undesirable to lower the general level of rates, which were reasonable, to accomplish the purpose in view. It was clearly undesirable from the railroad standpoint to accord the commodity in question a lower classification because there was no necessity for special treatment in other districts.

VIII. SUMMARY AND CONCLUSIONS

On the basis of the foregoing description and analysis, we reach the following conclusions:

1. Railroad freight rate levels declined but slightly from 1910 through 1916; rose sharply from 1917 to 1921; declined materially in 1922; declined slightly from 1923 to 1929; and fell appreciably from 1929 to 1932. The level of rates in 1931 was about 45 per cent higher than that of 1913.

2. The trend of passenger rates from 1910 to 1922 was similar to the course of freight rates. After 1923 passenger rates declined considerably more than freight rates. The level of passenger rates in 1931 was about 25 per cent above that of 1913.

3. Railroad earnings show very little correlation with railway rates. Factors other than rate changes are mainly responsible for the fluctuations in earnings during the past two decades.

4. Rate decisions of the Interstate Commerce Commission and the United States Railroad Administration greatly affected the level of both freight and passenger charges between 1917 and 1922. Rates on both classes of traffic were substantially increased in 1917, 1918, and

[40] *Traffic World*, Apr. 4, 1925, p. 867.

1920, and in 1922 freight rates were materially redu

5. Decisions of the Commission relating to the le of rates and to particular rates did not, between 1923 a 1929, appreciably reduce the general level of freight rates.

6. Since 1929 the Commission has granted some rate increases; but the increasing severity of the competition of other agencies of transportation, and the depression, have resulted in a reduction of the level of freight rates.

7. Under the Hoch-Smith resolution the Commission effected various readjustments of rate schedules; but owing to Supreme Court disapproval no important reductions of rates in the interest of depressed industries were put into effect. The policy of aiding depressed industry is difficult to administer and unsound in principle.

8. The Commission has placed several significant limitations on competition as a factor in rate making by: (1) giving increased attention to distance scales, (2) removing many large group and blanket rates, (3) allowing communities the benefits of natural advantages, (4) discouraging the wasteful transportation of property, and (5) employing many tests to determine the relative and absolute reasonableness of rates.

9. Although the Commission appreciates that it is logically and practically impossible to relate rates to costs with any degree of finality, it has made increasing use of the cost-of-service principle in rate making. This is evidenced by the doctrine that all rates should more than cover the direct outlays chargeable against particular traffic, and by the use of cost comparisons involving risk, special services, traffic conditions, physical conditions, and the distance hauled. An exception to this policy is found in the refusal to permit lower rates on train-load than on carload lots.

10. Both the law and the Commission's decisions make for confusion in connection with the long-and-short-haul problem. A definite policy should be formulated as to the importance that should be attached respectively to *alternative route* and *market competition*.

11. For a number of years the Commission has pursued a policy of greater standardization and uniformity with respect to classification and class and commodity rates. The Commission recognizes, however, that uniformity is impossible if not undesirable because of the lack of unity of operating and financial conditions as between territories and as between carriers.

CHAPTER VIII

OBSOLESCENT LINES

Among the factors affecting the net income of American railways in recent years is the increasing number of unprofitable branches and short independent lines.

I. THE EXTENT OF RAILWAY ABANDONMENTS

Before attempting to estimate the probable amount of obsolescent railway mileage, we shall examine the extent of the abandonments already effected.

1. *Abandonments authorized by the Interstate Commerce Commission, 1920-1932.* By the terms of the Interstate Commerce Act, as amended in 1920,[1] Congress authorized the issuance by the Interstate Commerce Commission of certificates of public convenience and necessity for the extension of existing lines of railroad, the construction of new lines, and the abandonment of all or any portion of a line of railroad or the operation thereof. As the law stands, no line of railroad operating in interstate commerce may be abandoned except by specific authority of the Commission. Such permission is granted only after a public hearing, in which both the railroad making application for abandonment and the individuals and communities whose interests would presumably be adversely affected by such abandonment are given an opportunity to present their case.

During the twelve years ending October 31, 1932, about 740 formal applications have been made to the Commission seeking permission for the abandonment

---

[1] Paragraphs 18 to 22 of Section 1 of the act; see *Annual Report of the Interstate Commerce Commission*, 1920, p. 26.

of approximately 12,000 miles of railway line. Certificates authorizing abandonment, in whole or in part, were issued by the Commission during the same period in 616 of these cases, covering 8,772 miles, while 84 applications involving about 1,600 miles of road have been denied, dismissed, or withdrawn.[2] Authorization of abandonment has proceeded, therefore, at an average rate of slightly over 730 miles per year. Compared with the total mileage of railway line in the United States at the end of 1920, namely, 252,845 miles, the abandonments authorized over the past twelve years represent less than three per cent.[3] There has been a tendency, however, to speed up the rate of abandonment in recent years.

2. *Character and location of abandoned lines.* Most of the abandonments authorized by the Commission have been for very short pieces of railroad line. In very few instances has the Commission sanctioned the abandonment of entire railroads. The longest of these, the Chicago, Peoria, and St. Louis, did not exceed 235 miles,[4] and in only 26 other cases have certificates been granted for the abandonment of lines, in whole or in part, in excess of 50 miles. The average for all cases over 50 miles between 1920 and 1932 was about 81 miles, while for the entire 616 authorizations the general average was 14 miles. Excluding the 28 cases involving 50 miles or more, the average for the remainder is slightly above 11 miles.

[2] The above statements cannot be made more exact, since complete data for 1921 are not available. There are some duplications in these cases.

[3] See *Annual Reports of the Interstate Commerce Commission*, 1920-1932.

[4] This line was not, in fact, abandoned in the physical sense, most of its mileage having been absorbed into other lines of railway.

It is obvious that most of the abandonment of railway lines already effected represents properties which are more in the nature of stubs or spurs than fully developed branch line "feeders." A considerable proportion, indeed, consists of extensions built to serve single "industries" or single plants. While the 84 applications for abandonment which have been denied, dismissed, or withdrawn, involved lines of somewhat greater average length—approximately 19 miles as against about 14 miles for the applications approved—the general average for 693 applications filed since 1922 is less than 17 miles. This seems to indicate that in the view of responsible railway managements the problem of pruning off unprofitable lines could best be approached by starting with the smaller and less obviously necessary properties, whether independent roads or parts of larger systems. Whether the time has now come for more radical surgery is a question concerning which there appears to be considerable difference of opinion among railway operating people. This question, however, is reserved for more adequate discussion in the next section. It is significant, perhaps, that several of the larger railway systems have embarked upon a vigorous policy of abandonment within the past two years, so far as can be judged from the number and sponsorship of the applications which the Commission has approved.

Railway mileage abandoned during the period 1921-1932 was very unevenly distributed as to geographical location. Abandonment was disproportionately large in the southeastern and north central groups of states and disproportionately small in the northeastern, western, and southwestern areas. The following table shows the mileage of abandoned lines in the several geographical areas and their percentage relation to the total miles of line and to the total mileage of abandonments authorized:

MILEAGE ABANDONED BY GEOGRAPHICAL AREAS, 1920–1932

Region	Region Mileage[a]	Mileage Abandoned		
		In Miles	Per Cent of Region Mileage	Per Cent of U. S. Mileage Abandoned
New England....	7,598	200.70	2.6	2.5
Middle Atlantic..	32,117	590.80	1.8	7.4
Southeastern.....	38,731	1,845.60	4.8	23.1
Southwestern....	41,124	1,150.10	2.8	14.4
North Central....	62,248	2,600.00	4.2	32.5
Western.........	67,228	1,609.05	2.4	20.1
Total........	249,046	7,996.25	3.2	100.0

[a] Dec. 31, 1930.

The lines included in the New England and Middle Atlantic groups on the one hand, and in the Western and Southwestern groups on the other, apparently resisted the general tendency towards abandonment, or at least failed to persuade the Commission of its need, to anything like the same degree as those in the Southeastern and North Central groups.

3. *Causes cited for unprofitableness of lines abandoned.* The numerous factors which have been assigned for the financial losses occasioned by the operation of lines sought to be abandoned fall into three or four groups. These have to do respectively with: (1) the exhaustion of local tributary natural resources, the destruction, abandonment, or removal of local industrial plants or resorts, or the failure of local projects to develop as originally anticipated; (2) motor vehicle competition; (3) competition by other forms of transport; (4) miscellaneous causes.

An analysis of 565 cases in which authorization was given by the Interstate Commerce Commission for abandonment of 7,997 miles of line during the period 1920 to 1932 has been made by Mr. R. E. Westmeyer of Rice Institute. The results of this analysis, which eliminates all duplications or rehearings, are incorporated, with the permission of the author, in the subsequent discussion. Mr. Westmeyer's results have been summarized in the table on the next page which groups into a few inclusive classifications the various causes cited and indicates their relative importance as affecting the number of abandonments authorized and the mileage involved.

The overwhelming importance of the exhaustion of natural resources as a factor causing obsolescence of short lines or branches of railway is clearly brought out by this tabulation. Alone or in combination with the destruction or abandonment of local industries or the failure of projects to develop—both of which are closely analogous to the exhaustion factor—it accounted for nearly one-half of all the cases and for more than one-third of the mileage for which the Commission has authorized abandonment.

The second important factor has been motor vehicle competition. In Mr. Westmeyer's analysis motor vehicle competition was cited as the primary factor accounting for abandonment in about 13 per cent of the cases, which represented somewhat over 20 per cent of the mileage abandoned. Together with other factors, motor competition played a more or less important part in an additional 10 per cent of the mileage. The cases in which it was the sole cause of abandonment, however, were distinctly less numerous than those where it was only one factor, even though a dominant one, among other influences.

REASONS FOR ABANDONMENT 1920–1932[a]

Reasons Given	Number	Per Cent of Cases	Mile-age	Per Cent of Mile-age
(1) Exhaustion of natural resources.....	190	*33.8*	2,165	*27.1*
(2) Destruction or abandonment of plant or resort.....................	34	*6.0*	267	*3.3*
(3) Failure of project to develop........	20	*3.5*	256	*3.2*
(4) Combinations of above factors......	10	*1.8*	150	*1.9*
(5) Exhaustion and motor competition..	35	*6.0*	729	*9.1*
(6) Exhaustion and miscellaneous......	12	*2.1*	192	*2.4*
(7) Plant destruction and miscellaneous.	5	*1.0*	69	*0.8*
(8) Failure of project and motor competition.........................	1	*0.2*	15	*0.2*
(9) Motor competition................	34	*6.0*	608	*7.6*
(10) Motor and other competition.......	15	*2.7*	294	*3.7*
(11) Motor competition and miscellaneous	23	*4.0*	722	*9.1*
(12) Steam railway, electric, and water competition...................	18	*3.2*	336	*4.2*
(13) Depression and motor competition..	3	*0.5*	65	*0.8*
(14) All other factors assigned[b].........	165	*29.4*	2,129	*26.6*
Total, all factors.............	565	*100.0*	7,997	*100.0.*

[a] As assigned by railroads receiving permission of Interstate Commerce Commission to abandon unprofitable mileage. (Based on an analysis by R. E. Westmeyer of 565 cases involving 7,997 miles of line.)

[b] Includes lines abandoned to aid in city planning developments, or to relieve railway congestion in certain areas.

II. ESTIMATES OF UNPROFITABLE MILEAGE AND ITS FINANCIAL BURDEN

The task of determining the probable mileage of obsolescent railway lines and the extent of the financial burden it imposes on the railway system as a whole may be approached from two different angles. One way is to estimate, on the basis of relative traffic densities, the mileage of railway line whose traffic is so thin as to justify the inference that the mileage in question does not pay its way. The other way is to go directly to railway operating officials and ask their judgment as to the extent of this problem in each individual case. Both methods have been used in this study.

1. *Estimate derived from study of traffic density.* The concept of freight traffic density means the average number of ton miles per mile of line. Traffic density is, in general, the most significant single index of the earning power of a railroad or of the relative earning power of different roads. The fundamental importance of freight traffic density in relation to the profitableness of railway operations has been indicated in Chapter IV. The charts on pp. 80 and 83 show that unit cost varies inversely with the density of traffic.

If the Class I steam railways of the United States are grouped on the basis of relative freight traffic density, it will be found that those among them which regularly report annual operating deficits are almost without exception those falling into the light traffic groups. Roads reporting net operating incomes are distributed, with respect to income per mile of line, in practically the same proportion as they are with respect to freight traffic densities. This relationship is illustrated by the summary statement on page 154 in which the 133 Class I roads, for which comparative operating averages for the three years 1927, 1928, and 1929 are available, are classified on the basis of freight density and net railway operating income per mile of line.

All the roads reporting deficits were in the light traffic groups. About a dozen roads managed to save some of their gross revenues for net, even though having a traffic density of less than 500,000 net ton miles, but only a handful earned more than $3,000 per mile of line whose density was not at least 500,000 to 1,000,000 net

FREIGHT TRAFFIC DENSITY AND NET RAILWAY OPERATING INCOME PER MILE OF ROAD[a]
(Based on average of three years 1927, 1928, 1929)

Traffic Density Net Ton Miles Per Mile of Road Annually[b]	Total Number of Roads	Number Reporting Specified Net Operating Income per Mile of Road Annually[c]					
		Operating Deficit	Under $1,000	$1,000 to $3,000	$3,000 to $5,000	$5,000 to $10,000	Over $10,000
Under 250,000	5	2	2	1	—	—	—
250,000— 500,000	13	3	6	3	—	—	1
500,000— 1,000,000	32	4	5	20	1	2	—
1,000,000— 1,500,000	31	2	—	15	12	2	—
1,500,000— 2,000,000	15	—	—	5	4	4	2
2,000,000— 3,000,000	12	—	—	2	5	4	1
3,000,000— 4,000,000	10	—	—	—	1	6	3
4,000,000— 5,000,000	5	—	—	—	—	3	2
5,000,000— 10,000,000	8	—	—	—	—	—	8
Over 10,000,000	2	—	—	—	—	—	2
Totals............	133	11	13	46	23	21	19

[a] Compiled from Interstate Commerce Commission, Bureau of Statistics, *Statement No. 32200, Comparative Statement of Operating Averages of Class I Steam Railways, Years 1931–1927.*

[b] Revenue and non-revenue freight.

[c] Net railway operating *income* as shown in this table, differs from net operating *revenue*, as given in the preceding table, since from the latter must be deducted taxes, and equipment and joint facility rents, in order to determine net operating income.

ton miles—a figure about one-third of the national average for the years 1927 to 1929. Only one road with a freight density below 500,000 earned more than $10,000 per mile of line. This was the Long Island, which enjoys the most lucrative passenger commutation business of any road in the United States. Among the other roads falling into the group earning above $10,000 per mile were practically all the outstanding coal and ore hauling roads, characterized by high traffic density, as well as certain lines, such as the New Haven, whose freight density is not above the general average but which enjoy high revenues per ton mile as well as a profitable passenger business.

The above figures suggest that there may be a fairly definite point in the scale of descending freight traffic densities below which a railroad cannot, under normal operating conditions, earn a net income. The figure of 250,000 net ton miles of revenue freight per mile of line annually has been given wide publicity as marking the dividing line between profitable and unprofitable operations. While it is probably impossible to set up any rigid formula equally applicable to railroads operating under such a wide diversity of conditions as those which characterize the various parts of the United States, it is believed that the figure named may be considered as at least a danger signal. It is distinctly worth while, at any rate, to determine as nearly as possible how extensive the light traffic density lines are in relation to the total railway mileage.

This analysis has been worked out with considerable care by Mr. E. S. Butler, of the Kansas City Southern Railway. According to Mr. Butler's studies, which were based on data relating to various years from 1919 to

1928 for the different railroads, but emphasizing particularly the years following 1924, the total mileage falling in the designation of "light traffic density" lines was as follows:

MILES OF RAILROAD OF SPECIFIED FREIGHT TRAFFIC DENSITY

Density[a]	Class I Roads	Class II Roads	Class III Roads	Total All Roads
Under 50,000	12,912	3,233	3,936	20,081
50,000–100,000	15,467	3,054	813	19,334
100,000–150,000	12,988	1,921	252	15,161
150,000–200,000	10,514	1,116	99	11,729
200,000–250,000	5,861	1,134	11	7,006
Totals	57,742	10,458	5,111	73,311
Total miles of line operated in 1928	238,994	14,219	5,580	258,793
Ratio, light traffic lines to total...	24.0 per cent	73.5 per cent	91.5 per cent	28.3 per cent

[a] Net revenue and non-revenue ton miles for Class I roads; net revenue ton miles for Class II and Class III roads.

This total of 73,311 miles of light traffic lines represents slightly over 28 per cent of the total mileage of line operated in 1928 by the three classes of railroads specified. These 73,311 miles were estimated to have carried less than two per cent of the total freight traffic of the country in 1928, which was about an "average" year for the railroads as a whole.

The average freight traffic density of these lines was only a trifle over 102,000 net ton miles per mile of line annually, or, say 2,000 ton miles per week. This is roughly equivalent to the movement of ten cars of freight per day, at an average car-loading of 35 tons, over each mile of line of the whole 73,000 miles. For a large part of the mileage the density was, of course, much lower. Some 20,000 miles, or more than a quarter of the total, had a traffic density of less than five loaded freight cars per day. Approximately as much more—19,334 miles—had from five to ten cars per day.

The geographical distribution of the light traffic mileage is very uneven. The detailed distribution in terms of miles is indicated by the table on page 158. The figures are based on results for the years 1924 to 1928 inclusive.

The regions where the percentage of light traffic lines is high relatively to the total are in New England and in the Northwestern and Central Western states. The excessively thin traffic in the two latter regions is attributable in no small degree to the competitive overbuilding of former days.

Using the data of the table on page 158, an estimated figure has been built up for the total ton mileage of freight service performed by these lines during an assumed normal year (based on the results of the five years from 1924 to 1928 inclusive). This figure is then multiplied, in each case, by the average freight revenue per ton mile realized by the roads in each of the several regions, on the assumption that the light traffic lines enjoyed the same average revenue per ton mile as all the lines included within the region. This assumption is unduly favorable to the light traffic lines, even if allowance be made for any extra allocation of revenues on account of the service of the branch lines in originating tonnage. Practically the only case in which this procedure penalizes the light traffic lines is in the Pocahontas region, where it may be safely assumed that the average revenue per ton mile is lower on the heavy traffic divisions, owing to the overwhelming preponderance of coal tonnage, than on the light traffic lines. In the

REGIONAL DISTRIBUTION OF LIGHT TRAFFIC DENSITY MILEAGE OPERATED BY CLASS I ROADS
(Classified according to net ton miles of revenue and non-revenue freight per mile of road annually)

Region	Mileage of Line Operated	Under 50,000 net Ton Miles	50,000 to 100,000	100,000 to 150,000	150,000 to 200,000	200,000 to 250,000	Total under 250,000
New England	7,379	905	647	648	245	150	2,595
Great Lakes	27,725	601	732	728	594	369	3,024
Central Eastern	23,669	788	962	817	542	447	3,556
Pocahontas	5,959	219	201	65	83	25	593
Southern	39,809	1,747	2,080	2,015	1,629	745	8,216
Northwestern	48,501	3,112	3,961	3,877	2,741	1,525	15,216
Central Western	53,008	4,152	4,818	3,776	2,624	1,765	17,135
Southwestern	32,548	1,388	2,066	1,062	2,056	835	7,407
United States	238,598	12,912	15,467	12,988	10,514	5,861	57,742

Central Western region the reverse situation probably obtains, because of the high average revenues accruing on the main lines from the long distance "bridge" traffic in perishable foodstuffs. Without attempting any refinements, however, the results may be accepted as at least a first approximation of the gross freight revenues earned by the light traffic lines. The results of this estimate are indicated by the summary statement on page 160.

The total figure obtained by this procedure is about $74,375,000, representing the estimated gross freight revenues directly accruing on the business done by the 57,742 miles of light traffic lines operated by the Class I roads in a typical pre-depression year. This total is equivalent to an annual average of about $1,288 per mile of road of such light traffic lines. The average annual cost of maintenance of way for light traffic, single track branch lines, approximates $800 to $1000 a mile, and taxes frequently run from $150 to $300 per mile. When to these costs are added the expense involved in care of equipment, conducting transportation, and soliciting traffic, not to mention overhead expenses, it is difficult to see how any considerable proportion of mileage having a traffic density of less than 100,000 ton miles per year can be economically justified.

This does not mean, of course, that any such general average figure can be applied indiscriminately to any or all of the numerous questionable branch line or light traffic line situations. Each local problem has to be worked out according to the facts peculiar to the local situation. It does mean, however, that taking the picture "by and large," railway management must make a showing to the effect that substantial reasons exist other than

ESTIMATED ANNUAL FREIGHT REVENUES ACCRUING ON LIGHT TRAFFIC DENSITY MILEAGE, CLASS I ROADS BY REGIONS

Region	Mileage of Line Operated	Freight Density[a] (Thousands of ton miles per mile)	Light Density Mileage[b]	Estimated Traffic on Light Density Lines (Millions of ton miles)	Average Freight Revenue per Ton Mile (Mills)	Estimated Freight Revenues, Light Density Lines	
						Total (Thousands of dollars)	Per Mile (Dollars)
New England..........	7,379	1,357	2,595	242	17.87	4,331	1,669
Great Lakes..........	27,725	3,275	3,024	357	11.08	3,995	1,307
Central Eastern......	23,669	3,995	3,556	400	10.18	4,074	1,145
Pocahontas..........	5,959	7,029	593	52	6.43	335	565
Southern............	39,809	1,577	8,216	930	10.17	9,463	1,151
Northwestern........	48,501	1,194	15,216	1,729	11.14	19,261	1,265
Central Western......	53,008	1,457	17,135	1,855	11.92	22,109	1,290
Southwestern........	32,548	1,200	7,407	901	12.04	10,847	1,464
United States.......	238,598	1,995	57,742	6,467	11.50	74,375	1,288

a Average of 1927-29.
b Under 250,000.

the direct estimated gross earnings of $1,288 per mile to justify the continued retention and operation of many thousands of miles of light traffic lines.

In passing it may be of interest to compare this estimate of $1,288 with the general average freight operating revenues per mile of road for all Class I roads. The latter figure fluctuated between $18,401 and $20,275 during the six years from 1924 to 1929, and for the three years 1927, 1928, and 1929, averaged $19,628, or roughly fifteen times as much as the above estimated freight earnings on the light traffic mileage, even though these latter are included in the general average. If the 57,742 miles of light traffic lines and their estimated earnings are deducted from the total, the remaining 181,000 miles—more or less—would show average freight earnings for 1927-29 of approximately $25,800 per mile of road, or practically twenty times as high an average rate as the estimated figure for the light traffic lines.

No credit has been given the light traffic lines in the above estimate on account of passenger earnings or miscellaneous sources of revenue. The almost universal testimony is to the effect that on the overwhelming majority of the thin traffic branch lines passenger revenues have practically disappeared. On many branch lines, in fact, passenger train service has been completely abandoned; on many others passenger service is furnished by "mixed trains," many of which are operated on a less than daily basis. It is not believed, therefore, that any very substantial inaccuracy, generally speaking, results from ignoring incidental passenger service revenues when considering the potential earnings of the light traffic lines.

The so-called short lines require some additional analysis. Upwards of 70 per cent of the total mileage of the Class II roads and over 90 per cent of that of the Class III roads is included in the designation of light traffic density lines, that is, those having an annual freight density of less than 250,000 net tons of revenue freight per mile of road. Taken as a whole, the entire group of nearly 600 Class II and Class III roads make a poor showing, as is indicated by the following table:

OPERATING AND FINANCIAL DATA OF CLASS II AND CLASS III RAILWAYS
1927–1930[a]
(Per mile of road)

Year	Ton Miles Revenue Freight	Net Railway Operating Income	Net Income After Interest	Capital Stock	Long Term Debt	Corporate Surplus
Class II roads						
1927	199,437	$710	−44	$16,280	$18,374	−$2,092
1928	200,747	671	−11	15,753	17,276	−2,480
1929	192,640	870	111	15,521	17,421	−2,667
1930	162,958	457	−221	15,879	17,589	−2,766
Class III roads						
1927	44,950	−$156	−$433	$9,748	$7,143	−$3,622
1928	51,640	−10	−301	9,552	7,187	−3,892
1929	48,721	11	−318	8,785	7,195	−3,457
1930	44,952	−135	−437	8,593	6,831	−3,307

[a] Compiled from Interstate Commerce Commission, *Statistics of Railways*, 1927–1930.

Of the 255 Class II roads reporting to the Commission in 1928, at least 79 failed to earn their operating expenses and taxes. For the 336 Class III roads the corresponding number was 157. These two groups of deficit roads operated about 5,197 and 2,029 miles of line respectively, or a total of 8,000 out of the aggregate of 20,000 miles of road included in the Class II and Class

III lines. It is believed that this figure of approximately 8000 miles may be taken as a conservative estimate of the short line mileage which is definitely unprofitable. The roads in question, it should be noticed, had incurred these deficits before meeting interest charges. This analysis clearly supports the foregoing estimate of about 11,000 miles of obsolescent mileage on Class II and Class III roads.

In summary: If we assume 250,000 ton miles of freight per mile of line annually to be essential to profitable operation, 73,311 miles were obsolete before the depression began, of which 57,742 miles were on Class I roads. If we assumed 100,000 ton miles to mark the dividing line, 39,415 miles would be in the obsolete category, of which 28,379 miles belonged to Class I roads. These estimates, it should be borne in mind, are for predepression years.

2. *Estimate derived from testimony of railway officials.* In order to secure the viewpoint of responsible railway operating officials as to the seriousness of the problem presented by obsolescent branch lines, an inquiry was addressed to 36 of the larger Class I railroads. These railroads which have supplied information in response to specific questions on obsolescent branch lines embrace most of the larger "systems" as well as several roads of intermediate size. Collectively they operate approximately 200,000 miles of line, or nearly five-sixths of the entire mileage of the Class I roads, and a slightly higher proportion of the estimated branch line mileage.

The responses of these executives give a fairly good indication of the significance they attach to the branch line problem and also permit a rough estimate of the mileage of questionable lines and of the financial burden they occasion the parent systems. It should be stated in advance, however, that no precise line of demarcation between a profitable and an unprofitable branch line operation can be drawn. It is only in the clear case where *all* the expenses of operation and overhead fairly chargeable *against the branch* exceed the *total system revenues* accruing from business originating upon or destined to that branch, or fairly allocable to it on account of "overhead" or "bridge" traffic, that an unequivocal answer can be obtained to the question whether the branch line pays its way or not. Obviously there are relatively few such cases. These are the cases in which abandonment procedure has been instituted or where it is clearly indicated as the appropriate remedy.

Far more numerous and much more difficult of determination are these cases where some surplus revenue remains above "out of pocket" expenses of branch line operation, plus a reasonable allocation of certain items of general system expense, some share of which the branch lines may reasonably be expected to absorb. The amount of such surplus revenues in relation to the *estimated* cost to the main line of handling the traffic originated on or destined to the branch is the crux of the problem. Railway cost accounting has not yet progressed to the point where precise answers are to be had to questions of this kind; indeed it may be inherently impossible to attain such a degree of precision. The most that can be expected, as a practical matter, is a reasonable balance of probabilities, giving due consideration to all the relevant factors in each individual situation.

Moreover, operating conditions or emergencies, which may require the utilization of the branch in question as a "relief" or "detour" line for traffic ordinarily routed

over other lines, are frequently controlling in the decision to continue a branch line, regardless of the dis-
appearance of its local traffic. More remote considerations, such as the possibility of abandoned branch lines
being acquired by rival or unfriendly roads, or even by
local interests which might persuade the regulatory
commissions to accord them a relatively high division
of through rates, are also sometimes present. It is not
improbable that the cumulative influence of these intangibles have in many instances retarded the systematic
analysis by railway operating officials of the purely financial aspects of branch line operation. In any event, their
attitude in numerous cases is probably colored at least
as much by general considerations of high policy as by
the immediate dollars and cents aspect.

The questions to which answers were solicited in the
investigation were designed to develop the matured
opinion of railway managements with respect to the
mileage of questionable branch lines in their respective systems, the seriousness of its financial drain, the
extent to which operating economies have been effected
in conducting branch line traffic, and the possibilities of
additional economies short of abandonment, the experience of the several roads with respect to abandoning
unprofitable mileage, and the potentialities of additional
savings which might be expected to accrue from a program of further abandonment. In general, effort was
made to secure the judgment of the respective railway
managements as to the essential importance of the whole
branch line problem, rather than to obtain precise data
which could be used in formulating an independent
estimate with respect to the several questions raised.
Thus, instead of asking the direct question as to the ex-

tent of the current deficit incurred in operating branch lines, an attempt was made to ascertain whether a given railway system would be better off without a particular branch line than with it. This type of question involves, of course, the balancing of intangibles, and often does not permit an unqualified answer.

Some railway officers were frank to admit that their roads contained a fairly large mileage of branch lines whose value to their systems was at least questionable, while others seemed to avoid the implications of such an admission and sought rather to indicate the various reasons why light traffic lines should not or could not be surrendered. These differences are illuminating, not only because they illustrate opposing attitudes or differences in individual temperament, but also as indicating differences in the thoroughness with which this phase of the railway management problem has been thought through by those who are responsible for decisions of fundamental policy.

It may be in order to make one further general observation. This is to the effect that radically different conclusions will probably be reached as to the unprofitableness of much branch line mileage according as one starts from the premise of railway competition or that of consolidation. If an indefinite continuance of the traditional policy of competition between rival railway systems is to be taken for granted, it is extremely improbable that railway managements will bring themselves to sanction the abandonment of more than a very minor fraction of their respective branch lines, even in those areas where the traffic is of the leanest. In this respect the branch line problem is quite of a piece with various other competitive railway practices; no one wants to surrender even the slightest appearance of an advantage to his rival, even though his stockholders, and indirectly the general public, may be paying a totally disproportionate price for the privilege of competitive service.

About one-third of the co-operating railway executives denied the existence of *any* unprofitable mileage in their respective systems, or at least gave no clear-cut indication of its quantitative extent or of the amount of financial drain imposed thereby upon total system revenues. In a number of instances where the fact of unprofitable branch lines was conceded it was not found practicable to attempt an estimate of their financial significance. In very few cases would the responding officers commit themselves to an estimate of the potential savings which might be expected from abandonment of branch lines as to whose value to the system they were frankly doubtful. These omissions reduce somewhat the basis of specific information available for an estimate of unprofitable branch line mileage. Taking the figures as reported, however, the general results are as shown in the table on the next page.

These results, for reasons already sufficiently indicated, are believed to err on the side of conservatism. Particularly in the Western district is the unprofitable branch line mileage probably understated—this because two large systems failed to name any definite figure, although the general tenor of their returns left no doubt that they were affected by the condition to no less an extent than their neighboring systems. If it may be assumed that approximately the same percentage relation of unprofitable branches to total branch mileage, or to total system mileage, holds in these two cases as in the other Western roads, an estimated 600 miles, more or

BRANCH LINE MILEAGE ADMITTED TO BE UNPROFITABLE
(Based chiefly upon results for 1929, or an equally good year)

District	(1) Number of Roads	(2) Total System Mileage	(3) Total Branch Mileage	(4) Unprofitable Branch Mileage	(5) Percentage Col. (4) to Col. (3)	(6) Percentage Col. (4) to Col. (2)
Roads Reporting Some Unprofitable Branches						
Eastern District............	7	27,217	5,503	907	16.5	3.3
Southern District...........	7	34,553	10,216	1,608	15.7	4.7
Western District............	11	95,491	39,830	3,360	8.4	3.5
United States...............	25	157,261	55,549	5,875	10.6	3.7
All Reporting Roads						
Eastern District............	12	42,497	11,954	907	7.6	2.1
Southern District...........	8	35,756	10,718	1,608	15.0	4.5
Western District............	16	120,582	51,274	3,360	6.6	2.8
United States...............	36	199,435	74,251	5,875	7.9	2.9

less, may be added to the reported figure for the group of 16 roads in the Western district, making an estimated total of 3,960 miles. This still leaves two roads in this group which do not admit any unprofitable mileage.

Similarly in the Eastern district, there is little reasonable room for doubt that some unprofitable branch mileage may be charged against one of the larger systems which reports a considerable number of very short branch lines, many of which are characterized by extremely thin traffic density. This road did not give any specific figure for unprofitable branch mileage, although it was clear that reasons other than purely financial explain the determination to retain at least some of these questionable branch lines. No attempt has been made in this instance, however, to adjust the returns, nor in one or two other cases of Eastern roads whose reported figures for unprofitable branch mileage are obviously too conservative.

The proportion of unprofitable branch mileage to total system mileage reported in the South, 4.6 per cent, is higher than in either of the other two districts, despite the fact that one large system reported a figure below one-half of one per cent. With but one exception, and that a relatively small road, all the railroads in the Southern district admitted having some unprofitable branch lines, the figure running as high, in one case, as one-third of the total branch line mileage of the system.

If the figure for unprofitable mileage reported by the Western group of roads is adjusted as was indicated above, the total for the 36 systems is raised to approximately 6475 miles, or a trifle over 3 per cent of their total system mileage. This, to repeat, is believed to be

an extremely conservative figure. If the same ratio—
3.2 per cent—is applied to the mileage of all the Class
I roads of the United States, an estimated aggregate
figure is obtained of approximately 7900 miles.

This figure may be compared with approximately
39,415 miles of obsolete lines as measured by traffic
density of less than 100,000 ton miles per mile of line
annually (p. 156). The difference is perhaps largely attributable to the natural reluctance of railway officials to
consider properties as obsolete so long as there is reasonable hope that revenues may be increased or so long as the
mileage in question is counted as an investment asset by
the Commission in its valuation data and is of possible
value in connection with consolidation agreements.

It is impossible to compute the amount of the financial
drain imposed upon the railroads by unprofitable mileage. This is because the railway accounts do not show the
operating deficits separately for branch lines. Accordingly, we make no effort to present an estimate of the annual losses sustained. It may, however, be useful to indicate the extent of the capital investment in obsolete
branch and short line mileage.

The capital investment in the unprofitable branch
lines of the 13 large railway systems which supplied such
information in response to the Committee's inquiry averaged about $23,700 per mile of road. While the figures
for individual roads differed more or less, the regional
averages for the three major districts varied less than 6
per cent from this figure. For the Class II roads as a
whole the average figure for investment in railway property at the end of 1928 was $35,163 per mile of road.
This figure exceeds the average investment per mile of

road in the unprofitable branch lines of the 13 large systems, since it includes *all* railway property—equipment, terminals, shops, general offices, etc.—and not merely the track and necessary appurtenant structures connected with the operation of the branch lines as such. For the Class III roads the corresponding figure for investment per mile of road was $17,107.

Applying these investment figures to the foregoing estimates of obsolescent mileage, we obtain the following results: Class I roads (officials' estimate), $187,467,000; Class II roads, $182,848,000; Class III roads, $47,900,000—or a total of $418,215,000. If we take the larger estimate of 39,000 miles and assume the same ratio of investment per mile the total invested capital would equal about $1,160,000,000. This is approximately 4 per cent of the total railway investment.

The writing off of so substantial an investment in obsolescent railway property may at first glance seem a rather formidable undertaking. In the case of the short lines—Class II and III roads—the problem is comparatively simple. It is not a question of curtailing operations or of writing down the value of the investment, but of discontinuing operations and liquidating the corporation. Inclusion of these roads in our list of mileage which ought to be abandoned is a recommendation, not that these roads should be required to discontinue service, but that they be permitted to do so whenever the security holders are convinced that they have nothing to gain by continued operation. The maintenance of service on these roads does not constitute a burden on the transportation system as a whole.

In the case of the unprofitable branch lines of the large railway systems, the situation is somewhat different.

Maintenance of service involves a dilution of the earnings of the entire system and impairs the capacity of the road to render services in the fields in which such service is economically justified.

Retirement of railway property abandoned and not replaced does not necessitate a charge against current earnings. It is accounted for by a direct charge to profit and loss account with offsetting credits to the appropriate property investment accounts. In some cases, however, the profit and loss accounts may not be large enough to absorb the charge.

Another factor which occasionally, though not often, gives rise to difficulty in efforts to secure abandonment is the mixed character of owner and creditor relationship as between the holders of the various classes of equities in main lines and branch lines. Generally speaking, it seems probable that the majority of the branch lines, or at least the majority of those here under discussion, are included within the coverage of general system mortgages, or of mortgages covering substantial parts of the entire system mileage. In these cases, while it might be true as a technical matter that the abandonment of a particular bit of railway property would diminish the legal security of the loan, as a practical matter the effect would be directly the opposite. The bondholder's security is fundamentally the earning power of the road as a whole. Anything which operates to increase the aggregate net earnings—and abandonment of unprofitable branches surely does that—really enhances rather than reduces the bond holder's interest.

III. ATTITUDE OF THE INTERSTATE COMMERCE COMMISSION TOWARD ABANDONMENTS

The obsolete road has presented to the Commission an important question of public policy. The problem is simple enough in the case of exhausted resources, where the need for the facilities in question practically ceases. In most cases of this kind there has been no opposition to the application for authority to abandon and practically without exception these applications have been granted.

A much more difficult situation confronts the Commission in those cases where a local population has gathered about the line in question, which is dependent, to some degree at least, upon the continued operation of the road. The basic problem here is essentially that of balancing the effect of abandonment upon the local shipping and traveling public against the effect of continued unprofitable operation upon the railroad and its owners. As the Commission has put it, with respect to the first of these alternatives: "Practically every abandonment of a line of railroad injures or inconveniences some of the people who have been served by it."[5] And again: "The test established by the statute is not whether the public convenience and necessity 'require' abandonment but whether the public convenience and necessity 'permit' abandonment."[6] With respect to the second alternative, the Supreme Court of the United States declared in 1925: "A railway may be compelled to continue the service of a branch or part of a line, although the operation involves a loss . . . this is true even where the system as a whole fails to earn a fair return upon the value of the property."[7]

Generally speaking, the Commission has exercised its authority very cautiously in sanctioning abandonment in contested cases. Permission to abandon has, on the

[5] *Abandonment by Northern Pacific Ry.,* 138 I.C.C. 213, 219 (1928).
[6] *Southern Pacific Co. Abandonment,* 158 I.C.C. 439, 443 (1929).
[7] *Fort Smith Traction Co.* v. *Bourland,* 267 U. S. 330; see also *St. Louis and San Francisco Ry. Co.* v. *Gill,* 156 U. S. 649; and *Puget Sound Traction Co.* v. *Reynolds,* 244 U. S. 574.

whole, been granted only in those instances where a clear showing has been made that the facilities in question no longer serve a useful purpose, either because the original traffic has disappeared or other facilities are available to serve the public, or where the railroad has been continuously operated at a loss and had no prospect of improving its position. The Commission has given little encouragement, however, to the doctrine that branch line abandonments are to be permitted solely on the ground that such operations are unprofitable, while the road as a whole is prospering, or even, in some cases, where it is not. The public convenience must govern in such instances.

Thus, in disposing of a set of applications made by the Boston and Maine in 1925 to abandon some 90 miles of branch lines in New Hampshire, part of which were granted and part denied, the Commission declared:

. . . This railroad and the people it serves are peculiarly interdependent and in these abandonment cases there must be kept constantly in view the necessity of the preservation of as much as possible of the present mileage in the service of the greatest number of the people. The evidence seems to be conclusive that not a few of the lines which it is now proposed to abandon should never have been built. Under present conditions they would not be built. At the time of their projection as independent enterprises it seems to have been understood that some of them were built for purely competitive or strategic reasons.

But irrespective of the origin of an existing line, people gather about it and create for themselves an interest in and a dependence upon it. Under these circumstances abandonment brings about the kind of hardships with which it is so difficult to deal. The sufferers in such cases have no redress against those guilty of the original error, nor were they responsible for that error. In some of the instant cases the extent of hardship which would probably follow abandonment would be very great, while in other cases it would be negligible. . . . The serious and difficult problem is how to sustain both the railroad system and New England territory as a whole without undue hardship on particular local territories. Benefits to the system of particular abandonments must be weighed against the inconveniences and losses which those abandonments will inflict upon the communities immediately affected. Benefits to particular communities of continued operation must be weighed against the burdens and retarding effect of such operation upon the development of the Boston and Maine system as a whole. . . .[8]

In granting relief to roads burdened with unprofitable branch lines the Commission has usually insisted that *alternative facilities* be available for the service of the public, either supplied by other railroads or by adequate highways. The absence of such alternative facilities was one of the principal obstacles blocking the attempt of the Boston and Maine to abandon the bulk of its unprofitable New Hampshire lines, referred to in the preceding paragraph. The decision in numerous other cases has depended upon the same point.[9] In an increasing proportion of abandonment applications in recent years the carrier seeking relief from the burden of continued operation of unprofitable lines has itself offered to provide substitute service in the form of motor transportation by public highways. Generally speaking, however, the railroads have been loath to engage in this form of transport, particularly in those cases where it may still be necessary to maintain the local line of railway in order to take care of occasional carload shipments of low

[8] *Abandonment of Branches by B. & M. R.R.*, 105 I.C.C. 13, 15-16 (1925).
[9] *Public-Convenience Certificate to S. and B. C. Ry.*, 67 I.C.C. 384 (1921); *Public-Convenience Certificate to P. M. Ry.*, 70 I.C.C. 324 (1921); *Abandonment of Branch Lines of C. and G. R.R.*, 71 I.C.C. 725 (1922).

grade freight. A railroad operating as a public carrier may not, like the private operator of a motor trucking service, choose its customers or select the type of tonnage it prefers to handle. It must serve all comers and accept whatever freight is offered, whether profitable to handle by motor transport or not.

While the Commission has insisted that the burden of proof very definitely rests upon the carrier to show that continued operation of the line sought to be abandoned would presumably result in further losses, and while it is the duty of the road to make every reasonable effort, through all practicable economies, to continue operations, even if on the basis of drastically reduced service, the public is also not without its obligations. As the Commission declared in refusing the Pere Marquette permission to abandon its Freeport branch: ". . . The mere desire to have a railroad is not enough. There must exist the will to co-operate in its operation and the ability to support it adequately."[10] Again, in relieving railroad traffic departments from the necessity of having to importune people to patronize a particular road, the Commission has said: "Shippers who must be coaxed to use any line of railroad evidently have no urgent need of that line."[11] In any event, the Commission must be convinced that the possibility of a future increase of traffic is a real one. In sanctioning the proposed abandonment of the Hawkinsville and Florida Southern, an independent 93-mile road which had fallen on evil days,

[10] *Abandonment of Branch by Pere Marquette*, 72 I.C.C. 267, 271 (1922); see also *Abandonment of Branch by Pere Marquette*, 72 I.C.C. 303 (1922); *Colorado and Southern Ry. Co. Abandonment*, 166 I.C.C. 470 (1930); *Abandonment by Hill City Ry. Co.*, 150 I.C.C. 159 (1928).

[11] *Abandonment by Miss. Valley Co.*, 145 I.C.C. 289, 293 (1928); see also 170 I.C.C. 269; 184 I.C.C. 575; 184 I.C.C. 754.

the Commission declared: "It is obvious . . . that the hope of increased business in the future can hardly prevail against the results of actual experience in the operation of the line."[12] In a number of instances in authorizing abandonment the Commission has suggested the sale of the property, either in whole or in part, to whatever local interests would assume responsibility for continued operation. Several of the longer independent roads which have been "abandoned" have, as a matter of fact, been acquired in this way by local interests, or by other railroads, usually in separate sections rather than as "going concerns," and their mileage thus kept in service. Short branches of larger roads have also been sold off to local industries at their salvage value and operated as industrial subsidiaries, relinquishing their status as common carriers.

With respect to the public preference for highway transportation, the Commission in 1931 stated its viewpoint thus:

That every community is entitled to use those means of transportation which it prefers cannot properly be questioned by any one, we think. Those who prefer a steam railroad and can support it have a right to their choice. Those who prefer a line of motor trucks have the same right. Similarly those who prefer still other forms of transportation have also this right. However, when a community has at its disposal, as many or most communities have, several means of transportation and it has exercised its choice in the form of patronage, it must realize that those means of transportation which its choice has eliminated from patronage may not be able to continue to exist without such patronage and that abandonment must follow as a last resort. A community which can support every known

---

[12] *Abandonment of Hawkinsville and Florida Southern Ry.*, 70 I.C.C. 566, 568 (1921); see also 71 I.C.C. 26; 150 I.C.C. 159; 180 I.C.C. 4; 184 I.C.C. 103; 184 I.C.C. 642.

means of transportation is unquestionably entitled to them all; but a community which can support only one cannot insist upon the retention of two if the patronage accorded to the least favored one is not sufficient to enable it to live.

As we have already seen, the Commission has, in fact, granted the majority of the applications for abandonments. This indicates that the failure to abandon a larger mileage is attributable rather to the management than to any failure of the Commission to co-operate. However this may be, our analysis indicates that unless a clear demonstration can be made that these light traffic lines are essential to the railway system as a whole from the standpoint of their value as "feeders" in originating traffic for "main line" operations, or as distributors of tonnage delivered to them, both the railway management and the Commission assume a burden of proof to justify their continued operation. The communities which they serve can, as a rule, in these days of improved highways be served more economically by other means of transport.

CHAPTER IX

RAILROAD WAGES AND OPERATING COSTS

The most important item in the cost of operating the American railway system is the compensation of labor. The operating payroll has aggregated as much as $3,424,000,000 in a single calendar year (1920), and during the ensuing decade varied between that figure and a minimum of $2,468,000,000 (1922). In 1931 the operating payroll fell to $1,965,000,000 and for 1932 it is estimated to have been less than $1,500,000,000. The payroll chargeable to operation comprises approximately 60 per cent of total operating expenditures. As compared with revenues, it represents over a period of years an average of approximately 44 per cent of the operating income.

I. THE WAGE BILL OF THE RAILROADS

During the past two decades the total wage bill of the steam railroads of the United States has followed an erratic course. Data showing payroll chargeable to operating expenses are not available for the period from 1910 to 1920; hence we must use here *total* compensation. It should be borne in mind that the term "compensation" includes not only the wages of labor employed in operating the roads, but also the salaries of officials and executives and the portion of the payroll that is chargeable to the capital account. On the average, the latter item comprises approximately 7 per cent of the total compensation bill.

Starting at a level of $1,144,000,000 in 1910, total compensation rose gradually during the next five years at an average rate of about $60,000,000, took a sudden jump of $276,000,000 during the first year of our participation in the World War and another jump of $883,000,000 during the first year of federal control. By 1920 it reached the peak of $3,754,000,000, an amount which was 328 per cent larger than the 1910 figure. The wage bill of the railroads during the years 1910-1931 is shown below, the amounts being given in millions of dollars.[1]

Railroad Wage Bill, 1910-31

Year	Amount	Index 1910=100	Year	Amount	Index 1910=100
1910	$1,144	100.0	1921	$2,824	246.9
1911	1,208	105.6	1922	2,693	235.4
1912	1,252	109.4	1923	3,062	267.7
1913	1,374	120.1	1924	2,883	252.0
1914	1,381	120.7	1925	2,916	254.9
1915	1,278	111.7	1926	3,002	262.4
1916	1,404	122.7	1927	2,963	259.0
1916	1,507	131.7	1928	2,874	251.2
1917	1,783	155.9	1929	2,940	257.0
1918	2,665	233.0	1930	2,589	226.3
1919	2,898	253.3	1931	2,125	185.8
1920	3,754	328.1			

Following a severe wage cut and an appreciable shrinkage in employment, the total compensation bill for 1921 declined by $930,000,000 to $2,824,000,000. Further wage declines coupled with additional curtailment in the number of employees, resulted in another drop of $131,000,000 in 1922, the total compensation paid out in that year being $2,693,000,000. Within two years the amount expended for wages shrunk by

[1] For all operating carriers. Data are from *Statistics of Railways,* Interstate Commerce Commission, 1930, p. S-9. For 1910-16 the data are for years ended June 30; for 1916-31, for years ended December 31.

$1,061,000,000, or 28 per cent. With the advent of re-
newed industrial activity the wage bill started upward
again, and in 1923 reached $3,062,000,000. In 1924 it
fell to $2,883,000,000 and thereafter maintained a more
or less stable level, fluctuating within a maximum range
of but 4 per cent between 1924 and 1929. With the coming of the depression in 1930, payrolls dropped to
$2,589,000,000, followed by a further decline to
$2,125,000,000 in 1931. In the latter year the com-
pensation bill of the carriers was 85 per cent above that
for 1910.

II. THE STATUS OF RAILROAD LABOR

The labor costs in the operation of the carriers are a
function of two factors: wage rates and working rules.
Both of these are in turn affected by the organization that
prevails among the membership of the railroad labor
force and by various laws, both federal and state, some of
which affect the number of workers required in certain
branches of the service and others in a measure the manner in which negotiation between the carriers and their
employees is carried on. Since any attempt to adjust labor
costs must always take into consideration the existing
labor organizations, a brief statement is here given of
their extent and negotiating practices.

1. Collective bargaining. Approximately three-fourths
of the employees of the carriers are affiliated with labor
organizations.[2] Like the employees of most other American industries in which trade unions are recognized, these
workers are organized into separate craft groups. Thus,
the engineers are affiliated with the Brotherhood of Locomotive Engineers, the telegraphers with the Order of
Railroad Telegraphers, and the switchmen with the

[2] On some roads virtually all employees are organized.

Switchmen's Union of North America. Many of these organizations are recognized universally by the carriers. In some instances, however, individual carriers do not negotiate with the national representatives of certain trade unions, and on some of such roads collective bargaining for certain classes of labor is restricted to independent company unions which cover the employees of the particular carriers. Several of the groups duplicate each other in the same field, as for example, the American Railway Agents and the Brotherhood of Railroad Station Employees. In all, there are some 40 different unions representing the various labor groups employed on the railroads, varying in size from small local unions to big national brotherhoods.

The bulk of the organized employees are affiliated with the 21 "standard railway unions,"[3] some of which, like the Brotherhood of Locomotive Engineers, the

[3] These unions are as follows:
Brotherhood of Locomotive Engineers
Brotherhood of Locomotive Firemen and Enginemen
Order of Railway Conductors of America
Brotherhood of Railroad Trainmen
Switchmen's Union of North America
Order of Railroad Telegraphers
American Train Dispatchers' Association
International Association of Machinists
International Brotherhood of Boilermakers, Iron Ship Builders and Helpers of America
International Brotherhood of Blacksmiths, Drop Forgers and Helpers
Sheet Metal Workers' International Association
International Brotherhood of Electrical Workers
Brotherhood Railway Carmen of America
International Brotherhood of Firemen and Oilers
Brotherhood of Railway and Steamship Clerks, Freight Handlers, Express and Station Employees
Brotherhood of Maintenance of Way Employees
Brotherhood of Railroad Signalmen of America
National Organization Masters, Mates and Pilots of America
National Marine Engineers' Beneficial Association
International Longshoremen's Association
Order of Sleeping Car Conductors

Brotherhood of Locomotive Firemen and Enginemen, the Brotherhood of Railway Trainmen, and the Order of Railroad Conductors of America, have their entire membership employed by the carriers. Others, like the Sheet Metal Workers International Association and the International Brotherhood of Electrical Workers, have only a limited proportion of their members engaged in railroad work.

The organizations of the train service employees are among the oldest in the United States, the Brotherhood of Locomotive Engineers dating from 1863.[4] Like the Conductors' and the Firemen's brotherhoods it was originally founded as a mutual benefit society. Of the four organizations, only one, the Brotherhood of Railroad Trainmen, started as a purely trade union body. From the very beginning, all four brotherhoods have provided life insurance for their members and their strength has been due in a measure to the favorable insurance rates they have been able to give to their members. They have always remained independent of the American Federation of Labor. Together they have an estimated aggregate membership of about 400,000.

Of the other unions with membership among railroad employees, 16 are affiliated with the American Federation of Labor. Like the brotherhoods these unions for the most part trace their origin to the latter part of the last century. The non-affiliated unions are mostly of recent origin, having secured a foothold either shortly prior to or during the war period. With but few exceptions they have a relatively small membership and their jurisdiction is recognized by a rather limited number of carriers.

These separate and distinct organizations usually act

[4] Helen Marot, *American Labor Unions*, 1914, p. 30.

independently of one another in their negotiations with the carriers.[5] Bargaining with separate carriers is the general practice for most of the crafts and in some instances the rates paid for the same type of work vary between different carriers in the same territory. Indeed, the wage rate for certain groups sometimes varies between different geographic areas on the same system.[6]

Independent bargaining by individual organizations is also generally characteristic of the "Big Four Brotherhoods." Unlike the other unions, however, they usually submit their demands, not to single carriers, but simultaneously to all systems in a given territory. On various occasions they have co-operated with one another in wage negotiations. Originally executed through federated committees representing their locals on individual systems, co-operative action was later extended through the formation of joint committees which at times have made joint demands for the co-operating unions.[7] In 1916 the

[5] Exceptions are to be found among certain organizations which are affiliated with one another through the Railway Employees Department of the American Federation of Labor which consists of nine international unions. Section one of the Railway Employees Department is composed of the Switchmen's Union; section two of the six shop crafts—the blacksmiths, boiler makers, carmen, machinists, sheet metal workers and electrical workers. Section three includes the stationary firemen and oilers and the maintenance-of-way employees. The department charters system federations on the various railroads to represent the common interests of the shop craft employees, and where such system federations prevail "no single craft can make a separate wage agreement without the consent of the president and executive council of the department." See Louis Lorwin, *The American Federation of Labor*, Brookings Institution, 1933 (in press).

[6] Thus, for example, the wage rates of telegraphers may vary from station to station on the same road. The rates paid to maintenance-of-way men frequently vary from district to district.

[7] Such co-operation as has taken place has in most instances been between the conductors and the trainmen. The engineers and firemen have also on occasion presented joint demands for wage changes.

four brotherhoods joined in presenting their demand for an eight-hour day to all the roads in the country at the same time. This was the first occasion on which all four of these organizations combined for purposes of submitting demands on a national rather than a local or regional basis.

During the period of federal railroad operation, changes in wages for all classes of labor were made on a national basis. Working rules and wage rates for given classes, which had formerly varied from road to road, were standardized through national agreements and made applicable to all carriers under the control of the Railroad Administration.

In granting wage increases after the return to private operation in 1920, the Railroad Labor Board dealt with all employees, irrespective of class, at the same time, and the advances granted were made applicable to all carriers. A similar practice was followed when wage decreases were authorized in 1921.

Although national agreements were nominally terminated by a decision of the Railroad Labor Board in 1921, it was not until the spring of 1922 when the Labor Board ordered a second wage reduction for all classes of workers other than engine, train, and telegraph service employees, that they in fact all came to an end. This wage order led to a shopmen's strike which was ultimately settled by the "Baltimore Agreement," and led eventually to individual settlements between the shopmen and individual carriers. Some of the roads refused to negotiate with the unions after the strike and to date have declined to recognize the jurisdiction of the shopmen's organization. The practice of dealing with individual carriers was also temporarily adopted by engine and train service employees for a short time after 1922 when they, like some of the carriers, virtually refused to recognize the jurisdiction of the Labor Board.

Changes in wage rates made between 1923 and 1926 were largely the result of negotiation between representatives of the employees and individual roads. This practice has remained in effect down to the present in the case of most of the organized employees. In the engine and train services, negotiations since 1926 have usually been on a regional basis.

Thus organized labor on the railroads still maintains its craft character, and collective bargaining for the majority of the workers is for the most part an individual matter between system committees of individual unions and single carriers. Recently, however, the various unions have co-operated with one another for the protection of their mutual interests. Such occasions were the wage negotiations of 1931 and 1932 when the 21 standard unions were represented as a unit through the Railway Labor Executives' Association in negotiating a 10 per cent cut for all of the members of the co-operating organizations.

2. *Methods of wage payment.* Through long years of negotiation with the carriers some of the employees' organizations have established elaborate schedules of wages and rules governing their working conditions. By and large, wage rates are fixed on an hourly basis. For the professional, clerical and general services, station masters, yard masters, certain types of foremen, and for a number of other groups of inconsequential size, the daily basis of payment prevails. In all, less than 10 per cent of the employees are on a daily wage basis. Piece work,

which prevails primarily among the shop employees of those roads which do not recognize the shopmen's unions, is of relatively little importance in the industry, the payroll for this method of payment aggregating but 2 per cent of the total.

In the train and engine service, wage payments are made on the so-called "dual" basis. This system, which applies to engineers, conductors, firemen, and trainmen, is in effect a combination of piece and day compensation. Originally instituted in the place of straight time payments by one of the Western roads over 50 years ago, the dual basis was put into effect as an incentive to the crews to speed up the movement of their trains. To-day this method of wage payment prevails on all but one railroad system.[8]

Under the dual system a fixed output is set for a standard day. In the road freight service, for example, 100 miles or less constitute a day's work for engineers, firemen, conductors, and trainmen. In terms of hourly output this means that 12-1/2 miles constitute the standard unit of production. Taking a concrete example of a freight engineer on a given class of engine on one of the Southeastern roads, the wage rate is fixed at $8.05 per day, $1.07 per hour, or 8.05 cents per mile.[9] When this engineer has rendered a standard day's work, that is,

[8] Recently the Delaware and Hudson Railroad negotiated agreements with the brotherhoods whereby the train service men are paid on a straight hourly basis, with a monthly guarantee of a minimum number of hours. In determining the wage rates under this agreement the hourly rate was fixed at a level which tended to approximate the actual hourly earnings of the employees under the discarded dual basis.

[9] This rate applies for engines with 200,000 to 250,000 pounds on drivers. Rates for enginemen and firemen vary with the weight on the drivers of the engine.

a 100-mile run in eight hours or less, he receives his standard day's pay of $8.05, irrespective of the number of hours consumed in making the trip. Should the time in making the 100-mile run be more than eight hours, over-time is paid at time-and-a-half rates for all hours in excess of eight. In the event that a run exceeds the standard day's work of one hundred miles, the engineer receives additional pay at a proportionate rate for every mile over and above the fixed day's standard. In other words, a 125-mile run completed in eight hours or less yields a wage of $10.06.

Standard day's wage (100 miles at 8.05
    cents per mile) . . . . $ 8.05
25 additional miles at 8.05 cents a mile 2.01
                                                    ———
    Total wage $10.06

Over-time rates are computed on a speed basis and come into effect at the end of the standard eight-hour day only in the event that the standard hourly unit of output (12-1/2 miles) is not realized. That is to say, whenever on runs of more than one hundred miles that consume more than eight hours, conditions are such that the engineer cannot average an output of 12-1/2 miles per hour he is paid on a mileage basis, plus over-time for the hours in excess of eight. Concretely, if the 125-mile run mentioned above consumes nine hours, that is, an average output of 13.9 miles per hour, the straight mileage basis alone prevails and no extra payment is made for the extra hour. The same would be true if ten hours (one hour for each 12-1/2 miles) were consumed. But once the average time consumed per unit of output (12-1/2 miles) exceeds one hour, over-time pay begins. Thus eleven hours for a 125-mile run would yield a total wage of $11.57.[10]

125 miles at 8.05 cents per mile $10.06
One hour overtime (1½ x $1.07) 1.51

Total wage $11.57

The dual basis of payment, which in reality is nothing but a piece-rate system with a guaranteed day rate,[11] and the provision for overtime in the event that conditions make it impossible for the employee to average a standard hourly output within the standard day, have been the subject of no little criticism. It has given rise to many "extra payments" such as compensation for switching or picking up cars from sidings. Such operations, the employees contend, are not included in their piece rates, and they insist upon "extras" for such additional work.

Criticism has always been directed toward this system of payments because it enables individual employees to make relatively large earnings in a comparatively short number of hours.[12] It also naturally gives the impression

[10] In the passenger engine service the basis of payment is 100 miles or less, five hours or less, for runs of more than 80 miles in one direction, making the standard hourly unit of output 20 miles. If the 100 miles are covered in five hours or less the full day rate is paid, irrespective of the actual time consumed. There are no penalty over-time rates in the passenger engine service and pro rata rates are paid for all over-time hours.

Conductors and trainmen in through passenger service are paid on a basis of 150 miles or less, 7.5 hours or less, the standard unit of hourly output being 20 miles. Overtime is paid for at the standard hourly rates.

[11] The guaranteed day rate is necessitated by the fact that the train crew's output is frequently affected by conditions over which they have no control, as for example, the length and weight of trains and dispatcher's orders.

[12] The following quotation from an official report rendered in 1901 is of interest in revealing that even 30 years ago the ability of the train service workers to earn a day's wages in less than the standard time was the subject of criticism:

"There is, from the very nature of the occupation, the greatest varia-

that the worker is receiving compensation for a greater number of hours than he actually works. It must not be overlooked, however, that payment is primarily based on piece rates, the unit being the train mile. In considering this problem, therefore, it should be borne in mind that anomalies of this sort are found in greater or lesser degree in any wage system involving piece-work payments.

In most industrial plants where piece rates are in effect, experience has proved that such a system of wage payments almost inevitably leads to greater output per unit of time and consequently to large earnings. Indeed such earnings have time and again been used as a justification for the continued lowering of piece rates, a practice which has caused this method of remuneration to be opposed by organized labor everywhere.

The high earnings which are obtained under this system by individual employees are not due to the dual system of wage payments as such. If criticism is to be levied, it should obviously be directed against the prevailing unit wage rates and the size of the standard unit of output; for the dual system does not necessarily involve the existing wage rates and speed bases. These are the results of negotiation between the carriers and the employees.

It should be borne in mind further that the dual wage basis does stimulate the speeding up of freight traffic. By cutting the running time whenever conditions so permit the train service crews not only increase their own leisure but, equally important, they at the same time increase the availability of both tracks and locomotives

tion in the hours of labor in the different grades of service. On fast express trains there are many cases where trainmen do not work more than five or six hours a day, including their lay-over, and receive a full day's wages." *Report of the Industrial Commission*, Vol. XVII, p. 737 (1901).

for other traffic with a consequent saving to the carriers.

3. *Working rules.* As a result of collective bargaining the railroad employees have secured the adoption of numerous working rules which bear upon their working conditions and earning capacity. To a considerable extent these rules came into being as a means of protecting the workers against unjust practices on the part of management. Some of them also are the result of "trades" between the management and the men whereby the employees have agreed to the acceptance of a given rule in place of a wage increase.[13]

Many complaints have been raised because of the undue burden which many of these working rules impose upon the carriers. In many cases, it is claimed the original cause for the adoption of a rule has been eliminated but the rule itself tends to remain. A case in point which is occasionally cited is a jurisdictional rule in effect on many of the carriers which does not permit any but specified employees to handle train orders at telegraph or telephone offices "where an operator is employed and is available or can be promptly located, except in an emergency," and provides that when train orders are handled by others in emergencies, a telegrapher shall be paid for the call. As a result of this rule, it is claimed, telegraphers are paid when telephone calls to the dispatcher are made by conductors, even though the telegrapher played no part in the operation itself.

In other cases the necessity for certain rules is generally accepted but complaint is made against their strin-

---

[13] In some instances minor officials have been known to accept certain rules in return for the employees' relinquishing certain wage demands. In this way such officials were in a position to report to their superiors that the demands for wage increases had been overcome, although in the long run the cost of the rule might add more to the cost of operation than the acceptance of the wage demands.

gency. The "call" rule, which provides that a shopman called or notified to work outside of bulletin hours shall receive pay for not less than five hours, is frequently mentioned as such an instance. When so called the workers are "required to do only such work as called for, or work of equal importance while they are on duty." This rule was originally adopted to abolish the abuses that arose in calling a man back to work at any time of the day or night to do a minor repair job. The accepted theory underlying it is that if the employee has to come back to the shop outside of working hours his recompense should bear some relation to the inconvenience to which he is put. The carriers accept this theory, but contend that once a man has completed the job for which he has been called they should be allowed to employ him on any other work that may be available during the remainder of the time for which he is paid.

In 1928 the "double-header" rule was the subject of negotiation between the Western carriers and the conductors and trainmen. This rule, which has been in effect since 1903, aims to prohibit the operation of long or heavy freight trains with two or more engines except on certain grades where "helper" engines are used, and this is in the main accomplished by placing a limitation on the tonnage or number of cars that may be handled on such trains. The employees contend that the rule makes for safety and better working conditions; the carriers contend that it hampers economical and efficient operation, and that its elimination would not add to the hazards of the men.[14] The carriers offered their men a one per

<hr />

[14] Report of the Emergency Board appointed by the President of the United States, September 29, 1928, under Section 10 of the Railway Labor Act. (*Footnote continued on p. 193.*)

cent increase in wages if they would eliminate this rule, but the employees have preferred to maintain it.

Jurisdictional shop rules, which specify the class of work to be done by each craft, have also been criticized as involving the excessive employment of men and extra expense. There is evidence, however, that in those instances where amicable working relations prevail these rules are not rigidly enforced by the employees.[15]

The extent of the financial burden imposed on the carriers by the various working rules is not subject to measurement. Informed opinion among the carriers estimates the total savings that might accrue from the elimination of what they consider "unjustifiable" working rules at a slight fraction of the total operating wage bill. Indeed, it is agreed that the extent of this saving would vary from road to road depending in large part upon the status of labor relations.[16] These rules are nevertheless of increasing moment in the consideration of railroad officials. From the point of view of the employees they go hand-in-hand with the wage rates and have a material bearing on their earnings. In addition, many working

---

In discussing the rules in question the Board stated: "These rules, however, involve technical questions involving working conditions, over a wide range of territory, which cannot be adequately understood or appraised in the brief time open to this board in making its report. . . .

"We believe that this phase of the controversy can be settled only after an investigation by men skilled in technical and practical operation of railroads and suggest that the matter be laid before the Interstate Commerce Commission for their advice and report."

[15] Representatives of some of the carriers have stated to the writer that these jurisdictional rules impose no unjustifiable burden on their roads.

[16] Many instances where working rules are observed in the breach more often than in their enforcement have been cited to us by management representatives. This is particularly true of those roads where amicable labor relations make possible necessary adjustments as occasions demand.

rules, entirely aside from their so-called money value, are highly cherished by them as safeguards which they deem essential to the maintenance of their industrial status.

4. *Legislation and labor relations.* The vital importance of the continuous operation of our transportation system to the public welfare has led to the development of federal machinery for the orderly adjustment of labor disputes.[17] This machinery has assumed great significance for two reasons. First, it has played an important part in preventing interruptions of interstate commerce. Second, and of importance from the point of view of this report, it has been through this machinery that many of the wage changes that have taken place in the railroad industry during the past generation have actually been determined. Indeed, it would be no exaggeration to state that, excepting the eight-hour day controversy of 1916 and the period of federal control, virtually every important change in wage rates, particularly for train service employees, has been effected through arbitration and mediation machinery established by the federal government, on which carriers, employees, and neutral third parties have been represented.

The first measure of this sort, the Arbitration Act of 1888, provided the machinery for voluntary arbitration in the event that a dispute between carriers and their em-

---

[17] Certain states have enacted legislation which has increased the labor cost of operation. Thus, for example, in order to promote safety of operation, 17 states have laws covering the number of employees required on trains. Arizona has a law limiting the number of cars on a single train. Just how far such legislation is necessary for safety is a matter of dispute. The carriers insist that they are unnecessary and do nothing more than add an undue burden to operating costs. See also Chapter X below, and *Hearings on Full Train Crews*, House Committee on Interstate and Foreign Commerce, 72d Congress, January, 1933.

ployees threatened interference with interstate commerce, and made provision for compulsory investigation of labor disputes by commissions to be appointed by
the President of the United States. This act was a dead
letter and, with the exception of one investigation made
on order of the President, its machinery was never utilized in settling controversies. Its failure to avert labor
difficulties led to the passage of the Erdman Act in 1898.
This act was applicable only to those employees directly
engaged in the movement of trains. It provided for voluntary mediation and arbitration and made illegal any
strike or lock-out by the parties accepting the arbitration
provisions of the law within three months of the arbitration award. The machinery created by this act resulted in
the settlement of numerous controversies, many of which
were of considerable importance. Virtually every significant dispute between 1906 and 1912 was peacefully
adjusted under its provisions and most of the important
changes in wages and working hours in those six years
were arrived at through the machinery it created.

The Newlands Act,[18] passed in 1913, strengthened the
existing mediation and arbitration machinery. It proved
inadequate, however, in the settlement of the eight-hour
day dispute in 1916, and "not until Congress constituted
itself an arbitration body, and without investigation,
granted the demands of the workers,"[19] was a strike
averted.

[18] In 1913 a strike by the conductors and trainmen on the Eastern
roads was averted only by the intercession of President Wilson. This action was the stimulus to the immediate passage of the Newlands Act.
[19] I. L. Sharfman, *The American Railroad Problem*, p. 334.
In 1913 and 1914 two strikes were averted under the Newlands Act
through the influence of President Wilson. In one case he persuaded the
parties to a dispute to agree to arbitration. In the other he persuaded
the Eastern railroad managers to grant the demands of their employees.

Under the Transportation Act of 1920, the Railroad Labor Board was established and given authority to adjust and decide disputes, and "establish rates of wages, salaries and standards of working conditions [for every class of employees] which in the opinion of the Board are just and reasonable." No provision, however, was made for the enforcement of its decisions. During its régime, the Board awarded a national wage increase aggregating $600,000,000, followed later by a wage decrease of $300,000,000. The refusal of certain roads, as well as certain employees' organizations, to abide by its decisions and the refusal on the part of the more powerful labor groups to recognize its jurisdiction led to the Board's end. In 1926, it was superseded under the Railway Labor Act by the United States Board of Mediation.

The Railway Labor Act now in effect establishes machinery for mediation and arbitration for all classes of employees and specifies that proposed changes in existing labor contracts must be preceded by 30 days' notice, during which period conferences between the interested parties must be held. Changes in rates of pay or working conditions by carriers are prohibited during such periods as the Board of Mediation is engaged in an attempt to settle controversies or to induce the parties to submit their difficulties to arbitration. In the event of failure by the Board to secure a peaceful settlement or an acceptance of arbitration proceedings, and if in its judgment a threatened controversy promises seriously to interrupt interstate commerce, the Board may advise the President to that effect and the President is empowered to create an "Emergency Board" to investigate and report concerning the dispute in question. After the creation of such an Emergency Board, and for 30 days after it has reported to the President, no change can be made by either party in the conditions out of which the dispute arose, except by mutual agreement.

The most important provision of the Railway Labor Act is that which requires that arbitration awards rendered under the act shall be legally final and conclusive on the parties involved unless impeached by a federal district court or appealed to a Circuit Court of Appeals. For the first time in railway labor history the parties to an arbitration proceeding under the law are legally bound to abide by its award.

The effectiveness of the Railway Labor Act is evidenced by the fact that during the six and one-half years of its history, despite 29 strike ballots among railway employees, only two insignificant strikes have occurred,[20] neither of which was attended by any substantial interruption of interstate commerce. Within this period the Board has disposed of 515 cases through mediation agreements and 229 other agreements to arbitrate. In five instances the threat of interference with interstate commerce has resulted in the appointment of special emergency boards by the President of the United States.

III. THE TREND OF RAILROAD WAGE RATES

In common with the rates for other organized labor the wage rates of railroad employees have shown a gradual upward trend during the last two decades. With the exception of the reductions ordered by the Railway Labor Board in 1921 and 1922, and those negotiated in 1932 and 1933, there were practically no other general wage cuts throughout the period.

---

[20] One of these strikes occurred on the Toledo, Peoria and Western Railroad in November 1929. According to the 1930 report of the Board of Mediation, it did not interrupt interstate commerce. The other, in the railway express service, was confined to New York City and was of less than a day's duration.

Prior to federal control there was little or no uniformity in the railroad wage structure. Approximately two-thirds of the carriers' employees were unorganized, and questions of wages were for the most part handled by each railroad directly with its own employees. With occasional exceptions, collective bargaining was restricted primarily to the engine and train service workers and the telegraphers. In the shop services wage rates varied from system to system and from shop to shop on the same system. Nor was there any uniformity in the matter of granting wage increases. As stated by the Railroad Wage Commission in its report on the wage situation for 1916-17: "Not all of the railroads made increases to the same classes, and no two made awards in the same percentages, even within the same groups of employments."[21]

The large variety of rates for the same job, the wide prevalence of piece work[22] and the absence of definite labor classifications during the pre-war period vitiate comparisons of wage rates for many classes of workers in pre-war days with those in the federal control and post-war periods. Such wage data as prevail for the pre-war period for the shop crafts, for example, represent for the most part conglomerates of nominal hourly rates for groups which include wage earners doing more or less similar work, frequently on a piece basis, and do not portray either actual wage rates or earnings. With federal control and national wage agreements came a definite

---

[21] *Report of the Railroad Wage Commission to the Director General of Railroads*, Apr. 30, 1918, p. 17, Washington, 1918.

Commenting further the Commission stated: "The investigation of the Commission disclosed many inequalities of pay in the same branch of the service, not only as between different sections of the country, but in the same section." (p. 39).

[22] It is estimated that something like one-half of the shop workers were on a piece-work basis prior to 1918.

classification of workers by groups, and basic hourly rates were established. This classification has, for the most part, been retained, particularly on those roads where wage rates are determined by collective bargaining, and makes possible a survey of the actual rates that have been in effect for all classes since 1918. The charts on the following page portray the changes in classified wage rates on a typical carrier in the southeastern part of the United States for selected classes of workers.[23]

It will be seen from these charts that all of the major wage rate increases on the railroads occurred between 1915 and 1920 when advances ranging from 40 per cent to 114 per cent were made for the various classes of labor. Indeed, the increases granted during this period account for most of the rise of approximately 90 per cent that took place in the rates of those classes for which comparable data are available between 1915 and 1929.

After the wage decrease of 1921, railroad wage rates with few exceptions did not again rise to their 1920 levels until 1928-29. In the case of the shopmen and maintenance of way section laborers, who also suffered a wage cut in 1922,[24] wage rates never again attained the heights reached in 1920. Increases granted between 1924 and 1929 eventually brought the machinists' and blacksmiths' rates within 6 per cent of what they had been at their peak, while the hourly rates for maintenance of way section laborers never rose above 75 per cent of the 1920 level. After the wage reduction of 1932 the rates paid

[23] These charts depict the fluctuations of general trade union wage rates for the country as a whole, as well as the fluctuations of rates for selected groups of railroad workers. In each case the base is the average rate for 1923. Data from carriers and from Bureau of Labor Statistics.

[24] It should be added that changes in working rules in 1921, although not affecting the wage rates themselves, did, in fact, affect actual hourly earnings.

GENERAL TRADE UNION WAGES COMPARED WITH RAILROAD WAGES, 1915-32

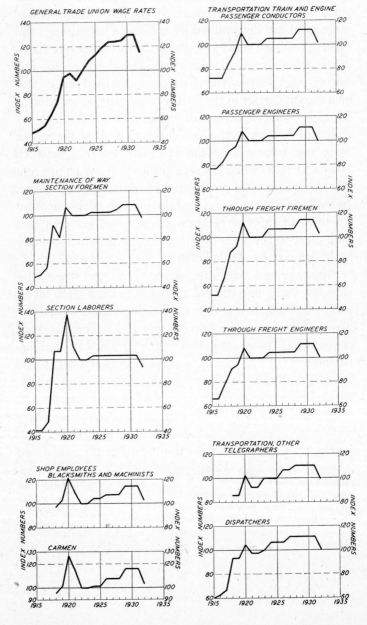

to the shopmen were about 2 per cent above, and those paid to maintenance of way laborers about 7 per cent below, where they had been a decade earlier.

In the train and engine services the movement of wage rates shows considerable variation as between the different classes for the years 1915 to 1920. After 1920 the rates for various classes tended to move in unison, the average for the group in 1929 slightly exceeding the post-war maximum. Like most other rates depicted in the charts, they were, in 1932, slightly above what they had been in 1920.

It is significant to note that between 1915 and 1920 the hourly wage rates for railroad labor increased by a considerably larger percentage than the average, rates for organized labor in general, as reported by the United States Bureau of Labor Statistics.[25] After 1920, general trade union rates increased much faster than wage rates on the railroads, rising to 32 per cent above the 1920 level in 1929 as compared with an average rise of less than 2 per cent for railroad employees. Between 1923 and 1929 the rates for the various groups of railway labor rose from 10 to 18 per cent, while general trade union rates advanced by 24 per cent. In 1932 the average union rates were approximately 20 per cent above where they had been in 1920,[26] while railroad wage rates for most classes had fallen by about 9 per cent below the 1920 level.

Surveying the entire period from 1915 to 1932, one finds that reported general trade union wage rates advanced by approximately 150 per cent between 1915 and

[25] "Union Scales of Wages and Hours of Labor," *Bureau of Labor Statistics Bulletin No. 566*, U. S. Department of Labor, May 15, 1931, p. 15.
[26] *Monthly Labor Review*, Bureau of Labor Statistics, U. S. Department of Labor, Vol. XXXV, No. 5, November 1932, p. 1153.

1929, while wage rates for most classes on the railroads rose by approximately 90 per cent. Between 1929 and 1932 general trade union rates declined by about 8 per cent, in comparison with a 10 per cent fall for railroad employees. There is good reason to believe, however, that in many of the industries the 1932 trade union rates were merely nominal and that they frequently bore little relation to the rates actually paid. From such isolated data as are available, it seems safe to conclude that the difference between the nominal and actual rates averages something like 20 per cent. On the basis of such an estimate, it appears that the actual union rates in 1932 were about 90 per cent above the 1915 level, while railroad wage rates were on the average approximately 70 per cent above.

IV. LABOR COSTS AND RAILROAD OPERATION

In surveying the relation of labor costs to the cost of moving railroad traffic, and to the carriers' revenues, the period 1911-1932 is here divided into two parts. The first, covering the years 1911-1920, traces the course of the compensation bill of the roads through the relatively stable period 1911-1915 and the hectic years of the immediate pre-war and federal control eras. The second period covers the years of deflation which followed immediately upon the return of the carriers to private ownership; the six years of increasing traffic accompanied by a declining labor force which ended in 1929; and the three years of declining traffic, contracting labor forces and falling wage bill which began in 1930.

1. *The pre-war and federal control periods.* In the consideration of railway labor costs, the years 1911 to 1920 logically divide themselves into two distinct periods. The first—1911-15—was one of comparative sta-

bility; the second, one of violent wage changes and increasing labor costs.

The years 1911 to 1913 saw a significant increase both in the number of railroad employees and in the pay-rolls. In this short period the average working force grew from 1,600,000 to 1,759,000, or by almost 10 per cent.[27] This increase, however, was but temporary. With the advent of the depression of 1914-15 the average number on the payroll fell to 1,640,000 in 1914 and to 1,492,000 in 1915; this decline of more than a quarter of a million bringing the working force down to almost 7 per cent below the level of 1911.

Accompanying the 10 per cent growth in personnel between 1911 and 1913 was a 14.6 per cent increase in the carriers' compensation bill, the difference being partly accounted for by wage advances that were granted during the period.[28] The effect of these advances is particularly evident in the payroll figures for 1914 when, despite a contraction of 119,000 in the working force, the wage and salary bill aggregated $1,337,000,000, or as much as in the year preceding. Indeed, it was not until 1915, when the number of employees had declined by a further 150,000, that the compensation outlay showed any appreciable fall. In that year $1,236,000,000[29] was

[27] The data in this and the following sections refer only to Class I roads. These roads operate approximately 92 per cent of the total mileage of railway line in the United States, employ 95 per cent of the railway personnel, and earn about 96 per cent of the aggregate gross revenues.

[28] On three occasions within the period here discussed the possibility of railroad strikes was sufficiently real to cause the President of the United States to take a hand in bringing about adjustments between the contending parties.

[29] (See table on p. 204.) The compensation data used here for the period 1911 to 1920 cover total compensation. These data include not only the part of the payroll chargeable to operation but also the salaries of general and division officers and the portion which is chargeable to capital account. Data showing operating payrolls are not available prior

RAILWAY EMPLOYEES' COMPENSATION AND RAILWAY REVENUES, CLASS I CARRIERS, 1911–15

Year[a]	Average Number of Employees[b]		Total Compensation[b]		Gross Ton Miles of Freight[c]		Compensation per Gross Ton Mile of Freight		Total Revenue[b]		Revenue per Gross Ton Mile		Percentage Ratio of Compensation to Revenue
	Average Number (In thousands)	Index Number[d]	Amount (In millions)	Index Number[d]	Number (In millions)	Index Number[d]	Amount (In cents)	Index Number[d]	Amount (In millions)	Index Number[d]	Amount (In cents)	Index Number[d]	
1911	1,600	100.0	$1,168	100.0	598,299	100.0	.1952	100.0	$2,752	100.0	.4600	100.0	42.43
1912	1,642	102.6	1,210	103.6	621,583	103.9	.1947	99.7	2,805	101.9	.4513	98.1	43.12
1913	1,759	109.9	1,339	114.6	701,816	117.3	.1907	97.7	3,108	112.9	.4429	96.3	43.06
1914	1,640	102.5	1,337	114.5	693,846	116.0	.1927	98.7	3,031	110.1	.4365	94.9	44.12
1915	1,492	93.3	1,236	105.9	674,184	112.7	.1833	93.9	2,872	104.3	.4260	92.6	43.05

[a] Year ending June 30.
[b] *Statistics of Railways*, Interstate Commerce Commission, 1911–1915.
[c] Data from *Report of Joint Commission of Agricultural Inquiry*, 1922, Pt. III, Table B-35, p. 614. Data include gross ton miles of loaded and empty freight cars.
[d] 1911 = 100.

paid out in salaries and wages, an amount which still exceeded the 1911 expenditure by 5.9 per cent.

Because of the increasing output per employee, the growing compensation bill of the carriers was not reflected in the unit labor costs of moving traffic. Gross ton freight mileage[30] grew by 17 per cent in the first two years of the period here discussed and in 1915 showed but little decline as compared with the shrinkage in the payroll. The result was a fall in compensation per gross ton freight mile from .1952 cents in 1911 to .1907 cents in 1913, followed by a slight rise in 1914 and a further decline to .1833 cents in 1915. At the end of the four years, in other words, when the payroll was 6 per cent above the 1911 level, the payroll cost of moving a unit of freight was 6 per cent below it.

The decline in unit costs, however, was not sufficiently large to offset the falling unit revenues. Although total revenues increased, their rise was not proportionate to either the increase in ton mileage or the growth in payrolls. Revenues per ton mile fell steadily and in 1915 were equal to but 92.6 per cent of what they had been four years previously. Thus the increasing compensation bill made serious inroads into operating revenues and the percentage of the latter which went to pay wages and salaries increased from 42.4 in 1911 to 44.1 in 1914. In 1915 the relatively greater fall in compensation reversed

---

to 1920. For the period subsequent to 1920 the non-operating payroll averaged approximately 7 per cent of the total.

[30] The unit of output used for the period 1911 to 1920 is a gross ton mile of freight. This unit represents the tonnage of loaded and empty freight cars moved one mile. In terms of actual work done by the labor force it is, in our opinion, a better measure than revenue ton mileage, which portrays the movement of loaded freight cars only. The data for gross ton miles herein used were taken from the *Report of the Joint Committee of Agricultural Inquiry*, 67 Cong. 1 sess., H. rept. 408, Pt. III (1922).

the upward trend and the ratio of payrolls to revenues dropped to 43.0 per cent.

The changes in the status of railroad labor which occurred during the last half of the second decade—1916-1920—have no counterpart in any other five years of railroad history. In this period the Adamson Act, passed under presidential pressure to avoid a transportation tie-up, granted to the train service employees a legal eight-hour day. In these five years the number of railroad workers grew by over 300,000, or by 22 per cent; national wage agreements and uniform working conditions were for the first time attained for all organized employees; wage rates were raised; the compensation outlay of the roads increased to heights previously unthought of.

With the abnormal stimulation of industry in 1916 resulting from allied purchases of American products, the demands on the railroad system became unprecedented. Gross ton freight mileage grew at a hitherto unknown rate, the increase in the two years 1915 to 1917 aggregating approximately 200 billion ton miles, or 30 per cent. At the same time rising wages in other industries were attracting great numbers of workers from the railroads and late in 1917 the carriers were threatened with a shortage of labor, some of the roads reporting "a net shortage of one-eighth of their entire labor force."[31]

The extent of labor turnover also reached unprecedented heights, running to four times the normal rate on some of the larger systems. Generally increased living costs, unaccompanied by corresponding wage increases, further accentuated the situation, and dissatisfaction reigned throughout the rank and file of railroad

[31] I. L. Sharfman, *The American Railroad Problem*, p. 98.

employees. As described by the Railroad Wage Commission, appointed by the Director-General of Railroads to investigate wage conditions on the roads in 1918, the situation on the advent of governmental control was such that "another three months of private management and we would have seen much more extensive concessions in wages, or there would have followed an unfortunate series of labor disturbances."[32]

Although wage increases aggregating $380,000,000 had been made in 1916 and 1917, such increases had not been "in any way uniform, either as to employments, or as to amounts, or as to roads, so that one class of labor benefited much more than another on the same road, and as between roads there was the greatest divergence."[33] As reported by the Lane Commission, more than half of all employees during December 1917 received $75 a month or less, and 80 per cent $100 per month or less. "Even among the locomotive engineers, commonly spoken of as highly paid, a preponderating number receives less than $175 a month, and this compensation they have obtained by the most compact and complete organization, handled with a full appreciation of all strategic values. Between the groups receiving from $150 to $250 per month, there is included less than 3 per cent of all employees (excluding officials) and these aggregate less than 60,000 men out of a grand total of 2,000,000."[34]

In May 1918, shortly after the federal government assumed control of the railroads, a graduated wage in-

---

[32] *Report of the Railroad Wage Commission to the Director-General of Railroads*, Washington, 1918, p. 14. This body was known as the Lane Commission because of its chairman, Franklin K. Lane.

[33] The same, p. 13.

[34] The same, p. 18.

crease varying from one dollar per month for those earning $250, to 43 per cent for those earning less than $46, was put into effect. This advance, estimated to have added $360,000,000 to the operating wage bill, was supplemented later in the year by other increases for certain classes. The total operating payroll advance for the entire year is estimated to have been $784,000,000.[35] Further wage adjustments in 1919, which added an estimated $181,000,000 to the operating payroll, brought the total wage increases under federal control to $965,000,000.[36]

Simultaneously with the return of the roads to private ownership in March 1920, the Railroad Labor Board was set up. Within a month there was submitted to it a demand for further wage advances to which some 90 per cent of the railways' employees were parties. Some of these demands had originally been made as far back as early 1919 and had been held in abeyance at the request of the President. In June the Board granted the railroad employees a $600,000,000 wage increase, equal to about 22 per cent of the payroll, and retroactive to May 1, 1920.

The results of the increasing wage rates and the growing size of the labor force between 1916 and 1920 are portrayed in the table on page 209. Compensation outlays expanded from $1,469,000,000 to $3,682,000,000, an increase of more than 150 per cent. The $270,000,000 increase from 1916 to 1917 brought with it a rise from .177 cents to .199 cents in the labor cost per gross ton mile of freight, while the $875,000,000 increase of 1918, in the face of a very slight growth in freight movement,

[35] I. L. Sharfman, *The American Railroad Problem*, p. 151.
[36] Testimony of Walker D. Hines, House Hearings on Deficiency Appropriations, 66 Cong., 2 sess., p. 210. See also Sharfman, I. L., p. 151.

RAILWAY EMPLOYEES' COMPENSATION AND RAILWAY REVENUES, CLASS I CARRIERS, 1916–20

Year	Average Number of Employees[a] (In thousands)		Total Compensation[a]		Gross Ton Miles of Freight[b]		Compensation per Gross Ton Mile of Freight		Total Revenue[c]		Revenue per Gross Ton Mile		Percentage Ratio of Compensation to Revenue
	Average Number (In thousands)	Index Number[d]	Amount (In millions)	Index Number[d]	Number (In millions)	Index Number[d]	Amount (In cents)	Index Number[d]	Amount (In millions)	Index Number[d]	Amount (In cents)	Index Number[d]	
1916e	1,599	97.1	$1,366	93.0	792,033	95.8	.1725	97.1	$3,382	94.0	.4270	98.1	40.40
1916f	1,647	100.0	1,469	100.0	826,765	100.0	.1777	100.0	3,597	100.0	.4351	100.0	40.83
1917f	1,733	105.2	1,739	118.4	873,656	105.7	.1990	112.0	4,014	111.6	.4594	105.6	43.33
1918f	1,842	111.8	2,614	177.9	884,764	107.0	.2954	166.2	4,881	135.7	.5517	126.8	53.55
1919f	1,913	116.1	2,843	193.5	821,699	99.4	.3460	194.7	5,145	143.1	.6261	143.9	55.26
1920f	2,023	122.8	3,682	250.6	914,224	110.6	.4027	226.6	6,178	171.8	.6758	155.3	59.59

[a] *Statistics of Railways*, Interstate Commerce Commission, 1930, p. S-9.
[b] *Report of Joint Commission of Agricultural Inquiry*, 1922, Pt. III, Table B-35, p. 614. Data include gross ton miles of loaded and empty freight cars.
[c] *Statistics of Railways*, Interstate Commerce Commission, 1930, p. S-96.
[d] 1916 = 100.
[e] Year ends June 30.
[f] Year ends December 31.

sent unit labor costs up to .295 cents. The advances of 1919, accompanied by a falling off in gross ton mileage and an increase in the number of employees, raised unit labor costs still further to .346 cents. By 1920 compensation per gross ton mile had risen to .402 cents, that is, to 127 per cent above what it had been in 1916.

During this year, as is shown in the table, revenues grew by 72 per cent. The largest increases took place in 1918, when a rate advance aggregating 28 per cent for freight and 18 per cent for passengers was put into effect by the Railroad Administration and, in 1920, when the Interstate Commerce Commission granted a further advance of 25 to 40 per cent for freight and 20 per cent for passengers. Neither of these advances, however, enabled revenues to keep pace with the mounting labor costs, and the ratio of payrolls to revenues rose from 43.3 per cent in 1917 to 53.5 per cent in 1918 and 59.6 per cent in 1920.

Within a short period of five years the share of gross revenues going to wages and salaries increased almost by one-half,[37] reaching the highest point which has ever been attained in the history of the railroads. Sixty cents out of every dolllar of revenue was being absorbed in labor costs.

2. *The post-war decade.* The first two years of the decade 1921-1930 were marked by fluctuations in railroad employment and compensation almost as violent as those which had occurred between 1916 and 1920. The wage increase of 1920 had hardly been granted when the business world was overtaken by a depression. The gross ton mileage of traffic on Class I roads fell by almost 162

---

[37] "The aggregate operating deficit for the 26 months of federal control was less by about $65,000,000 than the amount of annual wage increases." I. L. Sharfman, *The American Railroad Problem*, p. 152.

billion tons and in 1921 was almost one-sixth smaller than in 1920.[38] This decline was reflected in an 11 per cent fall in operating revenues from $6,178,000,000 to $5,517,000,000. Employment was also radically curtailed, the number of workers falling by 363,000 or 18 per cent.

The year 1921 also witnessed the first general wage cut that had occurred on the roads in many years. On the complaint of the carriers the Railroad Labor Board in the spring of 1921 ordered a reduction averaging 12 per cent, its decision being based on changed business conditions, the decreased cost of living, and the wage situation in other industries. This reduction was estimated to save the roads approximately $400,000,000 annually.[39] In addition, many of the working rules were modified with a consequent saving of millions of dollars. These awards, combined with the lessened employ-

[38] The radical differences between the data available for 1911-1919 and those available for 1920-1932 vitiate comparisons between these periods for certain items. Thus the only payroll figures available for the earlier period cover total compensation (see footnote 29). For the period 1920 to 1932, on the other hand, data are available which segregate that part of the compensation bill that is chargeable to the actual operation of the railroads as contrasted with total compensation which includes salaries and wages chargeable to capital account. In the table on pp. 216-17, covering the period 1920 to 1932, data dealing with compensation refer only to operating compensation and not to total compensation as in the tables on pages 204 and 209.

This change in the use of payroll figures makes it necessary to emphasize that the ratios between payrolls and operating revenues used for 1920-1932 show the percentage of revenue that went to *operating* compensation, while those for 1911-1920, in the tables on pages 204 and 209, show revenues paid out for *total* compensation.

The gross ton mileage data used for the later period are likewise not comparable with those used in the earlier tables, since they represent not merely freight car ton miles but all passenger car ton miles as well. These data give a much more accurate picture of the actual work done by the labor force than freight car ton miles taken alone. Like the operating payroll figures, they are not available for the years prior to 1920.

[39] *Railway Age*, Vol. LXX, June 3, 1921, p. 1254.

ment, brought about a decline of $835,000,000, or 25 per cent in the operating payroll.[40] Since revenues had fallen by a much smaller proportion the percentage of railway income that went to cover the wage bill in 1921 showed a large decline, the ratio of operating wages to operating revenues for 1921 being 46.9 per cent as compared with 55.4 in 1920.

In 1922 a turn in business activity revived traffic and operating revenues started upward again. With the pick-up in traffic, however, came also a 2 per cent drop in the number of employees. This decline in employment and another wage reduction, authorized by the Railroad Labor Board for most employees outside of the train services,[41] resulted in a further decline of $122,000,000 in the operating wage bill of 1922, a reduction which brought the operating compensation bill down to 5 per cent below that for 1921. Thus the ratio of the operating payroll to operating revenues dropped once more, the percentage for the year averaging 44.4.

The spurt in business activity which in 1923 sent the index of manufacturing and mining output to a level of 102 as compared with the previous maximum of 87 in 1920, resulted in the railroads being called upon to move more traffic than ever before in their history. In terms of gross ton miles of freight and passenger traffic, the output of the carriers aggregated some 74,000,000,000 ton miles more in 1923 than in 1920, the previous peak year. Operating revenues reached a point which has been exceeded but once in subsequent years. To render this service the roads, within twelve

[40] See pages 216-17.
[41] The workers affected by the wage order of 1922 were maintenance-of-way men, the shop crafts, the clerical and signal employees, the stationary firemen and oilers, and certain miscellaneous employees.

months, increased the number of workers on the payroll by a quarter of a million, or to a total of 1,858,000. Excepting the years 1919 and 1920, this labor force is the largest that has even been employed by the carriers.

This large increase in personnel, and wage increases granted by many of the roads to certain classes of employees, resulted in a $317,000,000 advance in operating payrolls. But this added cost was more than offset by increased operating receipts, with the consequence that the percentage of revenues that went to cover operating labor charges in 1923 showed a slight decline to 44.28 as compared with 44.4 in 1922.

After 1923 railroad history was for six years characterized by a steady tendency toward greater output and stabilized revenues. The record traffic movement of 1923 was soon surpassed. Indeed, with the exception of 1924, the high point of 1923 was regularly exceeded throughout the remainder of the decade. Such declines as occurred in traffic movements from one year to another were relatively small, the maximum for any 12-month period being slightly in excess of 3 per cent. In 1929 the combined gross freight and passenger ton mileage was 16 per cent larger than six years before.

This increasing traffic was moved by a steadily declining number of workers. By 1929 the average number of employees had fallen to 1,661,000, or by almost 200,000 below the average for 1923. Indeed, in the last year of the third decade there were fewer men employed on the roads than in 1910 and this smaller working force was moving 75 per cent more traffic than had been moved 20 years earlier.

Although operating payrolls showed a downward trend in the period here discussed, increasing wage rates and fuller employment for the labor force that was retained, kept the operating compensation bill from declining as rapidly as the number of employees. Like the labor force, operating compensation never again reached the level of 1923. The 1924 payroll was 6 per cent smaller than that for the year preceding, and in 1926, when the traffic movement attained new heights, it was 2.4 per cent smaller. By 1929 payrolls had fallen to 96 per cent of the 1923 figure.

The declining payroll was in a large measure made possible by the marked growth in the carriers' investments in plant and equipment. These admitted of a growing output per unit of labor employed[42] and in terms of hourly output the gross ton mileage of freight and

OUTPUT PER LABOR HOUR, CLASS I RAILWAYS, 1920–32[a]

Year	Gross Ton Miles of Freight and Passenger Traffic (Millions)	Hours Paid For (Millions)	Ton Miles Per Hour Paid For	Index of Ton Miles Per Hour (1923 = 100)
1920.........	1,107,970	5,447	203.41	85.1
1921.........	945,339	4,147	227.96	95.4
1922.........	997,357	4,318	230.98	96.6
1923.........	1,181,565	4,943	239.04	100.0
1924.........	1,152,843	4,556	253.04	105.9
1925.........	1,229,438	4,546	270.44	113.1
1926.........	1,311,595	4,697	279.24	116.8
1927.........	1,299,382	4,544	285.96	119.6
1928.........	1,324,198	4,329	305.89	128.0
1929.........	1,371,351	4,368	313.95	131.3
1930.........	1,226,450	3,773	325.06	136.0
1931.........	1,034,825	3,046	339.73	142.1
1931[b]......	885,161	2,610	339.14	141.9
1932[b]......	688,366	2,007	342.98	143.5

[a] Data for gross ton miles from Bureau of Statistics, Interstate Commerce Commission (see note b, of table on pages 216-17). Hours paid for, from *Wage Statistics*, Interstate Commerce Commission, Statement no. M-300.
[b] First ten months.

[42] As is shown by the accompanying table.

passenger car movement grew from 239 per man hour in 1923 to 314 in 1929, or by 31 per cent. This increase, together with a declining trend in operating payrolls, led to a continuous fall in the operating compensation cost per unit of output. As will be seen from the table on pages 216-17, compensation per gross ton mile of freight and passenger mile movement declined from .236 cents in 1923, to .195 cents in 1929, that is, by 17 per cent, as compared with a drop of but 4 per cent in total operating payrolls.

Revenues, in the meantime, had remained relatively stable. In 1926, as is shown in the table just referred to, they exceeded those of 1923 and in 1929 they just about equalled the level of six years earlier. Accordingly the ratio of operating payrolls to operating revenues continued with few interruptions the downward trend it had started in 1921, ending the decade at 42.6 per cent as compared with 44.2 per cent in 1923.

The effects of the present depression upon the carriers' operating labor costs are also portrayed in the table on pages 216-17. An 11 per cent decline in gross ton mileage between 1929 and 1930 was accompanied by a 16 per cent drop in revenues. Labor forces were further curtailed by 11 per cent and the number of employees fell to the lowest point in 27 years of railroad history.

Accompanying this decline in employment was an 11 per cent drop in operating payrolls which for the first time since 1917 brought the annual wage bill of the carriers to less than two billion dollars. This drop in payrolls and a significant increase in hourly labor output were not sufficient, however, to offset the disappearing revenues and despite a further decline in unit labor costs, the ratio of wages to operating receipts rose to a height which surpassed that of any year since 1921.

EMPLOYEES' COMPENSATION, RAILWAY REVENUES AND

Year	Average Number of Employees[a]		Gross Ton Miles of Freight and Passenger Traffic[b]		Compensation Chargeable to Operating Expenses[c]	
	(Thousands)	Index 1923 = 100	(Millions)	Index 1923 = 100	(Millions)	Index 1923 = 100
1920...	2,023	108.88	1,107,970	93.81	$3,425	122.98
1921...	1,660	89.34	945,339	80.01	2,590	93.00
1922...	1,627	87.57	997,357	84.41	2,468	88.62
1923...	1,858	100.00	1,181,565	100.00	2,785	100.00
1924...	1,751	94.24	1,152,843	97.57	2,625	94.25
1925...	1,744	93.86	1,229,438	104.05	2,646	95.01
1926...	1,779	95.75	1,311,595	111.00	2,718	97.59
1927...	1,735	93.38	1,299,382	109.97	2,691	96.62
1928...	1,656	89.13	1,324,198	112.07	2,630	94.43
1929...	1,661	89.40	1,371,351	116.06	2,674	96.01
1930...	1,488	80.09	1,226,450	103.80	2,367	84.99
1931...	1,259	67.76	1,034,825	87.58	1,965	70.56
1931[e]..	1,284		885,161		1,708[f]	
1932[e]..	1,041	81.07[g]	688,366	77.77[g]	1,218[f]	71.31

[a] Data for 1921–1930 inclusive from *Statistics of Railways*, Interstate Commerce Commission, 1930, p. S-9; for 1931 from *Preliminary Abstract of Statistics of Common Carriers*, Interstate Commerce Commission, 1931, p. 14; for first ten months 1931 and 1932 from *Wage Statistics, Class I Steam Railways* Interstate Commerce Commission, Monthly Statement No. M-300.

[b] Data based on gross ton miles of loaded and empty freight cars and product of average car weights and car miles of passenger cars, sleeping, parlor and observation cars, dining cars, and other passenger train cars. Passenger train car weights other than Pullman as of 1926 as prepared by the Bureau of Statistics, Interstate Commerce Commission.

The divergence between labor costs and revenues was still further accentuated in 1931 when the labor force was further cut by 220,000 men, or 16 per cent;[43] the operating compensation bill declined by 18 per cent and

[43] The average working force of the carriers in 1931 was 1,259,000 as compared with 2,023,000 in 1920 and 1,661,000 in 1929. A decline equal to that which took place between 1929 and 1931 has never been experienced in the entire history of the roads. The average number of employees in 1931 was smaller than that for any year since 1902, when the ton mileage of the roads was slightly more than half of what it was in 1931.

UNIT COMPENSATION COSTS, CLASS I ROADS, 1920-32

Operating Compensation per Gross Ton Mile of Freight and Passenger Traffic		Revenue[d]		Revenue per Gross Ton Mile of Freight and Passenger Traffic		Ratio of Compensation Chargeable to Operating Expenses to Revenue (Per Cent)
(Cents)	Index 1923=100	(Millions)	Index 1923=100	(Cents)	Index 1923=100	
.3091	131.14	$6,178	98.22	.5576	104.75	55.44
.2740	116.25	5,517	87.71	.5836	109.64	46.95
.2475	105.01	5,559	88.38	.5574	104.72	44.40
.2357	100.00	6,290	100.00	.5323	100.00	44.28
.2277	96.61	5,921	94.13	.5136	96.49	44.33
.2152	91.30	6,123	97.34	.4980	93.56	43.21
.2072	87.91	6,383	101.48	.4867	91.43	42.58
.2071	87.87	6,136	97.55	.4722	88.71	43.86
.1986	84.26	6,112	97.17	.4616	86.72	43.03
.1950	82.73	6,280	99.84	.4579	86.02	42.58
.1930	81.88	5,281	83.96	.4306	80.89	44.82
.1899	80.57	4,188	66.58	.4047	76.03	46.92
.1930		3,642		.4115		46.90
.1871	96.94[g]	2,662	73.09[g]	.3867	93.97[g]	45.76

[c] Data from *Statistics of Railways*, Interstate Commerce Commission, and 1931 *Preliminary Abstract of Statistics of Common Carriers*, Interstate Commerce Commission, 1931, p. 14.

[d] Data for 1921–1930 inclusive from *Statistics of Railways*, Interstate Commerce Commission, 1930, p. S-96.

[e] First ten months.

[f] Estimated on basis of compensation chargeable to operating expenses equalling 94 per cent of total compensation.

[g] Per cent of first ten months of 1931.

gross revenues dropped by more than $1,000,000,000, or 21 per cent. As in 1930, the continued fall in operating payrolls was far from sufficient to offset the accelerated contraction in operating revenues and the ratio of compensation to revenues rose to the level of 1921, namely, 46.9 per cent.

In view of the fact that the carriers' interest centers in the "productive" output of their labor force, namely the amount of revenue traffic that is moved, the trend of

LABOR OUTPUT AND COMPENSATION COST FOR REVENUE TRAFFIC, CLASS I ROADS, 1920–31[a]

Year	Tons Carried One Mile (Revenue Freight) (Millions)	Hours Paid For (Millions)	Tons Carried One Mile per Hour Paid For	Index Number (1923=100)	Compensation Chargeable to Operating Expenses (Millions)	Compensation Cost per Revenue Ton Mile (Cents)	Index Number (1923=100)
1920	410,306	5,447	75.3	90.2	$3,425	.835	123.7
1921	306,840	4,147	74.0	88.6	2,590	.844	125.0
1922	339,285	4,318	78.6	94.1	2,468	.727	107.7
1923	412,727	4,943	83.5	100.0	2,785	.675	100.0
1924	388,415	4,556	85.3	102.2	2,625	.676	100.1
1925	413,814	4,546	91.0	109.0	2,646	.639	94.7
1926	443,746	4,697	94.5	113.2	2,718	.613	90.8
1927	428,737	4,544	94.4	113.1	2,691	.628	93.0
1928	432,915	4,329	100.0	119.8	2,630	.608	90.1
1929	447,322	4,368	102.4	122.6	2,674	.598	88.6
1930	383,450	3,773	101.6	121.7	2,367	.617	91.4
1931	309,225	3,046	101.5	121.6	1,965	.635	94.1

[a] Compiled from *Statistics of Railways*, Interstate Commerce Commission, 1930, except 1931 which is from the *Preliminary Abstract of Statistics of Common Carriers*, Interstate Commerce Commission, 1931.

labor output per revenue ton mile of freight for Class I roads is here also portrayed. It will be noted that through 1929 the same steady upward trend prevails for the hourly output of ton miles of revenue freight as for gross ton mileage of freight and passenger car movements. (Compare the table on page 218 with that on page 214.) Between 1923 and 1929 the ton miles of revenue freight moved per hour paid for increased by 22 per cent as compared with a 31 per cent increase in the hourly output of gross freight and passenger ton mileage.

Unit labor costs per revenue freight ton mile also show a trend similar to that which prevailed for costs per gross freight and passenger ton mile. The former fell from .675 cents per ton mile in 1923 to .598 cents in 1929, or by 11.4 per cent, while the gross ton mileage output per labor hour fell by 17.3 per cent. In 1930 and 1931 the large decline in revenue freight tonnage, unaccompanied by a proportionate fall in the movement of empties caused the hourly labor output, as measured in revenue ton-miles, to decrease, while gross ton mileage, which represents the actual work done, continued to rise.

The failure of the sharp curtailment of the labor force and compensation bill to offset the radical decline in revenues in 1930 and 1931 led the carriers to serve formal notice on their employees in December 1931, advising of their intention to reduce rates of pay by 15 per cent. This notice served as a basis of negotiation between a committee of the carriers and the Railroad Labor Executives' Association at a meeting in January 1932,[44] where it was mutually agreed that the roads would withdraw their demand for a 15 per cent wage

---

[44] This meeting succeeded one held in November 1931 at which the Railway Labor Executives' Association presented to the carriers a program

reduction in return for a 10 per cent wage cut for 12 months ending January 31, 1933.[45] In addition, "without attaching any limitation upon the use of funds derived from the payroll reduction" the roads undertook to "make an earnest and sympathetic effort to maintain and increase railroad employment."

The agreement had hardly been concluded when the continued decline in traffic forced a further reduction of the labor force. As compared with an average monthly employment of 1,259,000 in 1931, the average for the first ten months of 1932 aggregated 1,041,000. Together with the 10 per cent wage reduction this decline caused the operating wage bill for the ten months ending October 1932 to fall to an estimated $1,218,000,000, or by 29 per cent, as compared with $1,708,000,000 for the same period of 1931.[46] In terms of units of output the reduction in the payroll during the first ten months of 1932 caused gross ton mileage labor cost to fall less than 5 per cent below that for the corresponding period in 1931. The 10 per cent wage cut, in other words, had been only partially reflected in unit labor costs. Indeed, it was only by means of an increase in freight rates that the growing margin between revenues and the wage

---

of unemployment relief and employment stabilization. This program, which called for the guarantee of annual employment for certain classes of workers, shortened hours, compulsory retirement insurance, and other undertakings for the relief of unemployment, was the subject of discussion at the January meeting. Although some of its provisions were accepted in principle by the carriers, to date the program has yielded no concrete results.

[45] This agreement provided that basic wage rates were to remain unchanged, the wage cut taking the form of a 10 per cent deduction from pay checks.

[46] The total compensation bill, including executives' salaries and wages chargeable to the capital account, for the first ten months of 1932 aggregated $1,296,000,000. It is estimated that approximately 94 per cent of this amount represented operating compensation.

bill was offset. Such a rate increase granted in 1932 checked the upward movement of the ratio of the wage bill to revenues, and the first ten months of 1932 saw a slight drop from 46.9 to 45.8 in the percentage of revenues that went to cover payrolls.[47]

The post-war period can be summarized in the following words. With the aid of increased and more effective equipment, a declining labor force has been rendering a steadily increasing output. In terms of gross ton miles of freight and passenger car movement output per man grew by 36 per cent between 1923 and 1929 and continued to increase even during the recent depression years, when the ton mileage underwent a marked decline.

Prior to 1929 the growth of output, despite various increases in wage rates, brought with it declining unit labor costs which more than offset the falling unit revenue receipts. But in 1930 and 1931 the decline in unit payroll costs was not sufficient to offset the sharp drop in revenues, and wages and salaries absorbed a larger proportion of the revenues than in any year since 1921. Nor was the 10 per cent wage reduction which brought with it a 5 per cent decline in unit labor costs for the first 10 months of 1932 sufficient to bring the operating payroll back to its former relationship to revenues. Notwithstanding a freight rate increase, revenues continued downward to 73 per cent of where they had been in the first ten months of 1931 and the period ended with 45.7 cents out of every dollar of operating revenues going to the payroll.

[47] The failure of the 10 per cent wage cut of 1932 radically to improve the plight of the carriers led them to press for further wage reductions in December of that year. Their attempt yielded no result other than the continuance of the 10 per cent reduction granted in 1932 for an additional nine months in 1933.

CHAPTER X

UNPRODUCTIVE EXPENDITURES

Like other owners of property, railroads are subject to certain general public requirements for the common good. These include assessments levied for the benefit of improvement projects—highway, drainage, levee, etc. —undertaken by special districts; also compulsory expenditures in connection with municipal park and boulevard developments. As a result of such improvements they are often compelled to make improvements to their own property. They are also subject to special requirements, sometimes involving the investment of large sums, because of their peculiar relationship to the public authority as public service undertakings.

Outlays to meet the requirements that are imposed upon property owners generally are payments for the privilege of owning property under the protection of government. Certainly, they are productive of neither revenues nor operating economies, but the railroad has no particular ground for complaint on that account, provided, (1) the improvement is not projected to mulct it as perhaps the largest owner of property within the district or municipality; (2) the requirements are fair in themselves and in the public interest; and (3) the burden is equitably apportioned among the property owners similarly affected. Nor may it complain because, incident to such improvements, it is compelled to comply with special requirements, such as relocation of yards and freight terminals, elimination of obstructions or nuisances, change of type of motive power, or installation of utilitarian facilities of somewhat more attractive appearance. If such requirements are unreasonable, the courts may be expected to take appropriate action.

A railroad cannot escape the fact that in most of the communities which it serves, its property occupies a conspicuous place and gives rise to especially difficult problems of town and city betterment. And in justice to American railroad managers it should be said that they were numbered among the first to make use of the professional landscape architect, and that they have a good record as sponsors and supporters of movements for civic improvement and beautification.

As a corporation affected with a public interest the railroad is subject to a variety of particular requirements. Some are imposed by legislation, others by administrative tribunals. A few of the direct legislative requirements may represent "strike bills" which were not called off; some are covertly or openly designed in the real or assumed interest of railroad labor; some are calculated to promote the safety and convenience of employees, passengers, or the public at large; some—an indeterminate number—represent attempts to impose restrictions upon specific matters of management, ostensibly in some phase of the public interest. The administrative requirements are generally those imposed by a regulatory commission or other public authority, whether to promote safety or to procure information needed for administrative use.

Numbered among these specific requirements are those designed to reduce or to remove the hazard or the inconvenience of highway crossings, and those made necessary by the construction of a navigable waterway intersecting the railroad right-of-way, as well as those specifying the complement of train service crews, limiting the number of cars in a train, or providing for the installation of certain appliances or facilities on equipment or elsewhere. Compliance with such requirements sometimes results in increased revenues or reduced operating costs, but the net result in the aggregate is unproductive.

Of these particular requirements those relating to highway crossings are most burdensome and perhaps most important. Certainly, the need is most obvious and obviously increasing. The situation in Wisconsin is typical. In that state, on June 30, 1932, there were 9,469 highway crossings, 713 at separate grades and 8,756 at grade. Of the grade crossings, 7,433 were unprotected except for statutory warning signs, and the nature of protection at the others was as follows: wigwag 600, flagman 198, flashlight 149, bell and lights 140, gates 119, and bell 117.[1] In view of increasing density of highway traffic and increasing mileage of improved roads, these figures indicate a contingent liability that must be faced.

The nature of the type of protection needed in connection with a particular crossing is usually determined by the state railroad or public service commission upon petition of an interested party, whether state highway commission, local government authority, local freeholders, or the railroad itself. In case the situation can be remedied by the installation of gates or other safety devices or by the assignment of a flagman, the burden of expense is borne solely by the railroad. If a separation of grades is deemed necessary, the procedure is similar but the allocation of costs is different. Thirty states have statutes providing for an even division of costs between the railroad and the public. In the case of state highways the public half of the expense is generally borne by the state. In the case of a local road the public burden is

[1] *Biennial Report of the Public Service Commission,* 1932, p. 59.

shared by the state and the particular local government concerned, according to ratios fixed by statute. In Maine, for example, the prescribed ratios are 50, 40, and 10. In New York they were 50, 25, and 25; by recent legislation they have been fixed at 50, 49, and 1. In some states, notably, California, Idaho, New Hampshire, and Wisconsin, the statute authorizes the state commission to determine the apportionment of the total expense burden among the several parties in interest. This represents an advance in legislation, since informal agreements are made possible and provision is made for the exercise of discretion by a responsible public body which is in a position to inform itself as to the equities involved in each particular case. The present New York law seems doubly defective; first, in its rigidity, and second, in the inducement which it offers to local authorities to initiate projects without incurring liability for more than a negligible share of costs.

Even if the railroads were to be fairly treated in the matter of crossing eliminations, they would still be subject to heavy burdens for installation and maintenance of safety appliances and also for the wages of flagmen, whose service is quite as directly for the public benefit as is that of the traffic officer on the public payroll.

It should be observed, however, that the lessening of the hazard incident to operation is of direct but indeterminate benefit to the railroads, since it relieves them of a heavy potential liability for damage and personal injury claims. An expenditure, itself unproductive of either revenue or operating economy, may be counterbalanced in part by the hidden element of liability insurance.

The need for track elevation generally arises from the growth of cities, to which the railroad has contributed and from which it has already benefited. Each project gives rise to special problems. Many are initiated by the railroads themselves, and there is an element of benefit to the railroad in all of them, whether undertaken voluntarily or under compulsion. That they include some items of expense not directly productive, is immaterial, assuming that the courts may be relied upon to protect the railroad from undue exactions.

To impose upon a railroad the costs of construction or alteration of bridges made necessary by the opening or improvement of waterways intersecting its line is difficult to defend. Disregarding the fact that the chief beneficiary is a direct competitor for traffic, here is a disturbance of an established physical arrangement for which the railroad is in no way responsible and one which the prudent investor in railroad securities could not be expected to anticipate.

The extra expenditures required by train-limit and full-crew laws represent a forced railroad contribution to railroad labor. Most of them go out through the payroll. As to the operative justification for assigning an adequate number of train-service men to train crews, there can be no question; but this is the proper function of management. If there is need for an official check upon the judgment of the management in this matter, the state regulatory commissions are available for that purpose. Certainly, the proper way to decide the question is not through legislative prescription, enacted in response to the concentrated pressure of group interests.

Train-limit laws are even less justifiable. Arizona has such a law which is now the subject of attack. Its effect is to require the breaking down of freight trains at the state line, operating across the state in two sections instead of one, and reassembling at the other state line. The anticipated effect of this measure in lower accident figures has not appeared.

Published official statistics are not helpful as a source of information as to the extent of expenditures deemed unproductive in nature. In the accounts from which they are derived such a distinction is not called for. Therefore, the desired information is available only through a process of analysis and appraisal. Such an analysis has been made at the request of the Advisory Committee of the Association of Railway Executives and the result has been presented in a report published by the Association.[2] This report is frankly intended as the basis of a special plea, but it is nevertheless valuable as indicating to the public the managers' estimate of the burden which their railroads have to bear. The total figures (Class I railroads) from that report are given below in round amounts, classified as to capital and current outlays:

UNPRODUCTIVE PROPORTION OF COST OF PROPERTY
CHANGES AND UNPRODUCTIVE CHARGES FOR
MAINTENANCE AND OPERATION, 1927-31

	Capital Outlays	Current Expenditures
Grade Crossing Elimination	$122,857,000	$ 29,901,000
Other Crossing Protection	10,134,000	98,277,000
Grading, Paving Sidewalks etc.	6,573,000	14,457,000
Track Elevation	24,514,000	2,286,000

[2] *Nonproductive Railway Expenditures, 1927-1931*, October 24, 1932, 4 pp.

	Capital Outlays	Current Expenditures
Civic and Public Improvements	25,126,000	9,777,000
Navigation Requirements	19,732,000	5,556,000
Train-limit and Full-Crew Laws	———	33,310,000
Other Items	14,927,000	19,302,000
Totals	$223,866,000	$212,871,000

Excluded from this table is an item of $9,564,000, representing the aggregate estimate by twenty railroads of the unproductive expenditures made by them for the installation of automatic train control systems. This item, in the opinion of the Association, is in "the twilight zone of doubt"; it is, moreover, incomplete, for some reporting carriers having such systems failed to classify it among the unproductive figures in their returns.

The railroad can no longer serve as almoner-at-large. Whatever the facts, the idea persists in a section of the public mind that the railroad is a monopoly—that monopoly implies ability to accumulate large funds, and that the possession of large funds carries with it the power to evade the payment of an equitable share toward the support of government. However these assumptions may have been justified in the past with reference to particular railroads under particular circumstances, they are not true to-day. Public regulation has been effective in preventing unreasonable charges for service; competing agencies of transportation have arisen to take away business; and the tax-gathering arm of government has become strengthened. Railroad accounts are now matters of public record, and they disclose no swollen surpluses out of which unreasonable demands may be met.

A railroad, therefore, can no longer be regarded as an ever-available source of financial support to projects for the sole or chief benefit of other interests. Assessment of railroad property at valuations out of line with those placed upon similar property otherwise owned, cannot be continued indefinitely. Creation of special taxing districts paralleling a right-of-way will sometime come to be regarded as a poor way to provide schools and other agencies of social betterment. A realistic examination of the system of preferential fares for clergymen and other favored groups would at once reveal its essential inequity toward the non-privileged passenger as well as the carrier.

Singly these abuses may have little effect upon revenues as a whole; but authorized as they may be by law and sanctioned by usage, they are unjust in themselves and inconsistent with that principle of the Transportation Act of 1920 that it is the proper business of government to see that railroad revenues be conserved and that railroad credit be maintained.

Protection of the traveling public may be expected sometime to force recognition of a new principle of sharing the cost of grade-crossing elimination upon a fair basis, perhaps that of relative benefits as measured by relative use.

There is need for a new public policy in this matter to meet the needs of the present transportation situation. So long as we had unimproved roads, used by horse-drawn vehicles, and railroads inadequately equipped with safety appliances, there was no question as to which user of an intersection was responsible for the hazard, and an equal sharing of the costs of separation of grades may have been even too favorable to the railroads. Train operation to-day is safeguarded by a multiplicity of control devices, while on the modern highways, the density of high speed motor traffic is productive of hazards that are reflected in the mounting figures of accident reports. Common fairness would indicate that since the highway user is becoming increasingly responsible for creating a hazard, it is incumbent upon the state, representing the police power, to assume a greater share of the burden incident to its elimination and to apportion the public share fairly among the several levels of government within its jurisdiction. Hazard, however, is not the sole reason for crossing-elimination projects; there is also the impatience of motorists at the delay of highway traffic occasioned by the closing of crossing gates or by the normal stopping of trains at intersections.

CHAPTER XI

TAXATION

Of all items of business costs, taxes are farthest removed from the direct control of business management. Other expenses and charges are incurred under contractual arrangements which are made in accordance with the financial and operating policies of the various industries. Taxes are compulsory exactions, the amounts and characteristics of which depend upon the revenue needs and tax policies of the governments levying them. Adjustment of tax costs, therefore, would necessitate a change in government policy with respect either to expenditures or to the apportionment of the tax burden, or in tax administration.

In the pre-war period, competition of other transportation agencies with the railroads was of such small proportions that it was generally believed to be a matter of relative indifference to the railroad companies themselves whether their taxes were large or small, since they could be covered, along with a reasonable return to capital, by rates fixed within the limits of what the traffic would bear. Demand for railroad service was relatively inelastic and increases in the taxes were presumed to be shifted to passengers and shippers in the form of higher rates. Tax policy with respect to railroads focused on the proportioning of the tax burden between the patrons of the railroads and the general body of taxpayers.

Developments of the last decade have brought a contraction of the range within which railroad rates may be varied without exceeding what the traffic will bear, and have reduced the monopolistic advantages which the railroads formerly enjoyed. Serious competition in the form of motor and water transportation has come into existence, and tax increases are not easily absorbed by rate increases. This introduces a new aspect into the railroad tax problem. It means that the railroad companies themselves must be prepared to absorb all or part of the present tax burden, or of any increase in the tax burden. It injects the competitive element into the formulation of tax policies relating to the railroads. No longer can tax measures be judged with reference solely to their effects upon railroad patrons. Their effects on the financial standing of the railroad companies as private industries must be considered and this involves the competitive relation of the railroads and other forms of transportation.

Depression has intensified the acuteness of the railroad tax problem which had been developing over a longer period. Even in normal times, tax systems cannot be formulated to attain the ideal of producing the needed revenues within the minimum dislocation of private interests, but changes in the financial fortunes of various classes of taxpayers are sufficiently gradual to permit adjustments in tax laws or business arrangements which will overcome the most acute tax problems. In a business depression the distribution of tax burdens among industries is subject to violent dislocations, occasioned not so much by changes in the amount of taxes to be paid as by the rapid and irregular variations in earnings.

This chapter will consider the relation of existing taxes to the earnings and property of the railroads and appraise the railroad tax burden in the light of the tax burdens on other industries and property. Attention will also be given to geographical variations. For this study,

the period 1911 to 1931, excluding the abnormal years
of government control 1918 to 1920, will be employed.

I. TRENDS OF FEDERAL AND STATE TAXATION: 1911-1931

In this section we make a comparison of the character
and amount of the taxes collected from the railways by

RAILWAY TAX ACCRUALS, FEDERAL AND LOCAL, 1911–31[a]
(In thousands)

Year[b]	U. S. Government[c]	State and Local	Total[d]
1911	$ 4,871	$ 99,939	$104,810
1912	4,862	111,357	116,219
1913	4,908	119,294	124,202
1914	4,770	132,336	137,106
1915	4,273	131,169	135,442
1916	5,970	141,084	147,054
1917	57,957	157,189	215,146
1918	53,508	170,087	223,595
1919	41,742	190,641	232,383
1920	50,542	232,208	282,750
1921	38,898	238,257	277,155
1922	52,649	248,765	301,414
1923	77,700	254,370	332,070
1924	74,964	266,563	341,527
1925	87,680	271,690	359,370
1926	109,817	279,935	389,753
1927	86,031	291,007	377,039
1928	89,277	300,715	389,992
1929	90,691	306,565	397,256
1930	40,986	308,221	349,207
1931	10,404	293,100	303,504

[a] Compiled from *Statistics of Railways in the United States*, 1911–31. Data
are for Class I railways and their non-operating subsidiaries except that prior
to 1917 switching and terminal companies are not included. Data for 1911
and 1912 include non-operating subsidiaries of all roads. Those for 1913–16
include non-operating subsidiaries of Class II carriers.

[b] Years ending June 30, prior to 1917; beginning with 1917 calendar years.

[c] U. S. Government taxes prior to 1917 are chiefly special excise taxes.

[d] Excludes taxes paid to foreign governments, and a few very small items
not allocated to state or federal government.

the United States Government, with those collected by
the states, municipalities, and other local taxing units.
Railroad financial reports classify railway tax accruals as "due to the United States government" and

"all other."[1] The preceding table shows the growth of two types of taxes for the years since 1911.

1. *Federal taxes.* During the last 20 years, federal taxes have included levies on net income, excess profits, capital stock, security issuance, and miscellaneous activities. Taxes on some form of net earnings, however, have contributed the bulk of federal railroad taxes and now constitute practically the whole amount.

It will be seen from the table above that in the period of business expansion extending from 1911 to 1926, federal taxes increased more rapidly than state and local taxes. This was partly because of the increase in railroad net income and partly because of upward adjustments in the federal tax rates. On the other hand, federal taxes account for the major part of the reduction of railroad taxes from 1929 to 1931. Preliminary figures of 1932 do not separate federal from other tax accruals but it is certain that federal taxes will show a decline in 1932 even below the modest figure of 1931.

Federal taxes place on the railroads a burden of a different character from that of state and local taxes. The amounts of the federal income taxes vary with the profits of the roads. The property and gross earnings taxes of states and localities continue at about the same amount whether profits are large or small. Even if the amounts of the two classes of taxes were the same for a relatively long period, the burden of the net income

---

[1] Aggregate taxes of Class I railways—"total tax accruals"—include "railway tax accruals," "taxes on miscellaneous operating property," and "miscellaneous tax accruals." "Railway tax accruals" constitute the main item; taxes on miscellaneous operating property and miscellaneous tax accruals at the maximum (1921) amounted to only $7,000,000 and have averaged about $5,000,000 since that time. The railroads as property owners also pay special benefit assessments for street paving, sewers, drainage, irrigation, etc. These charges are considered in Chapter X.

taxes is easier to bear because of its automatic adjustment to the ability of the railroads to pay.

By their automatic adjustment to the profits of industries and individual companies, federal income taxes result in a minimum of disturbance to existing competitive relations. Under the federal income tax, railroads are given the same tax treatment as their competitors and other corporations according to the profit test of private finance. But, because they require large investments in tangible property and because their operating ratios are comparatively high, railroads are subject to disproportionate burdens on their net earnings under property or gross earnings taxes, as compared with industries which use relatively little fixed capital.

Measures of the burden of federal taxes on the earnings of the railroads as an industry have a peculiarity not present in those of state and local taxes. Federal income taxes are paid only when there is net income, and only by the railroads making net income. Unprofitable roads pay no federal income tax whether their deficits are small or large. For the railroad industry as a whole, the net income is the difference between the profits and losses of the individual railroad companies. Thus, if the net income and federal income taxes of the profitable roads remain the same in two successive years, the burden of federal taxes on the net income of the industry may be increased or decreased by the variations in the amount of loss suffered by the unprofitable roads. Taxes on property and gross earnings, on the other hand, are paid by all operating railroads, whether they earn profits or suffer losses, and the burden of these taxes on the net income of the industry is the resultant of the combined relation of the taxes of all companies to their net income.

In the period 1911-1915 and again in 1931, federal taxes amounted to about 3.5 per cent of the total taxes on Class I railways. In the intervening period, however, there was first an expansion and then a drastic contraction in the relative importance of the federal taxes. They increased from 3.5 per cent of the total tax bill in 1911-15 to 22 per cent in 1926-30 and declined to 3.5 per cent again in 1931.

Although federal taxes have amounted to substantial sums during the last 20 years, they are a factor of secondary importance in the railroad tax problem. They have never amounted to more than one-fourth of the taxes paid by Class I railways, and during the depression they have been reduced to less than $10,000,000 and to only 3.5 per cent of the taxes imposed on railroad companies. Even when substantial in amount, federal taxes are derived only from those companies able to pay them and consequently do not aggravate the financial difficulties of the industry, which largely center upon the unprofitable companies.

2. *State and local taxes.* State and local taxes are the principal factor in the railroad tax problem. For 20 years, they have amounted to three-fourths or more of all taxes paid by the railroads. As long as it continues to operate, no railroad can escape these exactions. While no taxes, whether federal, state, or local, are easily borne, state and local taxes because of their magnitude and their disregard of variations in earnings give rise to most of the tax troubles of the railroad companies. This is particularly so in these times of financial emergency.

The great bulk of state and local taxes—well over 90 per cent—are ad valorem property taxes or gross earnings taxes levied in lieu of ad valorem taxes. While rail-roads pay capital stock, net income, mileage, and other miscellaneous taxes to the states, they are not large in the aggregate and amount to only a small percentage of the state and local tax burden.

With characteristic inflexibility toward changes in busi-ness conditions, state and local taxes increased in every year, except 1915, from 1912 to 1930 inclusive. In spite of the depression, they were $1,000,000 higher in 1930 than in 1929 and in 1931 fell below the level of 1929 by only $14,000,000. Only preliminary figures for 1932 are now available and these show a further reduction in all railway taxes of $29,000,000 from 1931 to 1932.

II. TAX BURDEN OF CLASS I RAILWAYS: 1911-1931

Whether the tax burden on a railway company is heavy or light depends not only upon the amount of taxes paid but also upon the relation of the taxes to the earnings, business and property of the road. The tax burden may be reduced in spite of an increase in taxes by a greater increase in earnings or property. Moreover, no one meas-ure of the tax burden is adequate for a sound judgment on all considerations involved. Net earnings are the most significant measure of the tax burden from the point of view of the financial interest of the railroads. But prop-erty investment or the volume of business must be taken into consideration if appraisal is being made of the fair-ness of the railroad tax burden according to the prin-ciples of existing tax laws or according to the tax burden on other property and business.

For these reasons, the tax burden of the railroads should be studied in the light of all pertinent measures of railroad finance and operations. An additional reason for such a broad study is the fact that it will disclose the character of the influences which have affected the railroad tax burden. The factual information for such a study has been derived from the financial reports of the railroads, published by the Interstate Commerce Commission.[2] The most important adjustment in the data has been the segregation of all items of railroad taxes into a separate category which is treated as the last deduction in the income or operating statement. Thus, all earnings items considered below, except net income after taxes, are amounts before deducting tax payments.[3] Property investment consists of the investment in road and equipment, improvements on leased property, materials and supplies, and cash, less accrued depreciation, of both Class I railways and their non-operating subsidiaries. Taxes which are compared with property investment include both the taxes of Class I railways and the railway tax accruals of their non-operating subsidiaries.

[2] No serious lack of comparability in the data is occasioned by the changing number of Class I railways, first because the railways which pass into and out of Class I are of relatively small importance, and second because the tax burden is measured by the relation of taxes to the various earnings and property investment items of the same years. The absolute figures for taxes and for financial items are, however, slightly affected by variations in the number of railroads included in Class I from year to year.

[3] Other statistical adjustments which should be noted for a proper understanding of the following comparisons are: Revenues from miscellaneous operations have been combined with railway operating revenues, expenses of miscellaneous operations have been combined with railway operating expenses, and uncollectible railway revenues have been included in operating expenses. No adjustment has been made for depreciation which is reported as an operating expense. The accounting for depreciation varies among the roads, but, generally speaking, substantial depreciation is charged against equipment but only a small allowance is made for depreciation of other types of railroad property. It was thought that less error would be involved in retaining depreciation as an operating expense than in shifting it to deductions from gross income although other industries with which comparison is made have a substantial charge for depreciation of real property in their deductions.

Taxes, Earnings, Property Investment, and Traffic
Class I Railways, 1911-1931

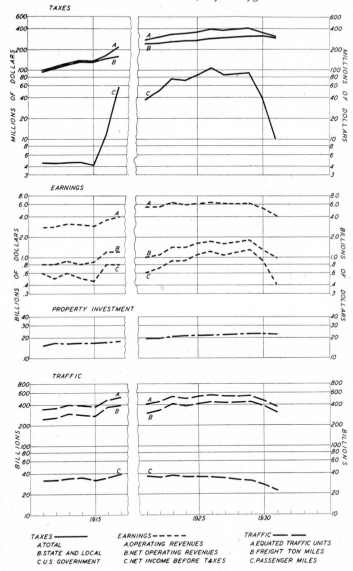

TAXES ———
  A. TOTAL
  B. STATE AND LOCAL
  C. U.S. GOVERNMENT

EARNINGS – – – –
  A. OPERATING REVENUES
  B. NET OPERATING REVENUES
  C. NET INCOME BEFORE TAXES

TRAFFIC —— —
  A. EQUATED TRAFFIC UNITS
  B. FREIGHT TON MILES
  C. PASSENGER MILES

1. *General trends*. Except for passenger traffic, the taxes, earnings, traffic and property investment of railroads have generally increased over the last twenty years. Not all items have had precisely similar trends, but the characteristic movement, as indicated by the chart on page 239, has been a steady increase from 1911 to a peak in 1926, a flattening of the trends from 1927 to 1929, and a sharp downward movement in 1930 and 1931.

Certain of the items do not share in the characteristic trend mentioned above. Passenger mileage, for example, reached a peak in 1917 and thereafter declined steadily to a lower level in the last three years than existed prior to the World War. Revenue freight ton mileage, taxes, and property investment, on the other hand, continued their upward movement until 1929.

During and immediately after the war, the adjustments which took place in the rates and business of the railroads changed the pre-war relationship of revenues and expenses. While operating revenues and operating expenses increased together to a maximum in 1926, their rates of increase were dissimilar. These differences in rates of increase and unequal increases of non-operating income and deductions from gross income had important effects upon the net operating revenues and net income of the railroads during the last decade.

Differences in the rates of change of the several revenue and expense items account for a substantial part of the variations in the railroad tax burden during the last twenty years. Taxes increased 298 per cent from 1911 to 1926, but operating revenues increased only 132 per cent and non-operating income only 32 per cent. Operating expenses increased only 146 per cent and deductions from gross income only 61 per cent. During the period 1911 to 1926, therefore, the growth of taxes greatly exceeded that of other items of revenue and expense and the tax burden was thereby greatly increased. But the tax burden was further aggravated by a more rapid increase of expenses than of revenues.

In the period of declining business after 1926, the differences in the changes of taxes and other items are even more marked. By 1931, the net increase of taxes over 1911 was 212 per cent as compared with 298 per cent in 1926. Property investment, non-operating income and deductions from gross income continued at approximately the 1926 level, but freight traffic, and operating revenues were at a level in 1931 almost two-thirds below that of 1926. Consequently the railroad tax *burden* has risen rapidly to higher levels in the last five years.

2. *Taxes compared with operating revenues and net operating income.* These differences in the changes in the items entering into the income statement of the railroads have affected most acutely the tax burden on the net earnings. To indicate the relative influence of operating expenses and of taxes upon the net operating income of the railroads, the chart on page 242 is presented.

In this chart, both operating expenses and railway tax accruals are shown as percentages of the operating revenues. The space between the two curves represents the percentage of operating revenues which was left after payment of operating expenses and taxes for a return on the capital invested in the railroad industry. It is evident that variations in the operating expenses have accounted for more of the variation in net operating income than have taxes. As a percentage of operating revenues, operating expenses have varied widely from year to year.

Taxes have increased steadily but, as compared with operating expenses, the increase of taxes has been gradual and steady. Thus, variations in the tax burden on net operating revenues, or on net operating income have resulted largely from the different proportions of operat-

RELATION OF TAX ACCRUALS, OPERATING EXPENSES AND NET OPERATING INCOME TO OPERATING REVENUES, CLASS I RAILWAYS, 1911-31

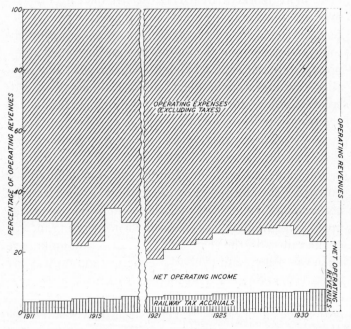

ing revenues absorbed by operating expenses from year to year. The improvement in operating efficiency indicated by the decreasing percentage of operating expenses to operating revenues from 1921 to 1929 tended to reduce the tax burden on net operating revenues in spite of the steady increases in taxes. From 1929 to 1931, on the other hand, operating expenses took increasing percentages of the operating revenues and drastically reduced the net operating revenues available to pay taxes.

Taking the last decade as a whole, the railroad tax burden has been placed on a higher level on account of the larger proportion of operating revenues needed for operating expenses than was the case before the war. In spite of the decline in the percentage of operating expenses to operating revenues from 1921 to 1929, it did not fall below what it had been before the war. Rate increases during and immediately after the war, therefore, did not increase operating revenues proportionally with operating expenses, and tax burdens on net earnings have been on a higher level in the post war period not only because of higher taxes but also because of the smaller percentage of operating revenues left for net operating revenues after the payment of operating expenses.

While the tax burden on the net earnings of any industry is higher than that on the gross earnings, it is worth while to emphasize the degree to which this is true in the case of the railroads. From 1921 to 1931, only from 5.6 to 29.4 per cent of the operating revenue was left for net operating revenue, out of which taxes were still to be paid. So large a proportion of operating revenue is required for operating expenses that small changes in the tax burden on property investment or gross earnings are necessarily multiplied into burdens three or four times as heavy on net operating revenue.

3. *Ratios of taxes to earnings, property investment, and traffic.* By means of the percentage ratios of taxes to the significant items of earnings, property investment, and traffic, the variations in the tax burden on railroads resulting from the trends and relationships noted above

may be studied in more detail. The chart below presents the ratios of different categories of railroad taxes to selected financial items for the period 1911-31.

RATIOS OF TAXES TO EARNINGS AND PROPERTY INVESTMENT
CLASS I RAILWAYS, 1911-31

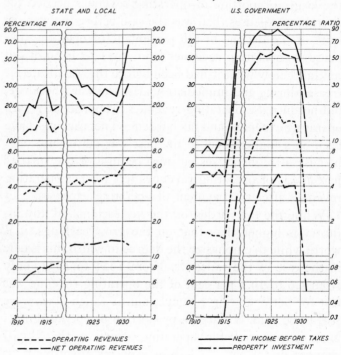

During the last decade, the state and local tax burden on property has varied little. The burden on operating revenues has gradually increased. Yet, the burden on net operating revenues and net income declined until 1929, and then moved rapidly upward. The wide variations in the state and local tax burden during the entire period have therefore come not from similarly wide variations in tax payments but from the changing relationships between operating expenses and operating revenues, and between fixed charges and net operating revenues.

Over this 20-year period, state and local tax burdens have largely controlled the trends in the total tax burden. Moreover, the federal tax burden is essentially different from the state and local tax burden. There is a similarity in the movement of the federal tax burden on all items of earnings and on property investment throughout the period. Varying with the net income of the railroad industry, federal taxes ignore the inflexibility of operating earnings and property investment. State and local tax burdens, on the other hand, generally move oppositely to the movement of railroad net earnings. From 1921 to 1929, state and local tax burdens on earnings declined while the federal tax burden on earnings was generally increasing. From 1929 to 1931, state and local burdens rose rapidly while federal tax burdens declined even more rapidly. The relative stability of the state and local tax burden on property is translated into a burden which increases when earnings decline and decreases when earnings rise.

Summarizing the foregoing analysis, it is clear that the increases in taxes levied against the railroads have not been offset by commensurate increases in earnings or property investment. The principal factor in the problem is the state and local taxes which make up the bulk of the railroad tax bill, and which do not adjust themselves to the changes in railroad earnings. The tax liability has gradually absorbed more and more of the earnings available for capital charges and has thus been an aggravating influence in the financial difficulties of the industry.

These data do not provide, of course, any convincing answer to the important question as to whether the railroads can continue to carry their present tax load and continue as a private enterprise. It is certainly true that the inflexible tax requirements imposed under property or gross earnings taxes constitute a more serious threat to the continuance of net operating revenues at a level adequate to sustain the capitalized values of outstanding securities in the railroad industry than in industries which pay largely net income taxes and which have relatively low operating ratios. However, rehabilitation of the finances of the railroads cannot be effected by tax reform alone but involves the other more difficult and important problems of readjustment in operating expenses and fixed charges to the reduced levels of traffic and operating revenues.

III. COMPARATIVE TAX BURDEN: RAILROADS AND OTHER INDUSTRIES

From the standpoint of government finance, railroads are but one class of taxpayers, and tax systems are formulated to produce the needed revenues by levies apportioned equitably among all classes of taxpayers. Whether railroad tax burdens are high or low is one question when viewed from the standpoint of railroad finance and another when viewed from the standpoint of government finance. In the latter case, the question depends on whether the burdens on railroads are higher, lower, or equal to those on other property and business. Even if the tax burden is equitable it remains to consider whether the tax burden as a whole, because of its sheer magnitude, is beyond the ability of private industry to bear.

Comparison of the tax burden on the railroads with that on other industries has definite limitations. Statistics are available for only a limited number of industries and types of property. Where statistics are available, their comparability is affected by the accounting procedures by which they were compiled and consolidated. Furthermore, an appraisal of the tax burdens of two or more industries must take into account the incidence of different taxes. Where taxes are passed on in higher prices, as the federal tobacco tax is, the tax burden on an industry may be lower than that on another industry which is forced to absorb its taxes. The measures of the tax burden of the two industries are identical, but the incidence of the taxes obviously is not the same, even though we cannot measure the difference statistically.

The greatest difficulty in the comparison of the tax burdens of different industries is presented by the burden on property values. So large a part of railroad taxes are assessed according to property owned that omission of comparisons of burdens on property would be unfortunate, but it is here that our statistical difficulties are the greatest. Property tax laws in general provide for assessment according to the true cash value of the property taxed, that is, the value determined by the bargaining of able and willing buyers and sellers in free and open markets. For the property of railroads and other incorporated large-scale industries no such value exists; hence tax administrators are forced to substitute constructive market values for actual market values in assessing companies in these industries. No statistics of these constructive market values have ever been compiled. In comparing tax burdens of railroads with other public utilities, we have used the book values of the properties, since these data are reasonably comparable with one another.

But in the case of farms our statistics of value are based on market values which fluctuate from year to year with changing market conditions; hence they are not at all comparable with book values of the property of the railroads which are not adjusted for changes in the price level of similar properties. Likewise current estimates of national wealth reflect year-to-year changes in prices and are not comparable with any figures we have for the value of railway properties we have therefore made no

TAX BURDEN ON CLASS I RAILROADS COMPARED WITH THE TAX BURDEN ON NATIONAL INCOME, 1913, 1921–30

Year	Percentage Ratios		Index Numbers	
	All Taxes to National Income[a]	Railway Tax Accruals to Net Value Product[b]	All Taxes to National Income (1913=100)	Railway Tax Accruals to Net Value Product
1913....	6.4	4.6	100.0	100.0
1921....	16.2	6.2	253.1	134.8
1922....	12.4	7.0	193.8	152.2
1923....	10.1	6.6	157.8	143.5
1924....	10.9	7.1	170.3	154.3
1925....	10.0	7.2	156.2	156.5
1926....	10.7	7.5	167.2	163.0
1927....	11.4	7.6	178.1	165.2
1928....	11.3	7.8	176.6	169.6
1929....	11.5	7.7	179.7	167.4
1930....	14.4	8.1	225.0	176.1

[a] Based on estimates of the National Industrial Conference Board.

[b] Net value product is difference between operating revenues and expenditures for materials, supplies, and miscellaneous. Railway tax accruals include those of non-operating subsidiaries.

comparisons of the ratio of taxation to property value as between railways and farms, or railway property and national wealth.

1. *Tax burden on railroads and on national income.* There is presented in the table above a comparison of the ratios of railway tax accruals to the net value product of Class I railways and of the ratios of all federal, state, and local taxes to the estimated national income of the United States for the period 1913 to 1930. The railway

tax accruals of the railroads include the amounts of these items reported by non-operating subsidiaries. Net value product represents the contribution of the railroad industry to the national income. It consists of the difference between operating revenues of Class I railways and the amounts of their purchases of materials and supplies from other industries. This item for the railroads corresponds to the "net value added by manufacture" reported in the Census of Manufactures. It provides the most significant measure of the tax burden on the railroad industry for comparison with that on the national income, since the national income as a total consists of the sum of the net value of the products and services produced by all kinds of productive enterprise.

In none of the years shown are the ratios of taxes to the net value product of the railroads as high as the tax burden on national income. Generally, the railroad tax burden was less than three-fourths that on national income. While this discrepancy in levels of burden is substantial, its significance is small, since it may be due entirely to the differences in the measures employed. The comparison of significance is between the trends of these burdens. The railroad tax burden increased less from 1913 to 1921 than did the burdens on national income. This may be partly explained by the greater fall in national income in the depression of 1920-21 than in railroad net value product.

There is a somewhat different relationship during the last decade. Measuring from 1913, the railroad tax burden had increased less by 1921 than the general burden on national income. However, the wide spread between the index numbers of 1921 and 1922 was gradually narrowed by a less rapid decline in the railroad burden than in the general burden until about the same level was reached in 1925. From that year on, however, the tax burden on national income increased more rapidly than did the railroad tax burden on net value product.

These comparisons are chiefly of value to indicate that, although the railroad tax burden has been rapidly increasing, there is no evidence that the increase has been disproportionate to the increase in the tax burdens on all national income. The differences in the levels and trends which have been pointed out are subject to a wide margin of error because of the nature of the underlying data used for measurement. This is particularly true of the marked divergencies of the data from 1929 to 1930, a period in which critical business conditions are undoubtedly more adequately reflected by the estimates of national income than by net value product, but in a general way, study of these data fails to show any marked divergence in the movement of the railroad tax burden from that of the general tax burden.

2. *Railroad and farm tax burdens.* As owners of large amounts of real property, railroads stand in about the same relation to the state and local property taxes as do farmers. For the agricultural industry as a whole, there are available data compiled by the United States Department of Agriculture for the gross income, certain items of expense, and the current value of agricultural capital.[4] Of these data, only gross income provides a suitable measure for comparing the levels of railroad and farm tax burdens.

In 1912, farm taxes amounted to 4.1 per cent of the gross income of the agricultural industry; total tax accruals were 3.9 per cent of railroad operating revenues.

---

[4] Yearbook of Agriculture, 1932, p. 893.

In 1930, farm taxes were 8.3 per cent of gross income; railroad taxes were 6.7 per cent of operating revenues. The burden of farm taxes on gross income increased 60 per cent from 1912 to 1929, and another 27 per cent from 1929 to 1930. The burden of railroad taxes on operating revenues increased 64 per cent from 1912 to 1929, and only 5 per cent from 1929 to 1930.

According to this comparison, the tax situation of the railroads as measured by gross earnings is no more serious than that of the farms. Farm taxes have required a percentage of agricultural gross income higher than the percentage of operating revenues required by railroad taxes. Both burdens increased about proportionately from 1912 to 1929, and the crisis of 1929 forced the burden of farm taxes to a level much higher than that attained by the railroad tax burden.

Financial statistics of an industry whose ownership and management is as decentralized as that of agriculture cannot be more than rough approximations. The gross income of the agricultural industry used in the above comparison was estimated from the market prices and quantities of agricultural products sold in each year, and the taxes were estimated by means of average real estate taxes per acre of land. For a relatively small group of owner-operated farms, financial statistics based on reports of the owners themselves are published by the United States Department of Agriculture.[5] From 1923 to 1930, the number of owner-operated farms covered by these statistics varied from 16,183 in 1923 to 6,228 in 1930. While this is a small group in comparison with the total number of owner-operated farms in the country, it provides the only reliable data available for a com-

[5] The same, pp. 894-95.

parison of the farm and railroad tax burden on other bases than gross income.

From the published statistics of these owner-operated farms, there have been derived the total receipts by combining cash receipts and the value of food produced and consumed on the farms; total expenses by combining cash outlays with the value of family labor including the own-

Tax Burdens: Class I Railways and Group of Owner Operated Farms, 1923-30

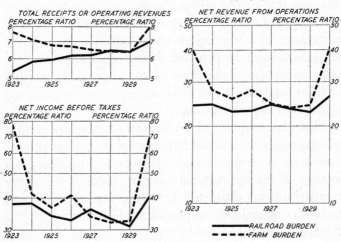

er; net revenues from operations by subtracting total expenses from total receipts; and net income before taxes by deducting interest from the net operating revenues.

In the accompanying chart, the ratio of farm taxes to farm earnings is compared with the corresponding ratios for the Class I railways. Measured by every item of earnings, the farm tax burden is higher than the burden on the corresponding items of railroads.

In their general trends, the tax burdens of the two industries are similar. However, from 1924 to 1929, the farm tax burden on total receipts was declining and the railroad tax burden on operating revenues was increasing. From 1929 to 1930, the farm tax burden on total receipts increased about 25 per cent, the railroad tax burden on operating revenues rose only 5 per cent; the farm tax burden on net operating revenues increased 68 per cent, the railroad burden only 15 per cent; the farm tax burden on net income before taxes increased 114 per cent, the railroad burden only 30 per cent; the farm burden on net income after taxes increased 373 per cent, the railroad burden only 51 per cent.

Another approach to the relation of railroad and farm tax burdens is to compare the farm real estate taxes per acre of land with the state and local railway taxes per mile of road. This comparison eliminates the influences of different accounting methods and valuation procedures on the measures of the tax burden. On the other hand, it can be used only for an appraisal of the trends of the two burdens since the physical units employed are not comparable for the purposes of appraising the differences in the levels of the burdens. Moreover, the comparison is limited to the 31 states for which the Department of Agriculture has thus far computed the farm real estate taxes per acre of farm land. These states, however, constitute five of the United States Census geographical regions. The railroad taxes per mile of road for each of the five regions have been estimated by adding together the taxes per mile of road of the states in each region and dividing the total by the number of states.

From 1913 to 1930, farm real estate taxes per acre in New England increased 150 per cent and state and local railway taxes per mile of road 73 per cent; in the East North Central region the farm taxes increased 140 per cent, the railroad taxes 169 per cent; in the West North Central region the farm taxes increased 151 per cent, the railroad taxes 114 per cent; in the West South Central region the farm taxes increased 162 per cent, the railroad taxes 119 per cent, and in the Pacific region, the farm taxes increased 155 per cent and the railroad taxes 109 per cent. In four of these five regions, therefore, farm real estate taxes per acre increased more rapidly from 1913 to 1930 than the state and local railway taxes per mile. The same relationship generally holds for the periods 1913 to 1922, 1913 to 1927, 1913 to 1928, and 1913 to 1929.

In addition to the 25 states included in the regional comparison, state comparisons may be made for the six states, Delaware, Virginia, West Virginia, Florida, Mississippi and Idaho. In 26 of the 31 states, the farm real estate taxes per acre increased more from 1913 to 1930 than the state and local railway taxes per mile of road. Only in Ohio, Indiana, Illinois and Michigan, and Iowa did the farm real estate tax per acre increase less than the railroad tax.

3. *Tax Burdens on railroads and electrical industries, 1912 to 1927.* Economically, railroads are generally grouped with the public utilities as public service corporations. These corporations are subject to some form of public regulation and are generally affected with a public interest. They have similar monopolistic characteristics and generally employ a substantial amount of tangible property in carrying on their activities. In the U. S. Census of Electrical Industries, taken quinquennially, there are presented financial data which permit a comparison of the tax burden on these industries and on the railroads for the years 1912, 1917, 1922, and 1927.

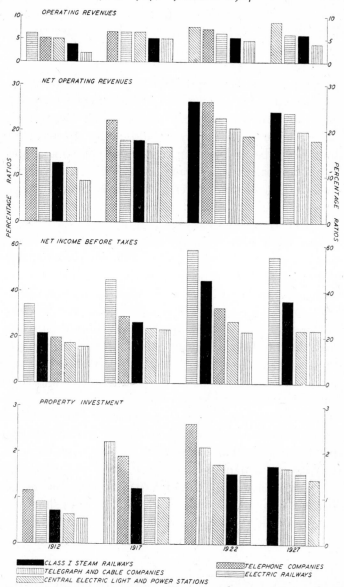

TAX BURDENS: RAILROADS AND ELECTRICAL INDUSTRIES
1912, 1917, 1922 AND 1927

OPERATING REVENUES

NET OPERATING REVENUES

NET INCOME BEFORE TAXES

PROPERTY INVESTMENT

PERCENTAGE RATIOS

1912   1917   1922   1927

CLASS I STEAM RAILWAYS
TELEGRAPH AND CABLE COMPANIES
CENTRAL ELECTRIC LIGHT AND POWER STATIONS
TELEPHONE COMPANIES
ELECTRIC RAILWAYS

The necessary data of the finances of the telephone industry were not compiled for 1927 but data for central electric light and power stations (commercial stations), telegraph and cable companies, and electric railways are available for all four years, and are summarized in the chart on page 255.

Measured either by property investment or operating revenues, the tax burden on railroads is not out of line with the burdens on these other industries. The railroad burden on property generally held middle ground in all four years, being less than that on telephone and telegraph companies and greater than that on electric railways and the electric power industry. On operating revenues the railroad burden was higher only than that of telegraph companies.

In the tax burdens on net operating revenues and net income before taxes the railroads take a position among the highest group, especially in the post-war years. In both 1922 and 1927, the railroad burden on net operating revenues was highest of the group, but on net income before taxes the railroad burden was substantially less than that of electric railways, although still higher than those on telephone, telegraph, and electric power companies. The severity of the railroad tax burden as compared with that of these other companies thus arises from the relatively heavy railroad requirements for operating expenses and fixed charges rather than from any disproportion in the relationship of tax requirements to property investment and operating revenues.

In this connection, the effects of the war on the tax burdens of the railroads and electric railways should be noted. While the burdens of industries increased on account of war developments, and while the increases in the burdens on property investment and operating revenues were relatively uniform for all industries, the tax burdens on net operating revenues and net income before taxes of electric railways and Class I railways rose much more than did those of the other industries. This is the result of two conditions, first the failure of rate increases to produce revenues adequate to offset the war-time increases in operating expenses and fixed charges of the transportation companies, and second, the failure of the transportation companies to achieve reductions in costs commensurate with the reductions in the costs of the more recently developed electrical industries such as the power companies.

There is no denying that taxes have developed into substantial burdens for all class of public service corporations. In comparison to the burdens of the electrical industries, however, the railroad tax burden is rendered acute primarily by the relatively large proportions of operating revenues required for operating expenses and fixed charges rather than by any disproportionate burden on property investment and operating revenues.

4. *Tax burdens on railroads and other companies reporting to the Interstate Commerce Commission, 1925-31.* Another comparison of the tax burden on railroads and other classes of public service corporations can be made for the period from 1925 to 1931 on the basis of financial statistics compiled by the Interstate Commerce Commission. These data are compiled by uniform accounting methods and relate the comparison to the developments of recent years. They cover Class I railways, Class A telephone companies, telegraph and cable companies, electric railways, pipe lines and water carriers reporting to the Interstate Commerce Commission

TAX BURDENS: CLASS I RAILWAYS AND OTHER COMPANIES
REPORTING TO INTERSTATE COMMERCE
COMMISSION, 1925-31

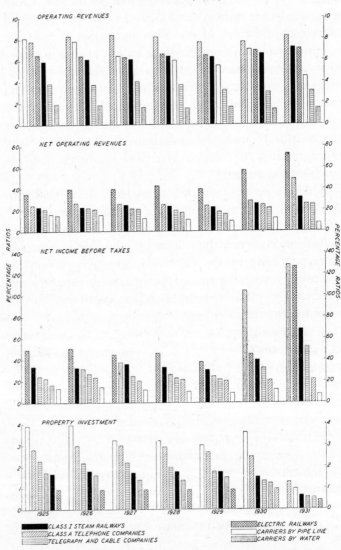

CLASS I STEAM RAILWAYS
CLASS A TELEPHONE COMPANIES
TELEGRAPH AND CABLE COMPANIES

ELECTRIC RAILWAYS
CARRIERS BY PIPE LINE
CARRIERS BY WATER

for the period 1925 to 1931. Analysis of the tax burdens of these classes of companies during this period involves both the relation of the burdens of the industries in the period and the trends in the burdens of the industries during the period.

Measured by operating revenues, the railroad tax burden has been consistently higher than that of water carriers and telegraph companies, about equal that of electric railways, and lower than that on telephone companies. The railroad burden was below that of pipe lines from 1925 to 1927, and in 1930, but above it in 1928, 1929, and 1931.

On net operating revenues, the railroad burden was generally higher than that of pipe lines, water carriers, and telegraph companies, but lower than that on telephone companies and electric railways.

On net income before taxes, the railroad burden was generally higher than that of any of the other industries, except electric railways.

On property investment, the railroad burden was higher than that of electric railways or water carriers but lower than that of telephone companies and pipe lines. The railroad burden was below that of telegraph companies from 1925 to 1927 but above it in the other years.

Differences in the tax burdens of the railroads and these other companies are partially explained by the inherent variations in the relation of earnings to the property investment of the several industries. Telegraph companies, water carriers, and pipe lines derive more operating revenues from a given investment in property than do the railroads so that an equal or higher tax burden on the property of these companies produces a lower or equal burden on operating revenues as compared with the railroads. From 1925 to 1930, the property burden of pipe lines was substantially above that of the railroads, but their taxes amounted to the same burden on operating revenues as those of the railroads. Electric railways, with a slower rate of capital turnover, carried a burden on operating revenues about equal to that of the railroads in spite of the fact that the tax burden on property investment was not much more than half that of the railroads. Property taxes constitute such a large proportion of the taxes of these companies that they bring to bear a dominating influence on the character of their tax burdens. With the existing diversity in the rates of capital turnover among even such homogeneous industries as public service industries, small variations or even equality in property burdens result in substantial variations in their burdens on operating revenues. In more acute form, the same condition holds for the relationship of property burdens and burdens on net operating revenues, and on net income before taxes. In the comparative tax burdens of the several industries, there are involved not only the amount of taxes paid but also the relationships of capital turnover, operating ratios, and overhead burdens.

In the trends of the burdens on these industries from 1925 to 1931, the railroads do not hold an especially unique position. It is true that the railroad burden on operating revenues from 1925 to 1929 was increasing while the burdens of the other companies either remained constant or declined, and that the burden of the electric railways and railroads on property investment remained practically constant while those of the other companies gradually declined, but on net operating revenues, where the railroad tax burden is most severe, the burdens on electric railways and water carriers as well as the burden of the railroads increased, and only those of telephone and telegraph companies and pipe lines declined. And from 1929 to 1931, the upward trend of the railroad burden on operating revenues was accompanied by increases in the similar burdens of telephone companies and electric railways and the increases of the railroad burden on net operating revenues by increases in the same burdens of all industries except pipe lines. After 1929, the burden of taxes on the property investment of railroads and of all other industries declined.

This comparison of the tax burdens of the railroads and other transportation and transmission companies from 1925 does not reveal any especially significant difference between either the level or the trend of the tax burdens of railroads and these other companies. If any generalization is warranted, it is that the tax burden of railroads on property investment and earnings, both gross and net, was higher than that of telegraph companies, pipe lines, and water carriers but less than that on telephone companies; and that on net operating revenues and net income before taxes the railroads had a tax burden less only than that of electric railways.

5. *Tax burdens of railroads and corporations reporting for the federal income tax, 1917 to 1930.* Comparison of the tax burden of railroads with a broader range of industries than is represented by the public utilities is made by means of the financial statistics of corporations compiled from federal income tax returns.[6]

[6] Adjustments made in the income tax data in order to make them reasonably comparable with the railroad data are as follows: For the transportation and other public utility corporations the item reported as "gross profits from operations other than those reported as gross sales" was taken to represent the item comparable with railroad operating rev-

Since the accounting procedures by which these data are compiled and classified are necessarily adjusted to the accounting practice of each type of industry, the comparisons are subject to a larger degree of inaccuracy than the preceding comparison because of lack of uniformity in the basic data. However, in a general way they provide a basis for appraising the status of the railroad tax burden in relation to the burden on other classes of corporations.

Ratios of both total and state and local taxes to the gross sales (operating revenues), net revenues from operations, and net income before taxes of the railroads and the agricultural, mining, manufacturing, trade, construction, and transportation and other public utility corporations reported for the federal income tax in the years 1917, 1922, 1927, 1929, and 1930 are shown in the accompanying chart.

According to all measures and in all years, the total tax burden of the railroads, transportation and other public utility corporations, agricultural and mining corporations are at the higher end of the scale while those of manufacturing, trading, and construction corporations are grouped together at the lower end of the scale. On gross sales and net revenues from operations, railroads and the transportation and other public utility

---

enues. For other corporations, "gross sales" was used. "Cost of goods sold," "compensation of officers" and "bad debts" were combined to represent operating expenses, except that for transportation and public utility corporations "miscellaneous deductions" were considered operating expenses. "Taxes other than the federal income taxes" have been taken to represent state and local taxes. Since the published statistics do not separate the railroads from other corporations in the transportation and other public utility business, the tax ratios of railroads based on the statistics of the Interstate Commerce Commission are used in the comparison.

Tax Burdens: Railroads and Corporations Reporting for Federal Income Tax, 1917-30

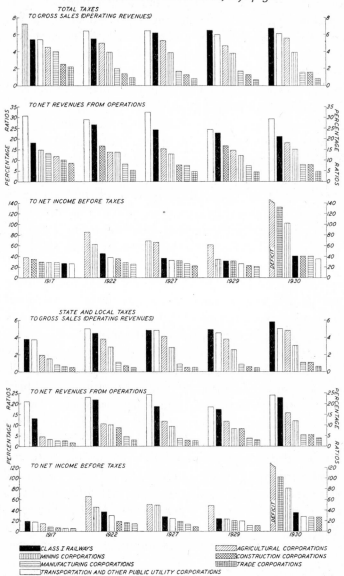

CLASS I RAILWAYS
MINING CORPORATIONS
MANUFACTURING CORPORATIONS
TRANSPORTATION AND OTHER PUBLIC UTILITY CORPORATIONS
AGRICULTURAL CORPORATIONS
CONSTRUCTION CORPORATIONS
TRADE CORPORATIONS

corporations have higher total burdens than any of the other classes of corporations, but on net income before taxes, agricultural and mining corporations show the highest burdens. The corporations with the highest burdens are those employing a substantial investment in tangible property and having a relatively slow turnover of their capital investment. Manufacturing, trade, and construction hold an advantageous position with relation to existing tax systems in that the amount of property investment is relatively small as compared with their gross revenues.

State and local tax burdens are largely responsible for the difference in total tax burdens of these classes of corporations, since a larger proportion of the tax burden on the public utility, agricultural, and mining corporations is state and local tax burden than is the case with manufacturing, trade, and construction corporations. In 1927, for example, 71 to 77 per cent of the total burden on the first group of industries was the state and local burden, as compared with only from 40 to 59 per cent for the manufacturing, trade, and construction corporations.

During the last decade, the tax burdens on public utility, agricultural and mining corporations have been raised more than those of the other corporations by the more rapid increase in state and local than in federal tax burdens. From 1922 to 1930, the railroad burden on operating revenues increased 22 per cent, the state and local burden 30 per cent. During the same period, the state and local tax burden on gross sales of agricultural corporations increased 26 per cent, the total 12 per cent; of mining corporations 7 and zero per cent; manufacturing corporations zero and minus 20 per cent; construction corporations 57 and 14 per cent; and trading corporations 20 and minus 11 per cent. In each instance, the burden of state and local taxes became relatively more heavy from 1922 to 1930 than the burden of total taxes. The same relationship of the burden of state and local taxes and of total taxes generally holds according to the other measures of the tax burdens.

Railroads are not alone in the difficulty of bearing a heavy tax burden because of their large property investments but share with all industries similarly situated the problems presented by the apportionment of the tax burden according to capital value rather than according to earnings.

IV. GEOGRAPHICAL VARIATIONS OF THE RAILROAD TAX BURDEN

Since the major factor in the railroad tax problem is the state and local taxes, it is desirable to indicate the geographical variations in the railroad tax burden. This is an aspect of the railroad tax problem, which, while fundamental to its proper understanding, can only be touched upon within the scope of this study. One of the problems raised by any geographical investigation of the railroad tax burdens is the allocation of the property, business, or earnings of the railroads among the states. Railroads are national in character, owning property and carrying on business in the several states. Their earning power, and consequently the sources from which their property and business derive their value, inheres in the operation of the railroads as going concerns without reference to geographical allocation. For many years, the conflict between the character of the railroad business and the necessity of determining tax bases within state boundaries has raised a very difficult problem of allocation for which only arbitrary techniques have as yet been devised. These techniques are not applicable in connection with the problem of ascertaining the differences in the actual tax burdens of the railroads among the states.

1. *By regions.* Problems of state allocation may be obviated by a study of the differences in the railroad tax burdens of the Interstate Commerce Commission regional groups of railroad companies. Within each region are included only entire railroad systems for which separate accounting is available. In the following table there

COMPARISON OF TAXES AND PROPERTY VALUES, CLASS I
RAILROADS,[a] BY REGIONS, 1930

Region	Ratio Taxes to Book Value of Investment	Ratio Taxes to Valuation[b]
Pocahontas	2.05	1.52
Central Eastern	1.66	1.32
Central Western	1.58	1.58
New England	1.50	1.11
Southern	1.49	1.57
Great Lakes	1.46	1.54
Northwestern	1.40	1.38
Southwestern	1.09	1.38

[a] Includes non-operating subsidiaries.
[b] Reproduction cost data of Interstate Commerce Commission.

are presented the ratios of railway tax accruals of Class I railways and their non-operating subsidiaries to the book value of their property investment, and the ratios of the railway tax accruals reported by Class I railways to the Interstate Commerce Commission reproduction cost valuation of these roads.

In the ranking of the regions according to the two burdens, there is little uniformity. New England, for example, shows the fourth highest burden on book value of investment and the lowest burden on physical valuation, and other regions are equally erratic in their rankings. There are indications in the data that the Pocahontas region has a high burden on property because of a high earning power, while New England has only an average railroad burden because of the relatively low earning power of New England roads.

State and local tax accruals are related to the operating revenues, net operating revenues, and net income before taxes of Class I Railways in 1927 and 1930 in the following table:

PERCENTAGE RATIOS, STATE AND LOCAL TAX ACCRUALS TO EARNINGS, CLASS I RAILWAYS, BY REGIONS

Region	1927			1930		
	Operating Revenues	Net Operating Revenues	Net Income Before Taxes	Operating Revenues	Net Operating Revenues	Net Income Before Taxes
New England...	4.1	16.9	40.1	4.6	16.0	28.9
Great Lakes....	4.5	18.7	25.0	5.8	26.4	43.6
Central Eastern.	4.0	16.7	25.8	5.1	20.3	30.6
Pocahontas.....	4.1	11.8	13.0	5.2	13.6	14.5
Southern.......	5.2	21.6	32.7	6.6	30.6	57.3
Northwestern...	6.3	25.2	43.3	7.3	30.5	52.1
Central Western.	5.4	18.9	23.3	6.3	21.9	26.9
Southwestern...	3.9	16.2	41.8	4.8	17.7	47.4

Comparison of these data with those relating to the property burdens of the railroads previously discussed shows that the relation of earnings to property investment is not by any means uniform and high burdens on property do not always mean correspondingly high burdens on earnings. The Northwestern, Southern, and Great Lakes regions were found to have relatively low tax burdens on property in 1930, but these regions had

the highest burdens on operating revenues, and net operating revenues in the same year. At the other extreme the
Pocahontas region with the highest property burden has
the lowest burden on earnings. The Southwestern region
had the lowest burden on property in 1930, the second
lowest burden on operating revenues, the third lowest
burden on net operating revenues, and the third highest
burden on net income before taxes. Determination of the
geographical centers of high and low tax burdens on the
railroads, therefore, depends largely upon the purpose
for which the determination is made and the measure of
the burden employed.

Net operating revenue probably provides the most
pertinent measure of the acuteness of the tax burden
from the point of view of the capital invested in the
railroad industry, and therefore of the relation of the
tax burden to the financial rehabilitation of the railroad
industry. Although the burden on net operating revenue
was generally higher in 1930 than in 1927, there were
no radical shifts in the geographical variations of this
burden. In 1930, therefore, and in the preceding three-
year period, the tax burden on net operating revenues
was most severe in the Southern, Northwestern, Great
Lakes, and Central Western regions in order, and least
severe in the Pocahontas, New England, Southwestern,
and Central Eastern regions in order. But the variable
relationship of fixed charges to net operating revenues
among the regions changes somewhat the geographical
distribution of the tax burden as measured by net income
before taxes. Yet the Southern, Northwestern, and
Great Lakes regions are found in the group of high
burdens on net income and the Pocahontas, New England, and Central Eastern regions in the group of low-

est burdens. The Southwestern roads appear to be adversely affected in their tax burden on net income principally by the heavy fixed charges which they have accumulated. From the standpoint of railroad finance, the tax burden presents the most acute problem in the Southern, Northwestern, and Great Lakes regions.

2. *By individual railroads.* In the final analysis, the railroad tax problem is one which touches most directly the individual railroad company. In the following table the ratios of total tax accruals to the earnings of the railroad having the largest operating revenues in each of the eight Interstate Commerce Commission regions are shown for the years 1922 and 1930:

PERCENTAGE RATIOS, TAXES TO EARNINGS OF SELECTED RAILROADS

Region	1922			1930		
	Operating Revenue	Net Operating Revenue	Net Income Before Taxes	Operating Revenue	Net Operating Revenue	Net Income Before Taxes
New Haven.....	3.8	20.1	—[a]	5.8	17.8	30.4
New York Central..........	5.6	27.6	49.5	7.5	35.4	50.1
Pennsylvania...	4.6	26.3	37.4	6.3	25.0	34.2
Chesapeake and Ohio.........	4.0	19.0	33.2	7.5	20.2	22.3
Louisville and Nashville.....	3.9	21.9	32.7	5.6	31.4	48.6
Milwaukee.....	6.3	36.3	252.9	6.7	31.5	204.9
Southern Pacific.	8.2	28.1	39.2	7.8	27.7	28.6
Missouri Pacific.	4.0	26.5	153.9	4.5	17.5	44.8

[a] Deficit.

There are wide variations in the tax burdens carried by these eight roads. In the relationships of earnings to property, operating expenses to operating revenues, and deductions from gross income to net operating revenues there are wide differences which result in an erratic distribution of the tax burden among the companies. In 1930, the tax burden on net operating revenues varied from 18 to 25 per cent, and on net income before taxes from 22 to 205 per cent. After payment of taxes the Milwaukee had a deficit while the Chesapeake and Ohio paid taxes amounting to only 29 per cent of its net income before taxes.

From 1922 to 1930, the tax burden on operating revenues of all companies except the Southern Pacific increased, but because of improvements in operating efficiency the burden on net operating revenues was relatively constant during the period. Some of the roads, particularly the New Haven, the Missouri Pacific, and the Chesapeake and Ohio effected changes in their financial structures which made the higher taxes of 1930 a lower burden on their net income than in 1922.

No geographical localization of the heavy burdens nor any relationship between the burdens on gross and net earnings are indicated by the comparison. Roads with high ratios of taxes to operating revenues may fall within the high or low burden group according to net income and vice versa. In the final analysis, the tax burden is a peculiar problem to each company involving the status of the business and finances of each individual road quite as much as the kinds, amounts, and administration of the taxes which it is forced to pay.

V. CONCLUSIONS

Taxation of the railroads is a problem which involves not only the financial condition of the roads but also the revenue needs and tax policies of the taxing governments. From the standpoint of railroad finance, the rapid growth of taxes for twenty years has developed into a burden which has placed an increasing strain on the earnings of the roads and which has been rendered more acute by drastic reductions in operating revenues without commensurate cuts in expenses and fixed charges during the last three years. The railroads, however, do not appear to be carrying disproportionate burdens on property investment or operating revenues as compared with other industries, but their heavy investment in tangible property, high operating ratios, and large fixed charges result in burdens on net operating revenues and net income before taxes which are more severe than on all other industries except agriculture and possibly mining. These results flow largely from the high burdens of state and local taxes on railroads, agriculture, and mines as a result of their large holdings of tangible property. The state and local property taxes on these industries do not vary with earnings and thus become heavier when earnings decline and lighter when earnings rise. Solution of the railroad tax problem must be sought, therefore, either in a reconstruction of the financial structure of the railroad industry or general adjustments in state and local taxes.

On the other hand, government activities and expenditures have been persistently increasing at a rapid rate for the last thirty years, and the depression has forced on governments of all grades the necessity for large new expenditures. It does not appear that the railroads have been treated with any marked inequality under the principles of existing tax laws as compared with other industries. But such a large proportion of the cost of government is now apportioned according to property ownership that the railroads, which must necessarily employ large amounts of tangible property in their business, are subjected to more severe burdens on their earnings than other industries in times of drastically reduced business.

In view of these conditions, the solution of the railroad tax problem under present conditions necessitates one or more of the following adjustments. First, the acute character of the existing problem will be alleviated by the financial adjustments, recommended elsewhere, which are designed to reduce operating costs and fixed charges. Second, reduction in the amount of railroad taxes, in so far as it may be achieved through reductions in the total tax burden on all industries, depends primarily upon a reduction in the costs of state and local governments. Third, reduction of the disproportionate burden on the railroads, along with agriculture and other large property holding industries, requires a modification of state and local tax systems for the purpose of distributing a smaller proportion of the costs of state and local governments according to the ownership of property.

For particular geographical areas, and for particular railroad companies additional relief from excessive tax burdens may depend upon the elimination of tax discrimination consisting of overassessment, abuse of special districts, discriminatory tax laws, double taxation, or illegal administrative practices.

PART III

FINANCIAL STRUCTURE AND FINANCIAL POLICIES

CHAPTER XII

FINANCIAL STRUCTURE AND OWNERSHIP OF THE RAILWAYS

The financial structure of American railways is more complicated than that of most industrial corporations, partly because our railroad systems have been built up by the consolidation of great numbers of pre-existing companies, each of which has contributed its quota of bonds, minority stocks or leasehold obligations; partly because nearly all major companies have passed through one or more financial reorganizations, and a reorganization procedure is usually characterized by the issuance of securities of types which are not used in ordinary corporate financing.

Typically, the financial structure of a major railroad consists of several issues of mortgage bonds, some of which constitute first or second liens on parts of the property, others of which are general mortgages covering all the properties subject to the lien of the various divisional bonds. Frequently a general mortgage contains an "after acquired property clause" which automatically extends it over property later acquired, subject, of course, to the lien of purchase money mortgages and any other liens which may already be attached to the property. Extensive use is also made of collateral trust bonds, the collateral usually consisting of the stock and bonds of subsidiary railroad properties which are independently organized. Sometimes the collateral trust bond is issued to secure funds to purchase the securities of independent properties which are then pledged under the collateral trust bond; in other cases the collateral trust bond is a means of raising funds on the security of a miscellaneous lot of stocks and bonds of subsidiary corporations already owned by the issuing company, which are individually not well enough known to command a market. Sometimes the purpose of the maintenance of subsidiary corporations and the issuance of collateral trust bonds against their securities is to avoid bringing newly acquired property under the lien of a previously existing general mortgage.

Another large block of railroad securities consists of "income" or "adjustment" bonds issued in connection with reorganization proceedings. The outstanding characteristic of this type of security is that the interest does not constitute an obligation unless it is earned. Sometimes the unpaid interest accumulates as a charge against future earnings, sometimes it is non-cumulative, and often it is non-cumulative to a certain date and cumulative thereafter. Sometimes the adjustment bond is secured by mortgage; sometimes it is merely a debenture.

The financial structure of the railways is further complicated by the presence of considerable amounts of convertible bonds, that is, bonds which carry the right of conversion into common stock at fixed ratios and between fixed dates. There is also a considerable volume of leased line securities, that is, stocks and bonds of roads whose property has been leased for a long-term or in perpetuity to some other railway corporation. In such cases the operating company ordinarily guarantees a fixed dividend on the stock of the leased line and assumes responsibility for maintenance, additions, and betterments. There are some unsecured debentures, but comparatively few railroad obligations lack the nominal security afforded by a pledge of some special asset.

One other type of security which distinguishes railroads from other types of corporate financing is the equipment trust. This is a device whereby a railroad buys cars and locomotives on the instalment plan, title to the equipment being vested in a trustee for the benefit of the security holders until payment is completed. In case of insolvency the equipment can, theoretically, be repossessed by the trustee and sold to some other road. Since the purchasing road has no title to the equipment pledged under an issue of equipment trust bonds, a receivership does not estop repossession by the trustee; hence no reorganization plan, so far, has enforced any material sacrifice on the equipment bondholders. Because of the peculiarly strong position of the equipment bondholders, which rests on the fact that equipment can be separated from the rest of the property of the road without destroying its value, it is possible to finance on equipment trust certificates up to practically 100 per cent of the cost of new equipment. The rate of interest on such securities is comparatively low, though, of course, the rapid rate of amortization (most frequently 10 years) necessitates a comparatively high addition to the fixed charges. Equipment obligations at the end of 1930 made up about 9 per cent of the total funded debt.

Another considerable element in the capitalization consists of short-term, that is, three- to five-year, notes. These are generally issued in order to meet a maturity or provide for some other capital expenditure at a time when market conditions are not considered favorable to the issuance of long-time securities.

Preferred stock, which makes up about 9 per cent of the nominal capitalization of the railways of the country, is of two principal kinds. Most of the preferred stocks are non-cumulative and have no claim against earnings except at the discretion of the Board of Directors. These non-cumulative preferred stocks in every case originated in some past reorganization in which they were issued in replacement of bonds in order to reduce the fixed charges. Ordinarily they constitute closed issues, and even if authority to issue additional amounts existed, they would be of no value as a means of further financing, since the non-cumulative feature leaves the stockholder too much at the mercy of the Board of Directors to make the security an attractive investment. The rate of dividend on these stocks ranges from 4 to 7 per cent.

The second group of preferred stocks, most of them of comparatively recent origin, are securities which have been sold on their merits as investments. They carry with them claims to cumulative dividends of 6 or 7 per cent. Most of them have been issued under authorizations which permit the issuance of additional blocks from time to time to meet the capital needs of the companies.

Railroad preferred stocks as a rule have equal voting power with the common stock, a feature which is not common in other types of corporate financing in this country.

Common stock makes up nominally 33 per cent of the capitalization of the railroads, and nearly 80 per cent of the total amount of stock. Typically, the par value is $100, though $50 par values are not uncommon. No-par stock has had a considerable vogue during the past decade, chiefly in connection with reorganization proceedings.

The accompanying table shows the amounts of the more important types of securities which were outstanding at the end of 1931.

RAILWAY CAPITALIZATION, DEC. 31, 1931[a]
(In millions of dollars)

Mortgage bonds	9,993	
Collateral trust bonds	576	
Income bonds	347	
Equipment trust obligations	881	
Miscellaneous obligations	942	
Total funded debt		12,739
Common stock	7,974	
Preferred stock	2,034	
Total stock		10,008
Total capitalization		22,747
Corporate surplus		4,993

[a] Classes I, II, and III railways and their non-operating subsidiaries. From Interstate Commerce Commission, *Statistics of Railways in the United States,* 1931, pp. S-27, S-122, S-124. Does not include securities owned by or for the issuing corporation.

This table fails to give a clear picture of the situation, however, because it does not distinguish railroad securities owned by other railroads from those actually outstanding in the hands of the public, and also because the par values of the common stocks are not an accurate measure of the actual importance of the common stock in the capitalization. We have no data by which to classify separately the securities not owned by railways.

The ownership of railroad securities. As to ownership of railroad stocks very little information is available, a fact which itself indicates that the stock is predominantly in the hands of private individuals rather than of institutions which make the facts of ownership public. About 2,900 million dollars par value, or 29 per cent of the outstanding stock of railroads, is owned by other railroads. Of the remaining 7,111 millions, about 260 million dollars worth (in par value), or 3.7 per cent, is accounted for by the holdings of the Pennroad Corporation, the Alleghany Corporation, and the Chesapeake Corporation—holding companies closely affiliated with railroad corporations. Investment trusts probably hold between 200 and 300 million dollars worth.[1]

Class I railroads at the end of 1929 had over 800,000 stockholders of record—this figure of course involving much duplication because the same person holds stock in more than one railroad. Foreign holdings are known to be large. The Department of Commerce estimates that at the end of 1931 foreigners held 2,250 million dollars worth (market value) of American securities. Before the war it was estimated that about four-fifths of the foreign holdings of our securities consisted of railroad stocks and bonds. The proportion would now undoubtedly be considerably lower, but even if it has fallen to 50 per cent it would appear that there must be two billion dollars par value of American railway securities in foreign hands.

Most individual holdings of stock are small in proportion to the total amount of railway stock outstanding. A compilation which we have made from data accumulated in a recent Congressional investigation[2] shows that at the end of 1929 the holdings of individuals, families and estates in blocks of over 5,000 shares of a single road aggregated over 500,000 shares, or perhaps 6 per cent of

[1] A check of the portfolios of 35 of the largest investment trusts whose holdings are reported in Poor's Manual, showed 107 million dollars in railroad securities. Several of the larger trusts give only their security lists, without indicating the amounts held, and a great many fixed trusts report only the number of shares of different stocks which are held against each "unit" but do not report the number of units outstanding.

[2] "Regulation of Stock Ownership in Railroads," 71 Cong. 3d Sess. H.R. 2789. Data refer to the end of 1929.

the total outstanding stock. Holdings in blocks of over 25,000 shares aggregated about 130,000 shares, or between 1 and 2 per cent of the total outstanding.

The table on page 282 groups the Class I roads according to the character of their controlling interests.

Of the 13 railroads controlled by industrial corporations, five are controlled by iron and steel companies (three by the United States Steel Corporation); two by power and light companies; three by copper companies; two by coal companies; and one by the American Tobacco Company. Of the railroads wholly or largely controlled by single individuals or families, by far the most important are the Van Sweringen roads. No other company in this group operates as much as 400 miles of road except the Virginian, which is controlled by the H. H. Rogers estate; the Florida East Coast, controlled by the Flagler estate; and the Western Pacific, controlled by Arthur Curtiss James. The classification "held in large part by one or more interests" comprises chiefly cases where a large block of stock has been acquired by another road, but not enough to establish permanent control. For instance, at the date of the report, 29 per cent of the stock of the Boston and Maine was controlled by the New Haven, and 13 per cent of the New Haven by the Pennsylvania and its affiliate the Pennroad Corporation. Ten per cent of the stock of the Delaware, Lackawanna and Western was registered in the names of George F. Baker and George F. Baker, Jr., and 38 per cent of the stock of the Chicago and Eastern Illinois was held by the estate of Thomas F. Ryan.

The roads of which there is "no marked concentration of ownership" includes most of the largest companies. The largest single interest in the Atchison, Topeka and

CLASSIFICATION OF CLASS I RAILROADS ACCORDING TO MANNER OF CONTROL[a]

Group	Number of Companies	Per Cent of Total	Road Mileage Operated	Per Cent of Total
I. Railroads controlled by an industry....................	13	8.12	3,282.37	1.36
II. Railroads wholly or largely controlled by an individual or family....................	18	—	21,137.52	—
Railroads subsidiary to companies in Group II.........	13	—	8,689.76	—
Total.................	31	19.38	29,827.28	12.32
IV. Railroads whose securities are held in large part by one or more interests.............	18	—	32,875.97	—
Railroads subsidiary to companies in Group IV........	14	—	14,225.72	—
Total.................	32	20.00	47,101.69	19.47
V. Railroads of which there is no marked concentration of ownership................	16	—	97,569.25	—
Railroads subsidiary to companies in Group V.........	46	—	48,896.03	—
Total.................	62	38.75	146,465.28	60.54
VI. Miscellaneous—Control held by investment syndicates, voting trustees, etc.........	6	3.75	6,381.26	2.64
VII. Unassigned—Railroads subsidiary to more than 1 group or to Canadian or Mexican railways...................	16	10.00	8,876.87	3.67
Total.................	160	100.00	241,934.75	100.00

[a] "Regulation of Stock Ownership in Railroads," 71 Cong. 3d. Sess. H.R. 2789, p. LI. (Original table has no Section III.)

Santa Fe holds only .76 of 1 per cent of the stock; the largest holder of Union Pacific stock is a Dutch investment trust with 2.27 per cent. The largest holding of Baltimore and Ohio stock is that of the Union Pacific with 2.56 per cent.

The bonded debt of the railroads is in very large part held by financial and fiduciary institutions and by other railroads. The following table[3] shows the estimated holdings of various types of institutions, as of the end of 1931 (in millions of dollars):

Railroads (other than issuing company)	909
Legal reserve life insurance companies	3,103
Fraternal life insurance companies	35
Other insurance companies	760
National banks	720
Mutual savings banks	1,025
Other banks	428
Educational institutions	275
Foundations	280
United States Treasury	40
Total	7,575

[3] Sources of data are as follows:

Railroads: *Statistics of Railways in the United States.*

Legal reserve life insurance companies: Estimated on the basis of figures given in Proceedings of the Twenty-Sixth Annual Convention of the Association of Life Insurance Presidents, December 8 and 9, 1932, pp. 108-9, for companies having 91.9 per cent of total admitted assets of legal reserve insurance companies.

Fraternal life insurance companies: Our own estimate, based on analysis of fraternal benefit orders and societies, reporting to the New York State Superintendent of Insurance.

Other insurance companies: Our own estimate; based primarily on analysis of reports of companies made to the New York State Superintendent of Insurance, and checked against data for fire companies in *Best's Insurance News,* July 20, 1932.

Banks: *Annual Report of the Comptroller of the Currency,* for 1931. Data are as of June 30, 1931. For mutual savings banks the data given by the Comptroller are for railroads and public utility bonds; we have

We have but scanty information concerning the ownership of the remaining 5,164 million dollars of railway funded debt. Foreign holdings, as was noted above, are known to be large. American investment trust holdings of bonds are small. Churches, hospitals, trade unions, and miscellaneous trusteeships of a public character undoubtedly account for a considerable volume, but data for an estimate are lacking.

These data are sufficient to show that the financial interests involved in the maintenance of the stability and earning power of American railroads are substantially those of the entire community. Any program of financial reconstruction must take into account not only transportation needs, and the interests of railroad labor but must be planned with cognizance of its probable repercussions on banks, life insurance companies, and trusteeships, and through them on the savings of all those whose savings these institutions safeguard.

---

assumed arbitrarily that 75 per cent of these holdings are railroad bonds. For other banks we have assumed that the relation between railroad bonds and public utility bonds is the same as for national banks.

Educational institutions: Railroad bonds estimated to make up 20 per cent of the total productive funds. A questionnaire returned to the Bureau of Railway Economics by 65 educational institutions showed that at the end of 1924, 24 per cent of their productive funds were in railroad bonds. An analysis of 30 large institutions made in 1931 by Wood, Struthers and Company showed 16.2 per cent of productive funds in railroad bonds. In the latter study securities were valued at the market; consequently the figures are probably considerably lower than the par values involved. On the other hand, the smaller colleges probably carry a smaller proportion of railroad bonds than do the large institutions whose portfolios have been analyzed.

Foundations: Estimate based on annual reports of six foundations having a total of 52 per cent of the assets of 108 foundations for social welfare compiled by the Twentieth Century Fund.

U. S. Treasury: *Annual Report of the Secretary of the Treasury,* 1931, p. 544.

CHAPTER XIII

RAILROAD CAPITALIZATION

During recent months there has been a revival of interest in the question whether the railroads are over-capitalized; a question which attracted a great deal of attention in the latter part of the pre-war period. In this chapter we consider the question from the standpoint of the public interest; the question whether a decrease in railway capitalization is desirable from the standpoint of efficient railway management is considered in Section IV of the next chapter.

In the pre-war period, public interest in the amount of railroads' capitalization centered in the determination of the proper base with which to compare earnings of the railroads, for the purpose of determining whether they were making more than a "fair" return. It was assumed that in the absence of restrictive control the monopolistic character of the railroads would enable them to earn more than a fair return on their investment, and since no valuation of the property had been made, discussion centered on the book values of the investment and on the capitalization.

As is pointed out in Part IV of this study, one of the primary purposes of the valuation law was to test the relationship between the face value of the outstanding railroad securities and the "value" of the property devoted to railroad uses. Quite apart from the question discussed in Chapter XX whether the valuation figures can be put to any practical use, it is obvious that the tentative valuations have served a useful purpose in dispelling the illusion that the railroads as a whole are grossly overcapitalized—so far as inventory values constitute a test. Whichever of the conflicting methods of valuation we employ, the results are roughly in line with the actual capitalization.[1]

I. THE CONTROL OF CAPITALIZATION

Since the passage of the Transportation Act the Interstate Commerce Commission has had a veto power over the issuance of securities by all railroads subject to its jurisdiction. In the exercise of this authority the Commission has been guided to a very considerable extent by a purpose to prevent overcapitalization. In general, aside from reorganization cases, capital issues are permitted only (a) to refund existing capital issues of equal or larger amount; (b) to acquire additional "capital assets"; and (c) to reimburse the treasury for the previous expenditure of free funds in the acquisition of capital assets.

Capital assets may be broadly defined as investments of a permanent character which are intended for continuing productive use in the service of transportation. They include right-of-way, track, structures, equipment, securities of other railways if held for purpose of permanent control (but not securities held merely as investments or for bargaining purposes), improvements on leased lines, organization expenses, and a reasonable amount of working capital.

It is not necessary for our purposes to analyze in detail the way in which these principles are applied.[2] Ordinarily the issuance of securities to refund or replace other securities is permitted even if a condition of over-

[1] See data in Chapter XX.
[2] Compare D. B. Locklin, *Regulation of Security Issues by the Interstate Commerce Commission*, 1927, Chapters V and VII.

capitalization is thereby perpetuated. In reorganization cases, however, the general policy of the Commission is unfriendly to the issuance of securities in excess of capital assets, even though capitalization is thereby reduced.[3]

In valuing the capital assets no single principle is followed consistently. Actual cost is the test most frequently applied, and is the regular rule in the case of property newly constructed. Where a carrier is issuing securities in connection with the acquisition of property which is already used for railroad purposes, the tentative or final valuations made under the valuation act of 1913 are always mentioned, but seem in most cases to be given little weight. Prospective earning capacity is given much weight in cases where the point at issue is the total amount of securities and not the propriety of an individual issue. Stock dividends are regarded unfavorably, but are sometimes permitted where capital assets have been accumulated out of earnings.

II. THE SIGNIFICANCE OF THE AMOUNT OF CAPITALIZATION

As the law now stands, the question whether the roads are overcapitalized in terms of their present and prospective earning power is of little practical importance. The base on which the roads are supposed to be allowed to earn a fair return, if they can, is determined by the value of the property, and the value of the property is independent of the capitalization. Lower rates might necessitate a capital readjustment; but a capital readjustment could not of itself result in lower rates. Nor is capitalization recognized as a basis for valuing property

[3] As is shown in Chapter XV, however, in actual practice the Commission frequently sanctions wide departures from the principle here indicated.

when it is acquired by another line. The courts give gross capitalization no weight in confiscation cases, and the investing public certainly does not gauge the value of a corporation's securities by their nominal amount. Finally, even if present laws regarding the rate base were to be abolished, we do not see any way in which a revision of the capitalization would be helpful. We cannot base rates on capitalization without some standard by which to determine the capitalization, and that standard will be the significant thing; not the capitalization based on it. In short, the nominal capitalization of a railroad has no real significance.

Nevertheless we do not suggest what may seem to be the logical conclusion; namely, that the Interstate Commerce Commission should cease to interest itself in the prevention of an overexpansion of the capital structure of the railroads. It is right that supervising authorities should insist on the maintenance of a reasonable proportion between changes in capitalization of the carrier companies and changes in the actual investment in carrier property. Neglect of this issue would lay the Commission open to the charge of collusion in practices designed to mislead investors, and would create a plausible basis for excessive claims for compensation in the event that the roads are ultimately taken over by the government. But the whole issue is of minor importance.[4]

III. SHOULD THERE BE A GENERAL DECAPITALIZATION?

Within the last year or so the question of overcapitalization has come up in a form entirely different from the traditional issue. It is now urged that the railroads

[4] This, it must be noted, refers to the gross capitalization, not the bond issues. Compare below, Section IV.

are overcapitalized, not in the sense of having a volume of stocks and bonds which is excessive in proportion to the original cost or reproduction value of the properties, but in the sense that the actual investment is greater than is justified by the current and prospective levels of traffic and of commodity prices—partly because of the increased competition of other types of transportation and partly because of the decreased ability of industry to pay rates that were once deemed just and reasonable. We are told that owners of railway securities must face the necessity of a drastic scaling down of the face value of their holdings. The railway-using public, it is argued, cannot be expected to pay for an indefinite period to a declining industry the capital charges which were appropriate to that industry in the days of its prosperity. In other words, the railroad business is overcapitalized on the basis of the going or commercial value of its plant and equipment.

Now it is obvious that if this view is correct the capitalization of the railroads will sooner or later be scaled down, if not in nominal amount at least in the market values by which the present and prospective income is actually capitalized. The question with which we are concerned here is whether it is in the public interest that this process be expedited and systematized.

So far as the stock is concerned the issue is easily disposed of. A reduction of the nominal capitalization of the railways would not in any way promote the objectives aimed at by the proponents of decapitalization. What is wanted is a reduction of the amount of income which goes to the owners of railway securities—to the end that rates may be lowered and wages maintained. But stock capitalization has no bearing on earnings even in the limited sense in which earnings are dependent on rate regulation.

Legally, the rate level is a function of the property valuation, or will be when the valuations are completed. We shall show in Part IV that the valuations as a matter of fact have had little importance in rate fixing.

But even if the valuations did control the rate level, the face value of the stock has no bearing on the valuation. Only 73 per cent of railway stocks paid dividends in 1931, and the average rate paid on all stock was 4.01 per cent. It is probably now running at less than 1 per cent. It is obvious that when a road is paying no dividends nothing can be saved for the shipper or the railway worker by cutting the nominal amount of the stock. And in the cases where the road does pay dividends the amount of stock is equally irrelevant. It is as easy and as legal to pay 12 per cent on a million shares as it is to pay 6 per cent on two million.

To be sure, very high nominal dividends advertise the prosperity of those who pay them and invite attack from all sides. It is therefore desirable that the number of shares shall be such that the funds available for dividends work out at about the customary amount per share— anywhere from $1.00 to $10.00 a year. In other words, the capitalization should be adjusted roughly to the earning power. But this is a very different thing from changing the capitalization with a view to changing the earning power.

Our conclusion is that if the question is viewed from the standpoint of the equities, either of the employees or of the rate-paying public as against the owners, there is no force in the suggestion that the stock capitalization of the roads should be cut down. The bearing of the capitalization on the financial policy of the roads is considered in Chapter XIV.

IV. SHOULD THERE BE A DEVALUATION OF THE FUNDED DEBT?

Sometimes the decapitalization idea takes the form of a plea for a horizontal scaling down of the bonded debt, by means of some novel and summary legal procedure.[5] It is argued that the bondholder has no equitable claim to exemption from the general sacrifices of the deflation era, and that a concomitant scaling down of bonded debt, valuation, and rates, would be no more than an equitable recognition of the changed earning capacity of the industry.

This contention is not without some force. It does seem at first glance ethically indefensible that the bond interest charges of the railroads[6] should have increased from 1928 to 1931 by 1 per cent, when compensation to employees declined 32 per cent, operating revenues 31 per cent, dividends 23 per cent, and the income of the shipping and consuming public by an average of perhaps 50 per cent.

So far as the question of equity is concerned this issue is between bondholders and stockholders; not between bondholders and the patrons of the railroads. The significant fact from the standpoint of the railway-using public is the *total* amount paid for the use of capital, not the allocation of the shrinkage between stockholders and bondholders. Between 1928 and 1931 the net earnings plus interest on funded debt, which is the total amount earned for capital, declined by 37 per cent. This is the figure which is significant for a comparison of the sacrifices of security owners and of other groups interested in the transportation problem. That the distribution of

[5] Reduction of bonded debt by reorganization of individual companies is discussed in Chapter XV.

[6] Railroad data in this paragraph refer to Class I roads only.

this loss between stockholders and bondholders has been unequal does not interest the shipping and consuming public except in so far as it may affect the railroads' ability to obtain capital which may be needed in the future.

The claim of the holders of railroad bonds for the maintenance of their income position at the expense of the stockholders is, of course, a corollary of the claims of stockholders to all the benefit of the increase in return to capital which occurs in periods of growing prosperity. From 1923 to 1930 the average rate of dividends on all outstanding railroad stock increased from 4.53 to 6.02 per cent, while the rate of interest on funded debt did not increase at all.

It is argued, however, that in extreme periods of falling prices which could not be foreseen when bonds were issued, stockholders have an equitable claim that fixed monetary obligations be scaled down to correspond to the increased purchasing power of the dollar. In the writer's judgment there is considerable force in this suggestion if presented as part of a general scheme for scaling down all debts. But there is no equity in applying it to railroad securities alone. Moreover, account must be taken of the fact that a large proportion of railroad debt (probably a larger proportion than that of any other important class of debt) was incurred at a time when the price level was lower than it is now.

The really cogent argument from the standpoint of public interest, for reducing the proportion of funded debt to stock equity lies in its bearing, not on the level of rates, but on their flexibility. One of the most unfortunate aspects of the railroad situation lies in the rigidity of the whole structure of railroad rates, wages, and charges in the face of changing business conditions. Railroad rates do not come down with prices; if they did, other things remaining as they are, all the roads in the country would be bankrupt in every major depression. On the other hand, the failure of rates to come down greatly increases the burden of deflation on industries producing bulk goods for distant markets, especially agriculture and coal mining, and makes it impossible to apply to industry the stimulus of reduced costs at a point where it would mean much more than it does at the place where it is generally applied—namely the cost of bank credit.

Railroad rates are a far more important element in the cost of doing business than is short-term bank credit, yet public authorities go on year after year trying to stimulate business recovery by forcing down money rates (while banks fail on every hand). At the same time railway rates are held up or actually increased lest railway credit be undermined.

Without going into the controversial issue of the underlying cause of business fluctuations, our judgment is that one of the most serious aggravating factors is the rigidity with which certain major costs of doing business stay up in the face of a general liquidation—and among these rigid costs railway rates are conspicuous.

Now it is obviously impracticable to throw on the railway managements the burden of stimulating business recovery by lowered rates in times of business depression (and presumably checking booms by raising rates when business appears to be over done) unless flexibility is introduced into other elements of their financial set-up. We discuss elsewhere the question of wages and the prices of the materials which the railroads buy; here we only point out that if the railroad rates are to be made responsive to the swings of business activity and the purchasing power of the dollar, it is imperative that their capital charges shall also be made less rigid.

If railroads were capitalized chiefly on stock and were permitted to earn and pay liberal dividends in periods of prosperity, they could attract capital for necessary expansion, even though it was well understood that in bad times they would be unable to keep up dividend payments. Such elasticity in the return on capital is highly desirable so long as the activity of business and the level of prices and incomes remains subject to wide and unpredictable variations.

These considerations are reinforced by the probability that the railroad financial structure may be subject to large changes during the coming decade because of new developments in the type of competition which they have to meet, and the amount of capital which they must invest in order to meet this competition and to render the types of service appropriate to the new transportation era. It seems to us therefore highly desirable, from the public standpoint, that stock issues should be the chief reliance of the railroads for new capital.

To be sure, in strict legal and economic theory, as was indicated above, the capital structure has no bearing on the question, even in acute depressions. The bondholder has no direct claim whatever against the travelling and shipping public. He has a claim against the corporation and the corporation has a claim against the public. But the fact is that public authorities do recognize in the bonded debt a financial claim against the public superior to that of the stockholders, regardless of the fact that the latter has made an equal contribution to the common cause—indeed is often a former bondholder who has been converted into a stockholder against his will. They also seem to recognize a vested right on the part of the management to protection against the legal consequences of inability to pay fixed charges. The most conspicuous evidence of this at the moment is the fact that the Reconstruction Finance Corporation and the Railroad Credit Corporation are providing funds to pay interest on funded debt, but none for dividend purposes.

There is considerable justification for measures intended to prevent a wholesale epidemic of bankruptcies in a basic industry in a period of acute depression—even though the patrons of a railroad are generally as well served by receivers as by the managements which they replace. But there are other evidences of a special solicitude for the bondholder, even in times of ordinary prosperity. In the Western Rate Case of 1926 an increase of rates was denied in the face of clear evidence that the applicant carriers could not earn the statutory fair return, and without any denial that the increased rates would actually yield increased revenue, on the ground that no *financial emergency* existed—in other words, because the creditors of the roads were not in danger though the stockholders had no prospect of getting the return contemplated by law.[7]

[7] To be sure, the Commission claimed that in this case the application for a rate increase was predicated on the claim that a financial emergency existed (though admitting that at the hearings this aspect of the question was not stressed by the carriers). Though no definition of an emergency was offered, it is clear that in this case creditors of the railroads were admitted to have a claim against the public not possessed by stockholders —and in our judgment not sanctioned by law. In the New England Divisions case, on the contrary, the decision was formally based on the inability of the New England roads to earn their fair return—whatever weight the fixed charges may have had in shaping the minds of those responsible for the decision.

In the Fifteen Per Cent Case the Interstate Commerce Commission said:

The applicants apparently recognize that at this time it is futile to increase rates with the object of reaching 5.75 per cent on the value of their properties as a whole. The practical limitation of what the traffic will bear and continue to move by rail must be given consideration. Clearly any practicable increase, unaccompanied by a pooling provision, might not prevent threatened default in the fixed interest obligations of some of the carriers. On the other hand, a smaller increase in the aggregate revenue, marshalled for the benefit of the carriers in need, will tend to stabilize the industry. We shall provide for such marshalling.

We do not find that we are justified on this record to attempt, by a rate increase, to protect the margin of one and one-half times fixed charges set by the New York law. To provide so far as practicable that actual interest charges be met is justified.[8]

There are also indications that the Commission has occasionally taken into consideration the amount of bonded debt in valuing properties under the provisions of the valuation act of 1913.[9]

If this line of reasoning is to prevail in the future, it is clear that railroad managers will have the duty to their stockholders to do as much financing as possible on bonds, while the Commission, as guardian of the interests of the shipper, will have a duty to keep the funded debt as low as possible.

Our judgment is that there is neither a legal nor an economic basis for this tacit recognition of a quasi-preferred status of the bonded debt as against the stock

[8] *Fifteen Per Cent Case of 1931*, Interstate Commerce Commission, Vol. 178, p. 579.

[9] See Vanderblue and Burgess, *Railroads: Rates, Service, Management*, p. 349, for discussion of valuation cases where the valuation of the property was apparently stretched to cover the bond issues.

equity of the railroads. As we have noted, there can be no objection to a policy of preventing wholesale bankruptcies in a public emergency, either by loans or by moratoriums. But as a standing policy the *form* of capitalization should have no bearing on the amount which a railroad is allowed to earn, or the treatment which it receives from public authority. The financial structure of a railway has merely to do with the distribution among its owners and creditors of the amount which, rightly or wrongly, the road is able to earn. If this structure is such that the bondholders are entitled to more than the road can earn—apart from wholly abnormal conditions created by war or depression—the road's capital structure is in need of reorganization.

CHAPTER XIV

FINANCIAL POLICIES

In Chapter II we showed in some detail that the railways have been able, in the period since 1920, to attract capital at a rate which seems fully proportionate to their importance in the national economy. The question whether the roads have not in fact attracted too much capital for their own and the public's best interest was also raised, the tentative conclusion being that the increase in railroad capital was probably justified by the reduction in operating costs, not only as measured in dollars but as gauged by physical tests, such as pounds of coal consumed and employees' time spent in proportion to the output of freight and passenger service.

This tentative conclusion is confirmed by a comparison of the records of the Eastern and Western districts.[1] The investment of the Eastern Class I roads increased between the end of 1923 and the end of 1929 by 23 per cent; that of the Western roads by only 12 per cent. The net amount earned on investment (net income plus interest on funded debt) increased 37 per cent in the East, as against 36 per cent in the West—this in spite of the fact that operating revenues increased 3½ per cent in the West and decreased 3½ per cent in the East. Operating ratios declined in the same proportion in both sections.

These figures seem to confirm the conclusion that the added investment in railway properties did justify itself in terms of the reduction of operating costs. However,

[1] The Southern district is omitted from the comparison because of the disturbing influence of changes in traffic density associated with the rise and collapse of the Florida land speculation.

a permanent investment of funds can, of course, be justified only in terms of a long time use of the resulting capital, and in this case it is obvious that the new investment under present conditions cannot pay its way. In other words, if railway managers had foreseen the coming of the present depression it would have been wise for them to have kept the new investment at a minimum, paying for a few years the higher operating costs which went with less adequate equipment, and saving the overhead during the recent years of comparative idleness.

But such reasoning after the event is of little significance. All industries, and most government units, are burdened with capital investments which they would not have made if they had foreknown the slackened rate of business activity of 1931 and 1932. So far as we can see now, there was no other alternative field of investment for the new capital which went into the railroads where it would have justified itself by a greater productivity than in the railways.

Assuming, then, that the total amount of capital raised recently by the railroads has not been out of line with what a sound public policy would have encouraged, what about the form of financing?

It is frequently stated that the railroads have been doing too large a share of their financing through issuance of bonds rather than stock; and that this is because the credit of the railroads has not been good enough to enable them to sell stock. It is also widely believed that the dividend policy of the railroads has been too liberal, so that they have not accumulated adequate cash reserves for contingencies or reinvested a surplus large enough to serve as a proper cushion in periods of declining revenue.

CAPITALIZATION AND SURPLUS OF RAILWAYS, DEC 31, 1924–1929.

(Millions of dollars)

Year	Corporate Surplus	Total Capitalization	Stock			Funded Debt					
			Total	Common	Preferred	Total	Mortgage Bonds	Collateral Trust	Income	Miscellaneous	Equipment Obligations
1924	3,786	21,681	9,300	7,399	1,901	12,381	9,210	1,125	369	620	1,057
1925	4,128	21,734	9,413	7,491	1,921	12,321	9,271	1,119	336	515	1,079
1926	4,555	21,749	9,365	7,451	1,915	12,384	9,383	1,062	314	528	1,097
1927	4,694	21,849	9,539	7,575	1,965	12,309	9,550	886	299	511	1,064
1928	5,051	22,026	9,722	7,703	2,019	12,304	9,631	795	378	520	980
1929	5,474	22,307	9,847	7,797	2,050	12,459	9,677	700	366	722	995

ª *Statistics of Railways of the United States* for the years indicated; Statement No. 17, except corporate surplus, which is computed from Statements 42 and 43 and Section A, Parts II and III.

Our conclusions are as follows: (a) the railroads have actually done a much smaller proportion of their financing through bond issues since 1924 than is generally supposed; (b) they could have done a considerably larger volume of their financing by stock sales during the period since 1921 if their managements had considered it desirable to do so; (c) it would not have been a sound policy for the roads, viewed as private profitmaking corporations, to do a much larger proportion of their financing through the sale of stock; (d) there is no basis for the current idea that railroad dividend policies were unduly liberal in 1922-29, but there is a basis for the criticism with regard to 1931; (e) under the conditions which appear likely to prevail over the next decade a much greater proportionate use of stock is desirable.

I. RAILWAY FINANCING, 1925-29

The table on page 300 shows the volume of various kinds of securities outstanding during recent years. The changes were as follows:

CHANGES IN OUTSTANDING SECURITIES AND CORPORATE
SURPLUS, DEC. 31, 1924 TO DEC. 31, 1929
(Millions of dollars)

Funded Debt
Mortgage Bonds	+467	
Collateral Trust Bonds	—425	
Income Bonds	— 3	
Equipment Trust Certificates	— 62	
Miscellaneous	+102	
Total		+ 78

Stock
Common	+398	
Preferred	+149	
Total		+ 547
Surplus		+1,688
Total Capitalization and Surplus		+2,314

It will be seen that from the end of 1924 to the end of 1929 two-thirds of the increase in the capital and surplus of railways consisted of reinvested surplus and nearly all the rest resulted from stock issuance. With the collapse of the stock market boom and the decline in railroad earnings, the tide turned the other way, as may be seen from the following statement of the changes during 1930 and 1931 (millions of dollars):

	Funded Debt	Stock	Surplus
1930	+184	+165	—1,117
1931[2]	+ 16	— 3	— 594

The data just presented refer to all railroad securities, including those owned by the issuing company and by other railroads. Our information regarding the amounts of securities in the hands of the public is less detailed but perhaps more significant. The table on p. 303 shows, for 1920 to 1931 inclusive, the amounts of railway stocks and railway bonds held at the end of the year by others than railways.

This table shows strikingly the way in which the method of railroad financing has responded to changed money market conditions. During the years from 1920 to 1924 bonds were very popular with investors. In these four years the railroads issued bonds in such great quantities as to make up the deficiency of financing in the six preceding years. The railway bonds owned by the general public increased by 1,108 million dollars, while stock in the hands of the public increased by only 100 million. On the other hand, in the period after 1924, and especially in 1927 and 1928, common stocks enjoyed unprecedented popularity; and between the end of 1924

[2] Class I roads and their non-operating subsidiaries only.

and the end of 1929 stock in public hands increased by 407 million dollars, while bonds increased by only 71 million.

Nevertheless, the swing toward the issuance of stocks was much less marked in the case of railways than it was with industrials during the same years. The chart on page 304 shows the change in the proportion of stocks to bonds in the public financing of railways and in the market for corporate issues as a whole. The much higher

SECURITIES OWNED BY THE PUBLIC, 1921–31[a]
(In millions of dollars)

Year	Stock	Funded Debt	Total	Percentage Funded Debt to Total
1921	6,673	10,409	17,083	60.9
1922	6,751	10,528	17,280	60.9
1923	6,847	10,963	17,810	61.6
1924	6,806	11,396	18,202	62.6
1925	6,886	11,305	18,191	62.1
1926	6,829	11,404	18,234	62.6
1927	6,756	11,381	18,137	62.1
1928	7,084	11,427	18,511	61.7
1929	7,213	11,467	18,680	61.4
1930	7,185	11,880	19,066	62.3
1931	7,111	11,830	18,941	62.5

[a] Computed from Statement No. 53, *Statistics of Railways in the United States*, 1931. Data refer to December 31 of year indicated.

proportion of bonds shown in the charted data than in the table on page 301 is due to the fact that the chart covers refunding operations, and not merely net additions to capital. This chart, combined with the preceding data, shows plainly that though the railroads got their new capital during the stock market boom largely in the form of stock issues, they did not take advantage of the great strength of the stock market to effect an extensive substitution of stock for bonds in their capital structure.

In spite of the popularity of stocks during the five-year period from the end of 1924 through 1929, a number of important roads did their financing in this period exclusively on stock, while others used the stock market for only a part of their need of new capital. Only a very few roads, of which the New York Central and the St. Louis-San Francisco were the most conspicuous, issued

RAILROAD AND OTHER CORPORATE SECURITY ISSUES
1919-29

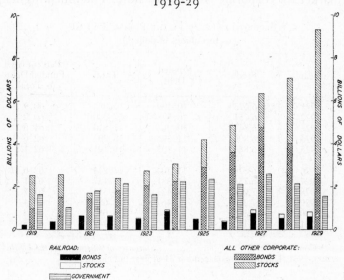

stock in such amount as not only to provide for their new capital needs, but to effect a substantial reduction in their funded debt. The table opposite classifies most of the more important roads in accordance with the extent to which they relied on the stock market and the bond market, respectively, for their new capital needs.

A considerable number of roads which sold no stock between 1925 and 1929 could have done so. Some

LEADING INDEPENDENT RAILROADS CLASSIFIED ACCORDING TO THEIR USE OF STOCK OR BONDS IN NEW FINANCING, 1926–30

Financed Chiefly Through Stock Issues	Financed Chiefly Through Bond Issues	Financed Through Both Stock and Bond Issues	No Important New Financing
Atlantic Coast Line Bangor and Aroostook Delaware & Hudson[a] Missouri-Kansas-Texas[a] New York Central Pennsylvania St. Louis-San Francisco Southern	Chicago, Rock Island and Pacific Great Northern Kansas City Southern Lehigh Valley Missouri Pacific Pere Marquette Pittsburgh and West Virginia Reading Southern Pacific Wabash	Atchison Baltimore and Ohio Boston and Maine Chesapeake and Ohio Erie[a] Illinois Central New Haven Nickel Plate Seaboard Air Line	Central of New Jersey Chicago Great Western Chicago and North Western Delaware, Lackawanna and Western Louisville and Nashville Maine Central Minneapolis, St. Paul and S. Ste. Marie. Norfolk and Western Northern Pacific Rutland St. Louis Southwestern Union Pacific Virginian Western Maryland Wheeling and Lake Erie

[a] Stock issued to refund bonds, not for new capital.
[b] Issued bonds bearing fixed charge to refund income bonds.

roads, such as the Southern Pacific and the Lehigh Valley, had outstanding common stocks which sold well above par most of the time. Others, such as the Great Northern and the Northern Pacific, whose stocks sold below par or too close to it to make stock financing safe, had substantial earnings above their fixed charges which would have enabled them to sell stock by shifting to a no-par basis, or reducing the par values. The use of bonds in the financial operations of these roads was therefore a matter of policy rather than of necessity.

That is not to say, however, that the stock market would have absorbed enough stock to make possible a radical reduction of the proportion of bonds in the capital structure of the railways. The mass of outstanding railroad capital is so great that even if all new capital were raised by stock issues the proportion of funded debt to total capitalization would change very slowly. A drastic reorganization of the financial set-up would have to be brought about either through an epidemic of receiverships and reorganization proceedings or through a recapitalization program instituted by governmental authority. The question whether such a recapitalization of the railways is desirable is wholly distinct from the question whether railway managements have on the whole been justified in the financial policies pursued during the past decade. Let us consider briefly some of the factors which have been responsible for the creation of the present capital structure.

II. STOCKS VERSUS BONDS: CONTROLLING FACTORS

The general rule of corporate finance is that an industry which issues only stock, or one which secures only a very small proportion of its capital through bond issues, does so from necessity. If an industry is speculative in character, investors consider that the risk of losing their capital must be compensated by an opportunity to share in the profits of success. In fact the railroad industry is the only one of which it is ever said that it sells bonds because it cannot sell stock; other industries sell stock when they cannot sell bonds.

Is this a fallacy, or is there some peculiarity about the railroad business which justifies a reversal of the ordinary way of appraising strength and weakness? One point may be suggested in partial justification of the current idea that railroads can finance on bonds when they cannot sell stock. The railroad capital structure of many roads is such that it is possible to issue bonds which will take precedence over a part of the already existing funded debt. In some previous reorganization an "open end" mortgage was created, and then one or more closed issues of junior bonds (debentures or income bonds) and preferred stocks were created to take care of existing interests. Henceforward if the corporation tries to finance on stock issues the securities it has to offer are junior to big intermediate fixed or contingent obligations, whereas if it finances on bonds the new security holder can be given a lien prior to that of these issues.[3]

In such cases there is real pressure to finance on bond issues, but the pressure arises from a faulty capital structure and is quite independent of the strength or weakness of the general income position of the road in question. In general, however, when bonds are issued it is because it is cheaper to finance in this way than through stock issues. The data presented in Chapter II showed that

[3] The Chicago, Milwaukee and St. Paul reorganization of 1928 furnishes a case in point. Compare Chapter XV.

railroads have been able to secure new capital through bond issues more cheaply than have most other industries. The cost of capital secured through stock issues cannot be computed with precision, but it is obvious that at least in the good years in which financial expansion chiefly occurs, more must be received, or at least reasonably expected, by the investor in stocks than it is necessary to offer to the bondholder.

This consideration is especially important in the case of numerous railroads whose voting stock is owned in large part by other roads. The value of a controlled road to a parent company consists in large part of the opportunity which it affords to control the flow of traffic. A subsidiary which furnishes traffic to the parent may be worth many times the amount invested in its stock, even if it pays no dividend. If bonds of the subsidiary are sold, the parent company need not buy them; if stock is sold the parent must either buy its proportionate share or see its control diluted, and must permit the payment of dividends not only on the new capital but also on the old minority stock. Obviously, from the standpoint of the controlling company, the more the subsidiary is financed on bonds the better.[4]

The obvious argument for a materially larger use of stock in the financing of railroads, assuming that the bond market remains open to them, is the fact that if the capitalization is largely in the form of stock, disbursements to owners of the capital can be curtailed much more rapidly and with less embarrassment in periods of adversity.

[4] This consideration is rendered more cogent by the fact that in cases where railroad corporations controlled by other railroads get into financial difficulties the courts and the Interstate Commerce Commission are likely to approve a reorganization plan which will scale down the bonded debt without wiping out the controlling stock interest. See Chapter XV.

How much weight railroad managers should give to this question depends on the anticipated variability of earnings. How severe and protracted a depression should a road be prepared to face without distress?

Looking backward now, it is easy to say of many roads that if they had taken advantage of the investment situation in 1925-29 to float stocks they would be in better financial shape now. Better, that is, from the standpoint of the managements. But we can hardly take the position that managements of railroads ought to have foreseen the coming of the greatest depression in history, and to have learned of it by methods not available to those to whom it was proposed to sell the stocks. For, obviously, foresight would have been of no avail to the roads as sellers of securities if what they foresaw had been known also to the prospective buyers of those securities.

So far we have discussed the question of funded debt solely from the standpoint of the fixed charges which it entails. Another and a more serious question is involved, however.

Funded debt not only involves fixed charges but, under American practice, it involves meeting maturities. Now capital which has been invested in railway properties cannot be converted at will to some other form. The promise of a railway to pay back at a fixed date a substantial portion of its capital is a promise which in the nature of the case it cannot fulfill, except by borrowing elsewhere or selling stock. And there is no sound reason why it should do so, unless the securities are issued to finance wasting assets.

Railway property may be classed into three types: first, fuel and miscellaneous supplies which are immediately destroyed in use; second, rapidly wasting capital assets like locomotives and cars; and, third, permanent assets like right-of-way and structures.

The purchase of property of the first class can properly be financed only out of working capital funds; the second may appropriately be financed by bonds or trust certificates of serial maturity; the third type of assets should be financed in such a way that there will be no maturity—other than that involved in an amortization rate which corresponds to the depreciation of the property. This means logically either stock or perpetual bonds.

It is not merely illogical that the *permanent* fixed capital of a railroad should be in such a form that the railroad is under legal obligation to repay it in large blocks at fixed dates; it is a financial peril. Often a road which has had no serious difficulty in paying its fixed charges has been very seriously embarrassed by the necessity of finding funds to pay off obligations which represent a permanent investment in the properties. The Missouri, Kansas and Texas in 1915 and the Baltimore and Ohio in 1932-33 are cases in point. The history of the railroad industry is strewn with the wrecks of companies which have had to refund bonds at a time when for reasons pertaining to the general investment situation rather than to the soundness of the particular enterprise, it was impossible for its management to refinance.

If perpetual interest-bearing obligations (substantially equivalent to the guaranteed leased line stocks now outstanding in limited amount) were substituted for obligations with a fixed maturity date, a large part of the objection to funded debt would disappear. A very large part of the present distress of the railroads is the result, not of excessive interest charges, but of inconvenient maturities.

It is within the power of railway managements to reduce greatly, if not to eliminate, the menace to financial
stability which lies in our present system of capitalizing
permanent investment on bonds of fixed maturity. The
practice of financing on short-term notes in the hope that
they will mature at a time when market conditions are
more favorable to the floating of long-term securities is
speculative and dangerous in the extreme. It cannot be
done away with in summary fashion, for there is outstanding a great mass of securities with a fixed maturity
date, and some of them are bound to mature at times
when it is practically impossible to refund them without the use of short-term notes. But the practice of financing new capital needs on short-term notes ought to
be definitely abandoned,[5] and capital instruments without maturity should be substituted for the outstanding
debt as rapidly as maturities and reorganizations make it
possible.

III. FUTURE FINANCING

From what has been said in the two preceding sections it is clear that there is no basis for a blanket indict-
ment of inefficiency against railway managements for the
creation and maintenance of the present proportions of
bonds in their capital structure. Looking forward, however, we believe that an intelligent financial policy will
look to a marked reduction of the proportion of fixed
charges to income—for the sake, not of economy, but of
safety. A proper balance between stocks and bonds depends on the variability of the earnings, and it seems clear
that the variability of railroad business, as well as that
of other forms of business, is likely to be greater than

---

[5] Still more emphatically the practice of issuing notes or terminable
bonds to buy the stocks of other companies.

was supposed in the years from 1925 to 1929. In spite of statistical evidence that the fluctuations of prices and business activity were actually greater than before the war, there was at that time a widespread belief that business had been stabilized, or at least that the violence of the swings of the cycle had been mitigated. It is now obvious that there was no basis whatever for this assumption. Moreover, so far as the railroad business is concerned the uncertainty is aggravated by the rise of newer forms of transportation and the unsettled state of the regulatory policy. It is therefore clear that the proportion of fixed charges to total income which would meet the test of a sound and conservative railroad financial policy is considerably smaller than it appeared to be before 1930.

Apart from a possible *general* revaluation of debt in which the railroads might share along with other debtors, there are only three ways in which the railroads can cut down their fixed charges. One is by selling stock to refund bonds—a solution which is out of the picture for the time being. Should financial market conditions again make it possible, prudence demands that it be utilized to the full. Second, there is the slow process of amortizing debt out of earnings. The practicability of this procedure, like that of the first, depends largely on the revival of the stock market. For it will be of little avail to amortize existing debt out of earnings if new capital has to be obtained by selling new funded debt. The third way out is by reorganization of the individual road on the basis of its individual financial difficulties.

If the roads are to secure new capital from time to time it is essential that there be some process of adjusting fixed charges downward in line with any permanent diminution of income below capacity to pay—or else of giving the new capital priority over the old.

Both of these results are accomplished, under our present system, by the procedure of reorganization and judicial sale, or occasionally by a voluntary readjustment. We describe in Chapters XV and XVI the methods which have been practiced in recent years in effecting reorganizations and consider some proposals for improving them.

IV. DECAPITALIZATION AS A FINANCIAL EXPEDIENT

We consider next, from the standpoint of the management of the railways the questions which were dealt with in Chapter XIII from the standpoint of the public —that is, reduction of the total capitalization and reduction of the funded debt. Our conclusion there was that the public has a considerable interest in encouraging the reduction of the funded debt, but only a remote and intangible interest in the size of the stock capitalization. Our conclusion here is that a considerable number of individual railroads would benefit by a scaling down of the par values of their common stocks or by a shift to no-par stock.[6] Par values of railroad stocks are in most cases fictions, accidents of the history of some half-forgotten reorganization or still more ancient original issuance of capital. When they are substantially above any reasonable prospective value as investments, they constitute a true overcapitalization.

Common stocks make up about one-third of the total railroad capitalization, and roads which still have a mar-

[6] Obviously they would all, viewed as private corporations, benefit by a scaling down or obliteration of their indebtedness, especially if it could be done without impairment of their future borrowing capacity. This, however, is beyond the horizon of practicability.

gin of earnings beyond their fixed charges might gain and could not lose by a scaling down of this part of the capital. It is as easy to stop dividends in bad years on 5 million dollars of stock as it is on 10 millions, and if conditions justify the payment of some dividend it looks better to pay 3 per cent on 5 million dollars than to pay 1½ per cent on 10 millions.

Moreover, under the laws of the states in which many of the railroads are incorporated, stock cannot be sold for less than its par value. Hence, in order to finance through the sale of common stock it is necessary that the number of shares be kept down to where the stock can be sold at or above par. While, as we have shown, a large number of railroads were able to sell stock during the period from 1923 through 1929, there was also a considerable number of roads which had a satisfactory rate of earning on the stockholders' equity but could not have sold common stock at par. In a number of cases the par value of stock was so high that in order to earn a return on a market value above par it would have been necessary for the road to earn an amount substantially greater than the statutory fair return on the tentative valuation of their properties.

In industrial corporation finance it is not unusual to effect a reduction of par value, or a change to no-par stock of low book value, in order to legalize the sale of new stock at its market value. Such a decapitalization would improve the financial set-up of a number of roads.

To be sure, all this is mere hocus-pocus. An intelligent system of regulation of corporate security issuance would permit the sale of stock below par, provided the stockholders were protected against the dilution of their holdings, for example, by the provision that the new stock must be offered pro rata to the old stockholders. But it is easier to recapitalize downward in order to bring the value of the stock above its new par than it is to get changes in the archaic laws which govern the issuance of stock.

The converse case of readjustment of capitalization to take care of greatly increased earning capacity is of less pressing interest but equally important as a matter of long-run policy. When a road's earnings become disproportionately large in relation to its capitalization, the argument for permitting it to recapitalize through stock dividends or through issuance of rights to purchase stock at par is very similar to the argument in favor of recapitalization downward in the case of shrunken earnings. The dilution of the stock equity does not in any way change the amount which a sound public policy will permit the regulated utility to earn, but it adds flexibility to the financial program.

We see no basis for the doctrine laid down by the Interstate Commerce Commission in 1928 in connection with the application of the Chesapeake and Ohio for permission to sell stock at par,[7] to the effect that such action would "place a burden on the carrier."[8] (This decision was later reversed.)[9]

The "melon" distributed by issuing rights to subscribe at par was nothing but the equity of the stockholders in

[7] 138 I.C.C. 535.

[8] It is to be emphasized, of course, that a decision as to whether a road should be permitted to increase its capital by stock dividends or by selling stock below its book value has nothing to do with the question whether the earnings which suggest and are expected to support this expanded capitalization are in fact excessive. Decision as to whether the carrier is charging more for its services than they are worth should be kept wholly distinct from the question of its capitalization.

[9] 150 I.C.C. 755 (1929).

the undistributed past earnings, and anticipated future earnings of their property. The stockholder was given a convenient opportunity to sell part of his equity if he was not willing and able to make his pro rata contribution to the capital needs of the company. There is no sounder method of financing than this. Certainly if it is desired to encourage financing by stock issuance there is no sense in regulations which hamper such financing and obstruct the efforts of stockholders to withdraw from the business a part of the earnings which have accrued as part of their equity.

V. DIVIDEND POLICY

We turn next to the question whether the dividend policy pursued by the railroads during the last few years has been sound. We have noted already that a very large share of the investment of new capital in the railroads during the past decade was reinvested surplus. In spite of this policy of reinvestment, earnings were large enough to make possible a very substantial increase in dividend payments. The record for the years 1922-31 is shown in the accompanying table. Payments made by one railroad to another railroad are excluded from both sides of this account, since the inclusion of such payments would involve much double counting—funds received by a railroad as dividends entering into the total from which its own dividends are paid.

We see nothing in this record to justify a conclusion that in 1922-29 the railroad managements were guilty of excessive liberality in the payment of dividends, no matter whether the question be viewed from the standpoint of private finance or from that of the public interest. After all, Congress deliberately decided in 1920 to recommit the railways to private ownership, and to

Year	Net Amount Available for Interest on Funded Debt[b]	Interest on Funded Debt	Net Income	Dividends	Ratio of Interest Plus Dividends to Income Available for Interest	Ratio of Dividends to Net Income
1922	$ 895	$515	$380	$273	88.0	71.8
1923	1,095	526	569	342	79.3	60.1
1924	1,113	564	549	306	78.2	55.7
1925	1,259	563	696	324	70.5	46.6
1926	1,352	564	788	369	69.0	46.8
1927	1,198	563	635	455	85.0	71.7
1928	1,313	558	755	402	73.1	53.2
1929	1,418	557	861	441	70.4	51.2
1930	1,034	569	465	492	102.6	105.8
1931	655	580	75	311	136.0	414.7

[a] Computed from data in Table 34, *Statistics of Railways*.
[b] This is figured as though all "other deductions" including interest on floating debt came ahead of interest on funded debt.

look to private initiative to secure the necessary capital to provide for their needed growth. At that time it was everywhere urged that the transportation system of the country was overloaded and in dire need of expansion. Stockholders' money has been attracted to the industry by the prospect of a return, and no restriction has been put on the right of stockholders to withdraw from the business whatever they can earn for themselves, within the rate structure approved by the Interstate Commerce Commission and subject to the other restrictions imposed by law and by administrative authority.

So far as stockholders control the situation, it is reasonably to be expected that they will withdraw from the railroads all the net income they can expect in so far as they are induced to leave surplus in the business in the expectation that future dividends will be increased or made more secure by so doing. There is no moral obligation on the stockholders to furnish capital for less than the full amount which it earns; the only question is one of sound financial practice. Obviously, it would be risky in a business which has large fixed indebtedness, and in which the calculation of earnings can at best be only approximate,[10] to withdraw regularly every penny of the earnings. But it is equally unsound finance to leave money in the business if it is likely that it can be used more profitably elsewhere.

It is clear too that if there is any merit in the plea that railroads should finance more largely on stock issues, there is equal merit in a liberal dividend policy; we cannot at the same time require that railroad managers shall meet their capital requirements by appealing to the profit-seeking instinct of prospective stock buyers, and condemn them for making stock investments attractive by making them remunerative.[11]

There is, however, just ground for criticism of the dividend record of 1931. It is to be expected, of course, that the ratio of dividends paid to earnings will rise in a period of declining earnings; partly because dividends are paid on the basis of the previous year's as well as the current year's record, and partly because a record by

[10] For instance, because of (a) the factor of judgment in setting up depreciation; (b) the uncertain amount of obsolescence; and (c) the large amount of unproductive investment which is really not investment at all but payment for the privilege of doing business.

[11] The case of the New York Central may serve as an illustration. There has been some disposition in recent months to criticize the management of this road for having paid out in dividends funds which it would now like to have for other uses. It is true that during the years 1926-29 the company paid out nearly 130 million dollars in dividends. But during this same period it earned about 243 million dollars. On the strength of these earnings and dividends it sold 120 million dollars worth of stock and retired nearly 50 million dollars worth of bonds.

calendar year obscures the extent to which the dividends have been declared in the first part of the year while the decline of earnings occurred in the last part. Nevertheless, there are cases where dividend payments were continued well into 1931 by railroads which were bound to need the money for fixed charges if the course of the depression was not quickly reversed.[12]

In connection with their dividend policy it has been suggested that the railroads have made a mistake in not carrying more ample reserves which could be drawn upon to meet interest charges during the lean years. This, however, does not point to a practical solution of the difficulty which arises from financing on bonds. Cash reserves have been drawn on heavily to meet fixed charges during the past two years, and bank loans have been expanded, as the following data show:

CURRENT ASSETS AND CURRENT LIABILITIES OF THE RAILROADS
Dec. 31, 1929–31[a]
(Millions of dollars)

	1928	1929	1930	1931
Current Assets:				
Cash.....................	503	515	438	329
Demand loans and deposits ..	139	107	58	51
Time drafts and deposits.....	107	55	96	40
Special deposits............	81	80	85	49
Other current assets.........	960	958	834	544
Total................	1,790	1,718	1,511	1,213
Current Liabilities:				
Loans and bills payable......	32	71	115	246
Other current liabilities......	1,119	1,130	1,047	901
Total................	1,151	1,201	1,162	1,147

[a] Class I railroads only. Table 42, *Statistics of Railways* for the years indicated.

[12] Conspicuous cases are the Frisco, which paid dividends on its common stock up to January 1931, and preferred up to November of that

We do not believe it would be sound policy for a railroad, or any other corporation, to carry cash balances large enough to take care of its charges during financial collapses such as occur only once in a generation. Nor is it practicable to accumulate reserves of securities for sale in such periods. A security reserve may be drawn upon in the case of a temporary emergency involving a single road or the roads of a limited section, but in a major depression the market for securities dries up. Forced sales of bonds by banks during the past year and a half have been a major cause of the demoralization of the financial structure of the country; if the railroads had attempted to market securities amounting to hundreds of millions at a time when the banks were in no position to buy them, the crisis would have been aggravated and the financial losses of the roads would have been increased by vast losses in their trading accounts.

---

year. This road was borrowing from the Reconstruction Finance Corporation in the early spring of 1932 to pay taxes and interest, and has now gone into receivership for the purpose of enforcing large sacrifices on its bondholders. The Southern Railway in 1931 paid three quarterly dividends at full 1929 rates, and four on its non-cumulative preferred; though it incurred a deficit for the year of $6.87 a common share. The Nickel Plate in 1931 paid three quarterly dividends on its common stock, or $4.50, and showed a deficit of $7.00 a share.

CHAPTER XV

REORGANIZATION PROCEDURE: CURRENT PRACTICE

In this chapter we examine the recent tendencies in the methods by which insolvent railroad corporations are reorganized. This is practically equivalent to examining the way in which railroad corporations now come into being, since practically all new railroad corporations in recent years are the outgrowth of financial reorganizations.

The necessity for an elaborate special procedure arises from the fact that in the case of a large railway, or a very large industrial or public utility corporation, it is usually not feasible to sell the property in the open market and distribute the proceeds to the creditors in the proper order of precedence. This is true because there is no competitive market in which to sell such large pieces of property and because breaking up the property and selling the items out piecemeal would sacrifice whatever value inheres in the property as a going concern, many of the items having no value except as parts of the major unit.

The fundamental purpose of a railroad reorganization is to cut down the fixed charges to a figure within the capacity of the road to earn them. This of itself, however, is comparatively easy. All that is necessary is to substitute stock or income bonds for a sufficient proportion of the bonds bearing a fixed charge. The difficult problem is to see that substantial justice is done between different classes of security holders. Theoretically, the purpose of the reorganization is not to take something away from one security holder and give it to another, but to apportion equitably the joint loss. In general this means that senior charges or claims which fall within the demonstrated earning capacity of the road should not be disturbed; junior claims which are covered by problematical earning power should be converted into contingent claims; and claims for which there is no prospect that earnings will be available should be wiped out or revalidated by substantial assessment. As we shall see, however, there is very wide variation in the practice actually followed.

I. REORGANIZATION PROCEDURE

The technique of reorganization of railway financial structures, which is not materially different from that used in the reorganization of other large business enterprises, was worked out many years ago and has not undergone significant change during recent years. The standard procedure is first, the appointment of a receiver to operate the properties during the period of insolvency for the benefit of the creditors; second, the appointment of committees to represent the various classes of security holders; third, the establishment of a reorganization committee which undertakes to work out a plan of recapitalization which will meet the approval of the committees representing the security holders, or such of these committees as are able to make their views effective; fourth, the deposit with the reorganization committees of securities owned by those holders who are willing to accede to the plan; fifth, approval of the plan by the court of proper jurisdiction; sixth, judicial sale of the property to a representative of the security holders who have accepted the plan; seventh, issuance of securities in the purchaser corporation to the various security holders in the proportions stipulated in the plan. In the case of railroads, approval of the plan by the Interstate Commerce Commission is also necessary, since no long-term securities can be issued by railway companies subject to the jurisdiction of the Commission, without its prior approval.

It is necessary also that some provision be made for liquidating the claims of those security holders who do not assent to the reorganization plan. This purpose is accomplished through a judicial sale of the property.[1] Since there is ordinarily only one bidder, the price is arranged in advance and must be approved by the court. The representative of those security holders who accept the plan pays this price in securities of the insolvent road, to the extent that they have been deposited with him. The holders of the securities who do not deposit are entitled to receive in cash their proportion of the "upset price." Cash must be found for this purpose, and usually also to pay other preferred claims such as taxes, a part or all of the expenses of the receivership and the reorganization, and miscellaneous minor items.

If there is only one class of securities outstanding, or if the securities represent claims to the same property, which can be ranked in a definite order of priority, the task of reorganization is comparatively simple. If, however, as is always the case with the larger railroads, the property has been built up out of units previously mort-

---

[1] In several recent cases, however, plans have been put into effect by judicial decree without a sale of the property. See *Phipps* v. *Chicago Rock Island and Pacific Railway Company*, 284 Fed. 945 (C.C.A. 8th, 1922). There are also several cases in which no provision whatever was made for non-assenting security holders. Compare cases of Atlanta, Birmingham and Atlantic, 117 I.C.C. 187 (1926), and Chicago and Eastern Illinois, 67 I.C.C. 61 (1921).

gaged, and then later subordinated to other lines, the task of apportioning the loss equitably becomes very complicated. A given bond may be secured by a first mortgage on one part of the property, a second lien on another part, and no lien at all on another part. There may be collateral trust bonds secured by part of an issue of mortgage bonds, the rest of which have been sold. Frequently there are bank loans which are secured by pledge of miscellaneous lots of securities with differing priorities. Under such conditions there is a real problem in determining the equitable claims of the holders of different securities against the price paid for the property as a unit.

In the majority of cases the committee which formulates the reorganization plan is virtually self-appointed. In the case of an important corporation the committee is usually set up and controlled by some large financial house which has previously floated the corporation's securities. In an important case the bankers also are likely to control some or all the security holders' committees. Sometimes there are two or more rival committees representing the same class of bondholders, and occasionally two rival reorganization committees are formed. In such a case the individual security holder may have a choice as to which of two plans he will support. Usually, however, he has no choice but to accept the plan as set up by the "official" committee, or else take his share in the "upset price." And, customarily, this upset price is so low as to bring strong pressure on most security holders to accept the plan. As different classes of securities are often represented by the same or interlocking committees, the strength of the position of the individual holders of securities bears only a remote relation to the guarantees and priorities stipulated in the mortgage indentures or the terms on which different classes of stock were issued. The relative treatment of different classes of investors is settled by bargaining within or before the reorganization committee, which is controlled only by the possibilities that a grossly inequitable plan may be set aside by the court, and that one which creates too weak a capital structure might be rejected by the Interstate Commerce Commission.

In the cases which have come up since the carriers were required to secure approval of the Commission for security issuance, the Commission has usually based its decision upon such points as the size of the total capitalization, the proportion of fixed charges to probable revenues, public interest in proposals for abandonment of parts of the system, and the relation of proposed transfers of lines from one system to another to the consolidation program.

In other words, the Commission has usually interpreted its responsibility as that of protecting the public interest in the maintenance of transportation, rather than of protecting the rights of security holders. On the other hand, the courts are interested primarily in the protection of the equities of security holders rather than in the reorganization of a transportation machine. The line is by no means a sharp one, however, and there is considerable inconsistency in the practice followed in different cases.

The Commission has not in fact rejected outright a single one of the forty-odd plans which have been submitted to it since 1920, though in a few cases it has required minor changes. In several cases where a reorganization was approved, the Commission has criticized the plan severely. It does not seem necessary for us to analyze case by case each of the reorganization plans which have been approved since the passage of the Transportation Act. Instead, we shall consider the subject topically, indicating in connection with each major issue the principal cases in which it has arisen.

II. SIZE OF CAPITALIZATION

Chief emphasis—in our opinion an undue emphasis —in the Commission's rulings has been laid by the Commission on the amount of securities to be issued. Even in cases where it is not proposed to issue any funded debt or preferred stock, the Commission scrutinizes the amount of common stock which it is proposed to issue, and in a number of cases has required that it be cut down. However, the Commission has never formulated a definite standard by which reorganization managers can determine in advance whether a given capitalization will be regarded as overcapitalization, and the precedents it has set vary widely.

The test most often applied is "investment," that is, the cost to the corporation of the capital assets. But this is an inadequate test in the case of a reorganized corporation, for the cost of property to the new company is whatever amount of securities are issued in exchange and the problem is to determine that amount. Other factors which are considered include valuation of the property, previous capitalization, book value, and probable earning capacity. The latter factor, however, has more bearing on the form of capitalization than on the amount.

1. *Investment.* When property is sold to a security holders' committee at an upset price fixed by a court as

a means of eliminating the non-assenting bondholders, this price is apparently never regarded as an index of appropriate capitalization. But when property has been sold outright for cash and the new owners are organizing an operating company, the Commission in recent years has usually insisted on capitalization based on this sale price.[2]

Whether actual investment is as important as the Commission's rulings imply, depends on the use to be made of the capitalization. The Commission has never, so far as we have noted, indicated the reason why it deems it so important that capitalization shall conform to the actual investment. If the idea is that an excess of capitalization over investment may afford a basis for later claims to the right to earn a return on the excess, the equity of the procedure seems to us ethically doubtful, as well as only remotely relevant to its purpose. There is much force in the following remarks of Commissioner Potter in the case of the Louisiana Railway and Navigation Company of Texas—or there would be if capitalization had any bearing on the return received by the owners of the property:

[2] See, for instance, Louisiana Railway and Navigation Co. of Texas (90 I.C.C. 229, 1924, and 99 I.C.C. 357, 1924); Toledo, Peoria and Western (124 I.C.C. 181, 1927); the Detroit, Caro and Sandusky (99 I.C.C. 783, 1925); Santa Fe, San Juan and Northern (154 I.C.C. 741, 1929); San Luis Valley Southern (145 I.C.C. 71, 1928).

There are some inscrutable exceptions. In the case of the Columbus and Greenville (86 I.C.C. 153, 1923) allowance was actually made for such intangible services as inducing people along the right of way to keep their livestock off the tracks, and inducing a state tax commission to lower the road's assessment. The total capitalization was three times the cost. In the case of the Tennessee, Alabama and Georgia Railway (72 I.C.C. 565, 1922) the purchase price of the old property and the new capital invested were both fully covered by preferred stock and common stock was issued to promoters in addition. Compare also the Missouri-Illinois case (67 I.C.C. 65, 1921).

The limit of $1,150,000 to securities authorized is applied because it represents the amount of cash paid by the present owner for the property, plus subsequent expenditures and plus necessary working capital. There is no warrant for arriving at authorized capitalization in this fashion. The question is what the property is worth, not what the owner paid for it. The buyer of a property is entitled to the benefit of his bargain. The majority report denies this to him.[3]

However, so long as rates are not based on capitalization the issue is rather academic. If the purpose of the Commission in cutting down the capitalization of reorganized companies is to protect the rate base one would expect to find much attention paid to valuation. Such, however, is not usually the case.

2. *Valuation data.* During the earlier years after the passage of the Transportation Act when the Commission's final valuations were not available there were frequent statements which seemed to imply that when the final valuations became available they would be taken seriously into account. For instance:

. . . Obviously, we can not upon an application for authority to issue securities give to those reports [the underlying reports of the Bureau of Valuation] the force and effect of final valuation, because of the fact that they are subject to revision and correction before they become a tentative valuation of the property covered, and because such tentative valuation, when made, will be subject, by the express terms of section 19a, to protest and change.[4]

In the Knoxville and Carolina case[5] the tentative valuation was definitely used as a basis for determining capitalization. But this was an isolated case, and there

---

[3] 90 I.C.C. 233 (1924).
[4] Denver and Rio Grande Western, 90 I.C.C. 144 (1924).
[5] 72 I.C.C. 221 (1922).

were others in which the maximum capitalization permitted was obviously far below the lowest valuation which could be justified on the basis of the accepted principles of valuation. For instance, in the Poteau and Cavanal Mountain Railroad Company case[6] the Commission refused to sanction the issuance of securities in excess of $40,000 against property valued by engineers employed by the company at $75,000. This case is the more striking in that the entire proposed capitalization consisted of common stock, so that no question of ability to earn fixed charges was involved. In the Toledo, Peoria and Western case, decided in 1927,[7] a total capitalization of $1,065,000 was permitted, the Commission's tentative valuation of the property being over $6,000,000.

On the other hand, in the Missouri-Kansas-Texas case it seemed almost certain that the capitalization approved was greater than the valuation, if a reasonable allowance was made for the no-par common stock, and probably greater than the total of bonds and preferred stock.[8] Also in the second reorganization of the Denver and Rio Grande Western,[9] the capitalization permitted was greatly in excess of the figure indicated by the tentative valuations. The underlying reports of the Bureau of Valuation indicated the value of the property as

[6] 86 I.C.C. 419 (1924).

[7] 124 I.C.C. 181.

[8] "From our preliminary study of the cost of reproduction new of the lines comprising the present Missouri, Kansas and Texas system, it would seem that the principal amount of bonds and par value of preferred stock to be issued will be not far short of, and may be in excess of, the cost of reproduction new of the properties of the acquired, allowing for current assets and the book value of securities of affiliated companies." 76 I.C.C. 103, 1922.

[9] 90 I.C.C. 99 (1924).

about 90 million dollars, to which about 23 million was added for property not included in the valuation. The capitalization permitted was 142 million dollars, exclusive of the no-par stock.

In recent years, when the final valuations have been available in an increasing proportion of cases, the Commission has taken a rather definite stand against their use as a test of proper capitalization. Their attitude was summarized in a recent case thus:

> We have held in a number of cases that the amount of a carrier's actual investment, not the value of its property, should be the measure by which to determine the amount of securities that may be issued by the carrier.[10]

But in this same case the Commission held that in the absence of reliable data as to the original cost of construction to the contractors the final valuation (plus net capital expenditures since the valuation date) was the best available measure—rejecting the "cost" paid by the railroad to the contractors in the form of securities.

In other recent cases where the final valuations were available they have not been used. In the case of the Ashland Railway, decided in 1928, the amount of capital stock was limited by the Commission to the investment of the stock subscribers of the new company, $6,000, although the final valuation was $88,000.[11]

3. *Previous capitalization.* In numerous cases stress is laid on the fact that the capitalization of the new company is substantially less than that of the old com-

[10] Roscoe, Snyder and Pacific Railway. 170 I.C.C. 407 (1931). This case is not a reorganization, but a readjustment of capital, virtually a stock dividend.

[11] 117 I.C.C. 723. For similar rulings see cases cited above in footnote 2.

pany. Usually this point is made when the capitalization by other tests appears to be high. No attempt is made, however, to enforce a general rule. In most cases where the Commission has cut capitalization below the figure asked by the applicant, the proposed figures were in fact below the former capitalization. But in the cases of the Chicago, Milwaukee, St. Paul and Pacific[12] and the International Great Northern[13] plans were approved which involved substantial increases in capitalization, and in the first reorganization of the Chicago and Eastern Illinois the nominal decrease becomes evident as an actual increase if accrued interest on indebtedness of the old company is eliminated from the capital assets and deduction is made for property not included in the reorganization.[14]

4. *Book value.* Book value is occasionally mentioned in cases where it is necessary to defend an apparently high capitalization[15] but there is no indication that it is taken seriously as a basis for determining the proper amount at which a road should be capitalized.

III. AMOUNT OF FIXED CHARGES

Next in prominence to the gross amount of the capitalization, among the factors discussed by the Com-

[12] 131 I.C.C. 673 (1928).

[13] 72 I.C.C. 722 (1922).

[14] Compare discussion of this case in D. P. Locklin, *Regulation of Security Issues by the Interstate Commerce Commission*, Urbana, 1925, p. 101.

[15] For example in the third reorganization of the Denver and Rio Grande Western (90 I.C.C. 99, 1924). Also in the case of the Missouri-Kansas-Texas Railway of Texas the fact is pointed out that "it appears that the total capitalization of the applicant will be equal to the book value of the properties and the net value of the other assets to be acquired." (76 I.C.C. 660, 1923.) One wonders whether the promoters of a new corporation ever submit a balance sheet in which the asset and liability sides do not balance.

mission in passing on reorganization cases, is the relationship between proposed fixed charges and probable
earning capacity. Thus the Commission said in 1924:

> The public interests require that before an issue of securities
> by a carrier is authorized, the probability of earnings sufficient
> to pay the costs of operation and of fixed charges be reasonably
> established with some surplus for dividends and other purposes.[16]

As a rule, the plan worked out by a reorganization
committee provides for a substantial reduction of fixed
charges, and is accompanied by an estimate showing
that probable earnings are sufficient to take care of them.
In such cases, this feature of the reorganization receives
favorable mention in the Commission's findings. But in
cases where no reduction is effected or where there does
not appear to be a reasonable chance that the charges can
be met, the Commission is not likely to withhold its
approval, unless the road is very small.[17]

Thus in the Georgia and Florida case[18] the Commission approved a plan though expressing the judgment
that the ability of the new company to carry its fixed
charges was "more than usually problematical." In the
Fort Smith and Western case[19] the Commission insisted
on a reduction of interest on bonds and a lengthening of
the period for which interest on certain income bonds
was to be non-cumulative. As thus revised the reorganization plan resulted in an increase of interest charges,
through the conversion of about $250,000 of mortgage

[16] Denver and Rio Grande Western, 90 I.C.C. 148.

[17] Cases where the proposed bond debt was cut down or wiped out
because the Commission did not believe the fixed charges could be
earned include Peoria Terminal (117 I.C.C. 377, 1926); San Luis Valley Southern (145 I.C.C. 71, 1928); Elkin and Alleghany (138 I.C.C.
341, 1928).

[18] 117 I.C.C. 473 (1927).

[19] 70 I.C.C. 777-782 (1921).

bond interest into $90,000 of mortgage bond interest and $187,000 of contingent interest on income bonds, non-cumulative for ten years. This "set-up" was approved on the ground that the evidence tended to show that for these ten years the *fixed* charges would be within the earning capacity of the road. There was apparently no suggestion that the interest on the income bonds could be earned.

In the Milwaukee case[20] there was an increase of interest charges from 21.5 million dollars to 22.8 million, inclusive of interest on income bonds. In the case of the Denver and Rio Grande Western three successive reorganization plans were approved within the space of three years.[21] The first effected no reduction of fixed charges, and the second did not bring them within the probable earning capacity of the road, as was admitted in connection with the third reorganization, less than a year later.

IV. REORGANIZATION EXPENSES

The present methods of reorganizing involve interminable delay and excessive expense. Reorganization managers are allowed a large measure of freedom in fixing their own compensation and that of their counsel. The amounts which are levied for this purpose on the security holders or charged against the capital account of the new road vary enormously from case to case and these differences do not seem to reflect corresponding differences in the work. They are subject, of course, to adjustment by the court which reviews the reorganization plan, and also by the Interstate Commerce Commission

[20] 154 I.C.C. 586 (1929).
[21] 70 I.C.C. 102 (1921); 82 I.C.C. 745 (1923); and 90 I.C.C. 141 (1924).

in case the expenses are to be covered by the issuance of new securities, but there seems to be a general understanding that the reorganization committees and their counsel have a vested right to profit enormously by the distress of the railroad.

In the case of the Missouri-Kansas-Texas, the Interstate Commerce Commission delayed its approval of the reorganization plan in order to secure a more satisfactory accounting of the reorganization expense, and succeeded in getting compensation of the reorganization committee reduced from $1,600,000 to $900,000.[22]

In later cases the Commission has shown some interest in the amount of expenses and has sometimes required detailed statements of the expense where it is proposed to include it in the capitalization of the new road. We have noted no cases in which it has insisted upon a reduction of the amounts proposed as compensation for the reorganization committee's services and for other expenses of reorganization. It is quite possible, however, that in the absence of the Commission's scrutiny and its attendant publicity the fees exacted would have been even larger than they were. In any event there is certainly an opportunity for a very large further saving in the costs of reorganization, without sacrifice of efficiency.

In the second Atlanta, Birmingham and Atlantic case the cost of the reorganization was over $600,000, in-

---

[22] These figures do not cover the entire expense of the reorganization. Trustees under the mortgages and their counsel got over $650,000 in connection with the foreclosure of mortgages. There was also an item of nearly a million dollars for underwriting commissions and profits, a share of which went to the reorganization managers. The receiver's salary and the fees of his counsel are not included in the figure given for reorganization expense. Moreover, much of the committee's work was done by employees of the railroad.

cluding a special fee to the receiver, but not including his salary of $12,000 a year.

In the Milwaukee case (1928) a fund of 3½ million dollars was set aside for reorganization expenses, out of the assessment levied on the stockholders. The attempt of the Interstate Commerce Commission to control the expenditure of this fund was overruled by the Supreme Court which held that the money was paid by the stockholders to the reorganization committee, and not to the railroad; hence was not under the jurisdiction of the commission.[23]

The length of time consumed in preparing reorganization plans and putting them into effect is quite as striking as the amount of money expended; indeed it would be impossible to run up more than a small fraction of the reorganization expense if the labors of the reorganization committee were not customarily prolonged over many years. The Milwaukee was in receivers' hand over three years; the Missouri-Kansas-Texas seven years; the Texas and Pacific eight years; the Chicago and Alton eight years. On the other hand, the reorganization plan of the St. Louis-San Francisco, which was prepared in an effort to avert receivership, was published in less than three months after the Interstate Commerce Commission stipulated that the fixed charges of the road should be cut down. And this reorganization plan was much more complicated and effected a much more drastic reduction of the railways' fixed charges than has been the case with most of the plans that have emerged from the prolonged deliberations of well-paid reorganization committees. We cannot avoid the impression that some of these reorganizations have

[23] 282 U.S. 311 (1931).

been delayed much longer than they would have been if no one had had a financial interest in prolonging the receivership and in magnifying the jobs of the various committees.

V. THE MAINTENANCE OF EQUITY

The Commission in passing upon reorganization plans has never, so far as we have noted, accepted full responsibility for the fairness of the redistribution of equities which the reorganization brings about, or intervened to require a different adjustment. In 1921 the Commission expressly disclaimed such responsibility, saying:

> Holders of small blocks of bonds have protested against the plan of exchanging bonds for stock. This is a matter properly to be brought before the court having jurisdiction in the premises, which has expressly reserved the determination of the equities in the receivership proceedings.[24]

On the other hand in 1926 the Commission seemed to accept a certain amount of responsibility for the justice of the plan, saying:

> . . . earliest approval should therefore be given unless there is something in the terms and conditions of the proposed acquisition or in the consideration, so inequitable as to require modification in the public interest.[25]

In later cases the Commission has given some consideration to equity, though we have not found a reorganization case in which its deliberations on this phase of the plan have had any tangible result.

In our judgment the courts and the Commission are jointly responsible for a situation in which substantial

---

[24] Chicago and Eastern Illinois, 67 I.C.C. 61.
[25] Atlanta, Birmingham and Atlantic, 117 I.C.C. 187.

denial of justice occurs frequently, and one for which there is neither necessity nor justification. In view of the importance of this issue it seems worth while to analyze the fairness of several of the more important recent cases, taking into account the possible necessity of some compromise with strict justice in order to bring down the fixed charges of the insolvent roads and find cash for their pressing needs.

1. *Chicago, Milwaukee, St. Paul and Pacific.*[26] This reorganization involved a substantial readjustment of the equities of bondholders and stockholders. The holders of all general and refunding bonds were given equal treatment. For each $1,000 bond deposited, the holder was given $200 of new 5 per cent second mortgage bonds and $800 of adjustment bonds, all the arrears of interest being paid in cash. A new open mortgage was thrust in ahead of them to provide for future financing. The old stockholders were given an opportunity to maintain their position in the new company on condition of paying an assessment of $4.00 a share and buying at par $24 worth of the 5 per cent second mortgage bonds for each share of preferred stock owned, and $28 worth for each share of common.

That the plan effected a substantial transfer of value from the junior bondholders to the stockholders cannot be denied. For the bondholders made a substantial sacrifice while the stockholders were allowed to pay in 12 million dollars and receive stock in the new company with a market value of about 80 million dollars. No opportunity was given the bondholders to subscribe

---

[26] 131 I.C.C. 673 (1928). The responsibility in this case belongs to the courts rather than the Commission as the Federal Court had held the plan to be equitable before it was presented to the Commission for approval.

to the new bonds and stock on the terms that were offered to the old stockholders.

It was desirable that stockholders should make a substantial contribution to the finances of the new company but it was not necessary for that purpose that the holders of the new stock should be the same as the holders of the old stock. If the right to pay $32 for $28 of bonds and one share of stock was valuable, and the market quotations of the period indicated that it was worth a very substantial amount, the bondholders had a right to it. Only if they failed to take it up could the offer made to the stockholders be defended on the ground of the primary necessity to raise the money, which is the ground always alleged for the refusal to wipe out stockholders' equities.

In this respect this settlement violated the principle that a sound reorganization must redistribute the existing values in the order of the claims against them; it amounted to a substantial expropriation of the bondholders for the benefit of the stockholders. The reason alleged for allowing the stockholders to retain their position was the necessity of finding cash, but no opportunity was given the bondholders to contribute the cash.[27]

Since the rate on the income bonds was as high as that on the old bonds exchanged for them, it might appear that the bondholders suffered no real loss. But the indenture securing the adjustment bonds contained a pecu-

[27] In this case, moreover, the necessity for cash was largely due to the exorbitant expenses of the reorganization. The chief use made of cash, aside from reorganization expenses, was to pay a debt to the United States which was incurred after the property was subjected to the lien of the mortgage bonds. In a later case the Supreme Court held that the government was not entitled to preference over the claims of other creditors for advances made under the terms of the Transportation Act.

liar provision whereby the management was free for five years to withhold from the adjustment bondholders, for reinvestment, two-thirds of the available net income, up to 5 million dollars. As the adjustment bonds were non-cumulative, this meant simply that income otherwise available to meet charges on the adjustment bonds could be used for additions and betterments and thereby become the property of the stockholders.

The solicitude shown for the interests of the stockholders is the more extraordinary, since the difficulties of the Chicago, Milwaukee and St. Paul were in an unusual degree the result of bad management.

2. *Denver and Rio Grande Western*[28] (*second reorganization*). In this reorganization the point of interest is the treatment of the 5 per cent mortgage bonds of 1955 and the adjustment bonds of 1932. The 5 per cents were undeniably senior to the adjustments, but both received exactly the same treatment. For each $1,000 of bonds of these issues, together with unpaid interest,[29] there were issued $725 of "general mortgage" 5 per cent bonds and $400 of cumulative preferred stock. The common stockholders (who were the Western Pacific and Missouri Pacific Railways) paid assessments totalling 10 million dollars.

So far as the company was concerned, the benefit of the reorganization consisted entirely of the assessment on the stock. The amount of 5 per cent bonds was reduced only from 31.1 million dollars to 29.8 million,[30]

---

[28] 82 I.C.C. 745 (1923).

[29] Including in the case of the adjustment bonds interest which was not yet due because not yet earned.

[30] The new general mortgage bonds had substantially the same priority as the old 5 per cents, as the underlying bonds amounting to 85 million dollars were not disturbed, though there was a slight improvement be-

while the 10 million of adjustment bonds were replaced by over 16.4 million dollars of preferred stock, the contingent charges rising from $700,000 to $986,700.

Since there was no significant difference between the claims of the new preferred stockholder and the old adjustment bondholder except that the rate was 6 per cent instead of 7, a change which was more than offset by the increase in the amount, it is obvious that the financial structure of the new company would have been substantially as good as it actually was if the stockholders had simply contributed this $10,000,000, and out of it the receivers' certificates and the back interest on the mortgage bonds had been paid off.

But though the company derived little benefit, the reorganization effected a substantial readjustment in the relative positions of the holders of the mortgage bonds and the adjustment bonds. Consider first the adjustment bondholders. In place of $10,000,000 of adjustment bonds which were substantially equivalent to preferred stock, and $1,983,000 of accrued interest, they got $4,000,000 of preferred stock which had just as good a priority as the adjustment bonds had previously had, and $7,250,000 of bonds which were much superior.[31] Thus the holder of a $1,000 bond who had been entitled to $70 of interest if and as earned, now had an absolute claim to $36.25 and a contingent claim to $24. On the other hand the holder of a refunding bond gave up $1,000 principal and $125.00 accrued interest, and got $725 of securities which were of substantially the same priority as those he had before, and $400 of

cause 5 million dollars of receivership certificates were paid off out of funds contributed by the stockholders.

[31] $85,000,000 of securities were to have priority over them as compared with $122,000,000 before the reorganization.

stock which was junior to $115,000,000 of securities as against $85,000,000 under the old "set-up." His position was weakened; that of the adjustment bondholders was strengthened.

This juggling of the equities of different classes of security holders did not materially improve the financial structure of the road, but took value away from one class of bondholders to improve the position of another class.

3. *Atlanta, Birmingham and Atlantic.*[32] In this case there were two issues of bonds, $4,090,000 first mortgage bonds and $4,544,000 income bonds, besides 300,000 shares of stock. The reorganization committee sold the control of the road to the Atlantic Coast Line for about $8,800,000, of which $3,600,000 was paid in cash and the balance in the form of a guarantee of 5 per cent dividends on $5,200,000 of new preferred stock. The Atlantic Coast Line took all the common stock, no provision being made for common stockholders of the old company. The cash was used for settling claims which were given priority over the first mortgage bonds, and the preferred stock was distributed to holders of both classes of bonds in the ratio of $60 of stock for $100 of bonds.

On the face of things, this settlement expropriated the first mortgage bondholders for the benefit of the holders of income bonds. The preferred stock was more than sufficient in face value to cover the claim of the first mortgage bondholders and there appears to be no sound reason why they should have been required to accept 60 cents on the dollar in stock, in order that income bondholders might have a larger share. If there was any

[32] 117 I.C.C. 181 (1926).

doubt as to whether a dollar for dollar settlement in preferred stock would have over-paid the first mortgage bondholders, it would have been proper to offer the holders of income bonds an opportunity to buy the preferred stock at approximately 80, using the money to pay off the mortgage bonds and distributing stock to the mortgage bondholders only to the extent that income bondholders failed to take up the stock offered them.

4. *St. Louis-San Francisco proposed reorganization (1932).* This company was incorporated in 1916 as the result of a reorganization procedure. It has outstanding in the hands of the public 25 million dollars in guaranteed bonds of the Kansas City, Fort Scott and Memphis Railroad, secured by a first mortgage on about one-half of the main line of the railway and a second mortgage on most of the rest, 6 million other divisional bonds, and 21 million equipment obligations. Next in seniority are 117 million prior lien mortgage bonds, and junior to these are about 120 million of "consolidated mortgage" bonds.

The interest on this indebtedness, together with some other miscellaneous fixed obligations, amounts to $13,700,000. The fixed charges were earned twice over from 1924 to 1927 inclusive, about 1.8 times in 1928 and 1929, 1.44 times in 1930, and about three-fourths of the charges were earned in 1931. As was noted in Chapter XIV, dividends were paid on the 49 million of 6 per cent preferred stock through 1931, and the 2 per cent quarterly dividend on 65 million of common stock was paid in January, 1931.

While the proportion of funded debt to total capitalization is high—about 71 per cent as compared with

59 per cent for the average railroad—the margin of safety over the fixed charges has been adequate to give the two larger issues a good rating as junior railway bonds go. As recently as 1928 it was able to sell its consolidated bonds—secured by a third mortgage on the best mileage—at a yield below 5 per cent, and to refund a large block of its bonds with preferred stock. In 1931, and especially in 1932, the company's income fell off rapidly, as did that of most other railroads. A bank debt of 6 million dollars was incurred, and then the company was forced to apply for a loan from the Reconstruction Finance Corporation. The Interstate Commerce Commission stipulated as a condition of its approval of the major part of the loan that the road should submit a plan of financial readjustment which would cut down its fixed charges.

The plan which was worked out in response to this suggestion provides that for five years interest on the prior lien and consolidated mortgage bonds shall be paid in interest "certificates" instead of cash. These interest certificates are to bear interest on a sliding scale which rises to 3 per cent after four years. For this period the fixed charges are reduced by about three-quarters, that is, to about $3,500,000. For the next five years, that is from July 1, 1937, to July 1, 1942, interest on the prior lien bonds is to be 50 per cent fixed and 50 per cent contingent, and on the consolidated bonds 40 per cent fixed and 60 per cent contingent.

Net income available after fixed charges is to be disposed of as follows, subject to the power of the directors to maintain a contingency reserve fund not exceeding 2 million dollars:

(a) Three million dollars may be appropriated for

capital expenditures; if not so used it is to be added to the sinking fund and applied to purchase of bonds.

(b) The next 3 million dollars goes to sinking funds. Of this amount one-quarter goes to retire short-term notes, three-eighths to retire prior lien bonds, and consolidated bonds (one-half for each) and three-eighths to retire prior lien and consolidated interest certificates (one-half for each).

(c) The balance, after July 1, 1937, goes next to pay contingent interest, including accruals thereof.

(d) Of the remainder, one-quarter, up to 1 million dollars, goes to retire short-term notes, three-eighths to retire interest certificates, and three-eighths to retire bonds.

A stock bonus is given to bondholders, the total thus distributed aggregating 23 per cent of preferred stock and 26 per cent of the common. Control is vested in a voting trust for ten years, the trustees being selected by the committee which drew up the plan. Working control of the road is apparently not shifted. A new mortgage is authorized prior to the existing prior lien and consolidated mortgages, the funds to be used for general corporate purposes.

It was hoped that this plan would be accepted by a sufficient number of security holders to make possible its execution without a receivership, but so much dissent developed that the management in the early autumn applied for a receivership, with the avowed purpose of using the receivership to force the execution of the plan. On November 2 the president of the company was appointed as receiver, and on the same day the plan was declared operative, without foreclosure of any of the mortgages.

As railroad reorganization plans go, the readjustment contemplated is not particularly drastic. If the earning capacity of the road returns to anywhere near pre-depression figures, the holders of the principal bond issues will ultimately be in substantially their previous position, while a continuance of earnings around the 1932 level will necessitate a further reorganization at the expiration of the five-year period. This is a reasonable arrangement in view of the uncertainty as to how permanent are the conditions which have caused the insolvency. However, in certain features the plan is open to the criticism which we have made of various plans promulgated under the auspices of the courts, namely, that it shifts the equities so as to deprive certain security-holders of rights for which they have paid without thereby forwarding the ostensible purposes of the reorganization. The following points must be noted:

First, the position of the holders of the consolidated mortgage bonds is unduly protected, as to both principal and interest, at the expense of the prior lien issue. As to the interest, income which would otherwise be available for paying the interest on the prior lien bonds will be applied to pay interest on certificates issued in redemption of consolidated mortgage bond coupons. As to the principal, the sinking fund is to be applied to retire consolidated bonds at the same rate as prior lien bonds, and to retire consolidated interest certificates at the same rate as prior lien interest certificates—a clear diversion of income from the holders of the senior to the holders of the junior securities.

These consolidated mortgage bonds were sold in 1928, chiefly to raise funds to pay off income bonds which carried a contingent charge. The prior lien mortgages were already outstanding and derived no substantial benefit from this transaction. There is therefore no equitable reason why consolidated mortgage bondholders should be paid anything if there is not enough to pay the prior lien bondholders in full—no reason, that is, except the necessity of securing consents from the consolidated mortgage bondholders to get any plan into operation.

Second, holders of the bank debt, which is legally junior to all of the bond issues except in so far as it is protected by mortgage bonds as collateral, are to get 3 per cent interest in cash for the first five years, while holders of the bonds get only 1 per cent interest on interest for two years, and 2 per cent interest on interest for the next two years. Moreover, the bank loans get one-quarter of the sinking fund, although they make up less than 3 per cent of the indebtedness for the service of which the sinking fund is created.

Third, the stockholders, whose interest would obviously be wiped out by the enforcement of the legal rights of the bondholders, are not called on to pay any assessment, their only concession being a dilution of their equity by the issuance of stock to the bondholders— stock which at present market prices they could buy back for less than half a million dollars. The valuable right to use the road as a means of controlling traffic is effectively protected from claims of creditors by the device of the voting trust.

The initial action of the Interstate Commerce Commission in making its approval of the Reconstruction Finance Corporation's loan contingent upon a capital reorganization seems to us questionable. The difficulties of the road are chiefly an outgrowth of the depression, and as such can appropriately be handled by the machinery of the Reconstruction Finance Corporation. At the time the recapitalization was suggested by the Commission, the road had been incurring a deficit for less than a year and that in a time of unprecedented depression. To set up a plan which deprives bondholders of three-fourths of their interest for five years, no matter what the road may earn, reflects a degree of pessimism in regard to this road which does not seem to be warranted by its record, as compared with that of other roads. The proposal that a road should be reorganized to the extent of cutting off three-fourths of fixed charges when its deficiency was only one-fourth as recently as 1931 seems to us arbitrary and calculated to destroy the confidence of possible future investors in the good faith with which railroad bond indentures are drawn.

Finally, if there is any reasonable basis for so drastic a cutting down of fixed charges it seems quite inexplicable that such elaborate pains should be taken to protect the position of the management which paid out in 1931 over 4 million dollars in dividends. One of the purposes of a mortgage is to give the holders of bonds secured by it a claim on the value represented by the control of the road. In this case, as in many others, the management is allowed to retain this equity without adequate compensation to the bondholders. It is seldom the case, however, that the dominant interests are permitted to retain control of a road without any assessment on the voting stock.

At the time of this writing the plan has been neither approved nor disapproved by the Interstate Commerce Commission. Nevertheless, it has been declared operative by the receiver, and interest on the prior lien and general mortgage bonds has been defaulted. Apparent-

ly, unless dissenting creditors take positive steps to secure an injunction against it, the provisions of the plan
as to the disposition of the roads' income will become
operative without such approval.

In the next chapter we consider possible ways of in-
troducing greater economy, efficiency and equity into
reorganization procedure.

CHAPTER XVI

REORGANIZATION PROCEDURE:
PROPOSALS FOR CHANGE

During the past year, because of the general financial distress of the railroads, the defects of the present reorganization technique have taken on greater importance than they have had since the close of the nineteenth century. It is generally recognized that present procedure is unduly expensive and dilatory, and there is considerable prospect of speedy legislation designed to simplify reorganization procedure and lessen its cost. This prospect is commendable. It would be unfortunate, however, that in framing this legislation no attention should be given to the other fundamental weakness of the present system—the lack of an adequate safeguard of the rights of those who have committed their capital to the railroads on the assurance of priority of their claims over those which are contractually inferior in lien.

The costliness, inequity, and a large part of the complexity of modern reorganization procedure are due chiefly to the intrusion into the practice of the courts, with the tacit approval of the Interstate Commerce Commission, of three principles, none of which has any sound basis in economic theory or, we believe, in law. One of these unsound principles is the so-called doctrine of relative priority or relative income position; the second is the power of the majority of the holders of a given security to commit the minority to the acceptance of a plan which transfers part of their rights to others; the third is a tendency to discriminate against holders of securities who have bought their holdings recently at

349

prices which reflect the road's financial distress. A fourth bad feature of the usual procedure is the fact that the various committees which make the plan are neither independent nor disinterested.

Let us consider first the relative priority doctrine. The general principle of the law is that the position of a secured creditor cannot be impaired by the creation of unsecured indebtedness, or the creation of indebtedness with a lien specifically junior to that of the first class. Likewise the position of the unsecured creditor cannot be impaired by the sale of securities to preferred or common stockholders. Those who buy junior bonds, unsecured debentures, or stock, risk both their principal and the stability of their incomes in consideration of larger prospective returns.

There is a long line of Supreme Court decisions which seem to the layman to support the absolute priority of creditors to whom priority has been assured by contract.[1] In the Louisville Trust Company case[2] the Court said:

> Any arrangement of the parties by which the subordinate rights and interests of stockholders are attempted to be secured at the expense of the prior rights of either class of creditors comes under judicial denunciation.

In the Kansas City Terminal Railway case[3] the following question was submitted:

> Is a plan of reorganization sufficient as to unsecured creditors and binding upon them which does not give precedence to

[1] Compare A. J. Buscheck, "A Formula for the Judicial Reorganization of Public Service Corporations," *Columbia Law Review*, 1932, Vol. 32, pp. 964-98; Bonbright and Bergerman, "Two Rival Theories of Priority Rights," the same, 1928, Vol. 28, page 127, and other studies cited in these articles.

[2] 174 U.S. 674, 19 Sup. Ct. 827 (1899).

[3] *Kansas City Railway Co.* v. *Guardian Trust Co.* 240 U.S.

the entire claim of the creditor over any part or interests of a stockholder in the old company?

The Court's answer was in the negative.

On the other hand, there is a line of cases in which lower courts have set up the doctrine that when all classes of security holders are involved in a common misfortune the right of the senior creditor is merely to have his relative priority maintained in the reorganized corporation but not to have his entire claim protected to the exclusion of junior creditors, or even stockholders. This doctrine seems to have originated in the supposed necessity, in certain cases, of securing funds to safeguard the value of the corporation as a going concern by permitting stockholders to maintain their position in the new company on the payment of an assessment smaller than would be necessary to pay off the creditors in full.

In some cases the control of the corporation is undoubtedly worth more to the existing stockholders than it would be to the bondholders or to possible outside bidders. In such a case there is no sound objection to permitting the stockholders to protect themselves by paying an assessment somewhat larger than could be obtained by selling the property in the open market, if such procedure actually gives the bondholders a better settlement than they could get by taking over the control of the property themselves. In practice, however, the doctrine is generally applied (as it was in the Milwaukee, the Missouri-Kansas-Texas, and Denver, Rio Grande and Western cases described above) in such a way as to give no assurance that stockholders have made anything like the contribution they would have been willing to make to protect their position, and without any investigation as to whether bondholders would have preferred to pay the same assessment and take the stock for themselves.

The courts seem to reason that since it may be impossible to obtain funds unless stockholders are permitted to contribute them and retain their interest, the presumption is that such necessity exists in every case where the reorganization committee submits a plan involving an assessment of stockholders which has been accepted by a substantial majority of the bondholders. Whether the bondholders have actually been offered the alternative of contributing the funds themselves much less the alternative of selling out in the open market the stock which is offered to the old stockholders the courts do not seem to inquire. Indeed the position taken by the court in the Phipps case[4] seems to amount to this: that any offer to creditors is fair, just, and timely if it gives them more than is given the stockholders.

We suggest that any revision of present law relative to reorganization procedure should include an unequivocal statement of the doctrine of absolute priority, that is, a provision that a reorganization plan, to be made effective under the proposed new procedure, must be such as to conserve for holders of each successive lien whatever equity remains in the property subjected to the lien of the mortgage after the full payment of prior lien claimants, together with a similar provision for the protection of unsecured creditors against diversion of their equity to the stockholders.[5]

This proposal implies a definite repudiation of the idea that an unsecured creditor has a claim superior to that

[4] *Phipps* v. *Chicago, Rock Island and Pacific Ry. Co.* 284, Fed. 945 (C.C.A., 1922).

[5] An ingenious plan for accomplishing this is suggested by Buscheck in the article cited above in footnote 1.

of the secured creditors. In a number of cases plans have been approved which involve cash payment to certain claimants who had no claim against anything except the unmortgaged assets and against those a claim co-ordinate with the deficiency claim of the mortgage bondholders.

The second element which obstructs the attainment of the most equitable solution of the reorganization problem is the undue weight which has come to be attached to the fact that a majority, or two-thirds, or 90 per cent, of the holders of a given security have assented to a modification of their claims.

No reform of the process of reorganization is adequate which does not eliminate this feature entirely. We do not question that under the present procedure such consents are necessary. They serve to prevent small minorities from securing undue advantages for themselves by holding up a beneficial reorganization, with a view to compelling the majority to buy them out on exorbitant terms. The opportunity of the minority to do this arises from the fact that nominally the individual bondholder has certain rights the actual enforcement of which would give rise to intolerable confusion. The holder of a single bond secured by first mortgage on a given piece of railway property often has a legal right to take possession of that property in event of default. Since it would be out of the question to enforce the provisions of the mortgage which authorize separate operation or separate sale of what have become integral parts of a unified system, some way must be found to abrogate the rights of the bondholders. Technically, of course, the situation is not changed as to the minority by the consent of any majority, however large, but for many years it has been an established practice of the courts to disregard the nominal rights of minority security holders when a large majority have waived their rights.

If, however, a new system of reorganization were set up in which the Interstate Commerce Commission, or some other public agency, was authorized to formulate a plan and put it into effect, subject of course to court review, the conditions which have engendered the rule of respect for the assent of the majority would no longer exist. If different groups of security holders suggested different plans an arbitration tribunal with adequate powers need not choose between them on the basis of the number of votes that could be marshalled in favor of one or the other plan, but on the basis of the inherent merits of the plans themselves. Minority as well as majority interests would have an opportunity to present arguments in favor of one or another plan and the decision could be made on the basis of the soundness of the proposed financial structure and the extent to which the equities of the various parts were protected.

Theoretically intended to protect the interest of the security holder, the rule of majorities operates in practice to the disadvantage of creditors and especially the holder of the prior lien security.[6] The holder of a fixed prior lien security has everything to lose and nothing to gain in bargaining with junior interests. He cannot hope that in a reorganization he will be given anything at the expense of junior claimants because junior claimants are not entitled to anything until he is paid in full.

---

[6] In the larger reorganizations it is often the case that the securities which rank first are relatively small in amount and are not disturbed at all. But as between the different groups which are disturbed the statement in the text as to the disadvantage of the prior lien security holds good.

The junior security holder, on the other hand, always has a chance of getting part of his claim paid at the expense of the senior claimant. He has a nuisance value because if he withholds his consent he may be able to cause the senior security holder great cost and delay in getting any sort of settlement.

Moreover, the majorities which are rolled up in favor of reorganization plans are rarely representative of the genuine judgment and genuine preference of the security holders. It would be quite possible under present procedure, or under the procedure proposed in various bills now before Congress, for unsecured creditors, stockholders, or other junior interests to buy up two-thirds of an outstanding prior lien issue and vote it in favor of a plan which gouged this issue for the benefit of their other interests.

In practice, moreover, it is not necessary that the controlling interest own anything like the full amount which is to be voted in favor of a plan. Strong pressure is always brought to bear on security holders to deposit their securities and accept the plan, and the alternative in case they refuse to do so is always indefinite and unattractive. The procedure necessary to obtain the assent of security holders to a plan puts a premium on qualifications that are essentially political in character.

We suggest therefore that the whole system of majority rule should be wiped out. It arises from a circumstance which would no longer exist under a reformed reorganization procedure; namely, the necessity of preventing the enforcement of certain technical rights of the individual stockholder.

A revised reorganization procedure should definitely repudiate the doctrine that the time when the holders of securities bought them, or the price they paid, has any bearing on their rights. In a number of reorganization cases the Commission and the courts have obviously been influenced by the fact that certain groups of security holders are known to have bought up their securities at large discounts after the financial distress of the road became apparent. This is a totally irrelevant consideration. To hold otherwise is to hold that the claims of an original or a later buyer are not fully transferable, but are in part destroyed by sale.

The point at issue is not merely the rights of the recent buyer, but the right of the earlier holder to sell his claims. One of the features of modern corporate finance which has been most important in mobilizing small savings for use in big enterprises is the transferability of equities. If the principle is established that when A transfers his claim to B, B's claim is not as good as A's, then the marketability of A's claim is impaired. In the long run the losses will not fall on the last holder but will be discounted in the price at which he buys.[7]

Finally, the situation is made worse by the fact that the committees which are formed to represent the separate security issues are not independent of the body before which they have to plead the cause of their claimants, and that body is not disinterested. The members of reorganization committees which make the plans are often also members of the committees representing certain security issues. Members of the committee set up

[7] Even if there were general agreement that the speculator ought to be squeezed, there is no reason why the stockholders or junior creditors should get the benefit of the abridgment of his claim. If it should be decided that the recent purchaser has actually acquired something less than the full claim of the earlier investor, surely the difference should accrue to the public and not to the stockholders or the other creditors.

to protect a certain security have to look to the reorganization plan for compensation for their own efforts; a situation which certainly does not make for independence of attitude if it becomes their duty to oppose the dominant group.

It has been possible to obtain the consent of the security holders who were mulcted in such reorganizations as are described above, chiefly because their only practicable alternative is to prolong the delay and increase the expense. The senior security holder has the choice between making unwarranted concessions to the junior holder in order to obtain his support for a reorganization plan, or else to face an unpredictable continuance of the process of nibbling away the property through the fees and expense accounts of lawyers, bankers, and accountants. Much of the gain from a simplified procedure consists in the fact that it would make such sacrifices unnecessary.

Concretely, we suggest that legislation should be enacted along the following lines:

1. *Receivership.* When a road confessed insolvency, or defaulted on its interest charges, or failed to pay its obligations at maturity, its affairs would be put in charge of two receivers appointed by the Interstate Commerce Commission from its professional staff who would be paid salaries appropriate to their technical qualifications. One of these receivers would ordinarily be a man with a background of railroad operating experience, and the other primarily a lawyer. The staff from which these men are drawn would be a permanent staff and when not engaged in this sort of work its members should be assigned other duties in connection with the Commission's work. The Commission might bill the road for

the expense of administration, but the receivers would be on the payroll of the Commission. It would probably be well to call the receivers by a new name, say, public comptrollers, to avoid the disturbing influence of receiverships on the public mind.

2. *Task of the receivers.* The first task of the receivers would be to test out thoroughly the question whether a reorganization was really necessary. No road would be reorganized merely because it was temporarily unable either to meet its interest charges or to repay obligations at maturity. In case of default on its obligations, it would be operated by the receivers for a reasonable period in order to determine whether its default is due to temporary conditions or to fundamental weaknesses in its capital structure. Particularly, reorganizations would not be carried through merely because a road had not made adequate provision for meeting its financial responsibilities in an unprecedented depression. A road which had a good record through 1930 but was unable in 1933 to meet its maturities or pay its fixed charges would be operated under a receiver without reorganization until it became clear whether there had been a permanent shrinkage of traffic to anything like the 1931-32 level.

3. *The planning of the reorganization.* When it became clear that a road could not carry the burden of its indebtedness, the responsibility for making a reorganization plan would rest with a disinterested public body, preferably a division of the Interstate Commerce Commission. This body would investigate the legal status of the various security issues, hear evidence as to the desirability of alternative procedures, draw up a plan, and put it into effect. Dissatisfied security holders would

have a right to apply to the Supreme Court of the District of Columbia for an injunction but only on the ground that the plan was inequitable; the Commission being the final judge as to whether in other regards the plan was in the public interest. If the court found that the protests were justified the plan would be remanded to the Commission for revision.

4. *Objectives.* The objectives aimed at by the arbitral tribunal would be (a) to provide a capital structure under which the road could function efficiently in the public service and obtain capital for future needs; (b) to distribute the ownership of the securities of the reconstructed corporation in such a way as to conserve for each class of security holders all that remained of the equity assured them in the contract.

It is frequently stated that since the paramount consideration in a railroad reorganization is to secure necessary cash and reduce fixed charges to a point where the road can continue to function in the public service, considerations of equity cannot be allowed to interfere with the success of a plan which has been worked out by a responsible reorganization committee and approved by a majority of the security holders interested. The fact is, however, that the securing of needed cash and the reduction of fixed charges are almost never matters of difficulty. Aside from small roads where the maintenance of service under any financial structure is a matter of difficulty, the problem set the reorganization committee is not to raise money but to raise it in such a way as to bring about the minimum dislocation of existing property rights. In practice, in fact, the problem of the·managers seems to be how to devise a plausible way of protecting the controlling interest from the necessity

either of giving up control or of paying to the bondholders what the control is worth in the market.

5. *Priority*. There would be a definite repudiation
of the doctrine of relative priority[8] both with reference to the relative position of bondholders and stockholders and also with reference to the relative claims of
creditors who are protected by different types of securities. There would also be a definite repudiation of the
idea that the claims of individual security holders are in
any way affected by the time at which they bought their
securities or the prices they paid for them.

6. *Consent of majorities*. The whole procedure of
depositing securities and obtaining consents to modification of the rights of security holders would be abolished.
The reorganization could be put into effect through a
judicial sale or otherwise, as the plan might provide.

7. *Committees of security holders*. Security holders
would be represented before the Commission in connection with the preparation of the plan, but the expenses
of such representation would be borne by the parties concerned. There would be no presumption in favor of the
plan which happened to be backed by a larger group as
against one backed by a smaller group; each plan being
considered on its merits. The Commission would not be
obliged to accept any plan submitted to it; it might
utilize the material submitted in order to draw up a
plan of its own.

[8] See above, pp. 349-51.

PART IV

REGULATION OF THE LEVEL OF
RAILWAY RATES

INTRODUCTORY STATEMENT

The regulation of railroad rates has always had a two-fold purpose—to prevent unfair or inequitable particular rates, and to prevent the roads from obtaining excessive earnings for their services in the aggregate. The latter involves consideration of the rate of return both of particular roads and of the railroad system as a whole. During the earlier years of federal regulation, discussions of discriminatory tariffs and rebates to favorite shippers overshadowed consideration of the level of rates, and it was not until 25 years after the inauguration of federal legislation that a real effort to regulate the general level of rates on some fair and equitable basis was undertaken by the Interstate Commerce Commission.

In 1913 there was passed the so-called Valuation Act which directed the Commission to "investigate, ascertain, and report the value of all property owned and used by every common carrier" subject to the Commission's jurisdiction. Until 1920, however, the use to which these valuations might be devoted was left undetermined. The origin of the Transportation Act of 1920 is explained as follows:

Toward the close of the period of federal operation of railroads (1918 to 1920) investors in railroad securities were becoming uneasy over the effects of regulation by the Interstate Commerce Commission. The machinery of regulation, it was charged, was unduly oppressive and likely to result in the carriers' receiving less than a reasonable return upon their investment. Whether any individual railroad company could earn a fair return upon the value of its property was usually dependent upon the general level of rates. Under the Constitution any given road is guaranteed against confiscatory rates; but such a guarantee, it was seen, might be utterly ineffective for the simple reason that an individual road cannot adjust its rates independently of the general rate structure. Thus it was contended that the general level of rates must be such that the carriers as a whole would be able to earn a reasonable return on their property as a whole.

This consideration led security owners to sponsor what has become Section 15a of the Interstate Commerce Act as amended in 1920. Under this act the Commission was instructed to "adjust rates so that carriers as a whole (or as a whole in each of such rate groups or territories as the Commission may from time to time designate) will, under honest, efficient and economical management and reasonable expenditures for maintenance of way, structures, and equipment, earn an aggregate annual net railway operating income equal, as nearly as may be, to a fair return upon the aggregate value of the railway property of such carriers held for and used in the service of transportation."

Under this authorization it was assumed, though not explicitly stated, that the Commission would use the valuation findings for the purpose of rate regulation. This act also provided that if the earnings of any road should exceed a certain fixed minimum, one-half of the excess should be subject to recapture by the government and used as a general railroad contingent fund. The determination of this rate of return on particular roads also involved the use of the Commission's valuation data.

In this division of our study we shall first describe the origin of the valuation idea and the procedure followed by the Commission in making valuations. Second, we shall show how the recapture provision has worked in practice. In the third chapter we give an appraisal of the various theories as to the proper basis of rate regulation. Fourth, we shall inquire whether the valuation data obtained by the Commission has been, or can be, put to significant uses. In the final chapter we shall set forth certain constructive suggestions for dealing with the difficult problem of general rate regulation.

CHAPTER XVII

THE VALUATION PLAN

Perhaps the most ambitious task ever undertaken by the Interstate Commerce Commission was that which involved the physical valuation of railroad properties as a basis for the regulation of earnings. When the Valuation Act was passed in 1913 the magnitude of the undertaking was not foreseen. The Commission estimated the cost at $3,000,000 and the time required for completion at three years. Senator LaFollette in his three-day speech on the floor of the Senate in 1910 put the cost at $2,400,000, while Senator Elkins ventured to predict an outlay of as much as $5,000,000 and that five years would be required to complete the project.

To the end of 1932 the cost to the government had been nearly $45,000,000 and very large sums had also been expended by the railroads.[1] It is now estimated that all the work will be completed by June 30, 1934, and that the total cost will be approximately $48,000,000.[2]

I. THE ANTECEDENTS OF THE VALUATION ACT

The undertaking of the federal valuation of railroads is popularly ascribed to the efforts of a few individuals who, with great persuasiveness, urged in the halls of Congress that the railroads were over-capitalized and their rates exorbitant. Picture conditions as they were in 1906,

[1] 72 Cong. 1 sess., *Railroad Legislation*, Hearings on H. R. 7116 and 7117 before Committee on Interstate and Foreign Commerce (1932), pp. 322, 477-79, 534-35. Alfred P. Thom, general counsel of the Association of Railway Executives, and others testified that the railways had spent approximately $138,000,000.

[2] The same, p. 538.

when the late Senator LaFollette first proposed a valuation in the form of an amendment to the Hepburn bill, then under consideration. Living costs were rising; concentration of industrial and railroad control had made great headway since the turn of the century; a "trust buster" was in the White House; the Interstate Commerce Commission was seeking restoration of the power to prescribe reasonable maximum rates of which it had been deprived by a Supreme Court decision in 1897; control of railroad accounting and capitalization was lacking; and rates could be advanced by the carriers without suspension, pending investigation of their reasonableness by the Commission.

It was under these circumstances that Senator LaFollette, fresh from tilts with the railroads during his governorship in Wisconsin, advanced the propositions that rates were excessive and that the railroads had unlimited power to go on taxing the people without let or hindrance. This power, he said, could be curbed only by a showing that the railroads were earning an exorbitant rate of return on the value of their property. And such a showing could be made only by a physical valuation of the railroads along the lines developed in the pioneering work of Michigan and Wisconsin.

The proposal, he later recalled, "seemed to break upon the Senate as a startling idea." The ground was unprepared and the measure found little support. Senator Newlands alone seems to have gone as far in his thinking on this subject as had the junior senator from Wisconsin. But as the bill was reintroduced from time to time, others gathered to the LaFollette standard. Railroad officials at first opposed the measure with all the power at their disposal, but gradually became reconciled to the idea as the conviction grew among their leaders that, owing to increased land values and reinvestment of earnings, a valuation made on a reproduction cost basis would amply support existing capitalization. The advantage of settling the persistent question whether, in fact, the railroads were overcapitalized seemed to have appealed at last to all parties concerned.

Such in brief is the popular explanation of the launching of the valuation project. Few realize that before this problem was discussed in the Senate the Interstate Commerce Commission was on record in favor of valuation. The powers conferred on the Commission by the original Act to Regulate Commerce were inadequate for the purpose of effective regulation of railroads. To make conditions worse, the courts nullified some of the vital powers which the Commission had thought were granted it by the Act of 1887.[3] Under the circumstances the Commission was powerless to remedy the varied evils which the Cullom Committee had disclosed during its country-wide investigation of railroad practices. The railroads stubbornly resisted further grants of what they regarded as inquisitorial powers. Manipulation, under-statement of earnings, creation of secret reserves, and other signal failures of the accounts to reflect the facts persisted.

The search for a proper method of determining the investment figures of the roads began, as a matter of fact, as early as 1888, for in the Commission's first annual statistical report the impracticability of building this cost item up to a sound basis from carriers' records was clearly set forth. In the meantime additions to the investment accounts continued to be made as the carriers saw fit. In

[3] See I. L. Sharfman, *The Interstate Commerce Commission*, 1931, Pt. I, Chap. I.

1900 beginnings in the development of a valuation technique were being made in Michigan (for taxation purposes, to be sure), and shortly thereafter in a number of other states—in some of which the purpose was specifically the regulation of rates.

The Commission's first official recommendation of a valuation came in its annual report for 1903, and it was repeated in 1905. As a result of the Hepburn amendment of 1906, which gave the Commission power to fix maximum reasonable rates and to supervise the setting up of depreciation and other accounts, the Commission, in its annual reports for 1907 and 1908, strongly recommended the undertaking of a valuation of the physical property of the railroads. The making of a valuation, the findings of which were to be incorporated into the carriers' primary investment accounts, became from this time on indissolubly linked with the regulation of capitalization.

During this period there came before the Commission several cases of a character which rendered the question of valuation of immediate practical importance. In the so-called Spokane case,[4] the Great Northern and the Northern Pacific confronted the Commission with valuations of their property made painstakingly by their engineers and experts to prove that the rates complained of were reasonable. While this case was under advisement, the Commission noted in its annual report for 1908 that "there is a growing tendency on the part of the carriers to meet attacks upon their rates by making proof, through their own experts and officials, of the value of or the cost of reproducing their physical properties."[5] In the ab-

[4] 15 I.C.C. 376 (1909).
[5] P. 84.

sence of an official valuation, both the Commission and the shippers were powerless to refute the data offered in evidence by the carriers concerned. It was impossible for shippers, observed the Commission, even intelligently to "cross-examine the railroad witnesses by whom such proof is made."[6]

In 1910 Eastern and Western carriers came before the Commission seeking authority for general rate advances. The Commission pointed out that it lacked information on which to base a judgment as to whether railway revenues were unduly low. Capitalization, according to the Commission's view, could not be accepted as representing the true value of the investment unless it could be shown that there was no watered stock.[7] But there was no way of judging the condition of overcapitalization except by a valuation of the physical property. Observing that it lacked authority to evaluate the carriers' property, such as some of the state commissions had, the Commission reiterated its belief in the need for a valuation:

This Commission has several times urged Congress to authorize a reproductive valuation of those railroads subject to federal jurisdiction. It is reported that certain railroad companies are making such valuations themselves, and the results may at any time be urged upon this Commission and the courts as a justification for higher rates. The interest of the public ought not to depend upon a valuation made entirely by the owners of these properties, no matter how honestly the work may be prosecuted.[8]

Such then are the events which culminated in the passage of the Valuation Act in 1913. Senator LaFollette's impassioned plea for a valuation to prove over-

---

[6] The same.

[7] *Advances in Rates—Western Case*, 20 I.C.C. 307, 320 (1911).

[8] *Advances in Rates—Eastern Case*, 20 I.C.C. 243, 305 (1911). See also p. 256.

capitalization and the excessiveness of rates, the Commission's long-standing belief in the advantages of such a valuation as an aid to effective regulation, and the practical issues presented by cases before the Commission, all contributed in proportions which can never be separately weighed to the passage of this legislation. Valuation, in short, was conceived as an essential step in the development of effective regulation of our railroads. As the Commission observed in its annual report for 1907:

From whatever point of view this question of valuation be regarded, whether of reasonable capitalization, of a reasonable schedule of rates, of effective administration of the depreciation accounts, or of the correct interpretation of the balance sheet, one is forced to conclude that an authoritative valuation of railway property is the next important step in the development of governmental supervision over railway administration. (P. 150)

II. THE PROCESS OF MAKING VALUATIONS

The Valuation Act did not prescribe the utilization of any single principle in arriving at the value of our railroad properties. As the purpose was evidently to arrive at a "fair value" for the properties, the general procedure indicated by the Supreme Court in 1898 in the famous case of *Smyth* v. *Ames*[9] was followed. The Commission was required "to ascertain and report in detail as to each piece of property other than land . . . the original cost to date, and cost of reproduction new, the cost of reproduction less depreciation, and present an analysis of the methods by which these several costs were obtained, and the reason for the differences, if any." It was assumed that on the basis of the figures thus derived a lump sum fair value figure might be obtained.

Insuperable difficulties were encountered in ascertain-

[9] 169 U. S. 466, 546 (1898).

ing a significant original cost figure. Strictly speaking, the original cost called for was the cost of every specific unit of property then used in the service. In only unusual cases, however, could recorded costs be traced to particular units of property, and all too frequently records of cost were entirely lacking. This was particularly the case where numerous amalgamations had occurred in the course of the development of a railroad system.

Another difficulty was found in the fact that costs had been incurred under widely differing price conditions. Many important railroads had held title to a substantial part of their property for the better part of a century. They had incurred costs in the decade 1830-40, as well as in the decade 1915-25. Does the addition of $1,000,000 expended in 1925 to the same amount expended in 1840 mean the same thing as $2,000,000 expended, let us say, at the war-time price peak? Only if prices remained relatively stable would costs incurred at widely different periods have the same significance. The appearance of exactness and reality which attaches to cost figures was thus seen to be quite misleading.

After some experimentation the Commission gave up the attempt to get original cost for specific pieces of property, except in the case of land and equipment. In lieu of detailed identification of property items the Commission made rough estimates and supplemented these in each case by a full statement of the financial history of the road, including the issuance of securities. These data were believed to give the maximum amount of money which could have been put into each railroad.

The act also required the Commission to prepare an inventory of the entire property of every common carrier subject to the Interstate Commerce Act. For carrying out this provision, and also the one which required the ascertainment of the cost of reproduction, the Commission organized an engineering section. The engineering inventory enumerated all the operating physical property of the carrier then in existence.

Once the physical inventory was completed, a cost figure had to be obtained by applying prices to the inventory units. The determination of the proper prices to be used involved much difference of opinion; but it was finally decided by the Commission that, instead of relying upon expert opinion, it was safer to take actual prices of some past period. For this purpose it was held that the range of prices over a period of five years, and in some cases ten years, previous to June 30, 1914 should be consulted in order to arrive at an average or normal price. In the determination of these average prices the carriers were asked to supply price data, accompanied by sworn statements as to their accuracy, and a check was made by consulting manufacturers of railway supplies and materials. On the basis of all this information the engineers of the Commission decided upon the price to be applied to the inventoried units.

The cost of installing materials and equipment in the actual railroad properties presented an even more difficult problem because of the uncertainty and variability of labor costs. An average cost over a period of years preceding June 30, 1914 was, however, again taken. The estimate of reproduction cost arrived at in this manner, as the Commission points out,

does not correspond with the original cost of producing the property as it was in fact produced. The present railroads of this country are the product of a process of gradual development. The narrow gauge road has passed into the standard gauge, the low class into the high class, the single track into the double track. Grades have been improved, curves eliminated. In the estimate of reproduction, all this is disregarded, and it is assumed that the existing property is reproduced by a single continuous impulse.[10]

The determination of a single lump sum value for the property as a whole presented the most difficult task of all. In the original act the Commission was not required to go further than to assemble all the data arrived at by the different methods and to explain the reason for the different results obtained by the different methods. Under the terms of the Transportation Act of 1920, however, it became necessary for the Commission to arrive at a lump sum value for each railroad which could be utilized as a basis for rate regulation and for the operation of the principle of recapturing excess earnings. In the determination of a single lump sum figure should the reproduction cost data alone be used, or should attention also be given to inventory values and to original cost and other financial data, even though the latter were admittedly incomplete? Should attention be given to market values of the outstanding securities? If attention were to be given to all these various factors what weight should be attached to each?

In the light of the Supreme Court decision in the case of *Smyth* v. *Ames,* decided in 1898, and subsequently followed, it appeared necessary for the Commission, if the rate base which it derived was to have any standing before the courts, to take into account all the elements which would be involved in the determination of a "fair value." The Supreme Court in that case laid down the following doctrine:

[10] *Texas Midland Railroad*, 1 Valuation Report 1, 115 (1918).

The original cost of construction, the amount expended in permanent improvements, the amount and market value of its bonds and stock, the present as compared with the original cost of construction, the probable earning capacity of the property under particular rates prescribed by statute, and the sum required to meet operating expenses are all matters for consideration, and are to be given such weight as may be just and right in each case. We do not say that there may not be other matters to be regarded in estimating the value of the property. What the company is entitled to ask is a fair return upon the value of that which it employs for the public convenience. On the other hand, what the public is entitled to demand is that no more be exacted from it for the use of a public highway than the services rendered by it are reasonably worth.[11]

It will be observed that in this statement as to the factors that enter into the determination of a fair value no *weights* were suggested as to the relative importance of the several elements of value. It was incumbent upon the Commission, however, if it was to arrive at a lump sum figure for the value of each road, to decide for itself what weights should be given to the various elements.

The method employed by the Commission prior to the Supreme Court decision in the O'Fallon case of 1929 consisted of valuing at 1914 unit prices all property, other than land, acquired before June 30, 1914 and still being used. The units installed after that date, but prior to June 30, 1919, were valued by means of indexes representing the relative price changes on the basis of the 1914 unit prices. The units installed in the third period, after June 30, 1919, were valued at net cost of additions less retirements. All land was to have value as of the current valuation year, measured by the value of neighboring lands. The single sum value of each of the

---

[11] 169 U.S., 466, 546.

railroads of the country was to be made up on this composite basis of reproduction cost as of 1914, estimated original cost from 1914 to 1919, ascertained original cost from 1919 on, current value on all land, and certain allowances for going value.[12]

Thus in the valuation of all property acquired prior to June 30, 1914, except land, allowance was made for reproduction cost as of that date, but that the reproduction costs of subsequent years were not given weight. Market values of bonds and stocks were not considered.

A discussion of the efforts of the Commission to make use of these basic valuation data is reserved to the fourth chapter of this division. This is because the difficulties which have been confronted by the Commission can best be understood in the light of the recapture experiment and of an analysis of the valuation theories which have for so long been the subject of legal and economic controversy.

[12] See *Excess Income of St. Louis and O'Fallon Railway Company*, 124 I.C.C. 3 (1927).

CHAPTER XVIII

THE RECAPTURE EXPERIMENT

The recapture principle incorporated in the Transportation Act of 1920 was, as indicated in the preceding chapter, an outgrowth of the plan to adjust the general level of rates so that the railroads as a whole would earn a fair return upon the fair value of their properties. It was seen that if the carriers as a whole were to earn a fair return on the railroad property as a whole, some individual roads, favorably situated, would inevitably earn more than a fair return, while others would be certain to earn less. What to do with the excess thus realized by certain roads presented a nice question, as did also the question of what could be done about the roads that obtained less than a fair return. As a solution of this problem a novel plan, said to have originated with President Warfield of the Seaboard Air Line Railway, was suggested.

This proposal, which subsequently became known as the Recapture Clause of Section 15a, provided that if any carrier "receives for any year a net railway operating income in excess of 6 per centum of the value of the railway property held for and used by it in the service of transportation, one-half of such excess shall be placed in a reserve fund established and maintained by such carrier, and the remaining one-half thereof shall . . . be recoverable by and paid to the Commission for the purpose of establishing and maintaining a general railroad contingent fund. . . ." The fund thus recaptured by the government was to be used "in furtherance of the public interest in railway transportation either by making loans

377

to carriers to meet expenditures for capital account or to refund maturing securities originally issued for capital account, or by purchasing transportation equipment and facilities and leasing the same to carriers."

The principle involved in this plan also appealed to those who were interested in preventing the railroads from obtaining excessive earnings. It constituted a restriction upon the total returns which favorably situated roads might expect to receive, and it promised to provide funds for the alleviation of the financial situation of weaker roads. In figuring the amount of income subject to recapture, the Commission undertook to use its lump sum valuation for each road as a base.

How this plan worked out between 1921 and 1930 is indicated below. In the accompanying table we show the aggregate earnings and rate of return of Class I roads and the amount of the earnings subject to recapture. The act specified 5.5 per cent as a fair rate of return for the years 1920 and 1921, and this amount was guaranteed for a six-month period following the return of the railroads to private management. It was left to the Commission to determine a fair rate for the future, and in 1922 the Commission set 5.75 per cent as a proper rate.

It will be seen that the rate of return for the carriers as a whole ranged from a low of 3.44 to a high of 5.96. Nevertheless in every year some roads earned in excess of 6 per cent, as is evident from the figures of income subject to recapture, shown in the last column of the table. The estimated aggregate liability of carriers in connection with the recapture provision for the years from 1920 to 1930 inclusive is $359,459,141.

Turning now to the way in which this principle has affected particular roads, we find unexpected results. It has turned out that many of the strongest roads show no recapturable income, while some of the weaker ones show

RATE OF RETURN REALIZED BY CARRIERS ON THE VALUE OF
THEIR PROPERTY[a]

(Class I roads only)

Calendar Year	Valuation of Carriers' Property[b] (In thousands of dollars)	Net Railway Operating Income (In thousands of dollars)	Rate of Return	Income Subject to Recapture (In thousands of dollars)
1921......	19,388,000	615,946	3.44	7,276
1922......	19,519,000	776,881	4.31	14,484
1923......	20,464,000	983,736	5.18	34,299
1924......	21,168,000	986,718	5.01	22,199
1925......	21,645,000	1,138,632	5.65	47,003
1926......	22,176,000	1,233,003	5.96	61,810
1927......	22,593,000	1,085,142	5.14	29,959
1928......	22,926,000	1,194,488	5.57	35,473
1929......	23,448,000	1,274,595	5.80	51,891
1930......	23,734,000	885,011	3.98	17,350

[a] Prepared by the Bureau of Statistics, Interstate Commerce Commission.

[b] Based on Interstate Commerce Commission's primary values as found under Section 19a, adjusted annually by adding the net increase in the carriers' book value of investment and an allowance for working capital, and deducting the annual increase in accrued depreciation. This, in short, is the method followed in the original O'Fallon case. When the valuation estimate found by the Commission in *Ex Parte 74*, 58 I.C.C. 220 (1920), adjusted for subsequent years by adding net additions and betterments at cost, is taken as the base value, the rates of return run about 0.4 per cent lower than those given in the table above.

A tabulation made by the Bureau of Railway Economics based on the Commission's valuation in *Ex Parte 74* gives rates of return which run from 0.01 to 0.1 per cent below those yielded by the Commission's calculations on the same *Ex Parte 74* basis. The discrepancy is attributable to a deduction in the Commission's calculation of annual accrued depreciation since 1921, and an inclusion of operating income from certain roads which are not covered in the tabulation of the Bureau of Railway Economics.

a substantial amount subject to recapture. For example, the Pennsylvania, the Burlington, the Northern Pacific, the Illinois Central, the Chicago and Northwestern, the

Lehigh Valley, and the Rock Island show no excess income available for recapture, while numerous roads now in receivership, such as the Seaboard Air Line, the Wabash, and the Ann Arbor, have substantial liabilities on this account.[1] This result is attributable to the fact that the basis of computing the excess earnings is the Commission's physical property valuation rather than the amount of capital stock and funded debt outstanding, which, in the case of these "weaker roads," is in excess of the physical valuation. While these roads have really been paying the penalty for having a bad capital structure, the result was none the less unanticipated. The operation of the principle has clearly not given to those roads whose financial position was precarious the relief that had been contemplated, and it has not served to increase the financial stability of the railroads as a whole.

The principle has also worked to the disadvantage of roads which showed large fluctuations in earnings from year to year. For example, the Denver and Rio Grande Western, regarded as one of the most difficult roads to operate, was for many years in receivership; in some years it barely met the operating expenses; and for five out of the eleven years in the period from 1920 to 1930 it made less than 2 per cent on the investment. Yet during the same period, thanks to a few good seasons, the recapture claim against it amounted to over $1,000,000.

Again, certain small roads, built for specific purposes, had large earnings for a few years, but having outgrown

---

[1] See the Interstate Commerce Commission's statement of estimated recapture liability of railroads from 1920 to 1930, 72 Cong. 1 Sess., *Railroad Legislation*, Hearings on H. R. 7116 and 7117 before Committee on Interstate and Foreign Commerce (1932), pp. 556-57; also pp. 8, 30, 99, 106, 502, 552.

their usefulness are now in a position where they can barely meet operating expenses. The case of the Yosemite Valley Railroad is a good illustration. It was built in 1907 to give access to the Yosemite National Park, but the tourist travel over it has never come up to expectations. During all but three of the years from 1907 to 1931 the road did not even earn its interest charges. In 1916, the year of the World's Fair in San Francisco, and in 1925 and 1926 when the construction of a large dam and a power plant at Exchequer, California, provided extra traffic, the road had sufficient revenue to meet the interest on its first and second mortgage bonds. There is no prospect of another such prosperous year, and the supply of timber in the territory served by this carrier— the freight revenue of the road is derived almost exclusively from forest products—is estimated to last at the most just 15 more years. Yet the road has a recapture liability for 1925 of $164,401.[2]

Two objections in principle have been made to the recapture plan. In the first place, it is argued that, so long as we have private ownership and management of independent railroad systems, there is no justice in taking property away from successful roads and lending it, or giving it, as was suggested in the *Fifteen Per Cent Case* of 1931,[3] to weaker roads. So long as investors buy securities of individual roads, it is urged that they must take the risks involved in that particular investment, and that they are entitled to the profits that are realized by that road— no more and no less. It is pointed out that the plan moreover involves an artificial and presumably wasteful di-

[2] See 72 Cong. 1 sess., *Railroad Legislation*, Hearings on H. R. 7116 and 7117, p. 94. For other illustrations, see the same, pp. 105, 106, 223-24, 256-61, 288, 295-96.

[3] 178 I. C. C. 539, 578-80 (1931).

version of capital into unremunerative channels. In any event, it is held that the principle could be justified only provided all railroad earnings were pooled or the existing independent companies were merged into one unified national transportation corporation.

The second objection, which would perhaps meet with more general agreement, is that the plan takes excess income away from a given road in good years and makes no provision for lean years. As Commissioner Eastman said, when speaking for the Commission before the House Committee on Interstate and Foreign Commerce: "It seems utterly unfair . . . if a carrier has earned excess income . . . in certain years when there was good traffic to penalize it and leave out of consideration years when earnings have been or will be deficient."[4] This policy is not only unfair, but may have economically ruinous results. It ignores a fundamental necessity in all business of setting up reserves in good times to provide for bad years to follow.

The shortcomings of this plan would be minimized if, instead of recapturing excess income on a yearly basis, a five- or ten-year basis were substituted. But there is no reason to assume that merely because a road has had a *net* excess of earnings for a given ten-year period it will be able to achieve the same results in the succeeding ten years. The net excess may have been the result of two or three years of substantial excess followed by several years in which there was a slight deficiency.

Another objection to this plan of using a ten-year average as a basis for computing excess earnings is that it would materially increase the work imposed upon the Commission. As Commissioner Eastman has pointed out:

[4] See 72 Cong. 1 sess., *Railroad Legislation*, Hearings on H. R. 7116 and 7117, p. 446.

It would be necessary for the Commission not only to ascertain the excess in every year, when there was an excess, but also to ascertain with equal precision the deficiency in every year when there was a deficiency, in order to determine the average result. That would, in the case of a good many carriers, increase the work imposed on the Commission. Of course there would be certain carriers that could be eliminated by inspection of returns . . . but wherever there was doubt about it it would be necessary to make a detailed investigation for each and every year.[5]

Aside from these issues of principle the recapture plan is open to numerous practical objections. The first of these is the endless litigation which is inevitably involved. This arises from the fact that the basis of computing excess earnings is the Commission's valuation of the property. Since the Commission's valuation has not been accepted by the courts as an adequate basis for rate regulation, the recapture of excess incomes as determined by the Commission can be contested in the courts. There are many legal issues which the carriers can raise in court with reference to the valuation base, and they could prolong through court litigation the payment of the recapturable income over a long period of years. This fact is cited by Commissioner Eastman as one of the most important practical objections to the recapture clause itself.

This possibility of contesting the amount of the excess earnings determined on the basis of the Commission's valuation is one reason why the railroads have not made special provision for meeting recapture obligations. A second reason is that the roads usually did not know until some years after the alleged excess had been earned precisely how much it would be on the basis of the Commission's computations. Whether or not this practice is defensible is immaterial now; the fact is that the railroads

[5] The same.

have not set aside funds with which to meet their liabilities. The result is often anomalous: in 1931, for instance, the Commission authorized the abandonment of a tap-line because it was not paying even its operating expenses, yet at the same time the Commission was forced to demand the payment of one-half of the excess income which the road had earned in 1922.[6]

The difficulties involved in collecting the money are shown by the following facts. The recapture clause has been in operation for over a decade. The total recapture liability of the carriers over the eleven-year period from 1920 to 1930 is estimated by the Commission to be in excess of $359,000,000.[7] Of this amount, up to December 17, 1931, only $10,717,922.97 has been paid by the carriers, and most of it under protest. This money is invested in government bonds and is held by the Commission in a special account. No use has been or can be made of it so long as it is subject to court litigation.

As matters now stand, the attempt to recapture the unpaid excess income, even if approved by the courts, would be as fruitless as it would be ridiculous. As Mr. Eastman, speaking for the Commission before the Committee on Interstate and Foreign Commerce, said:

For the moment practically all the railroads are financially

---

[6] There are many other minor grounds on which the recapture clause can be assailed. The requirements for the use of the recapture fund are too stringent for the fund to benefit weak carriers. Before a loan can be made from the fund, the Commission is enjoined to find that the applicant has adequate earning power to repay the principal and interest at 6 per cent. In normal times, any road that can meet the requirements can borrow from other sources at less than 6 per cent. The recapture clause, moreover, encourages wasteful expenditures on maintenance, for it is more profitable for a road facing recapture to reduce its net income by increasing its operating expenses chargeable to maintenance than to pay the excess to the government. (See the same, pp. 11 and 84.)

[7] The same, p. 568.

weak, and nobody knows how long this condition will continue. It is probable that the revival of their credit will lag considerably behind the revival of business conditions. . . . To the extent that we find amounts of any considerable size due in the proceedings now pending, there are few, if any, railroads which have cash enough on hand to pay them. . . . To obtain the necessary cash it would for the most part be necessary to issue securities to replenish their treasuries, and there are few which are now able to issue securities on reasonable terms, if at all. . . . There are better uses to which the slender railroad credit, so far as it is available, can be put than to raise cash to pay to the government excess income of the past which in most cases is more than balanced by the income deficiencies of the present. . . . Summing up the situation we [the Commission] are of the opinion that the difficulties, disadvantages, and dangers of recapture far outweigh its possible advantages.[8]

There is another complicating factor in the problem at this particular juncture which should be mentioned. When liability has been definitely established, the Commission requires the deposit of collateral security pending final payment. In some cases this collateral, originally adequate, is now greatly depreciated; but the Commission is nevertheless obliged to sell this collateral if the road does not meet the liability. Under the circumstances a road inevitably seeks in the courts a restraint against the enforcement of the Commission's orders. It will be seen also that even though the collateral were not sold at distressed prices, so long as it is on deposit with the Commission it is unavailable for other uses by the railroad.

The case against the recapture clause has recently been summarized by the Interstate Commerce Commission as follows:

. . . The present recapture provisions impose in their enforce-

[8] The same, pp. 9-11.

ment a vast expenditure of time and money upon both the government and the railroads, they provoke litigation over complicated questions of valuation and accounting, they encourage extravagant expenditures by the more prosperous companies when times are good, they hang like a cloud over the credit of many companies when times are bad, and under the present law there is no effective way of using the funds to public advantage if they are recaptured.[9]

In the light of the foregoing analysis of the principles involved and of the way in which the recapture plan works in practice, the conclusion appears reasonably clear that the clause should not only be repealed for the future but that the repeal should be retroactive in its effect. There is no prospect that any considerable proportion of the sums due could ever be collected. Moreover, the cost of collection, all factors considered, might well exceed the sums obtained. The whole thing should be written off as an engaging experiment which worked in unexpected ways and turned out badly.[10]

[9] *Fifteen Per Cent Case*, 178 I.C.C. 581 (1931).

[10] It may be of interest to note that not only the Commission but all the other interested parties have reached this conclusion. Among these may be mentioned the organization representing all the state regulatory commissions, shippers' organizations, the official representatives of all Class I railroads, the Short Line Railway Association, the Railroad Security Owners' Association, the association of industrial, business, engineering, and construction companies furnishing goods and services to the railroads, the Brotherhood of Locomotive Firemen and Enginemen, and the Association of Railway Labor Executives.

CHAPTER XIX

ANALYSIS OF VALUATION PRINCIPLES

In discussions of the problem of the regulation of the rate of return of railroads and other public utilities several different principles or bases have been given consideration. The primary bases are the market value of the properties concerned; the cost of, or investment in, the properties; and the cost of reproducing the existing properties as of the current date. In connection with some of these bases there are variations or refinements which will need consideration. The first suggested base may be summarily disposed of but the other two require more extended discussion. We shall seek to determine whether either of the other principles provides an adequate or fair basis for rate regulation.

I. MARKET VALUES AS A BASIS OF RATES

The regulation of the level of railway rates on the basis of existing market values involves, as has often been pointed out, an obvious fallacy. The value of the outstanding securities of a railway at the date on which regulation would be undertaken would represent a capitalization of existing earnings at the prevailing market rate of return on capital. If the earnings were $1,000,000 and the rate of capitalization were, say, 5 per cent, the value of the securities outstanding would be $20,000,000. If as a result of an increase in freight rates the earnings in the above case were increased to $2,000,000, the value of the property would become $40,000,000—on the basis of which the earnings are still 5 per cent. Similarly, if rates were cut in two and the earnings declined to

$500,000 the value of the securities would decline to $10,000,000.

Since the value of the properties thus represents merely a capitalization of the earnings, market value obviously cannot be used as a basis for judging the fairness of the earnings themselves. The value of outstanding securities is in fact no longer seriously advocated as a basis of rate making.

II. THE COST OF REPRODUCTION THEORY

The principle that the general level of rates should be based not on what railroads may have cost at the time they were constructed but upon what it would cost to reproduce them in any later year has had many supporters. Its justification is based upon certain general considerations as to the factors which determine values in competitive industries in a changing world. With fluctuations in the arts or methods of production, or with changes in the general level of prices, the cost of constructing a factory, let us say, varies accordingly. The values of existing factories, moreover, tend to move up or down more or less automatically with the changes in the cost of producing new factories.

The explanation is as follows: If conditions justify the building of additional enterprises at higher cost, existing establishments will receive a differential profit by virtue of the fact that their cost of construction has been lower. If, on the other hand, new competing establishments can be constructed at lower cost, then those already in operation will be at a disadvantage and suffer accordingly. Thus purchasers of securities of existing establishments will be willing to pay more for such securities at a time when the cost of construction is rising and they will not be willing to pay as much at a time when the cost of construction is falling. The explanation is sometimes put in the following terms: In considering the price which he will pay for any piece of property, a purchaser would weigh, along with other factors, what he thinks it would cost him to construct such a property new—this because such an alternative is usually open to him.

This general principle as to the considerations which govern value is well substantiated in general legal theory. It is perhaps not surprising, therefore, that the courts have been disposed to attach great weight to this reasoning and to hold that a railroad company, like any other business, is *entitled in law* to estimate value on the basis of the cost of producing the enterprise at any given date.

The most common objection to this principle is that the conditions under which the railway industry operates are different from those of private competitive industry. The assumed purchaser of a railroad does not, in fact, have the alternative of building another railroad in the same locality and according to the same model. As a financial venture the building of a competing line would be altogether hazardous, and the consent of the Interstate Commerce Commission for such a duplication of facilities would undoubtedly be withheld.

Moreover, although values in competitive industries may tend to adjust themselves more or less automatically to changes in the cost of producing new competing establishments, the situation is essentially different in an industry such as the railroads. Since we do not permit the building of new lines for the purpose of competing with existing routes, a line once constructed usually remains a permanent carrier and is protected in large measure from the competition of other roads.[1] Because of this

---

[1] There were, of course, conspicuous exceptions to this in the days of uncontrolled railroad development.

semi-monopolistic position it is argued that the theory of automatic value adjustment does not operate in anything like the same degree that it does in competitive private enterprise. It should be borne in mind, however, that the development of other forms of competition has measurably affected this situation.

It is also contended that under the operation of this principle security owners would receive an excessive return upon actual investment in periods of rising prices. Why give to railway owners an added return—at the expense of the users of railway service—when they have incurred no new costs? This argument sounds convincing, but there is another aspect of the matter which must be borne in mind. When prices and costs of reproduction are falling, instead of rising, the utilization of this principle would accrue to the advantage of the shipping and travelling public, and to the disadvantage of the railway owners. Unless it can be shown that the trend of costs is permanently upward, it cannot well be argued that the security owners would be certain to benefit from the reproduction principle.

The fact that the application of this principle produces different results in periods of rising and falling prices is responsible for an interesting and significant shifting of views on the subject on the part of the groups directly involved. In the nineties the cost of producing railroads fell sharply, in part because of the general decline in prices and in part because of improvements in methods of railway construction. When it became apparent that railways could be reproduced for less than their original cost the public adopted the view that the benefits of progress should be passed on to them in the form of lower freight rates. In the leading case of *Smyth* v. *Ames*, decided in 1898, the counsel for the appellants, William J. Bryan, argued vigorously for the reproduction cost theory. The railroads, on the other hand, though formerly favoring the cost of reproduction theory, contended that the important consideration was the actual amount of investment in existing roads.

With the subsequent rise in prices, particularly during the World War period, the views of both the railroads and the shipping public underwent another change. The carriers became staunch advocates of reproduction cost as the proper basis for rates, whereas the representatives of the public contended that such a principle was indefensible.

Since costs of reproduction remained relatively high, even after the decline of prices in 1920, the attitude of the public and the railroads remained unchanged for some years. But since the drastic price declines which began in 1929 the balance of advantage has again shifted. While no formal admissions have as yet been made it is clear that it would now be advantageous for the railroads to utilize investment as a basis for rates and for the shippers to have rates based upon the cost of reproduction.

While this evidence that neither the general public nor the railways are without bias has no bearing on the validity of the principle itself, it nevertheless serves to clarify the nature of the problem. If we were sure to have only very gradual changes in prices, neither side would at any time derive any material advantages from the application of this theory. With stable prices the cost of reproduction would not differ widely from actual cost. The significance of this aspect of the problem will be considered in connection with the study of the cost, or investment, theory, to a discussion of which we now turn.

III. THE COST, OR INVESTMENT, THEORY

The principle which has perhaps had the greatest support from students of the problem is that if rates are to be fair they must be based upon the cost of the railway enterprise. There is a certain simplicity of appeal in the proposition that a property is worth what it cost and that the return permitted to the owners of a railway should be determined on the basis of their actual investment. The advantage of this principle is stated as follows by Mr. Justice Brandeis:

Where the financing has been proper, the cost to the utility of the capital required to construct, equip, and operate its plant, should measure the rate of return which the Constitution guarantees opportunity to earn. . . . The rate base would be ascertained as a fact, not determined as matter of opinion. It would not fluctuate with the market price of labor, or materials, or money. It would not change with hard times or shifting populations. It would not be distorted by the fickle and varying judgments of appraisers, commissions, or courts. It would, when once made in respect to any utility, be fixed, for all time, subject only to increases to represent additions to plant, after allowance for the depreciation included in the annual operating charges.[2]

The ideal condition for the utilization of the cost or investment principle would be one in which it would be applied from the beginning of railroad construction. Then it would be possible to include in the investment all the original outlays, plus the additions necessary with the passage of years, with proper allowance for depreciation, etc. But as a practical matter, the movement for the regulation of rates arose at a time when a large part of our railway system was already constructed, and in consequence numerous complications presented themselves.

[2] See *Southwestern Bell Telephone Co.* v. *Public Service Commission of Missouri*, 262 U. S. 276, 306-07 (1923).

Cost records, back to the beginning, were not available, and in the process of the upbuilding of railroad systems there had been many amalgamations and many transfers in the ownership of securities.

In the absence of complete cost data, and in view of the fact that the investment of existing security owners was a very different matter from the money that had actually been put into the properties at successive stages over a long period of time, it was necessary to let bygones be bygones to a considerable degree and to start on some compromise investment base. Actual costs incurred in the future could thereafter be added to the base cost.[3] In such an investment base there should, of course, be no place for fictitious, or watered, capitalization; for by very definition the conception of actual investment eliminates all fictitious elements.

The conception of "prudent investment" projects itself in this connection. It is contended that in many cases, particularly in our early railroad history, investments have been made which could not be justified by considerations of ordinary business prudence. Why then should the public be asked permanently to pay rates which would yield a return upon imprudent expenditures?

There are two interpretations of the term "prudent investment," varying widely in their significance. The first is that in determining the investment *base* all costs incurred in the past which represented fraudulent purchases or obviously inflated cost entries should be excluded. Such a conception of course represents a mere refinement of the plain investment theory. There can be little dissent from this refinement as a matter of prin-

[3] For the actual procedures followed by the Commission under the Valuation Act of 1913, see the following chapter.

ciple—though in practice there may be real difference of opinion as to the merits of any particular cost item under consideration.

Under the second interpretation, investments, however honestly made, which later prove to have been ill-conceived, would be excluded from the rate base. It is urged that the public should not be expected to pay rates which would yield a return upon such investments. Under this interpretation the Commission, in determining the original rate base, would eliminate not only fraudulent or flagrantly excessive items but also costs which later events had proved to be unwise, that is, unprofitable. As for future additions, this "prudent investment" theory might mean either that the Commission would at the time pass judgment upon the wisdom or prudence of every particular investment, or that in subsequent years it would judge whether, in the light of events, these investments had been prudently made. There is much vagueness among writers on the subject as to just how far they would go in the utilization of this theory. The position of Justice Brandeis is, however, perfectly clear from the quotation above. Once determined as having been prudently made the investment is to remain fixed *for all time*. The Interstate Commerce Commission has been equally explicit.[4]

IV. APPRAISAL OF ALTERNATIVE PRINCIPLES

The primary fact to be remembered in beginning an appraisal of these valuation principles is that it would not make any essential difference which was used if it were not for changes in the general level of prices and in

[4] *Excess Income of St. Louis and O'Fallon Railway Co.*, 124 I. C. C. 3, 37 (1927).

the cost of constructing railways. If prices and costs were stable the original cost of production and the cost of reproduction would remain the same. Since, however, the general level of prices fluctuates, the utilization of the cost of reproduction principle would, as we have seen, yield values that differ materially from the original cost. The advocates of the original cost theory properly contend that such a principle would give in a period of rising prices a valuation base and a level of rates higher than necessary to induce the railroads to render adequate railway service.

The adherents of the original cost or "prudent investment" theory do not, however, escape the dilemma presented by price changes. Apparently neither Justice Brandeis in the statement quoted above, nor Commissioner Eastman in his statement as to the inherent fairness of the principle of reasonable original cost[5] as a permanent basis of rate making, is aware of the implications of this principle in a period of falling prices. In the case with which they were concerned in 1929, namely the O'Fallon case, the cost of reproduction principle would have yielded higher values than would the original cost principle. But at present price levels the utilization of original cost as a basis for rate making might result in rates substantially higher than if the reproduction cost principle were employed. The application of the original cost theory in a period of rapidly falling prices would give the railroads larger returns than would be necessary to procure adequate capital.

The weakness of the investment theory is even more apparent when one recognizes that the cost of railroads

[5] *Excess Income of Richmond, Fredericksburg, and Potomac Railroad Company*, 170 I.C.C. 451, 535 (1931).

may decline over a period of years because of technological improvements as well as because of changes in the general level of prices. Assuming that the general price level remains stable in the future the utilization of the cost of production principle would still mean that the benefits of progress would accrue not to the shipping and travelling public but to the owners of railroad securities. In his dissenting opinion in the O'Fallon case Justice Brandeis argued very cogently that, as an offset to high reproduction costs, allowance should be made for what he called "functional depreciation," resulting from progress in the arts of railroad construction, from competition, etc.[6] This is on the theory that the public is as much entitled to receive the benefits of progress in a monopolistic industry as it is in industries where competition prevails.

It is just as important, however, to make allowances for technological changes in connection with the cost, or investment, theory as it is with the cost of reproduction theory. In either case, as a matter of policy, it is necessary to face squarely the question whether the public is entitled to receive the benefits of progress in the arts and sciences. To accept the principle enunciated by Justice Brandeis, that prudent investment would give a rate base which would "be fixed for all time," is certainly to take one's stand against giving to the public the benefits of progress. To agree with the Commission's statement in the O'Fallon case, that this principle "would recognize and protect every dollar invested in railroad property, whether at high prices or low prices,"[7] would be to hold that railroad rates at this juncture (1933) should be high

[6] *St. Louis and O'Fallon Railway Company* v. *U. S.,* 279 U. S. 461, 516-534 (1929).

[7] *Excess Income of St. Louis and O'Fallon Railway Company,* 124 I. C. C. 3, 37 (1927).

enough to cover costs incurred during the period of highest construction costs.

In its statement in this case the Commission at one place did take account of the effects of changing prices on the investment theory and stated:

> By reason of the replacements of units of railroad property which are continually taking place, such a system would tend to adjust itself to changes in the general price level, but this tendency would be manifested so gradually and slowly that changes in rates necessitated by value changes could be made without violent disruption to business or any other interests.[8]

This is equivalent to saying that between 1913 and 1923, for example, replacements at higher price levels were sufficient to make the actual cost to the road equivalent to the cost of reproduction in 1923; or that within the last three years the railroads have been so nearly reproduced at the lower cost now prevailing as to nullify the effects of the price decline on the original cost theory.

In other words, when the cost of reproduction theory is attacked, the significance of price changes is accepted at full value, but when the original cost theory is being supported it is held that offsetting replacements render price changes of little consequence. If the Commission's contention in this statement were valid, it would not make the slightest difference whether production or reproduction cost were utilized.

The truth is that under no single principle of valuation can we escape the effects of the problems produced by general price fluctuations and by technological changes. Although it has shortcomings of its own, the reproduction principle has at least the merit of yielding

[8] The same.

to the public the benefits of technological improvements. Similarly, it is impossible to escape the effects of competition, of population shifts, and of changes in industrial and agricultural organization. The acceptance of either the investment or the reproduction cost principle as the sole basis of value for rate regulation would mean that owners of obsolete lines should somehow be permitted a return upon "every dollar invested."

There is another assumed advantage of the investment theory which requires analysis. Reference is made to the doctrine that the utilization of this principle would make the values of railroad securities stable, regardless of whether prices were rising or falling. If rates were readjusted upwards in a period of rising prices it is pointed out that the value of railway securities would obviously rise, and if adjusted downwards when prices were falling security values would decline. This is undoubtedly true, but it does not follow that *real* stability of security values is achieved when, in a period of rising prices, rates remain adjusted on a basis of original cost. In such a period it is taken for granted that money wages must be raised if *real* wages are to be maintained—that is, if the purchasing power of the laborer is to remain stable. Similarly, in a period of rising prices the returns from the investment in stock ought to rise if the stockholders' purchasing power is to remain stable. The difficulty with bonds in a period of rising prices is precisely that the money return remains fixed and the real income of the bondholder declines in consequence. Assuming that fluctuations in prices are to continue, the principle that railroad rates should be adjusted so as to prevent changes in the prices of stock is thus open to serious question.

When one views this problem in historical perspective,

it is clear that the emphasis upon original cost or "prudent investment" as the proper and altogether sufficient basis for rate regulation is the result of conditions existing in a particular era. The whole movement for the adjustment of rates on the basis of actual investment in connection with railways and public utilities generally came during a period when prices were rising. The railroads were, on the whole, in a prosperous condition, and the view naturally prevailed that the great problem was to insure that a public service industry would not take from the public, in the form of rates and fares, more than it was entitled to take. Under the conditions prevailing the utilization of the original cost or investment theory afforded the surest means of protecting the interests of the public from a potential octopus. As has already been indicated, the implications of this principle in a period of falling prices and declining costs were ignored.

The conditions under which these principles of valuation arose, and under which the Valuation Act was passed, no longer exist, and there is no telling when they will again exist. Not only has the cost and value situation been profoundly altered, but the railroads have come to be subjected to new forms of competition, which are undermining a large part of the railroad rate structure that had been built up over many years by the railroads with the sanction of state and federal regulatory commissions. As a result the problem has become not so much one of protecting the public against extortionate rates as one of stabilizing the financial condition of a great industry in which the American people are interested as shippers, investors, laborers, and taxpayers.

CHAPTER XX

THE UTILITY OF PHYSICAL VALUATION

In this chapter we shall review our experience in attempting to utilize the physical valuation data obtained by the Interstate Commerce Commission. It was assumed that the valuation thus determined might be used as a basis of rate regulation and for sundry other purposes. In connection with regulation the data were supposed to be used to ascertain, first, whether any particular road had obtained in any given year an excess of income subject to recapture by the government; and, second, whether the roads as a whole were earning a fair return, 5.75 per cent subsequently being fixed as a reasonable rate.

I. PHYSICAL VALUATION AND THE EARNINGS OF INDIVIDUAL ROADS

The valuation data obtained by the Interstate Commerce Commission were in fact utilized as a basis for computing the income of individual railroads which was subject to recapture under the terms of the Transportation Act of 1920. The payment of the excess income thus determined was, however, protested by the railroads mainly on the ground that the Commission's valuation data did not take into account all the elements which should be considered in the determination of a "fair value," as laid down by the Supreme Court of the United States.[1] In particular it was contended that insufficient weight had been given to current costs of reproduction in determining the values of 1920 and of subsequent

[1] See statement in case of *Smyth* v. *Ames,* 169 U.S. 466 (1898).

years. In due course a test case, involving an inconsequential road near St. Louis known as the St. Louis and O'Fallon Railway, was presented to the courts.

The Supreme Court of the United States decided, in a split five-to-three decision, that the Commission had not taken sufficiently into account all elements of value. The Court observed:

The report of the Commission is long and argumentative. Much of it is devoted to general observations relative to the method and purpose of making valuations; many objections are urged to doctrine approved by us; and the superiority of another view is stoutly asserted. It carefully refrains from stating that any consideration whatever was given to present or reproduction costs in estimating the value of the carrier's property. Four dissenting commissioners declare that reproduction costs were not considered; and the report itself confirms their view. Two of the majority avow a like understanding of the course pursued. . . . The Commission disregarded the approved rule and has thereby failed to discharge the definite duty imposed by Congress.[2]

Two issues are involved in the controversy over this decision. The first is that of original cost or prudent investment as an adequate basis of fair value; and the second is whether the Commission did in fact give sufficient attention to other elements of value. The Commission, and also dissenting members of the Court, did "stoutly assert" that prudent investment was a satisfactory sole basis of value, one which would be fixed for all time.[3] This the majority of the Court denied, citing the rule laid down in *Smyth* v. *Ames*, which prescribes that all elements of value must be considered.

As a matter of fact, however, the physical valuation

[2] *St. Louis and O'Fallon Railway Co.*, v. *U.S.* 279 U.S. 461, 485-87 (1929).

[3] See quotation from Justice Brandeis, above, p. 392.

data of the Commission are by no means the precise equivalent of prudent investment. They represent reproduction cost as of 1914, with land valued at current market prices in each succeeding year. Justice Brandeis in the dissenting opinion argued that the Commission had thus given sufficient weight to reconstruction cost, and he further found that the Commission may reasonably have concluded that "functional depreciation" as a result of technological improvements, competition, etc., counterbalanced fully what might otherwise have been the higher value of the plant. The issue was thus confused. If prudent investment was the proper *sole* basis of value why contend that *sufficient* weight had been given to other elements of value?

In any event, the moment it is admitted that other elements of value should be considered the question arises as to how much importance should be attached to each element; and this is a matter of judgment in which men will differ in accordance with their personal views as to the merits or justice of one theory of value as compared with another.

It is contended by many that if the Court insists that no single basis of valuation will suffice, it is then incumbent upon the Court to lay down a formula which would give the proper weights to be attached to the various elements entering into value. Otherwise, it is pointed out, it will be impossible for the Commission to establish a basic valuation which can be utilized in the regulation of rates. But the Court is opposed to the establishment of any binding formula, and holds that each case must be decided on its merits in the light of evidence then and there presented and weighed. The soundness of this position may be indicated by assuming that in 1910 the

Court had decided that original cost should always count for 30 per cent, reproduction cost for 60 per cent, and other factors for 10 per cent. In 1920 this formula would have resulted in a very high value, but in 1933 it would give a very low one. To establish a formula means abandoning the opportunity of judging a case in the light of existing conditions.

In the absence of a formula, and in the light of the O'Fallon decision, the Commission made another effort to arrive at a valuation base that would meet the test imposed by the Court. This effort is found in *Excess Income of Richmond, Fredericksburg, and Potomac Railroad Co.*[4] In this case much more weight was evidently given to the cost of reproduction in determining a final lump sum value. The original cost of the property, including land appraised at the 1920 value, was $25,012,663, to which the Commission added $1,513,000 for working capital, making a total figure of $26,526,000. The Bureau of Valuation of the Commission estimated the cost of reproduction, less depreciation and including land and working capital, at $31,827,000. After presenting these data, the Commission stated:

Upon consideration of the foregoing and all other facts of record pertaining to the value of the respondent's property as an economically developed, well maintained, and seasoned railroad, in operation as a going concern, we find the value thereof for rate-making purposes during the period March 1, 1920, to December 31, 1920, to be $29,600,000.[5]

This figure is just slightly closer to the reproduction cost than to the original cost figure. This is perhaps what

[4] 170 I.C.C. 451 (1931).
[5] The same, p. 509.

led Commissioner Mahaffie to say that "values found in this report have been determined largely from consideration of reproduction cost estimates prepared by our Bureau of Valuation."[6]

It is evident that in this case the Commission, like the Supreme Court, sought to weigh all elements of value and to arrive at a reasonable figure, all things considered. That the figure arrived at is, however, a mere matter of judgment is evidenced by the fact that the estimate did not meet with the unanimous approval of the Commission. It would not, therefore, be surprising if the members of the Supreme Court in reviewing the case might find themselves divided, and possibly again in disagreement with the majority of the Commission.

It is clear that the Commission cannot act effectively as an administrative agency unless it has definite rules of procedure—either a single basis of value or a combination basis that has definite proportions. It is equally clear that the Court will not—and should not—lay down an unchanging formula to meet the requirements of a changing world.

Another possible alternative is for the Court to delegate to the Commission the power to determine value in each case as it arises, the Commission's decision being binding and not subject to judicial review. Under this alternative the Commission, as now constituted, would undoubtedly have given little, if any, consideration to reproduction cost or market values, adhering strictly to prudent investment. Inasmuch, however, as such a procedure might mean confiscation of property, the property owners concerned have the right under the "due process" clause of the Constitution to have the case re-

[6] The same, p. 538.

viewed in the Courts. "The ascertainment of compensation is a judicial function and no power exists in any department of the government to declare what the compensation shall be or to prescribe any binding rule in that regard."[7]

The Commission is therefore apparently unable to utilize either its original valuation data, or revisions thereof to allow more adequately for other elements of value, as an automatic measure of a railroad's earnings which are subject to recapture. The same legal considerations of course apply to the utilization of physical valuation data for the regulation of the earnings of the railroads as a whole. Anyone who contends that this situation is unfortunate, and that the Commission should be given final power to determine fair value, is of course really arguing that the Constitution should be amended. So long as the due process clause exists the Court cannot delegate its responsibility. At least this is the view of the Court; and we cannot go back of that.

II. PHYSICAL VALUATION AND THE REGULATION OF THE LEVEL OF RATES

The constructive part of Section 15a of the Transportation Act of 1920 was supposed to be that which placed upon the Commission the responsibility of adjusting rates so that the roads as a whole would earn an aggregate *annual* income which would represent a fair return upon their properties as a whole. It was assumed that, on the basis of physical valuation data, the Commission would adjust the general level of rates upward or downward from year to year with a view to providing adequate

[7] Justice Butler in *U.S.* v. *New River Collieries Co.* 262 U.S. 341, 343-44 (1923).

earnings for the railroad system as a whole. We must now inquire how this plan has worked in practice.

Within a few months of the passage of the Transportation Act, the Commission made a genuine effort to adjust rates with a view to increasing railroad income. The carriers sought authority to "increase their freight revenues to a basis that will enable them to earn an aggregate annual net railway operating income equal, as nearly as may be, to 6 per cent upon the aggregate value of the railway property."[8] The Commission, after considering the high costs of labor and materials obtaining at that time, the probable volume of traffic, and other factors, granted increases averaging about $33\frac{1}{3}$ per cent for freight traffic and 20 per cent for passenger traffic. It was expected that this would give a return of $5\frac{1}{2}$ per cent. The effect of this general increase was, however, promptly nullified by the severe industrial depression which began in the summer of 1920 and continued until 1922.

The next case involving a readjustment of rates was instituted by the Commission on its own motion in November 1921 and resulted in a reduction of rates the following spring. The Commission observed that the recent increases in freight rates and passenger fares, which had been granted when business was active, were proving a burden. It was discovered that "high rates do not necessarily mean high revenues, for, if the public can not or will not ship in normal volume, less revenues may result from higher rates."[9] The rates were therefore reduced in spite of the fact that the carriers were not earning a fair return—on the theory that general business and the vol-

---

[8] *Increased Rates, 1920*, 58 I.C.C. 220, 246.
[9] *Reduced Rates, 1922*, 68 I.C.C. 676, 732.

ume of traffic would be stimulated by lower railroad rates more than sufficiently to counter-balance the losses incident to lower unit charges.

The next two cases to come before the Commission related not to the railroads as a whole but to those of a particular region. Carriers in the Western district applied in 1926 for rate increases on the ground that their income had for some years been below the equivalent of a 5.75 per cent return, and that their financial condition was seriously prejudiced. Although the Commission did not deny that the rates of return were below and were likely to continue below 5.75 per cent, it refused to grant increases on the ground that no financial emergency had been established, the roads apparently being in good condition.[10] This decision obviously laid down a new basis for determining the need for rate increases, one not in accord with the principles enunciated in the Transportation Act.

In 1930 the Commission granted an increase in class rates "to carriers in the Western group as distinguished from the Western district."[11] The decision was based on the established fact that these roads were not earning a fair return, that their financial condition necessitated higher rates, and on the ground that "this class rate traffic can reasonably bear such rates." It was, however, admitted that "the revenues obtainable from the increases in class rates herein authorized will not augment the earnings sufficiently to produce a fair return upon the carriers' property in the Western group as a whole. There is a limit to the maximum reasonableness of class rates if traffic thereunder is to move freely." Again factors other than "fair return" governed the decision.

[10] *Revenues in Western District*, 113 I.C.C. 3 (1926).
[11] *Western Trunk Line Class Rates*, 164 I.C.C. 1 (1930).

The final case involving a horizontal change of rates was the *Fifteen Per Cent Case* of 1931. Railroad earnings had been seriously impaired and the roads sought a general increase of 15 per cent. It was not expected that this increase would enable the roads to earn 5.75 per cent on the value of their properties as a whole, but it was hoped that the increase would enable them at least to maintain financial solvency.

The Commission permitted some increases but denied the roads a horizontal advance on the ground that it would probably do more harm than good. The Commission stated that:

> ... The facts set forth above show beyond question that there are elements of plain peril to the railroads in such an increase in freight rates as they propose at the present time. The chief dangers are (1) that at a time when transportation costs are of vital consequence to every industry it will stimulate new competitive forces already rapidly developing; (2) that it will alienate or impair the friendly feeling toward the railroads on the part of the people of the country which is essential to adequate legislation for their protection and the proper regulation of all forms of transportation in the public interest, and (3) that it will disturb business conditions and an already shell-shocked industry, and accelerate the tendency toward a localization of production.[12]

Physical valuation, it will be seen, played little, if any, role in the adjustment of rates during this whole period. Although in the first case it was considered in estimating the rate advances required, other factors also had to be taken into account; and other factors, moreover, determined the outcome of the experiment. The reductions in 1922 were not made with a view to decreasing excessive railroad earnings, but in the hope that lower rates might

---

[12] *Fifteen Per Cent Case, 1931,* 178 I.C.C. 539, 575.

increase traffic and revenue. In 1926 physical valuation was ignored and rate increases were denied on the ground that the financial condition of the roads in question was not precarious. The trunk-line class rate advances of 1930 were based on the twofold consideration of financial need and capacity of the traffic to bear some increase. The 1931 case was determined by general considerations in which physical valuation played no part.

During these years the level of rates was also reduced to some extent by changes in individual rates. These individual rate changes were initiated not with a view to affecting the general level of rates but merely for the purpose of establishing more satisfactory individual rates. The most important of these changes were carried out under the Hoch-Smith resolution, which directed the Commission to adjust rates with a view to relieving depressed industries.[13]

Experience has shown conclusively that it is impossible to adjust rates from year to year so as to produce stable earnings. In view of the changes which occur in the volume of traffic and operating costs it is impossible to determine with any precision what level of rates would be necessary to yield a given return. It will be seen that if, in the year 1925, for example, rates were to be adjusted so that during that year earnings would be satisfactory, they would have to be increased or decreased, as the case might be, at the very beginning of the year—otherwise it might be too late. To do this would necessitate gauging in advance, with a fair degree of accuracy, operating costs and the volume of traffic, and also the effects of rate changes upon the volume of traffic.

This basic difficulty has been clearly recognized by the

[13] For a full discussion of these cases see Chapter VII.

Commission. In the hearings before the House Committee in 1932, Commissioner Eastman testified as follows:[14]

I have gone over this history, not by way of apology for the Commission, but merely to show the great practical difficulties in attempting to maintain, even approximately, a constant level of railroad net earnings, regardless of changes of one sort or another in economic conditions. We believe, as this committee did in 1919, that it is impracticable to do this. That being so, we further believe that it is unwise and undesirable to continue provisions of law which create the impression that railroad net earnings can and will be brought up to a certain standard in periods when traffic is light for one reason or another, and that they should and will be brought down to that standard when conditions are favorable and traffic is heavy.

No effort was made to adjust the level of rates so as to yield a "fair return" over a period of years. Between 1921 and 1931 there were only two years (1926 and 1929) in which the roads as a whole earned as much as 5.75 per cent on the basis of the Commission's valuation. Nevertheless the Commission did not grant any general increase. It appears to have been assumed that, inasmuch as the act prescribed that the rates should be adjusted so as to produce a satisfactory *annual* return, there was no occasion for considering the average return over a period of years. Inasmuch as it was not deemed necessary to permit in prosperous years earnings large enough to make up for losses in less favorable times, the rates were as a practical matter almost certain to average less than 5.75 per cent over a period of years.

It is evident that the Commission assumed, between the years 1922 and 1930, that the railroads were faring well enough even though the average return was well

[14] 72 Cong. 1 Sess., *Railroad Legislation*, Hearings on H.R. 7116 and 7117 before Committee on Interstate and Foreign Commerce, 1932, p. 14.

below the rate that had been established. It should be noted also that on the whole the railroads were apparently satisfied with conditions, for it was only the Western group that applied for a general increase during this period. The significant fact in this connection is that the Commission was not using the valuation data as a basis for its policy, but rather the financial condition of the roads and what the traffic would bear.

We found in a preceding chapter that in the years from 1923 to 1929 the earnings of the roads as a whole, although averaging less than 5.75 per cent, were nevertheless high enough to attract an adequate volume of capital to the industry. It would appear, therefore, that the rate of 5.75 per cent, which was set in 1922 as a fair rate, was somewhat higher than necessary. The security owners contend, however, that the ability of the roads to attract capital was determined not merely by the existing rate of return but by the belief that the Transportation Act of 1920 gave assurance that the railroads would be maintained upon a sound financial basis in the future. This belief might well have been influential in the early years; but it could hardly account for the continued flow of capital to the railroad industry after it had become apparent that the rate level persistently yielded less than 5.75 per cent and that the Commission was not endeavoring to adjust the level of rates so as to yield a higher return. We must conclude, therefore, that fiduciary institutions and other furnishers of capital regarded railway securities as a good investment, relatively speaking, even though the roads were not earning the so-called fair return.

The real weakness of the situation is found in the fact that it was only in the good years from 1923 to 1929 that one could with assurance say that the return to the railroads was high enough to attract adequate capital. In 1921 and 1922 the rate of return on the Commission's valuation was 3.44 and 4.31 per cent respectively, while on the basis of investment it was only 3.09 and 3.87 respectively. For the period 1930-31 the return was 3.98 per cent and 2.46 per cent on the basis of the Commission's valuation, and only 3.64 and 2.25 respectively on the basis of investment.

The principle of not permitting the roads to earn more than a fair return in good years when they are certain, as a practical matter, to have less than that amount in bad years, inevitably results in financial difficulties whenever the lean years occur. If it were possible, as had been naively assumed when the act was passed, to raise rates in a period of depression and thereby obtain more revenue, it would be proper to restrict earnings in good years to the minimum set as a fair return; but since it is impossible to obtain an increase of revenue in depressed years it is obviously necessary to enable the roads—if this is possible—to build up reserves in good years with which to tide themselves over periods of restricted earnings.

Other issues are involved in this problem, such as the financial policies of railroads in connection with their capital structures generally; the payment of high dividends; and failure to provide for adequate amortization of bonds. These issues are discussed in other chapters.

We conclude from this section of the analysis that physical valuation data have not been used by the Commission during the past twelve years as a means of adjusting the general level of rates from year to year so as to yield the railroads a fair return. We agree with the Commission, moreover, that it is wholly impracticable to adjust rates so as to yield annually a given return, and that it is accordingly unwise and undesirable to continue these provisions of law. We conclude further that the Commission made no significant use of the valuation data in adjusting the rate level so that the roads as a whole might earn a fair return over a period of years, rate readjustments being governed by other considerations.

III. OTHER USES OF VALUATION DATA

Aside from rate regulation there are a number of other possible uses to which the Commission's basic valuation data have been or may be put. The principal uses are in connection with (1) taxation assessment; (2) acquisition of railroad properties; (3) condemnation proceedings; (4) determining proper capitalization in reorganization cases; and (5) loans by the Reconstruction Finance Corporation.

1. For taxation purposes. There are two ways in which it is contended that the Bureau of Valuation is important in connection with taxation: First, the Commission's valuation engineers are sometimes borrowed by states to make appraisals of railroad and other property for taxation purposes. While this may be regarded as a convenience it is not a proper function of the Commission to maintain engineers at public expense merely because they might, on occasion, be loaned for useful purposes. In any event experience shows that the training and experience of these valuation experts is not of a character to make them particularly well equipped for the purpose of taxation valuation, which involves techniques distinct from those involved in ascertaining physical values for rate-making purposes.

Second, it is said that the Commission's valuation data

are frequently called for by state commissions as an aid in determining the amount of railroad taxation. Let us see whether the data are important in this connection. Railroad tax laws require that the assessment be based upon commercial values rather than upon original cost or reproduction cost. Inasmuch as the valuation data of the Commission are not based upon commercial considerations, and in view of the fact that they disregard entirely the value of the so-called franchise, which depends upon earning power, their usefulness in the determination of taxation is negligible.

The Commission's property inventories are, however, of some slight use in allocating unit taxation assessments between different states. The assessment of railroad property for state taxation involves, first, the determination of the value of each railroad system as a unit, and second, the allocation of this unit valuation among the states in which the property of the railroad is located. The Commission's data may here sometimes be useful in enabling a state tax commission to apportion the assessment between different states, but even here numerous other factors must be taken into consideration.[15]

2. In acquisition cases. Many cases come before the Commission involving the purchase of one road by another in connection with merger operations. Experience shows, however, that the Commission's valuation figures are seldom of any use in determining a fair price. To cite a few cases:

The Ulster and Delaware Railway Company was valued by the Commission at $6,648,019. When taken over

[15] This statement with reference to taxation was prepared by Benjamin P. Whitaker, who is the author of the section of this report which deals with railroad taxation.

by the New York Central, the Commission, after extended hearings and arbitration proceedings, agreed to a price of $2,500,000. The Boyne City, Gaylord, and Alpena Railroad was valued at $1,706,500, but the Commission tentatively fixed $230,000 as the amount to be paid by the New York Central for that road. The Chicago, Attica and Southern Railroad was valued at $3,382,104. The Commission's examiner has recommended that the Commission fix a price of $215,000, but no final decision has been rendered. In the *Connecting Terminal Railroad Company Control Case*, the physical value of the terminal in question was $1,176,071; its purchase was authorized at $885,013.86. In all these cases commercial considerations obviously dominated the decision as to value. The physical inventories of the Commission, however, afford evidence as to the existence of the properties involved.

3. In condemnation proceedings. Where railroad properties are condemned by public authority one might assume that valuation data of the Commission would constitute a sound basis for payment. As a matter of fact, in cases of this kind the properties seldom have a commercial value closely related to the physical valuation, and when this is the case commercial considerations are likely to be given primary weight. Here again, however, the existence of physical inventories is useful.

Similar considerations would be involved in case the government should eventually take over the ownership of the railroads. The public would wish to obtain as good a bargain as possible, regardless of physical valuation. Inasmuch as government ownership is most likely to come at a time when the railroads are having difficulties, it would naturally be urged that the government should not pay for the properties more than they are *worth*. The price paid would be the result of bargaining.

4. In determining proper capitalization in reorganization cases. Thus far the Commission's valuation of carrier property has been given little weight in cases of this kind. In fact the only instance where it has been definitely used as a basis for determining capitalization was in the inconsequential *Knoxville and Carolina* case in 1922. In some cases the capitalization approved was much below what the physical values showed, and in other cases it was considerably above.[16]

5. In passing on loans by the Reconstruction Finance Corporation. In the hearings before the House Committee on Interstate and Foreign Commerce, Commissioner Lewis testified that, in passing upon carriers' applications for loans from the Reconstruction Finance Corporation "those in charge of that work state that this value record is one of the most valuable things available to us to measure the unencumbered equity in the property of a particular carrier."[17] If primary importance is attached to the valuation data in this connection the Commission is using an unsound basis for judging the safety of loans—for all experience shows that the only sound basis for credit extension is earning power. The fact that a road may a decade ago have been given a valuation by the Commission of $100,000,000 affords no basis for belief that a loan made now will be repaid; the fact that the physical valuation in 1922 of some unencumbered division was set at $10,000,000 does not indicate that a loan of, say, $2,500,000, would now be safe. If the earnings fail to materialize the value of the property declines propor-

[16] See Chapter XV.
[17] 72 Cong. 1 Sess., Hearings on H.R. 7116 and 7117, p. 544.

tionally; and in any case it is seldom possible to sell a division of a railroad property.

It goes without saying that in these various cases valuation data, when available, will be submitted in evidence. But the mere fact that the valuation records are referred to does not mean that they are actually used in arriving at a decision. Even assuming that they are used, it does not follow that the use is a wise one. In any event we must conclude from this brief survey that the use of the valuation data in these miscellaneous ways has been incidental rather than primary.

This is a convenient place to point out that the Commission's valuation data have performed one very important service, namely, in answering the question whether or not the railroads were overcapitalized. It will be recalled that the belief that the railroads were greatly overcapitalized was one of the reasons which led to the Valuation Act of 1913. The accompanying table shows the investment in Class I railroads as revealed by the books of the companies, the capitalization as represented by the par value of the stocks and bonds outstanding, and the Commission's valuation of the railroad property.

It will be seen that the roads as a whole are substantially undercapitalized and that the Commission's valuation figures vary but little from the railroads' own book values. While many roads were undoubtedly overcapitalized in earlier days surplus earnings have been put back into the properties in sufficient amounts to absorb all of the water and to provide a substantial margin of investment over and above the par value of outstanding securities. It remains true, of course, that there are certain roads whose capitalization is excessive in comparison with the fair value of their properties.

IV. SHOULD VALUATION BE CONTINUED?

It is clear from the preceding analysis that the valuation data have not served the primary purposes for which they were intended, namely, the determination of recapture liability and the adjustment of rates so as to give

INVESTMENT, CAPITALIZATION, AND VALUATION OF CLASS I RAILROADS
(In thousands of dollars)

Year	Investment in Road and Equipment[a]	Capitalization (Par value of stocks and bonds)	Commission's Valuation of Property[b]
1923......	20,673,220	17,591,135	20,464,000
1924......	21,484,888	18,177,399	21,168,000
1925......	22,058,034	18,098,164	21,645,000
1926......	22,375,334	18,256,527	22,176,000
1927......	22,873,060	18,297,036	22,593,000
1928......	23,248,298	18,607,051	22,926,000
1929......	23,835,519	18,822,429	23,448,000
1930......	24,393,164	19,006,276	23,734,000

[a] This book value does not include working capital and good-will. Investment and capitalization figures taken from *Statistics of Railways in the U. S.* Interstate Commerce Commission, 1930, p. S-7.

[b] Includes working capital. For a more detailed explanation, see footnote b to table on p. 379. Working capital accounts for from 2 to 4 per cent of the total value.

the roads as a whole a fair return. It is clear also that miscellaneous uses to which the value figures have been devoted have been of negligible significance. The question whether it is desirable to complete the valuation and to keep the figures thereafter up to date must therefore be squarely faced. It is estimated by the Commission that the valuation project upon which it has been engaged for so long, will be virtually completed by June 30,

1934.[18] After that date the task would be one of keeping the existing records up to date.

The first question to be considered is the nature of the unfinished work of valuation. To understand what is lacking it is necessary to recall briefly the history of the project. The first stage involved the making of physical inventories of all existing properties, and the field work on this task was practically completed by 1920. After that it was necessary to evaluate these physical properties in accordance with the principles previously determined, and also to take account of the net changes in property account year by year thereafter. For all of the important roads this task has been completed up to 1928. For the years since that time, however, the work of bringing the net changes in property accounts up to date is still unfinished—even for some of the more important roads. The unfinished work is therefore an integral part of the project as a whole.

When the task is finished we shall have a virtually complete physical inventory of actual units of railroad property; and we shall also have for each road an aggregate valuation which represents, since 1920, actual cost for all items except land, with reproduction cost playing a role in the valuation figures prior to 1914.[19]

What would be involved after 1934 is merely the compilation of net changes in inventories. It would be necessary for the Commission to check the accuracy of the accounts of each railroad as submitted, and also to check from time to time the actual physical units of property.

[18] It is necessary to say *virtually* because in some cases it may prove impossible to obtain promptly the necessary records.

[19] It is estimated that 66 per cent of the valuation figures now represent definitely established cost.

In keeping the physical inventory, allowance must of course be made for physical depreciation, which involves the use of appraisers of property if the depreciation account is to be kept with a maximum of accuracy. This supervisory function is closely analogous to that performed by the Comptroller of the Currency in connection with the national banks. Reports are required periodically from all banks and in addition the national bank examiners visit the banks and check over the loans and collateral.

It would not be necessary, however, to revalue the property from year to year to take account of changes in the level of prices. All that is necessary in this connection is for the Commission to keep up to date its price index of railway materials for the different sections of the country—which is a routine matter. With such an index available it is then a simple matter in case of need for the Commission to apply the index to its valuation figures in order to arrive at an estimate of the cost of reproduction of any given road, or, for that matter, of the railroads as a whole.

Our conclusion is that it is important that the valuation work of the Commission be completed and that thereafter the inventories be kept up to date. We say this notwithstanding the fact that experience has shown that the recapture provision should be repealed, that the general level of rates cannot be adjusted so as to yield a fair return from year to year, and that the Commission has not used its valuation data in regulating earnings over a period of years. The primary reason for this conclusion is that in cases where the railroads contend that established rates are confiscatory the inventories of physical property and the Commission's cost data are of genuine importance.

While few cases involving confiscation have come before the courts except in connection with the recapture plan, which involved the actual taking away of property from given railroads, and while it is not likely that many confiscation cases will arise in the future, particularly if the roads are consolidated into a few large systems, there is always the possibility that some railroads might appeal to the courts on the ground that individual rates or rates in general are so low as to amount to confiscation. Whenever a confiscation case arose the railroads would present evidence before the courts to show that they were not receiving a fair return. Although the court under its procedure would presumably take into account various elements entering into fair value, it would be important for them to have the Commission's data as to physical valuation and also its estimate as to reproduction cost as a check upon the data submitted by the roads. One does not need to adhere to the view that cost of production is a satisfactory single basis of value to recognize the importance of the Commission's data in arriving at a fair value.

If we should eventually have government ownership, naturally no further confiscation cases would arise. Even so, it would be desirable for us to have an inventory of the units of railroad property. An accurate inventory of physical properties is essential to effective business administration, whether the business is run by private enterprise or by the government.

V. CONCLUSIONS

The analysis of this division of our study shows how and why the attempt to regulate the general level of rates on the basis of valuation data as provided under the

Transportation Act of 1920 has failed. The Commission has not been able to make effective use of its valuation data either for the purpose of determining recapture liability or in adjusting the rate level so as to yield a fair return on railway property. We have found, moreover, that no single principle of valuation, either original cost (prudent investment), or reproduction cost, or market valuations of securities, can be used as a definite permanent basis of rate adjustment. We live in a dynamic world and we must accordingly have a pragmatic theory of rates.

Such a theory of rates in fact underlies the suggestion by the Interstate Commerce Commission for a new rule of rate making, and it is also embodied in the Rayburn bill for the amendment of the Interstate Commerce Act which was introduced in the House of Representatives on April 27, 1932. This bill reads:

In the exercise of its power to prescribe just and reasonable rates the commission shall give due consideration, among other factors, to the effect of rates on the movement of traffic; to the need, in the public interest, of adequate and efficient railway transportation service at the lowest cost consistent with the furnishing of such service; and to the need of revenues sufficient to enable the carriers, under honest, economical, and efficient management, to provide such service.

The Commission's suggested rule is that "in regulating the general level of rates, fares, and charges the Commission shall, among other things, be guided by the need for producing, so far as possible, revenues which will be sufficient for the maintenance of an adequate national railway transportation system; and also to recognize the principle that the railroads may justly earn a

surplus in times of prosperity as a safeguard against deficiencies in times of depression."

Both of these suggested rules of rate making allow for
flexibility in administration, emphasize the duty of the
carriers to provide the most efficient possible transportation service, and recognize the necessity of providing revenues sufficient to permit the roads to obtain the capital
that is necessary for the efficient conduct of transportation.

We have discussed in previous chapters the problem
presented by the unbalanced capital structure of certain
railroad corporations, and we have also shown the obsolete character of many railroad properties.[20] We shall
discuss in a later chapter the problems involved in increasing railroad efficiency.[21] Given a railroad system
without obsolete lines, with properly adjusted capital
structure, and with increased efficiency of operation, this
rule of rate making will amply safeguard the public
interest.

[20] See Chapter VIII and Part III.
[21] See Chapter XXXVI.

PART V
WATER TRANSPORTATION

INTRODUCTORY STATEMENT

It is the purpose of this division of our study to determine the place of waterways, particularly inland canals and rivers, in our national transportation system. The analysis is divided into three parts. We give first a brief account of American waterway history and policy, indicating the nature and extent of the country's waterway program at the present time; second, we compare in general terms the cost of water and rail transportation; and, third, we study certain specific projects with a view to determining the inclusive cost of transportation on these waterways.

Before beginning this analysis of the relative cost of rail and water transportation, it is necessary to make a differentiation between the various types of water transportation.

The ocean and the Great Lakes are highways ready made by nature—the only construction costs involved pertaining to the provision of harbor facilities. Such agencies, of course, stand in a class apart so far as costs are concerned. In a second class of waterways may be placed such short connecting channels as the Suez, the Panama, and the Soo canals. In the first and second cases the provision of a relatively short artificial channel saves an ocean journey of several thousand miles; in the case of the Soo a channel little more than a mile in length makes possible without transshipment a long uninterrupted journey from the head of Lake Superior to the lower lakes. Such canals are obviously not analogous to railways or long inland water routes. In a third class are a few naturally navigable rivers which require little dredging or other improvement, the best example of which is perhaps the Rhine river of Europe. A fourth type consists of canalized rivers and canals, which, like the railroads, involve large initial construction costs for the highway itself and also large annual maintenance charges. Practically all of the American streams unfortunately require extensive canalization work to render them navigable for purposes of commerce. It is this fourth class alone which requires analysis here, for it is only where there are large construction costs that the economic feasibility of waterways has been called in question.

CHAPTER XXI

WATERWAY HISTORY AND POLICY

Inland water transportation played a role of tremendous importance in the early development of this country. Until almost the middle of the nineteenth century, in fact, our economic expansion was primarily determined by the location of rivers and canals. In the third quarter of the nineteenth century, however, river transportation began to decline rapidly in importance, and before the end of the century a large part of the canal mileage had been abandoned. The result was that in the decade of the nineties a movement was inaugurated for the rehabilitation of our numerous inland waterways under the leadership of the national government. In this chapter we present a brief survey of this history and indicate the present status of the waterway development, thus preparing the way for the economic analysis of the following chapter.

I. WATER TRANSPORTATION TO 1890

Canal construction began in a small way in Virginia and the New England states shortly before 1800, but it was not until the second quarter of the nineteenth century that canal transportation became important. The completion of the Erie Canal in 1825 led to a period of very rapid canal development. The movement for the construction of canals spread not only to those states which were in need of lines of communication with the West but it led to comprehensive water transportation plans within the Western states themselves. By 1838 indebtedness had been incurred by eighteen states to the extent of $60,201,551 for canals, $42,871,084 for railways, and $6,618,868 for public roads.[1] In a few states, notably New Jersey and Delaware, canals were constructed by private enterprise.

With all these early canals it was assumed, as had been the case with turnpike roads, that the full cost of transportation should be borne by the shipper. Accordingly, tolls were levied for the use of property constructed and maintained by the state. Few, if any,[2] of the canals, however, yielded returns sufficient to cover both capital charges and maintenance expenses. The panic of 1837 and the ensuing depression wrecked the hopes that had been entertained of deriving large financial revenues from state canal (and railway) systems. The Pennsylvania canals proved a complete financial failure. Almost the entire system was sold to railroad companies in 1857 and 1858, the net loss to the state being put at $59,440,078.[3]

The New York system of canals, which included the Erie and numerous connecting channels, made a much better showing. However, even this system had to be supported in substantial part from general tax resources. This system was constructed in four stages: (a) 1817 to 1836; (b) 1836 to 1862; (c) 1862 to 1882; and (d) 1894 to 1897. (The new barge system was authorized in

[1] E. L. Bogart, *Economic History of the United States*, p. 206.

[2] The Illinois and Michigan Canal is reported by the Illinois Canal Commissioners as having paid for itself and yielded a profit to the state up to 1871 of $97,742.41 (*Annual Report*, 1872, p. 4), but included in the revenues were the proceeds of land grant sales. The total cost of the project was $9,513,021.50. Up to 1885 the net receipts from operation had been $2,919,040.61, while receipts from land grant sales amounted to $5,892,707.96. (*Preliminary Report of Inland Waterway Commission*, 1908, p. 249). It was the land subsidy, therefore, which made it possible for the canal nominally to pay out.

[3] *Tenth Census of the United States*, 1880, Vol. IV, pp. 7-8.

1903.) In no single period did the revenues from the project cover all of the overhead and maintenance charges. Up to September 30, 1882, taxpayers had contributed $27,272,538 net; and there remained a capital debt of $6,259,661, the liquidation of which remained a permanent charge against the taxpayers. To September 30, 1902 the net cost of the canals to the taxpayers was $67,055,666.[4]

In general it may be said that the canal system reached its high point of development in the decade of the fifties, though in some cases the peak of traffic was reached much later. The New York canal system, for example, carried its greatest traffic in 1872, while 1882 was the peak year on the Illinois and Michigan Canal. Abandonments began before the Civil War and as many as 314 miles had been given up as early as 1860. In summarizing the condition of the canals in 1880 the Tenth Census states that "1956.56 miles are now abandoned and a large portion of the remaining 2515.04 miles is not paying expenses."[5]

The deepening and improving of river channels did not become important until after the advent of the steamboat. So long as commerce was handled by canoes, keelboats, and barks, river obstructions were of no great importance. Fulton and Livingston established a regular steamboat service on the Mississippi in 1817. Three years later Congress called for a survey of the Ohio and Mississippi rivers with a view to determining the most practical method of improving these streams for navigation purposes. The first federal appropriation for

---

[4] These figures are taken from *Annual Report of the Comptroller of the State of New York, year ending Sept. 30, 1909.*
[5] *Tenth Census of the United States,* p. 731.

river improvements amounting to $75,000 was made in 1824. Until after 1880, however, the expenditures on river improvements were comparatively small. Down to 1879 expenditures for all purposes on the lower Mississippi and its tributaries did not exceed $5,000,000, while those on the upper Mississippi approximated $11,500,000.[6]

River transportation reached its peak about the same time as did canal transportation. On the Ohio and Mississippi there was virtually no competition until 1850. New Orleans was the great entrepot of traffic for the interior of the country, while Cincinnati and St. Louis were the primary assembling points for traffic moving out. In 1840 New Orleans was the fourth port in the world, while as late as 1850 the population of Cincinnati was nearly four times, and that of St. Louis nearly three times, greater than that of Chicago.

After the Civil War the railroads became active competitors for the traffic handled by the rivers. Within the next 20 years most of the high grade traffic was lost to the river carriers, though low grade commodities continued to move in large quantities for a longer period. Before the end of the century, however, canal and river transportation in general had come to be relatively insignificant—the one important exception being coal traffic on the Monongahela and Ohio rivers. Transportation on the Great Lakes is, of course, another story.

It is commonly contended by advocates of waterway development that the sole explanation of the decline of water transportation in the period following the Civil War was the unfair competition offered by the railways. As a matter of fact, the railroads did commonly cut their

[6] *Eleventh Census of the United States,* 1890.

rates where water competition existed, raising them later when the competition had been effectively suppressed. They also refused to co-operate where traffic might move by a combined rail and water route; and in other cases they secured control of boat lines as a means of eliminating competition.

In fairness, however, it must be noted that the tolls on waterways charged by the state to cover interest and annual maintenance charges—inadequate at best—were steadily reduced and were shortly abolished altogether. In 1883 the State of New York abolished tolls on its state canal system, and in 1884 Congress abolished tolls on all federal rivers and canals, with the exception of the Panama.[7] The plain purpose of abandoning tolls, thereby shifting *all* of the capital costs and maintenance charges from the shipper to the general taxpayer, was to make it possible for the waterways to retain traffic in competition with railways which shouldered their own capital and maintenance charges.

During this first era of our waterway history—ending about 1890—the role of the federal government in connection with river and canal transportation was secondary to that of the states. The aggregate federal expenditures for waterway development to 1890 were approximately as shown on the next page.[8]

In presenting the amount of state government expenditures on waterways up to 1890 allowance must be made for the fact that in some cases the gross outlays were materially reduced by the receipt of tolls. Precise figures are not available, but after studying the relevant

[7] See p. 4.
[8] Table from Bureau of the Census, *Transportation by Water, 1906*, p. 47.

data, we estimate that the net outlays of state governments amounted to approximately $200,000,000.[9] This figure compares with about $100,000,000, expended by the federal government on rivers and canals.

FEDERAL EXPENDITURES FOR WATERWAY DEVELOPMENT TO 1890

Mississippi system [including all tributaries]	$ 84,211,783
Seacoast harbors, rivers, and channels	87,763,503
Great Lakes harbors and connecting channels	37,522,937
Lake Champlain	1,133,660
Unallocated	3,408,903
Total	$214,040,786

II. THE PROGRAM OF WATERWAY REHABILITATION

The great decline of water transportation after the coming of the railways was not accepted by the public as evidence that rail transportation was inherently superior. It was believed that all that was necessary to revive canal and river traffic was to rehabilitate the waterways—make them deeper and provide them with better equipment. In recent years it has also been urged that they need to be articulated into a comprehensive national transportation system.

The main arguments in support of the rehabilitation of inland water transportation were as follows: First, it was believed that water transportation is inherently much cheaper than transportation by rail. It was contended that on the new barge canal traffic could be car-

---

[9] This estimate has been obtained by analyzing the financial results of all the important state canal projects for which data are readily available. Some of the funds used by the states were obtained from the national government. In 1836 and 1837, the federal treasury distributed to the states a little over $28,000,000 of surplus revenue derived from the proceeds of public land sales. A considerable part of this money was used by the states in promoting canal projects.

ried at a rate of .52 mills per ton mile as compared with 7.5 mills per ton mile received by the railroads—which indicated that rail transportation was something like fourteen times as costly as that by water. One of the most common statements was that a dollar would carry a ton of traffic 127 miles on the railways, 333 miles on the old Erie Canal, 1,250 miles on the Great Lakes, and 2,000 miles on the improved Erie Barge Canal.

The benefits to accrue to all classes of society as a result of this cheaper transportation were repeatedly set forth in language such as the following:

To your entire business interests it means cheaper freight rates. To the manufacturer it means direct touch with the great markets by a cheap, dependable, competing, and at all times freight-regulating route for their finished output and the cheaper assembling of their raw materials.

To the wholesaler and jobber it means opportunity for the extension of trade. It means that the great markets of commerce will be open to them to make of such opportunity what they will.

To the retailer it means increased population, increased opportunity and an expansion in business beyond any limit now possible.

To the wage-earner it means dwelling in a prosperous district under most advantageous conditions; an increase of opportunity and lower cost of living. To the man who owns a little home would come a rise in value that would make him more independent, and, with greater security of steady and remunerative employment, he could further improve his surroundings.

To the landowner and real-estate dealer there will come a greater demand, and with greater demand greater valuation and greater sales. It will mean that your city will be a greater and more prosperous city, a better one to live in.

Much as it will mean to all other classes the farming interests will be the greatest beneficiary. Indeed, as agriculture is the foundation of all industrial and commercial growth, it is first affected. It will mean increased markets and better and surer prices; it will mean greater earning capacity; greater social and educational advantages, through increased wealth. The growth of the cities will ever assure a home market for home produce and elimination of freight charges now deducted from receipts for long hauls over the railroads.[10]

The second purpose of the rehabilitation of waterways was to provide effective regulation of railway rates. It was pointed out that wherever railways were subjected to water competition the rates were substantially lower than elsewhere. To quote from President Roosevelt in a Memphis address in 1907: "Wherever a navigable river runs beside railroads the problem of regulating the rates on the railroads becomes far easier, because river regulation *is* rate regulation."[11] It appeared to follow that whether the waterways enjoyed any commerce or not the potential competition would force the railroads to carry traffic at lower rates, to the benefit of American shippers.

The third major argument was that the railways needed relief from an excessive volume of traffic, particularly in the form of low grade bulky commodities. This argument was first advanced strongly in 1906 and 1907 when, for a brief period, there was a shortage of railroad cars. In 1920 this argument was again advanced as a major reason why the St. Lawrence waterway should be constructed.

The second and third of these arguments do not merit consideration. It is economically indefensible to

[10] *Proceedings of the Fifteenth Annual Convention of the Ohio Valley Improvement Association*, Cincinnati, Ohio, Oct. 14 and 15, 1909, p. 9.
[11] *Annals of the American Academy of Political and Social Science*, Vol. 31, p. 3.

spend millions of dollars for the purpose of providing "potential" competition when we have available an infinitely less costly means of regulation. In the early days when it was uncertain how effective the Interstate Commerce Commission might be in the regulation of railroad rates, there may have been some point to the argument that waterways were needed for the purpose of preventing the railways from charging excessive rates; but this argument cannot be seriously advanced under present conditions.

With reference to congestion of railway traffic it may merely be noted that there has been none since the abnormal conditions which prevailed immediately after the war. Since 1924 there have been continuously large car surpluses, and railway facilities are adequate to take care of any probable growth of traffic over the next decade.[12] Even if a deficiency of railroad facilities existed it would not necessarily follow that the deficiency should be made good by turning to an alternative form of transport. There are no serious physical obstacles to the indefinite expansion of railway tracks and equipment. The practical question from the standpoint of the railroads is always whether there is sufficient traffic to justify an increase in facilities. And if perchance the additional facilities required were not provided by private enterprise and it became necessary for the government to supply the deficiency, the guiding principle as to what form the additional facilities should take should be determined by considerations of comparative cost.

The ultimate economic test to be applied to any particular form of transportation is its ability to render the

---

[12] For a detailed analysis see H. G. Moulton, C. S. Morgan, and A. L. Lee, *The St. Lawrence Navigation and Power Project*, pp. 159-67.

service required more cheaply than it can be rendered by other agencies. If waterways can carry many classes of freight traffic more economically than can railways, highways, or pipe lines they should obviously play an important role in a national transportation system. All other considerations are beside the point.

Before turning to a consideration of the relative costs of transportation by water and by rail under modern conditions it will be of interest to set forth the extent of our expenditures under the new inland waterway program since 1890. The trend of traffic growth is shown on page 471. Between 1890 and 1931 the total expenditures, federal and state, upon inland waterways were as shown in the table below. The figures cover maintenance as well as construction costs. They do not include any expenditures for flood control, for hydro-electric projects, or for the Panama Canal.[13]

FEDERAL EXPENDITURES ON WATERWAYS, 1890-1931

Mississippi system	$ 472,984,507
Intra-coastal canals and other waterways	104,903,915
Operation and care of canals	104,487,905
Examinations and surveys	8,221,374
Seacoast harbors and channels	515,954,872
Great Lakes harbors and channels	163,303,189
	$1,369,855,762

[13] The primary source of these data is the *Annual Report of the Chief of Engineers, U. S. Army*, 1931. Since the engineers' figures, however, include expenditures from the very beginning of federal appropriations, it has been necessary to deduct those made prior to 1890. For this purpose we have used the census of 1890 as adjusted in Bureau of the Census, *Transportation by Water, 1906*. The costs of maintenance and operation of the Soo Canal and of the works on the St. Clair River have been transferred from "Operation and care of canals," to "Great Lakes harbors and channels." For method of obtaining navigation expenses on the lower Mississippi, see below, pp. 498-503.

The item "Operation and care of canals" does not cover all the operation and maintenance charges for canals, for a figure of $26,052,456 is included for maintenance under "Intra-coastal canals and other waterways." The explanation of the separate operation item is apparently the method of making appropriations. The item "Seacoast harbors and channels" includes such inland canals as the Houston Ship Channel, and apparently all coastal rivers connecting with improved harbors. Without making a detailed analysis of every harbor project it is impossible to separate the expenditures on harbors proper from connecting channels. Accordingly, we are not able to present a precise figure as to the total expenditures of the federal government on inland waterways, exclusive of seacoast harbors and Great Lakes harbors and channels.

The first four items in the table above, however, give a total of $690,597,701, to which should be added perhaps $100,000,000 for expenditures on seacoast rivers and channels, making a total of something like $790,000,000 for inland waterway development, exclusive of ocean harbors and the Great Lakes.

Since these expenditures are made out of annual appropriations rather than from the proceeds of bond issues the federal government has had to meet no out-of-pocket interest charges in this connection. On the other hand, the government has received no interest on its investment.

Certain state governments have also made large expenditures for waterway development since 1890. The State of New York expended $9,000,000 on new construction on the old Erie Canal system between 1894 and 1897, and something like $25,000,000 on maintenance and interest between 1890 and 1905. Construction costs on the new state barge canal system between 1903 and 1931 aggregated $176,747,841, and maintenance and interest charges aggregated well over $100,000,000.[14]

The State of Illinois has expended on the Illinois River project $16,000,000 up to June 30, 1931.[15] In addition $18,000,000 out of the total construction costs on the Chicago Sanitary Ship Canal is ascribed to navigation.[16] Other states have also expended small sums on canal and river improvements. On the basis of these incomplete data we estimate the total state expenditures since 1890 at something approximating $330,000,000.

In addition to these expenditures on navigation channels, substantial outlays have also had to be made for the provision of terminals. In some cases terminal facilities are provided by municipalities or by private industries making use of waterways. In New York, however, the state has constructed terminals for the barge canal system. In connection with the Mississippi River the federal government has loaned a part of the money required by cities in providing terminal facilities. In all these cases a charge is made for the use of the terminals; but the revenues thus derived have defrayed but a small portion of the cost.

The data are not available to give an accurate figure for total expenditures upon terminal facilities. The 66 terminals and grain elevators provided by the State of New York cost over $26,000,000. Since this figure has

[14] For detailed figures, see below, pp. 473-76.
[15] *Report of the Chief of Engineers,* 1931, p. 1269.
[16] *Report of the Deep Waterway Committee of the Chicago Commercial Association,* 1906, p. 20.

already been included in the cost of the Barge Canal system, it should not be counted again; but it is useful here in indicating the magnitude of the terminal problem. On the Mississippi River, there are at least 48 points where some sort of terminal facilities have been provided, but no inclusive cost estimates are available. A special study that has been made indicates, however, that in 11 of the larger cities approximately $6,000,000 has been expended during the last ten years for terminal facilities.[17] Expenditures on terminals for the entire Mississippi River since 1890 must have run several times this amount.

No data are available as to the amount of expenditures for terminal facilities on the Ohio River system, most of which have been provided by private enterprise. There are as many as 255 terminals on the Ohio proper, only ten of which have been provided by municipalities, the remainder being owned and operated by private companies.[18] Since the traffic is composed largely of bulky, heavy commodities, very expensive mechanical appliances are required, such as electrically operated gentry and hoisting cranes, overhead steel barge unloaders, mechanical yard loaders, elevators with chute dumps, etc. Inasmuch as the traffic on the Ohio is about six times that on the Erie, the terminal facilities undoubtedly represent an investment of a good many millions of dollars.

There are no available data with reference to terminal facilities on other rivers and canals, nor is there any in-

[17] F. J. Lisman, *Analysis of the Inland Waterways Corporation's Annual Report for 1931*, p. 27.

[18] *Transportation in the Mississippi and Ohio Valleys*, Corps of Engineers, U. S. Army, and U. S. Shipping Board, 1929, pp. 123-38. The list above excludes terminals owned by railroad companies.

formation as to the value of land sites which have been contributed by localities. For the entire country, exclusive of the New York Barge Canal system, it would seem that an estimate of $60,000,000 would be conservative.

Mention should also be made here of the fact that lighting facilities on inland waterways are provided at public expense by the Bureau of Lighthouses of the United States Department of Commerce. Capital cost data are not available, but the annual outlay for the fiscal year ending June 30, 1932, for rivers was $407,762.[19]

Summarizing the foregoing data, we find that there has been spent upon internal waterway development since 1890 roughly $1,177,000,000. This is exclusive of expenditures on the Great Lakes and seacoast harbors.

III. THE FUTURE PROGRAM OF WATERWAY DEVELOPMENT

The program of waterway development, begun a generation ago, is still far from complete. In fact, the present program of development, if carried out, will apparently involve expenditures over the next five or ten years exceeding the total outlays by the federal government for navigation for the entire period from 1890 to 1931, namely, about $790,000,000. The program calls for canalization not only of so-called trunk line waterways, such as the Ohio and Mississippi systems, but also of the branches and sub-branches thereof and of a large number of other separate projects. Without an exhaustive study of the United States Army Engineers' reports it would not be possible to give a complete list of waterway improvements now being made by the federal government. The following list gives *authorized* projects for which allotments were made for the fiscal year 1931-32 and an

---

[19] Data furnished by the Bureau of Lighthouses.

incomplete list of allotments for the year 1932-33. In order to present a complete picture we include ocean and lake harbors. The amounts given indicate the extent and character of expenditures rather than direct outlays, since a certain number of allotments made each year are subsequently transferred to other projects.

1. PRINCIPAL OCEAN HARBORS[a]

	Allotments 1931-32	Allotments 1932-33
New York Bay and Harbor:		
Supervisor, New York Harbor ....$	193,500	$ 320,000
New York Harbor	415,000	120,000
Bay Ridge and Red Hook Channels	492,200	561,200
Buttermilk Channel	45,000	9,100
East River	11,135,800	444,000
Harlem River	80,000	9,000
Newtown Creek	130,000	103,000
Hudson River Channel	386,000	330,000
West Chester Creek	—	33,600
East Chester Creek	—	150,000
Collection and removal of drift	122,000	38,000
Portland, Maine	—	65,000
Boston	32,500	34,000
Philadelphia:		
Delaware River at Camden	267,410	34,910
Delaware River to sea	2,452,960	3,381,000
Baltimore	1,378,360	917,200
Norfolk	917,400	—
Charleston	8,000	49,205
Savannah	905,300	300,000
Jacksonville:		
St. John's River to sea	449,000	543,550
Mobile	612,000	228,500
New Orleans, Louisiana:		
Southwest Pass—Mississippi	290,000	100,000
Galveston	126,000	23,000
Los Angeles	401,500	700,000
San Diego	395,000	154,000
San Francisco	368,000	413,000
Portland, Oregon:		
Columbia River at mouth	610,000	710,000
Columbia River and Lower Willamette River	975,000	675,200
Seattle	95,000	22,000

2. GREAT LAKES HARBORS AND TRIBUTARY STREAMS

Survey Northern and Northwestern Lakes	197,300	143,250
Grand Marais, Minnesota	10,000	47,000

	Allotments 1931-32	Allotments 1932-33
Duluth-Superior, Minnesota, Wisconsin ....$	284,241	$ 49,000
Ashland, Wisconsin	230,000	62,500
Ontonagon Harbor, Michigan	55,000	—
Keweenaw Waterway, Michigan	60,000	1,285,000
Marquette, Michigan	14,300	26,000
Warroad Harbor and River, Minnesota	13,500	12,000
Manistique, Michigan	4,500	6,000
Menominee Harbor and River, Michigan	29,000	10,000
Oconto, Wisconsin	—	8,000
Green Bay, Wisconsin	37,000	12,000
Fox River, Wisconsin	151,000	165,000
Sturgeon Bay, Wisconsin	100,000	1,500
Algoma, Wisconsin	5,500	96,000
Kewaunee, Wisconsin	10,000	2,000
Two Rivers, Wisconsin	45,000	1,000
Manitowoc, Wisconsin	7,000	4,000
Sheboygan, Wisconsin	18,000	9,000
Port Washington, Wisconsin	6,000	—
Milwaukee	485,000	50,500
Racine, Wisconsin	12,500	4,000
Kenosha, Wisconsin	4,000	—
St. Joseph, Michigan	127,000	5,000
South Haven, Michigan	7,000	—
Saugatuck and Kalamazoo River, Michigan	—	20,000
Holland, Michigan	4,000	192,500
Grand Haven and Grand River	95,000	80,650
Muskegon, Michigan	679,100	139,100
White Lake, Michigan	4,000	3,500
Eagle, Michigan	6,000	—
Ludington, Michigan	42,000	6,000
Manistee, Michigan	11,000	16,700
Charlevoix, Michigan	—	3,000
Portage Lake, Michigan	4,000	5,000
Frankfort, Michigan	395,000	142,000
Monroe, Michigan	20,755	617,000
Waukeegan, Illinois	306,000	149,000
Chicago	34,550	16,748
Chicago River, Illinois	61,511	4,000
Calumet Harbor and River, Illinois	394,246	—
Indiana Harbor	286,000	63,000
Michigan City, Indiana	113,000	—
St. Marys River, Michigan	2,009,338	1,879,338
St. Clair River, Michigan	11,000	230,000
Channels in Lake St. Clair, Michigan	196,000	125,000
Detroit River, Michigan	18,000	1,334,534
Harbor of Refuge, Harbor Beach, Michigan	22,500	2,000
Black River, Michigan	24,000	—

	Allotments 1931-32	Allotments 1932-33
Saginaw River, Michigan ....$	—	$ 362,000
Rogue River, Michigan	33,000	20,000
Toledo, Ohio	—	74,000
Alpena, Michigan	—	30,000
Sandusky, Ohio	15,000	19,600
Huron, Ohio	18,300	—
Vermillion, Ohio	14,500	—
Lorain, Ohio	69,500	95,000
Cleveland, Ohio	227,900	146,000
Fairport, Ohio	300,000	446,000
Ashtabula, Ohio	10,000	52,724
Conneaut, Ohio	60,000	10,000
Erie, Pennsylvania	42,500	—
Dunkirk, Pennsylvania	60,000	—
Buffalo	1,104,998	46,500
Olcott, New York	—	14,000
Rochester (Charlotte) New York	16,000	—
Great Sodus Bay, New York	31,000	—
Little Sodus Bay, New York	7,000	—
Oswego, New York	1,316,000	712,000

3. Intracoastal Waterway

Cape Cod Canal	140,481	52,000
Raritan River	329,359	94,069
Washington Canal and South River, N.J.	90,218	—
Delaware River to Chesapeake Bay	490,000	—
Chincoteaque Bay, Virginia	500	—
Norfolk to Beaufort Inlet, North Carolina	284,000	177,400
Beaufort, N.C. to Cape Fear River, N.C.	186,000	—
Cape Fear River, N.C. to Winyah Bay, S.C.........	996,000	105,000
Winyah Bay, S.C. to Charleston, S.C.	21,850	7,100
Charleston to Beaufort, South Carolina	11,000	—
Beaufort, S.C. to St. Johns River	106,000	16,000
Jacksonville, Florida to Miami, Florida	1,642,210	447,000
Pensacola Bay, Florida to Mobile Bay	275,000	150,000
Mobile, Alabama to New Orleans	15,432	52,844
New Orleans to Sabine River	246,900	1,023,000
Sabine River to Corpus Christi	90,000	485,000

4. All Other[b]

Kennebunk River, Maine	—	32,000
Lynn Harbor, Massachusetts	150,000	302,000
Salem Harbor, Massachusetts	36,587	—
Nantucket Sound, Massachusetts	27,000	150,931
New Bedford and Fairhaven Harbor, Massachusetts..	357,931	152,624
Taunton River, Massachusetts	110,000	81,000
Fall River Harbor, Massachusetts	125,492	18,700
Connecticut River	19,500	—

	Allotments 1931-32	Allotments 1932-33
Bridgeport Harbor, Connecticut ....$	138,000	$ 45,000
Thames River, Connecticut	23,000	152,000
Stamford Harbor, Connecticut	34,500	29,000
Greenwich Harbor, Connecticut	16,000	—
Harbor Refuge, Block Island, R.I.	7,000	—
Flushing Bay Harbor, N.Y.	—	20,000
Hay (West) Harbor, N.Y.	8,401	—
Jamaica Bay, N.Y.	566,158	384,329
Tarrytown Harbor, N.Y.	11,341	15,000
Woodbridge Creek, N.Y.	30,000	—
Hudson River, N.Y.	135,800	—
Rondout Harbor, N.Y.	1,000	—
Mamaroneck Harbor, N.Y.	—	21,600
Narrows of Lake Champlain, N.Y.	500	500
New York to New Jersey Channels	66,800	—
Newark Bay, Hackensack and Passaic Rivers, N.J. ..	382,500	240,000
Shoal Harbor and Compton Creek, N.J.	13,500	—
Shrewsbury River, New Jersey	11,007	10,000
Mispillion River, New Jersey	15,000	—
Manasquan River, New Jersey	202,000	79,460
Cold Spring Inlet, New Jersey	—	52,000
Raccoon Creek, New Jersey	—	26,500
Delaware River, Philadelphia to Trenton	1,025,230	355,000
Schuylkill River, Pennsylvania	1,038,500	220,000
Little Machipongo River, Delaware	13,500	—
St. Johns River, Delaware	—	25,200
Wilmington Harbor, Delaware	100,000	150,000
Murderkill River, Delaware	13,500	—
Potomac River at Washington	5,000	237,917
Thimble Shoal Channel, Virginia	65,113	15,158
James River, Virginia	687,179	894,500
Pagan River, Virginia	37,000	—
Onancock River, Virginia	8,000	8,000
Blackwater River, Virginia	3,000	—
Monroe Bay and Creek, Virginia	12,450	2,750
Smith Creek, Maryland	5,250	250
Rappahannock River, Virginia	19,000	1,520
Mattaponi River, Virginia	—	300
Pamunkey River, Virginia	—	400
Nandua Creek, Virginia	—	2,000
Occohannock Creek, Virginia	42,000	—
Nansemond Creek, Virginia	86,300	33,458
Urbanna Creek, Virginia	10,000	—
Willoughby Channel, Virginia	8,500	—
Claiborne Harbor, Maryland	13,100	—
Choptank River, Maryland	5,300	—
Wicomico River, Maryland	73,000	—
Switch Cove, Maryland	9,500	—
Herring Bay, Maryland	6,300	—

	Allotments 1931-32	Allotments 1932-33
Broad Creek, Maryland ....$	6,000	$ —
Elk and Little Elk River, Maryland	6,000	1,600
Meherrin River, North Carolina	—	3,000
Edenton Harbor, North Carolina	—	10,000
Roanoke River, North Carolina	24,000	26,400
Mackay Creek, North Carolina	1,100	—
Far Creek, North Carolina	34,500	—
Morehead City Harbor, North Carolina	36,500	—
Pamlico and Tar Rivers, North Carolina	241,000	21,500
Knobbs Creek, North Carolina	80,500	4,000
Belhaven Harbor, North Carolina	53,500	2,500
Neuse River, North Carolina	—	3,500
Silver Lake Creek, North Carolina	11,000	—
Contentnea Creek, North Carolina	1,000	1,000
Shipyard Creek, North Carolina	20,000	—
Trent River, North Carolina	2,000	1,000
Beaufort Inlet, North Carolina	71,350	30,500
Waterway between Cove Sound and Beaufort, N.C...	3,700	
Cape Fear River, N.C., below Wilmington	270,000	431,900
Cape Fear River, N.C., above Wilmington	627,500	8,000
Northeast (Cape Fear) River, North Carolina	—	2,700
Black River, North Carolina	1,500	1,200
Waccamaw River, N.C. and S.C.	16,000	3,000
Winyah Bay, South Carolina	27,000	50,000
Great Pedee River, South Carolina	4,500	4,700
Savannah River below Augusta, Georgia	51,900	170,500
Altamaha, Oconee, and Ocmulgee Rivers, Georgia ..	39,000	9,000
Brunswick Harbor, Georgia	653,000	73,000
Fancy Bluff Creek, Georgia	—	3,500
Satilla River, Georgia	—	8,000
Flint River, Georgia	48,500	—
St. Mary's River, Georgia and Florida	—	8,450
Fernandina Harbor, Florida	55,000	—
St. Johns River, Palatka to Lake Harney	27,000	—
Hollywood Harbor, Florida	44,000	—
Oklawaha River, Florida	13,500	10,000
Miami River, Florida	—	686,000
Miami Harbor (Biscayne Bay)	100,000	150,000
Caloosahatchee River and Lake Okeechobee	742,545	2,140,546
Key West Harbor	25,000	—
Charlotte Harbor, Florida	29,000	—
Tampa Harbor, Florida	181,440	266,550
Cedar Keys Harbor, Florida	59,500	—
Carrabelle Bar and Harbor, Florida	44,797	11,000
Apalachicola Bay, Florida	22,500	35,000
Channel, Apalachicola River to St. Andrews	5,000	—
Apalachicola River, Lee Slough and Lower Chipola River	—	10,000
Upper Chipola River	12,000	—
St. Andrews Bay, Florida	45,000	25,000

	Allotments 1931-32	Allotments 1932-33
St. Marks River, Florida ....$	11,000	$ —
Narrows in Santa Rosa Sound, Florida	3,500	—
Pensacola Harbor, Florida	36,000	—
Removal of water hyacinths, Florida	6,000	9,500
Choctawhatchee River, Florida and Georgia	11,000	12,800
East Pass Channel Gulf of Mexico to Choctawhatchee River, Alabama	8,657	—
Alabama River, Alabama	154,000	121,257
Black Warrior River, Warrior and Tombigee Rivers, Alabama	51,000	84,000
Tombigee River, Demopolis, Alabama to Walkers Bridge, Mississippi	2,500	—
Bayou La Batre, Alabama	10,000	—
East Pearl River, Mississippi	—	1,037
Pascagoula Harbor, Mississippi	2,500	20,000
Biloxi Harbor, Mississippi	52,000	—
Channel Mobile Bay and Mississippi Sound	52,700	—
Gulfport Harbor and Ship Is. Pass	123,000	40,000
Mississippi River, Baton Rouge to New Orleans	20,000	—
Bayou Terrebonne, Louisiana	60,000	—
Bayou Grossetete, Louisiana	6,000	—
Bayou Teche, Louisiana	75,983	31,908
Johnsons Bayou, Louisiana	7,000	—
Bayou Bonfouca, Louisiana	10,000	—
Tickfaw and other rivers, Louisiana	3,000	—
Amite River, Louisiana	4,000	—
Barataria Bay, Louisiana	21,500	—
Mermentau River, Louisiana	4,000	—
Bayou Plague mine Brule, Louisiana	2,000	—
Calcasieu River, Louisiana	20,000	—
Tangipahoa River, Louisiana	2,000	—
Pass Manchac, Louisiana	1,000	—
Removing water hyacinths, Louisiana	32,000	29,000
Sabine—Neches Waterway	496,300	496,300
Dickinson Bayou, Texas	19,000	—
Galveston Channel, Texas	200,000	—
Galveston Harbor—Texas City—Channel	1,155,525	171,000
Port Olivar Channel, Texas	24,000	8,000
Double Bayou	9,000	—
Freeport Harbor, Texas	130,000	65,000
Anahuac Channel, Texas	11,000	—
Cedar Bayou, Texas	17,200	—
Clear Creek, Texas	7,000	—
Arkansas Pass—Corpus Christi Channel, Texas	350,000	115,000
Channel from Pass Cavallo to Port Lavaca, Texas ..	—	10,000
Port Arkansas, Texas	190,000	50,000
Brazos Is. Harbor, Texas	9,000	—
Houston Ship Channel, Texas	894,000	321,000
Red River below Fulton, Arkansas	160,300	55,000
Ouachita and Black Rivers, Arkansas and La.	445,200	102,500

	Allotments 1931-32	Allotments 1932-33
Tensas River and Bayou Macon, Louisiana ....$	5,000	$ 7,791
Boeuf River, Louisiana	5,000	—
Bayou d'Arbonne and Carney, Louisiana	2,500	—
Tallahatchee and Colwater Rivers, Miss.	2,500	—
Big Sunflower River, Mississippi	15,000	2,000
Yazoo River, Louisiana	40,000	6,000
Mouth of Yazoo River, Mississippi	615	3,000
Arkansas River, Ark. and Okla.	51,750	3,110
White River, Arkansas	66,750	43,500
Black River, Ark. and Mo.	32,500	1,500
Current River, Ark. and Mo.	2,750	3,500
St. Francis and L'Auguille River and Blackfish Bayou, Arkansas	9,750	10,964
Ohio River:		
Open channel	3,037,858	1,678,360
Lock and dam construction	321,500	1,494,133
Monongahela River	1,670,000	398,000
Allegheny River, Pennsylvania:		
Open channel work	2,500	2,500
Lock and dam construction	154,000	4,626,442
Youghiogheny River, Pennsylvania	17,000	4,500
Green and Barren, Kentucky	5,000	—
Kanawha River, West Virginia	2,050,000	3,427,000
Cumberland River, Tenn. and Ky.	6,000	19,000
Tennessee River:		
Above Riverton	387,000	275,000
Below Riverton	126,600	1,629,000
Tradewater River, Ky.	2,500	—
Mississippi River:		
Mouth of Illinois to Minneapolis	5,093,193	7,605,000
Mouth of Illinois to mouth of Ohio	4,466,000	4,761,579
Missouri River:		
Kansas City to mouth	15,896,139	8,908,576
Sioux City to Kansas City	1,930,000	5,893,000
Illinois River:		
Mouth to Utica	—	450,000
Utica to Lockport	3,390,000	4,560,000
Minnesota River	—	8,000
St. Croix River, Wisconsin and Minnesota	5,500	10,000
Ogdensburg Harbor, N.Y.	—	60,500
Richmond Harbor, California	—	28,246
Petaluma Creek, California	44,400	166,500
Redwood Creek, California	26,000	—
Oakland Harbor, California	220,000	45,000
Noyo River, California	190,000	15,000
San Pablo Bay and Mare Is. Strait	100,000	50,000
Suisun Bay Channel	76,000	22,500
San Rafael Creek, California	13,000	30,000
Humboldt Bay and Harbor, California	260,000	185,506
Monterey Harbor, California	200,000	245,000

	Allotments 1931-32	Allotments 1932-33
Stockton and Mormon Channels, California ....$	—	$ 5,000
Mokelume River, California	3,700	2,000
Yuba River, California	13,500	15,000
San Joaquin River, California	250,000	691,000
Feather River, California	1,500	1,500
Middle River and Empire Cut, California	1,600	800
Coquille River, California	63,000	—
Coos Bay, Oregon	75,000	92,000
Umpqua River, Oregon	110,000	450,000
Yaquima Bay and Harbor, Oregon	100,000	100,000
Yaquima River, Oregon	9,500	—
Suilaw River, Oregon	1,000	—
Tillamook Bay and Bar, Oregon	458,000	110,000
Skipanon Channel, Oregon	124,000	—
Willamette River above Portland	85,000	224,000
Snake River, Idaho, Oregon, Washington	6,000	—
Lake River, Washington	3,700	—
Skamokawa Creek, Washington	—	2,000
Lewis River, Washington	1,000	—
Cowlitz River, Washington	18,000	—
Willapa River and Harbor, Washington	60,000	125,000
Skagit River, Washington	3,000	—
Hoquiam River, Washington	3,500	49,500
Grays Harbor and Bar, Washington	180,000	56,000
Grays Harbor, inner and Chehalis River	50,000	—
Quillayute River, Washington	72,000	35,000
Puget Sound and tributaries	20,000	8,000
Kootenai River, Idaho, Montana	3,500	—
Bellingham Harbor, Washington	28,484	—
Everett Harbor, Washington	132,000	—
Lake Washington Ship Canal, Washington	11,000	—
Olympia Harbor, Washington	46,000	—
Tacoma Harbor, Washington	161,000	—
Swinomish Slough, Washington	8,000	—

[a] Figures for 1931-32 include allotments from the War Dept. appropriation act of Feb. 23, 1931; the emergency construction act of Dec. 20, 1930; and the unallotted balance from the War Dept. appropriation act of May 28, 1930 plus reallotments. See *Report of the Chief of Engineers*, 1931, pp. 13-24.

Figures for 1932-33 include allotments from the War Dept. appropriation act of July 14, 1932, as released in mimeograph July 15, 1932; the Emergency Construction Act of 1932 (mimeograph release of Sept. 13, 1932); amounts unallotted and reallotments from the War Dept. appropriation act of Feb. 23, 1931; and reallotments from the emergency act of 1931. See *Report of the Chief of Engineers*, 1932, pp. 17-22.

[b] Excludes allotments for waterways in noncontiguous territories.

Inasmuch as the surveys on some of these projects have not yet been completed, and since in many cases the necessary depth of channel hàs not been determined, it is impossible to give precise estimates of the cost of completing this program. In hearings before Congress in connection with the appropriation bill for 1932, Brigadier General G. B. Pillsbury, Assistant Chief of Engineers, made the following statement:

The total estimated cost of completing all projects, including new authorizations, is $307,000,000. In addition to this there will be required approximately $200,000,000 to complete certain work on the upper Mississippi, the Tennessee, and the Missouri Rivers for which partial authorizations only have been granted. This makes a gross total of $507,000,000 to complete all authorized projects.[20]

In addition to these authorized projects surveys are being made on many other rivers. The latest annual report of the Chief of Engineers states:

The comprehensive surveys of nearly 200 rivers with a view to the formulation of general plans for the most effective improvement of such streams for the purposes of navigation, in combination with the most efficient development of potential water power, the control of floods, and the needs of irrigation, have been continued. During the year reports on 47 of these rivers have been completed and transmitted to Congress, making a total of 110 such investigations that have been completed.[21]

In addressing the Ohio Valley Improvement Association in October 1929, President Hoover estimated that we should complete the entire Mississippi system within the next five years and the intra-coastal canals in the next ten years. As to the probable cost he stated:

[20] 71 Cong. 3 sess., Hearings before the Sub-Committee of House Committee on Appropriations in charge of War Department appropriation bill for 1932, p. 154.
[21] *Report of the Chief of Engineers*, 1932, p. 6.

At the present time we are expending approximately $85,000,000 per annum on new construction and maintenance of these works. To complete these programs within the periods I have mentioned will require an increase in the government outlay by about $10,000,000 per annum, not including the St. Lawrence.

The estimate of $85,000,000 given above includes flood control. The actual appropriations, exclusive of flood control, since 1929 have been as follows:

1930-31	$75,386,906
1931-32	90,913,227
1932-33	98,649,187

It is clear from this analysis that, apart from the St. Lawrence project, the program of internal waterway development calls for expenditures by the federal government during the next ten years of at least $800,000,000.

This does not, of course, measure the full cost of waterway development to the country. With many projects the federal government requires state and local government agencies to participate in the development of the enterprise. For example, in the project for providing a 12-foot channel between Beaufort, North Carolina, and the Cape Fear River, a distance of 93.5 miles, the Rivers and Harbors Act of 1927 "imposes the conditions that local interests furnish, without cost to the United States, a right of way 1000 feet wide, and give assurances that they will take over the highway bridge on its completion and maintain and operate it in perpetuity."[22]

---

[22] *Report of the Chief of Engineers*, 1932, p. 556.

It is also required in some instances that terminal facilities and railway connections shall be provided at local expense. In any event, whether specifically required or not adequate terminal facilities must obviously be provided if the waterways are to be used.

CHAPTER XXII

COMPARATIVE COST OF WATER AND RAIL TRANSPORTATION

The usual method of comparing the costs of transportation by rail and water is to cite the relative *rates* paid by shippers. Since the freight *rates* paid by waterway shippers are commonly lower than those by rail, it is not unnaturally assumed that water transportation costs less than rail. Prior to 1884 when tolls were paid by waterway shippers for the purpose of meeting capital and maintenance charges borne by the government, a comparison of rates was a proper means of measuring the relative costs of water and rail transportation. But since the abolition of tolls, the costs allocable to capital investment and maintenance charges are paid by the general taxpayers. These costs are concealed from public view, being absorbed in the general budget figures of the government. The *rates* paid by shippers are therefore obviously only a portion of the story.

I. ANALYSIS OF GENERAL COST ELEMENTS

The shortcomings of the method of comparing *rates* as a measure of cost may be illustrated as follows.

Railway rates must provide the means of meeting:

1. Interest and dividends on investment in railway properties and rolling stock.
2. Maintenance of roadbed, track, and terminals.
3. Maintenance of equipment.
4. Taxes on real estate properties, and equipment.
5. Corporation income taxes.
6. The out-of-pocket costs of transporting goods.

Water rates must provide the means of meeting:
1. Interest and dividends on investment in boats only.
2. Maintenance of boats only.
3. Taxes on boats and on boat company income, if any.
4. Out-of-pocket costs of transporting goods.

In other words, in the one case the rates must cover all of the so-called overhead costs of the transportation agency, and also provide tax revenues for the government; whereas in the other case all of the overhead costs attributable to the highway itself, are borne by the government—which means, of course, by the taxpayers.

It may be useful in this connection to see what would be involved if the situation were exactly reversed. Suppose the New York State Barge Canal, for example, were constructed at private expense and that the rates charged to shippers had to cover interest and dividends on the capital investment in the waterway, annual maintenance charges, taxes for the support of the state, and the direct cost of moving goods over the canal. Suppose, second, that the State of New York constructed a parallel railroad and maintained it in first class operating condition, enabling a New York Central Railroad *Operating* Company to make rates merely sufficient to cover the out-of-pocket costs of transportation and interest and dividends on the investment in rolling stock. Would a comparison of rates that the railroad charged with those that would have to be charged by the canal prove anything as to the inclusive cost of transportation by rail and water respectively?

It is an elementary principle of transportation that the costs which are of overwhelming importance are the so-called overhead or indirect costs. Accordingly, to exclude such costs when estimating the cost of transportation by water and to include them when estimating the cost by rail is to invalidate the comparison completely. All items of cost must be included on both sides of the equation if we are to arrive at a true measure of the relative costs of transportation by rail and by water.

To determine the relative cost of transportation by rail and by water one must give consideration to four factors: (1) the original cost of construction, (2) capacity, (3) maintenance expenses, and (4) direct transport costs. While no thoroughgoing comparison of these factors has ever been made on a theoretical basis, much pertinent evidence is fortunately available on each aspect of the problem.

1. *Original costs.* The original cost of construction of canals naturally varies materially with the character of the project. The New York State Barge Canal will, however, serve as a fair illustration of the cost of a long inland canal and the Ohio River for a canalized stream.

The enlargement and improvement of the New York canal system, authorized in 1903, cost the state $192,803,467, exclusive of outlays on the old Erie Canal system, and of accumulating interest and maintenance charges since the new canal was opened for traffic in 1918.[1] The cost per mile has been nearly $370,000. This figure may be compared with an investment in all railroads of the Eastern district of $188,000 per mile of road. This figure includes investment in second, third, and fourth tracks, the expensive terminal properties in metropolitan areas, and rolling stock and equipment of every kind. Of the total investment in railroads more than 25 per cent is, moreover, assigned to passenger traf-

---

[1] See below, pp. 473-76.

fic. For the United States as a whole the investment per mile of road is $108,000. The physical valuation data of the Interstate Commerce Commission show almost the same figure.

Since 1890 federal expenditures for new work on the Ohio River have aggregated about $120,000,000 for a distance of 981 miles. This is equal to about $122,000 a mile. Since the railroad distance between Pittsburgh and the mouth of the Ohio River is, however, only 648 miles, the cost per mile, for purposes of comparison with the railroad, is really about $200,000. This may be compared with about $189,000 per mile of investment on the Chesapeake and Ohio Railroad, and $205,000 on the Norfolk and Western.[2]

So far as capital cost is concerned, it is clear that the railways have a very great advantage, as compared with the New York State Barge canal. The capital charges per mile on the New York canal system are more than double those on a railroad, even with double and quadruple tracks and passenger terminals included. Similarly, taxes on capital invested in the canal would—if levied—be more than double those on a similar railroad mileage. The disadvantage is less marked in the case of the Ohio River.

2. *Carrying capacities.* While the original cost of a waterway may be greater than that of a railroad, is not its carrying capacity so much greater as to more than offset this disadvantage? The answer to this question is in the negative. In the case of a canal or canalized river requiring locks there is a neck of the bottle which greatly reduces the volume of goods that can be moved in a given

---

[2] Investment per mile of road based on mileage owned by company plus investment in non-operating subsidiaries.

time. The number of boats of a given size that can pass through a lock in a day determines the rate of movement and, in effect, the distance apart at which the boats must travel. That is to say, if it takes fifteen minutes for a lockage, the boats may as well be fifteen minutes apart. The limiting factor in the case of a railroad is the space required between trains in the interests of safety. The answer is that 1500-ton freight trains can move much more quickly past a given point than 1500-ton barges can move through canal locks. Moreover, the right of way on the railway is not closed by ice for several months each season.

It has been shown elsewhere that the potential capacity of a railroad is in fact several times as great as that of a waterway requiring locks.[3] Moreover, the actual movement of traffic over some of our railroads has actually exceeded the theoretical maximum capacity of the Erie Canal and of the Ohio River. The estimated maximum capacity of the Erie Canal is 100,000 tons a day,[4] and of the Ohio River 320,000 tons.[5] These figures assume a continuous stream of traffic in one direction and the utilization of the locks to maximum capacity. This theoretical possible movement may be compared with an actual freight movement over the Pennsylvania Railroad through the city of Altoona on two tracks—with two other tracks accommodating forty passenger trains the same day—amounting to nearly 500,000 tons. This

[3] H. G. Moulton, *Waterways Versus Railways*, pp. 432-34, for Erie Canal; and H. G. Moulton, C. S. Morgan, and A. L. Lee, *The St. Lawrence Navigation and Power Project*, pp. 173-80, for St. Lawrence waterway.

[4] John A. Fairlie, "The New York Canals," *Quarterly Journal of Economics*, 1900, p. 234.

[5] "Examination of the Ohio River," *Report of Special Board of U. S. Army Engineers*, 1908, p. 112.

is at the rate of a 50-car freight train every five minutes.[6] The theoretical maximum capacity of the St. Lawrence waterway with its gigantic locks is only 216,000 tons per day.[7]

3. *Maintenance charges.* It is often assumed that in the case of a waterway maintenance charges are of negligible importance since, unlike a railway road bed, a waterway does not wear out. The truth is, however, that both canals and rivers, if they are to be kept in good navigable condition, require large maintenance outlays every year. The primary source of difficulty is the silt which accumulates every season both in canals and rivers. Constant dredging is required if channels are to be kept navigable; and in addition there are large annual outlays in connection with the maintenance of terminal facilities and the repair and operation of locks.

We may compare the maintenance charges on the New York Barge Canal system with those on the Erie Railroad, which is located in the same section of the country and, like the canal, carries mainly bulky traffic. The maintenance charges on the canal system in 1930 amounted to $3,300,363, or $6,286 per mile of canal. Expenses on maintenance of way and structures on the Erie Railroad amounted in the same year to $6,097 per mile of road operated. This figure of course includes maintenance charges attributable to passenger traffic, which contributed 18 per cent of the revenues. The ton mileage of traffic per mile of canal was only 2,586,000 as compared with 5,055,000 ton miles of freight traffic per mile of line on the Erie Railroad.

[6] See statement of Mr. Fisher, general superintendent of transportation of the Pennsylvania Railroad, as given in the *Proceedings of Great Lakes Regional Advisory Board*, Feb. 11, 1926, p. 38.

[7] See *The St. Lawrence Navigation and Power Project*, pp. 172-74.

A similar comparison may be made between the Ohio River, where the bulk of the traffic is mineral products, with that on the Norfolk and Western and the Chesapeake and Ohio, where a large part of the traffic also consists of products of the mines. On the Ohio River maintenance charges amounted in 1929-30 to $6,559,305,[8] or $6,800 per mile of river. This does not include maintenance costs of terminals, but is for the river proper. Expenses for maintenance of way and structures on the Norfolk and Western Railway, including terminals, amounted to $5,282 per mile of road operated. The passenger revenues on this road amounted to about 6 per cent of the total. The traffic on the Ohio River amounted to 1,500,000 ton miles per mile of river. The Norfolk and Western in 1929 carried 7,973,000 ton miles of freight per mile of line. Maintenance charges on the Chesapeake and Ohio average $5,644 per mile, passenger traffic accounting for 6 per cent of the revenue. The ton mileage of freight per mile of line on the Chesapeake and Ohio was 7,540,000.

4. *Direct transport costs.* In this respect, also, it is almost universally believed that a waterway has a tremendous advantage over a railroad. Will a boat not glide through the water with infinitely less friction than is encountered by a car moving over steel rails? Certain experiments have recently been made which throw very interesting light upon this problem. It appears to have been definitely established by dynamometer tests that up to three or four miles per hour a given number of tons may be moved in a boat through the water with fewer foot pounds of effort than the same number of tons can be moved over a smooth steel track—but that for any speed

[8] For method of computation, see pages 482-85.

exceeding three or four miles per hour the advantage is with the railway steel track. The reason is that the speed resistance in the water increases rapidly, while on the rails it increases but gradually. It is therefore only in the case of traffic where speed is a matter of no consequence that the waterway has an advantage even in direct haulage costs.

Further evidence that the direct cost of moving traffic by water is high relatively to that by rail is found in the fact that the railways manage to compete even though their rates have to cover other than out-of-pocket costs. The fact is that waterway rates, although they contribute nothing toward overhead, maintenance, or taxes, are typically only about 20 per cent below rail rates. While rates charged by the railways on competitive traffic may not, typically speaking, cover a proportionate share of overhead expenses, they do undoubtedly more than cover out-of-pocket costs.

Attention should also be called to the fact that wages on waterways are substantially lower than those on railways. The average yearly compensation per employee during the years 1923-30 was $893 on water carriers (Mississippi River and tributaries) and $1,685 on Class I railroads; wages having accounted for 46.7 per cent of operating costs on the railways compared with 41.9 per cent on the waterways. In spite of low wages the operating ratio of the water carriers on the Mississippi River and tributaries was much less favorable than on the railways. The average operating ratio for the years 1923-30 inclusive on the Mississippi River and tributaries was 100.5, as compared with 74.3 on Class I railways. The dividends declared during this period by the carriers on the Mississippi River and tributaries amounted to only

$287,000, or about one-fourth of one per cent annually on the average capital investment.[9]

There are two other factors bearing upon the relative cost of transportation by rail and water which should be mentioned here. The first is that the distance by water between given points is commonly much greater than that by rail. For example, the distance from Chicago to New Orleans via the Illinois and Mississippi rivers is 1,534 miles, as compared with 921 miles by the Illinois Central Railroad. The distance from St. Louis to Kansas City by the Missouri River is 398 miles, while by rail the distance is only 278 miles.

The second factor is that of transshipment. In some instances a water route saves a transshipment; but much more frequently an extra handling of the goods is required. This is particularly the case in connection with the assembling of traffic from producing areas, particularly from agricultural and mining regions. As the National Waterways Commission pointed out many years ago, "When grain began to be produced away from the waterways, it had to be loaded first into railroad cars, and, once in the cars, it remained there until it reached its market."[10] The same consideration is frequently of decisive importance in the movement of raw materials and industrial products. Wherever the traffic does not originate directly on a water route the cost of transshipment to water commonly proves a serious handicap to its movement that way. The experience of other countries, as well as the United States, demonstrates that in the main

[9] Compiled from annual *Statistics of Railways in the United States.* For the operating results of the Inland Waterways Corporation, see below, pp. 498-503.

[10] *Report of National Waterways Commission, 1910,* Document 11, p. 48.

water traffic is confined to traffic having its origin and destination on the water route—although there are some exceptions to this rule.

The fact that rivers and canals lack the ability of the railways to permeate the areas where traffic is assembled, and also, by means of spur tracks and sidings, to lay it down near the place of use in terminal centers is a serious handicap. Waterways lack the flexibility of the railways in this regard, even as the latter lack the flexibility of truck transportation. As we show elsewhere, the one important competitive advantage of the truck is its ability to pick up traffic anywhere and to lay it down precisely where needed.[11]

Whether we look at the problem of relative costs from the standpoint of construction costs, maintenance charges, or direct transport costs, the advantage is with the railways as compared with canals or canalized rivers. On a combined basis, including all elements of costs, the advantage of the railway is decisive. The alleged relative cheapness of canal and river transportation is attained, as was already indicated, only by omitting, in the case of a waterway, all overhead and maintenance costs from the computation while including them in the case of a railway.

II. MISSISSIPPI VALLEY ASSOCIATION'S COST COMPUTATION

An attempt has recently been made by the Mississippi Valley Association to prove that transportation by rivers and canals is cheaper than railroad transportation when capital investment is taken into account.[12] The method employed is as follows: An estimate is first made of the

---

[11] See Chapters XXVIII and XXIX.

[12] In statement of the Mississippi Valley Association before the National Transportation Committee, Dec. 9, 1932.

investment in rivers, canals, and connecting channels, as compared with the investment in railroads that is allocated to freight transport. Annual interest is then figured on these investments and compared with the tons of freight carried. The figures, in condensed form (for 1930) are as follows:

	Railroads (for freight only)	Rivers, Canals, and Connecting Channels
Investment	$19,133,502,226[13]	$804,989,618
Tons freight originated	1,153,196,636	226,760,000
Investment per ton	$16.59	$3.55

The conclusion is reached from this analysis that water transportation, even when overhead expenses are included, is only about one-fifth as costly as that by rail.

The method here employed in showing that water transportation is cheaper than that by rail is, however, unsound. In the first place transportation service is measured, not simply by tons of freight *originated*, but by the distance that the freight is carried. The average length of haul on the railways is about eight times that on the waterways. The railway ton mileage in 1930 was 383,449,588,491, the waterway ton mileage 9,087,513,000. On a ton-mileage basis the investment works out at 5 cents by railroad and 14 cents by water. Moreover, the ton-mileage figure on the waterway is materially increased by virtue of the fact that the water

[13] The method of computing this figure was to add to the book value of the investment of Class I roads an item of 915 million dollars for land grants and other subsidies from federal, state, and local governments; then reduce the total by a percentage based on the ratio of passenger expenses to total expenses, so as to get the investment for freight purposes. Since the land and other property donated to the railroads, and the assets purchased with the proceeds of sales of such property, are included in carriers' investment accounts, there is extensive duplication.

distance between given points, as already indicated, is typically much greater than the distance by rail.

Several other shortcomings of this analysis may also be noted: First, the cost of rivers, canals, and connecting channels includes only federal expenditures; but the tonnage figures include traffic on waterways constructed by states as well. This omission would increase the investment figure by over $300,000,000. Second, the waterway tonnage includes traffic through the Soo and other connecting channels on the Great Lakes. The Soo, as we have seen elsewhere, is in a special class by itself; and the traffic through the St. Clair flats is really a part of the Great Lakes traffic proper. The traffic through the Soo alone amounted to approximately one-third of the total waterway tonnage. Third, non-revenue traffic, amounting to about 10 per cent of the total, is excluded from the railway tonnage figure, but such tonnage is included in the case of waterways. In many cases where large construction operations are now under way, nearly all the water traffic is non-commercial.[14] Finally, the waterway tonnage consists primarily of heavy, bulky commodities, the package freight amounting to only 12,747,000 tons. The railroad traffic, on the other hand, consists in substantial part of high grade traffic requiring rapid service and costly terminal facilities. Whereas in terms of tonnage the water traffic is equal to 19.7 per cent of the railway traffic, in terms of value it is equal to only 6.1 per cent.

In so far, therefore, as investment may be used as a basis for measuring relative costs it shows conclusively that railway freight transportation is very much cheaper than inland canal and river transportation. This method

[14] See below, pp. 481, 489.

of measurement does not, however, include the direct costs of transportation. In the following chapter we shall compare the *inclusive* costs on particular water routes with the cost by rail for comparable service.

III. RAILWAY SUBSIDIES

In the foregoing analysis we have pointed out that waterways are subsidized by federal and state governments. Attention must now be called to the fact that the railroads have also received since the beginning of their development substantial subsidies from federal, state, and local governments. There has been so much controversy over this subject that it is desirable here to present as accurate a statement as possible as to the character and extent of these aids.

In the decade of the thirties, as has already been pointed out, state governments, with some assistance from the national government, promoted and gave financial assistance to comprehensive transportation development plans, involving turnpikes, canals, and railroads. The subsidies consisted chiefly of stock and bond subscriptions, cash contributions, and land grants. The period of extensive land grants by the federal government to the railroads, however, was in the period from 1850 to 1871. These land grants consisted both of right-of-way and of adjoining lands, and it was understood that the latter would shortly be sold by the railroads to settlers. The land grants were made principally to Middle Western and Western roads as a means of promoting the more rapid settlement of the country.

Data compiled by the Bureau of Valuation of the Interstate Commerce Commission, as of December 31, 1930, show that the total land grants to the railways by federal and state governments aggregated 176,030,259 acres. Of this total the records show that 148,579,360 acres were sold, yielding a return of $376,314,484—an average price of $2.54 an acre. Lands were forfeited or otherwise disposed of to the extent of 8,999,542 acres. The donated lands still owned by the railroads amount to 18,470,003 acres. At an average price of $2.54—the price at which the other land was sold—the value of this land near the time of its acquisition was about $46,000,000. The total value of the land *received* was thus approximately $422,000,000.

There are no precise data as to the value of the contributions made by federal and state governments through stock and bond subscriptions, cash donations, and in miscellaneous ways. The Mississippi Valley Association has, however, compiled an estimate from Interstate Commerce Commission reports showing a total of $194,002,531—including an item of $7,253,631 for tax aids.[15]

Total contributions by the federal and state governments thus approximate roughly $616,000,000. As an offset to this we find that the Interstate Commerce Commission has given the railways credits for transportation services to the government amounting to $41,447,248, leaving the government's net contribution at $573,000,000. In every land grant there was a clause which provided that the railroads should perpetually transport mail, troops, and government supplies at reduced rates. The railroads contend that the value of these services already exceeds the value of the land grants.

---

[15] For want of other data this figure may be tentatively accepted. See statement of Mississippi Valley Association to the National Transportation Committee.

It remains to call attention to the present value of the land which the railroads received as grants and which remain undisposed of. The Bureau of Valuation of the Interstate Commerce Commission carries railway land at the current market price of adjacent property. The Bureau's figures show the *commercial* value of lands acquired by all Class I carriers "through aids, gifts, grants, or donations from federal, state, and local governments, corporations, and individuals" to be $500,234,389, as of December 31, 1930.[16] As a result of the shrinkage in real estate values since 1930 this figure would of course now be materially reduced. Taking the figure as of 1930, however, we find that the total value of the aids received by the Class I railways was $376,000,000 (lands sold) plus $194,000,000 (other aids) plus $500,000,000 (lands on hand) or $1,070,000,000.

The subsidies to the railways thus represent about 4 per cent of the investment in the Class I railways as a whole. This may be compared with a subsidy of at least 85 per cent in the case of waterways. The only private investment in waterway properties is that which (in some cases) is put into terminal facilities, and the investment in boats. The railways pay taxes on their subsidized investment, while the waterways do not.

[16] All the foregoing data are for Class I railroads. The figures are not greatly modified by the inclusion of the minor carriers. The land value figure is, however, raised to $516,465,195.

CHAPTER XXIII

ANALYSIS OF SPECIFIC PROJECTS

Thus far our analysis of the costs of transportation by rail and water has been in general terms. We shall now study certain specific projects, adopting the method of converting overhead, capital, and maintenance charges, borne by the government, into a ton-mile cost and adding this figure to the rate paid by shippers in order to obtain the inclusive cost. In figuring the cost of these projects we shall omit from consideration all capital costs incurred prior to 1890, and, in the case of the New York State Barge Canal system, all prior to 1905. We make this elimination because the modern era of water transportation, as we have already indicated, begins about 1890, and it is hardly fair to charge against present waterways the cost of earlier improvements, the value of which has been largely lost.

I. THE NEW YORK STATE BARGE CANAL SYSTEM

Since this project has already been discussed to some extent for illustrative purposes, only a very brief summary of its history and present status is here required. In 1903 the state appropriated $101,000,000 for deepening and improving the old canal system, utilizing a new route for a considerable part of the distance. The new route was opened for navigation in May 1918, though the construction was still far from complete. Up to June 30, 1931 the total construction costs have been $176,747,841, of which $26,610,988 was for terminals not provided for under the original appropriation. In addition, the cost of carrying the bonds issued in connection with the project had aggregated $63,210,572; and maintenance charges from 1918 to 1931 amounted to $46,755,215. Even yet, however, the construction costs are not complete and every year there are substantial outlays for new works. In recent years there has been a movement to get the federal government to spend large sums in deepening and widening the route in order to accommodate larger boats. The federal government has, moreover, already expended approximately $10,000,000 for the development of barge canal facilities at Troy, at Oswego, and at Tonawanda and Black Rock channel.[1]

1. Traffic development. The traffic development on the Barge Canal system has been disappointing. As the chart on the following page indicates, the traffic on the canal since it was opened to operation in 1918 has averaged less than half the volume that was carried during the seventies and eighties. In fact, the traffic during the last six years prior to the abolition of tolls on the old canal—1877 to 1882—averaged 5,434,474 tons as compared with an average of 3,040,814 tons from 1925 to 1931 inclusive. The volume of traffic annually since 1922 has been as follows:

TON MILES OF TRAFFIC, NEW YORK BARGE CANAL SYSTEM, 1922–1931

1922	362,442,277	1927	581,832,903
1923	405,925,906	1928	741,878,620
1924	448,399,607	1929	715,551,472
1925	543,860,257	1930	922,933,819
1926	552,208,134	1931	1,358,048,539

The traffic consists primarily of bulky, low grade commodities. The most important items are grain moving east; petroleum and other oils, sugar, sulphur, and fertilizers moving west from the port of New York; and

[1] Compiled from *Annual Report of the Chief of Engineers, U. S. Army*, 1932.

WATER-BORNE TRAFFIC ON SELECTED ROUTES[a]

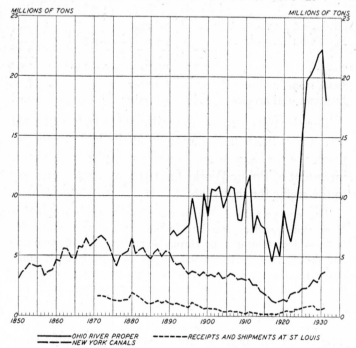

[a] The sources of the data used are as follows:

Ohio River: *Transportation in the Mississippi and Ohio Valleys*, Corps of Engineers, U. S. Army, and U. S. Shipping Board, 1929. For correction of Ohio River data, see below, pp. 481-82.

New York Canals: *Annual Reports of the Superintendent of Public Works*.

Receipts and shipments at St. Louis: *Annual Statements of the Trade and Commerce of St. Louis*, Merchants Exchange of St. Louis (for years 1871-1923); *Reports of the Chief of Engineers* (1923-1931).

sand, stone and gravel, which are mainly local traffic. The distribution of tonnage by commodities in 1931 was as follows:[2]

[2] *Annual Report of the Superintendent of Public Works, New York*, 1931.

	Percentage of Total		Percentage of Total
Grain, except flaxseed	32.5	Sulphur	3.37
Petroleum and other		Chemicals, drugs	3.29
oils	23.9	Fertilizers	2.25
Sugar	8.17	Pig iron and billets	1.95
Sand, stone, and gravel	6.9	Lumber	1.88
Iron and steel articles	5.38	All other	10.41

The sharp increases in ton mileage for 1930 and 1931 are, curiously enough, primarily attributable to the influence of the depression. The report of the State Superintendent of Public Works for 1930 says, with reference to the traffic for that year:

The unexpectedly heavy movement of wheat via the New York State canal appears largely the result of the world-wide business depression existing throughout the year. European and British buyers have purchased mostly in comparatively small quantities, the rapid fluctuation of prices deterring them from large commitments. This has resulted in comparatively few cargo lot shipments, the greater portion being what is commonly called "berth tonnage."[3]

The result has been to divert much grain traffic from Montreal cargo boats to liners out of New York. The grain traffic over the St. Lawrence to Montreal shows a decline of over 40 per cent between 1928 and 1931.

Cut rates on coastal and inter-coastal traffic, and also on the barge canal, have diverted some traffic destined for inland distributing centers of the East to the New York City-barge route. This rate cutting is, however, of a ruinous character and both the Canal Lines' Executives' Committee and the Intercoastal Conference are now in favor of the regulation of minimum rates by the government. At the hearing before the National Transportation

[3] The same, 1930, p. 38.

Committee the Canal Executives expressed themselves as favoring "constructive water line regulation, which should from the beginning be comprehensive, complete, and carefully planned."[4]

Another factor responsible for stimulating the water traffic is discrimination against the railways in the use of state elevators at Oswego. Grain destined to move by rail is charged more than when moving by water.

2. *The inclusive cost of transportation.* Since a number of boat companies operate on the canal, and since they are not officially required to publish rates, no precise figure is available as to the average rates paid by the shippers on canal traffic. The federal barge line on the Mississippi, however, reports an average of 4.91 mills per ton mile in 1929 and 5.05 mills in 1930. An average rate of 4.5 mills per ton mills for the New York canal system would seem to be a conservative figure.[5] To this freight rate must be added the costs borne by the tax-payers in the form of overhead and maintenance expenditures.

The State of New York had outstanding bonds against this project at the end of 1931 amounting to $151,440,000 which bear interest on the average at slightly more than 4 per cent. The actual out-of-pocket expenditures by the state treasury in connection with this project in 1931 for interest on bonds outstanding was $6,057,600.[6] This figure, however, does not include in-

---

[4] Brief in behalf of Canal Lines' Executives' Committee before the National Transportation Committee, New York, December 1932, p. 4.

[5] See below, p. 502.

[6] Since 1927 the interest figure is not given separately in the Annual Reports of the Comptroller, but is lumped with other charges for public works. For the 1931 figure we have taken a flat 4 per cent on the bonds outstanding.

terest on the full construction cost. At the least we should figure interest on the full $176,747,841 of construction cost, and it is also proper to include with capital costs interest charges during the period of construction.[7] While about $25,000,000 has been expended upon additional construction since the canal was nominally completed in 1918, we will include in capital cost—in order to be conservative—only the interest accumulation on the investment up to 1918, namely, $16,055,626. The interest at 4 per cent on this total of $192,803,467 gives an annual interest cost of $7,712,183. (This does not include interest on improvements made by the federal government, noted above.)

Maintenance charges by the state government amounted in 1931 to $2,794,832 net.[8] In addition, the maintenance charges allocable to the barge canal in connection with federal improvements at Troy, Oswego, and Black Rock Channel amounted to approximately $140,000.[9] This makes total maintenance charges of $2,934,832.

The minimum annual overhead cost for interest and maintenance, borne by the taxpayers, aggregates $10,646,970. Inasmuch as the total traffic carried over the canals amounted in 1931 to 3,722,012 tons, the contribution of the taxpayers amounted to approximately

[7] This is in accordance with commercial practice and is followed by the federal government in connection with the Panama Canal.

[8] The state receives some income from terminals, warehouses, and water power leases; this amount has been subtracted from the gross maintenance. In 1930 the state expended also $291,072 on new construction, and $133,106 in 1931.

[9] This figure has been computed by taking 60 per cent of maintenance costs for Black Rock Channel and for Oswego Harbor (barge canal traffic accounting for 60 per cent of the totals attributable to these improvements) plus the total maintenance cost for Troy Harbor.

$2.88 per ton. In terms of a rate per ton mile the tax-payers' subsidy to the shippers amounted to about 7.84 mills per ton mile. Adding 4.50 mills, the shippers' rate, gives 12.34 mills per ton mile. For purposes of comparison with railway charges this figure has to be increased by virtue of the fact that the distance between Buffalo and Albany by water is 363 miles as compared with 303 miles by rail. The water rate in terms of the rail mileage is equal to approximately 14.81 mills. This cost figure does not, it should be observed, include any provision for taxes on the capital invested in the canal improvements or make any allowance for depreciation of canal property.

We may now compare this figure with the actual rates charged by the railways. The average freight rate per ton mile on the New York Central Railroad in 1931 was 9.87 mills; on the Erie Railroad 9.72 mills, and in the Central Eastern region as a whole 10.32 mills. These rates represent the average on all classes of freight, high as well as low grade traffic. Rates on grain, petroleum, sand, stone, and gravel, and other bulky products are naturally very much lower than those on high grade freight. It will serve to clarify the problem, therefore, if we cite rates on certain railroads, the traffic of which is primarily bulk tonnage. The average rate per ton mile on the Chesapeake and Ohio in 1931 was 5.97 and on the Norfolk and Western 6.84 mills. The bulk of the traffic on these roads is mineral products. The road which has the highest percentage of its traffic in products of agriculture is the Canadian Pacific Lines in Maine. In 1931 agricultural traffic comprised 50 per cent of the total. The average rate per ton mile was 8.79 mills.

The rail rates must provide sufficient revenue to cover local, state and federal taxes. If the railroads were relieved of these taxes their rates could of course be somewhat reduced. For the purpose of computing the amount of taxes imputable to freight service, and hence to the freight rate per ton mile, we take 1928, rather than the peak traffic year, 1929, or the depressed years which have followed. The tax was equivalent to .79 mills per ton mile.[10]

It is clear from these figures that the inclusive cost of transportation on the New York Barge Canal system is nearly double that on railways for similar types of traffic. The taxpayers of the State of New York contribute over 10 mills per ton mile in order to make possible a slight reduction—amounting to 1 or 2 mills at the most—in freight rates to shippers. If the canal were abandoned and the railroads were permitted to handle the traffic the increased tonnage would make possible a reduction in rail charges and/or increased tax contributions to the government. At the same time the abandonment of the canal would save the taxpayers the annual maintenance charges.

II. THE OHIO RIVER

The Ohio River and its tributaries have always constituted a most important—in many ways the most important—link in our inland water transportation system. The Ohio River never suffered any severe decline in traffic during the period of waterway decadence, though there was a marked shift in the character of traffic. In the early days the commerce on the Ohio River consisted of a wide variety of commodities, including grain,

[10] Taxes apportioned to freight service on the basis of the ratio of freight expenses to total operating expenses.

lumber, fruit, and general merchandise, as well as products of the mines. In the decade of the eighties, however, Ohio River steamers carrying miscellaneous packet freight largely disappeared from the river and were replaced by barges carrying mainly coal and lumber. By 1887 only one regular steamboat line remained in operation between Cincinnati and New Orleans.

The federal government had expended on improvements and maintenance of the Ohio River up to 1890 about $8,482,000, while from 1890 to 1910 expenditures for new construction and maintenance aggregated something over $20,000,000.[11] In 1908 a special board of Army engineers made an examination of the river and recommended its improvement by a system of locks and movable dams, 54 in number, which would give the river a limiting depth of nine feet. The estimated cost was $63,731,485 for river improvements and $5,000,000 for the necessary dredging plant.[12] The completion of this project was formally celebrated in 1929. The cost, excluding maintenance charges, and terminal facilities which were provided by private interests and municipalities, had amounted to a little less than $100,000,000. From 1890 to June 30, 1930 total expenditures by the federal government for construction and maintenance upon the Ohio River aggregated $150,205,927. Expenditures upon tributaries of the Ohio during the same period amounted to $88,141,524—making a total for the Ohio River system of $238,347,451.[13]

[11] The published reports of the United States Army Engineers for this period do not enable one to give precise figures.
[12] "Examination of Ohio River," *Report of the Special Board of U. S. Army Engineers,* 1908, pp. 35, 39.
[13] Compiled from *Annual Reports of the Chief of Engineers,* and the *Eleventh Census of the United States,* 1890.

OHIO RIVER TRAFFIC, 1927–1931[a]

(000 omitted)

Commodity	1927		1928		1929		1930		1931	
	Tons	Per Cent	Tons	Per Cent	Tons	Per Cent	Tons	Per Cent	Tons	Per Cent
Coal and coke.........	8,518	44.1	9,161	43.7	9,751	44.4	9,769	43.7	8,519	47.1
Sand, stone, and gravel...	9,574	47.5	9,177	43.8	9,074	41.3	9,526	41.3	7,083	39.2
Iron and steel.........	982	4.9	[b]	—	1,595	7.3	1,630	7.3	902	5.0
Petroleum............	206	1.0	323	1.5	590	2.7	449	2.0	416	2.3
All other.............	847	2.5	2,270	11.0	944	4.3	964	5.7	1,151	6.4
Total.........	20,127	100.0	20,931	100.0	21,954	100.0	22,338	100.0	18,071	100.0

[a] Compiled from *Annual Reports of the Chief of Engineers*. Traffic on the Ohio River is divided into three classes: local traffic, which moves up and down the river between cities located on the river; traffic which originates at river points and is shipped out of the river over tributaries or the Mississippi; and traffic which originates on other streams and moves inbound to Ohio River points. These figures should not be compared with traffic moving over other streams unless allowances are made for duplications.

[b] Not shown separately.

1. Character of traffic. Traffic moving over the Ohio River at the present time consists chiefly of coal and coke received from tributaries, and sand, gravel, and stone originating along its banks. As is shown in the table opposite, these two classes of commodities comprise more than 85 per cent of Ohio River traffic.

The coal and coke trade originates in mines adjacent to the Monongahela and Allegheny Rivers in Pennsylvania and in the middle Appalachian coal fields of West Virginia. The mines of Pennsylvania are so close to the Monongahela and Allegheny Rivers that transshipment to the river is not required. About two-thirds of the coal traffic from the middle Appalachian field moves by rail to Huntington, West Virginia, and about one-third by the Kanawha River.

Prior to 1900 a substantial part of the coal moving over the Ohio was shipped to Mississippi River points. In recent years, however, only a small percentage of the Ohio River coal moved to Mississippi points. About one-half of the Monongahela and Allegheny coal and coke which passes down the Ohio is destined for Woodlawn, Pennsylvania, only 18 miles below Pittsburgh, while the other half is distributed between Pittsburgh and Follansbee, West Virginia, 71 miles below Pittsburgh. Some 80 per cent of the coal and coke tonnage originating in the upper Kanawha is shipped as far as Cincinnati.

The sand, stone, and gravel trade is almost entirely local traffic, and comprises the bulk of all traffic which originates on the Ohio. This traffic, in fact, originates in the river and moves short distances to wharves where it is transshipped to truck or railway car. This traffic in 1930 comprised 77 per cent of the upstream tonnage originating on the river and 59 per cent of that moving downstream. Moreover, of the traffic passing from the Ohio into the Mississippi or into the tributaries of the Ohio 77 per cent consisted of sand, gravel, and stone. The average length of haul for sand and gravel moving on the Ohio in 1930 was only 14.9 miles.

The iron and steel traffic on the river consists of two principal movements. The first is the down-bound movement of partially fabricated materials from steel plants located above Pittsburgh to their subsidiaries just below Pittsburgh. The second important movement, amounting to about 20 per cent of the total, is outbound traffic to Mississippi River points. The principal movement is to Memphis, Tennessee, but a small amount moves as far as Vicksburg and New Orleans. This traffic, however, has shown a decrease in recent years. The traffic in petroleum products is largely local—an upstream movement from Parkersburg, West Virginia, to Wheeling, and a down stream movement from Catlettsburg, Kentucky (mouth of Big Sandy River) to Louisville.

The traffic situation on the tributaries may be very briefly summarized. Water-borne commerce has declined steadily since 1890 on all the tributaries except those which are adjacent to the coal mines and on the Tennessee and Little Kanawha rivers, which have a growing volume of local traffic in sand and gravel. As we have already seen, it is the coal traffic originating on these tributaries which accounts for the largest volume of the Ohio River traffic. The following data show the traffic trends on the above mentioned group of tributaries where traffic is increasing and upon all other tributaries by decades since 1890:[14]

---

[14] Compiled from *Annual Reports of the Chief of Engineers*, and the *Eleventh Census of the United States*, 1890.

	1890	1900	1910	1920	1930
Tributaries with increasing traffic	7,138,770	9,579,939	15,006,233	32,169,737	34,667,739
Tributaries with decreasing traffic	3,370,968	2,609,788	1,373,305	821,875	1,559,464

The chart on page 471 gives the impression that commercial traffic on the Ohio River has been increasing very rapidly in recent years. The data there given are the official figures presented by the United States Army Engineers. The increase is, however, primarily attributable to the fact that the method of compiling statistics of sand and gravel shipments was changed in 1925. Prior to that date sand and gravel dredged from the channel—on this and other rivers—were not included as tonnage. Since 1925 they are included as tonnage, even though they may not be shipped out of the pool in which they are dredged. The inclusion of this non-commercial traffic, during a period when the expenditures upon improvements of our waterways have been increasing very rapidly, has served greatly to increase the nominal tonnage.

The chart on page 482 shows the changes in tonnage on the Ohio River for various classes of freight from 1905 to 1930. It will be seen that the bulk of the increase in recent years is attributable to the inclusion of this illegitimate sand and gravel traffic. With this traffic eliminated, the traffic on the river in 1930 was not appreciably greater than in 1905.

Very little of the commercial traffic, moreover, is common carrier business. About 95 per cent of the terminals are owned by private enterprise and the bulk of the traffic is moved by private industries in their own boats and barges. The route is mainly of advantage to iron and steel industries of the Pittsburgh region. The advantage of subsidized cheap transportation on the Ohio River system goes not to the ultimate consumers of iron and steel products but, mainly at least, to the particular iron and steel companies which are so situated as to take advantage of these low water costs.

FREIGHT TONNAGE ON THE OHIO RIVER
1905-1930[a]

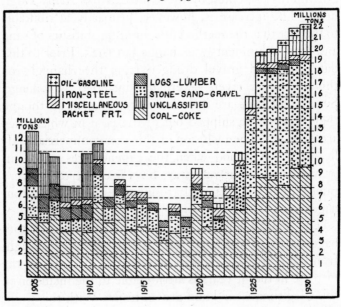

[a] Chart taken from J. E. Switzer, "The Completed Ohio River Project," *Proceedings of Indiana Academy of Science*, Vol. 41, 1931, p. 346.

2. *The inclusive cost of transportation.* Inasmuch as the traffic is so largely handled by private companies it is difficult to ascertain the direct transport costs on the river. We are informed that the rate on coal for the short hauls in the Pittsburgh district is 25 cents a short ton, which

gives an average ton-mile rate of about 8 mills. Sand and gravel rates are similar. Allowing for lower rates on the traffic which moves longer distances, we might have an average rate as low as 6 mills. To this rate must be added the cost borne by the taxpayers.

Of the $150,000,000 expended upon the Ohio River, approximately $120,000,000 was for new construction costs and about $30,000,000 was for maintenance and operation. These outlays for maintenance and operation are continuous in character. There are more than 50 locks on the river which require constant repairs and frequent rebuilding. Reporting on the condition of locks and dams for 1931, the United States Army Engineers state that "[Locks] Numbers 4 and 5 are so deteriorated as to require excessive maintenance and repair. Investigation is in progress with a view to replacing these structures and Number 6 with one new fixed dam located at Montgomery Island."[15] Likewise, it is necessary to dredge the river continuously in order to maintain the necessary channel depth.

The sums expended for the maintenance and operation of the Ohio River and its system of locks and dams for the years 1930-31 and 1931-32 were as follows. The figures are taken from the annual reports of the Chief of Engineers:

	1930-31	1931-32
Operation of locks and dams	$2,733,368	$3,041,666
Repairs and betterments of locks and dams	681,976	985,161
Operating snag boats	49,362	50,000
Open channel—dredging	278,861	970,922
Open channel—new work	1,962,276	1,161,226
	$5,705,843	$6,208,975

[15] *Report of the Chief of Engineers,* 1931, p. 1339.

The average expenditure for the two years is $5,957,409; and the expenditure for the year 1932-33 will probably exceed this amount. Appropriations for the current year, exclusive of those for operation and care of locks and dams which are met from permanent, indefinite appropriations, amount to $4,408,838. With the operation of locks and dams included the total will approach $7,000,000. It appears, therefore, that although the canal was formally completed in 1929 expenditures are continuing at much the same rate as in preceding years. In fact, the expenditures for the last three years exceed the average for the whole period from 1910 to 1929.

A portion of the cost is allocated to "open channel— new work"—which raises the question as to whether the improvements were really completed in 1929. On this point the engineers have stated that "owing to the fact that a part of the work to be done is the removal of deposits that form annually, and that recent surveys of all bars are not yet available, no reliable estimate can be made as to what proportion of the work is completed."[16] If these bars form annually it would seem clear that their removal is a proper charge against maintenance. If there are any bars that have not been dredged at all these should obviously be regarded as a part of the original cost; but it is not clear that there are any such. Since the history of river canalization in general indicates that new bars are always forming it seems reasonable to regard all these dredging charges as allocable to the continued maintenance of the Ohio River in a proper condition for navigation.

The foregoing figures relate only to maintenance ex-

---

[16] *Report of the Chief of Engineers.* 1931, p. 1343.

penditures incurred by the Army engineers. Navigation aids in the form of fixed lights, buoys, and channel markers are provided by the United States Bureau of Lighthouses. The total outlay for such aids on the Ohio River system in the fiscal year 1931-32 was $118,766. We do not have figures for the Ohio proper but $80,000 may be taken as a rough approximation.

Unlike the State of New York, in connection with the Barge Canal system, the United States government has not issued bonds for the improvement of rivers but has financed the projects out of annual appropriations. The $120,000,000 referred to above nevertheless represents an investment by the federal government in the Ohio River. Since this money might be invested elsewhere in a profitable way, we must include the interest on this amount as an element in the cost of transportation on the Ohio. At 4 per cent, the annual interest charge would amount to $4,800,000. The total subsidy to shippers on the Ohio River, in 1931-32, was $6,208,975 (river maintenance), $80,000 (navigation aids) and $4,800,000 (interest on investment)—a total of $11,088,975.

In terms of a rate per ton mile the taxpayers' subsidy to the shippers on the Ohio River proper amounted to 7.46 mills. This figure is computed on the basis of the *total* traffic, including the non-commercial sand and gravel tonnage. The addition of, say, 6 mills for the cost of moving traffic gives a total of 13.46 mills. The distance between river points is typically from 40 to 50 per cent greater than the distance by rail between the same points. Between Pittsburgh and Cairo, Illinois, the water distance is 981 miles and the rail distance 648; between Pittsburgh and Bellaire, Ohio, where the traffic is heaviest, the water distance is 94 miles and the rail distance 69 miles. The ton-mile rate by water must, therefore, be increased by 40 per cent for purposes of comparison with rail rates, making a rate of 18.84 mills as the inclusive cost of transporting bulky commodities consisting almost entirely of the lowest grade of traffic. This cost may be compared with rates per ton mile on the Chesapeake and Ohio Railroad for the same year of 5.97 mills, on the Norfolk and Western of 6.84 mills, and on the railroads of the Central Eastern region 10.32 mills.

III. THE MISSOURI RIVER IMPROVEMENT

In 1906 the Missouri River Improvement Association was organized for the purpose of "educating the public" as to the possibilities of commerce on the river, particularly between Kansas City and St. Louis, and for securing federal appropriations for the improvement of the channel. In 1908 the Board of Engineers, United States Army, after a two years' examination and survey, estimated that a permanent navigable channel of 6 feet depth and a minimum width of 200 feet between Kansas City and St. Louis could be procured at a cost of $3,500,000. A re-examination of the problem in 1912 led the Engineers to a revised estimate of $20,000,000 and the project was then launched in a systematic way.

In 1915 the District Engineer in charge of the Missouri River recommended that further development of the project be abandoned on the ground that the expense was disproportionate to any possible gains that might be realized. The publication of this report, which threatened a serious setback to the waterway movement in general, led to a great conference of waterway interests in Kansas City in August 1915 which was attended by over 200 delegates representing 10 states and 48 cities. The Board of Engineers finally yielded to the pressure of public opinion and recommended the completion of the project.[17]

The total expenditures upon the Missouri River system prior to 1890 were $5,692,310. From 1890 to 1932 inclusive the expenditures upon the Missouri River system aggregated, including maintenance, $76,193,494, of which $1,364,020 was spent on four tributaries, the Yellowstone, Kansas, Osage, and Gasconade rivers.

The construction costs, excluding maintenance, on the St. Louis-Kansas City division, which the Board of Engineers estimated at $20,000,000, had amounted, up to June 30, 1932, to $47,945,328. On June 30, 1932 the Board said: "At ordinary stages there exists a depth of 6 feet from Kansas City to the mouth. Some additional construction is necessary to stabilize and maintain the channel."[18] The amount estimated for completing the project is $7,720,000, inclusive of available appropriated balances on hand amounting to $5,558,522, part of which would perhaps be used for maintenance.[19] (Including construction costs prior to 1910, the total figure for capital outlay is approximately $62,000,000.) In addition to these federal expenditures, local interests in the Missouri Valley have contributed from 1912 to 1932 as much as $2,090,682 toward general improvements on the Missouri.

Maintenance charges on the Missouri River have increased similarly with the capital cost. The Engineers

[17] For a full analysis of the economic significance of the project as it appeared at that time the reader may be referred to an article by H. G. Moulton in the *Journal of Political Economy*, December 1915, pp. 961-70.

[18] *Report of the Chief of Engineers*, 1932, p. 1152.

[19] The same, p. 1157.

estimated in 1908 an annual maintenance charge of $147,500;[20] in 1912, $500,000;[21] in 1928 they reported that "it was impracticable to estimate the cost of annual maintenance";[22] in 1931 the estimated outlay was put at $1,000,000;[23] in 1932 it rose to $2,876,204.66;[24] and the estimate for the fiscal year ending June 30, 1934 is $2,330,000.[25]

The difficulty of providing satisfactory navigating conditions on the river is indicated by the following statement:

The stream is notorious for instability of channel, shifting sand bars and shore accretions, and extensive erosion of its alluvial banks by swift, undercutting currents. Low-water stages occur in the late fall and winter, succeeded by a secondary flood in April and the annual June high water. Navigation is halted or seriously impeded from three to five months by ice and low stages.[26]

1. Traffic. The traffic moved on the river declined somewhat between 1911 and 1922. Since 1924 the commerce has increased, as shown by the table on the following page.

The figures of total tonnage have commonly been cited as evidence of the beneficial results of the improvements made on the river.[27] Practically the entire tonnage, however, is an incident of the construction work itself. The large increases in tonnage in recent years is due sole-

[20] 60th Cong., House doc. 1120, p. 37.

[21] *Report of the Chief of Engineers*, 1927, p. 1110.

[22] The same, 1928, p. 1146.

[23] The same, 1931, p. 1244.

[24] The same, p. 1247-51.

[25] The same, 1932, p. 1157.

[26] *Transportation in the Mississippi and Ohio Valleys*, Corps of Engineers, U. S. Army, and U. S. Shipping Board, 1929, p. 35.

[27] Among other places in testimony before Congress when soliciting appropriations.

ly to the enlarged scope of the construction and dredging work which was being undertaken on the river during those years. Private commerce has almost disappeared.

TRAFFIC ON THE MISSOURI RIVER

Year	Commercial Traffic	Government Materials	All Traffic
1924	181,813	165,511	347,324
1925	249,899	161,000	410,899
1926	343,815	170,609	514,424
1927	196,971	354,310	551,281
1928	3,484	809,717	813,201
1929	779	1,157,553	1,158,332
1930[a]	____	____	1,828,439
1931[b]	____	____	1,377,860

[a] Volume of materials used in government work not shown separately.
[b] "A large percentage of the traffic reported was for river improvement work." *Report of the Chief of Engineers*, 1932, Pt. II, p. 689.

The traffic moves only a few miles. Seventy-eight per cent of the total is sand, stone, and gravel and 21 per cent is "wood and paper," consisting largely of pilings, logs, and other lumber. Nearly all of the commercial traffic reported for the years 1924-27 consisted of sand, stone, and gravel. In view of the fact that no commercial traffic in sand and gravel has been reported since 1928 one may presume this trade was not really "commercial" in earlier years. The 779 tons of commercial traffic in 1929 consisted of 750 tons of logs, 10 tons of horses and mules, 6 tons of cattle and hogs, 6 tons of corn, 4 tons of machinery, and 3 tons of "all other."

2. *The inclusive cost of transport.* A brief statement will suffice to show the contributions of the taxpayers for transportation on this section of the Missouri River. In the year 1932 the interest on the capital investment at 4

per cent, amounted to, roughly, $4,000,000. Maintenance charges amounted to $2,090,293.[28] This makes a total of $6,090,294. Estimating that the genuine *commercial* traffic is as large as it was in 1928, the transportation cost borne by the taxpayer amounted to $1720 a ton. On the basis of 1929 commercial traffic the subsidy is $7900 a ton.

3. Contemplated improvements on the upper Missouri. The program of Missouri River development also calls for the provision of a depth of 6 feet from Kansas City to Sioux City, a distance of 417 miles, and the improvement of the river by the removal of snags and dredging operations from Sioux City to Fort Benton, Montana, a distance of 807 miles. There was expended on the Kansas City-Sioux City stretch up to 1927 for new work $2,987,000. Revised estimates in 1932 called for an additional expenditure of $77,000,000. Twenty-seven million dollars has been appropriated under acts of January 1, 1927 and July 30, 1930. Maintenance costs for the year 1933-34 are estimated at $250,000.

The traffic on this stretch of the river amounted, in 1929, to 208,800 tons, of which only 489 tons was commercial traffic. The traffic on the river above Sioux City amounts to only a few thousand tons annually.

In concluding this account of the Missouri River development mention may be made of the fact that local interests in the valley are becoming disillusioned about the benefits that were to be conferred on agricultural traffic. The Board of Trade of Kansas City has recently passed a resolution against government operation of

---

[28] Lights have not as yet been provided, but a large item on this account was included in the 1933-34 budget of the Bureau of Lighthouses.

barge lines. "Reports dated November 30, 1929 and February 10, 1930, by the district engineer, and December 26, 1929 and February 20, 1930 by the division engineer, on preliminary examination and survey [of a 9-foot project in the lower Missouri] are held in abeyance indefinitely by the Board of Engineers for Rivers and Harbors at the request of local interests."[29] The railway rate on grain from Kansas City to the Gulf (Port Arthur) is 4.76 mills per ton mile (11 cents a bushel). Since the water distance from Kansas City to New Orleans is 1556 miles as compared with 789 miles from Kansas City to Port Arthur by rail, the waterway has no possibility of competing for the only important type of potential water traffic originating in territory tributary to the Missouri valley.

IV. THE MISSISSIPPI RIVER

The golden era of transportation on the Mississippi, romantically depicted by Mark Twain, came to an end before the close of the last century. Shortly after the Civil War passenger and general merchandise traffic declined rapidly, leaving in the main only lumber products on the upper river and cotton, grain, and coal on the lower stretches. The maximum traffic was probably reached in 1889. Traffic on the upper river declined from 3,947,000 tons in 1889 to 1,836,000 in 1910, and to 630,951 in 1920. On the lower Mississippi the traffic for all sections, including duplications, declined from 6,701,000 in 1890 to 3,742,000 in 1910; and then increased, during the war period, reaching 5,364,000 in 1920. No data are available which show traffic on any one section of the Mississippi (or the river as a whole) over a long period of years. Receipts and shipments at

[29] *Report of the Chief of Engineers*, 1932, p. 1171.

St. Louis—the best measure of river traffic we have—are shown in the chart on p. 471.

During the World War the United States Railroad Administration commandeered all privately owned floating equipment on the Mississippi and Warrior Rivers, alloted $12,000,000 for new floating equipment, and took over the operation of the boats. Under authorization of the Transportation Act of 1920 which among other things was intended "to promote, encourage, and develop water transportation, service, and facilities and to foster and preserve in full vigor both rail and water transportation," this Mississippi service was transferred to the jurisdiction of the War Department.

The officers in charge in due course contended that the operating losses were the result of hampering regulations and restrictions, and that if the service were set up on a satisfactory business basis it would be possible to demonstrate the inherent advantages of water transportation. Accordingly, Congress in 1924 created the Inland Waterways Corporation to be operated as a separate unit under the War Department. In reporting the bill favorably to the House of Representatives, the Committee on Interstate and Foreign Commerce stated that:

The Committee believes . . . that if this bill becomes a law the Government can and will within the next five years demonstrate not only the practicability of water transportation, but the great advantage and economy to shippers, and the profitable results that will reward private capital invested in transportation facilities on our rivers. And when that time comes, it is the judgment of the Committee that the Government can dispose of its properties to private capital to an advantage and withdraw entirely from such activities.

After the enactment of this bill the Secretary of War can operate the barge lines in accordance with the same business principles that would be followed by a private transportation company. And it is the opinion of the Committee that if they cannot then operate it successfully and at a fair profit, private capital could not do so; that further expenditure of government funds for the improvement of our inland waterways would be useless and should be stopped.[30]

A new national policy was thus launched. Although the water carriers were provided with a toll-free highway, on which maintenance costs were met by the government, private capital had not evinced any considerable interest in developing river transport. The remedy appeared to be to have the government demonstrate the short-sightedness of private enterprise in not taking advantage of the profit-making opportunities which the river afforded. Before analyzing the results of this experiment we must consider briefly the costs that have been incurred by the government in the construction and maintenance of the navigation channel itself.

1. *Expenditures on the river.* Since 1879 expenditures for all purposes on the lower Mississippi River—that is, from St. Louis to Head of Passes at New Orleans—have been met out of special appropriations and administered by a permanent Mississippi River Commission. On the upper Mississippi, however, as well as on the Ohio and the Missouri River systems, they are handled by the United States Army Engineers. The expenditures made by the Mississippi River Commission include those for flood control as well as for navigation; but unfortunately neither the Mississippi River Commission nor the United States Army Engineers, who report outlays on the Mississippi, attempt to separate the expenditures for flood control from those assignable to navigation. The accounts

[30] 68 Cong. 1 sess. H.R. 375.

of the Commission are classified according to the character of the work, while the United States Army Engineers, in their summary statement[31] simply list all expenditures under the one heading "Flood Control." It is therefore necessary for us to make the best allocation possible from the data available.

The Commission reports the following sub-classes: levees, revetments, dredging and miscellaneous, and gaging waters. The levees are clearly flood control works, but it would seem that expenditures for dredging and snagging primarily benefit navigation, as do also those for revetments and contractions. After discussing the flood control aspects of the project the Annual Report of the Mississippi River Commission for 1932 goes on to say: "The adopted project *also* provides for revetting to stabilize the river channel and prevent excessive caving of banks; this supplemented by contraction works and dredging will insure a navigable channel 300 feet wide and 9 feet deep."[32] While these navigation improvements may contribute somewhat to flood control, it is probably equally true that navigation also benefits from flood control works.

Out of the total federal expenditures on the lower Mississippi system, amounting to $268,000,000, the expenditures assignable to navigation on this basis of allocation would be $137,454,000; those assignable to flood control $131,000,000.[33] In addition to these federal expenditures local interests along the river have contributed $3,491,283[34] assignable to navigation purposes. Lo-

[31] See, for example, *Report of the Chief of Engineers*, 1932, p. 13.

[32] The same, 1932, p. 1928.

[33] It is necessary to use a figure including some allocated funds because no other total gives a satisfactory classification of expenditures. Amount taken from *Report of the Chief of Engineers*, 1930, p. 2102.

[34] *Report of the Chief of Engineers*, 1930, p. 2108.

cal contributions for the purposes of flood control since 1882 amount to $202,258,496.[35] The expenditures on the tributaries of the lower Mississippi are handled by the United States Army Engineers and involve no flood control outlays. Prior to 1890 these expenditures amounted to $4,830,000; between 1890 and 1930 they aggregated $18,676,000.[36]

Federal expenditures, including maintenance, on the upper Mississippi River System, that is above the mouth of the Ohio River, amounted between 1890 and 1930 to $78,993,937 and on the tributaries to $13,263,994. These expenditures were incident to the provision of a 6-foot channel. Under authority of the Rivers and Harbors Act of 1927 a special board of engineers made a new survey of the upper Mississippi with a view to securing a channel depth of 9 feet at low water between the mouth of the Missouri and Minneapolis in order to provide a uniform depth with that on the lower Mississippi and the Ohio. The Rivers and Harbors Act of 1930 authorized the new project for a 9-foot channel between the mouth of the Illinois River and Minneapolis, the required depth to be secured by means of locks and dams, such locks to be "of not less than Ohio River standard dimensions." The estimated cost of the new work is put at $124,000,000, while maintenance charges for a 9-foot channel are estimated at $1,000,000 annually.[37]

2. *Traffic.* During the post-war period, traffic on the Mississippi River from the Twin Cities to New Orleans has increased from 5,994,972 tons in 1920 to 13,969,537 tons in 1930. The figure for 1930 includes materials used

[35] The same, p. 2073.
[36] Compiled from *Annual Reports of the Chief of Engineers* and the *Eleventh Census of the United States.*
[37] *Report of the Chief of Engineers,* 1932, p. 1112.

in government construction work, brush for river improvements, rafted logs, and the Baton Rouge coastwise and foreign petroleum trade, which is not considered by the United States Engineers as a part of Mississippi River traffic. With these items eliminated we have for 1930 a total of 9,245,031 tons which benefits from Mississippi River improvements. The detailed figures are as follows:[38]

		Short Tons
Total*		13,969,537
Less		
Material used in government work	1,042,552	
Brush (river work)	83,658	
Rafted logs	226,576	
Baton Rouge coastwise and foreign petroleum trade	3,371,720	4,724,506
Net traffic interested in Mississippi River improvements		9,245,031

* Net tonnage, all known duplications having been eliminated.

About 43 per cent of the traffic is a local petroleum movement between Vicksburg and New Orleans, and 17 per cent is sand, stone, and gravel. The following table shows the principal traffic classified by commodities and direction of movement:

	Tons
Principal northbound traffic:	
Sugar	352,059
Sulphur	85,886
Burlap and bagging	31,730
Coffee	21,927
Sisal	17,533
	509,135

[38] Compiled from *Report of the Chief of Engineers*, 1931, Pt. II.

Principal southbound traffic:		Tons
Heavy iron and steel	457,472	
Wheat	174,802	
Cotton	109,201	
Tobacco	17,226	
		758,701
Petroleum products		
Vicksburg-New Orleans[a]		4,027,449
Sand, stone, and gravel		1,635,389
Barged logs		457,472
Coal and coke		226,979
All other		1,629,906
Total		9,245,031

[a] Not included in the coastwise and foreign trade noted above.

3. *Extent of the subsidy for river improvement.* In reducing the taxpayers' contribution for river improvement to a rate per ton mile it will be desirable to consider the upper and lower river separately. The construction costs on the upper Mississippi from the beginning have amounted to about $70,000,000.[39] Total expenditures prior to 1890 amounted to $16,642,000, of which perhaps $10,000,000 may be assigned to capital. The capital outlays since 1890 may therefore be put at roughly $60,000,000. The interest on $60,000,000 at 4 per cent equals $2,400,000 annually. Maintenance charges in 1930 amounted to $2,648,759,[40] making a total outlay of $5,048,759. The traffic on the upper Mississippi in 1930 amounted to 153,639,152 ton miles. This amounts to approximately 33 mills per ton mile contributed by the taxpayers for overhead expenses.

[39] *Report of the Chief of Engineers,* 1930, p. 1201. For cost of reservoirs at head waters, see p. 1207.

[40] In 1931 these charges amounted to $3,777,019 and in 1932 to $2,471,984.

On the lower Mississippi capital costs since 1890, computed on the basis indicated above, have been approximately $72,000,000. Interest on this sum at 4 per cent is $2,880,000. Maintenance charges for navigation purposes amounted in 1930 to $2,394,380.[41] In addition, *new work* for navigation purposes, which is difficult to distinguish from maintenance because of its recurrent character, amounted to $7,436,793.[42] The annual costs for capital, maintenance, and continuous construction thus aggregate something like $12,700,000 annually.

The traffic on the lower Mississippi amounted in 1930 to approximately 1,570,000,000 ton miles.[43] The overhead contributions of the taxpayers, therefore, amounts to roughly 8 mills per ton mile. If the recurrent construction for new work be eliminated from the annual costs, the ton mile contribution of the taxpayers amounts to approximately 3 mills. Since the distance by water on the lower Mississippi is about 60 per cent greater than by rail this is the equivalent of 4.8 mills by rail.

4. *Extent of subsidy to Inland Waterways Corporation.* We turn now to a consideration of the Inland Waterways Corporation which operates barges on the subsidized Mississippi and Warrior Rivers. On June 1, 1924 the War Department transferred to the Corporation assets in the form of barges and other floating equip-

[41] Expense for navigation aids incurred by the Bureau of Lighthouses for the river as a whole was $289,996 for the year ending June 30, 1932.

[42] These data have been compiled from the accounts of the Mississippi River Commission as reported by the Chief of Engineers, U. S. Army.

[43] This figure is computed by eliminating from the over-all ton mileage figure given by the engineers the seacoast traffic and that in government improvements as shown on p. 496 above. In computing ton mileage for Baton Rouge traffic we used the distance between Baton Rouge and New Orleans; for the government material we assumed that it moved the average ton mile distance for the given division of the river on which it was transported.

ment appraised at $10,236,684, and Congress appropriated $5,000,000 for additional capital. In 1928 Congress authorized the appropriation of an additional $10,000,000 as necessary—$4,000,000 of which was actually contributed in 1929 and $3,000,000 in 1930. The growth of traffic has been as follows:

	Tons		Tons
1924 (7 months)	591,815	1928	1,872,597
1925	1,152,794	1929	1,653,381
1926	1,342,556	1930	1,490,624
1927	1,650,207	1931	1,533,915

The slow rate of development of traffic was ascribed in part to the failure of the railroads to co-operate in the matter of through rates. Accordingly, in 1928 Congress passed the Denison Act which provides that the railroads must join with inland waterway carriers in through routes and joint rates with reasonable division of revenue between the rail and water carriers.

As was indicated above, it was the intention to demonstrate the commercial feasibility of water transportation on the Mississippi River—given a toll-free route constructed, maintained, and lighted at the expense of the government. The operating corporation gave the government stock for the cash advanced—though not for the $10,236,684 of property which was donated—and it was expected that dividends would be paid to the government on this stock.

The President of the Corporation states that for the period June 1, 1924 to September 30, 1932 the Corporation had a "net income" of $922,871.34.[44] Analysis of the Corporation's accounts, however, shows that this

[44] Statement before the National Transportation Committee and elsewhere.

statement is quite misleading. This figure of $922,871.34 is listed as being "net income of operating subsidiaries." But under "debits" we find an item called "losses assumed on equipment retired" amounting to $809,427. The official explanation of the failure to provide adequate depreciation on this equipment is that much of the equipment received from the War Department was already obsolete and unfit for use at the time it was taken over and that it was greatly overvalued. We find, however, that the year before these properties were taken over the present head of the Inland Waterways Corporation, who was then in charge of the barge fleet for the War Department, said "It was fortunate indeed that the demands of war brought into being the present magnificent fleets operated by this service."[45] In 1925, in pointing out what a good bargain had been made, he stated that "the total appraised value of the physical assets of this Corporation, as a going concern (exclusive of any value for good will, which usually is valued at 10 per cent) is almost $10,000,000. This valuation was made by the American Appraisal Company of Milwaukee."[46]

Aside from the operation of boats the Corporation's statement shows one important item of expense and one important item of income. The cost of operating the Washington office was $454,339.56. On the income side there was interest on Corporation funds deposited in banks amounting to $310,495 and interest on long-term loans to local communities for the purpose of developing

[45] *Annual Report of the Chief of Inland and Coastwise Waterways Service*, 1923, p. 8.

[46] Brig. Gen. T. Q. Ashburn, *Waterways and Inland Seaports* (issued by the War Dept.), 1925, p. 25.

barge line terminals amounting to $69,363. This large income from bank deposits has evidently been made possible largely by the fact that the government advanced to the Corporation in 1929 and 1930 $7,000,000 of new capital, much of which was not immediately required for the purchase of new equipment. This is evident from the cash balance on hand at the end of successive years. Including this income contributed by the government and counting the losses on equipment retired, the Corporation's statement shows a net income from the whole period to September 30, 1932 of $38,962.84.

As a government agency the Corporation has certain cost advantages that would not be enjoyed by a private company, such as free postage and wireless service, free legal services, and government rates on telegrams. There is also free office space to the extent of 2200 square feet. Nor does the Corporation pay taxes on its property assets valued at $24,000,000, except $8,490 (1931) to the State of Alabama for property in that state. At the low rate of $2.00 per hundred taxes would amount to $480,000 per year.

Since the President of the Corporation claims that *in effect* it pays substantial taxes, the issue involved must be briefly considered. The so-called taxes are in reality funds paid by the Corporation to municipal terminals for the use of their facilities. "We paid the municipalities last year $228,952 which was available to them to pay taxes."[47] Of course this is nothing but rent; it is no more to be called a tax than is the rent which an individual pays for his apartment or a business corporation pays for its office space or warehouse. These terminals are, more-

[47] Brig. Gen. T. Q. Ashburn, Address before Mississippi Valley Association, St. Louis, Nov. 21-22, 1932.

over, operated by the municipalities at a substantial deficit, and this represents another subsidy to river traffic.

It is impossible to determine from the Corporation's accounts whether with the Warrior River operations eliminated the Corporation would have earned a return on the capital investment.

Although the original purpose of the Corporation was to demonstrate to private enterprise that money could be made from water transportation, the president of the Corporation now insists that it is unnecessary to earn any return on capital in order to demonstrate the value of the enterprise. He points to the savings to the shippers as being far more significant than any dividends on capital invested. He regards the entire population of this country as being in a sense stockholders in this enterprise, receiving their dividends in the form of low transportation charges. Unfortunately private enterprise which was to be shown how to make *real dividends* cannot operate on this basis. Interest at 4 per cent on $24,000,000 of property and cash furnished by the government would be $960,000 a year.

The transportation charges averaged approximately 5 mills per ton mile in the year 1931, having increased about 1 mill since 1928. A differential of from 10 to 20 per cent below rail rates is regarded as necessary in order to induce traffic to move by water. There is thus little, if any, real saving, if the convenience and time factor in transportation be allowed for. A rate of 5 mills per ton mile on the Mississippi is not a low transportation rate for low grade traffic. Because of the extra distance by river it is the equivalent of about 8 mills per ton mile by rail.

The Committee on Interstate and Foreign Commerce, as was noted above, stated in 1924 that if the War Department cannot in five years "operate it [the barge line] successfully and at a fair profit, private capital could not do so; and that further expenditures of government funds for the improvement of our inland waterways would be useless and should be dropped." The experience of the last eight years does not appear to have proved the enterprise an economic success.

In appraising this Mississippi River transportation experiment, it will be useful to the reader to contrast our policy on the Mississippi with that in connection with the Panama Canal. In the administration of the Panama Canal it is not assumed that the taxpayers should subsidize the shippers. Both the original cost of the project, including interest throughout the period of construction, and the annual costs of maintenance, are regarded as transportation charges assessable against the shippers, and tolls are levied for the purpose of covering these overhead costs. During the five-year period 1928-32 the earnings amounted to slightly more than 3 per cent. The accounting principles followed by the War Department in connection with its administration of the Panama Canal project may well serve as a model for use in connection with our internal waterways generally.

V. THE INTRACOASTAL WATERWAY

The character and economic significance of the intracoastal waterway may be very briefly summarized. This waterway is planned to extend along the coast from Boston to Corpus Christi, Texas. It is being surveyed and constructed in a haphazard manner. The Cape Cod Canal has a controlling depth of 23 feet. A 25-foot channel is under survey by the United States Engineers to connect up open water at New York harbor with the Delaware River. A 12-foot canal, 19 miles long, is being provided between the Delaware River and Chesapeake Bay. From Norfolk, Virginia, to Beaufort, South Carolina, the route involves 424 miles of tortuous inland navigation, with depths varying from 4 to 12 feet. South of Beaufort there is a 7-foot route following tidal channels to Jacksonville, Florida; and an 8-foot channel is proposed from Jacksonville to Miami via rivers and canals. Between Miami and Corpus Christi disconnected sections are now under improvement.

The character of much of the route may be indicated by the following description of the 94-mile section from the Cape Fear River, North Carolina, to Winyah Bay, South Carolina:

The waterway begins at Southport, N.C., and follows in general a route from the Cape Fear River up Elizabeth River 6.7 miles to a point near its headwaters; thence through high ground 2.6 miles to the headwaters of Davis Creek; thence down Davis Creek to the sounds and salt marshes [having a depth of about 1½ feet at high water] and through the latter to Little River, S.C., a distance of 24.2 miles; thence up Little River 5.7 miles to its headwaters; thence through high ground 21.8 miles to the head of Socastee Creek; thence down Socastee Creek 6.5 miles to the Waccamaw River (which is maintained at 12 feet depth) and down the latter 27 miles to Winyah Bay.[48]

Over $40,000,000 has already been expended upon the various divisions of this project for new work. Contemplated improvements on other sections will involve the expenditure of vast additional sums. For example, the Chief Engineer now recommends the deepening and widening of the Cape Cod Canal at an estimated cost of

[48] *Report of the Chief of Engineers*, 1931, pp. 635-36.

$23,500,000. The appropriations for 1931-33, for the various divisions of the project, aggregating $7,534,363, are shown on page 445.

The only important service which this canal now renders is to provide a sheltered yacht route from the northern states to Florida and Gulf waters. This class of traffic has declined materially since 1929. There is no through commercial traffic on the route and very little local traffic except in one or two sections. It has as competitors the railways along the Atlantic coast and also the coastwise shipping routes. The long distances involved and the slow movement will always make successful through-route competition with coastwise vessels impossible. It is, moreover, of no value from a naval point of view.

VI. THE ST. LAWRENCE PROJECT

This project was conceived at the close of the war when there was a temporary shortage of railroad facilities. The main arguments advanced in its support were that (1) it was necessary to relieve traffic congestion; (2) it would greatly reduce transportation costs, bringing much needed relief to the interior of the country; and (3) it would lead to the development of vast water power resources. Inasmuch as this project was thoroughly analyzed in a separate study published in 1929,[49] it is necessary here merely to summarize the issues and call attention to certain recent developments. Since we are here concerned only with transportation, the power aspect of the problem will be omitted from consideration.

The project calls for the construction of a 27-foot channel in the St. Lawrence River. The Welland Canal,

[49] Moulton, Morgan, and Lee, *The St. Lawrence Navigation and Power Project*, The Brookings Institution, 1929.

recently completed by Canada, would be used for passing Niagara Falls. A 27-foot depth would have to be provided for other connecting lake channels, and the lake harbors would have to be proportionally deepened.

The public mind has been greatly confused as to the cost of this project mainly because the cost figures which have been presented usually relate only to certain phases of the project. The Joint Board of Engineers was under instructions to report only on the cost of the improvements in the St. Lawrence River and inter-connecting lake channels; the costs of constructing the Welland Canal and of providing suitable lake harbors and the requisite port facilities did not come within their field of inquiry. The cost of improving the Great Lakes harbors must, however, be assigned to this seaway project because a greater depth than now exists is not necessary for efficient lake boat transportation. Whether or not these expenditures are borne exclusively by the Federal government is immaterial, in any case the costs will have to be paid by the taxpayers of the United States and Canada. The Welland Canal must be included as a part of the project as a whole, even though it was already under construction, for the reason that it is an indispensable link in the route. It is, moreover, generally agreed that Canada is entitled to credit for the costs incurred in connection with this part of the seaway.

The engineers' tentative estimates of the cost of constructing the St. Lawrence channel (for the two countries) assignable to navigation is $184,659,000,[50] exclusive of interest during construction. Interest at 4 per

[50] This is for a single stage improvement and assumes a fifty-fifty allocation on works jointly for navigation and power. The same, p. 87.

cent would add about $30,000,000 to the cost of the project. The engineers estimate the cost of inter-connecting lake channels at $65,100,000, which must be raised to $75,000,000 to include interest during construction. The fact is that although the St. Lawrence project has not been approved large additional appropriations have already been made for the inter-connecting channels in anticipation of the deepening of the St. Lawrence.

The cost of deepening outer and inner harbors on the lakes and developing the necessary port facilities we have estimated at $250,000,000 for ten harbors. As the table on pp. 443-45 indicates, there are a large number of lake harbors, all of which would undoubtedly ask for deeper water in order to give them the advantages of the seaway. The cost of the Welland Canal was originally estimated at $50,000,000. After the war the estimate was raised to $115,000,000. But the cost has proved to be $128,000,000, not counting interest during the period of construction which would amount to at least $25,000,000.

In our computation of the inclusive cost of this project, assignable to navigation, of slightly more than $600,000,000 (nearly a billion including the power development) we made only one modification of the engineers' cost figures. We assumed that the cost might exceed the *tentative* estimate of the Board by as much as 20 per cent. In view of the fact that the costs of waterway projects in this country have usually run from fifty to several hundred per cent above the estimates, we increased the Board's *tentative* figure by 20 per cent, or about $58,000,000.

The basic argument for the St. Lawrence seaway is that it would greatly reduce the cost of transportation between the interior and tidewater, particularly on grain. The project was, in fact, commended to the interior of the country largely on the ground that the savings on grain shipments would amount to from 8 cents to 12 cents a bushel and that this would be reflected in the price of the *entire* product of the farmer, whether exported or not. Savings on the grain trade alone were variously estimated at from $240,000,000 to $366,000,000 annually.

Inasmuch as the entire cost of moving grain from the head of the lakes to Montreal, including transshipping charges, is considerably less than 8 cents for the season's average, a reduction of from 8 to 12 cents a bushel is obviously impossible. In our study of the project we arrived at the conclusion that the maximum reduction that might be effected, on the basis of rates existing in 1928, was 4 cents a bushel; and that this would be accomplished not by bringing ocean vessels into the lakes but by extending the trip of lake vessels as far as Montreal. Recent evidence submitted by lake carriers indicates that lake boats carrying 725,000 bushels could navigate a 27-foot channel to Montreal and that there might be a "theoretical" saving of as much as 2.49 cents a bushel as compared with present costs for smaller boats. It is pointed out, however, that these savings might be materially reduced by delays resulting from bad weather and by accidents or trade conditions such as waiting to load or unload.[51] It appears also that there is doubt in the minds of some lake navigators as to whether the lake vessels would go to Montreal, owing to the heavy

[51] William H. Coverdale, President, Canada Steamship Lines, Ltd.

insurance charges that would be involved on lake vessels navigating difficult channels.[52]

Our analysis indicated that ocean vessels were much less efficient carriers than the specially constructed shallow-draft lake boats, and we concluded that the only vessels which might enter the lakes for the grain trade would be trampers at the peak of the season when the rates were at the highest point. Recent evidence submitted by lake carriers indicates that the cost of shipping grain in large lake vessels, carrying 572,000 bushels, would be one-third less than the cost of moving grain in ocean tramp steamships carrying 280,000 bushels, the largest vessel which could operate over the route on a satisfactory time schedule. After considering the problem with the leading shipping companies of the world, we also reached the conclusion that ocean shipping companies would not establish on this route regular cargo service for miscellaneous freight.

Traffic estimates made by the Bureau of Foreign and Domestic Commerce in support of this project indicated potential traffic of from 18,600,000 tons to 23,700,000 tons annually.[53] Although this figure makes no allowance for the steady decline in American grain exports, forecast by the Department of Agriculture, let us nevertheless accept—for the moment—a total of 20,000,000 tons as a basis for computing the burden which the St. Lawrence seaway would impose upon the taxpayer. The annual interest and maintenance charges

[52] Capt. Joseph S. Wood, an experienced navigator on the lakes, so testified before the National Transportation Committee.

[53] Our own analyses, based upon a detailed study of every important commodity which might possibly use the St. Lawrence route, indicated total traffic possibilities of roughly half this amount. For criticism of the method used by the Department of Commerce, see *The St. Lawrence Navigation and Power Project*, pp. 285-90.

incident to the St. Lawrence navigation project as a whole, when figured on the most conservative basis, would amount to roughly $40,000,000 annually. This is equivalent to $2.00 a ton on the above greatly exaggerated traffic estimate. Taking the grain traffic as fairly typical of the tonnage that might use the route, we find that the taxpayers would be contributing $2.00 a ton in order that the shipper might save (at 2.50 cents a bushel) 83 cents a ton.

This project raises a fundamental question of national policy for both Canada and the United States. In neither country are present transportation facilities in any sense inadequate. In fact, the great need, even in normal times, and particularly in Canada, is for an increase in traffic on existing rail lines to the end that costs and rates may be reduced. To divert by means of heavy subsidy a portion of this traffic to a waterway route which is closed for several months each year means inevitably an increase in the difficulty of maintaining railroad financial stability. Since the water route is typically closed by ice from late November to May, the route cannot in any event eliminate the necessity for railroads; the most that it can do is to take a portion of the traffic away from the railroads during the season of open navigation.

If it is necessary to reduce the rates to the interior, either because of agricultural depression or a desire to restore the balance in the rate structure which was upset by the construction of the Panama Canal, this can be done by the simple expedient of reducing railroad rates to the seaboard and meeting the resulting deficit out of the federal treasury. The cost would be but a fraction of that involved in constructing a seaway for this purpose.

VII. CONCLUSION

The foregoing survey of our efforts to rehabilitate inland water transportation offers an excellent illustration of the confusion that arises in the public mind once fundamental principles have been lost sight of in the determination of public policy. So long as tolls were levied on waterways in order to cover capital costs and maintenance charges everyone could know, by reference to the rates paid by rail, water, or highway, which form of transportation was more economical. But once tolls were abolished and shippers by water were relieved of the larger part of the cost of transportation, the economic issues involved were completely obscured—this for the simple reason that a large portion of the cost was concealed from public view, being absorbed in the general budget figures of the government. The general public has for the most part been completely unaware of the costs which taxpayers have shouldered in connection with water transportation. From discussions of this problem extending over a period of more than twenty years with leaders of public opinion the writer knows that most of them are not aware of the hidden costs in water transportation, or, if aware of them, were completely in the dark as to their magnitude. It is only when one goes to the trouble of unearthing from government archives the subsidies involved, translating these into terms of ton mile water rates, that the true situation is revealed.

The situation in European countries has been directly analogous. After the coming of the railways the waterways quickly began to suffer a decline. Tolls were then abolished for the purpose of enabling the waterways to compete for certain classes of traffic, and rates by rail were fixed at a point roughly 20 per cent above the rates which were necessary to enable the waterways to obtain traffic. This was true in countries where the railways were owned by the government, as well as in those where private enterprise prevailed. In Germany, for example, the government operates the railroads at a profit and uses the excess revenues to offset the deficit on the waterways. If the deficit on German waterways, other than the Rhine River, is allocated on a ton mile basis to the traffic moved, the rates by water are found to be more than double those by rail.[54] But the public there as here is unaware of the extent of the subsidies to waterways.

It is easy to understand how shipping and commercial organizations, interested in lower transportation *rates* for their particular communities, should bring organized pressure to bear upon Congress for appropriations for specific projects. Even if they knew of the high *inclusive* costs of water transportation, it would seem advantageous to obtain local aid from the federal treasury. But these apparent gains to particular communities are usually nullified in the end. A glance at the list of waterway projects given on pages 443-50 shows that these expenditures are so widely diffused throughout the country that each local recipient of aid is at the same time contributing, through taxes, to subsidizing waterway projects elsewhere. This sort of thing, of course, never works out equitably; but that is only another objection to the pork-barrel system.

The "indirect benefits" in the form of lower rates and stimulated industry and trade, of which so much is made, are pure illusion, unless it can be shown that the *inclu-*

[54] For an extended analysis of the waterways of Germany and other European countries, see H. G. Moulton, *Waterways Versus Railways*.

sive cost of water transportation is lower than that by rail. This is because the gains to shippers are more than matched by the losses to taxpayers. After all the taxpayers in the mass are the very people who use transportation facilities, namely, manufacturers, farmers, merchants, and the public generally.

We subsidize the construction and maintenance of inland waterways for the purpose of diverting low grade traffic from railroads. Then, when difficulties arise for the railways, we look to the federal treasury, that is to the taxpayers, for more subsidy in order to prevent bankruptcy and the breakdown of essential transportation service. It is policies such as these which account in no small degree for the government's financial plight at the present time. The taxpayers can be saved $100,000,000 annually by abandoning uneconomic waterway enterprises, and at the same time the financial condition of distressed railroads will be materially improved. Moreover, it will be much easier to effect a reduction in freight rates if we cease to divide an insufficient volume of tonnage between duplicating transportation services.

PART VI
HIGHWAY TRANSPORTATION

CHAPTER XXIV

NATURE OF THE HIGHWAY TRANSPORT PROBLEM

The motor vehicle traffic which flows over the highway systems of the country is decidedly heterogeneous in character. Ordinary passenger car traffic predominates in terms of volume, but truck and bus operations, while constituting a relatively small portion of vehicular traffic, create special problems not only in the administration and financing of highway development, but in the co-ordination and regulation of various transportation agencies as well.

During the first two decades of development in the field of highway transportation no particularly complex problems of public policy arose. Both the buildings of roads and the building of motor vehicles were passing through experimental phases. The use of public highways for purely commercial purposes had not attained sufficient importance to cause any concern on the part of established transportation agencies.

But during the last decade the rapid expansion of improved highway mileage and the perfection of motor vehicle equipment have given rise to a substantial volume of commercial operations on the highways. This chapter is intended to indicate briefly the nature and the scope of operations of the various agencies which utilize the public highways.

I. GROWTH OF HIGHWAY TRANSPORT

In 1900 only 8,000 passenger cars were registered in the country and truck registrations did not appear in official records until 1904, when only 410 were registered. By 1918, passenger car registrations had increased to 5,621,617 and trucks to 525,000. Passenger car registrations reached the peak of 23,121,589 in 1929 but had declined to 22,347,800 by 1931. Truck registrations increased consistently between 1918 and 1930 at a somewhat faster rate of growth than passenger cars.[1] But in 1931 truck registrations also declined slightly.

Bus registrations increased rapidly between 1921 and 1926, followed by a slower increase during the ensuing five years. By the end of 1931 it is estimated that about 98,000 buses were in use, but only 50 per cent were in revenue service. Some 40 per cent of those in revenue service were limited to city operations.[2] Scattered information indicates that passenger car traffic accounts for between 85 and 90 per cent of the vehicle mileage traveled annually over the rural highway systems of the United States.[3] The growth of bus transportation is shown in the chart on page 17.

While the passenger car traffic is fairly homogeneous as to both character of traffic and type of equipment, no such uniformity exists in truck operations. In the latter, widely different types of vehicles are used, variations in ownership and operation exist, and various types of services are rendered by the several types of truck operations.

1. *Variations in types of vehicles.* Since 1928 significant shifts have occurred in the rated capacities of trucks produced in the United States. The term *rated capacity*

---

[1] Annual average rate of change for passenger car registrations between 1918 and 1930 = 12.94 per cent; for trucks, 16.15 per cent. Passenger car data include buses.

[2] From *Bus Transportation.*

[3] See Bureau of Public Roads reports on traffic surveys conducted in New Hampshire, Ohio, Pennsylvania, and eleven western states.

is useful for purposes of comparison, but the actual load carried does not in many cases coincide with rated capacity. Prior to 1929 about 85 per cent of the annual truck production was in the lightweight class (¾ to 1½ tons capacity) while by 1931 this group accounted for only 26 per cent. The bulk of the production had shifted to the medium capacity class (1½ to 3½ tons capacity) accounting in 1931 for about 70 per cent of truck production. At no time during recent years has production of the heavy class of truck (3½ tons capacity and over) accounted for more than 5 per cent of total truck output.[4] But these production data, of course, do not accurately reflect the number of motor trucks of the various weight classes actually in operation in the various states at the present. Truck registration data by weight classes are available for only 20 states. These states, however, are fairly well distributed geographically. They show that about 63 per cent of the trucks in operation during 1930 were registered in the light-weight class, something over 30 per cent in the medium-weight class, and about 3 per cent in the heavy-capacity group.

2. *Character of ownership and operation.* "The number of trucks engaged in either commercial or private hauling over the highways is not definitely known."[5] It has been estimated, however, that of the 3,500,000 trucks in use, approximately one million are farm owned and two million others are privately owned and not operated for hire. Of the remaining 500,000, approximately 200,000 are common carriers and 300,000 are contract carriers. That is, about 86 per cent of all trucks are owner

[4] National Automobile Chamber of Commerce, *Facts and Figures of the Automobile Industry*, 1932, p. 9.

[5] I.C.C. Docket 23400, "Co-ordination of Motor Transportation," p. 274.

operated, the load and the truck being owned by the same individual or agency; contract carriers, operating for hire or under hauling agreements with agencies and not observing fixed routes or schedule, account for about 9 per cent, and common carriers operating for hire over fixed routes on regular schedule at published rates account for the remaining 5 per cent.[6]

Approximately 70 per cent of all trucks using the highways are operated individually by individuals who own but one truck each, and the balance are distributed among approximately 272,000 fleets,[7] only 55 of which comprise more than 100 vehicles each.[8]

The geographic distribution of truck ownership shows a similar lack of uniformity. Nevada has a registration of 7,000 vehicles as compared with 331,000 in New York, and almost one-half of the trucks in use are owned in eight states. In 1931 eight states—New York, California, Pennsylvania, Texas, Illinois, Ohio, Michigan, and New Jersey—reported aggregate truck registrations of 1,686,263 out of a total for the country of 3,466,303, or 49 per cent of the total.

3. *Volume of traffic carried by trucks.* Information with regard to the volume of inter-city truck traffic is even less satisfactory than that concerning the distribution of truck ownership. The evidence available, however, indicates that about 4 per cent of the total volume of inland traffic is carried by trucks operating in inter-city service, and that the revenue derived from these

[6] Distribution based on U. S. Census of Agriculture, 1930, and a study of 180,000 trucks operating over the federal-aid roads of eleven western states, as reported in Bureau of Public Roads, *Survey of Traffic on the Federal-Aid Highway Systems of Eleven Western States,* 1930.

[7] National Automobile Chamber of Commerce estimates, based on census by the Reuben H. Donnelly Corporation.

[8] *Facts and Figures of the Automobile Industry,* 1932.

operations constitutes about 6 per cent of the total of inland traffic revenue. (See chart on page 17.) Of the inter-city truck traffic about 20 per cent is carried by common carrier operators, 30 per cent by contract carriers, and 50 per cent by trucks privately operated.[9] The evidence further indicates that from 20 to 30 per cent of motor truck operations are interstate in character.[10]

II. CHARACTER OF THE TRUCKING BUSINESS

Small scale operations and individual management are characteristic features of commercial trucking operations.[11] The rapid growth of the industry, the relatively small capital investment required to establish operations, and the ease with which these operations can be abandoned have all contributed to the instability of competitive conditions.

In view of the diversified character of truck ownership and the varied conditions of operation, no definite statement can be made as to the profitableness of the truck business in general or as to wages and working conditions. The better organized truck companies of course keep systematic accounts and set up adequate charges for depreciation. The same is more or less true of the contract carrier. But the individual owner may or may not be operating on a commercial basis.

Since the beginning of the depression the situation

[9] I.C.C. Docket 23400, "Co-ordination of Motor Transportation," p. 403.

[10] The same, pp. 274 and 405. See also U. S. Department of Commerce, *Motor Truck Freight Transportation*, Domestic Commerce Series, No. 66, 1932, p. 21.

[11] The recent study of motor freight transportation points out that although there is an apparent tendency toward consolidation and large-scale operation in the motor freight field, the industry is still predominantly one of small fleets and individual management. See *Motor Truck Freight Transportation*, p. 1.

within the industry has been complicated by the appearance of a large number of individual truckers for hire who are regarded as "fly-by-night" operators. That is to say, they secure possession of a truck on credit, and by virtue of the fact that they make no proper charges for depreciation are enabled through cut rates to eke out a living until such time as they lose possession of the truck. The process is then repeated by another temporary owner. It is this "cut-throat" competition which has led well organized truck companies to favor regulation of rates.

Wages and hours of work also show the widest conceivable variations. The individual owner who carries his own produce is, of course, not concerned with wages as such, and his hours may be limited only by his physical stamina. The contract carrier, operating under widely varying conditions with particular contracts, requires flexibility in hours, and the wages paid can be varied from time to time.

Among the common carrier trucking companies, wages and working conditions are more nearly standardized. The following table shows the truck wage situation in its most favorable light, since the wages are in all cases for organized workers employed by well established truck companies:

	Hours Per Week	Weekly Wage
New York City	48 to 54	$41.00 to $47.50
Chicago	57 to 60	31.00 to 46.00
Boston	48 to 52	30.00 to 36.50
St. Louis	57 to 67	28.00 to 42.00
San Francisco	48¾	33.00 to 48.00

The hours of work are somewhat longer than those on the railroad, where the standard is a 48-hour week. Truck drivers' wages on the largest trucks are in all cases much below the rates paid to locomotive engineers and firemen. Wages paid to the drivers of the light trucks are about the same as those paid to railway section bosses and signalmen helpers.

1. *Range of operations.* The truck has been adapted to a wide range of hauling tasks which vary from the delivery of light farm produce to the heavy service of logging camps, construction work, and the transportation of household goods. The distances over which these operations take place also vary widely. In common carrier and contract trucking operations, regularly scheduled runs in excess of 500 miles are reported. Occasional hauls up to 2,500 miles are not uncommon. Scattered sources of information indicate that a considerable amount of long-distance hauling of a variety of commodities is being done. A recent Department of Commerce study states:

> Tires, for example, are being shipped by truck from Ohio factories as far as Omaha, St. Paul, and New York. Fully assembled automobiles are transported on special semi-trailers for distances as great as 1,000 miles from the factory. Fish have been trucked from Seattle to San Francisco, and fruit and vegetables moved from the eastern shore of Maryland to New England.[12]

The great bulk of trucking operations, however, are for relatively short distances. Over 50 per cent of the routes operated by 182 motor trucking concerns in common carrier and contract carrier service in 37 states and the District of Columbia are shorter than 70 miles in length. Only 20 per cent have a length greater than 120 miles, 8 per cent greater than 200 miles, and 5 per cent greater than 250 miles.[13]

[12] The same, pp. 715-70.
[13] The same, p. 18.

The maximum effective operating range of from 200 to 250 miles is determined primarily by the radius within which overnight delivery is possible. This is much longer in regions of sparse traffic than in the dense traffic areas of the eastern states.[14] Annual mileages for commercial trucking operations vary from 4,000 to 75,000.

The flexibility of trucking operations, both as to operating ranges and adaptability to a variety of hauling tasks, has been made possible largely by two factors: the rapid expansion of improved highway facilities since 1918 and the advances in automotive engineering.

2. *Types of equipment*. During the past decade, advances in automotive design have greatly increased the economy of trucking operations. Changes in tire equipment and the use of trailers have been important contributors to this increased operating economy.

The rapid obsolescence of the solid tire is one of the most significant recent developments in motor transportation. Substitution of pneumatics and particularly of low-pressure tires make possible the carrying of heavier loads in lighter vehicles at greater speed and with less destructiveness both to vehicles and to road surfaces. Between 1921 and 1931 the proportion of annual truck production which was equipped with solid tires decreased from 28 per cent to 3.1 per cent.[15]

Dual pneumatic and balloon tires are now in common use on all types of trucks, and the single pneumatic tire equipment is rare on the larger trucking units operated by common carriers and contract haulers in inter-city movements.[16] Less than 5 per cent of the heavier trucks

[14] See Chapter XXVIII for detailed data in connection with the movement of agricultural products.

[15] *Facts and Figures of the Automobile Industry*, 1932, p. 39.

[16] *Motor Truck Freight Transportation*.

and buses manufactured and equipped with pneumatic tires in 1928 carried low-pressure tires, but by the end of 1931 about 90 per cent of these vehicles were so equipped.[17] The tendency in the matter of tire equipment is clearly toward the exclusive use of pneumatics with a preponderance of balloon tires in trucking operations which utilize the rural highways.

As might be expected, the proportion of the heavy-type trucks is higher among trucks used in commercial operation than among other trucks. The returns from a questionnaire circulated among the trucking industries in 1929 indicate that the percentages of light, medium, and heavy duty trucks in use by trucking concerns during that year were 58 per cent, 32 per cent, and 10 per cent respectively.[18] It appears that the two and a half ton capacity truck is best adapted to inter-city commercial operations. The actual load commonly carried by this type of truck, however, is roughly double the manufacturer's rated capacity.[19]

The utilization of trailers, together with improved tire equipment, has facilitated the carrying of greater gross weights per vehicle without increasing the destructive effects of the vehicle upon road surfaces. Vehicle and trailer combinations carrying 90,000 pounds on 30 balloon tires have been registered in some states. But this particular combination is no longer legally allowed, and the tendency in state legislation is definitely toward the limiting of gross weight as well as maximum over-all length of truck and trailer combinations. These limitations are designed for bridge protection, and also to elim-

[17] G. M. Sprowls (of the Goodyear Tire and Rubber Co.), *Motor Freight*, American Roadbuilders' Association, Bulletin No. 26, 1932, p. 56.
[18] General Motors Truck Co., *National Motor Truck Analysis*, 1929.
[19] *Motor Truck Freight Transportation*, p. 9.

inate the nuisance and danger factor created by unduly long combinations of vehicles.

In the following chapters of this division we shall attempt to clarify, in so far as the data will permit, the economic issues involved in highway transportation. The next two chapters are concerned with the question of highway development and financing and extent to which the costs are borne by highway users, while the fourth chapter discusses the problem of automobile and highway taxation. The fifth chapter shows the extent to which the truck has taken over the marketing of perishable agricultural products. The last chapter takes up the question of highway and railway competition in the terminal areas and analyzes the possibilities of a better co-ordination of the two types of service.

CHAPTER XXV

HIGHWAY DEVELOPMENT AND FINANCING

Highway development in the United States has passed through three distinct phases, each characterized by the administrative dominance of a different agency, or combination of agencies. In the early period, extending to the middle of the nineteenth century, the federal government assumed the initiative in furnishing major highway routes, but gradually relinquished the responsibility to separate states until finally, in 1856, all federal jurisdiction over national highway routes had been assumed by the states through which the routes passed.[1] In the meantime, various states had found the development of subsidiary highway routes excessively burdensome and had placed highway development on a commercial basis by granting charters to individuals and companies, empowering them to build and operate roads and to charge tolls for their use. The states, however, participated in the financing of these projects and retained the right to regulate their use. This first phase of highway development, then, was one of centralized control and semi-commercial operation.

The second phase in the evolution of highway transport embraces the era of rapid railroad building. During this period "the calamity of the railway" fell on toll-road operations; states transferred their official favors

---

[1] The Cumberland Road, leading through Maryland, Pennsylvania, Ohio, Indiana, and Illinois, was the most extensive of these routes. Thomas R. Agg and John E. Brindley, *Highway Administration and Finance*, 1927, p. 21.

to railroad development and highway transportation declined to a position of minor importance. As soon as transport over public roads became unnecessary and unprofitable except for short distances, the building and maintenance of roads was reduced to a matter of local concern and consequently was left to minor political subdivisions—the county, township, and road district.

Thus between the middle and the end of the nineteenth century only a relatively small portion of highway travel passed beyond county boundaries. Under such conditions the administrative and financial responsibility for furnishing highway facilities quite naturally narrowed down to the political units whose areas most nearly conformed to the economic limits of highway transportation.

At the turn of the century the transportation of goods and persons over public roads entered its third and present phase of development, characterized by a rapid increase in highway usage. As a result of the coming of the automobile it soon became apparent that the increased operating radius of highway travel was creating traffic which bore no relation in point of origin and destination to purely political boundaries, and that such traffic was of a basically different character from the type which moved wholly within a local area. It was further realized, vaguely at first, that the cost of highway facilities required by these different types of traffic could not with equity be assessed wholly against local property owners, but that a certain portion of the costs should be assessed against general state funds collected from taxpayers at large. From this recognition of the existence of dissimilar types of traffic there emerged the conception of general use highways and land utilization highways.

Legislative recognition of such a concept of highway development was first expressed in the State Aid Act (1891) of New Jersey.[2] This legislative provision marks the beginning of the swing back toward centralized control over highway activity, a movement which has gained acceleration during the last decade until now the state again occupies the central position in the field of highway development, with the federal and local governments participating in varying degrees.

The sections below are designed briefly to trace the trends in modern highway development and to establish the extent and physical characteristics of existing highway facilities as well as to indicate the changing methods by which the development of these facilities have been financed.

I. EXTENT AND CHARACTER OF HIGHWAY DEVELOPMENT

During the period from 1900 to 1920 passenger car registrations increased from 8,000 to 8,225,859; and motor truck registrations increased from 410 in 1904 to 1,006,082 in 1920.[3] No motor trucks were manufactured prior to 1904. Only 153,530 miles or 7.0 per cent of the 2,151,379 miles of rural highways existing in 1904 had any type of surfacing while by 1921 about 387,457 miles or 13.0 per cent of the rural highway mileage had been surfaced.[4]

With widely diffused vehicle ownership it was inevitable that pressure would be exerted upon government agencies to expand and improve highway facilities.

[2] See *Report of the State Highway Engineer to the New Jersey State Highway Commission*, 1926, p. 2.
[3] *Facts and Figures of the Automobile Industry*, 1932, p. 14, National Automobile Chamber of Commerce.
[4] From U. S. Bureau of Public Roads.

GROWTH AND CHARACTER OF RURAL ROAD SYSTEMS, 1921–1931[a]

| Year[b] | Mileage | | | Character of Surface | | | | | | | | |
| | Total | State | Local (County and Town) | State | | | | | Local (County and Town) | | | |
				Percentage State	High Type Surfaced[c]	Other Surfaced	Not Surfaced	Percentage Surfaced	High Type Surfaced[c]	Other Surfaced	Not Surfaced	Percentage Surfaced
1921	2,924,505	202,915	2,721,590	6.9	14,707	69,665	118,543	41.6	11,067	292,018	2,418,505	11.1
1923	2,995,727	251,611	2,744,116	8.4	25,339	86,061	140,211	44.3	13,077	314,864	2,416,175	12.0
1924	3,004,411	261,216	2,743,195	8.7	31,126	100,983	129,107	50.6	14,467	325,091	2,403,637	12.4
1925	3,006,183	274,911	2,731,172	9.1	36,244	108,610	130,057	52.7	17,506	358,900	2,354,766	13.8
1926	3,000,190	287,928	2,712,262	9.6	41,022	122,037	124,869	56.6	17,387	369,618	2,325,257	14.3
1927	3,013,584	293,353	2,720,231	9.7	46,642	129,924	116,787	60.2	18,272	393,883	2,308,076	15.2
1928	3,016,281	306,442	2,709,839	10.2	53,173	139,965	113,304	63.0	19,233	473,766	2,276,840	16.0
1929	3,024,233	314,136	2,710,097	10.4	61,070	147,254	105,812	66.3	20,649	433,462	2,255,986	16.8
1930	3,009,066	324,496	2,684,570	10.8	69,522	156,699	98,275	69.7	22,537	444,801	2,217,232	17.4
1931	3,034,893[d]	328,942	2,705,951[d]	10.8	80,985	161,715	86,242	73.8	[e]	[e]	2,332,851[d]	21.2

[a] Basic data from U. S. Bureau of Public Roads.
[b] Data not available for 1922.
[c] Includes Portland cement concrete, bituminous concrete, brick, and block.
[d] Preliminary estimates.
[e] Not available.

INDEX OF MILEAGE OF RURAL ROAD SYSTEMS, BY TYPES, 1921–1931[a]
[1921 = 100.0]

Year	Rural Road Mileage			Non-Surfaced Mileage		Surfaced Mileage		High Type Surfaced Mileage	
	Total	State System	Local System	State	Local	State	Local	State	Local
1921	100.0	100.0	100.0	100.0	100.0	100.0	100.0	100.0	100.0
1923	102.4	124.0	100.8	118.3	99.9	132.0	108.2	172.3	118.2
1924	102.7	128.7	100.8	108.9	99.4	156.6	112.0	211.7	130.7
1925	102.8	135.5	100.4	109.7	97.4	171.7	124.2	246.4	158.2
1926	102.6	141.9	99.7	105.3	96.1	193.3	127.7	278.9	157.1
1927	103.0	144.6	99.9	98.5	95.4	209.3	136.0	317.1	165.1
1928	103.1	151.0	99.6	95.6	94.1	228.9	142.9	361.5	173.8
1929	103.4	154.8	99.6	89.3	93.3	246.9	149.8	415.2	186.6
1930	102.9	159.9	98.6	82.9	91.7	268.1	154.2	472.7	203.6
1931	103.8	162.1	99.4	72.8	88.2	287.7	189.1	550.7	—

[a] See preceding table for actual data.

The general features of this physical expansion for the country as a whole, covering the period 1921-1931 are indicated in the table on page 530. For purposes of ready comparison an index of highway development based on the same data is shown in the table on page 531.

It will be noted that in these tables the aggregate data for rural road mileage are segregated according to *state highway* systems and *local road* systems. Rural road mileage includes all mileage not included in the streets of cities and incorporated places; state highway systems embrace all mileage over which state governments exercise primary administrative and financial control;[5] and local road systems include the mileage over which political subdivisions—counties and towns or townships—exercise primary administrative and financial control. These distinctions and definitions will be retained throughout.[6]

At the end of 1921 the highway system of the country contained 2,924,505 miles of roads, of which 202,915 miles or 6.9 per cent was included in the state systems. Only 84,372 miles or 41.6 per cent of this latter mileage were surfaced and of the surfaced mileage only 14,707 miles or 17.4 per cent were of the high type surface. In the same year only 11 per cent of the local road mileage was improved with any type of surface and only 3.7 per cent was of the high type.

[5] Several states, notably North Carolina and Virginia, have recently assumed both administrative and financial control over all or the bulk of rural road mileage. Official reports, however, still classify mileages formerly included in county systems as local roads.

[6] Mileage shown for state highway systems is based on accurate measurements, but the actual physical extent of local road systems is not precisely known. This is particularly true with reference to town road systems. These data, however, represent the most authentic estimate available.

By the end of 1931 significant shifts (as indicated in the accompanying chart) had occurred in this distribution. While the total rural highway mileage had expanded only 110,388 miles, or 3.8 per cent, state highway systems had added 126,027 miles—an increase of 62.1 per cent. At least 12 per cent of this increase in state mileage was occasioned by the transfer of local mileage to state systems, rather than by an expansion of the entire rural road mileage. In contrast, the extent of local road systems showed an absolute decrease of 15,639

CHARACTER OF SURFACE: STATE HIGHWAYS AND LOCAL HIGHWAYS

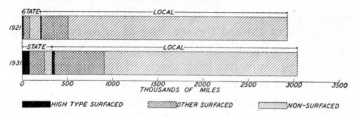

miles. Moreover, by the end of 1931, about 74 per cent of state highway systems mileage was surfaced—as contrasted with the 42 per cent of 1921. Of the surfaced mileage in 1931, over 33 per cent was high-type surfacing as compared with 17 per cent in 1921.

In the local systems only 21 per cent had been surfaced by the end of 1931, as compared with 11 per cent in 1921; and of the 1931 surfaced mileage not more than 5 per cent had been improved with high-type pavement, representing an insignificant percentage increase over the 3.7 per cent in 1921. Thus at the end of 1931, the state highway systems, comprising only 10.8 per cent of all rural road mileage, contained about one-third of all surfaced mileage in the country, and approximately 78 per cent of the mileage surfaced with high-type pavement. These ratios compare with corresponding per-centages of 6.9, 21.8, and 57.1 for the year 1921.

These data, showing the relative development in the physical extent of state and local highway systems and the rate of change in the character of highway facilities within each group of systems over the ten-year period, are highly significant. They indicate quite clearly that the forces—whether commercial or non-commercial—associated with the development of motor vehicle transportation during the past decade, which have exerted effective pressure to secure both increased volume and improved character of highway facilities, have directed that pressure toward the securing of primary highway routes; those included within state systems. No similarly effective pressure has been extended for the expansion of local road systems.

The quantitative analysis presented above serves only to indicate general trends in the direction and intensity of highway development for the country as a whole. Unfortunately, the rate of growth and the administrative procedure reflected in the existing systems of highway facilities have varied widely from state to state. In short, there is no national highway system in the United States. All of the problems which emerge from the development of modern highway transportation have their origin in the governmental activity of states and their political subdivisions. Consequently, it is impossible, because of the very nature of the problem, for any conclusions which are based solely upon an analysis of quantitative data for the country as a whole to be uniformly applicable to the actual operating conditions in all states.

Discussion of aggregate data is useful only as a point of departure. When we come to consider the question of how highway costs should be allocated between types of users we shall have to take account of the wide variations in different states.

II. HIGHWAY OUTLAYS AND METHODS OF FINANCING

Neither the expansion of highway mileage nor the increase in mileage of higher types of surfacing furnishes a complete picture of the growth of highway facilities. Improved maintenance of existing roads, reduced gradients and straightened alignment, stronger bridges and culverts, and widened roadways, all have contributed to the tremendously increased effectiveness of motor vehicle operation. In the aggregate these items have occasioned substantially increased outlays for highway development.

1. *Outlays.* Governmental outlays for all highway purposes during the period from 1921 to 1931 are shown below. The table on page 536 shows disbursement of highway funds by state highway departments and the one on page 537 gives a similar statement for local governments. The chart on page 538 brings out the changes which took place between 1921 and 1930 in state and in local disbursements for different purposes.

Total disbursements for state and for local highway purposes have shown widely different rates of growth. Between 1921 and 1930 outlays for state highway systems increased by 187 per cent and for local road systems by only 34 per cent. In 1921 outlays for state highway systems, comprising 6.9 per cent of rural mileage, accounted for 38 per cent of total outlays, while by 1930

DISBURSEMENTS OF ROAD FUNDS BY STATE HIGHWAY DEPARTMENTS
1921, 1926, 1930, and 1931[a]
(Dollar items in thousands)

Object of Expenditures	1921		1926		1930		1931	
	Amount	Per cent	Amount	Per cent	Amount	Per cent	Amount	Per cent
Current outlays:								
Maintenance[b]	$100,079	25.2	$219,842	35.4	$290,157	25.5	$269,807	24.7
Interest on bonds and notes	64,833	16.4	125,617	20.2	191,684	16.8	160,980	14.7
Machinery and equipment[c]	10,417	2.6	33,690	5.4	50,668	4.4	61,862	5.7
Miscellaneous[b]	8,412	2.1	22,285	3.6	22,302	2.0	21,482	2.0
Other obligations assumed[d]	16,417	4.1	38,250	6.2	2,227	0.2	4,313	0.4
				—	23,276	2.1	21,170	1.9
Funds transferred to counties or townships for local roads	6,451	1.6	23,848	3.8	66,898	5.9	32,969	3.0
Capital investment in construction and right of way[b]	284,303	71.5	356,175	57.3	713,117	62.5	730,955	67.0
Principal payments[b]	6,651	1.7	21,879	3.5	69,505	6.1	57,278	5.3
Total disbursements	$397,484	100.0	$621,744	100.0	$1,139,677	100.0	$1,091,009	100.0

a Compiled from records of the U.S. Bureau of Public Roads. State data in most cases are for the calendar year, but where calendar year figures are not available the fiscal year most nearly corresponding thereto, has been used.

b "Miscellaneous" from 1921 through 1927 includes administration and engineering when reported separately, also traffic control. From 1928 through 1931 the pro rata share of administration, engineering, materials, and supplies is included with "Capital investment in construction and right of way," and with "Maintenance."

c Covers purchase (a capital investment), rental, and repairs; the major part of these expenditures is applicable to maintenance.

d Includes items such as police patrol; expense of administration and collection of motor vehicle license fees and gasoline taxes (and refunds); construction of city streets as part of state highway, etc.

DISBURSEMENTS OF ROAD FUNDS BY LOCAL GOVERNMENTS
1921, 1926, and 1930[a]
(Dollar items in thousands)

Object of Expenditures	1921		1926		1930	
	Amount	Per cent	Amount	Per cent	Amount	Per cent
Current Outlays:						
Maintenance................	$271,852	42.8	$322,013	42.9	$403,901	47.4
Interest on bonds and notes[b]...	185,726	29.2	213,236	28.4	284,229	33.4
Miscellaneous[c].............	46,487	7.3	66,685	8.9	82,605	9.7
	39,639	6.3	42,092	5.6	37,067	4.3
Funds transferred to state......	—	—	72,769	9.7	38,615	4.5
Capital outlay for construction...	337,870	53.1	265,718	35.3	296,595	34.9
Principal payments[b].........	26,738	4.2	91,070	12.1	112,576	13.2
Total.............	$636,460	100.0	$751,570	100.0	$851,687	100.0

[a] Compiled from records of the U. S. Bureau of Public Roads. The Bureau states that "the data are partly estimates and approximations, but are the only available figures obtainable by this Bureau." Data for 1931 are not available.

[b] For 1921 bond interest is included with payments on principal; thereafter when reported in one amount it is approximately allocated.

[c] Includes administration and engineering, except when these items are allocated to construction and maintenance.

these outlays on state systems, comprising 10.8 per cent of rural road mileage, made up 57 per cent of all highway expenditures.

Capital outlays for new construction and expenditures for maintenance have accounted for a large portion of the increased expenditures on state highway systems. About 58 per cent of the increase is due to new construction and most of the remainder to maintenance operations. On the other hand, capital outlays for new con-

DISBURSEMENT OF ROAD FUNDS BY STATE AND BY
LOCAL GOVERNMENTS, 1921 AND 1930

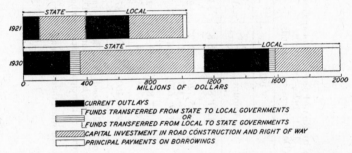

struction on local road systems have shown an absolute decrease. Thus the entire increase in total disbursements for local road facilities is accounted for by expanded outlays for maintenance and payment of interest and principal on outstanding debt.

In short, the trend in local road administration is merely to maintain a decreasing total mileage at a somewhat higher standard of serviceability and to pay off previously incurred debt. Again, as in the previous discussion of mileage expansion, it is apparent from an analysis of highway outlays on state and local systems that effective pressure for permanently improved highway facilities has been reflected largely in operations on state highway systems.

2. *Sources of highway income.* In the course of ten years the methods of financing highway development have undergone radical changes. The tables and charts on pages 540 to 543 show the sources of income by which state and local highway activities have been financed during the period from 1921 to 1931.

In final analysis all highway income is derived from three sources: state and local general funds, special motor vehicle tax levies, and federal aid allotments.

a. General Funds. Substantially all of the amounts shown in the following tables under the items "general taxation and appropriations," "local road tax levy and appropriations," and "transferred to state by local governments" come directly from general funds. In addition, proceeds from a portion of borrowing operations are eventually repaid from the general funds. Since tax systems differ widely from state to state, no unqualified statement can be made as to the types of tax levies which contribute to the general funds of state and local governments. In general, however, it can be said that revenues from property tax levies constitute the bulk of local government current income.

b. Special Motor Vehicle Tax Levies. These levies will be referred to in subsequent discussion as user taxes. They are composed of two types of levies: a fixed charge for motor vehicle license plates, and a per gallon tax on gasoline. The great bulk of user tax revenues, as contrasted with those which contribute to the general funds of state and local governments, are derived from a special class—motor vehicle users. Only nine states fail to make any provision for exemptions on refunds of

SOURCES OF HIGHWAY INCOME FOR EXPENDITURE BY STATE HIGHWAY DEPARTMENTS

1921, 1926, 1930, and 1931[a]

(Dollar items in thousands)

Source of Income	1921 Amount	1921 Per cent	1926 Amount	1926 Per cent	1930 Amount	1930 Per cent	1931 Amount	1931 Per cent
Revenues:	$179,870	44.5	$420,225	62.4	$761,313	67.0	$ 696,167	63.7
General taxation and appropriations[b]	67,233	16.6	48,147	7.1	43,318	3.8	35,438	3.3
User taxes:	104,558	25.9	358,855	53.3	700,911[c]	61.7	639,585	58.5
Motor vehicle fees	101,284	25.1	224,552	33.4	289,802	25.5	253,403	23.2
Gasoline taxes	3,274	0.8	134,303	19.9	411,109[c]	36.2	386,182	35.3
Miscellaneous income	8,079	2.0	13,223	2.0	17,083	1.5	21,144	1.9
Non-revenues:	224,198	55.5	252,983	37.6	375,360	33.0	396,470[d]	36.3[d]
Receipts from bond and note issues	111,397	27.6	103,846	15.4	222,288	19.6	130,614	11.9
Federal aid allotments	77,457	19.2	79,163	11.8	92,463	8.1	218,074	20.0[d]
Transferred to state by local governments	35,344	8.7	69,974	10.4	60,609	5.3	47,782	4.4
Total	$404,068	100.0	$673,208	100.0	$1,136,673	100.0	$1,092,637[d]	100.0

[a] Compiled from records of the U. S. Bureau of Public Roads. State data in most cases are for the calendar year, but where calendar year figures are not available the fiscal year most nearly corresponding thereto, has been used.

[b] State tax assessments and appropriations from state general fund are often made to cover bond obligations.

[c] Includes taxes of former years held by Illinois Court as follows: 1927, $6,310,565, and 1929, $11,659,778.

[d] Included are certain amounts from other federal funds as follows: For flood relief, Alabama $149,499; Arkansas, $801,301; Kentucky, $137,198; Louisiana, $786,271; New Hampshire, $29,158; South Carolina, $548,908; and Vermont, $163,258. For public lands highway construction: Arizona, $4,333; Idaho, $125,427; Utah, $211,206; and Wyoming, $43,577. (Total for 11 states is $3,000,136.) Emergency advance funds amounting to $62,730,289 are also included. This amount represents loans to the various states to be returned within five years (1933-38) to the United States Treasury by deductions from future federal aid apportionments. The percentage distribution of the federal aid allotments in 1931 is: flood relief, etc., 0.3;

SOURCE OF HIGHWAY INCOME FOR EXPENDITURE BY LOCAL GOVERNMENTS
1921, 1926, AND 1930[a]
(Dollar items in thousands)

Source of Income	1921		1926		1930	
	Amount	Per cent	Amount	Per cent	Amount	Per cent
Revenues:	$417,996	56.2	$576,884	74.4	$689,993	84.3
Local road tax levy and appropriations from general fund	348,514	46.9	443,047	57.1	494,633	60.4
User taxes:	15,356	2.0	77,594	10.0	162,022	19.8
Motor vehicle fees	15,117	2.0	37,861	4.9	54,911	6.7
Gasoline taxes	239	.0	39,733	5.1	107,111	13.1
Miscellaneous income	54,126	7.3	56,243	7.3	33,338	4.1
Non-revenues:	325,497	43.8	198,540	25.6	128,386	15.7
Receipts from sale of bonds	323,176	43.5	168,575	21.7	94,684	11.6
Transferred from state for local roads	2,321	0.3	29,965	3.9	33,702	4.1
Total	$743,493	100.0	$775,424	100.0	$818,379	100.0

[a] Compiled from records of U. S. Bureau of Public Roads. The data are partly estimates and approximations but are the only available figures obtainable by this Bureau. Data for 1931 are not available.

taxes on gasoline not consumed in highway operations.[7]

c. Federal Aid Allotments. An act of the sixty-fourth Congress provided—"that the United States shall aid the states in the construction of rural post roads."[8] This original act of 1916 commonly known as the Federal Aid Act has been amended and supplemented at various times. In general its provisions limit the mileage eligible for federal aid in any state to 7 per cent of the total rural

SOURCES OF STATE HIGHWAY INCOME

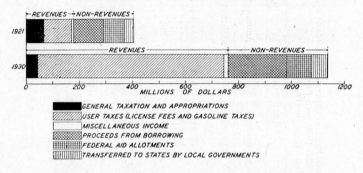

road mileage in that state. They also establish a distinction between primary, or interstate, highways, and secondary, or inter-county, highways, and provide "That in approving projects to receive federal aid . . . the Secretary of Agriculture shall give preference to such projects as will expedite the completion of an adequate and connected system of highways, interstate in character."[9] Acceptance of the provisions of the various federal aid acts is wholly optional with any state.

Highway projects on which the federal government

[7] I. G. Cramford, *The Administration of the Gasoline Tax in the United States*, 1932, p. 25.
[8] 39 Stat. L., 355.
[9] 42 Stat. L., 212.

participates with state highway departments are financed about half by federal funds and half by state funds. Federal participation in highway development is supervised by the Bureau of Public Roads of the Department of Agriculture. This bureau operates only through state highway departments.

SOURCES OF LOCAL HIGHWAY INCOME

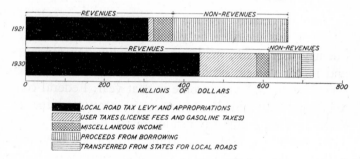

3. *Sources of state highway income.* In 1921 revenues derived either directly or indirectly from general tax sources accounted for 25.3 per cent of all state highway income. This figure is arrived at by combining the amounts derived from general taxation and appropriations and transfers to the state by local governments. An additional 27.6 per cent was obtained from the proceeds of note and bond issues. Data compiled by the Bureau of Public Roads show that all bonds issued since 1920 for state highway purposes which were outstanding at the end of 1931 were being serviced as follows:

	Amount	Per cent
From state general funds	$ 237,111,000	20.2
From motor user funds	935,414,150	79.8
	$1,172,525,150	100.0

In the single year 1930 all state highway bonds were issued against motor user revenues.[10] It seems certain then that general tax funds were pledged for the repayment of at least 20 per cent of the debt so incurred in the year 1921 and that in this year somewhere between one-third and one-half[11] of all state highway income was derived either directly from, or in anticipation of, general tax revenues.

Gasoline taxation was not introduced until 1919[12] and by 1921 was yielding only negligible amounts, consequently user taxes, made up of gasoline tax revenues and motor vehicle license fees constituted only 26 per cent of state highway income in that year. Federal contributions and miscellaneous sources accounted for 21 per cent of state highway income in 1921.

By 1930[13] the highway income pattern had been materially altered. General tax funds no longer were being called upon for any substantial contribution to state highway development. General taxation, together with transfers to the state, accounted for only 9 per cent of the total state highway income. Moreover, revenues from user taxes were pledged to cover interest and amorti-

[10] Evidence introduced by Bureau of Public Roads in Hearings on S. 2793, *Regulation of Motor Carrier Transportation*, Pt. 2, p. 212.

[11] These limits are arrived at by the following calculations: If in 1921, 20 per cent of state highway bonds were issued against general funds then 5.5 per cent (20 per cent of 27.6 per cent) plus 25.3 per cent, or 30.8, of all highway income was derived directly or indirectly from general funds. If all bonds in 1921 were issued against general tax revenues, then 27.6 per cent plus 25.3 per cent or 52.9 per cent of total state highway income was so derived.

[12] The first gasoline tax was introduced in Oregon in 1919 and by 1929 every state had adopted this form of tax levy as a means of financing highway development.

[13] The year 1930 is used here for two reasons: (1) federal unemployment relief advances to states during 1931 in form of federal aid road funds distort the trend of ordinary highway activities, and (2) financial data for local road activities are not available for 1931.

zation on all state borrowing for highway purposes, thereby relieving general property from all obligations on that score. Federal contributions had dropped from 19 per cent to 8 per cent of aggregate state highway income. As a result of the phenomenal growth of revenue derived from gasoline tax levies (from $3,273,988 in 1921 to $411,109,446 in 1930), user tax revenues accounted directly for 61.7 per cent of all state highway income in 1930 as compared with only 26 per cent in 1921. An additional 19.6 per cent was obtained from borrowings supported wholly by user taxes. Thus in 1930 motor vehicle users as a special class were responsible, either through direct or through anticipated payment, for 81 per cent of the income made available from all sources for state highway purposes.

As in the case of physical development wide variations exist in the methods of financing in different states. These must be taken account of in any attempt to allocate costs between different users.

4. *Local road systems.* By reference to the table on page 541 it will be seen that tendencies similar to those reflected in methods of financing state highway activities have influenced the financial procedure of local governments in developing local road systems. For example, in 1921, direct tax revenues derived largely from property taxation, together with proceeds from borrowing, accounted for $671,689,934, or 90 per cent of local highway income. By 1930, however, these sources of income contributed at the most only $589,317,806, or 72 per cent of local highway income.[14] User taxes in 1921 furnished only $15,356,409, or 2 per cent of local road in-

---

[14] While general funds were held responsible for the retirement of practically all bonds issued in 1921, substantial portions of the borrowings in 1930 were backed by gasoline tax levies.

come, but by 1930 this source of revenue produced $162,021,831, or about 20 per cent of all local highway funds. The decrease in both relative and absolute contributions by general taxpayers was, therefore, more than compensated for by a rapid increase in the contributions of motor vehicle users as a special class. Here again substantial variations from this average condition are found from state to state.

III. SUMMARY

The period from 1921 to 1931 shows an unmistakable trend in the methods of financing rural road development in the United States. State general funds have been progressively relieved from participation in highway development until by 1930 the maintenance of state highways and the creation of additional highway facilities was being financed exclusively by revenues derived from special motor vehicle taxation and by contribution from the federal government. This tendency was not limited to state highway programs. The relative importance of general fund revenues in the financing of local roads consistently decreased throughout the period, though at a slower rate than in the case of state financing. Thus at the beginning of the period, special user taxes accounted for only one-tenth of all income available for rural road work (state and local) while by the end of the period this source of revenue was producing more than one-half of the income available for rural road purposes.

All of the quantitative data presented in this chapter are designed solely to indicate general trends in the rapidly shifting methods by which the development of highway facilities has been financed during the past decade. They do not tell us whether user taxes are adequate to cover the highway costs properly allocable to them.

CHAPTER XXVI

WHO PAYS FOR THE HIGHWAYS?

Attention has already been called to the marked tendency toward the financing of all state highway operations by means of revenues derived from special fees levied on motor vehicle operation. It was pointed out that in 1921 these special user tax revenues accounted for only 26 per cent of all state highway income, but that by 1930 some 80 per cent of the income made available for expenditure on state highway systems was contributed by motor vehicle users in the form of gasoline tax levies and license fees. These data were introduced to establish trends in the methods of financing highway development. No effort was made to relate these special tax contributions to the annual costs of highway improvement and maintenance. The purpose of this chapter is to determine the extent to which the gasoline taxes and license fees paid to state governments by motor vehicle users have been adequate to meet the true costs of highway development during the last decade of rapid expansion in highway improvement.

It is impossible to make a thoroughly satisfactory answer to the question for two reasons: first, the lack of certain essential data, and, second, the lack of a satisfactory standard for allocating the user contributions between general use highways and so-called land utilization roads.

Legally, highways are classified in three groups, and these groupings do not correspond accurately to differences in the character of the traffic. The classes are: (1) state highways; (2) county highways; and (3) town or township highways. The purpose of state highways is to make possible inter-city transportation; the fact that owners of adjoining property derive benefits is a wholly secondary consideration. The cost of building and maintaining these highways is therefore properly chargeable to the general user. On the other hand, the town or township roads, commonly called land utilization roads, are maintained primarily for the benefit of the local land owner and the local community. While these roads serve some general use, this is incidental to their main purpose. County roads are intermediate in character between state and local roads, but in general resemble the former rather than the latter in that their main objective is to afford inter-community transportation. They do not primarily serve the owners and occupants of immediately adjacent land. In addition, certain city streets form parts of state highway systems.

I. DETERMINATION OF HIGHWAY COSTS

With reference to city streets included in state highway systems, we have no data covering either mileage or costs. With regard to the county roads, we have estimates of mileage, but costs of construction and maintenance cannot be separated from those of the town or township roads.

To compute directly the relationship between the costs of highway development and maintenance and the amount contributed for that purpose by users of the highways, we would have to have detailed information concerning the distribution of expenditures between the elements of the highway structure which are subject to rapid depreciation, such as surface, and those which are relatively permanent, such as right-of-way, grading, and draining. We also need information as to the proportionate mileage of the various types of surface.

No trustworthy data are available with reference to the distribution of expenditures between the different elements of cost, nor with respect to the salvage value of road surfaces. We cannot, therefore, compute the annual cost directly. The available information does, however, make possible an indirect computation which will show whether the amount which is being collected from highway users is sufficient to amortize the investment in state highways within a period which falls between reasonable upper and lower limits of the probable lifetime of the roads. No such computation can be made for county and town roads, however.

1. *State highways.* The method used in the computation is as follows: First, provision is made for the annual payment required to cover interest and amortization of the right of way, grading, and drainage structures built during the first year. It has been assumed that these items require a minimum of 25 per cent of the total outlay for new improvements,[1] and that they have an economic life of 100 years.[2] The balance of the first year's revenue is the amount available for interest on, and amortization of, the cost of that year's surfacing. We compute the number of years necessary to amortize the cost

---

[1] On federal aid projects paid for during 1930 and 1931, in seven states for which data are available, grading and drainage items ranged from 16.1 to 47.5 per cent of the total cost. In aggregate outlays for all highways, which include a larger proportion of low cost surfaces, grading and draining costs must comprise at least as large a proportion of the total as on these federal aid projects.

[2] For a discussion of this point see *Proceedings of the Highway Research Board*, 1930, p. 334.

of the year's surfacing, if this same amount is applied to it in each succeeding year. Funds available in the second year are allocated (a) to meet the second-year contributions to amortization of the first-year construction, and (b) to amortize the right-of-way, grading, and drainage costs incurred in the second year. The balance of revenue remaining is the amount available to amortize

STATE HIGHWAY FINANCING, 1921–1930[a]
(Dollar items in thousands)

Year	User Contributions Available	Net Current Outlay	User Contributions Available for Capital Outlay	Capital Outlay	Annual Average Interest Rate	Interest Charge on Construction Funds Used During Year
1921.....	$104,558	$ 89,662	$ 14,896	$289,349	3.55	$5,046
1922.....	113,112	107,387	5,725	293,038	3.88	5,577
1923.....	162,949	117,293	45,656	284,725	3.38	4,732
1924.....	222,628	155,764	66,864	389,218	3.60	6,882
1925.....	289,174	180,414	108,760	397,191	4.04	7,864
1926.....	358,855	186,152	172,703	363,708	4.23	7,533
1927.....	416,725	200,997	215,728	412,443	4.07	8,226
1928.....	493,299	191,683	301,616	548,562	3.91	10,519
1929.....	565,352	219,074	346,278	569,552	4.36	12,151
1930.....	700,911	239,489	461,422	728,342	4.27	15,225

[a] Basic data from U. S. Bureau of Public Roads.

the cost incurred in this second year for surfacing. Contributions collected in the third year are applied to amortizing first-year and second-year construction at the respective rates set up for those years, then to amortization of grading, draining, and right-of-way costs of the third year; the balance is the amount available for interest and amortization costs of the third year. Interest is figured on each year's construction at the rates actually paid in that year. No allowance is made for salvage values. The basic data are shown in the table on the opposite page.

In this table the "user contributions" column shows not the total collections but only the actual amount of gasoline tax and license fees allocated to state highway departments. The "net current outlay" column shows the amount applied each year to the recurring items of state highway department expense, maintenance of existing highways, administrative expense, and miscellaneous items. The "capital outlay" represents the total amounts to be funded at the end of each year because of investments in right of way and new construction made during the year. It includes not only amounts applied to the acquisition of right of way and to new construction, but also interest on the funds used in construction operations during the year. This amount is shown in the last column. The column headed "annual average interest rate" represents the actual rate of interest paid on the long-term borrowing operations of states during that year.

The table on page 552 shows in detail the results of our computation of the number of years required to amortize each year's capital investment on the basis of that year's revenue collections.

It will be seen that in the years just after 1919, when gasoline taxes were generally low, user contributions were not sufficient to amortize the investment except over very long periods. In the later years, on the other hand, the revenues available have been sufficient to pay off the investment in very short periods, assuming that payments on account of the earlier years were made at rates based on the revenues of the earlier years. While there is no specific agreement as to the economic life of various types of road surfaces it is quite generally agreed that the range varies from seven years for low-type surfaces, to 20 years for the high-type rigid surfaces. It seems clear, therefore, that during the first three years of the period, when gasoline tax rates were generally low, the amounts available were not sufficient to pay for the in-

ADEQUACY OF USER CONTRIBUTIONS TO AMORTIZE CAPITAL INVESTMENT IN STATE HIGHWAYS, 1921–30
(Dollar items in thousands)

Year	User Contributions Available for Capital[a]	Amortization of Previous Outlays	Amortization of Current Year Expenditures for Right-of-Way Grading and Structures[b]	Balance Available for Amortization of Current Year's Surfacing	Number of Years Required to Amortize Current Year's Surfacing
1921....	$ 14,896	—	$2,649	$ 12,247	25.3
1922....	5,725	$ 14,896	2,907	12,078[c]	—
1923....	33,578[d]	17,803	2,496	13,279	50.1
1924....	66,864	37,912	3,608	25,344	13.2
1925....	108,760	66,864	4,090	37,806	8.1
1926....	172,703	108,760	3,908	60,035	3.8
1927....	215,728	172,703	4,276	38,749	8.2
1928....	301,616	215,728	5,481	80,407	4.5
1929....	346,278	301,616	6,296	38,366	13.4
1930....	461,422	346,278	7,896	107,248	4.5

[a] From preceding table.
[b] Costs spread over 100 years; interest figured at rates shown on Page 550.
[c] Deficit.
[d] Balance after making up deficit for previous year.

vestment in road surfaces within the economic life of those surfaces, but that during the later years the user contributions have been adequate, so far as state highways are concerned, not only to cover the maintenance and interest costs and current depreciation, but also to make up a substantial part of the deficiency of collections in the earlier years.

It must be emphasized here that this conclusion is based on aggregate data for the country as a whole, and is not necessarily applicable without qualification to each individual state. Such qualification is essential because the wide variations between states are not limited to the physical characteristics of highway development. The methods by which highway activities are financed show a similar lack of uniformity from state to state. For example, 23 states in 1920 levied no general taxes for the support of state highways, while the remainder levied taxes which made up from 0.3 per cent to 64 per cent of their respective state highway incomes. In practically all such cases, however, the assessments were levied to cover previously incurred bonded obligations. There is a general correspondence between the states which make such levies and those in which special motor vehicle tax revenues account for the largest portions of county and town highway income.

In general, states which derive the largest percentages of state highway income from user contributions are operating largely on a pay-as-you-go basis, while proceeds of bond issues constitute substantial portions of the highway budget in those states which derive a relatively small percentage of state highway income from highway users. Direct collections from levies on users constitute over 60 per cent of total state highway income in only 24 states while user taxes combined with receipts from bonds and notes make up a similar portion of highway income in 41 of the 48 states.[3] In final analysis, then, user contributions, either current or anticipated, constitute a uniformly large portion of the state highway in-

---

[3] It will be recalled that gasoline tax revenues were pledged for the repayment of all bonds issued for state highway purposes during 1930.

come in about 85 per cent of the states, indicating that the conclusion reached above for the country as a whole would be applicable to a substantial portion of the individual states.

2. *Local highways.* Since gasoline taxes and license fees fall upon all owners of motor vehicles, whether or not they operate on state highway systems, it has been regarded as necessary to allocate a portion of the receipts, which are usually collected by the state government,[4] to counties and townships. We shall now indicate the extent of these contributions to local government units.

It has already been observed that the county roads are largely devoted to general traffic purposes. Accordingly we shall compare the income received from vehicle taxes with the maintenance charges and outlays for improved surfaces on county road systems during the period 1921-1930. Since the capital and maintenance costs of county and township highways are lumped together, it is necessary to estimate the amount attributable to county roads. This can be done on a rough basis for maintenance charges. Various state surveys indicate that the traffic density on county highways is very much heavier than on town roads. It may therefore be assumed that in 1930 the maintenance expenditures per mile are about double the average maintenance expenditures for county and town roads combined. Figured on this basis, about 45 per cent of total maintenance charges incurred by local governments is allocable to the county roads. Applying this percentage to the actual maintenance expenditures for each year in 1921-1930 we obtain the fol-

---

[4] In some states, however, local governments levy and collect their own vehicle taxes.

lowing figures for county road maintenance as compared
with contributions from highway users. The last column
gives the annual capital outlays on all local roads:

LOCAL HIGHWAY FINANCING
(In thousands)

Year	Mainte- nance Ex- penditures[a]	Estimated County Road Mainte- nance	User Con- tributions Allocated[a]	Estimated Amount Available for Capi- tal Outlay	Actual Capital Outlay[a]
1921	$185,726	$ 83,577	$ 15,356	$ −68,221	$337,870
1922[b]	—	—	—	—	—
1923	190,569	85,756	39,855	−45,901	239,047
1924	195,014	87,756	43,828	−43,928	255,836
1925	196,574	88,458	71,379	−17,079	264,966
1926	213,236	95,956	77,594	−18,362	265,718
1927	237,970	107,087	87,100	−19,987	289,180
1928	259,753	116,889	104,212	−12,677	282,315
1929	260,478	117,215	122,379	5,164	256,582
1930	284,229	127,903	162,022	34,119	296,595

[a] Data from U. S. Bureau of Public Roads.
[b] No data available.

During the greater part of the period, highway revenues allocated to local governments were clearly inadequate to meet even estimated maintenance charges on
county roads. The revenues, however, increased steadily
and by 1929 they exceeded maintenance charges. In 1930
the excess over maintenance was sufficient to amortize
within a reasonable period the capital outlay on both
county and town road system. It should be borne in mind
that this computation relates only to the current situation. Indebtedness incurred in previous years remains a
charge against present and future income.

These figures pertain to the country as a whole. The
situation, however, varies widely in different states. In
13 states the county and township governments received
no revenues from gasoline taxes and license fees, while
in 22 states over 20 per cent of all local road funds were

derived from this source. In a number of states these revenues from motor vehicles are sufficient to cover virtually the entire cost of all highways—state, county, and local. In North Carolina the state has assumed the responsibility for financing from this source the full cost of local as well as state highways.

We believe that the following principles should govern the allocation of highway costs between the various groups of society:

1. In general, the costs of highway development should be charged against the groups of society that demand highway facilities, and that presumably benefit directly from the facilities furnished by government agencies in response to that demand.

2. Specifically, the actual cost of all highway development provided because of highway user demand for improved facilities should be met from payments made to the government agencies by motor vehicle users as a special class of society.

3. All remaining road costs should be financed from the general tax funds collected by the governmental agencies which provide land utilization roads. While the fact that these roads most directly benefit land owners suggests general property revenues or special assessments as the most reasonable source of funds for this purpose, the determination of this point does not fall within the scope of the present study.

Over the last decade the practice has been coming progressively close to that indicated by these principles. During most of the period since 1920 the revenues received from highway users were not sufficient to cover the costs of all highways devoted to general usage, both state and county. The rapid development of the highways necessitated the extensive use of general tax revenues to meet maintenance costs and capital charges. But in due course the revenues collected from highway users increased rapidly, and by 1930 they were sufficient to cover both maintenance and current capital charges. Interest and amortization on previously accumulated indebtedness remains, however, as a charge against current tax receipts.

Looking forward, it is reasonable to assume that for the country as a whole, if not for all states, contributions from highway users will be sufficient to cover the full cost of state and county highways and an increasing portion of town roads.[5] We conclude, therefore, that on the whole highway users are now paying for those highways which are of general use. Local highways are still being paid for, in the main, by local beneficiaries.

Paying for the use of highways through gasoline taxes and license fees is, however, a very different thing from paying taxes for the general support of government. The gasoline taxes, so-called, and license fees, are devoted primarily to defraying highway costs. Only to the extent that they exceed the costs incurred by the government in providing the highways can they be regarded as taxes in the true sense. While in certain states some revenues

[5] In reaching this conclusion no account was taken of those portions of city streets which form integral parts of state highway system routes. It is only reasonable that the same funds which support state highway systems proper, should contribute to the maintenance of these through city streets. This principle has gained some acceptance during recent years. In 1931, about $20,000,000 (2 per cent of the total) of the revenue collected from license fees and gasoline taxes was applied to the upkeep of city streets. In some sections this problem is being solved directly by the building of by-passes around metropolitan areas which make it unnecessary for through traffic to utilize city streets.

from this source are diverted to purposes other than highway development, for the country as a whole, as we have seen, gasoline taxes and license fees are little if any more than sufficient to cover the cost of general use highways. The contribution of the motor vehicle operators to the general support of government is therefore measured by other forms of taxation applicable to motor vehicles and companies.[6]

II. ALLOCATION OF HIGHWAY COSTS BETWEEN TYPES OF VEHICLES

The discussion so far has been limited to a determination of the adequacy of motor vehicle user contributions to meet the total costs of general use highways. If all classes of motor vehicles required the same type of highway facility, no further problem would be involved. The fact remains, however, that the development of heavy truck and bus traffic has occasioned outlays for highway facilities substantially in excess of the requirements of ordinary passenger traffic. Since it has been stated as a principle that motor vehicle users as a class should pay the costs of all general use highways, it logically follows that this cost should be allocated among the various weight classes of motor vehicles in proportion to the differential cost of the types of highways required by each class of vehicle. That is, heavy vehicles should share equally with all vehicles in the basic cost of furnishing highways which meet the requirement of ordinary passenger car and light truck traffic and, in addition, should bear the entire cost of the additional facility required.

The elements of road construction cost are (1) right of way, (2) grading, (3) drainage structures, (4)

[6] See discussion in following chapter.

bridges, and (5) road surfaces. The first three of these cost elements are determined primarily by the requirements of ordinary passenger car traffic. The cost of bridges is determined largely by the requirements of occasional or possible movements of equipment whose gross weight exceeds that usually allowed for ordinary motor vehicle operation. The significant elements of differential cost appear mainly in the outlays required for various widths and thicknesses of road surfaces.

The minimum pavement width of a road containing only two lanes is determined by two factors—speed and vehicle clearance. The high rates of speed maintained by modern motor vehicles necessitate a substantial clearance between the two lines of traffic. Any factor which reduces this clearance reduces either the effective utilization of the road or the margin of operating safety, or both. Since the width of truck and bus bodies—as compared with the width of passenger car bodies—constitutes such a factor, it appears that a wider road is required for their operation in order to avoid the sacrifice, either of maximum utilization of the road, or of safety of operation for all traffic. It can therefore be stated as a principle that if all traffic, including heavy vehicles, requires a twenty-foot road surface in order to obtain the degree of utilization, safety, and convenience that could be obtained from an eighteen-foot pavement used exclusively by passenger cars and light truck traffic, the entire differential in cost between the eighteen-foot and the twenty-foot pavement should be borne by the heavy trucks and buses.

The minimum thickness or strength of road surfaces capable of supporting ordinary passenger car and light truck traffic is determined largely by climatic and subsoil conditions. It is an established fact that heavy bus and truck traffic requires added pavement strength. As a result of a long series of tests conducted by the United States Bureau of Public Roads, the approximate relationships have been established between vehicle wheel impacts[7] and the strength, or design, of pavements adequate to resist the impacts delivered to the pavement by various wheel loads.[8] It is therefore possible to determine the approximate additional cost required to construct a pavement that will not be destroyed by the maximum existing or potential volume of heavy-type vehicle traffic. These increments of cost, plus an equal participation with all other vehicles in the basic cost of constructing a road surface adequate to meet the requirements of ordinary vehicle traffic, should determine the contribution of each weight class of heavy-vehicle traffic to the cost of building road surfaces strong enough to support the heaviest type of vehicle which is permitted by law to operate over the highways.

It should be noted that the principle adopted here to govern the differential contributions of various weight classes of vehicles is based on the added cost of building road surfaces which will not be destroyed by the vehicular traffic they are designed to carry, and not on the cost of replacing surfaces which have been destroyed by loads which they were not designed or constructed to carry. One example will serve to illustrate the validity of this principle. A concrete pavement designed to carry a given volume of four-ton trucks may be structurally destroyed

[7] U. S. Bureau of Public Roads, *Public Roads*, March 1921.

[8] The Bureau of Public Roads has used these findings in developing a method for approximating the proper allocation of road costs to various types of vehicles classified by weight and by tire equipment. See 72 Cong. 1 sess., Hearings on S. 2793, Vol. 2, p. 231.

by the volume of five-ton truck traffic which uses it. Under the "wear and tear" principle the entire cost of replacing this destroyed surface would be assigned to the five-ton truck group. The fact remains, however, that this loss could have been prevented by adding a small increment of thickness to the road, thereby making it adequate to carry five-ton trucks.

Other considerations make it desirable to limit the maximum gross weight which a single vehicle is allowed to carry, as well as the maximum physical dimensions of the vehicle itself. Gross weight must be limited to the carrying capacities of bridges, and body lengths must be limited in order to minimize the nuisance factor and traffic hazards introduced by the "train" type of truck operation. If the proper relationships are to be maintained between the type of roads constructed and the physical characteristics of motor vehicles, highway officials must know in advance the width and strength of pavement required by the types of vehicles which are to be allowed to operate over the highways.

With these requirements in mind the American Association of State Highway Officials has proposed a set of uniform regulations to govern the gross weight, physical dimensions, and speeds for motor vehicles operating over the highways. These proposals appear to incorporate the best engineering thought and technical information available on the subject. The most significant limitations are on length, axle load, and gross weight. The length of single vehicles is limited to 35 feet over all, and of combinations to 45 feet over all (not more than two units). Axle load is limited to 16,000 pounds for high-pressure and 18,000 for low-pressure pneumatic tires. The formula for gross weight limitation is determined particularly by reference to bridge design requirements.[9]

The principle that should govern the allocation of additional highway costs against truck and bus traffic is clear; but it is impossible at the present time to discover whether truck traffic and bus traffic are in fact paying for the additional costs which are properly assignable to them. This is because data as to the contributions made through gasoline and license fees by the several types of motor traffic are not available.

We know that heavy vehicles do contribute substantially more in the form of gasoline taxes and license fees than do passenger cars and light trucks. But a specific statement as to the amount of the special tax contributions made by the various weight classes of motor vehicles in relation to the differential cost of highway facilities required by these various classes must await the development of additional quantitative data.

Three distinct types of information are needed for each state: (a) the number of registered vehicles in each weight class and the respective license fees paid, (b) the annual gasoline consumption by each weight class of vehicles, and (c) traffic density of each weight class in relation to the total volume of vehicular traffic. The data listed under the first of these items could be obtained from the motor vehicle departments of most states, but at present they are not reported to or collected by any federal government agency.

The second item involves a more difficult problem.

[9] Adopted by the American Association of State Highway Officials in convention at Washington, D.C., Nov. 17, 1932, and recommended for adoption by all states.

The annual mileage traveled and the gasoline consumption per mile for each weight class of vehicles must be accurately determined if the amount of special tax contributions made by these vehicles is to be known. The use of average gasoline consumption and mileage figures for all trucks and for the country as a whole obviously would furnish no answer to the problem. Conclusive quantitative data on this point must refer to the actual motor vehicle operating experience within each state, or at least within groups of states where operating conditions are similar.

The necessary traffic density information can be obtained only through traffic surveys conducted in each state. Traffic volume and the type of vehicular traffic vary widely over different sections of the general use highway in any state. Some sections require high-type concrete surfaces, some intermediate, and on other sections ordinary "treated gravel" surfaces meet in full the requirements of vehicular traffic. Specific knowledge of these variations is of course essential to an allocation of highway costs between the various classes of motor vehicles. The Bureau of Public Roads, in collaboration with various state highway departments, has devoted considerable attention to this problem, but information is at present available from only a few states.

At the present time, therefore, it is impossible to answer the question whether passenger automobile traffic is subsidizing the truck and the bus, or *vice-versa*. In some states the passenger car may be contributing disproportionately, while in other states the opposite may be true.

CHAPTER XXVII

MOTOR VEHICLE TAXATION

There exists no end of confusion in the public mind with reference to motor vehicle taxation. In discussions of the competitive status of motor carriers and railroads we find the widest diversity of opinion expressed as to relative tax burdens. It is frequently contended by railroad interests that the motor carriers contribute little or nothing to the general support of government; while, on the other hand, statistics are presented by motor interests which tend to show that highway transportation is loaded down with taxes and that the contribution which it makes to the support of government is, in fact, excessive.

The primary source of confusion is to be found in the fact that a large portion of the so-called motor vehicle taxes are of a special type, the proceeds of which are devoted not to the general support of government but to meeting costs incurred by the government in constructing and maintaining the highways. On the highways of a former day it was the practice of the operating company or franchise holder to levy tolls on all traffic passing over the highway for the purpose of securing the means with which to cover capital and maintenance costs. Such a procedure was, however, not feasible in connection with motor vehicle transportation, and in consequence special types of levies were eventually devised to accomplish the same purpose.

In current discussions these special levies are commonly regarded as identical in character with any other taxes, whereas as a matter of fact the proceeds are not, generally speaking, available for the general support of government. So important is this conception to an understanding of the taxation controversy in this field that we shall divide our analysis into two parts, the first dealing with these special taxes and the second with other motor vehicle taxes.

I. SPECIAL MOTOR VEHICLE TAXES FOR HIGHWAY SUPPORT

The demand of motor vehicle owners for improved highways forced upon governments, particularly state and local governments, enormous expenditures for highway development. Not until 1919 was an adequate plan devised for meeting the financial problem involved. In that year the State of Oregon first gave concrete expression to the principle, later accepted by all states, that the additional costs imposed upon state governments by motor vehicle users as a special class should be apportioned in justice to all upon the direct beneficiaries of this new service. Gasoline taxes and license fees, or registration taxes, were adopted as the instruments for applying this principle. Special studies were made and technique developed to combine these two forms of taxes into a system of special motor vehicle taxes which would apportion the costs of improvements in highways as equitably according to the benefits received as practical tax methods would permit. Revenues from the special motor vehicle taxes were generally segregated into a special fund dedicated to defraying the costs of construction and maintenance of the highway system.

While the purpose of these special levies for the support of the highway is the same as that of tolls, they are not, strictly speaking, tolls in form. As stated by the United States Supreme Court,

The present registration fees cannot be said to be tolls in the commonly accepted sense of a proprietor's charge for the passage over a highway or bridge, exacted when and as the privilege of passage is exercised. . . . The fact that registration fees are imposed generally upon all residents who use motor vehicles, without reference to any particular highways, or to the extent or frequency of the use, and that, as in California, they are not exacted of non-resident automobilists passing through the state . . . marks them as demands of sovereignty, not of proprietorship, and likens them to taxes rather than tolls.[1]

The same reasoning would appear to be applicable to gasoline taxes. These levies are not exactly rents, according to the accepted meaning of the term "rent" as the payment for the *exclusive* use of a physical unit of tangible property for a specified period of time, although they have some of the features of a rent payment. They conform more nearly to the requirements of a license or a fee, an exaction upon individuals for the granting of a privilege, or for services which, while provided in the public interest, are of direct and measurable benefit to the individual upon whom the levy is made. But licenses and fees are ordinarily associated with regulatory or supervisory services and their amounts are fixed at the nominal sums required to defray the cost of the regulation.

Whatever these special motor vehicle levies be called —taxes, rents, or fees—their special character may best be revealed by comparison with taxation in connection with railroads. The railroad company covers the cost of its right of way and the maintenance thereof out of revenues derived from freight and passenger traffic; and revenues which are allocated to interest and maintenance charges are not regarded as taxes. The railroad does, however, procure from its revenues funds with which to

[1] *Carley and Hamilton* v. *Snook*, 50 Sup. Ct. Rep. 207.

pay taxes for the general support of government, both on its physical properties and on income. The contributions of highway users in the form of gasoline taxes and license fees intended to cover capital cost and maintenance charges incurred by the state are thus the equivalent of interest and maintenance on right of way and structures among the items of railroad expense. Only such portion as may be in excess of these capital and maintenance charges, and hence available for general governmental purposes, may properly be regarded as general taxation. Inasmuch as only negligible amounts of these special levies, as was shown in the preceding chapter, are available for the general purposes of government, the genuine *tax* contributions of motor vehicles are to be measured only by the general motor vehicle taxes discussed below.

Two issues are involved in the question as to whether these special motor vehicle levies should contribute to the general support of government. If the value of land in public highways, which is used for commercial purposes by transportation agencies, is to be in effect withdrawn from taxation—as is the case if gasoline and license taxes cover only capital and maintenance charges —the tax burdens on other properties must be proportionally heavier. There is here involved a question of equity in taxation. The second issue relates to the competitive position of highway and other forms of transportation. If highway real estate property is untaxed while the railroads and pipe lines are taxed, the latter are clearly placed at a competitive disadvantage. This may mean —the question is one of fact—that traffic is diverted from one agency to another not because of greater transportation efficiency but merely because of unequal tax burdens. The fairness of the principle that users of highways should contribute to the general support of government proportionally with competing transportation agencies has been recognized by the National Automobile Chamber of Commerce.[2] In accordance with this principle there should be included in the cost of highways to be defrayed by the highway users a charge equivalent to the property taxes which would be imposed upon the real estate represented by the highways if the real estate were privately owned.

II. GENERAL MOTOR VEHICLE TAXES

General motor vehicle taxes are differentiated from the special taxes discussed above by the fact that they are levied for the general support of government rather than for the support of the highways which are provided for motor vehicle users. These taxes, which are related to the ownership and use of motor vehicles, consist of property taxes on motor vehicles and of business taxes on companies or individuals engaged in motor vehicle transportation.

It is true that this theoretical differentiation between special and general motor vehicle taxes is not always applied strictly in practice. Partly to simplify administration and partly because of the inevitable indefiniteness of principles in an evolving field of taxation, special and general motor vehicle taxes have been combined in a single levy in some states. Registration taxes have been enacted not solely as special taxes but also as taxes on motor vehicles as property or on business carried on by means of motor vehicles. Moreover, judicial decisions bearing upon the taxing power of the states with respect to interstate motor vehicle carriers have resulted in cast-

[2] Testimony of Mr. A. J. Brosseau before the National Transportation Committee.

ing what are essentially business taxes into the form of charges for the use of the highways as places of business.

Frequently business taxes are so intertwined with the registration taxes that it is impossible to segregate the two and identify that part of the levy which is exacted strictly for highway use and that part exacted as a general business tax. This difficulty is being gradually resolved as the distinction between general and special taxes is being more widely recognized by the enactment of separate statutes for the two types. While it is necessary to allow for the existing overlapping of these two forms of taxation, the difference is recognized in a sufficient number of states to justify the treatment of all forms of registration and gasoline taxes as special motor vehicle taxes and other levies as general business taxes.

Because these general taxes form integral parts of the general property and business tax systems of the various states, statistics of revenues and of other relevant aspects of general taxes on motor vehicles are not universally segregated from those of other property and business subject to the same taxes. It is not possible, therefore, to appraise quantitatively the general tax burdens on motor vehicles for the country as a whole. With the available information, these taxes can be studied only in relation to their position in and relation to the general tax measures under which they are imposed. With the limited time available, reliance has necessarily been placed upon available compilations of the state and local tax laws for this analysis.

1. *Property taxation of motor vehicles.* Instead of being exempted from all taxes other than special motor vehicle taxes, motor vehicles are generally taxed as personal property in accordance with the same principles govern-

ing the taxation of other types of property. Thirty states and the District of Columbia retain the general property tax on motor vehicles, although some of the states have devised more effective methods for discovering and valuing motor vehicles. Three states exempt motor vehicles along with most other classes of tangible personal property. Three states have substituted an equivalent excise tax for the personal property tax on motor vehicles. One state imposes a tax on the value of motor vehicles at a relatively high rate as a substitute for separate registration and personal property taxes. Of the remaining eleven states which levy registration taxes in lieu of personal property taxes, four include the value of motor vehicles as a measure of the registration tax on all or certain classes of motor vehicles. Of the 48 states and the District of Columbia, only seven jurisdictions have motor vehicle taxes among which the personal property tax or its equivalent cannot be definitely identified.

While official reports of the revenues derived from property taxes on motor vehicles are not available, the National Automobile Chamber of Commerce and the *Oregon Voter* have estimated these revenues in 1929 at $149,000,000 and $89,000,000 respectively.[3] Municipal taxes on motor vehicles are included in the first estimate but these revenues would not account for the wide difference in the estimates. According to either estimate, however, it is evident that a substantial property tax burden is laid on motor vehicles as personal property.

2. *Business taxation of motor vehicles.* Only within the last decade has transportation by motor vehicles

[3] N.A.C.C. *Facts and Figures of the Automobile Industry*, 1932, p. 22; Iowa Studies in Business, *Motor Vehicle Taxation for Highway Purposes*, 1932, pp. 9-10.

emerged as a significant form of business enterprise, and the industry is still in the stage of early expansion. All forms of business organization from the individual enterprise with one or two vehicles to the corporation with large fleets exist side by side in the industry. In a general way the carriers by motor vehicles have been classified as common carriers and contract carriers, and as carriers running over definite routes between fixed termini and carriers having no definite schedules, but the legal and economic principles relating to the different classes of carriers are still indefinite. Public policy with reference to the regulation or non-regulation of the rates, services, and finances of the carriers is still in the formative stage.

Taxation laws and principles applying to this new form of business reflect the indefiniteness of the legal and economic status of this developing field of transportation. Motor carriers have been generally brought under the existing system of state business taxes and federal corporation taxes, but neither the federal nor the state governments have developed business tax systems sufficiently broad in scope to handle an industry with the diversity of business organization, the range in size of individual units, and the geographical mobility which characterizes the present motor carrier industry. Judicial principles governing the taxing power of the states over interstate and intrastate carriers, and over common and contract carriers are only in the early stages of formulation. Consequently, taxation principles and methods covering motor vehicle business are essentially tentative and experimental in character.

It is more difficult to segregate and identify motor vehicle business taxes in existing systems of motor vehicle taxes than any other motor vehicle levy. There are many kinds of motor vehicle taxes in the several states, and frequently a state imposes taxes differentiated according to the types of carriers. Some states have included motor carriers in their systems of public utility corporation taxes, while others have subjected motor carriers to substantially higher registration taxes to take account of the use of highways as a place of business. Measures of the business of motor carriers, such as capacity, gross receipts, ton and passenger miles, have also been adopted as the measures of the use of the highways for which registration taxes are imposed.

In the light of these complications, it is not possible to determine accurately from the laws or the practice of motor vehicle taxation where business taxation or highway taxation was intended. This discussion, therefore, is intended not as a detailed and precise analysis of the status of motor vehicle business taxation but as a statement of general features of this field of taxation which can be quite clearly identified.

As a general rule, motor carriers are subject to the same general business taxes as are imposed on other types of business. General business taxes in most states are restricted to corporations, although some states have taxes applying to unincorporated business of certain types. California and Connecticut have gross earnings taxes upon public service corporations which fall upon all or certain classes of motor carriers. Although only a small proportion of the motor carriers are incorporated, those that are, are subject to the capital-stock and net-income taxes generally levied by the states on domestic and foreign corporations and by the federal government.

In addition to the general business taxes on motor

vehicles, there have been developed in a considerable number of states special taxes applying exclusively to specified classes of motor carriers. These taxes are in addition to registration taxes and appear to have been designed to exact a contribution for the use of the highways as a place of business, to supplement the business taxes on corporations by a tax on the business of the large number of unincorporated concerns engaged in motor vehicle transportation, or to place a tax on motor carriers roughly equivalent to the gross earnings taxes on all or certain classes of other public service corporations. Judicial decisions relating to state taxation of the interstate commerce of motor carriers, however, have so affected the form of certain of these taxes that their real intent is obscured. As was noted previously, certain states have preferred to achieve an approximation to a business tax by higher registration tax rates.

Separate taxes upon motor carriers probably designed to tax their business take two general forms, the traffic mileage taxes and the gross earnings taxes. Eighteen states have separate taxes based upon the passenger and ton mileage of all or specified classes of motor carriers. Nine states, other than Connecticut or California already mentioned, have gross earnings taxes on all or specified classes of motor carriers. New Jersey, which has a gross earnings tax on certain intrastate carriers and a passenger mileage tax on one class of interstate carriers, is included in both groups. Twenty-six states in all, therefore, have developed separate taxes on motor carriers which can probably be considered special business taxes. Four other states have separate taxes on the capacity of carriers for hire which cannot be classified either as registration or as business taxes.

Within less than 15 years, there have thus been developed among the 48 states systems of motor vehicle taxes which are reasonably well integrated and established on generally accepted principles. Such a rapid development of a new field of taxation has inevitably brought with it the diversity of methods characteristic of experimentation, and consequent vagueness in the formulation and application of taxation principles. No other development in American taxation, however, presents such a record of rapid and universal adoption as that of motor vehicle taxation.

CHAPTER XXVIII

TRUCK COMPETITION IN AGRICULTURAL PRODUCTS

As a direct competitor of the railroads the truck has made the largest inroads in connection with the movement of certain types of agricultural products. In this chapter we shall show the character and extent of truck transportation of agricultural commodities and analyze the economic considerations responsible for this development. In order to portray the situation as accurately as possible we present a survey of conditions in various parts of the country.

The great field of the truck in connection with the movement of agricultural products lies in the transportation of perishable commodities such as livestock, fruits and vegetables, and dairy and poultry products. The basic reasons why truck competition has become so important in these fields are the perishable character of the commodities which require rapid transportation, the large volume which is produced within truck haul of one or more markets, and the high scale of railroad rates and additional charges which raise the total cost of rail shipment to a level at which the truck may compete successfully.

Cotton is the most important non-perishable commodity which moves extensively by motor truck, although there has been increased shipment of wool, tobacco, hay, and canned goods. Reduced hauling charges by truck as compared with the rail rates have been the chief factor in shifting these commodities to the truck. These lower truck rates have largely been due to the lack of employment for trucks and men in normal activity.

Transportation of the perishable commodities by rail usually requires special equipment and the maintenance of expedited service on a schedule basis. While both long and short hauls are common with most of these commodities, the truck has achieved most of its success in transporting them over comparatively short distances. Because of their perishable character, these commodities are forwarded in successive daily shipments rather than in larger units. For this reason the marketing unit has usually been the carload.

The development of the refrigerator car permitted the railroads to participate in the handling of perishables. While the refrigerator car was first used in the transportation of meat, it was soon adapted to other perishable commodities. It is equally useful in protecting such products from cold during the winter and in cooling them during the summer. Other special forms of equipment include the livestock car, the live poultry car, and the tank car for the hauling of milk.

In the transportation of perishables numerous special services are required, among which are icing, heating, diversion, etc. However, additional charges are paid by shippers for these services, which increase the total cost of rail transportation. Special terminals are required in many of the cities in order to expedite the handling of such products. The ownership of such terminal facilities has been an effective method for securing shipments over the lines of certain carriers, especially on interline traffic. The competition between the railroads for perishable business indicates that it has been a profitable form of traffic.

Most of these commodities are handled for the shorter hauls on class rates, usually in the higher classes. Commodity rates have prevailed for the more important longer hauls, and blanket rates have been common from the Pacific coast to eastern markets. Short hauls in small quantities have been largely at less-than-carload express rates. Thus the entire rate structure has created a much higher level for the shorter hauls than for the longer distances. This was an ideal situation to induce the competition of the motor truck, which could operate most effectively and economically for the shorter distances.

While the real competition of the truck with the railroad is in the hauling of the products from country points to city markets, there are two uses of the truck which should be mentioned before discussing the competitive situation in detail.

The initial service required in the marketing of farm products is assembling for shipment in the producing districts. In the past the unit of shipment was usually the carlot, and stations and towns were located along the railroad at distances largely based upon the territory from which such assembling could be carried on most effectively with horse transportation. With the entrance of the motor truck, the area which might be served from one town was greatly increased. This was further enlarged by the improvement of roads, and thus the economic necessity for many of the country stations was eliminated.

The 1930 census reported that 900,385[1] trucks were owned on the farms of the country. These trucks are

---

[1] Fifteenth Census of the United States, Agriculture, Vol. II, Pt. I, p. 54.

mostly of small size and are commonly used in reaching the local assembling points or markets. With such a truck, the farmer is able to make a much wider selection than in the day of horse transportation, when little choice was possible. The entire system of assembling farm products in the rural districts has changed during the past decade and even greater adjustments are likely to occur in the near future.

The next most numerous group of trucks comprises those engaged in city and suburban distribution. These include the trucks used in wholesale distribution, and also the much larger number employed in the various forms of retail delivery. These do not compete with the railroad, except in a few instances where shipments from outlying suburban points were formerly handled by rail.

I. LIVESTOCK[2]

The trucking of livestock has grown more steadily and more consistently than the trucking of any other important agricultural commodity. The first records indicate that 1.61 per cent of the livestock received at 16 markets in 1916 was delivered by motor truck. Each

[2] Unless a specific reference is given the statistics used in this section are those of the U. S. Department of Agriculture—particularly those given in a mimeographed publication *"Driven-in Receipts of Livestock, 1931"* issued in February 1932. It must be recognized that there are some inaccuracies in these figures, as they are based upon the number of head received at public stockyards, divided into receipts by "rail" and "driven-in" (trucks). Animals delivered by either rail or truck to packing plants without passing through a stockyard are not included. It is impossible to secure information of this type for the entire country, but a recent Iowa study (D. H. Fitzgerald, "Statistics of Livestock Marketing and Livestock Trucking in Iowa in 1931," *Iowa Agricultural Experiment Station Circular 136*) reports that direct deliveries to packing plants from Iowa farms in 1931 amounted to 59.6 per cent of the hogs, 14.5 per cent of the cattle, 39.4 per cent of the calves, and 19.3 per cent of the sheep marketed. These figures would indicate that the percentage of truck movement to the total is even larger than stated.

year since that time this proportion has increased, until the percentage of truck receipts at 20 markets[8] during the first nine months of 1932 amounted to 38.36 per cent. During this period of nine months, 51.5 per cent of the hogs and calves, 34.8 per cent of the cattle, and 20.7 per cent of the sheep were received by motor truck. The continuous growth in the trucking of livestock during the period 1916-31 is shown in the accompanying table.

LIVESTOCK RECEIPTS BY TRUCK AS PERCENTAGES OF TOTAL RECEIPTS AT PRINCIPAL MARKETS, 1916–31

Year	Hogs	Cattle	Sheep	Calves	Total
1916.........	1.79	1.38	1.28	4.10	1.61
1917.........	2.97	1.56	1.64	6.41	2.42
1918.........	4.21	1.71	1.71	7.33	3.14
1919.........	5.75	1.91	2.20	8.33	4.08
1920.........	6.97	2.20	3.43	9.48	5.21
1921.........	7.71	2.44	4.14	8.83	5.85
1922.........	8.35	2.86	6.20	9.43	6.74
1923.........	8.19	2.90	6.08	10.22	6.85
1924.........	8.66	3.33	5.89	10.41	7.17
1925.........	10.87	4.62	6.05	13.17	8.60
1926.........	14.43	5.68	7.12	15.72	10.72
1927.........	17.71	7.27	9.43	17.84	13.49
1928.........	23.81	10.46	10.73	22.67	18.05
1929.........	28.86	13.47	12.79	28.61	21.85
1930.........	34.38	18.06	14.00	35.46	25.56
1931.........	42.98	24.03	17.01	44.91	31.39
1931 Animals received.	28,311,500	10,579,367	20,657,544	3,475,302	63,023,713
1931 Animals trucked in......	12,166,957	2,542,037	3,514,820	1,560,609	19,784,423

The Chicago livestock market is the largest in the country, but the actual farm area within practical truck haul of it is much smaller than is the case in the other centers. While it ranks eighth in the number of animals

[8] Includes Sioux Falls, Cleveland, Pittsburgh, and Lancaster in addition to the markets listed in the tables which follow.

received by truck in 1931, the 1,105,084 head of live-stock trucked in amounted to only 7.24 per cent of the total receipts. We can secure a more accurate picture of the conditions in the other 15 markets by eliminating Chicago. The following table shows truck receipts as percentages of total receipts in 1931, with and without the Chicago figures. It will be seen that about 40 per cent of the receipts at the larger markets outside of Chicago came by truck in 1931.

	Chicago Included	Chicago Excluded
Hogs	42.98	56.37
Calves	44.91	50.89
Cattle	24.03	28.45
Sheep	17.01	20.68
All species	31.39	39.11

LIVESTOCK RECEIPTS BY TRUCK AT SPECIFIED MARKETS, 1931

Market	Truck Receipts		Markets Ranked in Terms of	
	Number of Animals	As Percentage of Total Receipts	Animals Trucked	Percentage of Total Receipts Trucked
Omaha	3,180,198	36.45	1	9
Sioux City	2,947,595	61.72	2	3
St. Paul	2,243,439	35.30	3	11
Indianapolis	1,905,617	83.13	4	1
East St. Louis	1,797,524	37.43	5	8
St. Joseph	1,633,905	48.02	6	6
Kansas City	1,277,842	23.07	7	13
Chicago	1,105,084	7.24	8	16
Cincinnati	857,962	45.57	9	7
Milwaukee	494,794	35.49	10	10
Fort Worth	457,822	20.52	11	14
Wichita	457,746	51.15	12	5
Oklahoma City	434,101	66.87	13	2
Denver	420,584	11.68	14	15
Louisville	353,613	58.82	15	4
Portland	216,597	35.20	16	12
16 Markets	19,784,423	31.39		

GROWTH OF TRUCK TRANSPORTATION OF LIVESTOCK
1916-31

(Truck receipts expressed as percentages of the total supply
received at 16 markets)

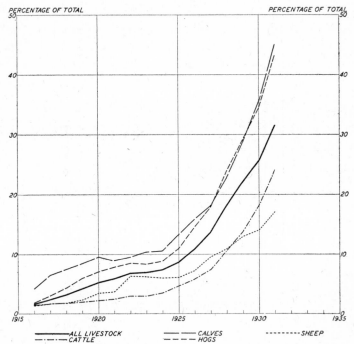

1. *Hog receipts by truck.* The real competition between the railroad and the motor truck in the livestock
industry has been in the transportation of hogs. In 1931
42.98 per cent of all hogs received at the 16 markets
came by truck; with Chicago excluded, the average for
the other 15 markets was 56.37 per cent. Indianapolis
led with 86.74 per cent and Sioux City was second with
81.81 per cent. With the exception of Chicago, every
market received over 25 per cent of its supply by truck.

LIVESTOCK RECEIPTS BY TRUCK AS PERCENTAGES OF TOTAL RECEIPTS AT INDIVIDUAL MARKETS

Market	Hogs				Cattle				Sheep			
	1924	1927	1930	1931	1924	1927	1930	1931	1924	1927	1930	1931
Chicago	0.52	1.92	5.88	8.60	0.63	1.92	5.77	7.97	0.23	1.02	2.91	3.79
Cincinnati	21.09	29.34	37.58	46.52	10.60	13.45	20.68	23.85	16.85	26.10	56.00	48.05
Denver	16.29	16.18	32.95	39.77	5.15	6.07	9.90	16.01	2.63	3.38	2.53	3.41
East St. Louis	2.02	6.13	27.16	39.22	.96	3.71	19.99	23.95	3.39	11.44	32.67	39.00
Fort Worth	11.23	27.42	34.43	35.11	4.62	6.38	13.66	22.53	6.79	9.41	12.63	13.69
Indianapolis	32.21	47.84	73.49	86.74	16.01	26.82	51.73	67.81	47.59	50.23	72.86	75.49
Kansas City	6.72	16.08	39.22	51.55	1.07	2.36	7.81	11.15	5.26	8.26	11.17	13.39
Louisville	26.49	43.44	47.06	39.52	14.42	20.15	37.56	47.54	27.32	45.36	68.81	78.95
Milwaukee	4.60	9.95	20.56	30.26	11.89	22.74	36.25	44.59	8.79	15.85	23.22	33.39
Oklahoma City	29.96	46.70	72.15	77.09	9.25	17.00	38.98	53.25	43.50	50.23	69.39	61.03
Omaha	10.43	28.27	46.78	58.11	2.86	10.60	24.95	31.47	8.92	10.48	12.45	16.80
Portland (Ore.)	10.55	23.04	22.73	25.86	3.13	8.72	14.91	15.43	9.86	23.41	47.67	54.45
St. Joseph	11.08	27.22	66.26	79.92	4.18	7.24	21.38	31.70	13.33	17.67	21.17	24.27
St. Paul	4.01	11.39	26.57	41.89	4.27	8.14	20.60	29.70	4.53	8.12	11.98	16.60
Sioux City	12.95	39.72	71.66	81.81	6.70	18.40	39.04	50.15	7.29	16.40	24.48	28.80
Wichita	17.75	29.55	55.22	54.64	6.83	14.57	30.84	41.39	21.22	28.39	62.19	59.75
Average (16 markets)	8.66	17.71	34.38	42.98	3.33	7.27	18.06	24.03	5.89	9.43	14.00	17.01
Total number of animals received	39,251,347	28,807,342	28,878,679	28,311,500	13,849,451	12,762,640	10,847,598	10,579,367	14,373,484	14,674,417	18,135,283	20,657,544
Total number of animals trucked in	3,401,036	5,101,517	9,927,779	12,166,957	461,250	928,479	1,958,585	2,542,037	846,950	1,384,463	2,538,178	3,514,820

Figures for the smaller markets which have not been included would show even higher percentages, as certain of these markets have developed because of truck hauling.

The production of hogs is largely concentrated in the Corn Belt states, and the animals are usually fattened on the farms where they were born. There are comparatively few farms in this area which are not within motor truck haul of a livestock market. Few farmers are in position to sell a carload at one time, and so a carload must be assembled from a number of farms. This additional expense, or the higher less-than-carload rate if the shipment is made separately, permits the motor truck to compete to a greater degree than in the case of cattle and sheep.

2. Cattle receipts by truck. The number of cattle received by truck in 1931 was 24.03 per cent of all cattle receipts. There are several reasons why this percentage was so much smaller than the one for hogs. A considerable portion of the cattle marketed is produced in the plains and mountain states and shipped relatively long distances. For such hauls the railroads have continued as the principal transportation agency. Feeder cattle are usually purchased and marketed in carlot units, since cattle feeding is conducted on a scale which makes the carload more practical than a smaller unit. Also, the feeding-in-transit privilege in effect at certain markets is a factor favorable to rail transportation. The marketing of dairy cattle for slaughter has largely been taken over by the truck, because a few head of such cattle are usually sold at a time.

While the average of the 16 markets was 24.03 per cent in 1931, the percentage at Chicago was only 7.97, while Kansas City, Portland, and Denver reported 11.15, 15.43, and 16.01 per cent respectively. At other markets, however, especially in the Corn Belt, the percentage was high, reaching 67.81 per cent at Indianapolis.

3. Sheep receipts by truck. Conditions here are similar to those for cattle. The movement by truck to the 16 markets was 17.01 per cent of all receipts in 1931, with wide variation between the different markets. Chicago and Denver, which handled 34 per cent of the entire receipts, received less than 4 per cent of their supply by truck. Louisville and Indianapolis, on the other hand, showed more than 75 per cent moving by truck.

As is the case with cattle, many of the sheep originally come from the mountain states. Because of the economy of rail transportation, owing to the long haul and the feeding-in-transit privilege, the bulk of this business is still handled over the railroads. Sheep produced in the farm areas of the Middle West appear to follow the same general practice of moving by truck as do hogs but do not form as large a portion of the total supply.

4. Calf receipts by truck. While calves are handled in much smaller volume than hogs, practically the same situation with regard to rail and truck competition prevails for both. The average truck receipts for the 16 markets in 1931 was 44.91 per cent of the total receipts, or 50.89 per cent with Chicago excluded. The highest percentage was 77.95 per cent at St. Joseph, and the smallest, except Chicago, at Kansas City, with 35.16 per cent.

5. Character of truckers. Persons operating trucks fall within four classes: Commercial truckers who charge fixed rates per hundredweight or per trip; country buyers who purchase stock from the producers; truckers who haul only for certain marketing agencies; and farmers who own their own trucks and do their own trucking. For the most part trucks of relatively small capacity are used. Since the initial investment is usually low, many individuals have been able to enter the trucking business. Most of the trucks are owned in the country and are available for hauling on short notice. The number of farmers who own their own trucks appears to be steadily increasing. In view of the small investment required, and of the choice of markets opened to farmers having trucks, the number is likely to continue to increase.

One of the greatest factors in the cost of trucking is the possibility of a return load. With the downward trend in rates, this must necessarily have a considerable influence on the railroads and other lines of business affected.

6. Length of haul by truck. Conditions vary so widely in the scattered areas where the trucking of livestock is highly developed that it is impossible to generalize concerning the length of haul. Analyses of receipts at individual markets, however, include reports on mileage zones which are typical of truck receipts at these markets.

A study of the truck receipts in 1927 at three Illinois markets—Chicago, Peoria, and East St. Louis—led to the following conclusions regarding the distance from which truck shipments came:

At Peoria the largest numbers of cattle and calves and of hogs came from Zone 2, a distance of 16 to 25 miles; while at Chicago, Zone 4, 36 to 45 miles, sent the greatest numbers. The largest sheep receipts came from Zone 1, 15 miles, at Peoria; from Zone 5, 46 to 55 miles, at East St. Louis; and from Zone 6, 56 to 65 miles at Chicago. Peoria drew 88 per cent of its cattle and calves, and over 95 per cent of its hogs and sheep from the first four zones, a radius of 45 miles. At Chicago 66 per cent of the cattle and calves, more than 51 per cent of the hogs, and more than 28 per cent of the sheep came from within this distance. At East St. Louis (National Stock Yards) 50 per cent of the cattle and calves, slightly over 51 per cent of the hogs, and about 27 per cent of the sheep came from such a radius.[4]

Data on length of haul at the South St. Paul market are given in the accompanying table. It will be seen that

LIVESTOCK TRUCKS AND TONNAGE ENTERING SOUTH ST. PAUL MARKET
JANUARY-NOVEMBER 1930[a]
(Classified according to length of haul)

Length of Haul (In miles)	Trucks			Tons of Livestock	
	Number	*Percentage Distribution*	*Accumulated Percentage*	Number	Average Truckload
0–15........	16,128	*17.2*	*17.2*	13,805.90	0.86
16–30.......	22,130	*23.6*	*40.8*	32,043.86	1.45
31–45.......	24,474	*26.1*	*66.9*	43,306.68	1.77
46–60.......	15,660	*16.7*	*83.6*	29,956.79	1.91
61–75.......	9,471	*10.1*	*93.7*	19,675.52	2.08
76–90.......	2,438	*2.6*	*96.3*	3,195.42	1.31
91–105......	1,594	*1.7*	*98.0*	4,080.87	2.56
106–120.....	656	*0.7*	*98.7*	1,443.40	2.20
121–135.....	563	*0.6*	*99.3*	1,580.96	2.81
136–150.....	469	*0.5*	*99.8*	1,066.66	2.27
151 and over	187	*0.2*	*100.0*	628.82	3.36

[a] Adopted from *Docket 23400, Co-ordination of Motor Transportation*, Interstate Commerce Commission, p. 288. This report also states that "the average haul into 17 markets in 1931 was 65 miles."

93.7 per cent of all trucks bringing livestock to this market in 1930 came a distance of less than 75 miles, and that the average load per truck did not reach two tons until the distance covered was over 60 miles.

[4] R. C. Ashby, "Livestock Truckage Rates in Illinois," *University of Illinois Experiment Station Bulletin 342*, p. 136.

A Missouri study based on 1930 shipments shows the mileage to market by rail and truck from Missouri towns for which both types of service were available.[5] The results are tabulated in the accompanying table.

COMPARISON OF LENGTH OF TRUCK AND RAIL HAULS TO THREE MISSOURI
LIVESTOCK MARKETS, 1930
(In miles)

Carrier	East St. Louis (Ill.)	Kansas City	St. Joseph	Average for Three Markets
Hogs:				
Truck	139	62	62	88
Railroad	152	76	68	99
Cattle:				
Truck	134	64	63	87
Railroad	146	80	67	98
Sheep:				
Truck	124	69	70	88
Railroad	138	84	78	100

The average distances to market by truck are well above those reported for other territories. The average haul to East St. Louis was nearly twice that to Kansas City and St. Joseph, raising the average for the state appreciably. From the figures available for other states, the averages for Kansas City and St. Joseph are much more representative for the Corn Belt as a whole than are the figures for East St. Louis.

The situation in the Corn Belt is well summarized in the following quotation:

From a recent Indiana study the facts would indicate that the bulk of the livestock arriving by truck at the Indianapolis market came from within 60 miles of that market. At all of these markets (Cleveland, Cincinnati, Indianapolis, Peoria, Chicago, East St. Louis, and South St. Paul) very little livestock at the

[5] F. L. Thomsen and W. R. Fankhanel, "Cost of Marketing Livestock by Truck and Rail," *Missouri Agricultural Experiment Station Research Bulletin 165*, p. 17.

time of the studies was coming from distances over 85 miles. On the other hand there was very definitely a tendency for livestock to be trucked further each year. The St. Paul study showed the average haul for all trucks for 1924 of 22 miles; for 1926, 31.6 miles; for 1928, 35.7 miles; and for 1929, 40.8 miles.[6]

The only available data showing the actual sources of supply of receipts by truck are those for the Chicago market during the period of June-October, for the three years 1930-32. The accompanying table, which gives the sources of hogs received by truck in Chicago, shows the rapid increase in truck hauling from the nearby area.

SOURCES OF HOG RECEIPTS BY TRUCK AT CHICAGO, JUNE-OCTOBER 1930–32

Source	Number of Hogs Received by Truck, 1932	Truck Receipts as Percentage of Total Receipts		
		1930	*1931*	*1932*
Illinois........	383,978	23.5	39.1	59.5
Iowa.........	38,929	—	0.6	5.8
Indiana.......	24,252	57.0	84.5	92.8
Wisconsin.....	6,058	0.7	1.7	8.3
4 States.....	453,217	9.3	14.9	32.1

The quantity received from Michigan and Ohio was less than 1 per cent of the receipts from the states listed in the table. While the very rapid increase from Illinois is the most important point brought out by these figures, the expansion of truck movement from Iowa, which involves a minimum distance of about 140 miles, is perhaps of greater significance as far as the future is concerned.

7. *Rates by motor truck.* The steady increase in the percentage of livestock hauled by motor truck developed

---

[6] G. F. Henning, "The Influence of the Truck in Marketing Corn Belt Livestock," *Journal of Farm Economics*, July 1931, p. 386.

while truck rates generally were higher than the corresponding rates by rail. This apparent disregard of costs can be explained by other factors of importance in livestock marketing.

Truck hauling of livestock is largely by contract carriers, and it is exceedingly difficult to determine the rates which are actually in use at any time. Information of this character can only be secured from detailed studies covering representative shipments to important markets. An Illinois study made in 1927 and 1928 is partially summarized as follows:[7]

Considering only truck shipments moving 45 miles or more, the apparent savings in marketing by rail instead of by truck, figured on the basis of the 1927 truckage and freight rates would have been as follows:

To Peoria, 53 cents a head, or 20 cents per cwt.

To East St. Louis, 57 cents a head, or 25 cents per cwt.

To Chicago, 26 cents a head, or 11 cents per cwt.

On the basis of 1928 truckage rates and 1927 freight rates, the apparent savings would have been:

To Peoria, 38 cents a head, or 14 cents per cwt.

To East St. Louis, 44 cents a head, or 19 cents per cwt.

To Chicago, 15 cents a head, or 6 cents per cwt.

Any comparison of the expense of marketing livestock by truck and by rail should include attention to risk, differences in terminal market charges, shrinkage, buyers' attitudes, and convenience to shipper. With the exception of buyers' attitude and convenience, these factors have been taken into consideration in the foregoing comparisons of marketing expense. From available data it appears that losses due to death or crippling in truck shipments are as heavy as in rail shipments, and heavier when shipping mileage is considered. More complete information, however, is needed on this subject. Terminal charges (yardage and commission) are higher on truck shipments than on rail at

[7] Ashby, *University of Illinois Experiment Station Bulletin 342*, p. 166.

the three markets here considered. Shrinkage is not greatly different on the two methods of shipment, judging by available data. Having allowed for all other factors, the cost of convenience may be measured by the net difference between the cost of two methods of transportation.

The comparative cost of marketing livestock by motor truck or by rail is largely determined by the total cost of marketing by each of the two methods rather than by the difference between the transportation rates alone. This fact is developed in a recent Missouri study[8] which compares the marketing costs by the two methods from the farm through to the livestock market. In this comparison the other costs of marketing, such as feed, yardage, commission, insurance, and association or local assembling charges, have been included in addition to the transportation rates. In order to make a fair comparison an allowance for the cost of hauling from the farm to the initial railroad station has also been included, as the truck movement begins at the farm rather than at the railroad station.

While the comparison includes data from only eleven points, it indicates that the truck rate was substantially above the railroad rate in every instance. On the other hand, when the total cost of marketing was determined, as outlined above, the difference between the two methods of transportation was much reduced. In several instances the cost of marketing by rail was slightly larger than the cost of marketing by truck when all of the cost items were included.

During the early period of expansion of truck transportation, livestock shippers were willing to use the

[8] Thomsen and Fankhanel, *Missouri Experiment Station Research Bulletin* 165, pp. 18 and 32.

new service because of its convenience rather than because of its relative cheapness. During the past two years
the low prices of livestock have forced economies in marketing which were not given consideration during the
earlier period. The number of trucks which were being
used for livestock hauling had increased very materially.
Because of the resulting keener competition there was a
distinct tendency to lower truck rates. Operating costs
were slightly lower but truck drivers were secured for
much lower wages because of the general labor situation.
For this reason the following quotation from the Missouri study is significant:

It is apparent that in 1931 the cost of marketing by truck was
considerably lower compared with rail than in 1930. For all
species to St. Joseph, and hogs to Kansas City, the cost was less
by truck than by rail. For hogs to St. Louis and cattle to Kansas
City, the costs were about the same, taking into account the
complete mileage range. For sheep to Kansas City and both
cattle and sheep to St. Louis, rail shipment was cheaper than
truck. These developments are very significant. They indicate
that no longer is convenience the main or only incentive to truck
shipments. Cost, the big argument previously used in support of
rail movement, now is generally in favor of the truck.

Certain of the indirect costs of marketing favor trucking and others favor rail. Thus commission, yard
charges, and other similar expenses are higher for truck
handling because of the smaller volume of each shipper.
On the other hand, shrinkage is probably less by truck
than by rail because of the shorter time on the road.
If the net costs of marketing are about the same, a further increase in the trucking of livestock can be expected
because of its convenience, this having been the deciding
factor up to the present time. The return of livestock
to the railroads for short hauls, say up to 75 or 100 miles,

is unlikely. Above these distances the railroads may be able to regain the traffic if proper steps are taken to encourage it.

The return of shipments to the railroads will not be secured through the enforcement of such rate schedules as were put into effect in January, 1932, concerning which the following comment is of interest:

> Rates on single-deck cars of livestock are now considerably higher than they have been since 1920. The increases were particularly large on shipments originating in western Iowa and moving east, for example, to Chicago. Rates on hogs shipped double-deck were not increased as much and in certain sections of the state were actually lowered. In the past, however, particularly from the local loading points in Iowa, the majority of the hogs have been shipped single-deck, many of the small shippers at these points not having enough hogs available at one time to ship double.
>
> At the same time the truck rates for hauling livestock have been declining, and in sections of the state where competition between truckers is more or less unregulated, rates are now very low, probably below the actual cost of giving this service.[9]

In the case of one railroad this 1932 rate increase has been stated to have resulted in almost a complete cessation of short-haul shipments which were subject to the new rates.

An attempt to regain business which has already gone to a competitor by increasing rates and minimum weights would seem to indicate poor judgment. The railroads are now a minor transportation factor in many sections and must make their service attractive to shippers or witness the complete loss of the livestock business to the motor truck in the competitive area. Unless there

---

[9] D. G. Fitzgerald, "Statistics of Livestock Marketing and Livestock Trucking in Iowa in 1931," *Iowa Agricultural Experiment Station Circular 136*, p. 11.

is a change of present railroad policies, a more rapid increase in truck hauling than has taken place up to the present time can be expected.

8. Combination of rail and truck transportation. The method which appears to offer most possibilities of success in restoring livestock business to the railroads, especially on the longer hauls, is the combination of truck hauling from the farm to a railroad point, and shipment by rail for the remainder of the way. Some effort is being made to bring this plan into operation through a tariff on the Western trunk lines[10] which became effective on December 10, 1932. This rule reads as follows:

> On shipments of livestock delivered to carriers' station by motor truck lines for shipment therefrom by rail, the carriers, upon request, will advance to the delivering motor truck line its charges for transporting the livestock to the carrier's station. Charges so advanced will be included as back charges on the waybill for collection from consignee.
>
> Exception: Will not apply on shipments delivered to carrier at public livestock markets or public stockyards, as named in Item 150, nor on shipments transferred from a station on one railroad to a station on another railroad.

This new rule indicates that the Middle Western carriers, including the lines operating both east and west of Chicago, are making an effort to work out a practical method for providing combined rail and truck service from the farm to market. This is not true of the Southwestern carriers, which recently disapproved a similar rule for their territory.[11]

9. Changes in the livestock industry. During the past decade factors other than the competition between the truck and the railroad have been operating to effect

---

[10] *Western Trunk Lines Freight Tariff No. 236-B, Item 65.*
[11] *Southwestern Freight Bureau Docket No. 25429.*

changes in the industry. Large packers have been shifting their slaughter operations closer to the producer. Likewise they have been buying a portion of their livestock in the country, directly from the producer. Consequently the volume passing through the stockyards records has not given as complete a picture of the entire industry as it formerly did. The farmer has also had his choice of markets widened by the establishment of a considerable number of independent packing plants in the producing areas, and by the prompt and complete market information now available over the radio. Each of these changes has tended to substitute the truck for the railroad as it has reduced the length of haul necessary to reach a buyer.

The transfer of livestock hauling to the truck in certain markets has reduced the volume of business handled by the railroads and has therefore resulted in a reduction of the number of trains operated. Such curtailment of service naturally has further reduced the ability of the railroad to compete with the truck. The decline in the total number of animals shipped by rail must ultimately be recognized in an adjustment of rates on other types of business, unless a considerable portion of the short-haul business is restored to the railroads.

10. Truck transportation in the distribution of packing-house products. With the improvement of truck equipment so that refrigeration is available for rather long trips, the distribution of meat products by some packers has been transferred to motor trucks, especially in the vicinity of the smaller packing plants. Distribution from branch houses into outlying districts also has been developed in replacement of the former "peddler car" service. Merchandising advantages favor the motor truck, as it permits the employee of the packer to make frequent personal contacts with the retailer and to fill his exact requirements at the time delivery is made.

II. FRUITS AND VEGETABLES[12]

Fruit and vegetable production is carried on commercially in every state of the Union. Because over 40 commodities are grouped under this general classification, the producing areas are scattered from coast to coast and from the Gulf of Mexico to the Canadian border. With the exception of citrus and other tropical fruits, which must be grown in districts relatively free from frost, the other crops are frequently grown in a large number of widely scattered states. The heavy shipping areas are usually of small size and have developed because of favorable soil, climatic, and water conditions.

In the period 1926-31 the total carlot shipments of fruits and vegetables by rail and boat were somewhat in excess of 1,000,000 cars annually. These shipments reached the high point in 1929, and declined about 5 per cent during the two following years. There was little change in production to justify this decline, which can largely be attributed to the motor truck. Shipments from areas which are a long distance from market have been

---

[12] In the remainder of this chapter most of the statistics of receipts at markets of various agricultural products have been compiled from numerous mimeographed reports of the Bureau of Agricultural Economics of the Department of Agriculture. The information regarding truck receipts was compiled from mail reports by individual dealers to the various branch offices of the Bureau. While every effort has been made to secure complete records, it is recognized that truck receipts are not as complete as railroad receipts. However, such errors represent omissions rather than duplications, and the totals are probably over 90 per cent complete. Several series of figures have been specially prepared for use in this report. Unless otherwise stated, the statistics should be credited to the Bureau of Agricultural Economics.

quite well maintained, while those from the area where truck hauling is important have shown a decline. Annual shipments of fruit and vegetables during the period 1922-32 are given in the following table:[13]

Year	Carlot Shipments	Year	Carlot Shipments
1922	850,011	1928	1,061,946
1923	905,960	1929	1,066,400
1924	944,045	1930	1,044,408
1925	952,033	1931	1,011,203
1926	1,012,012	1932	840,000
1927	1,017,098		

The complete records for 1932 are not available at the time this is written. The total loadings were approximately 840,000 cars, representing a decline of 171,203 cars from the preceding year. While part of this decline is attributable to the motor truck, reduced production of important crops in the Southern states and the generally low level of prices prevailing in the markets have also been important causal factors. The most important states from the standpoint of rail and boat carlot shipments in 1931 were the following:

	Carlot Shipments		Carlot Shipments
California	282,114	Maine	48,118
Florida	117,984	Virginia	46,127
Texas	58,274	Idaho	40,544
Washington	56,769	Georgia	34,156
New York	54,630	Colorado	27,543

About 20 commodities move in large quantities from the standpoint of railroad tonnage. The average annual

---

[13] The data include boat shipments reduced to carlot equivalents but do not include movement by motor truck. The 1932 figure is approximately complete.

railroad and boat shipments of these commodities for the period 1929-31 were as follows:

Commodity	Number of Carloads	Commodity	Number of Carloads
Potatoes	248,743	Mixed vegetables	30,784
Apples	103,051	Canteloupes	25,455
Oranges and satsumas	84,861	Celery	24,818
		Grapefruit	24,711
Grapes	61,307	Pears	23,255
Watermelons	54,530	Sweet potatoes	18,993
Lettuce and romaine	52,913	Lemons	16,234
		Strawberries	14,359
Cabbage	40,371	Mixed citrus	12,950
Peaches	40,022	Carrots	11,847
Onions	36,757		
Tomatoes	31,154		

1. The process of rail marketing. Under the normal system of rail transportation, the usual path of fruits and vegetables to market is approximately as follows: After harvesting, the produce is sized, graded, and packaged at some type of packing house. This may be located on the farm where the produce was grown, or may be a private or co-operatively owned house at a convenient railroad station. After the carload is completed at the local station, it is started on its way to market. If it has been sold, it is shipped to the buyer. If sale has not been completed, it is billed to some diversion point or large market so as to secure the advantage of through rates. Sale is usually completed while the car is in transit, and the commodity is diverted to its destination on the instructions of the buyer. If sale is not made, the produce may be turned over to a representative of the shipper for sale at the time of arrival.

When the carload arrives at market, the consignee

gives the railroad instructions for the handling of the car. It may be unloaded in a produce terminal by the railroad employees, placed on a team track for sale from the car, or carted to the store of the dealer for sale. Quantities less than a carload are usually purchased by a jobber, chain store, or large retailer and carted to the buyer's place of business. Most of this handling in the market is carried on during the night or early morning hours, so that the produce may reach the retail store during the morning hours for sale to the consumer on the same day.

During this process the railroad performs certain definite services. It maintains icing facilities along the route to market and an adequate supply of refrigerator cars in the shipping district, usually large enough to care for peak-load requirements. It handles the produce in scheduled trains, operated so as to arrive at hours best suited to market requirements. It provides a diversion service which permits the changing of destination of car-lots while en route to market. In many of the larger markets, yards are provided which allow for the accumulation and regulation of supplies in accordance with daily supply and demand. Frequently the produce terminal is owned by the railroad, or a subsidiary, and is used as the market place of the industry. In such instances the produce is unloaded by the railroad, displayed for sale, and the product delivered to the buyer on the written instructions of the seller. The number of cars unloaded each day is the measure of the available supply.

From the statement given above it can be seen that railroad activity is woven into the entire distribution structure for fruits and vegetables. Extra charges are made for many of these services, and the competition of the railroads to secure business of this character indicates that it is profitable.

2. *Development of the use of the motor truck*. Market gardeners who were located near every large or medium-sized city were among the first to utilize the motor truck. It enabled them to reduce the time spent in going to market with wagons. As soon as the truck had proved practical for this purpose, the market garden area of many cities shifted from just outside the built-up section of the city to points as far distant as 25 miles, where it was possible to secure lower-priced land.

Other farmers who were located in the new area or even farther from the city saw the opportunity of better markets which the truck gave them. By adjustment in farming operations, they were able to enter the market with one or more crops. Part of the hauling was done with farm-owned trucks, but there has been a steady growth in the proportion done by trucks sent by a city dealer for the produce of a particular farmer. The opening of new districts through the extension of good roads increased the amount of such hauling.

This development did not assume real importance until the pneumatic tire was adapted to the medium-sized truck and increased the speed of hauling. Although it is difficult to determine the exact amount of this type of trucking, most of the receipts at many markets during certain seasons are delivered in this way, and the truck dominates the transportation from many producing areas.

The importance of the motor truck as a transportation agency depends primarily upon whether one or more heavy producing areas are located within the range of economical truck haul. Thus New York City receives supplies from Long Island, New Jersey, and the Hudson River Valley by truck. Philadelphia draws on near-by areas in Pennsylvania, New Jersey, and Delaware for much of its total receipts. Boston, on the other hand, does not have any heavy producing area within truck haul at the present time, and so the truck receipts are relatively small. Chicago receives much of its supply from Illinois, Michigan, and Wisconsin, and the truck has become a very important factor in distribution there. Denver and Salt Lake City, being located close to ship-ping areas for many different varieties of produce, use the motor truck to a large degree in securing their sup-plies. Los Angeles and San Francisco are located within truck haul of very productive areas and receive much of their supply by motor truck rather than by rail. Records of truck and rail receipts for 1931 are available for all of the markets named except Chicago. They present in-teresting variations, which are shown in the following table:

PRODUCE RECEIPTS BY TRUCK AS PERCENTAGES OF TOTAL RECEIPTS AT SPECIFIED MARKETS, 1931

Market	Carlots Received			Truck Receipts as Percentage of Total Receipts
	By Rail and Boat	By Truck	Total	
Boston..........	36,345	4,355	39,700	10.9
New York.......	133,375	19,411	152,786	12.7
Philadelphia.....	39,182	15,077	54,259	27.8
Denver.........	5,715	1,391	7,106	24.3
Salt Lake City...	1,395	1,906	3,301	57.7
San Francisco....	11,983	5,577	17,560	31.7
Los Angeles......	22,244	40,012	62,256	64.3
Seven markets	249,239	87,729	336,968	26.0

Nearness to an important shipping area is essential if the percentage of truck receipts is to be high. In certain of the Northern cities the truck movement is large during the harvest season, but the percentage for the year is reduced because of the small local supply during the balance of the year. On the other hand, the heavy receipts at Los Angeles are due in part to the fact that production continues throughout the entire year within hauling distance of the city.

3. Recent rapid increase in truck receipts. Comparable figures for 1931 and the first nine months of 1932 are available for Boston, Los Angeles, New York, and Philadelphia. The period in 1932 includes the months during which the local production is most important, so that the percentage of truck movement for the entire year will probably not be as high as that shown in the accompanying table for the nine-months period.

COMPARISON OF 1931 AND 1932 PRODUCE RECEIPTS BY TRUCK AT SPECIFIED MARKETS

Market	Truck Receipts (Estimated carlots)		Truck Receipts as percentage of Total Receipts	
	1931 (12 months)	1932 (9 months)	*1931 (12 months)*	*1932 (9 months)*
Boston..........	4,355	8,898	*10.9*	*17.7*
Los Angeles......	40,012	33,504	*64.3*	*70.6*
New York[a]......	19,411	39,633	*12.7*	*23.6*
Philadelphia.....	15,077	23,604	*27.8*	*38.1*
4 Markets.....	78,855	105,639	*25.5*	*32.2*
Boston, New York, and Philadelphia.......	38,843	72,135	*15.7*	*25.7*

[a] Not complete.

It is evident from the table that the actual quantity of produce received by truck at the three Eastern markets has doubled within the past year, and that the figures for the entire twelve months of 1932 will show truck receipts substantially more than twice those of the preceding year. It is probable that the 1932 percentage for the Eastern cities will increase by half over the 1931 percentage. This ratio of increase did not hold for the four cities because truck receipts already formed such a large part of the total receipts at Los Angeles.

At New York during the months of August and September 1932, 47.7 per cent of the fruit and vegetable supply was received by motor truck as compared with 33.5 per cent in 1931.[14] The truck receipts for the first nine months of 1932 were equivalent to 39,633 carlots, or 23.6 per cent of the total receipts. Because of the incompleteness of the records of truck receipts, each of the above percentages should be increased somewhat to present the true facts.

The source of truck receipts is known by states, but the wide variation in the size of the states makes it impossible to analyze available figures satisfactorily. For example, Salisbury, Md., is nearer to New York City than Utica, N.Y., and Norfolk, Va., than Rochester, N.Y. The division of truck traffic shown in the accompanying table, which takes account of the districts where fruits and vegetables for New York originate, is probably as accurate a statement as can be made from available data.

Ten per cent or more of the 1932 supply came from outside the 200-mile limit, the exact percentage depending upon the quantity which moved more than 200 miles within the State of New York. Berries and beans were the two most important commodities hauled from more

---

[14] These figures include receipts at the jobbing market and at the Gansevoort and Wallabout markets, but do not include the Harlem market or scattered deliveries.

distant states. The Maryland receipts included many different commodities because the haul was not more than 250 miles.

SOURCES OF PRODUCE RECEIPTS BY TRUCK AT NEW YORK CITY,
JANUARY-SEPTEMBER 1932

Nearby States	Estimated Carlots		Distant States	Estimated Carlots	
	Number	*As Percentage of all Truck Receipts*		Number	*As Percentage of all Truck Receipts*
New Jersey......	15,054	*38.0*	Maryland.....	2,410	*6.1*
Long Island......	12,975	*32.8*	Virginia........	447	*1.1*
New York.......	5,357	*13.5*	N. Carolina....	476	*1.2*
Pennsylvania....	1,116	*2.8*	S. Carolina....	24	*0.1*
Delaware........	1,049	*2.6*	Florida........	10	—
Connecticut.....	477	*1.2*	Ohio..........	30	*0.1*
Massachusetts...	132	*0.3*	Vermont......	5	—
			Maine........	71	*0.2*
7 states.......	36,160	*91.2*	8 states.....	3,473	*8.8*

The situation at Philadelphia during the first nine months of 1932 was even more striking than that at New York. During this period 36,577 cars arrived by rail and the equivalent of 23,605 cars by truck, or 38.1 per cent of the total receipts. During August and September 1932 the percentage received by truck was 66.8 per cent of the total supply as compared with 57.4 percent in 1931. The sources of the quantity received by truck during the nine months is shown in the table on page 604.

Practically all of the movement from the first five states listed was within 200 miles of Philadelphia, and this included 95 per cent of the truck receipts. At least 80 per cent of the total receipts came from within the 100-mile limit, and represents tonnage which has undoubtedly left the railroad for good. Most of the North Carolina truck receipts consisted of berries, beans, and peas, while those from South Carolina were largely beans.

SOURCES OF PRODUCE RECEIPTS BY TRUCK AT PHILADELPHIA
JANUARY-SEPTEMBER 1932

Source	Estimated Carlots		Source	Estimated Carlots	
	Number	*Percent-age Distribu-tion*		Number	*Percent-age Distribu-tion*
New Jersey	12,696	*53.8*	Indiana	8	—
Pennsylvania	5,224	*22.1*	Long Island	6	—
Maryland	1,560	*6.6*	Miscellaneous	6	—
Virginia	1,501	*6.4*	New York City		
Delaware	1,466	*6.2*	(reshipments)	73	*0.3*
N. Carolina	650	*2.8*			
New York	301	*1.3*	All sources	23,605	*100.0*
S. Carolina	94	*0.4*			
Florida	20	*0.1*			

The available records for Boston are more complete than those of any other large city. While the total quantity received by truck during the nine months was estimated at 8,898 carlots, only 357.5 cars were classed as "long distance" hauling. Most of the latter were berries of various kinds, which were received from June to September. The truck receipts from outside the local producing area were only 4 per cent of the total truck movement, and were important only in one group of products.[15]

At Los Angeles during the year 1931 produce equivalent to 40,012 carloads arrived by motor truck. This was 64.3 per cent of the total supply.

---

[15] Data were obtained from the Bureau of Markets, Massachusetts Department of Agriculture.

TRANSPORTATION AGENCIES DELIVERING PRODUCE AT LOS ANGELES
JANUARY–SEPTEMBER 1930–32

Transportation Agency	Carlot Equivalents			*Percentage Distribution*		
	1932	1931	1930	*1932*	*1931*	*1930*
Boat..............	3,070	2,889	2,440	*6.4*	*5.9*	*5.4*
Express...........	623	487	589	*1.3*	*.9*	*1.3*
Railroad..........	10,340	13,196	14,301	*21.7*	*27.1*	*31.5*
Truck............	33,504	32,277	28,004	*70.6*	*66.1*	*61.8*
All agencies	47,504	48,277	45,334	*100.0*	*100.0*	*100.0*

About one-fifth of the rail receipts for 1931 shifted to the truck in 1932.

The chief reasons for the high percentage of truck receipts at Los Angeles are the wide variety of products grown within truck haul and the fact that production in this area continues throughout the year. The percentage of the total supply received by truck each month during 1932 varied from 53.4 per cent in January to 83.8 per cent in August. During the first nine months of 1932 this supply originated in the producing areas listed in the following table:

SOURCE OF PRODUCE RECEIPTS BY TRUCK AT LOS ANGELES
JANUARY–SEPTEMBER 1932

Producing Area	Approximate Haul (In miles)	Carlot Equivalents	*Percentage Distribution*
Local sources[a]	—	23,061	*68.8*
Beaumont-Yucaipa.....	90–100	424	*1.3*
Coachella Valley.......	100–140	713	*2.1*
Imperial Valley........	200–225	2,072	*6.2*
San Diego County......	85–130	946	*2.8*
Central Coast..........	100–425	3,423	*10.2*
San Joaquin Valley.....	175–400	2,716	*8.1*
Miscellaneous.........	—	149	*0.1*
Total..............	—	33,504	*100.0*

[a] Includes the counties of Los Angeles, Orange, Ventura, Riverside, and part of San Bernardino County.

Because of the large size of the Central Coast and San Joaquin Valley producing areas, it is impossible to determine the average length of haul within these areas. The truck receipts from over 100 miles were approximately 10,000 cars during the nine months, or about 30 per cent of the total.

There are no detailed records available from any of the Middle Western states where truck hauling is as highly developed as it is on either coast. Most of the southern Michigan fruit and vegetable traffic is now handled by truck, and regular distribution is carried on from Benton Harbor, Mich., to many markets such as Chicago, Indianapolis, Detroit, and cities in Ohio.

A comprehensive study made in 1928 and 1929 reached the following conclusion:

That between 150,000 and 200,000 carloads were trucked to market 20 miles or more in the United States during 1929, as compared with 1,068,745 carloads reported shipped by rail and boat.[16]

Detailed figures of the movement of strawberries and cantaloupes over the roads in that state are compiled by the state highway police in Delaware. These data necessarily include traffic originating in Maryland and Virginia as well as in Delaware. The totals for 1932 were 896,538 crates of strawberries and 366,123 crates of cantaloupes. In terms of carlots shipped from that district, the quantity hauled by truck was equivalent to 3,735 cars of strawberries and 916 cars of cantaloupes, and is believed to be the largest in any year.

4. *Decline in rail shipments in certain areas.* There has been a substantial decline in the number of cars

---

[16] "Marketing Fruits and Vegetables by Motor Truck," *U. S. Department of Agriculture Bulletin No. 272*, p. 87.

shipped by rail in certain of the areas where truck competition has become important. The accompanying table indicates the extent of this decline in certain Eastern and Middle Western states by giving the annual railroad shipments as percentages of the average shipments for the eight years from 1924 to 1931.

ANNUAL RAILROAD CARLOT SHIPMENTS AS PERCENTAGES OF
THE EIGHT-YEAR AVERAGE, 1924–31[a]

Year	United States	Six Eastern States[b]	Five Middle Western States[c]	All Other States
1924	93	121	125	88
1925	94	122	125	89
1926	100	119	123	97
1927	100	107	94	101
1928	105	90	98	108
1929	105	81	87	108
1930	103	87	70	105
1931	100	73	78	103

[a] Some boat shipments are included in the figures on which the percentages in this table and the accompanying chart are based.

[b] Massachusetts, New York, New Jersey, Pennsylvania, Delaware, and Maryland.

[c] Michigan, Ohio, Indiana, Illinois, and Missouri.

Since the trend of the United States as a whole and for the 37 states outside the two selected areas is upward, some factor peculiar to the Eastern and Middle Western states must account for the downward trend for these regions. Decline in production might do so, but production figures do not show a comparable decline. Since the states within these areas are those in which trucking is most highly developed (except in California) the motor truck seems the most logical explanation of the decline in rail shipments.

5. Products handled by truck. Although a wide variety of products may be carried by truck, highly perishable produce is being handled to a greater degree than other products. The elimination of the cost of refrigeration on the shorter hauls is an element of economy. The value of the product per pound appears to be an important factor in determining the extent to which a variety of fruit or vegetable may be handled by truck.

DECLINE OF RAILROAD SHIPMENTS OF FRUITS AND
VEGETABLES IN CERTAIN AREAS WHERE TRUCK
COMPETITION IS IMPORTANT[a]

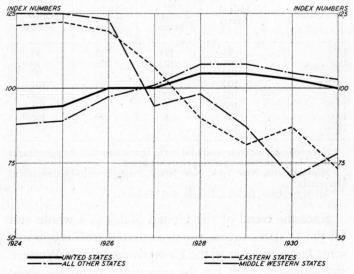

UNITED STATES EASTERN STATES
ALL OTHER STATES MIDDLE WESTERN STATES

[a] See the table on page 607 for data.

In the case of the perishable and high-value commodities such as berries and mushrooms, the truck is competing with a less-than-carload express rate higher than the comparable freight rate.

On the other hand, potatoes usually have not been trucked more than 50 miles until the last year or two, and even now they are rarely trucked for more than 100 miles. One exception is the truck haul from Aroostook County, Me., to the seacoast in the vicinity of Bangor in connection with water shipment to Atlantic and Gulf Coast points.

6. *Types of truckers.* The hauling of fruits and vegetables is carried on by three different groups. These are the producers themselves, contract truckers, and merchant truckmen of various types. Producers naturally haul their own products where the hauls are short and where marketing is carried on over a considerable period of time. Contract truckers usually operate from the markets and secure business through their relations with the dealers in the market. In this way they are able to shift from point to point as the marketing requires, and so maintain a satisfactory degree of employment which would not be possible if operations were confined to a single average producing district.

Merchant truckers are more common in the Middle West and combine the functions of dealer and transportation agency. They operate chiefly between the producing area and small towns or the suburbs of larger cities. Under these conditions, the merchant trucker reduces handling and selling expenses as well as time in transit, and therefore has advantages over the railroad that can hardly be offset. On the other hand, the merchant trucker presents one of the most difficult phases of the trucking problem since he establishes prices through his opportunity to deal directly with the individual farmer. If one or more truckers are able to purchase their supplies below the established market level, they may disturb the market in all of the consuming areas in which they operate. One of the most important problems in connection with the merchant trucker is the purchase of ungraded or partly graded produce which injures the outlet for well standardized produce in the market.

The farm-owned trucks are usually of the smaller sizes, although large producers who have need for the truck over a considerable period of the year are likely to use the medium sizes. The contract truckers and merchant truckers are usually equipped with medium-sized trucks of from two to three tons capacity. This size of truck is responsible for the large increase of produce trucked during the past few years. Formerly the ton and ton-and-a-half sizes were the most common for longer hauls, but these capacities were too small to be economical for most commodities.

Most of the trucks used in handling produce are of the open type, as heavy canvas covers are sufficient protection except during the coldest winter weather. When hauling is to be done in the Northern states during the winter months, enclosed bodies are used, frequently with sufficient heat to prevent damage to the produce. During most of the year the open body is an advantage as it permits the air to circulate through the load and reduces the need for refrigeration.

7. *Truck hauling as compared with express shipment.* The motor truck has made its greatest inroads into the express business of the railroads. Products such as berries, early vegetables, soft fruits, and mushrooms, which formerly moved by express (for the most part at less-than-carload rates), now move in large quantities by truck. The express charge included delivery to the consignee, a service the truck furnishes. The growth in regular service by motor truck for the handling of certain of these commodities shipped over long seasons of time indicates that real economies can be effected through

truck handling. The operation of a truck line for the transportation of mushrooms, for instance, has been profitable enough to permit substantial reductions in rates as well as to provide adequate maintenance and a surplus. Hothouse vegetables are moving in truck-load lots from the Cleveland area to the larger Eastern cities as well as to those of the Middle West. This truck service makes faster delivery than express and has permitted distribution to develop in a way which was not possible previously. Contract truck rates are stated to be below the rail express charge.[17]

As has been mentioned, the movement of strawberries for distances up to about 500 miles has largely shifted to the truck. This has been due to the time saved, the elimination of refrigeration costs, and the much wider direct distribution which was possible because of the smaller units of transportation which the motor truck permitted. The ability of the truck to save one day's time in getting certain early vegetables to market may mean that the increase in shipping cost will be more than offset by the increased selling price.

8. Advantages and disadvantages of the motor truck. The most detailed study[18] of the use of the motor truck in the marketing of fruits and vegetables was made in New Jersey, where trucking is important. This survey attempted to determine the advantages and disadvantages from the standpoint of the producers and the dealers in the market. There has been little change in conditions since the study was completed, except for improvements in truck construction and reductions in hauling rates.

[17] Letter. Cleveland Growers Marketing Co. No. 10, 1932.
[18] B. M. Price, "The Motor Truck as a Carrier of Fruit and Vegetables to Greater New York," *New Jersey Agricultural Experiment Station, Bulletin No. 503,* p. 21.

The advantages of the motor truck are stated as follows:

1. Faster service.
2. Convenience and saving in labor.
3. Better condition of product on arrival.
4. Early delivery to market with maximum time for preparing shipments.
5. Greater opportunity for diversion of product.
6. Less loss for shortages and damaged packages.
7. Promptness in payment of claims.
8. Lower transportation costs in local territory.
9. Agreements to pay for loss of early market.
10. Return of empty crates.
11. Increased sales to retailers.
12. Intimate touch with market through truckman.

The disadvantages of truck hauling are given as follows:

1. Lack of advance market information.
2. Absence of proper regulation of responsibility of operator, regularity of schedule, and standardization of rates.
3. Necessity for immediate sale or storage.
4. Terminal market congestion.
5. Rising transportation charge with increasing distance.
6. Lack of opportunity for shipping point inspection.
7. Interrupted service resulting from unfavorable weather.
8. Miscellaneous disadvantages such as break-downs, lack of insurance, delay in market, etc.

Although the reasons given apply specifically to the New York market, they are equally applicable to the other markets where the handling of produce by truck has become important. It is probable that at the present time, the advantage of lower costs to shippers would appear first in the list of advantages, because of the much lower level of prices prevailing for farm produce.

Another important advantage is the ability to make direct delivery in truck-load lots to smaller markets which cannot use carlots by rail shipment. Still another advantage is the possibility of distributing a lower grade of produce than could be sold satisfactorily through the regular trade channels by rail shipment.

In many instances the motor truck is able to make more direct delivery to the buyer, and thus saves handling and other costs which would otherwise be incurred. For example, the freight rate from Rochester, N.Y., to New York City is 45 cents per barrel on apples in carlots. The cartage charged to a point above 150th Street in New York is an additional 35 cents. Thus the total transportation charge by rail in this instance is 80 cents per barrel, although the less-than-carload truck rate for the same delivery is the fourth-class rate, or slightly less than 60 cents per barrel. Thus, while the rail rate itself is cheaper than the truck rate, the other costs which must be incurred raise the rate to such an amount that the truck has little difficulty in competing with the railroad.

9. *Disturbing influence of the motor truck in distribution.* The use of the motor truck in the transportation of fruits and vegetables has resulted in a number of improvements and economies, especially where it was possible to reduce or eliminate handling. However, these advantages have been offset by certain disadvantages which have resulted from the wide use of the motor truck.

An accurate knowledge of the supply of produce available at the beginning of each market period is an essential requirement to the determination of prices in line with supply and demand. When such products are received by railroad, the number of cars of each important product is usually posted at some central point so that all interested may have this information. The arrival of additional supplies is largely controlled by the railroad schedule, and the late arrivals were usually held over to the market period the following day. But with the general use of the motor truck, accurate information of this character is practically eliminated, as the number of trucks arriving in the market or the products contained in these shipments cannot be readily determined. When trucks are delayed and arrive after the opening of the market, dealers are not able to make delivery of the product on prior sales. Not infrequently, orders are refused for produce which may later arrive by truck without advance notice to the dealer. Thus the general use of the motor truck has made market information of little value, except in instances where all truck receipts are delivered to a single point. The direct delivery of produce to the suburban areas of many cities supplies retailers who would normally secure supplies from the central market. When such truck delivery is made regularly, operations are quickly adjusted to the new situation. But in numerous instances, direct delivery by truck is irregular and not dependable, and so disturbs both distributors and retailers.

A somewhat similar situation developed in many producing districts as a result of the entrance of the truck. If the trucker operated on a contract basis, there was comparatively little disturbance as the control of the grade and destination of the produce remained in the hands of the marketing agency. But in country districts where the truckers were operating as peddlers rather than as contract carriers, conditions were greatly upset. As peddlers, their primary desire was to purchase supplies as cheaply as possible, even to the acceptance of partly graded produce in order to secure a low price.

One of the most important improvements in the marketing of produce during recent years has been in the standardization of the product which was placed on the market. Through the use of the proper grades and grading facilities, a more dependable product was offered to both distributors and consumers. In seasons of abundant supply it was possible to withhold the lower grades from the market, while the same quality of fruit might be marketed freely in periods when the supply was smaller than usual.

The purchasing of partly graded produce by truck peddlers from farmers soon made it difficult to carry on the regular grading operations in many communities. The opportunity to sell ungraded or partly graded products led producers to lose sight of the importance of standardization in the marketing of produce. Thus the competition of truckers created confusion in many of the producing areas and complicated the operations of the numerous packing houses of both private and co-operative ownership. It produced the same confusion in markets where such products were sold, as the partly graded product became the dominating factor under weak demand conditions such as prevail at the present time.

Considerable progress has been made in certain parts of the country in solving the problems which have resulted from the increased use of the truck. One of the most successful methods has been the establishment of markets where trading may be carried on between producers and truckers. Such markets are now in operation in New Jersey, New York, Maryland, Michigan, and Utah, and prices paid to producers are established on the basis of competition, which is frequently absent when the transfer is made at the farm of the producer. The degree of competition and the supervision of grades have done much to eliminate the problems which have upset normal conditions.

The confused situation which may result from the general shift of marketing into the hands of the trucker merchant are well illustrated by the following extracts from a recent case in California.[19]

The operator of the so-called peddler truck buys farm products at the point of production and sells them in adjacent markets. He is an itinerant, moving from district to district of the state as the crops develop, or to the fields in adjoining states. Various types of peddler trucks use the highways of the state as the main adjunct of their business, not only hauling farm products to the market but also hauling whatever other commodities may be obtained for the return trip.

A representative of the State Department of Agriculture is quoted in the same decision as follows:

The trouble that the department has with the truckers is that the trucker is one day operating as a produce dealer within the meaning of our act, and the next day he is operating as a hauler of some other line of traffic. If they consistently operate as produce dealers within the meaning of our act, we could then put our finger on their operations and bring them within the law. However, we have exhausted all possible means of bringing these truckers under license and bond. As I stated before, if we had some way of finding out just what truckers were handling produce and on what basis they were handling produce it would save an untold amount of money to the growers of the State of California.

The situation in the Florida citrus area is somewhat similar. Trucks have taken over the bulk of the business to the Southeastern states and have made serious inroads on the existing distribution system. The growth of the trucking is indicated by a recent statement:

[19] *Docket 25243, Railroad Commission of California*, pp. 28-29.

The per cent of truck shipments to date is much higher than a year ago: 43.5 per cent of the total orange movement, including rail and truck, has been moved by truck, compared with 22.8 per cent last season; and 12.5 per cent grapefruit by truck this season as compared with 7.6 per cent last season.[20]

The Florida railroads established an emergency rate early in 1932, based on higher minimum weights, and have also endeavored to combat the truck competition with other modifications such as rates for shipments of fruit in bulk. These have not been in effect for a long enough time to determine their real value. A considerable portion of the truck shipments are in connection with water shipments to the Eastern Seaboard markets through several ports. Citrus fruits are probably hauled greater distances from California, Florida, and Texas than any other form of produce handled by motor truck.

The market at Benton Harbor, Mich., is one of the most successful of this type. During the 153 days of the 1931 marketing season 102,285 growers' loads containing 4,837,758 packages were sold, for which the producers received $3,235,461.95. Over four and one-half million packages were sold up to the middle of September 1932. The success of the market is stated to be largely due to the careful grading of the product so that the truckers may buy with confidence in the quality of the product.[21]

10. Redistribution by motor truck from terminal markets. Many dealers in small population centers previously found it most satisfactory to purchase part of the supply necessary for their businesses in the nearest large city market, shipment being made in a so-called "mixed

---

[20] *Florida Clearing House News*, Nov. 15, 1932, p. 5.
[21] *Michigan Farmer*, Nov. 15, 1932.

car." The order was usually loaded in the afternoon and was available to the local dealer the following morning. By this method it was possible to carry a fresh supply of all kinds of produce, many of which could not have been handled if it had been necessary to purchase in carload quantities. The length of haul of the "mixed car" was usually from 50 to 200 miles.

With the coming of the motor truck this situation has been entirely changed. The local dealer now goes to the large market with one or more trucks. These trucks are loaded at the time of the market and immediately driven back to the dealer's store. In many instances it is possible to save an entire day in transit. The demand for supplies for such out-of-town buyers has resulted in the establishment of "early markets" which make it possible for produce to be hauled a considerable distance in time for morning delivery to retailers.

The larger centers have become the most important points for this type of handling, as supplies of all kinds of fruits and vegetables are available there. Distribution of this character has been particularly important from Boston, New York, Philadelphia, Baltimore, and Pittsburgh, as there are numerous smaller cities within reach of these markets. The situation is well illustrated by the following comment regarding conditions at Pittsburgh in 1930:[22]

Fifty per cent of the total carlot unloads of fruits and vegetables at Pittsburgh, it is estimated, left the city by motor truck as against 12 per cent by express, less-than-carload, mixed cars, and by boat in 1930, and 38 per cent was consumed in the city proper. . . .

[22] Brice Edwards and J. W. Park, "Marketing Fruits and Vegetables by Motor Truck," *U. S. Department of Agriculture Technical Bulletin 272*, p. 78.

The approximate practical limit of motor truck reshipments from Pittsburgh was Altoona and Bellefonte, Pa., to the east; Cumberland, Md. and Clarksburg, W.Va. to the south; Cambridge and Canton, Ohio, to the west; and Meadville and Warren, Pa., to the north.

The large railroad produce terminal was opened in Pittsburgh in 1928. This lent impetus to the outbound motor truck movement, which about doubled in the two years after the terminal was opened. The long distance outbound motor truck movement became an important marketing factor during 1925 and 1926. An indication of the change lies in a railroad report that ten years ago (1920) the average weekly shipments of mixed cars to surrounding towns were from 150 to 200 cars a week, and in the spring of 1930 were only from 25 to 50 cars a week. Thus the rail redistribution is only about 25 per cent of its former volume, whereas the total redistribution from Pittsburgh has increased.

While there is no accurate information on the trend of these shipments since 1930, the proportion which then remained with the railroads was so small in volume that further decline would make little difference to the carriers.

The situation at Baltimore is quite similar, except that Baltimore receives much of its incoming supply from producing areas within motor truck haul of the city, whereas the greater portion of the Pittsburgh supply arrives by rail. Much of the redistribution out of Baltimore, therefore, consists of the transfer of produce from truck to truck. In 1930 it was estimated that 24 per cent of the wholesale trade left the city by motor truck, as compared with only 4 per cent by express, less-than-carload lots, and mixed cars.

Philadelphia is the source of supply for most of the area within a hundred miles, except in the directions of

New York and Baltimore. A large proportion of the supply comes from nearby producing areas. A considerable part of this business has shifted from the mixed-car shipment by rail to the motor truck, which makes possible much faster delivery to points in Eastern Pennsylvania such as Allentown, Reading, Lancaster, and Harrisburg.

New York is the largest market in the country and has always had a substantial trade to outlying points, either by rail or by boat. In recent years, however, it has been possible for a dealer with a motor truck to purchase on the "early market" (about midnight) and haul his produce 100 miles in time for morning sales. This has been one reason for the increase in truck hauling from the farm to New York, as it has made it possible to deliver produce for this early market with much greater certainty than by rail.

A new element which may have considerable effect in the future has recently appeared in redistribution from New York, Philadelphia, and other seaboard points. This is the shipment by water of fruits and vegetables from Florida and other Southern points, and the possible extension of this service in a large way to the heavy shipping areas of the Pacific coast. If fruits and vegetables are laid down at New York by boat at costs substantially less than rail costs, it is certain that truck distribution from the seaboard to inland points will be developed considerably beyond the present range of effective hauling. This will reduce direct rail carlot shipments to many markets. The probable economical haul will be longer than is usual in the produce industry, because return hauls should be available from most of these destinations. If such plans are carried out the railroads may lose a substantial amount of shipments direct to inland points unless a successful effort is made to meet this competition.

Conditions are similar in all of the important central markets of the country. Redistribution from them has largely been taken over or developed by the motor truck, which is usually able to render faster service than the railroad can expect to furnish for the short hauls involved.

III. DAIRY PRODUCTS

The dairy industry is one of the largest branches of agriculture. It is widely scattered over the entire country and its character varies in accordance with production factors and with the availability of markets in different districts.

The size of the area from which any city draws its supply of fluid milk depends primarily upon the population of the city and the character of the farm land adjacent to it. The cream supply may come from the same territory as the milk or it may be secured from distant points. Cream is milk in such concentrated form that it may be shipped for distances of a thousand miles or more without loss of quality and at practicable transportation costs.

Manufactured milk products are generally prepared in areas where production conditions are favorable and no local markets for fluid milk are available. The natural variation in the seasonal production cycle results in much larger volume during the spring months than during the remainder of the year. Any surplus above immediate consumption is held in storage until required in the period of smaller production, which usually comes during the fall months. Most dairy products are manufactured in the Northern states. Minnesota, Wisconsin, and Iowa are the chief source of our butter, cheese, and canned milk.

1. *Transportation of milk from the farm to the plant*. The first step in the transportation of milk is from the farm to the plant, either in the country or city. This is true whether the milk is destined for fluid consumption or for manufacture. The only important exception is the creameries to which shipment from the farm is in the form of cream.

Prior to the use of the motor truck, milk was hauled only a few miles by wagon to the nearest milk plant. Such plants were located at nearly every railroad station in milk producing areas. As the truck replaced the wagon in this field, the length of haul naturally increased. With the development of improved roads into the country districts, trucks operated for much longer distances. The present important limiting factors are road conditions, distance, and the time required for collection and hauling. The usual distance from the farm to most country plants is probably not more than 50 miles. When direct delivery is made from the farm to city plants, this distance may be increased substantially, with a maximum of about 100 miles. Truck shipments from country plant to city plant are made for longer distances although only infrequently over 200 miles.

In the handling of fluid milk, the service and rates include the return of empty containers. For this reason, back hauls of other commodities are practically impossible.

2. *Transportation of fluid milk by the railroad*. The rail service in the handling of fluid milk is almost en-

tirely of shuttle character, providing for a daily movement from the country plant to the city terminal. Milk traffic on the railroads is considered a part of the passenger business, as single cars are handled in passenger trains. Where the quantity handled by rail is sufficient, regular milk trains are operated. Because of the limitations of time and the adequate supplies available, there are comparatively few rail hauls of fluid milk of more than 300 miles.

Country milk plants are usually located on railroad lines and are able to load directly into the car. In the case of city plants this arrangement is much less common. Where country plants are not located on the railroad, two hauling charges are required in addition to the cost of the rail transportation. In other instances, branch-line service is not satisfactory. The quantity shipped from a single country plant is frequently so small that it is necessary to pay the less-than-carload rate on it. These higher rates give a wider margin for truck competition.

3. Railroad tank cars. In the past few years, there has been a substantial change in the method of handling large quantities of milk. The tank car, a form of special equipment usually operated as a privately owned car line has come into use. Each car contains two large insulated tanks holding from 300 to 350 cans each, so constructed as to carry the milk with a minimum of fluctuation in temperature while in transit. Tank cars greatly reduce the cost of handling in the plants, as no cans are required, but they introduce other problems which have an influence on the possible use of this new equipment. The capacity of tank cars is more than double the regular minimum carload quantity. Frequently milk from one plant is insufficient to allow economical use of the tank-car equipment. Present practice in such instances is to "pick up" milk from several plants, but this process delays the movement of the train and places many of the shipments in the less-than-carload rate group. Satisfactory utilization of the tank car is dependent upon the consolidation of sufficient quantities into one or two plants so as to permit loading at those points. Unless a city plant is located on the railroad, tank truck equipment is necessary in order to transfer the milk from the car to the plant. This increases the cost of the entire operation considerably, as such special equipment is usually not suitable for other uses.

4. Development of motor truck transportation of milk. The initial use of the motor truck as a substitute for the railroad occurred in transporting milk from country plants in nearby producing areas to the cities. This was especially true in those areas where there was sufficient supply in close proximity so that the entire transportation system could be developed on a motor truck basis. While the length of haul did not exceed about 50 miles in the earlier development, it has been extended to at least double that distance. With the exception of a few of the larger cities (discussed below on pages 626-29) the transportation of the milk supply has almost entirely left the railroads and has been transferred to the motor truck.

While most of the hauling of milk is by the ordinary truck, either with or without an enclosed body, the latest development is the tank truck. This is an adaptation of the tank-car principle which permits the hauling of milk in smaller units than with the tank car. The tank truck can only be operated between plants, but the reduction in labor requirements from its use results in appreciable saving in operating costs. Tank trucks are used for both inter-plant transfers in the country and hauls from the country plant to the city. In the latter case, the tank truck competes directly with the railroad. One of its chief advantages is direct delivery to city plants distant from the railroad terminal, or to points where the rail service is unsatisfactory or unusually expensive.

Most of the cities which had a population over 300,000 in 1930 now receive all or most of their milk supply by truck. Among these cities are the following, in the order of their population:

Detroit	Washington
Los Angeles	Minneapolis
Cleveland	New Orleans
St. Louis	Cincinnati
Baltimore	Kansas City
Pittsburgh	Seattle
San Francisco	Indianapolis
Milwaukee	Rochester
Buffalo	Portland, Oregon

Each of the cities named above is located within truck haul of a dairy district producing an adequate supply of milk for city consumption. For this reason it is not necessary to ship milk by rail for longer distances. The situation in most of these cities is well illustrated by a report on motor truck hauling into Rochester:

In a recent study of the Rochester Milk Market information was obtained concerning truck routes on which were located over 90 per cent of all the farms which produce and ship milk directly into the city. Rochester draws approximately 93 per cent of its total milk supply from such sources, the balance being handled through country milk plants. Probably less than 5 per cent of the producers bring in their own milk.

The study included 70 routes operated by 47 proprietors and their drivers. Thirteen haulers controlled 36 routes; the other 34 haulers had only one route each. About one-half of the 47 haulers were operating dairy farms and hauled their own milk with that hauled for other dairymen.

. . . The rated capacity for individual trucks ranged from 1.5 to 5 tons, averaging 2.4 tons. The maximum number of cans that could be carried per truck varied from 42 to 150. . . . Actual loads averaged about one-eighth more than the rated capacity in tons, but only a trifle more than half of the maximum capacity in cans. . . .

The average route had slightly less than 19 "shippers," producing a daily average for the year of about 45 full cans or 2.4 cans per shipper. On individual routes, the number of shippers varied from 3 to 40, the number of cans hauled daily from 15 to 94.

On the average the 1,322 farms on the 70 routes were 19.4 miles from the center of the city. The distance for individual farms varied from 4.5 to 45 miles. The total hauling distance covered by individual trucks in loading and delivering the milk varied from 13 to 92.5 miles and averaged 39.4 miles per route. . . . Less than 10 per cent comes from farms more than 30 miles away.[23]

The four metropolitan areas of New York, Chicago, Philadelphia, and Boston are the only large markets which the motor truck has not taken over from the railroads. Complete figures are available for three markets to indicate the extent to which the truck operates in these districts.

The records for New York include the metropolitan area as far as the Connecticut state line and most of the New Jersey suburban area.

[23] H. W. Mumford, Jr., "Milk Hauling to Rochester, N.Y.," *Farm Economics*, Cornell University, No. 74, pp. 1712-15.

MILK RECEIPTS AT NEW YORK, 1930–32
(40-quart cans)

Year	Total Receipts	Truck Receipts	Truck Receipts as Percentage of Total Receipts
1930............	36,469,791	2,141,514	5.9
1931............	35,534,977	3,370,129	9.5
1932[a]...........	25,896,294	3,939,817	15.2

[a] January–September inclusive.

While the rail receipts of milk at New York still include most of the supply, the truck receipts as percentages of all receipts have practically tripled since 1930. Further increases may be expected because of extension of truck operations during the last quarter of 1932.

The distances from which milk now moves by truck to New York City are indicated by the following extract from a discussion published early in 1932:

Previous to 1925 very little milk was brought to the New York market by truck or wagon from distances greater than 25 or 30 miles. About that time, long distance hauling of milk was started. Milk now is hauled from country plants as much as 100 miles or more from the city. During the past few years, the quantity of milk delivered to the market by truck has increased to a very great extent. No satisfactory system of reporting milk received by truck has yet been established.[24]

The center of production for the New York market is about 225 miles from the city, and a considerable portion of the supply from points nearer the city is being shifted over to the motor truck.

Philadelphia is located in the center of an important agricultural district, and the milk supply comes from the

[24] Leland Spencer, "Milk and Cream Receipts at the New York Market," *Farm Economics*, Cornell University, No. 74, p. 1711.

states of Pennsylvania, New Jersey, Delaware, and Maryland.

MILK RECEIPTS AT PHILADELPHIA, 1929–32
(40-quart cans)

Year	Total Receipts	Truck Receipts	Truck Receipts as Percentage of Total Receipts
1929.............	7,433,134	4,076,037	54.8
1930.............	7,395,317	4,120,595	55.7
1931.............	7,243,678	4,196,567	57.9
1932[a].............	5,154,365	3,151,959	61.1

[a] January–September inclusive.

While the total quantity received at Philadelphia has declined slightly during the period, the percentage hauled by trucks has increased slowly but steadily, and is now over 61 per cent of the total. During the first nine months of 1932, 96 per cent of the total came from the states immediately adjacent to the city—Pennsylvania, New Jersey, and Delaware.

The situation at Boston is substantially different. The figures for the Boston market are not indicative of the situation for Southern New England as a whole. The milk from distant points is concentrated in the Boston market, while the other cities and towns secure all or most of their supplies from local sources. The most important source of Boston's supply is Vermont.

At Chicago the production situation is comparable with that at Philadelphia. Immediately outside the suburban area lies an old dairy district in the three states of Illinois, Wisconsin, and Indiana. Much of this district is within a hundred miles of the city, and so well within the range of satisfactory trucking. Official figures are not available, but the following information has been fur-

Milk Receipts at Boston, 1930–32
(40-quart cans)

Year	Total Receipts	Truck Receipts	*Truck Receipts as Percentage of Total Receipts*
1930............	6,176,942	451,655	*7.3*
1931............	6,416,012	499,370	*7.7*
1932ᵃ...........	4,792,547	402,773	*8.4*

ᵃ January–September inclusive.

nished by the producers' organization operating in that market, and presents the daily receipts as of November 1, 1932:[25]

	Pounds	Percentage Distribution
Milk received in tank trucks	1,023,907	*37.8*
Milk received in cans by truck	725,000	*26.8*
Total by truck	1,748,907	*64.6*
Milk received by rail	956,788	*35.4*
Total receipts	2,705,695	*100.0*

That portion received in tank trucks had been handled through a country plant, while that received in cans represented direct deliveries from producers to city plants. The trucking operations cover an area within a radius of about 90 miles from Chicago, "although within the 90-mile circle many cars of milk are being handled by the railroads at greatly reduced rates which went into effect about two years ago."

5. *Shipment of cream by motor truck.* The cream supply of the larger centers of population is usually secured from the more distant portion of the milk-producing

[25] Letter from the Pure Milk Association, Nov. 8, 1932.

territory. Where the supply is not adequate for both purposes, cream is shipped into the market from some distant source of supply. Such shipments are usually from long distances and from the producing districts where butter, cheese, or canned milk are the normal outlet for the production. The cost of such long shipment would be prohibitive except for the fact that each can of cream is prepared from 10 to 12 cans of milk.

In most of the markets the cream supply comes from the same producing district as the milk, or from plants in the more distant portion if the production area is large. While there has been some tendency to increase the hauling of cream by truck into New York, only a small proportion of the cream supply received at the three large Eastern city markets is handled by truck, as is shown by the following percentage data:

Market	January-September 1932	January-September 1931
New York	4.0	0.5
Philadelphia	4.7	3.8
Boston	0.7	—

6. Type of trucks and truckers. The ownership of the trucks used in hauling milk is divided among farmers, milk distributors, and contract truckers. The initial delivery of milk is carried on by all three of these groups. After it passes through the first plant, most of the hauling is done by trucks owned and operated by the distributors themselves or under contract to them.

No special equipment is usually required in the hauling of milk in cans. In certain areas enclosed trucks are used which give additional protection in either summer or winter weather. Hauling has been in operation for a long enough time to establish the fact that it can be carried on satisfactorily even during severe winter weather.

As previously mentioned, the tank truck is the most recent development in this field. It is adapted to the hauling of a rather large quantity of milk from one plant to another with a minimum of handling expense. The contents may vary from 500 to 2,000 gallons, with the most common capacity from 1,000 to 1,400 gallons.[26] The tank truck is especially adapted to the hauling of milk between plants which are not located on the railroad, thus saving charges at both ends in addition to the rail rate.

7. *Cost of truck hauling.* In the collection of milk from the farm, the truck is usually operated with a load much below capacity. This is due to the necessary handling of partly filled cans and to the variation in the amount of daily production per farm, owing to the seasonal production cycle. As most of such hauling is of contract character, the rates vary greatly, depending upon length of haul, character of roads, size of loads, loading and unloading conditions, and the amount of local competition. Rates of 35 cents per hundredweight are reported for hauls of 100 miles in California. These rates probably represent the maximum distance and rate direct from the farm to the city.[27] In the vast majority of cases, however, the rate paid varies from 10 to 25 cents per hundredweight. If a direct haul from farm to city permits the closing of a country plant, it frequently provides a greater margin for hauling than the rail rate itself.

[26] R. P. Hotis, "Transporting and Handling Milk in Tanks," *U. S. Department of Agriculture Technical Bulletin No. 243*, p. 3.

[27] J. M. Tinley and Martin H. Blank, "An Analysis of the East Bay Milk Market," *University of California Experiment Station Bulletin No. 534*, p. 74.

The hauling of milk in cans between plants is generally done for amounts considerably less than the charge in the collection from the farm. The transfer usually consists of approximately a full load from one point and is over improved roads. Much of this work is done by contract haulers who specialize in this business. An important advantage of this system is the possibility of shifting trucks of various sizes between different routes, so as to adjust the size of truck to the load. In this way the most economical operation may be secured and reserve trucks are available whenever needed. While some inter-plant hauling is in direct competition with the railroads, much of it is the necessary assembling of supplies for manufacturing operations, as well as the accumulation of volume to secure minimum quantities for rail shipment.

Hauling from a country plant to a city plant is usually a substitution of the motor truck for the railroad. Transfer from the railroad to the truck is largely determined by convenience factors and by the cost of truck hauling as compared with rail charges plus necessary transfer costs.

8. *Length of motor truck haul of milk.* There is such wide variation in the length of motor truck haul of milk that it is impossible to make an average which might approximate the actual situation. The length of the usual haul from farm to country plant is not in excess of 50 miles. The haul from the country plant to the city is longer and the maximum distance is from 100 to 150 miles, although scattered instances up to 300 miles exist.

There are several factors which limit the distance milk can be hauled. The round trip must be made in less than

24 hours unless duplicate equipment is maintained. Another factor is the time limitation prescribed by the regulations governing the handling of milk in the particular city involved. Practically all milk hauling from the country must be done in the daylight hours, when there is more traffic than during the night when the long distance hauling of most commodities is carried on.

9. *Reasons for the use of the motor truck in milk transportation.* The motor truck has assumed its present general use in the collection of milk from the farm largely because of the convenience of the service which can be rendered at a fairly low cost. It is likely that this will increase with the further improvement of rural highways, the consolidation of country plant operations into a smaller number of plants, and the possible reduction in hauling charges which can be effected by the elimination of duplication in hauling routes and the more efficient organization of them.

The chief reason for the expansion of long distance hauling from the country to the city has been a reduction in the total cost of transportation, especially in the case of city plants without railroad facilities. The same situation has been true of country plants off the railroad. The elimination of the local transfer charge has increased the possible saving in transportation cost.

The country milk plant facilities were originally located on the basis of wagon delivery to the plant. Since truck hauling has become so general, plant operations could now be carried on much more economically if operations were concentrated in larger pants. This would produce economies in plant operating and transportation costs through the increased volume handled at each plant, but would necessarily increase the length and cost of haul from the farm.

Some of the increase in the hauling of milk directly to the city plants has been due to the elimination of country plant operations effected through direct delivery from the farm to the city plant. As country plant expense frequently exceeds the entire transportation charge, the economies which can be effected where conditions permit this type of adjustment are considerable.

The substitution of the motor truck for rail service between country and city plants has been made largely because of the saving in the cost of truck transportation as compared with the rail rate plus transfer charges in the city. One large distributor reports the hauling of milk in its own tank trucks in 1932 for an average cost of 26.5 cents per hundredweight, as compared with a rail cost of 55 cents, including a city transfer expense of from 2.5 to 8 cents per hundredweight. Reductions in rail rates may reduce or eliminate the possible saving which can be effected by truck, and thus tend to restore the traffic to the railroads. Reductions of this character have been or are now being made in a number of important milk producing regions.

Truck hauling may be used without reducing transportation costs. Because of the flexibility of the truck, it may be much more satisfactory from the standpoint of plant operating schedules and costs. The necessity for adjusting operations to railroad schedules can be entirely eliminated if the truck is substituted for the railroad. In some cases this may permit the delivery of milk one day earlier than if rail service were used. In those instances where the time required for truck hauling is much less than by rail, the condition of the milk may be improved sufficiently to justify the change.

7. *Truck transportation of butter.* The transportation of butter and cheese by motor truck on an extensive scale is a recent development. Comparatively little information of statistical character is available, but the growth of this kind of transportation into Chicago during 1931 and 1932 gives some indication of its possibilities. Incomplete reports of the truck receipts of butter during 1931 show that 8,190,549 pounds, or 3.4 per cent, of the total receipts were delivered by truck. With a much more complete system of reports this quantity had increased in the first nine months of 1932 to 30,515,183 pounds, or 17 per cent of the total receipts. While the real increase was not as large as the percentages would indicate, there has been a very definite trend toward motor truck hauling. Iowa and Wisconsin are the two important sources of truck shipments, with most of the remainder coming from Illinois, Michigan, and Indiana.

Butter has a high value per pound, and therefore will permit a rather high transportation charge. Because of the necessity for low temperatures, hauling by motor truck was not practical for longer hauls until special equipment was devised for that purpose. With the insulated truck body and the development of refrigerating materials and equipment to maintain low temperatures in transit, the truck hauling of butter is likely to increase in the near future for distances within the practical possibilities of the motor truck.

Aside from the question of relative cost as compared with rail service, one of the chief advantages of the motor truck is the frequency of delivery. Most butter is sold on a "quotation basis," and the ability to make frequent small shipments permits a closer relation to the average market quotation than does the accumulation of solid carloads for rail shipment at longer intervals.

Much butter is stored at central points on a transit basis when shipped by rail. Shipments by truck do not have this privilege and therefore are limited to the markets which can be reached by direct haul from the producing areas.

The development of the truck hauling of butter depends largely upon the relation between railroad rates and refrigeration charges as compared with the similar rates or costs by motor truck. With the rapid increase in the hauling of butter by truck, it would appear that savings are being effected by the use of the truck at the present time. Any substantial shift in either of these charges would change the present situation.

8. Truck transportation of cheese. As is the case with butter, the trucking of cheese is a comparatively recent development. Figures of the truck receipts of cheese at Chicago are available only for the last eight months of 1931 and the first nine months of 1932, and are admittedly incomplete for the 1931 period. Despite this fact, reported truck receipts in 1931 totalled 5,639,789 pounds, or 20.6 per cent of the total receipts. From January to September 1932, truck receipts were 11,733,334 pounds, or 36.4 per cent of all receipts. Nearly 87 per cent of the truck shipments came from the State of Wisconsin. The percentages for Chicago are not typical of other cities because of the proximity of Wisconsin, the most important cheese producing area in the country.

There appear to be no important advantages in truck hauling of cheese as compared with railroad shipment, except that the cheese factories are small and are usually located at points which are rather inaccessible to the railroads. Cheese is usually assembled into central warehouses from the factories for storage and rail shipment.

9. *Truck transportation of ice cream.* In the earlier development of the ice cream industry, distribution to outlying points was made by steam or electric railway express. With the improvement of the highways, the development of refrigeration materials and equipment, and the insulation of the truck body, much ice cream distribution has been shifted to the motor truck. By using truck delivery, the ice cream manufacturer is able to supply the exact needs of each dealer at the time that the delivery is made. In addition, he secures the immediate return of the empty cans and is able to re-ice the store equipment. Because this service is distribution to retailers, there appears to be no reason to expect that there will be a return of ice cream transportation to the railroads.

IV. POULTRY AND EGGS

The form of rail transportation used in the shipment of poultry and eggs depends largely upon the distance which the product will move. Shipments from the Middle Western states, the largest producing district, are forwarded by freight. Eggs and dressed poultry are moved in refrigerator cars and live poultry in special cars constructed for that purpose. Refrigerator cars are used for the transportation of eggs from the highly localized producing districts of the Pacific coast and the intermountain states to Eastern markets. Shipments from both Eastern and Middle Western producing areas to cities within several hundred miles were formerly made by express, largely at less-than-carload rates. Because of the overnight delivery usually secured by express, it was possible to handle both eggs and live poultry by this means.

Many of the producing districts in the Eastern states are quite restricted in area, and it has been possible to establish truck routes which can handle the eggs from an area as a unit and operate at rates below the less-than-carload express rate. The earlier hauling was largely done with small trucks; but as pneumatic tires were adopted on medium-size trucks, hauling was shifted to larger sizes in most instances. The continuous character of egg production and the need for regular service made it possible, even in the beginning, for the truck to compete successfully within distances of not more than 100 miles. Since that time there has been a gradual increase in the length of haul until the present general range of from 200 to 300 miles has been established. In certain areas, "pick-up" trucks are used to collect the eggs from the farms, thus permitting the maximum use of the larger truck for the trip to market. With the development of improved highways in the Middle West, the truck began to handle more of the movement to the nearby consuming markets, although the percentage of the total production involved was smaller than in the Eastern producing areas.

1. Transportation of poultry by truck. New York is the largest market for live poultry in the country, so that the receipts by the various methods of transportation at that city are significant. Freight receipts come from the Middle West, while truck and express receipts are from nearby states. The following table shows the distribution of live poultry receipts at New York among the different transportation agencies:

POULTRY RECEIPTS AT NEW YORK

	Pounds	Percentage Distribution
1930:		
Freight (rail)	192,006,000[23]	85.5
Express (rail)	7,611,679	3.4
Truck	24,945,134	11.1
Total	224,562,813	100.0
1931:		
Freight (rail)	182,736,000[23]	85.3
Express (rail)	4,568,003	2.1
Truck	26,964,668	12.6
Total	214,268,668	100.0

While truck receipts increased by one-twelfth during 1931, express receipts from the same general territory decreased two-fifths and combined truck and express receipts decreased 3.2 per cent. As the remaining express business amounted to only one-sixth of the truck receipts, there would appear to be little chance for much additional shift to the truck from this source.

Large quantities of live poultry are hauled to New York by truck from all of the Eastern states. The table on page 640 gives the quantity and percentage of the truck and express receipts from each important state, ranked in the order of truck receipts.

While there were ten states which shipped at least 500,000 pounds by truck, only two states forwarded that amount by express. These two states were New York and New Hampshire, and the amount forwarded from each by express was only one-third of the truck movement from the same state. Virginia and Vermont were the only states from which the express movement exceeded

---

[23] Computed on average carload of 18,000 pounds.

the truck movement. A fair proportion of the truck movement is from states which are entirely outside the 200-mile limit. This is also true of much of New York and Pennsylvania, so that it is impossible to estimate the average haul.

The Chicago market is close to the center of heavy poultry production in the Middle West, and truck haul-

SOURCES OF TRUCK AND EXPRESS SHIPMENTS OF LIVE POULTRY INTO NEW YORK, 1931

State	Truck Shipments		Express Shipments	
	Pounds	*Percentage Distribution*	Pounds	*Percentage Distribution*
Massachusetts...	5,301,794	*19.66*	393,423	*8.61*
New York.......	5,042,360	*18.78*	1,643,818	*35.99*
Delaware.......	5,042,360	*18.70*	6,389	*.14*
Maryland.......	2,345,728	*8.70*	86,558	*1.89*
New Hampshire..	2,159,647	*8.01*	692,930	*15.17*
Connecticut.....	1,716,680	*6.37*	59,359	*1.30*
New Jersey......	1,710,717	*6.35*	59,476	*1.30*
Rhode Island....	1,136,559	*4.21*	44,253	*.97*
Pennsylvania....	1,108,561	*4.11*	285,621	*6.25*
Maine..........	827,025	*3.07*	296,839	*6.50*
Virginia.........	337,517	*1.25*	421,864	*9.23*
West Virginia....	66,960	*.25*	14,672	*.32*
Vermont........	54,660	*.20*	470,027	*10.29*
Miscellaneous....	93,600	*.34*	99,163	*2.04*
All sources.....	26,964,668	*100.00*	4,568,003	*100.00*

ing into Chicago would be expected to be more important than at New York. The table and the chart on page 641 show the same general shift from express to truck as at New York, but at Chicago one-fifth of the freight receipts of live poultry as well have gone over to the truck.

The important sources of supply of express shipments to Chicago in 1931 were Illinois, Iowa, and Wisconsin (in the order named). Minnesota, South Dakota, and

	Carlots	Percentage Distribution
1930:		
Freight (rail)	1,141	21.2
Express (rail)	2,113	39.3
Truck	2,121	39.5
Total	5,375	100.0
1931:		
Freight (rail)	837	16.7
Express (rail)	1,277	25.4
Truck	2,902	57.9
Total	5,016	100.0

RELATIVE IMPORTANCE OF FORMS OF TRANSPORTATION
DELIVERING LIVE POULTRY AT THE NEW YORK
AND CHICAGO MARKETS, 1930-31

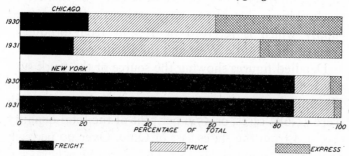

Iowa furnished over one-half of the total receipts by freight. Unfortunately information regarding the quantity received by truck from each state is not available. It is probable that the chief sources of supply are the same as those for express shipments, although Wisconsin might rank ahead of Iowa because of its comparative nearness to Chicago.

While figures are not available for the other centers,

in general it may be stated that receipts of live poultry by motor truck have largely replaced those formerly moved by express wherever there are poultry producing areas within motor truck haul of the city. As poultry appears to be hauled into New York greater distances than most commodities, it may be expected that the average haul to other cities is longer.

2. *Truck movement of eggs.* It is possible for eggs to move directly to the retailer by express or truck, making it difficult to secure records of truck receipts. Information regarding truck receipts of eggs has been available only during 1931 and 1932, and the figures for the former year are known to be incomplete. At New York these records show that only a small portion of the total supply, or from 5 to 7 per cent, reaches the market by truck. This is due to the large proportion of the total supply which is received by freight from producing areas of the Middle West and the Pacific coast.

Detailed figures showing the source of the truck supply for New York are available only for the month of December 1932. The total truck receipts for that month were 35,682 cases, or 57.6 per cent of the total quantity received from the states east of Ohio. Over 90 per cent of the eggs from Connecticut, Delaware, Maryland, and Virginia arrived by motor truck. About 80 per cent of the much larger volume from New Jersey and Pennsylvania came by truck, but only 33 per cent of the receipts from New York State were handled by truck. Considerable portions of the states of New York and Pennsylvania are outside the area within which truck operation is practicable at present. It is probable that at least 80 per cent of the eggs within over-night truck haul of

New York are being shipped by motor truck. Practically all of this business has been transferred from express to truck shipment during the past decade. In addition to the lower rate the advantage of pick-up at the farm and the reduction of breakage appear to be the chief reasons for this change of transportation methods.

At Philadelphia quite complete records of truck receipts have been compiled since 1929. These show that both the quantity and the percentage of eggs received by truck during 1931 and the first nine months of 1932 were substantially less than in 1929 and 1930.

EGG RECEIPTS BY TRUCK AT PHILADELPHIA, 1929–32
(In cases of 30 dozen)

Year	Total Receipts	Truck Receipts	*Truck Receipts as Percentage of Total Receipts*
1929............	1,697,122	323,676	19.1
1930............	1,758,781	338,575	19.2
1931............	1,730,059	232,471	13.4
1932[a]...........	1,221,130	174,742	14.4

[a] January–September inclusive.

Most of the decline in receipts appears to have been occasioned by the substitution of Middle Western supplies for those from Pennsylvania during 1931. This may have been partially due to market conditions rather than to any change in the transportation situation.

As is shown in the table on page 644, 80 per cent of the eggs from the territory within normal motor truck haul of Philadelphia were handled by motor truck. The immediately adjacent states of Pennsylvania, Maryland, and Delaware shipped over 85 per cent of their supply by truck.

The only dependable records for Chicago are those

for the first nine months of 1932. These show that 699,763 cases or 22 per cent of a total of 3,175,216 cases, were received by motor truck. Ninety per cent of the total truck movement was from the states of Iowa, Wisconsin, Illinois, Minnesota, Missouri, and Michigan. The four states immediately adjacent to Chicago (Illinois, Wisconsin, Indiana, and Michigan), supplied only

MAJOR SOURCES OF EGG RECEIPTS BY TRUCK AT PHILADELPHIA, 1931
(In cases of 30 dozen)

State	Total Receipts from State	Truck Receipts from State	*Percentage by Truck*
Pennsylvania....	176,618	150,638	85.3
Maryland........	32,929	27,298	82.9
Virginia.........	37,128	23,697	63.8
Delaware........	23,906	22,310	93.3
New York.......	19,591	7,627	38.9
6 states........	290,172	231,570	79.8

43.5 per cent of the truck receipts. Clinton, Iowa, is the nearest shipping point in any state not adjacent to Chicago, and it is 138 miles distant by direct rail mileage. Therefore, all eggs from the State of Iowa and other states not included in the four adjacent to Chicago, must have been hauled a minimum distance of 140 miles. The truck deliveries from these more distant states amounted to 56.5 per cent of the total truck supply. Since much of the area of the four adjacent states is more than 140 miles from Chicago, it is probable that at least two-thirds of the total supply trucked to the Chicago market was hauled more than 140 miles.

The percentage of the total shipments which arrived by motor truck varied with the state of origin, as the following table shows:

ORIGIN OF TOTAL AND TRUCK RECEIPTS OF EGGS AT CHICAGO
JANUARY–SEPTEMBER 1932

State of Origin	Total Receipts (30-dozen cases)	Truck Receipts (30-dozen cases)	*Percentage by Truck*
Michigan	51,468	49,018	95.2
Indiana	18,140	15,934	87.8
Wisconsin	228,911	130,012	56.8
Illinois	207,143	108,525	52.4
Iowa	675,459	202,749	30.0
Minnesota	376,672	71,699	19.0
Missouri	630,406	67,012	10.6
Nebraska	147,681	14,538	9.8
Kansas	279,969	20,231	7.2

Sixty per cent of the aggregate receipts from the four states of Illinois, Wisconsin, Indiana, and Michigan reached the Chicago market by truck during the nine months. That portion of the supply which was stored in transit was not primarily intended for consumption in Chicago, but was included in the total receipts for the market. Since 83.9 per cent of the eggs received from these four states during September arrived by truck, it appears that the percentage of the Chicago consumption received by motor truck during part of the year was considerably higher than was the percentage for nine months.

Although figures for the smaller cities are not available, it is known that most of the supply produced within truck haul of these cities is handled by motor truck. This is due to the smaller volume available, and to the fact that hauls of 200 miles or more are usually not necessary to supply these smaller markets.

V. COTTON

Cotton is a crop of major importance in the twelve states extending from North Carolina to Oklahoma and southward to the Gulf of Mexico. It is of minor importance in the next tier of states to the north, and also in certain irrigated areas of New Mexico, Arizona, and California. In recent years the production in Texas has expanded considerably, so that this state now provides about one-third of the total produced in the entire country. Most of the production is located within five hundred miles of the Atlantic, Gulf, and Pacific coasts. The movement of cotton is primarily to the coast for water shipment to foreign countries or to mills along the Atlantic seaboard. Because of its non-perishable character, cotton is readily held in storage for considerable periods of time without deterioration in quality. This tends to make the movement into consumption extend over the entire year, although the shipment from the farm to the warehouse is largely concentrated within the few months following harvesting.

In the ordinary process of handling, cotton is hauled in bulk from the farm to a nearby gin. After ginning, it is pressed into a low density bale weighing approximately 500 pounds and is then ready for movement to market. From that time on, the cotton in the bale maintains its identity, although it is usually reduced into a smaller size of bale (to standard density) at the nearest compress. The cost of such compression has usually been a part of the railroad rate on cotton. When the cotton reaches the seacoast, and is prepared for export shipment, it is usually further compressed to a high density bale so as to require the minimum amount of space on the ship. While the high density compresses were originally located only at the seaports, the installation of such facilities at interior points in recent years has had considerable influence on the transportation situation. The conflict of interest between the interior and seaboard compresses and warehouses has been one of the causes of the development of truck competition.

Some knowledge concerning the rates and services of the railroads in the handling of cotton is essential to an understanding of the problem of truck competition. The following extracts briefly summarize the situation as it had developed up to 1930:

Practically all cotton rates apply on "any quantity," as distinguished from "carlot" or "less-than-carlot," though under long established custom they have been made on entirely different bases in the territories east and west of the Mississippi River. . . .

Most of these rates include the carrier privilege, which means that if cotton is delivered to the carrier uncompressed, the carrier has the privilege of having it compressed, whether at origin or in transit, or carrying it flat. The charge for such compressing, which at present is 15 cents per 100 pounds except at certain Mississippi River points, where it is 18 cents, is paid by the carrier. This privilege generally applies only where the rate is 58 cents per 100 pounds, or more. In a few instances it is provided that where cotton is delivered to the carrier compressed, the carrier-privilege rate is abated by the amount of the compress charge, or by such portion of it as will leave the carrier a certain net amount. . . .

The effective date of the order (*Docket 17000, Part 3, Cotton*, 165 I.C.C. 595) of the Interstate Commerce Commission establishing the new rates was originally January 10, 1931, but it was postponed to June 15, 1931.

Under this recent decision the rates east and west of the Mississippi River are both based primarily on distance, but the difference in the matter of compression which formerly existed still prevails.

Because of the character of cotton itself and the methods of producing and distributing it that have developed through the years, there has evolved a system of special services adapted to the needs of cotton transportation.

Probably the most important of these is the comprehensive

scheme of transit privileges, under which practically all cotton is stopped at concentration points, where it is sorted and assembled into even-running lots and re-forwarded on the basis of the through rate from point of origin to destination. Cotton is usually compressed at the first compress point it touches, which may or may not be a concentration point also. . . .

The substitution of cotton at concentration points is inherent in the present system of distribution, which requires that cotton be assembled in even running lots as to staple and grade. The general restriction is imposed permitting the substitution of rail-borne cotton, except that in the Mississippi Valley local or "wagon" cotton may be substituted for rail cotton. . . .[29]

The establishment of the new rate structure in 1931 naturally disturbed many existing rates. Moreover, it coincided with a substantial drop in the price of cotton and with depressed conditions in the lumber and petroleum industries of the Southern states which utilized trucks to a considerable extent in their operations. As a result the effect of the proposed rates was not as expected.

In Rate Structure Investigation, Part 3, Cotton, (165 I.C.C. 595) rate scales were prescribed on cotton which increased the rates up to 300 miles and reduced the rates for distances beyond 300 miles. The railroads state that they cannot avail themselves of the increased rates authorized in that proceeding by reason of truck competition which is keenest on the short hauls.[30]

Thus the increase in the railroad rates in 1931 induced competition by trucks, especially in the shorter hauls where the cost factor was in favor of the trucks. The Commission authorized modifications of its order in two

[29] E. S. Moulton, "Cotton Production and Distribution in the Gulf Southwest," *U. S. Department of Commerce Series 49, Part III*, pp. 239-41.

[30] L. S. Flynn, "Co-ordination of Motor Transportation," *Docket 23400, Examiner's Report*, Interstate Commerce Commission. (72 Cong., S. Doc. 43, p. 51.)

subsequent proceedings,[31] which permitted the carriers to meet truck competition.

The recent improvement of the Mississippi River and the re-establishment of barge service have a direct bearing on the truck competition with the railroads. Certain large shippers have developed warehouse facilities at river points and use motor trucks for collection from inland points. In this way it has been possible substantially to increase the tonnage handled on the river. The chief advantage of river transportation has been its low rates, which have made it necessary for the railroads to reduce their rates in the competitive area.

1. Development of motor trucking of cotton. The hauling of cotton by motor truck began in the area immediately adjacent to the ports and interior cotton markets and resulted in some extension of the area. This was because longer hauls could be made with trucks than with horses and wagons. While there was a small increase in the percentage of total receipts which arrived by truck, this did not assume great importance until the 1930 crop. The available records indicate that truck receipts amounted to less than 10 per cent of the total in 1929, and in most instances to less than 5 per cent. But with the 1930 crop there was a considerable increase in the percentage received by truck, and with the 1931 crop there came a further increase at certain points.

Owing to the recent expansion of production in Texas, the ports of Galveston and Houston have become increasingly important in the assembling of cotton. Records of the truck receipts at Houston are available as far back as the 1919 crop, but the quantity did not equal 1 per cent of the total receipts until the crop of 1923.

[31] 174 I.C.C. 9 and 174 I.C.C. 249.

From the figures in the accompanying table it is readily apparent that the truck became an important factor

COTTON RECEIPTS BY TRUCK AT HOUSTON, 1923–32[a]

Season[b]	Total Receipts (In bales)	Truck or Wagon Receipts (In bales)	*Truck Receipts as Percentage of Total Receipts*
1923–24.........	1,816,883	17,383	*1.0*
1924–25.........	2,668,265	28,954	*1.1*
1925–26.........	2,617,929	50,671	*1.9*
1926–27.........	3,580,290	50,784	*1.4*
1927–28.........	2,543,212	95,335	*3.8*
1928–29.........	2,869,213	221,486	*7.7*
1929–30.........	2,629,467	226,617	*8.6*
1930–31.........	2,843,534	696,169	*24.5*
1931–32.........	3,185,943	1,410,580	*44.3*
1932–33[c].......	1,910,120	669,572	*35.1*

[a] Houston Cotton Statement, July 30, 1932. Issued by Houston Cotton Exchange and Board of Trade.
[b] From Aug. 1 of the year in which the crop is grown to July 31 of the following year.
[c] To Dec. 23, 1932.

in the transportation of the 1930 and 1931 crops. The sharp decline in 1932-33 is attributable in large part to state legislation restricting truck movement.

Galveston is within 50 miles of Houston and both ports receive the same railroad rate on shipments from points 100 miles or more inland from Houston. It would be expected, therefore, to find similar situations at the two markets.

COTTON RECEIPTS BY TRUCK AT GALVESTON, 1929–31[a]

Season	Total Receipts (In bales)	Truck Receipts (In bales)	*Truck Receipts as Percentage of Total Receipts*
1929–30.........	1,921,861	21,259	*1.1*
1930–31.........	1,563,875	149,347	*9.5*
1931–32.........	2,366,542	142,941	*5.1*

[a] *Shippers Digest of Galveston*, Aug. 10, 1932.

But despite the close proximity of the two markets, the truck receipts at Galveston are still of small volume and

Truck Receipts of Cotton at Certain Markets, 1923-32[a]

(Expressed as percentages of the total receipts of cotton at respective markets)

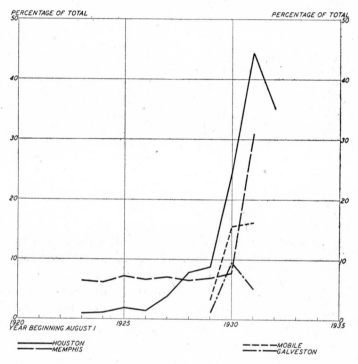

[a] For data see tables on pp. 650, 652, and 653.

showed a decline from the 1930 crop to the 1931 crop. This is probably due to the fact that most of the truck shipments to Galveston must pass through Houston.

Memphis is the largest interior market in the country

and assembles cotton from a considerable territory. It has the further advantage of being on the Mississippi River, and of enjoying more favorable rates than otherwise might be available. Wagon or truck receipts averaged 104,000 bales from 1918 to 1922. The receipts by truck or wagon since that time are shown in the following table:

TRUCK RECEIPTS AT MEMPHIS, 1923–31[a]

Season	Total Receipts (In bales)	Truck Receipts (In bales)	Truck Receipts as Percentage of Total Receipts
1923–24	926,310	58,935	6.4
1924–25	1,303,301	79,415	6.1
1925–26	1,999,630	143,056	7.2
1926–27	2,349,229	156,067	6.6
1927–28	1,512,313	105,285	7.0
1928–29	1,822,921	118,150	6.5
1929–30	1,994,716	136,625	6.8
1930–31	1,394,717	106,886	7.7
1931–32	2,091,716	646,116	30.9

[a] Data for the seasons through 1929–30 are from Moulton, *Cotton Production and Distribution in the Gulf Southwest*, p. 247. Later data are from *Weekly Statement of Memphis Cotton Exchange*.

It is apparent that truck receipts at Memphis did not become important until the 1931 crop, or one year later than the large increase at Houston.

Both water and rail transportation have been important factors in the movement of cotton into the Mobile market. The motor truck has become important since the 1930 crop but it has drawn its business from the railroads rather than the water carriers.

2. *Direct delivery to mills.* After mills were located in the cotton producing districts of the Southeastern states, a limited number of nearby producers could sell their crops direct to these mills. The motor truck has made it possible for a much larger number of producers

to make such direct deliveries. Direct marketing has now grown to such proportions that certain mills have placed buyers in their warehouses to handle such purchases.

This method of marketing seems likely to continue as long as it supplies the mills with a sufficient quantity of the proper types and grades of cotton for their manufacturing requirements. If the mills are willing to share the savings with the producers, truck hauling for direct marketing should increase in the future.

COTTON RECEIPTS AT MOBILE AND METHOD OF TRANSPORTATION, 1929–31[a]
I. Bales Received

Season	By Truck	By Water	By Rail	Total
1929–30.....	12,672	162,439	224,845	399,956
1930–31.....	93,554	300,852	207,682	602,088
1931–32.....	86,088	263,989	183,680	533,757

II. Percentage Transported

Season	By Truck	By Water	By Rail	Total
1929–30.....	3.2	40.6	56.2	100.0
1930–31.....	12.5	50.0	34.5	100.0
1931–32.....	16.1	49.5	34.4	100.0

[a] J. H. Goff, *Alabama Economic Review*, p. 19.

3. Direct delivery from ship to mill. The use of the motor truck has developed in the hauling of cotton from the ship to the mill as it has in the producing districts. This has become more common, because good roads have been available for a longer time in the manufacturing areas than in most of the producing states. In New England many of the mills are located within short truck haul from the seaports where the cotton is received by ship. Truck delivery from ship to mill has therefore become the common form of transportation. This is also true in the Southern manufacturing areas, in spite of the fact that longer hauls are necessary because of the greater distance of the mills from the seaports.

No detailed information appears to be available regarding the length of truck hauls of cotton. As in the case of other commodities, this must be secured from detailed surveys, which have not been made in the short period during which the truck has been an important factor.

Movements to the Gulf ports are from points as far distant as about 400 miles, but the bulk of the movement is for distances not exceeding 175 miles. Long distance movements are increasing, however. The Southern Pacific reports movements from Calexico to San Pedro, Calif., 250 miles. To the interior mills in the South and Southwest the movements are generally 100 miles or less.[82]

4. Explanation of growing truck competition. One of the reasons for the rapid increase in the amount of cotton hauled by truck was the considerable number of trucks which were made available because of the depression in the lumber and petroleum industries.[83] Many of the trucks used were of the cheapest possible construction, consisting of a pleasure-car power unit and an inexpensive semi-trailer. Only a small initial investment was required, and many men purchased trucks because of their inability to secure other employment. Loads carried were up to 20 bales, or 10,000 pounds.

Because of the large number of trucks which entered the business, rates declined quite rapidly and reached points considerably below the existing rail rates. In the absence of more detailed information, the following quotation gives some idea of the situation:

[82] *Docket No. 23400, Co-ordination of Motor Transportation,* Interstate Commerce Commission, p. 295. 182 I.C.C. 263, 295 (1932).

[83] The same, p. 295.

Truck rates on cotton generally lack a firm basis and are frequently adjusted to what the carrier can charge. They are materially lower than the rail rates in effect at the time that trucking became a factor in the situation. The Seaboard Air Line reports truck rates in North and South Carolina which range from 50 to 90 cents lower per bale than for single line rail hauls and from 85 to 120 cents lower than for joint line rail hauls. The truck rates in this instance range irregularly but generally upwardly from 35 per cent of the single line rail rate at 10 miles to 75 per cent at 200 miles.[34]

The ease with which trucks entered the cotton transportation field was partly due to the fact that carlot rates had never been developed in the handling of cotton despite their almost universal use in other commodities. As was mentioned previously, the "any quantity" rate had been the basis of the rate structure. This was essentially a less-than-carload rate and offered no financial inducement to the shipper to assemble the product and forward it in carload units.

Contract trucking is usually premised on the handling of a full load. Thus it has been possible for truckers, operating with truck loads, to haul at prices below rail rates established on a less-than-carload basis. This has been particularly true of those sections in which rates were to be increased on the order of the Interstate Commerce Commission.

The development of hauling was also related to the conflict of interest between the inland and seaboard compresses. Under the rail tariffs, the cotton was to be compressed to standard density at the first compress, which usually was an inland one. If the cotton was transported by truck, it could be delivered to the seaport compress in its original form, and the seaport compress and ware-

[34] The same, p. 295.

house thus secured a larger volume of business, at the expense of the inland compress and warehouse. One trade interest encouraged the trucking development while another was injured by it. The attitude of shippers was largely determined by trade affiliations.

The price of cotton is established on a world basis, and therefore the buying price at any shipping point is approximately the world price less the cost of transportation and marketing. If a dealer at any point was able to effect a reduction in transportation charges through truck hauling, his local competitors were forced to adopt the truck. As a result, the shift to truck hauling has been largely by communities and sections.

The price of cotton has declined substantially during the period in which truck hauling has developed and has forced every possible economy in handling. The proposal to increase rates for the shorter hauls, despite the low prices of cotton, undoubtedly increased the antagonism of shippers, who were able to protect their interest by the use of the trucks.

5. *Texas truck legislation.* Because of the importance of Texas as a cotton producing state, and because of the large amount of trucking which has developed into Houston and other markets, state legislation regulating trucks has been accorded considerable attention. Three acts were passed in 1931 and two of them have been upheld by decisions of the United States Supreme Court.[35] The most important direct provision is the limitation of the total load of any truck to 7,000 pounds, except under special permit. In addition, each contract carrier is required to secure a permit from the State

[35] U. S. Supreme Court, October Term, 1931, No. 826; October Term, 1932, No. 326.

Railroad Commission. Such a permit may be issued only if the proposed operation will not injure an existing common carrier, either rail or truck. The Commission is also given the right to establish minimum and maximum rates for contract carriers. Because of the uncertainty of the situation regarding this legislation the receipts by truck of the 1932 crop up to December 23, 1932 were 35.1 per cent as compared with 44.3 during the entire preceding marketing season. The new legislation greatly modified the conditions relating to long-time contracts for truck haulage. In effect the law provides that any load of more than 13 bales of cotton is illegal. This limitation automatically required an increase in truck rates because of the reduced loads which were allowed. If there is no change in the law, and it is enforced effectively, it appears certain that the quantity of cotton moving by truck in Texas will be reduced in the future.

6. *New carlot rail rates.* Another factor tending to reduce the amount of trucking is the establishment of a temporary tariff in the Mississippi Valley territory which provides for lower rates on carlot shipments with compression charges excluded.[36] For example, the rates shown at the top of the following page (effective September 6, 1932 and to expire July 31, 1933) are in effect from Arkansas, Southeastern Missouri, and Memphis to New Orleans.

This tariff gives the shipper who forwards his cotton in carlots with the heaviest minimum weight a substantial reduction in the freight charge to New Orleans. In this particular instance (Class D) the shipper secures a rate which is approximately equal to the river rate by

[36] J. E. Johanson, *Cotton Carload Tariff*, Interstate Commerce Commission No. 2437.

	Minimum Weight (In pounds)	Rate per cwt. (In cents)
For 40 ft. 7 in Cars		
Class A	25,000	45
Class B	35,000	36
Class C	50,000	30
Class D	65,000	25

barge. A somewhat similar tariff has been suggested in the Southwestern area,[37] and several tariffs are now in effect in the Southeastern territory. One of these new carlot tariffs[38] in the Southeastern area provides for the following rates and minimum weights:

	Minimum Weight (In pounds)	Rate per cwt. (In cents)
For 40. ft. 7 in Cars		
Class A	25,000	46
Class B	35,000	37
Class C	37,500	31

Thus the railroads have made temporary and belated recognition of the fact that the transportation of cotton requires carlot rates similar to those for other commodities. If permanent rates are established which provide for substantial reductions for carload shipments of cotton, part of the incentive to use the motor truck will have been removed.

7. *Advantages and disadvantages of truck hauling.* The chief advantage of the motor truck in the transportation of cotton appears to be its lower cost. In nearly all other respects, rail shipment is more advantageous. Rapid handling is usually not a necessity as it is in the case of perishables. Financing, insurance, claims, and

[37] *Docket No. 17000, Part 3, Cotton*, Interstate Commerce Commission. 165 I.C.C. 595.

[38] F. L. Speiden, *Southeastern Cotton Tariff*, Interstate Commerce Commission No. A-734, Supplement 69 (effective Oct. 10, 1932).

protection from exposure to the weather are all more satisfactory when shipment is made by railroad.

VI. SUMMARY AND CONCLUSIONS

It is impossible to make an accurate estimate of the amount of agricultural traffic which has been diverted from the railroads to the trucks. The records in the case of livestock indicate that at least 40 per cent of the movement into the stockyards is by truck at present. The information in the case of the other commodities is too incomplete to permit an estimate of the total truck movement; but it probably is not as great as is generally believed to be the case. The tremendous volume of agricultural products which must move for long distances require railroad service, and thus keep the proportion of the products moved by truck at a comparatively low percentage.

The tonnage and revenue of agricultural and livestock products moved by rail during recent years have been as follows:

Year	Tons Originated[39]	Revenues[39]
1928	143,656	$980,915
1929	140,250	958,085
1930	133,857	898,871
1931	119,119	820,894

These records show that farm products in 1931 furnished 82.9 per cent of the tonnage and 83.9 per cent of the revenue of 1928. During the first six months of 1932 there was a further decline to 81.3 per cent of the tonnage and 81.2 per cent of the revenue of the corresponding period of 1931.

[39] In thousands. Data relate to Class I roads only. From *Interstate Commerce Commission Freight Commodity Statistics.*

Despite the competition of trucks, the movement of agricultural products has been maintained to a much greater degree than the other business of the railroads. This is shown by the following comparisons, using the 1928 figures as 100.

	1928	1929	1930	1931
Products of Agriculture				
Tonnage	100	98	94	83
Revenue	100	98	91	81
Animals and Products				
Tonnage	100	97	90	84
Revenue	100	97	92	91
Total Freight				
Tonnage	100	104	90	70
Revenue	100	103	87	70

The real competition between the motor truck and the railroad in the transportation of farm products has taken place in those producing areas which are relatively close to consuming centers. While the development of motor truck hauling has been going on for over a decade, the greatest expansion has occurred during the past five years. This has been due to the increase in the number of farms located on improved roads, the greater distance over which the truck can be operated with pneumatic tires, and the obvious economies which are effected when a truck is loaded at the farm or country plant and direct delivery is made to the desired city destination without rehandling.

While the early development of trucking was limited to the hauling of livestock, fruit, vegetables, and milk, nearly all agricultural commodities are now being handled by truck for distances up to about 50 miles. Trucks are competing with the railroad for distances in excess of 50 miles chiefly in the transportation of livestock, fruits and vegetables, milk and other dairy products, poultry, eggs, and cotton. With the single exception of cotton, it will be noted that all of these commodities are of perishable character.

The expansion of trucking in the perishable commodities has been due to two important factors. First, these commodities have been included in the higher rate groups because of their perishable character, and the class rates on the shorter hauls have also increased the relative cost of rail transportation. Truck rates on agricultural products are primarily based upon truck-load units, while the competing rail rates are frequently those for less-than-carload freight or express shipment. Numerous additional expenses such as refrigeration, terminal charges, and cartage at either shipping point or destination, or both, must be paid by the shipper as a part of the cost of rail transportation.

In the earlier development, the truck charges were equal to or slightly below the cost of rail shipment including additional charges. But in recent years there have been numerous instances where the truck charge has declined to such an extent that the truck rate now is about equal to the rail rate alone. In some cases truck rates are below the competing rail rate, but these are probably based upon local competitive conditions rather than upon lower costs of operation. Certain shippers with a large volume of products have been able to effect substantial savings by the operation of their own trucks, but special conditions which are not representative of the general situation usually apply to these cases.

The other chief reason for the expansion of trucking has been the convenience of the service to the shipper. Shipments might be made or delivered at any time, without regard to the railroad schedule. Trucks could be sent to any point which had direct connection by highway, and much time saved as compared with the railroad service to the same point. Small markets have been able to secure more satisfactory supplies of perishables in truck-load units than was possible when carload shipments were necessary. In addition, much less time was spent in transit, which permitted the elimination of refrigeration expense. Direct delivery from farm or country plant to the city destination resulted in less damage as well as reduced cost through the elimination of handling.

Cotton is the chief non-perishable commodity which has been shipped in large quantities by truck. This development has been at certain markets where conditions were favorable rather than at all points in the cotton area. The truck has been co-ordinated with the barge in the Mississippi Valley area. Until the fall of 1932, the railroad rate structure did not provide carlot rates for cotton, but all rates were on an "any quantity," basis. Thus the truck rates, which were based on full loads, did not find much difficulty in competing with the railroads for the cotton business. Depression conditions also greatly increased the number of trucks competing for this business, and rates were further lowered because of this competition. A conflict of interest between seaport and inland compresses and warehouses has been an important factor in the increase in trucking to certain markets.

Legislation in Texas has had an appreciable influence in restricting cotton trucking during recent months. The establishment of temporary carlot rates in the Mississippi Valley and the Southeastern states should permit the railroads to compete more effectively with the trucks in those areas. On the other hand, there is every reason to expect a steady increase in direct hauling by truck to the mills of the Southeastern states because of the savings which this method effects.

An additional reason for the increased use of the motor truck has been the attitude of the shippers toward the railroad and the attitude of rail officials toward truck competition. During the past two years the price level for farm products has been considerably below the pre-war basis, and averaged 83 per cent of the 1913 base during 1931 and 60 per cent during 1932. Shippers naturally resented the payment of freight charges which were 145 per cent of the 1913 base, which was the level during 1931. In the past this resentment could only be shown through attacks upon the rate structure. But during the past few years the availability of the motor truck has made it possible for the shipper to divert all or a portion of his business away from the railroad. In those instances where the practice became general, railroad revenues were seriously affected. As truck shipments usually resulted in some saving as compared with the cost of rail shipment with its additional handling costs, the shipper was encouraged to make further use of the motor truck.

As a group the railroads have until very recently failed to recognize this situation. Little effort was made to speed up schedules to meet the faster service of the motor truck. Requests for higher rates because of the decline in the volume in traffic only served to act as additional incentive to shippers to develop every possible method for reducing the cost of transportation. From the experience of years, shippers had learned that improved service was usually secured at points where two railroads competed with each other. The motor truck created such competition at nearly every point, and the pressure of low prices of farm products frequently compelled its use.

The loss of business to the motor truck has probably been greatest in those products which formerly were shipped by less-than-carload express. In districts where there was a sufficient concentration of production, trucks have absorbed most of this business at rates which are lower than the express rates.

The trucks owned by farmers are usually of the smaller sizes, most of them not exceeding the ton and a half size. Medium-sized trucks predominate in the hauling of farm products for hire, with two to three and a half tons as the most common capacities. The larger units from the four-ton capacity upward are chiefly found in the hauling of milk and cotton and are relatively few in number. Within each group, the larger size is usually found making the longer hauls. In general it can be stated that there are comparatively few trucks of four tons or more which are engaged in the hauling of farm products on the highway.

Most of the trucking of farm products for hire is carried on by contract truckers who specialize in the hauling of a single class of goods or by truckers who purchase the products which they transport. In addition to presenting a problem of regulation as a transportation agency, the truck operator has become a most disturbing factor by functioning as a dealer. Numerous attempts have been made to control this situation with various types of licenses, but it will continue to be a difficult problem. Flexibility of operation, the chief asset of the motor truck, greatly increases the problem of regulation and supervision.

The general belief that motor truck hauling is being

carried on for long distances is not supported by the available facts. While it is true that there are instances where hauls of around 500 miles are being made, the vast proportion of the trucking is for much shorter distances. Accurate facts can only be secured by detailed studies of the actual truck receipts for a few markets. These studies indicate that something like three-fourths of such truck hauling over the highway is for distances which do not exceed about 100 miles. Most of the balance of the trucking is for distances which do not exceed 200 miles, and only a small percentage of the total is moving more than 200 miles. The hauls for livestock, milk, and potatoes are below the average in distance, while those for citrus fruits, berries, butter, cheese, poultry, and eggs are longer than the average. Cotton and most of the fruits and vegetables move about the average distances. However, the length of truck haul is still increasing. It is determined largely by the nearness of markets and the relative value per pound and perishability of the product. Return loads are comparatively few, but are likely to increase if truck rates continue to decline. *In general the present limit of effective trucking can be stated to be the distance covered in an over-night trip.*

While the diversion of traffic in carloads is not large in proportion to the total railroad tonnage the loss of revenue is important, because the trucks have taken over the short-haul business in the commodities which pay the higher rates. The loss of traffic and revenue is not great for the railroads as a whole, but the concentration of truck competition into limited areas makes the loss of revenue for the railroads involved most serious. Unless this loss can be spread over a considerable volume of other traffic, a continuance of the present situation must eventually force a greater abandonment of service on branches and short lines than has already been effected.

The truck has the fundamental advantage of being able to use the public highways for terminal purposes, thus eliminating the heavy costs which are necessary for the privately owned terminal facilities of the railroads. The ability of the truck to eliminate much rehandling in the city is also a factor of advantage to it from the cost standpoint. Each of these cost factors favors the use of the truck for hauls of comparatively short distances. The truck has already usurped practically all of the business up to about 50 miles, and it is probable that it will continue to hold its present dominant position on most hauls up to 100 miles.

In practice, truck costs increase with the distance of operation, while rail costs begin with fairly large terminal expenses, so that the rail rates are relatively high for the lower mileages, but do not rise in proportion as the distance increases. These two fundamental characteristics indicate that the truck will prevail as the dominant transportation agency for shorter distances, while the railroad will continue to retain the business for the longer distances. It is obviously impossible to make any definite line of demarcation between these two distances, as such a division in any given case will depend upon the commodity transported, the rates and costs of both transportation agencies, and the particular service which each agency is able to render.

The motor truck has greatly disturbed marketing methods and agencies dealing in commodities handled by truck. Many economies have been effected through the use of the truck, but losses have also resulted. These losses—for instance, those resulting from reduced standardization—are partly due to the demand conditions which have resulted from the depression and may disappear when more normal business conditions prevail. But it is certain that there will be continued disturbance in the marketing agencies until the truck has found its proper place and conditions have become adjusted to the new situation.

Both the motor truck and the railroad are essential parts of the facilities for the transportation of farm products. The motor truck now dominates the hauls of less than 50 miles, and in many instances up to 100 miles. It possesses natural advantages which make it unlikely that it will be easily replaced in this field of activity. On the other hand, the railroad has great advantages in the transportation of farm products for long distances, and it is now handling the great bulk of the business from 200 miles upward. Between these two limits there is a considerable volume of business which is now divided between the two carriers. Eventually, this will be handled by the agency which offers the best service at lowest cost, or perhaps by a combination of the two agencies. While the truck has made considerable inroad into the business in this field, there is good reason to believe that the railroads can retain the business that they now have and regain a considerable portion of that which has been lost.

This can only be done through a careful consideration of each district and each commodity so that the best possible service for the lowest possible cost may be given to the shipper. The rate structure should be systematically revised (especially for the shorter distances), following the principle that the greatest total revenue is most important to the railroad, whereas the lowest possible transportation cost per unit of product is the most important to the shipper. Increased total revenue appears to have been secured in instances where rates have been reduced recently.

A drastic revision of the charges which are made for services in addition to actual freight transportation will probably be one of the most productive methods for securing new tonnage or regaining old. This should include the question of collecting certain commodities, such as livestock, from the farm, as well as the possibility of reducing the high costs of delivery which now prevail in certain cities.[40] These two factors have been among the most important reasons for the expansion of truck hauling, and a satisfactory solution of the problems surrounding them would do much to permit the railroad to meet the competition of the truck.

Each form of transportation has its advantages and disadvantages. Each is essential to the maintenance of the most efficient distribution for the benefit of both producers and consumers. Each should be maintained in the field of its greatest usefulness to the public. The process of working out this relationship in any particular territory is dependent on factors which vary in each instance. Shippers must realize that their primary interest is in good transportation of all kinds, truck operators that stability of rates at profitable levels is essential to permanent success, and the railroads that the best possible service for the lowest practicable rate will produce the greatest total revenue.

[40] Compare Chapter XXIX.

CHAPTER XXIX

POSSIBILITIES OF CO-ORDINATION OF RAIL AND MOTOR TRANSPORT

Possibilities of the motor vehicle as a competing agency as well as a useful adjunct to the rail, for certain classes of traffic, were not fully realized by railroad officials prior to the World War. Since then they have been more or less divided in opinion, some belittling the value of the motor, while others have been alive to its possibilities. In the beginning the general railroad policy was to suppress highway transport. However, the motor vehicle developed in spite of this policy, and cut heavily into the rail business. The railroads as a whole have not been in a position to co-ordinate their service with that of the fast growing competitor. Consequently, there are at present two forms of transport, in some instances working together, but in general against each other.

There seem to be two avenues open to the railroads relative to the trucking business. They may confine their attention to rail transport, using the motor only as a means of bettering their own operating methods, or they may become land transport companies and render both rail and highway services. The second alternative seems the better one. It is logical to think of the railroad as part of the land transport scheme, as it is to-day, and of the present railroads as parts of huge land transport systems in the future. The new systems will consist of combinations of rail and highway transport. Railroads should prepare for a co-ordinated system which will meet the needs of the times and be flexible enough to meet them continually. The automobile has a legitimate field and when equipped with improved tires and perhaps the Diesel engine, the zone for its economic service is likely to be extended.

Co-ordination of rail and highway transport of freight can be realized when the railroads and the motor operators come to recognize the zones within which each can best render service. This would permit an intelligent form of competition within those twilight zones where either mode of transportation, or a combination of both, may be used.

Co-ordination involves such a harmonizing of transportation interests as will result in the moving of traffic either exclusively by one form of transport or by a combination of rail and motor, depending upon how it can be handled best or at the lowest cost. Complete co-ordination would require the merging of rail and highway agencies into unified transportation systems. It can be approximated without consolidation or agreements, provided the two agencies are placed upon the same plane of competition.

Railroads may make extensive use of trucks in terminal areas, in connection with replacement of certain line-haul service, and freight consolidation and transfer; or they may operate trucks over the highway in competition with independent motor lines. Buses are operated in both intra-city and long-distance service, and are sometimes substituted for unprofitable passenger trains.

Assuming that the railroads will become *land transport* companies, there are two general policies which they may adopt; namely, (1) to operate trucks directly, or through subsidiary or affiliated companies, or (2) to contract the work out to independent common carriers and private contract truckers. They may choose to do both.

I. IN TERMINAL FREIGHT MOVEMENT

By far the greatest opportunity for reduction in freight transportation costs lies in the terminal areas. Railway operating statistics show that terminal costs exceed those for line haul many times over. For example, in the case of less-than-carload freight, the line haul cost between New York and Chicago is little more than the cost of terminal handling at New York or Chicago.

Terminal costs are particularly heavy on less-than-carload freight, which requires the clerical labor of making out perhaps twenty-five bills per car instead of one, which loads at an average of five or six tons instead of fifteen, which requires breaking bulk at transfer points and often a great deal of extra switching. The cost of handling these small lots is also greater to the shipper because of the higher cost of terminal trucking.

A study of terminal costs at three hundred stations in the United States, which went back as far as 1916, showed a direct cost (platform, clerical, switching, etc.) of 5½ cents to over 10 cents per hundred pounds in less-than-carload handling. Such costs usually make up about 75 per cent of the total cost, which includes rent, investment, maintenance, taxes, and other overhead items. Direct costs had probably doubled by 1923.[1]

Recent studies at Eastern terminals have shown direct costs on less-than-carload merchandise freight of over $3.00 per ton, and total costs of $4.00 per ton. Handling carload freight in the New York terminals costs about half as much as less-than-carload lots.

An exhibit presented by the Pennsylvania Railroad in Interstate Commerce Commission Docket 21723, covering a test period in November 1928, gave the cost of

[1] W. C. Maxwell in *Railway Age*, June 26, 1926, p. 1971.

handling 682 tons of less-than-carload freight between two cities approximately 200 miles apart. It showed that clerical costs, platform costs, and switching costs at both terminals amounted to $4.80 per ton. This compares with the other selected cost items as follows:

	Per Ton	Per cent
Terminal and transfer (clerical, platform, and switching)	$4.80	74.8
Road haul, including empty movement	1.10	18.0
Car maintenance	.17	2.5
Freight claims	.30	4.7
Sum of above costs	$6.43	100.0

Direct terminal and transfer costs, according to this exhibit, were over four times as large as road haul costs.

Another exhibit filed in the same case by the New York Central Railroad showing movement in October 1928 of 257 tons of less-than-carload freight between two cities 400 miles apart, showed total clerical, platform, and switching costs at both terminals as $6.70. This compares with other selected items as follows:

	Per Ton	Per cent
Terminal and transfer (clerical, platform, and switching)	$6.70	71.0
Road haul, including empty movement	2.24	23.5
Car maintenance	.41	4.3
Freight claims	.12	1.2
Sum of above costs	$ .47	100.0

In this case direct terminal and transfer costs were three times as great as road haul costs.

The cost to shippers of terminal cartage on less-than-carload units is also high. In the New York metropolitan area minimum single package shipments cost 50 cents to

$1.00 a package to transport to or from railroad stations. In larger lots, which usually average 200 to 300 pounds per consignment, and 600 to 700 pounds per truck load destined to an average of three railroads, these rates run from 10 cents to 20 cents per hundred pounds.

The accompanying diagram shows allocated direct costs for moving a ton of merchandise less-than-carload freight from a door in one city to a door in another.

DIRECT COST PER TON OF DOOR-TO-DOOR HANDLING OF L.C.L. FREIGHT (LINE HAUL 450 MILES)

CITY"A"				LINE HAUL	CITY"B"			
PICK-UP	TERMINAL AND TRANSFER			LINE HAUL	TERMINAL AND TRANSFER			DELIVERY
CARTAGE	BILLING AND OTHER CLERICAL	PLATFORM	SWITCHING AND TRANSFER	LINE HAUL	SWITCHING AND TRANSFER	PLATFORM	BILLING AND OTHER CLERICAL	CARTAGE
$2.20	$1.52	$1.39	$1.11	$2.30	$0.74	$0.93	$1.01	$1.50

NOTE: These figures cover direct costs only. For total costs, including rent, taxes, depreciation, and overhead add 25 per cent for railroad items; for cartage add 40 per cent.

RATIO OF DIRECT TERMINAL COST TO LINE HAUL COST

I. Railroad only ....$\dfrac{6.70}{2.30} = 2.9$

II. Railroad and cartage ....$\dfrac{10.40}{2.30} = 4.5$

The two cities are located in the East. The railroad figures are based on an actual study made in 1928 to determine the cost of moving goods from the outbound station to the receiving station. The cartage figures are based on average costs for trucking in the two cities. The summary of the actual railroad study, from which the diagram figures are taken, did not show the cost for each terminal separately; it merely gave the combined cost for each item. Since the average operating costs of the terminals in the two cities may be considered in the ratio of 4:6, the diagram figures were obtained by breaking down the summarized costs in this ratio. To get total railroad costs including interest, depreciation, taxes, overhead items, etc., 25 per cent may be added to the figures shown. The total cartage costs may be obtained by adding 40 per cent. These percentages are in accord with actual data obtained.

The high cost and slow movement of freight at and through terminals are due in part to the awkward and antiquated layouts of terminals and their facilities; lack of unlimited terminal co-operation among the various railroads or railroad groups; certain unwarranted duplicate facilities; multiple handling of cars and goods; poor transfer set-ups; and large wasteful outlays on facilities built in an effort to attract traffic to individual roads or separate groups of roads. The general problem of terminal unification will be discussed in Chapter XXXIII. In this chapter consideration will be given to the ways in which a better co-ordination of rail and truck facilities would contribute toward a reduction of terminal costs.

1. Co-ordination through use of auxiliary transfer equipment. An ideal co-ordination of rail and highway transport beyond the zone where the truck may do the work alone more economically and with speedier service, would be an arrangement whereby the trucker might take the goods from the door of the shipper in some kind of container to a point on the railroad outside of the congested areas, and transfer the shipment for rail haul, then retransfer to highway, and thence to door of consignee. Means for doing this through use of the present forms of container, demountable truck body, rail wagon, etc., are satisfactory to some railroads, shippers,

FIGURE I

Transfer of containers from railroad car to motor vehicle

FIGURE 2

Transfer of lime containers

(Brick containers have same dimensions.)

and truckers; but others object to the size of the transfer vehicles, the method of placing them on flat cars, and the cost. It would seem that concentrated effort would develop standard equipment that would be suited to universal unit transfer service, from the point of view of cost, dimensions, capacity, weight, and mobility. Such equipment would save rehandling and sorting of goods. It is recognized that some truckers prefer to re-sort to suit their method of delivery to consignee. Whatever type of equipment is adopted it must provide safety and have standard features that will permit ready transfer to cars of different railroads.

Figures 1 and 2 show types of steel container in use today, while Figure 3 shows one type of demountable truck body.

The less-than-carload container is intended to provide a means of conveyance of smaller proportions than the box car, yet capable of taking suitable lots of less-than-carload freight as unit shipments. Its primary purpose is to give the shipper a more expeditious service and a cheaper rate. It has also come to be used by some railroads themselves. The so-called standard containers have a maximum capacity varying from 7,000 to something over 10,000 pounds but experience has demonstrated that 7,500 represents a high average load.

The container is placed at the door of the shipper or consignee for loading or unloading. Trucking is done by or for the user of this service, who must also provide facilities for transfer of the container to and from the truck. The shippers' packing and wrapping costs are reduced or entirely eliminated, loss and damage is practically eliminated, and the service is faster. The advantages to the railroads are: simplification of billing operations, reduction of light loading and increasingly expensive merchandise car movements, and fewer transfers in the rail movements.

The device first came into use between Cleveland and Chicago in 1921, and it was introduced between Buffalo and New York in 1922. Since then it has become available between a large number of cities in the eastern part of the country. The New York Central lines in 1922, 1927, and 1930 handled 278, 10,217, and 47,886 containers respectively. Between June 20, 1928 and January 3, 1931, the Pennsylvania Railroad handled 63,084 containers.[2] Forwarding companies have used containers to quite an extent. It has been said that the recent so-called "all commodity" rates have not been favorable to the extended use of the containers.

Use of containers by railroads themselves to replace box cars in station-to-station service makes for a reduction of sortings of less-than-carload freight and of expensive, lightly loaded car movements, as well as for speedier service. Containers have been used to a limited extent in handling such bulk freight as bricks, cement, and lime.

Container-concentrating points are sometimes used and wider development of the practice has been suggested. In some instances where this is done the containers themselves are trucked to such points; in others the contents are trucked for loading there.

The Pennsylvania Railroad makes use of containers in place of box cars between a considerable number of Eastern and Middle Western stations, and has eliminated a number of its transfer stations where formerly less-than-carload freight was transferred and consolidated en route.

[2] 182 I.C.C. 342.

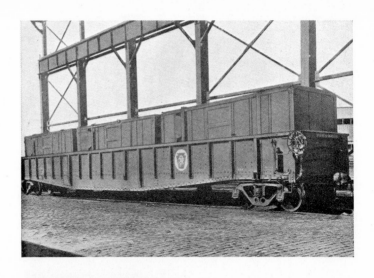

FIGURE 3

Top: Three truck bodies in a railroad car placed under crane for unloading

Bottom: Trailer with demountable body coupled to truck for movement over city street

Some railroad officers are not impressed with the present type of container, believing it to be too heavy and too small. Successful use of the container depends on a more or less universal use, which in turn requires standardization for easy exchange of equipment.

The demountable truck body was first used in 1917 in the Cincinnati terminal area, and since 1919 it has been used by all railroads at that terminal. It is used in effecting a more rapid and cheaper transfer of less-than-carload freight between main stations and sub-stations of each road, and stations of different roads.

Some railroad men look with favor upon the line hauling of truck bodies to save rehandling of unit loads and to obviate the necessity of expensive highway hauls. This provides means for linking up existing facilities of rail carriers and service of truck companies. The possibility of the demountable truck body as a device for holding traffic to the railroads has been suggested. Many believe that the demountable truck body is more suitable for handling small shipments than the smaller railroad cars which have been proposed.

The Pennsylvania Railroad has used demountable truck equipment between Philadelphia and New York. Rates for such movement between these points makes it profitable to the trucker to dispense with the line hauls in some cases and at the same time give as quick service as he can get through use of the highways.

Truck-body tariffs, effective November 5, 1931, were filed by the Pennsylvania, the Baltimore and Ohio, the Reading, the Central Railroad of New Jersey, and the Lackawanna for application between Baltimore and Jersey City, Baltimore, and Richmond, and Philadelphia and Jersey City. They were permitted to take effect without suspension by the Interstate Commerce Commission. Rates vary with size of body.[3]

The so-called rail wagon differs from the container and the demountable truck body in that the entire unit, which is equivalent to a trailer, is run on to a specially constructed under-car for inter-city movement. This feature is said to facilitate the making up and breaking down of trains, to effect quicker collections and deliveries, and to save railroad station and terminal expense. No lifting devices are required. An inexpensive concrete ramp is used to place the body on the car.

This type of equipment has been used since September 1930 by an electric railway running between Cleveland and Toledo. A somewhat similar arrangement, consisting of closed sealed trailers, is in use on the Chicago, North Shore and Milwaukee Railroad (electric) in connection with its ferry and truck service. Various types of rail wagons are being experimented with. It would seem that further development along this line might lead to a universally accepted mode of hauling unit shipments.[4]

Light trucks in the form of large platform trucks have been experimented with and used in a few places for picking up and distributing loads to points very near freight platforms.

2. *Co-ordination through pick-up and delivery service.* Except in one or two isolated cases[5] American rail-

[3] 182 I.C.C. 344.

[4] 182 I.C.C. 345.

[5] Store-door delivery was furnished for a number of years at Baltimore and Washington on higher class shipments from New England, New York, and Philadelphia. The service was instituted in 1883 in the case of Washington and earlier in the case of Baltimore. It was in every respect unique and was abolished by the carriers in 1913 on a finding by the Interstate Commerce Commission that withdrawal of the service in one place and its retention in another was unduly discriminatory. 27 I.C.C. 347.

roads have not rendered pick-up and delivery service. In England and Canada this form of service has been given for many years. One of the reasons why certain freight traffic has gone to the truck is the appeal which store-door delivery service has to some shippers. In an effort to retrieve this traffic certain railroads have developed a plan comprising truck pick-up and delivery with rail line-haul. This type of service may be complete from door of shipper to door of consignee; from door of shipper to freight station in the territory of the consignee; or from freight station of shipper to door of consignee. Some of the lines adopting the general plan are the St. Louis Southwestern, the Texas and Pacific, the Missouri Pacific in Arkansas and Texas, the Missouri-Kansas-Texas of Texas, the Spokane, Portland, and Seattle, the Pacific Electric, the Southern Pacific lines in Texas, the Pacific lines of the Southern Pacific, the Yazoo and Mississippi Valley, and the Long Island Railroad.

The Long Island Railroad inaugurated its service in conjunction with the Railway Express Agency a short time ago and finds that there is a clear indication of recovery of certain business formerly lost to the motor truck. In the near future all shippers in four boroughs of New York City and the Metropolitan district in New Jersey will be given optional pick-up and delivery service for carload and less-than-carload lots. The proposed charges, in addition to the rail rate, are 6 cents to 20 cents per hundred pounds, depending on the carload minimum weight of the official classification, with special rates for newsprint paper, flour, automobiles, and silk; and higher rates for less-than-carload lots. Under this arrangement the terminal trucking agency employed by the carrier distributes the inbound freight from the carrier's break-bulk station to store door and collects the tariff charge from the consignee. The reverse applies for outbound shipments. All railroads furnishing the services in the Southwest agreed to an arrangement which was made effective November 16, 1931, whereby pick-up and delivery service is provided at regular rail rates to distances in certain instances up to 300 miles and at a charge of 20 cents for 100 pounds at a greater distance. Trucking in general is contracted for by local draymen.[6] The Southern Pacific lines have found that they can give better service and at less cost by operating, to a large extent, their own trucks, through their subsidiary, the Pacific Motor Transport Company.

There seems to be general agreement among railroads and shippers that many shipments require the pick-up and delivery service. The general trend toward a new type of distribution made possible by the truck unconsciously makes people, including railroad men themselves, think less in terms of less-than-carload and carload lots, and more in terms of truck loads. This new thought is very pronounced in certain railroad circles. A wider use of pick-up and delivery service may revolutionize certain industries. Mr. J. R. Turney, traffic vice-president of the St. Louis Southwestern Railroad, envisages the possibility of obsolete industrial tracks for many on-rail shippers in the distant future.[7]

The inability of the so-called cartage service in Canada to stem the tide of motor competition illustrates the necessity of meeting trucking rates as well as service to make pick-up and delivery truly effective, at least from the present railroad point of view. In spite of the service the

[6] 182 I.C.C. 340.
[7] *Traffic World*, Nov. 26, 1932, p. 1040.

Canadian railroads have lost to truckers a large part of their less-than-carload business.

For the store-door service the usual arrangement is for the railroad to organize a subsidiary trucking company, which in turn contracts with local truckers for pick-up and delivery. Rates are quoted and bills of lading issued by the trucking subsidiaries. The rates are usually equal to the regular rail station-to-station rates, though in some cases they are made equal to those of certified highway competitors. Rates of the latter, as a rule, do not differ widely from the rail level. The subsidiary company remunerates the local trucker, pays the railroad for line haul, and after the deduction of a percentage for contingencies and other percentages for returns on investment, pays over the remainder of the gross receipts to the railroad.

3. Co-ordination through express and forwarding companies. The Railway Express Agency has an investment of about $9,500,000 in motor vehicle property. Recently it operated nearly nine thousand motor trucks and about 450 trailers in city service.[8] The management is giving consideration to the practicability of extending operations to include the handling of all less-than-carload freight of rail carriers.

As has been previously stated, the Agency and the Pennsylvania Railroad are experimenting with the express-freight service on Long Island. Should railroads in general co-ordinate with the Agency in this service, the company may contract with private truckers to handle a large bulk of the traffic. In this way the private truckmen would become potential solicitors for business.

[8] 182 I.C.C. 348.

Forwarding and consolidating freight companies, in recent years, have developed a pick-up and delivery service through the use of trucks under their control. They consolidate miscellaneous shipments of less-than-carload freight and divide with the shippers the difference between carload and less-than-carload rates. Several of the larger companies are under railroad control, and through their organizations effect a certain degree of co-ordination of rail-motor service.

4. Co-ordination through union off-rail freight stations and merchandise warehouses. Recently there has been considerable agitation to build inland or off-rail freight stations. The union inland off-rail freight station recently built by the Port of New York Authority at Fifteenth Street and Eighth Avenue, is an excellent example of a station operated by all trunk line railroads to handle less-than-carload freight in a large metropolitan area. The building is 14 stories high, the basement and first floor constituting the terminal, the upper stories being used for warehouse purposes, manufacturing, and general loft building space. Large elevators connect the various floors with the terminal. Goods manufactured in the building can be delivered by elevator directly to outbound platforms of the station. Local truckers can deliver their goods to the terminal and after clearing the goods are taken out by trucks connecting with particular railroad stations. A well planned and well managed layout of this type attracts truckers and through its use they can handle freight at a lower rate. Some truck rates have already been reduced because of relief from congestion and attendant saving of time in loading and unloading.

Of nearly three thousand warehouses listed in the 1931 Directory of Distribution and Warehouses, 430 reported some form of trucking activity. Truck lines were operated by 176 warehouses, truck terminals by 160, while 94 operated both truck lines and terminals.[9]

St. Louis, Grand Rapids, Louisville, Indianapolis, and Sioux City have central terminals where the greater part of the local freight is cleared. In one of the St. Louis terminals there are scheduled motor freight rates for 400 communities in six states. From this terminal, truck service is given by over forty companies.

Off-rail freight terminals and warehouses, both large and small, are located in many cities to act as transfer points for local and over-the-highway truck hauling. Co-ordination is effected through merchandise warehouses to which goods move by rail in carloads and from which the warehouseman, directly or by truck distribution, provides service to the local dealers or to nearby communities. Here, again, quicker service is provided than is available by rail alone. Forwarding companies and chain stores are consigning carload shipments directly to terminal warehouses.

In a number of cities there are truck depots for receiving and forwarding freight, and through these stations interline movement is handled. Sometimes the depots are built in conjunction with warehouses and storage plants; large trucks operating over the highway sometimes using them as central clearing stations, the light truck picking up and delivering at nearby points. The depots are generally used by common carrier operators who utilize them for picking up return loads. The following quotation indicates the activities of some depots:[10]

[9] R. E. Plimpton, "Distribution Advances with the Motor Truck," in *Journal of Land and Public Utility Economics*, August 1931.

[10] 72 Cong., S. doc. 43.

A truck depot was established at Sioux City, Iowa, in 1928 following upon the great increase in livestock trucked into Sioux City in order to afford return loads for such trucks. The Sioux City truck depot handled 49,180,481 pounds of outbound merchandise in 1930, an increase of 38 per cent over 1929. About 47 common-carrier operators using 250 trucks handle merchandise from this depot over a radius of 150 miles. They directly serve about 500 towns and connect with other truck lines radiating out of Sioux Falls, S.D., and Omaha, Neb. The Sioux City depot gives 24-hour service except on Saturdays and Sundays. The average amount per month handled by the trucks from January 1 to October 1, 1930, was 4,177,931 pounds. Besides the common-carrier trucks some 700 other truck operators bringing livestock into Sioux City compete for outbound merchandise.

At Indianapolis the union truck terminal handled about 78,000 tons inbound and outbound in 1930. A truck depot at Louisville, Ky., serves 33 common-carrier truck lines operating about 200 trucks within a radius of 150 miles.

One of three truck depots at Seattle handled 27,856 tons of freight in 1925 and 30,468 tons during the first 10 months of 1930. Facilities are provided for assembling shipments to other States and to Canada, Alaska, and the Orient. The truck terminal receives and checks all shipments, applies the rates, assumes responsibility for carriage and accounting, for loss and damage claims, and C.O.D. shipments. Shippers are not required to take up matters with the individual truck operator. Goods destined to Alaska or the Orient from Portland, Ore., and moved by truck from that point to the depot in Seattle and thence by truck to the dock, constitute a through shipment, Portland to the docks, and the rate is so made. From 80 to 115 trucks, varying with the season, use the terminal. The truck terminal is open from 8 A.M. until 6.30 P.M.; rail terminals at Seattle close at 4 or 4.30 P.M.

The off-rail inland freight station in New York is a railroad truck depot; in other words it is not designed to tie up to over-the-highway trucking. As co-ordinated service advances there is no reason why a motor truck freight depot cannot serve as part of a rail freight depot and warehouse.

The foregoing analysis indicates that improvements in terminal conditions resulting in great economies can be realized with a relatively small outlay of capital. The problem consists mainly of developing a high degree of rail and truck co-ordination through extensive terminal trucking. Certain minor changes in the present layout of freight houses and their facilities would be involved. The motor truck could be substituted more extensively for trap or peddler car service between freight stations and industries in terminal districts; it could replace freight car service between main freight stations and sub-stations located in metropolitan areas; it could be used in place of freight car service between freight stations on different railroads which have a steady interchange of less-than-carload business; and it could be used as a carrier of freight to consolidating stations located just outside of the busy terminal districts, thus relieving congestion. In many port cities trucking can be done in place of certain lighterage service. For various transfer operations within and outside of the terminal areas, almost unlimited use of the truck with proper auxiliary equipment could be made. These improvements are independent of those which might be realized by a general reorganization of railroad terminals, or by the complete unification of all terminal facilities. The possible economies in these directions are discussed in Chapters XXXIII and XXXVI.

II. IN LINE HAUL FREIGHT MOVEMENT

Railroad efficiency in line haul movement of carload freight, generally speaking, has increased greatly during the past decade. This is particularly true in the case of through service; but in the case of short haul movements, way-freight service, distribution near large cities, and movement in zones where general traffic is heavy, the rate of travel is slow and the costs run high.

1. *High cost and slow movement.* Operations involving short haul movements of less-than-carload lots and package freight have seldom proved profitable to railroads and in many instances have been conducted at a loss—the standard rail equipment and method of operation not being well suited to this class of business. For a number of years railroads have operated their local way-freight or so-called peddler train service at rising costs. These trains are slow moving, as they serve stations along the route. The tonnage is small, the handling of freight expensive, and the level of rates is kept low to prevent the loss of traffic. These trains hamper fast through-freight running in territory where traffic is heavy, causing an indirect loss. The slow movement and relatively higher cost of local service have permitted the truck to cut into the traffic and attempts to hold this unprofitable business to the rails have been ineffective.

In many cases the present facilities and equipment for handling small shipments are excessive and very expensive to operate, thereby creating an out-of-pocket cost that has been a disturbing factor to railroad management. In order to counteract this loss the rates on other services are necessarily higher than they would otherwise be.

2. *Co-ordinated motor service.* This includes trucking from station to station to replace certain way-freight trains, and trucking between selected distributing and concentrating centers for less-than-carload freight in order to eliminate station stops and permit straight car shipments.

Hauling traffic by rail from large merchandise shipping centers to well located zone stations, from which goods are immediately taken by trucks to other stations, has expedited shipments over some railroads. Before the truck came into use it was the practice to concentrate the rail traffic at important zone stations from which the freight was sent by local or peddler trains to its destination on the following day. This added an extra day from point of origin to destination. Saving this time and cutting down the period of transit by trucking through the terminal area at shipping centers has resulted in much better service.

For a number of years certain railroads, including the Pennsylvania, the New York Central, the St. Louis Southwestern, the New Haven, and the Boston and Maine, have been substituting motor service for line haul movements. The Pennsylvania and New York Central lines began experimenting with truck service in 1923. Recently the former operated 49 routes in replacement of local way-freights. The operations of the New York Central include station-to-station motor service in place of way-freight, service between stations on the same division to avoid the handling of freight at intermediate transfer stations, hauling by truck from smaller to larger stations to make straight car loading from the larger stations, hauling by truck from central delivery stations to small outlying stations where final delivery is made to consignees, interchange service between railroad and steamship lines in place of lighterage service, and use of containers.[11]

The Boston and Maine Railroad is making extensive

[11] G. L. Wilson, *Co-ordinated Motor-Rail-Steamship Transportation*, p. 97.

use of the motor to co-ordinate rail and highway transport. In 1925 it introduced motor trucking and since that time has extended its service, more or less as a by-product, to include store-door pick-up and delivery service of freight entirely by truck or by a combination of rail and truck. Its trucks replace certain way-freight trains besides acting as concentrating and distributing mediums to and from designated concentration points on its lines. A subsidiary company operates the motor service. The highway service was organized to compete with independent trucking companies as well as to replace certain trains.

The railroad has designated concentration points or depots at important cities for the collection of freight. Less-than-carload shipments are consolidated into straight car loads at these main depots, from which the freight is forwarded by rail freight service. For points within the zone of a concentration depot, inbound less-than-carload shipments are received and distributed by truck to local stations or doors of consignees. This cuts down the number of stops of certain way-freight trains and eliminates other trains entirely.

Other railroads operating trucks over the highway include the St. Louis Southwestern, Southern Pacific, Reading, and New Haven. Reports indicate that the advantage of truck co-ordination in some fields is lessened because of competitive practices which are resorted to by both railroad and trucking companies. If both agencies would face the problem squarely, a high degree of truck co-ordination seems entirely practical.

The basic policy of certain railroads relative to co-ordinating their truck activities with that of rail service seems to involve two principal objectives; namely, to increase rail revenue where there is a large volume of truck traffic by substituting freight train service for the road haul portion of truck service; and to decrease rail expense where there is a small amount of rail traffic by substituting trucks for light package freight trains. In working toward the first objective one railroad has a four-step program; namely, (1) to secure common carrier truck operating rights on the highway for its subsidiary trucking company; (2) to operate a reliable trucking service in such a manner as to secure all possible competitive truck traffic between commercial centers and intermediate points, both truck load and small lots; (3) to replace subsidiary trucking service by that of competitors on inter-line truck traffic to and from territory outside the railroad's operating areas; and (4) when truck traffic has been developed by the subsidiary company in sufficient volume, to divert a substantial amount of the road haul through the medium of demountable truck bodies or the so-called "box car" systems, by joint facility contract with the railroad on a car-mile or some other basis.

Shortage of box cars drove many railroads to the use of the truck in the first place. It was then that the special advantages of trucking became recognized. An extension of co-ordinated service by all railroads along the lines indicated should result in economies and improvement of service; some of the traffic which has left the rail would return. If the railroads want the business they may either operate trucks of their own, gain a financial interest in existing motor companies, or contract the work out to independent trucking concerns.

III. CO-ORDINATED RAILROAD BUS SERVICE

As we show in Chapter V there has been a great decrease in railroad passenger traffic since the war. The decline has been most marked on short independent lines on interurban railways, and on branch lines.

1. *High cost of hauling certain passenger traffic.* Today many railroads are maintaining standard equipment and facilities far in excess of the amount required for handling the present traffic; also, between many points various railroads have been practically duplicating one another's service, in spite of the decreasing amount of business. However, it is realized that in some instances the railroad lines diverge to a great extent between common termini, and what appears to be an inexcusable duplication may be somewhat justified on further investigation.

2. *Manner of effecting economies.* Real economy may be brought about by substituting bus service for all-rail operation on unprofitable branch lines where passenger traffic is light. The bus can also be made to replace local trains on main lines.

Bus operation in lieu of all-rail branch line and local main line service which railroads have found impossible or disadvantageous to abandon, has become quite common. The St. Louis Southwestern, Pennsylvania, Boston and Maine, and New Haven railroads are some of the lines which have achieved substantial operating economies by bus substitution as well as providing more frequent service. While the bus operations themselves have in many cases proved unprofitable, the substitution has eliminated greater losses in maintaining all-rail service. Improved high speed rail-motor cars, like the rubber tired highspeed Diesel-Electric Budd car now being experimented with by the Reading Railroad, may show important economies and that will show this type of equipment to be a good substitute for standard rail equipment, especially where mail, express, and baggage traffic is handled. In many cases where the bus has ultimately been used, the gasoline-electric rail-motor was first substituted for the regular steam trains.

Except for terminal convenience, as in the case of the Baltimore and Ohio Railroad service from Manhattan to Jersey City, and the furnishing of service to off-rail points, such as parks and resorts, bus operation as a supplementary feeder service seems to have gained but little headway. Experience seems to show that bus lines do not in general act as feeders for rail service. Usually bus lines tie in with one another rather than with the railway. When co-ordination develops to a certain point, however, it would seem that bus lines could act as substantial feeders and distributors from and to off-rail points.

Bus operation over the highways, that is, activities independent of rail service, are carried on by independent motor operators and also by companies controlled by railroads or in which the latter have a substantial interest. The St. Louis Southwestern operations in Texas, New Mexico, Tennessee, and Missouri; the operations of the Boston and Maine, the Reading, the Central Railroad of New Jersey, Union Pacific and the Chicago and North-Western through the Interstate Transit Lines between Chicago and Los Angeles, St. Louis and Kansas City, and Omaha, Minneapolis and St. Paul, are indicative of direct railroad activities in bus service. Among operations conducted by companies in which railroads have a substantial interest may be included the various Greyhound Lines. For example, the Pacific-Greyhound, in which the

Southern Pacific has one-third stock interest, operates along the Pacific coast and east to Salt Lake City and to El Paso; the Southland-Greyhound Lines, in which the Southern Pacific has 35 per cent stock interest, operating in Texas; the Pennsylvania-Greyhound Lines and its subsidiaries, in which the Pennsylvania Railroad has a half interest, etc. In general the principal bus lines parallel the railroads in which they are financially interested; in some cases they go into the territory of other railroads.[12]

While some of the principal bus lines are yielding a nice profit, many are not so fortunate. It would seem that the bus lines should profit by errors made by the railroads in the past; that they should not attempt to pyramid and duplicate to so great an extent. Through cooperation they should be able to build up systems where duplication and competitive wastes could be held to a minimum. Consolidation on the part of the railroads can bring this about, because of the railroads' direct interest in the motor bus service.

IV. RAILROAD USE OF MOTOR VEHICLES

In the preparation of data that were used in connection with Interstate Commerce Commission Docket 23400,[13] questionnaires brought out the following:

(a) Intercorporate relationships of rail and motor carriers

There are four ways in which carriers subject to the act engage or participate in motor-vehicle operations, (1) directly as part of their other operations, (2) through subsidiary companies, organized for the purpose or acquired by purchase of existing operations, (3) through acquiring a stock interest in independent

---

[12] 182 I.C.C. 351.
[13] 182 I.C.C. 263, 393.

companies, and (4) by means of contracts with independent operators.

Direct operations are limited in number and are illustrated by certain minor operations of the Monongahela Railway and Chicago, Milwaukee, St. Paul and Pacific Railroad. Here the investment in motor-vehicle facilities and the results of operations are merged with and made a part of the rail operations.

The second type is the most common. Examples are Boston and Maine Transportation Company of the Boston and Maine Railroad, New England Transportation Company of the New York, New Haven and Hartford Railroad, Southwestern Transportation Company, subsidiary of the St. Louis Southwestern Railroad, and Interstate Transit Lines, jointly owned by the Union Pacific and the Chicago and North Western. In this case the general practice is to maintain separate investment and operating accounts for the subsidiary, only the final results being taken into the books of the parent company. However, as indicated by part (d) below, there are instances in which the accounting is merged with that of the rail carrier. Provisions for the distribution of joint expenses and for intercompany payments for services rendered vary considerably. In some cases the subsidiary itself enters into contracts with independent operators.

The third type is illustrated by the interests which railroads have acquired in various of the Greyhound companies. In some instances the interest is held through the agency of a holding company. Thus through Pennsylvania Greyhound lines, Incorporated, the Pennsylvania Railroad has a half-interest in eight bus lines whose property investment totals $5,935,667, and through American Contract and Trust Company it has substantial interests in seven trucking companies.

Operations by contract with independent truck companies are especially numerous on the New York Central and the Pennsylvania.

(b) Extent of truck operations of Class I railroads,
January 1 to June 30, 1930

During the period January 1 to June 30, 1930, 18 Class I railroads engaged in intercity or terminal motor trucking operations on one or more of the three bases first indicated in (a) above. Operations were over about 8,865 miles of intrastate and 1,547 miles of interstate routes. Some 551 trucks and 115 trailers were used. (In 1927, 114 trucks and 34 trailers were in use.) The traffic reported by 13 of these companies totaled 413,259 tons, on which revenue of $1,385,369 was earned.

(c) Extent of bus operations of Class I railroads, January 1 to June 30, 1930

During the above period 34 Class I railroads conducted bus operations, directly through subsidiary companies or through companies in which a financial interest is held. Some 3,105 busses were used and operations were over 38,169 miles of intrastate and 27,632 miles of interstate route compared with 745 busses operated over 2,856 miles of intrastate and 1,051 miles of interstate route in 1927. In all, 35,931,000 passengers were carried or, excluding city operations, 20,007,554. The total passenger revenue accrued, including that from city service, was $16,182,029. (Excluding Southwestern Transportation Company, which did not report the number of passengers carried.)

(d) Financial results of truck and bus operations of Class I railroads, year ended December 31, 1929

Returns of the carriers to our questionnaire do not in all cases make it possible to show separately the results of their freight and passenger operations. . . . [Their] total investment on December 31, 1929, was $46,114,891. Of the companies for which complete information was returned 20 reported operating incomes ranging from $457 to $866,356 and aggregating $2,036,054, while 27 reported operating deficits ranging from $672 to $264,285 and aggregating $868,185. After making various corporate adjustments, 21 companies had net income totaling $1,547,967, and 26 had net deficits totaling $942,268. Offsetting many of the deficits shown are savings resulting from the removal of unprofitable train service.

Since the foregoing data were received by the Interstate Commerce Commission certain railroads have greatly increased their activities in the motor field, one case being that of the Reading through its subsidiary the Reading Transportation Company. While its activities are still in the development stage, it is doing pioneer work and gaining experience in anticipation of a more or less complete system of rail and motor co-ordination.

The managers of most railroads believe that it is highly necessary to set up a special division to oversee the motor operations of the company. The management and personnel of this motor division should be motor minded so that old railroad ideas will not hamper proper co-ordination. Such men are quick to grasp special advantages which the use of the truck may afford. While certain railroads, through strong subsidiary companies, operate their own motor vehicles, most railroads contract with independent concerns to perform trucking services. It is stated by some railroad men that the principal reason for utilizing the services of going motor companies has been to stimulate local good will rather than incur ill will by performing the service with railroad trucks. At the same time they avail themselves of the services of an experienced organization.

After three years' experience with the operation of pick-up and delivery service on the Southern Pacific Lines, the Pacific Motor Transport Company, a subsidiary, finds that it can give a better and cheaper service by operating its own trucks, with a few exceptions.[14] In its operations throughout the states of California, Arizona, Nevada, and Oregon, its pick-up and delivery service as far as physical operation is concerned is similar to that of the Railway Express Agency; that is, the haul between

[14] L. B. Young, V.P. and Gen. Manager, Pacific Motor Transport Company, "Cutting the Cost of Storedoor Delivery," *Railway Age*, Dec. 24, 1932.

cities and towns is performed by the railroad in railroad cars, while the pick-up and delivery is done by motor trucks. The Reading Railroad is also of the opinion that co-ordination, in general, can be kept under better control through operation of railroad owned equipment.

From evidence at hand it is more or less obvious that each railroad should set up a strong motor division in order to make co-ordinated rail-motor transport truly effective. Whether each railroad or group of railroads should organize a strong subsidiary motor company may be a question. Obviously, the railroads should control or at least hold a financial interest in certain strong and well organized key companies. It would seem that all possible use should be made of local truckers to handle part of the local business, since each one, through close personal contacts with business concerns, becomes a potential freight solicitor. Even though the railroads should arrange for the Railway Express Agency to handle certain less-than-carload business, the latter would do well to contract certain work out to independent local truckers for the solicitation and good will feature involved. The personal touch between responsible local draymen and shippers is a contact that should lead to a most satisfactory transport service.

V. SUMMARY

A survey and study of rail and highway transport—with co-ordination as the basic objective—to the end that the best possible system of land transportation be established at lowest cost, brings out the following points:

1. Co-ordination to a high degree, of rail and motor operation, should make possible an ideal form of land transport, joining the flexibility of trucks in terminal operations with the low cost of road haul by rail.

2. The motor vehicle may be used by railroads to improve their own rail operations; it may be used by independent operators or groups in competition with rail transport; or it may be employed by railroads themselves for the purpose of engaging in a general motor operating business. The highest degree of co-ordination is involved in the first case.

3. The greater the railroads' participation in motor transportation the greater may be the extent of co-ordination. Rail-motor co-ordination can best be accomplished through use and not through restriction. Thought should run along the line of rails *and* motors; not rails *versus* motors.

4. The rail and motor should co-ordinate more especially at points where railroad operations are most limited and expansion most difficult and costly; namely, in urban areas. A comprehensive use of the motor at terminals will relieve the railroads of various forms of costly and delayed service, such as trap car service and movements that require excessive switching, as well as a certain amount of lighterage and car floating in port cities. For transfer and consolidation of freight, the motor truck, trailer, and demountable truck body are admirably suited.

5. Proper co-ordination of rail and motor to the degree of setting up effective pick-up and delivery service should in most cases relieve congestion in terminal districts; greatly increasing the capacity of certain freight stations and permitting the elimination of others. Store-door delivery, however, is not to be regarded as a panacea.

6. In the unification of freight terminals or steps leading thereto, the truck can play an important part in in-

creased flexibility of operation. Unification in practically all cases is necessary for flexibility and expeditious terminal handling of goods at low costs to public, shipper, and carrier.

7. To secure the fullest benefit from co-ordinated rail and highway transport, there should be utilized and further developed practical auxiliary equipment along the line of containers, demountable truck bodies, and trailers. This would permit efficient handling of unit shipments.

8. The bus can be used to replace certain unprofitable branch line passenger service as well as that of local main line trains. The use of the motor will permit the pruning of railroad equipment and facilities, including stations and general structures, and create a great saving. Bus lines often serve a class of people who might not be able to travel by rail.

9. More extended use can be made of the motor to replace way-freight and peddler trains, and to consolidate freight at zone stations.

PART VII

OTHER TRANSPORTATION AGENCIES

CHAPTER XXX

OIL AND GASOLINE PIPE LINES

Pipe lines constitute a unique specialized transportation system developed by the petroleum industry for its own use. They serve the oil industry in three ways: (1) by assembling crude oil at central points for storage or shipment to a refinery; (2) by trunk line shipments of crude oil to refineries or marine shipping terminals; and (3) by long distance shipment of the principal refined product, gasoline, from field refineries or tidewater refineries or tank terminals. The "gathering" line pipes are laid on top of the ground and the common sizes are two, three, and four inches in diameter. The pipes of the trunk lines, commonly six to eight inches in diameter, with a tendency in recent years toward larger dimensions, are buried in the ground below the freezing level.

The railroads also engage in the movement of crude oil to refineries and of the various refined products to central distributing markets and widely scattered points of consumption. The present competitive situation is that pipe lines do virtually all of the gathering of crude and the great bulk of the overland moving of crude to refineries, while the larger part of the movement of refined products from refinery to retail distribution is by railroad tank car. Railroad pre-eminence in distributing refined products has been affected by truck and barge-line competition, and more recently by the building of pipe lines for gasoline.

The pipe-line mileage of the country is equal to almost 50 per cent of the railway main track mileage. Oil pipe lines measured 111,160 miles on May 1, 1931,[1] of which 58,020 consisted of trunk lines, and 53,640 of "gathering" lines. Gasoline lines (August 1, 1931) totalled 3,210 miles.[2] Thus pipe-line mileage equalled 45 per cent and the longer gasoline lines 1.3 per cent of the railway mileage of the country. Pipe lines are found in only 24 states, and 95 per cent of their principal mileage is in 12 states. The important trunk line mileage radiates out from the Gulf ports to the oil fields of New Mexico, Texas, Oklahoma, Arkansas, and Louisiana, and extends in a broad sweep northeastward from Kansas and the aforementioned oil pools across the states of Missouri, Iowa, Illinois, Indiana, Ohio, and Pennsylvania. The pipe lines of California constitute an entity in themselves.

I. DEVELOPMENT OF THE SYSTEM

The development of pipe lines was an integral part of the growth of the petroleum industry. The first oil well was drilled in Pennsylvania in 1859, and pipe lines appeared shortly thereafter. They were destroyed by teamsters, thousands of whom had developed a profitable business hauling oil to the nearest railroad. The matter culminated in the "Battle of the Teamsters" when the militia was called out. The first successful pipe line, four miles long, began operations among the oilpools of western Pennsylvania in December 1865.

In the earliest days of the industry the principal products were kerosene and lubricants, and refining was done almost entirely near the wells. In 1875 a four-inch line 60 miles long was laid to Pittsburgh, and the

[1] U. S. Bureau of Mines, *Release No. 10,945.*
[2] Bureau of Mines, *Technical Paper No. 517*

development of pipe-line construction increased rapidly after 1876, together with the location of refineries near such large consuming markets as Cleveland, Pittsburgh, Buffalo, Baltimore, Philadelphia, and New York.

Crude oil for these market refineries was gathered by pipe lines and then shipped over the railroads. The Erie, the New York Central, and the Pennsylvania railroads competed actively for the business through their branches in the oil fields. Even then Standard Oil interests were obtaining freight rate rebates of 40-50 per cent on crude oil and 25-45 per cent on refined products.[3]

In 1874 a combination including a number of pipe lines was formed by Pennsylvania Railroad interests. A contest ensued with Standard Oil interests, who presently acquired all of the Pennsylvania Railroad pipe lines and refineries. Although the first important trunk line was built by a group of independents in 1878 (the Tide Water Pipe Co., Ltd., line from the Pennsylvania fields to the Atlantic Coast near New York), the Standard later secured an interest in the line.

The Standard then organized a number of additional pipe line companies, many of which are still operating. Among these were the National Transit Co. in Pennsylvania in 1881; the Buckeye Pipe Line Co. in 1886, to reach the new Lima, Ohio, field; and the Indiana Pipe Line Co. in 1891, to connect this field with its Whiting, Indiana, refinery (built in 1890; the first refinery in the Chicago district). In the late eighties or early nineties the South West Pennsylvania Pipe Line and the Southern Pipe Line Co. built a trunk line to the Atlantic seaboard; the Northern Pipe Line Co. and the New

[3] *Report of Commissioner of Corporations*, 1907, Pt. I, pp. 347-48.

York Transit Co. built a line to the Atlantic coast, and the Eureka Pipe Line Co. built lines into West Virginia. In 1891 Pittsburgh interests built a trunk pipe line to Marcus Hook, Pennsylvania; this became a part of the Standard system in 1895.

Thus by 1892 (the date of the first automobile) there were numerous pipe lines, mostly six inches in diameter, and aggregating 3,000 miles in length, connecting the oil pools of western Pennsylvania with refineries in Eastern cities. With the major pipe line systems in the hands of Standard Oil, which also controlled over 90 per cent of the refining business, producers had to sell their oil to a single company. The railroads in the oil region commonly discriminated against independents in rates for crude and refined products through rebates given the large shipper not only on his own shipments, but also on those made by the independents.

The struggle of one group of independent producers of the Bradford, Pennsylvania, district, against Standard interests and the railroads is one of the epics of the industry. Organized in June 1891, they had a crude oil line from Coraopolis to Oil City and Titusville in operation by January 1893, but it took them ten years more to get their line to tidewater. They desired twin lines, one for crude and one for refined oil. When the line reached Williamsport, they began shipping over the Reading Railroad; this carrier first accepted their traffic, then reversed its policy, not wishing to disturb its relations with its chief oil shipper. The Erie Railroad sent an armed party to prevent the crossing of its right-of-way at Hancock, New York, despite a prior understanding. Nevertheless, the line was put through to Wilkes-Barre in 1893, whence oil was shipped over the Jersey

Central. A million-dollar war chest to aid refiners in the ensuing price war was formed in 1895 as the Pure Oil Company. The line was taken south to Marcus Hook, Pennsylvania, and the first export cargo was loaded in May 1901.

Prior to 1900, as much as 96 per cent of oil production was east of the Mississippi. Between 1901 and 1930, 66 per cent came from west of the Mississippi; and in the year 1930 four states, Texas, Oklahoma, Kansas, and California, together produced 86.5 per cent of all the crude oil in the United States. The first pipe lines in Kansas were laid down in 1903, and shortly thereafter were extended to Missouri and Oklahoma. By 1905 Kansas City was connected with Eastern pipe lines. In 1909-10 an extension across Arkansas gave connection through the Oklahoma Pipe Line Company and the line of the Standard Oil Company of Louisiana with the latter's refinery at North Baton Rouge. By 1914 the Gulf Oil refineries at Fort Worth and Port Arthur were drawing oil from the Mid-continent and Gulf (or coastal) fields of Texas and Louisiana. On January 1, 1914 there were five major companies operating in the Mid-continent field having total trunk lines of 6,059 miles, and total gathering lines of 3,956 miles.[4]

A few short pipe lines were constructed in California in the nineties, but the rapid development came with the opening of the San Joaquin Valley wells shortly after 1900. By 1919 there were five companies operating in California with lines extending 2,439 miles. Since 1920 the California mileage has more than doubled, and the area covered has been greatly widened. Whereas prior

[4] Federal Trade Commission, *Pipe Line Transport of Petroleum*, 1916.

to 1920 the principal movement of crude oil had been by pipe line from the Mid-continent field across the Central Western states, the swift rise of production in the Los Angeles basin in 1923 created a flow of cheaper oil to Atlantic coast refineries, and replaced a large part of the crude previously drawn from the Mid-continent field. The Eastern group of pipe line companies suffered successive losses of traffic as a result of large shipments from the Mexican field in 1920-22, the use of California oil in Eastern refineries beginning in 1923, and the growing volume of tanker shipments from the Gulf during the last few years.

The development since 1920 has been part of the growth of large integrated oil companies, both Standard and independent, distributing refined products over a wide area. Many companies have set up comprehensive transportation systems of their own, combining pipe lines, tankers or barges, and trucks. In the rise of several of the large independent oil companies, they first obtained advantageous production in the new fields as they were developed, and built pipe lines to the already existing transcontinental or Gulf coast lines, and shipped over these common carrier lines or the railroads to refineries which they established in the principal markets. With the numerous oil discoveries in recent years there came adequate oil reserves for all, and the competition shifted to the development of markets. The great growth of industrial, public utility, railroad, marine, and, especially, automotive uses for oil and its products had enormously increased the demands on the oil industry, and the various oil companies secured different positions in serving this market.

Gasoline pipe lines are the latest specialized transportation service developed by the oil industry. While pipe lines have been used to move refined oil and gasoline to tidewater shipping terminals for years, it is only recently that they have been utilized in distributing gasoline to marketing points. On February 1, 1930, the Tuscarora Pipe Line Co. (Standard Oil Company of New Jersey controlled) began transporting gasoline inward from the Bayway refinery on New York harbor; pre-

GROWTH OF INTERSTATE PIPE LINES, 1921–1931[a]
(Dollar figures in thousands)

Year	Miles[b]	Investment	Operating Revenues	Net Income	Dividends Declared
1921	55,260	$365,000	$115,900	$34,400	$32,096
1922	57,349	382,300	128,100	58,568	57,121
1923	64,760	432,100	131,200	62,639	42,962
1924	68,185	496,200	146,900	72,234	41,151
1925	70,009	511,100	164,600	88,495	72,209
1926	72,846	539,400	173,100	80,401	50,929
1927	76,070	609,400	195,600	93,239	74,131
1928	81,676	659,100	222,100	117,206	80,897
1929	85,796	741,000	251,400	142,216	125,314
1930	88,727	772,700	237,900	123,741	132,826
1931	93,090	845,050	222,900	120,738	125,281

[a] Interstate pipe lines reporting to Interstate Commerce Commission, *Statistics of Railways*.
[b] Trunk and gathering lines operated.

viously it had been solely a crude oil pipe line. Since then gasoline lines from tidewater refineries have been built by Socony-Vacuum in New England; by Sun Oil Co. and Atlantic Refining Co. through Pennsylvania to Pennsylvania-Ohio-New York, and Pennsylvania points, respectively; by Phillips Petroleum Co. northward from the Mid-continent field to Wichita, Kansas Cty, and St. Louis; and by a group of six oil companies from their Mid-continent refineries to Omaha, Minneapolis, and Chicago, with other extensions in prospect.

The growth and financial condition of the interstate pipe line industry (oil and gasoline) is shown by the preceding table.

As was already indicated, the total pipe line mileage, including intrastate lines, is 111,160. There are no precise data as to the ton mileage of pipe line traffic; but the Bureau of Railway Economics has made a rough estimate for 1928 of about 30,000,000,000 ton miles.[5] It will be seen from the table that the industry is very profitable and was not affected severely even in the depression year 1931. This is of course attributable to the well sustained demand for oil and gasoline.

II. REGULATION

The interstate pipe lines were made common carriers by the Hepburn Act of June 29, 1906. They were placed under the jurisdiction of the Interstate Commerce Commission, which requires such pipe line companies to file financial and statistical reports upon a standard form. These reports are public records.

A change in the control of pipe line companies resulted from the decree of the Supreme Court on May 15, 1911, dissolving the Standard Oil Trust. Stocks of the pipe line companies were distributed ratably to the shareholders of the old Standard Oil Company of New Jersey, beginning December 1, 1911.

The Interstate Commerce Commission then initiated formal proceedings to require the common carrier pipe lines to file schedules of rates charged. Decision was rendered in this case June 3, 1912, and orders were issued to the common carrier pipe lines to file their rate

[5] Bureau of Railway Economics, *An Economic Survey of Inland Waterway Transportation in the United States*, Special Series 56, 1930, p. 28.

schedules with the Commission on or before September 1, 1912. This order was carried through to the Supreme Court in order to establish the authority of the Commission in the matter. The decision was rendered June 22, 1914, in what are known as "The Pipe Line Cases."[6] The interstate pipe lines were declared to be common carriers in fact, with the single exception of a private line connecting oil wells in Oklahoma with a refinery in Kansas.

No interstate common carrier business had been done by any of the companies operating in the Mid-continent field prior to the *Pipe Line Cases* decision, although both the Texas Co. and the Gulf Oil Co. pipe line system had published tariffs soon after the passage of the Hepburn Act. Prior to this decision the Prairie Pipe Line Co. had refused to act as a common carrier. Soon after the decision, however, it issued tariffs in conjunction with connecting lines for shipments to the refineries east of the Mississippi River. The Oklahoma Pipe Line Co. had always acted as a common carrier for intrastate shipments under the Oklahoma state law, but prior to the decision Prairie Oil and Gas was the only shipper over its lines.

Even when tariffs had been filed with the Interstate Commerce Commission, the use of the Standard Oil pipe lines by independent refineries was precluded in most cases by the size of the minimum quantity required for shipment, and consequently the lines continued to serve only Standard refineries. This situation was attacked in 1922, and a 100,000-barrel minimum requirement was ordered reduced to 10,000 barrels to two points in Pennsylvania. In this case[7] the rates were found to be reasonable, but the minimum tender was reduced.

[6] 234 U. S. 548.
[7] *Brundred Bros.* vs. *Pennsylvania Pipe Line Co.*, 68 I.C.C. 458.

The Commission stated in a letter to the House Committee on Interstate and Foreign Commerce:

This is the one and only occasion on which the Interstate Commerce Commission has been asked to regulate these rates and charges. The Commission has prescribed accounting regulations for pipe line companies, secures periodical reports from them, and has required them to file published schedules of their rates and charges.

1. *Rebates and discriminations in the oil industry.* The history of pipe lines touched on conditions prevailing in the transportation of both crude petroleum and its refined products during the late 70's and early 80's. The Standard Oil interests controlled pipe line transportation, and secured price advantages over its competitors in railroad transportation. Local discrimination in freight rates and the practice of giving rebates to large shippers were common in all industries at this time. Although the enactment of the original Act to Regulate Commerce in 1887 was intended to provide federal regulation of railroad rates, the authority and jurisdiction of the Interstate Commerce Commission was not definitely established for some years, and discriminatory practices continued. Those used in the petroleum industry included rebates and allowance of fictitious claims; blind billing and false waybills; lower rates for tank car shipments; and discontinuance of prorating by connecting railroads.

2. *The "Commodities Clause."* According to the United States Supreme Court the Commodities Clause has for its object to prevent carriers engaged in interstate commerce from being associated in interest at the time of transportation with the commodities transported.[8] When this section of the present Interstate Commerce Act was being drawn, the inclusion of pipe lines with the

[8] 238 U.S. 516.

railroads under its provisions was considered; but as finally enacted May 1, 1908, the Commodities Clause covered the railroads, but specifically excepted all pipe lines. Common carrier status was enforced upon oil pipe lines, but not upon gas and water pipe lines. The specialized nature of pipe line carriers was obvious then, and the struggle of "independent" oil interests to free themselves from railroad discrimination by means of pipe lines was still fresh in the legislators' minds.

More recently there has been renewed agitation for the application of the Commodities Clause to pipe lines. Under date of November 20, 1930, the Association of Railway Executives issued a "Declaration of Policy" suggesting, among other means of equalizing competition between the railroads and other transportation agencies, "that pipe line common carriers be subjected to the same restrictions as to the transportation of commodities in which they are interested, directly or indirectly, as the railroads now are." This would mean that no oil company could own a pipe line, and that private capital would have to take over, or develop anew, this specialized transportation service.

On January 29, 1931, Congressman Hoch introduced a bill proposing to amend the Commodities Clause so as to make it applicable to "any common carrier subject to the provisions of this, the Interstate Commerce Act," rather than just to a "railroad company." At the hearings on this bill on February 17 and 18, 1931, some of the so-called independent oil companies produced witnesses, who offered in testimony the fact that large-scale production, continuous modernization of refineries, and development of markets to the point which justified the erection of lines gave large integrated companies an advantage over small independent producers.

The Interstate Commerce Commission had been asked to review the bill, but replied that it did not possess sufficient information to express an opinion as to whether pipe line conditions called for the application of the Commodities Clause; that while it had limited jurisdiction over pipe line carriers it had had little occasion to exercise this authority. Partly in the light of this situation the House Interstate and Foreign Commerce Committee, to which the Hoch bill was referred, instituted an investigation of pipe lines by sending questionnaires to all the pipe line companies to elicit information as to control, traffic, and charges. As yet the results of this investigation have not been published.

3. *State regulation.* Regulations applicable to pipe lines have been examined in 14 states[9] having the principal pipe line mileage of the country (97½% of total trunk line mileage as of May 1, 1931). All but four have declared oil pipe lines to be common carriers. West Virginia, Missouri, and Wyoming regulate them as they do common carriers by including them in their public utilities acts. Indiana has no specific regulations for pipe lines except that the right of eminent domain is given to them as such. In every state, pipe line companies have the right of eminent domain. In Texas and Oklahoma this may be exercised only after a written acceptance of common carrier status has been filed. In Illinois a certificate of convenience and necessity must be procured.

The regulating body with general powers of supervision and control is the railroad, public service, or public utilities commission, except in Illinois where it is the

[9] Texas, Oklahoma, Pennsylvania, Ohio, Kansas, California, West Virginia, Missouri, Illinois, Louisiana, Indiana, Kentucky, Arkansas, and Wyoming.

Commerce Commission and Oklahoma where it is the Corporation Commission. Oil pipe lines are not specifically subjected to the Railroad Commission of Kentucky or the Public Service Commission of Indiana. Among the specific powers of the regulating body is the power to fix rates after hearings on its own motion or on complaint. The power to require such reports, accounts, and information as the commission sees fit is specifically bestowed in every state except Texas and Arkansas where it would seem to be included in the commission's general powers. The laws of Ohio, Kansas, California, Illinois, and Wyoming specify that annual reports shall be made. Those of California and Louisiana require that reports made to the commission shall be kept confidential. In Illinois reports are published unless the commission withholds them, and in Ohio the commission may withhold them for a "reasonable" length of time.

III. COMPETITION BETWEEN RAILROADS AND PIPE LINES

The extent to which pipe line companies compete with the railroads is shown by the following table, which gives the revenues received by Class I railroads from oil traffic, crude and refined, and the revenues received by pipe line companies reporting to the Interstate Commerce Commission for the years 1928-1931:[10]

Year	Railway Revenues	Pipe Line Revenues
1928	$357,000,000	$222,000,000
1929	380,000,000	251,000,000
1930	367,000,000	238,000,000
1931	318,000,000	223,000,000

[10] Pipe line revenues from *Statistics of Railways*; railway revenues from Interstate Commerce Commission, *Freight Commodity Statistics*.

The pipe lines move the great bulk of the crude oil; for example, in December 1932, tank car movements constituted only 2.6 per cent of domestic refining receipts. Conversely, the railroads move most of the refined products; the pipe line movement of gasoline for the year 1932 (which was double that of 1931) being only 7.4 per cent of the total refinery production.

The data are not readily available with which to make a satisfactory comparison of railway and pipe line rates for identical services. Railroad rates for the long haul of crude oil from Mid-continent points to Eastern market refineries are approximately double those charged by pipe lines. Such rail rates are "paper" rates in the sense that they are probably very high. For some of the shorter hauls from the Texas fields to Gulf coast points, the railway rates are only about 50 per cent higher than pipe line rates. Since 1920 there have been a number of reductions in trunk pipe line rates; and the differential between pipe line and rail rates is now greater than it was before the war. The rate structure investigations conducted under the Hoch-Smith resolution covered, among other things, rates on petroleum and petroleum products. The rates on refined products agreed upon by the majority of the Commission were referred to by Commissioner Eastman, in a dissenting opinion as setting maximum rates, the thought being that if the railroads really wanted the oil industry's traffic they would do well to establish competitive rates well under these levels.[11]

The pipe lines have exerted a considerable influence on rail rates by controlling shipments of crude oil and gasoline. The effect of this significant development has

[11] 171 I.C.C. 286; and 171 I.C.C. 381.

been to influence not only the rates on rail movements of petroleum and its products but also the rates on bituminous and anthracite coal, which are competitors, in many respects, of petroleum products in both industrial and domestic markets. At the present time efforts are being made to procure a schedule of rates in Southwestern territory which will enable the railroads more effectively to meet severe competition which they are encountering from pipe lines and trucks.

Nor is it possible to compare the relative costs of pipe line and railroad transportation. On the one hand it is impossible to allocate railroad costs specifically to oil traffic; and on the other hand pipe line costs vary so widely that it is impossible to give an average that is significant. Inspection of the detailed reports of interstate pipe line companies indicates wide cost variations. Three items, however, always make up the bulk of the investment total. In order of importance they are pipe, construction, and station equipment, which together account for from 70 to 85 per cent of the total.

As compared with railroads, the costs of pipe line operations are relatively low mainly because of the simplicity of the operations and the comparatively small number of laborers required. The ratio of employees' compensation to operating expenses in 1931, for example, was 65 per cent on the railroads as compared with 38 per cent on the pipe lines. The wages per employee, however, differ only slightly. In 1930, the average amount earned per employee on the railroads was $1,714 and on the pipe lines $1,844. The relatively high wages of pipe line employees are doubtless attributable to the relatively high proportion of skilled workers. The pipe line companies, like the railways, are subject to property taxation on both fixed structures and equipment, and to corporate income taxes. The comparative weight of pipe line and railroad taxation is indicated in Chapter XI.

The pipe lines are the only form of transportation other than the railways which does not receive annual subsidies from the government; nor have they at any period received land grants.

CHAPTER XXXI

AIR TRANSPORT

Although air transport is not at present an important part of the national transportation system, it is growing rapidly enough to be worthy of careful study. This chapter will be devoted to a survey of the present scope of air transport, to a discussion of the various ways in which its development has been aided and regulated by the federal government, and to a consideration of the steps which should be taken to make it an efficient, self-supporting part of a co-ordinated national transportation system.

Expansion of air transport in the United States has been rapid since 1926. That year witnessed the establishment of the Aeronautics Branch of the Department of Commerce, and the beginning of its efforts to provide airways and aids to air navigation. The year also marked the establishment of the first domestic contract air mail routes.

From the beginning certain air mail carriers offered passenger services, at first in air mail airplanes, later in special equipment and on special schedules. Passenger air transport services independent of mail contracts became increasingly numerous in 1927, 1928, and 1929. The security markets of the period were favorable to the flotation of aviation issues; two aviation holding companies interested in air transport were created, each capitalized at more than $50,000,000, Aviation Corporation and United Aircraft and Transport Corporation.

The year 1930 witnessed the collapse of the aviation boom. The Post Office Department had already been seeking legislation designed to place air mail service on a more stable basis; the legislation sought in 1930 was broadened to include aid to distressed passenger air services. Legislation was obtained in the form of the so-called Watres Act of 1930, by which four-year air mail contracts were replaced by ten-year air mail route certificates, the compensation for mail carrying was changed from a poundage to a mileage basis, and the Postmaster General was given authority to determine the compensation for the transportation of air mail. Air mail carriers have since been required to furnish passenger service, and air mail and passenger routes have been greatly extended.

I. SIZE AND ORGANIZATION OF THE INDUSTRY

The accompanying map[1] of air passenger transport routes in the United States indicates the geographic scope of the industry. The air transport routes in the United States totaled 28,550 miles at the end of 1932, of which 27,458 miles were traversed by passenger service, 25,593 by mail service, and 27,058 by express service. Airplane miles scheduled daily averaged 132,476, indicating an average frequency of service of more than twice daily.[2] Miles flown by domestic scheduled air transport in 1932 exceeded 45,000,000. Transport airplanes to the number of 407 were in domestic use on June 30, 1932; pilots numbered 481, co-pilots 166, mechanics and riggers 1,488, hangar and field employees 954, and office personnel 803; a total of 3,892.[3] The capital privately invested in air transport probably amounted

---

[1] Supplied by the Aeronautics Branch of the Department of Commerce.
[2] *Air Commerce Bulletin*, Jan. 3, 1933, Vol. 4, p. 33.
[3] Information from the Department of Commerce.

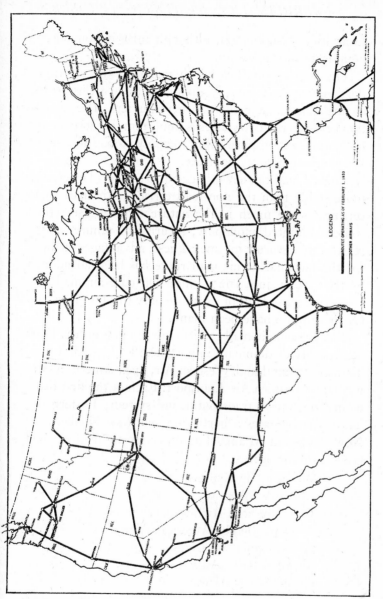

AIRWAY PASSENGER ROUTES OF THE UNITED STATES

to at least $50,000,000, although information on this point is difficult to obtain.

The business entities which make up the air transport industry are sharply divided into two classes, the air mail carriers and the non-mail carriers. The distinction between the two classes is important, because almost no generalization purporting to apply to both classes of operators may safely be made.

The air mail carriers as a group are older, larger, and more stable than the non-mail carriers. Air mail route certificates are much in the nature of franchises; they confer a limited monopoly, security of tenure, and a reasonably assured income. These advantages account for the fact that no air mail route has been abandoned by the carrier since 1927; since that date air mail carriers have passed out of existence only through mergers. Of these there have been many.

The present air mail carriers are ten in number. Four of these are of dominant importance: United Air Lines, Transcontinental and Western Air, Inc., American Airways, and Eastern Air Transport. Each of the first three named operates a transcontinental system; Eastern Air Transport operates a north and south system between New York and Miami. The other six air mail carriers are the following:

> Western Air Express
> Northwest Airways
> Transamerican Airlines Corporation
>   (controlled by American Airways)
> Pennsylvania Air Lines
> National Parks Airways
> United States Airways

The passenger air transport operators with no mail

contracts persist as a group, but the existence of the individual members of the group has been precarious. Non-mail passenger air transport companies have originated since 1924 and ceased operation, merged, or become mail carriers, as shown in the following table:

MORTALITY OF NON-MAIL PASSENGER AIRLINES[a]

Year Started	Number Started	Stopped, Merged, or Became Mail Carrier					Operating January 1, 1933
		1st Year	2nd Year	3rd Year	4th Year	5th Year	
1925	1	0	1	0	0	0	0
1926	2	1	0	0	0	1	0
1927	4	2	0	1	1	0	0
1928	10	5	4	1	0	0	0
1929	21	7	6	5	1	—	2
1930	19	6	4	3	—	—	6
1931	13	6	3	—	—	—	4
1932	7	2	—	—	—	—	5
Total	77	29	18	10	2	1	17

[a] *Domestic Air News*, May 30, 1929, p. 8; June 15, 1929, pp. 9–10. *Aeronautics Bulletin* No. 1, Mar. 15, 1928, p. 7. *Air Commerce Bulletin*, Dec. 2, 1929, p. 4; Dec. 16, 1929, p. 14; July 1, 1930, Vol. 2, pp. 11–13; Dec. 1, 1930, Vol. 2, pp. 281–83; Apr. 1, 1931, vol. 2, pp. 493–96; May 2, 1932, Vol. 3, pp. 532–36; current bulletins during 1932; and Jan. 3, 1933, Vol. 4, pp. 328–31. The table is not entirely accurate, because the Department of Commerce may never have obtained a record of some of the early companies; also it is frequently impossible to obtain accurate information as to the time operation ceased.

The number of years of operation refers to calendar years; that is, carriers ceasing operation during the calendar year of beginning are included as stopping during the first year, and so on.

Non-mail passenger airlines operating at the end of 1932 are shown in the table on the next page.

The development of air express services should be noted. The present volume of traffic is negligible in amount, but growing rapidly. Certain air mail carriers have long co-operated with the Railway Express Agency to provide facilities for handling air express. Two new air express organizations have come into existence during the past few months. One organization, known as

NON-MAIL PASSENGER AIRLINES, JANUARY 1, 1933[a]

Name	Year Started	Airway Miles	Airplane Miles Scheduled Daily
Bowen Air Lines..............	1930	1,028	2,596
Braniff Airways..............	1930	2,007	4,004
Commuters Air Service........	1932	24	192
G. & G. Airlines Co., Ltd.......	1930	128	768
Gorst Air Transport...........	1929	15	330
Hanfords Tri-State Air Lines...	1932	240	480
Inter-City Airlines, Inc........	1932	79	316
Kohler Aviation Corp.........	1929	259	1,040
Ludington Airlines, Inc........	1930	355	4,890
Martz Airlines, Inc...........	1930	323	646
Maine Air Transport Co., Inc...	1932	30	60
Rapid Air Transport, Inc.......	1930	644	1,288
Reed Airline.................	1931	124	248
Seattle-Vancouver Airways....	1932	123	246
Varney Air Service, Ltd........	1931	435	3,988
Wilmington Catalina Air Line..	1931	31	310
Wyoming Air Service, Inc......	1931	476	952
Total.................		6,321	22,354

[a] *Air Commerce Bulletin*, Jan. 3, 1933, Vol. 4, pp. 328–31, and information obtained from the Department of Commerce. Airway mileage duplications were not eliminated.

General Air Express, provides the interchange framework for several air mail and other carriers; pick-up and delivery service is provided by Postal Telegraph messengers. The second organization, Air Express Corporation, is a full-fledged transport company devoted only to air express, which it transmits between New York and Los Angeles in sealed airplanes.

II. ECONOMIC CHARACTERISTICS OF AIR TRANSPORT

Two economic characteristics of air transport are especially worthy of note: (1) the industry is one in which larger size is ordinarily accompanied by lower cost; (2) the industry is one in which rapid technological change is still in process.

Lower cost accompanies larger size in air transport because the industry is now so marked by unutilized capacity.

Some element of unused capacity is present in almost every cost incurred by the small airline, including costs for every kind of equipment and grade of personnel. These wastes are progressively reduced as the scale of operation increases. Waste caused by unused . . . space is glaring up to the point of the maximum attainable utilization of the minimum of capacity which can be scheduled. As the number of trips daily is increased, economy results from the larger number of flying hours per airplane and pilot, and from the lower proportion of reserve equipment and flying personnel. When trips are scheduled at close intervals, the frequency can be adjusted to volume of traffic, and a greater proportion of the capacity scheduled can be utilized. Finally, when traffic increases to the point where several airplanes are dispatched simultaneously on each flight, only the last will fly with a partial load.[4]

Possibly the practical limits of these economies will be reached when 30-passenger airplanes move over the airways at ten-minute intervals. That amount of traffic is many years in the future, particularly on airways of comparatively light traffic density. Meanwhile, the cost situation is such that competition between airlines operating over the same route appears undesirable.

The opportunities of the airplane as a vehicle are con-

[4] Paul T. David, "Federal Regulation of Airplane Common Carriers," *Journal of Land and Public Utility Economics*, Nov. 1930, Vol. 6, pp. 359-71. Reference may be made to this source for a more complete analysis.

stantly being widened by research and progress in design. The fundamental characteristics of the airplane have undergone little change in some years, but the constant pressure for improved performance is bringing forth results which are at times startling. Four fields of research are of special importance: aerodynamics, engine design, structures and materials, and problems of air navigation. Much is still expected from research seeking to minimize the drag of each component part of the airplane, and to reduce the drag resulting from aerodynamic interference between the parts. "Large drag reductions even for the most efficient existing airplanes still appear to be possible."[5]

In the field of engine design, phenomenal increases in power output per unit of engine displacement are being obtained by the use of super-chargers, the more perfect scavenging of exhaust gases in connection with fuel-injection systems, and the development of two-cycle engines. High-speed compression ignition (Diesel) engines promise much in the way of lower fuel consumption, and in the use of fuel of lower cost. Four different types of such engines are said to be under development here and abroad.[6]

Problems in connection with air navigation are of great importance to air transport, and remain in large part unsolved. Blind or instrument flying through clouds and fog passed from the experimental to the routine stage only recently; the landing of airplanes in thick fog is still decidedly in the experimental stage, although methods of some promise have been devised.[7] Such methods

[5] See National Advisory Committee for Aeronautics, *Annual Report*, 1932, p. 56.
[6] The same, pp. 56-59.
[7] The same, pp. 34-35.

when fully developed will require reliance on delicate instruments and also exceptional skill on the part of pilots, but without them air transport will remain weather-bound at frequent intervals.

III. FACTORS INFLUENCING THE COMPETITIVE POSITION OF AIR TRANSPORT

Air transport may be compared with other forms of transportation with respect to at least six criteria: cost, speed, safety, reliability, comfort, and convenience. In this section the present position of air transport in each of these matters will be summarized and the existing tendencies will be stated.

1. *Cost.* Air transport is at present a highly costly form of transportation. Exact statistics of cost are difficult to obtain, but information received from governmental agencies and individuals experienced in the industry indicates that costs as high as one dollar per capacity ton mile still occur.[8] The cost given includes depreciation and taxes. Capacity ton-mile costs of 60 to 75 cents are common; probably the lowest figures achieved in air mail service are a little below 50 cents per capacity ton mile. The Ludington Line, possibly the lowest cost airline in the world because of a favorable conjuncture of circumstances, reports a cost of approximately 40 cents per capacity ton mile.[9] The differences in cost of operation are principally due to differences in managerial ability, the frequency of schedules, the distance between stops, the kind of terrain, and the type of airplane used.

The capacity ton-mile costs indicated may readily be

[8] The cost indicated is that of moving a fully loaded one-ton airplane one mile; the "capacity ton mile" differs from the usual "ton mile" in that complete utilization of capacity is assumed.

[9] Information received from the company prior to its recent merger with Eastern Air Transport.

changed to seat-mile costs by dividing by ten.[10] Costs are then seen to range from four to ten cents per seat-mile.

Actual passenger-mile costs may be obtained by adjusting for the percentage of capacity which is utilized. Statistics compiled by the Department of Commerce for 13 months ended October 31, 1932 indicate 41.57 per cent utilization of the passenger capacity provided by American air transport.[11] During the fiscal year ended June 30, 1932, the comparable ratio for the passenger business of the domestic air mail carriers alone was 36.66 per cent.[12] The highest ratio for an air mail route was 59.49 per cent.[13] The Ludington Line, probably the highest ratio non-mail carrier, achieved a ratio of 64.5 per cent during the year ended August 31, 1931, but has not been able to maintain this record.[14] High percentages of utilization are likely to accompany low seat-mile costs; the reverse is also true. The range of passenger-mile costs is therefore much greater than the range of seat-mile costs. Passenger-mile costs in a few rare instances have been below seven cents, through low seat-mile cost and high utilization. The more common case of a seat-mile cost of eight cents and a utilization factor

---

[10] It is the custom of the industry to allow 200 pounds for the average passenger and baggage.

[11] *Air Commerce Bulletin,* Dec. 15, 1932, Vol. 4, p. 296. U. S. foreign air transport routes are included.

[12] Information from the Superintendent of Air Mail Service.

[13] From the same source. The lowest ratio was not released. One air mail carrier, National Parks Airways, is reported by the Department of Commerce as carrying an average passenger load of .58 passenger. This would represent 14.5 per cent utilization of a four passenger airplane. *Air Commerce Bulletin,* Sept. 1, 1932, Vol. 4, p. 118.

[14] Information received from the company. The recent lower ratio has resulted from inability completely to adjust schedules to the decline in business resulting from the depression.

of 40 per cent yields a passenger-mile cost of 20 cents a mile. At the high cost end of the scale, passenger-mile costs have recently exceeded 50 cents a mile. Airlines operating under such conditions are maintained in existence only through federal aid in the form of mail contracts.

Air transport costs have been coming down steadily during the past three years and will continue to do so, unless cost sacrifices are made to obtain speed. A capacity ton-mile cost of 35 cents seems within reach on several heavy traffic routes during the next five years. The small size of the air transport traffic unit facilitates the adjustment of capacity to traffic; utilization factors of 60 to 70 per cent should become common on the best routes. Unit costs of about five cents per passenger mile or fifty cents per ton mile are thus readily possible in the near future on the best routes.

The distinction between air transport costs and air passenger fares should be noted. The previous discussion has been confined to costs, on the assumption that eventually the fares actually charged will approximate the costs which in practice are incurred by the operators. So far, there has been little relation between costs and fares. The non-mail carriers have almost invariably been forced to quote fares below cost in order to obtain traffic, while in the case of the mail carriers, part of the cost has been met by their income from mail.

Air passenger fares averaged 6.2 cents per mile during 1932, according to the Department of Commerce. These fares apply only to the distance between airports; some additional expense must usually be met by the passenger in connection with transportation to and from airports, but on the other hand, airline distances are from

10 to 20 per cent shorter than the comparable distances by railroad. Air passenger fares usually include the transportation of 30 pounds of baggage and also usually include meals served en route. Round trip fares almost invariably are 10 per cent less than twice the one way fare. The present passenger fares by air and by rail with Pullman service are compared for several sample routes in the accompanying table.

AIR AND RAIL PASSENGER FARES ON SELECTED ROUTES

Route	Distance (In miles)		Time (In hours)		Fare	
	Air	Rail	Air	Rail	Air	Rail
New York–Chicago[a]	736	909	6½	18	$ 47.95	$ 51.70
New York–Los Angeles[a]	2,626	3,111	26½	108	160.00	152.40
New York–Miami	1,210	1,348	14¾	29¼	73.67	65.10
New York–Washington	204	227	2	5	12.95	10.02
Fort Worth–Oklahoma City	182	205	2	6⅓	12.50	9.26
San Francisco–Los Angeles	350	475	2¼	12	18.95	21.54

[a] Rail fare via extra fare trains.

2. *Speed.* The high cost of air transport is balanced by the high speeds it provides. During the fiscal year 1932, the average speed realized in practice by air mail carriers was 108.1 miles per hour. The general average was held down by old type single motor airplanes used only in mail service; the average speed of tri-motored equipment was more representative of the passenger service offered and amounted to 114.4 miles per hour.[15] Accurate statistics are not available for the non-mail carriers; in the main they operate two classes of airplanes: low speed tri-motors, cruising around 110 miles

[15] Information obtained from the Superintendent of Air Mail Service. The average is based upon time between stops, but is affected by time lost in landing.

per hour, and high speed single motor airplanes cruising from 140 to 175 miles per hour.

The future of air transport speed is much in doubt. It seems unlikely that new equipment will be purchased in the future unless capable of cruising at about 140 miles per hour; on this point there appears to be general agreement. With respect to higher speeds, well informed individuals are in disagreement. Some hold that speeds can be advanced to 175 miles an hour without increase in cost; others think a prohibitive increase in cost will occur, followed by a reaction to possibly 140 miles per hour.[16]

Large orders have recently been placed for equipment expected to cruise at more than 150 miles per hour, but it will take at least three years to raise the average of the industry to any such point.

3. *Safety*. The speed of air transport would be more attractive if accompanied by less risk. The hazard may be exaggerated in the mind of the public, but nevertheless is very real. American air transport accident experience since 1928 is summarized as follows:

SAFETY IN UNITED STATES SCHEDULED AIR TRANSPORT[a]

Year	Miles Flown per Pilot Fatality	Miles Flown per Fatal Accident	Passenger Miles per Passenger Fatality
1928	1,185,939	889,454	956,019
1929	1,197,214	1,047,562	2,408,403
1930	4,618,150	4,105,023	4,322,802
1931	4,307,817	3,529,929	4,770,876
1932	3,395,531	2,996,057	5,862,103

[a] *Aeronautics Bulletin* No. 13, July 1, 1932, p. 12; *Air Commerce Bulletin* May 16, 1932, Vol. 3, pp. 558–59. Passenger miles per passenger fatality in 1928 and 1929 were estimated, using 250 miles per average trip. Data for 1932 obtained from the Department of Commerce. The experience of U. S. foreign airlines is included.

[16] The latter view is held by Mr. Edward P. Warner, the editor of *Aviation*.

Comparison with foreign experience is difficult. This is because the volume of traffic in other countries is relatively small and therefore in any given year chance plays a large part in determining the percentage of fatal accidents. But the American record appears to be very much better than that of Germany, France, or Great Britain.[17]

On the railroads in 1932 the passenger miles to the passenger fatality averaged 548,333,624.[18] While such a record may never be approached by the airlines, the achievement of United Air Lines, which carries more than one-third of the domestic air passenger traffic, shows that the risk of air transportation by a well organized company compares not unfavorably with the risk in individual passenger automobiles. In 1931 and 1932 this company averaged 17,225,921 revenue passenger miles to the revenue passenger fatality.[19] This figure may be compared with 20,840,000 passenger miles to the passenger fatality in ordinary passenger automobile transportation.[20] It is well to bear in mind in comparing these figures, however, that the law of chance may have worked during this particular period to make the record of the United Air Lines better than it would be over a longer period. On the other hand, the enormous automobile passenger mileage virtually eliminates the element of chance.

Air transport seems destined to become steadily safer, unless flying in very bad weather is undertaken pre-

[17] *Aviation*, March 1932, Vol. 31, p. 138.
[18] Year ending June 30. *Annual Report of the Interstate Commerce Commission*, 1932, p. 72.
[19] Information received from the company.
[20] Estimate for 1929. *Transactions of the Actuarial Society of America*, May 1931, Vol. 32, p. 253.

maturely. Increased volume of traffic should lead to operation of a more routine type, with greater ease in the establishment of safety habits. Regulation may well become more stringent, and should bring the laggards up to the present status of the best companies.

The accident records of the mail carriers and the non-mail carriers compared as follows during the year which ended June 30, 1932:[21]

	Mail Carriers	Non-Mail Carriers
Pilot miles per pilot fatality	2,300,155	5,115,978
Passenger miles per passenger fatality	6,307,892	2,110,128

Air mail pilots frequently fly alone in weather so bad that passenger flights are not permitted, hence the greater risk to air mail pilots than to air mail passengers. The apparent difference in risk between non-mail pilots and non-mail passengers cannot be explained and probably would not be present if a larger sample were available; the non-mail pilots escaped in two of the four fatal crashes in non-mail transport during the period. The comparison in passenger risk so unfavorable to the non-mail carriers may exaggerate the difference between the two classes of operators. With all due allowance for chance variation, it lends much support to the view that the mail carriers as a group are safer because of their financial strength, better equipment, and longer experience.

4. *Reliability.* The index of reliability most used in the industry is the percentage of miles scheduled actually

[21] *Annual Report of the Post Office Department*, 1932, p. 30; *Air Commerce Bulletin*, Sept. 1, 1932, Vol. 4, p. 114; and information received from the Department of Commerce.

flown. In air mail service, the ratio was 93.34 per cent during the fiscal year 1931, and 93.31 per cent during the fiscal year 1932.[22] Similar ratios for passenger service by air mail carriers are not available but would be distinctly lower. The similar ratio for passenger service by non-mail carriers during the fiscal year 1932 was 81.8 per cent.[23] This ratio confirms statistically a fact of common observation, that the service of the non-mail carriers is less reliable than that of the mail carriers. Light passenger reservations usually coincide with bad weather, and the two factors together lead the non-mail carriers to cancel trips that a mail carrier would fly.

Comparison with other forms of transportation with respect to reliability requires recourse to additional criteria. It is difficult to obtain information as to the number of scheduled trips arriving late and the degree of lateness, but one investigator concluded that the following distribution would now be typical in air transport:[24]

	Per cent
Trips canceled	11.5
Trips not completed	6.6
Trips completed on time	43.8
Trips late less than 15 minutes	17.9
Trips late more than 15 minutes	20.2
	100.0

A high percentage of trips completed late because of adverse winds may be remedied by the simple expedient of revising schedules, but the trips uncompleted because

[22] Computed from *Annual Report of the Post Office Department*, 1932, p. 118.

[23] Computed by the Department of Commerce, using an estimate for miles scheduled based on trips scheduled, and disregarding mileage flown on uncompleted trips.

[24] Security Owners Association, *A Study of Transportation by Airway as Related to Competition with Rail Carriers*, p. 32.

of bad weather are a serious difficulty. The methods now proposed for meeting the problem seem hardly conducive to safety even when fully developed.

5. *Convenience and comfort.* These are less tangible factors of competitive importance. Airline tickets are now readily obtainable, and facilities for transportation to airports are rapidly being provided, although they add appreciably to the cost of the average air trip. Terminal facilities are reasonably comfortable and are being improved. Methods are now known by which airplane noise may be reduced to a level close to that obtaining in railroad trains, but the noise abatement methods are costly and are therefore only slowly coming into use. The newer airplanes are more commodious than the old, but for reasons of economy the airplane seems destined to remain a vehicle in which the passenger is rather cramped. An exception may be made for routes capable of supporting large flying boats.

Airsickness remains the greatest obstacle to comfort in air travel. To some extent it can be prevented by better ventilation and greater stability in flight, but it will be some time before the average passenger can look forward to an air trip in rough weather with any pleasure.

IV. AIR TRAFFIC LEVELS AND RATES OF GROWTH

Three classes of air traffic must be considered: passenger, mail, and express. Passenger traffic is now the most important class from the standpoint of physical volume and also of outlay by the public. Mail traffic continues to be the most important class from the standpoint of the revenues derived by the carriers.

1. *Passenger.* The growth in air transport passenger traffic since 1926 has been as follows:

UNITED STATES DOMESTIC AIR TRANSPORT PASSENGER TRAFFIC[a]

Year	Number of Passengers	Passenger Miles	Average Fare per Mile	Estimated Passenger Revenues
1926........	5,782	1,445,500	$0.12	$ 175,000
1927........	8,679	2,169,750	0.106	230,000
1928........	48,312	12,078,000	0.11	1,300,000
1929........	163,114	40,778,500	0.12	4,850,000
1930........	374,935	84,015,572	0.083	6,950,000
1931........	469,981	106,442,375	0.0674	7,150,000
1932	474,279	127,038,798	0.062	7,900,000

[a] Sources: Passengers, 1926 and 1927 from *Air Commerce Bulletin*, May 16, 1932, Vol. 3, p. 559; 1928 and 1929, the same, Dec. 2, 1929, p. 4, Dec. 16, 1929, p. 14, July 1, 1930, Vol. 2, p. 11, omitting Pan American and Pan American Grace Airways; 1930 and 1931, the same, July 15, 1931, Vol. 3, p. 40, and May 2, 1932, Vol. 3, p. 532. Passenger miles through 1929 were estimated, assuming an average trip of 250 miles. Passenger miles for 1930 and 1931 were from the same source as passengers. Average fares, *Air Commerce Bulletin*, May 16, 1932, Vol. 3, p. 559. All information for 1932 was obtained from the Department of Commerce.

During 1932, air passenger traffic was more than one per cent of average Pullman passenger traffic. During the four-year period 1928-31 Pullman passenger miles averaged 12,600,924,000 annually.[25]

Prediction of future air transport passenger traffic is dangerous for several reasons. Governmental support is important, and the industry is also too young to warrant trend extension. Assuming no sudden withdrawal of support on the routes now furnishing most of the traffic, an annual growth rate of 25 per cent would seem readily possible during the next few years. Compounded annually, that rate of growth would indicate a ten-fold increase in ten years, at the end of which period air transport might be carrying a passenger traffic equal to more than ten per cent of present Pullman traffic.

Air passenger traffic will not necessarily be drawn

[25] Information from the Pullman Company.

completely from the railroads. Some new passenger traffic may come into existence as speed leads to more trips and longer trips. More important is the fact that the flexibility and the tremendous speed advantage of air transport may draw passengers from private automobiles who at present find little advantage in railroad transportation.

2. *Air mail*. The growth in air mail traffic is shown in the following table:

UNITED STATES DOMESTIC AIR MAIL TRAFFIC[a]

Fiscal Year	Reported Pounds of Mail	Estimated Net Pounds of Mail	Reported Ton Miles of Mail	Estimated Ton Miles of Mail
1926.........	32,000	—	—	—
1927.........	473,102	—	—	—
1928.........	1,861,800	—	—	—
1929.........	5,635,680	—	—	—
1930.........	7,719,698	—	—	—
1931.........	8,579,422	3,845,109	—	3,297,550
1932.........	8,845,967	3,544,263	3,137,968	3,044,473

[a] Sources: Reported pounds of mail, estimated by the winter for 1926, for other years from *Annual Report of the Post Office Department*, 1932, p. 118. Estimated net pounds and estimated ton miles, Post Office Department, Appendix to the *Cost Ascertainment Report*, 1932, Tables 3 and 5. Reported ton miles were obtained from the Superintendent of Air Mail Service.

The fiscal year 1932 marked the first decline in the physical volume of air mail.[26] The fiscal year 1933 will probably witness a further decline, because of the increase in air mail postage rates effective July 6, 1932. During the fiscal year 1932, air mail ton miles amounted

[26] The increase in pounds as reported by the carriers may be disregarded, since a varying amount of duplication occurs as services are shifted. Unfortunately, the carriers did not report ton miles during all of the fiscal year 1931. The disagreement of the two ton-mile figures in 1932 may be accounted for by the fact that the total reported by the carriers includes the weight of mail sacks.

to approximately four per cent of the non-local first class mail ton miles.[27]

The future volume of air mail traffic depends almost entirely on the postage rate policy. The transportation of all long distance first class mail by air is sometimes advocated, but seems unlikely to occur for many years. A more reasonable policy would be the progressive reduction of the air mail postage rate from time to time until the air mail letter rate is only one cent higher than the normal first class letter rate. The excess revenue from air mail should then amount to about fifty cents per ton mile, a cost which transport operators should soon be able to achieve on heavy traffic routes.[28] Lower air mail postage rates would tend to divert a larger proportion of first class mail from the railroads, but first class mail is so minor a source of income to the railroads that the loss should not be appreciable. During the fiscal year 1932, the railroads were paid

[27] Post Office Department, Appendix to the *Cost Ascertainment Report*, 1932, Table 5.

[28] The July 1932, increase in air mail postage rates appears to be justifying itself by some increase in postal revenues, but the increased postage rates were accompanied by a vigorous program of traffic solicitation by the air mail carriers, the first in two years. In any case, high postage rates are not the way to encourage growth. Lower postage rates seem a more likely source of increased revenue through increased volume; the increased loads of air mail would not necessitate larger payments to carriers because of the large amount of unused space now being purchased. Lower air mail postage rates should not increase the loss on the service, and in time might reduce it.

The estimated excess revenue from a one cent differential was arrived at as follows: First class mail averages 37 letters to the pound. At the low rate, air mail would average no heavier than first class mail, and the excess revenue would be 37 cents a pound. This will equal 50 cents a ton mile if the average haul is no longer than 1480 miles. During the last fiscal year, the average haul was 1720 miles. A lower air mail rate should lower the average haul to a point nearer that for first class mail, which last year was 519 miles. See the source cited in the preceding footnote, Chart 3.

$23,754,091 for the transportation of first class mail.[29]

3. *Air express*. Domestic express traffic has developed since 1926 as follows:[30]

Year	Pounds	Year	Pounds
1926	3,555	1930	359,523
1927	45,959	1931	788,059
1928	210,404	1932	1,033,970
1929	250,034		

The present amount of air express is negligible, and the future of this class of traffic is much in doubt. The present shipments in almost all cases result from emergencies or are designed to obtain publicity for the shipper.[31] One investigator who hopes much for air express found no one who would predict future air express rates lower than three times the comparable rail rates.[32] At such rates, air express may provide an important source of revenue for the air carriers, yet certainly will be a negligible competitor of surface transportation.

V. CO-ORDINATION WITH OTHER TRANSPORTATION FACILITIES

Co-ordination of transportation facilities seldom becomes an important problem except in connection with the handling of freight. Air mail is the principal freight load of the airplanes; all necessary co-ordinating of air mail service occurs through the medium of the Post Office Department. The co-ordination of air express

[29] The same, Table 60.

[30] *Air Commerce Bulletin*, December 2, 1929, p. 4; December 16, 1929, p. 14; July 1, 1930, Vol. 2, pp. 11-13; July 15, 1931, Vol. 3, pp. 40-42; and information from the Department of Commerce.

[31] The larger volume of such traffic abroad appears to result from the desire of shippers to short-circuit the delays experienced by surface traffic at customs houses.

[32] Monte C. Abrams, "Perplexities of Air Express," *Aviation*, Nov. 1931, Vol. 30, pp. 651-53.

services is a more difficult problem. Surface pick-up and delivery services are prerequisite to the establishment of successful air express services. Co-operative arrangements have accordingly been entered into, in one case with the Railway Express Agency, in the other with the Postal Telegraph-Cable Company. Further experimentation is needed in order to determine the relative success of the two arrangements. Possibly in the end some joint solution will be reached by which small parcels will be handled by messenger and large parcels by the Express Agency. A single comprehensive air express service seems desirable, but possibly can only be achieved after a period of competitive experimentation.

Co-ordination of air passenger facilities is of less importance, because the passenger can do much of his own co-ordinating. However, the transfer of passengers from one form of transportation to another can be made much more convenient as soon as the volume of traffic warrants it. A cheap, rapid, and convenient form of transportation between airports and metropolitan centers is much to be desired, but present traffic levels do not warrant even the regular scheduling of small motor buses in most cases. Taxis are usually pressed into service, to be followed by small buses with growth in traffic, and possibly by rapid transit extensions to exceptionally busy airports. It is perhaps unfortunate that more airports have not been located adjacent to railroads, but steam railroads are not well adapted to supply the need for transportation between airports and metropolitan centers. Passenger interchange between railroads and airlines is of slight importance, and seems unlikely to become more important. In most cases the air traveler will be able to approach his destination closely enough to complete the trip by taxi, electric railway, or bus.

VI. EXTENT OF GOVERNMENT AID

The United States is unique among countries aiding civil aviation in the amount that it spends. In recent years the federal funds spent to aid civil aviation have aggregated about a third more than the total spent by France, Germany, and Great Britain. However, there is ample reason to believe that the United States receives more for its money in terms of the actual scheduled and non-scheduled traffic which is aided.[33]

The federal expenditures within the borders of the United States flow through three channels: the Air Mail Division of the Post Office Department, the Aeronautics Branch of the Department of Commerce, and the Weather Bureau of the Department of Agriculture. In this section, some attention will be paid to each class of expenditure and also to expenditures of local governmental units in the establishment of airports.

The financial history of the domestic contract air mail service is summarized in the following table:

UNITED STATES AIR MAIL REVENUES AND PAYMENT TO CARRIERS[a]

Fiscal Year	Estimated Postal Revenue	Payments to Air Mail Carriers	Excess of Payments Over Revenues	Revenues as a Percentage of Payments
1926	$ 118,407	$ 89,754	$ 28,653	132
1927	1,500,000	1,363,228	136,772	110
1928	3,640,000	4,042,777	402,777	90
1929	4,250,547	11,169,015	6,918,468	38
1930	5,272,616	14,618,231	9,345,615	36
1931	6,210,345	16,943,606	10,733,261	37
1932	6,016,280	19,938,123	13,921,843	30
	$27,008,195	$68,164,734	$41,156,538	40

[a] Estimated postal revenue for 1926, *Annual Report of the Post Office Department*, 1928, p. 132; for 1927 and 1928, estimated by the writer on the basis of information in hearings before Committee on Appropriations on Post Office appropriations bill, 1929, p. 301; for 1929–1932, Post Office Department, *Cost Ascertainment Reports*, 1929–1932, p. 9.

[33] For comparisons, see *Aviation*, March 1932, pp. 136-39.

The two striking features of this table are the decline in the proportion of self-support by the air mail service and the increase in the annual loss on air mail service. Under the original Air Mail Act of February 2, 1925, the carriers could be paid only four-fifths of the air mail postage.[34] The service was established with the definite intention that it should be self-supporting, and it was self-supporting during the first few months. The first amendment of the Air Mail Act[35] struck out the prohibition against payment of more than the postage receipts in order to avoid the necessity of counting the postage on air mail letters. A few months later, on February 1, 1927, air mail postage rates were simplified[36] and in effect reduced, with the result that the air mail service operated at a small loss during the fiscal year 1928, as shown in the table. The Air Mail Act was again amended in 1928, to provide for lower air mail postage rates and an extension of air mail contracts, with the expectation that the compensation of the carriers would be reduced.[37] Air mail postage rates were reduced from ten cents per half ounce to five cents for the first ounce on Aug. 1, 1928.[38] The volume of traffic at once doubled, but no immediate readjustment was made in the poundage rates paid the carriers, and the service operated at a loss of more than $7,000,000 in the fiscal year 1929.[39] After the third amendment of the Air Mail

[34] 43 Stat. L., 805.

[35] 44 Stat. L., 692, June 3, 1926.

[36] *Annual Report of the Post Office Department*, 1927, p. 29.

[37] 45 Stat. L., 594, May 17, 1928; *Congressional Record*, Jan. 6, 1928, v. 69:1111.

[38] *Annual Report of the Post Office Department*, 1929, p. 126.

[39] Allowing for an indeterminate amount of postal expense in addition to payments to carriers.

Act in 1930,[40] the compensation of the carriers was re-adjusted, but new policies were inaugurated. The Postmaster General undertook to foster air passenger service, and to bring about a national system of air mail and passenger routes. Air mail carriers have since been required to provide passenger service, and the loss on passenger service has been a material factor in determining the compensation for carrying mail. The results of this policy are apparent in the record for the fiscal year 1932. Air mail revenue amounted to only 30 per cent of the payments to carriers and to only 25 per cent of the total expenditures in connection with air mail, which amounted to $23,771,367.[41] The net loss for the year was $17,755,087.

The federal government thus appears to have spent 20 cents on the average five-cent air mail letter during the fiscal year 1932, or to have lost 15 cents each on such letters. In view of the motives underlying the expenditures, however, a portion of the loss may be allocated to the passenger traffic which indirectly was aided. During the fiscal year 1932 the air mail carriers were responsible for 3,137,968 ton miles of mail traffic,[42] and 8,635,942 ton miles of passenger traffic,[43] a total of 11,773,910 ton miles.[44] If the loss on air mail service

---

[40] The so-called Watres Act. 46 Stat. L., 259.

[41] *Annual Report of the Postmaster General*, 1932, p. 99. These expenditures include an apportioned share of the cost of collection, post office, railway mail, and delivery service, in addition to all direct expense, according to information received from the Post Office Department.

[42] Information from the Superintendent of Air Mail Service.

[43] Computed from *Air Commerce Bulletin*, Mar. 1, 1932, Vol. 3, p. 411, Sept. 1, 1932, Vol. 4, p. 119, and information supplied by the Department of Commerce.

[44] Air express and miscellaneous traffic are disregarded.

Carrier and Route	Passenger Ton Miles	Mail Ton Miles	Total Ton Miles
Transcontinental and Western Air			
New York–Los Angeles....	1,154,598[b]	659,209	1,813,807
United Air Lines			
New York–Chicago.......	1,060,208	447,605	1,507,813
Chicago–San Francisco....	1,024,061	949,678	1,973,739
Chicago–Dallas..........	432,801	143,042	575,843
Salt Lake City–Seattle....	122,506	101,916	224,422
San Diego–Seattle........	617,128	118,504	735,632
Total.................	3,256,704	1,760,746	5,017,450
Eastern Air Transport			
New York–Miami........	884,992	240,952	1,125,944
Western Air Express			
Salt Lake City–San Diego..	164,151	102,874	267,025
Cheyenne–El Paso........	56,767	12,098	68,865
Total.................	220,918	114,972	335,890
American Airways			
Atlanta–New Orleans.....	4,441	19,704	24,145
Boston–New York........	359,121	11,232	370,353
Omaha–Atlanta..........	53,711	54,044	107,755
Dallas–Brownsville.......	74,072	16,557	90,629
New Orleans–Houston....	2,388	7,571	9,959
New York–Fort Worth....	387,449	49,252	436,701
Atlanta–Los Angeles......	473,080	93,686	566,766
Chicago–Cincinnati.......	107,453	7,279	114,732
Dallas–Galveston.........	27,418	4,349	31,767
Chicago–Memphis........	205,328[b]	9,979	215,307
Total.................	1,694,461	273,653	1,968,114
Northwest Airways			
Chicago–Pembina........	416,770	46,448	463,218
Pennsylvania Airlines			
Washington–Cleveland....	160,862	10,856	171,718
U. S. Airways			
Kansas City–Denver......	87,409	5,388	92,797
Transamerican Airlines			
Bay City–Chicago........	383,161	16,783	399,944
National Parks Airways			
Salt Lake City–Great Falls.	44,099	8,961	53,060
Total, all carriers.......	8,303,974[c]	3,137,968	11,441,942

[a] Passenger ton miles were computed on the basis of ten passengers and baggage to the ton from *Air Commerce Bulletin*, Mar. 1, 1932, Vol. 3, pp. 409–11, and Sept. 1, 1932, Vol. 4, pp. 117–19. Mail ton miles were obtained from the Superintendent of Air Mail Service. Mail payments are from the *Annual Report of the Postmaster General*, 1932, p. 118, supplemented by information from the Superintendent of Air Mail Service. Mail revenues were apportioned among the routes on the basis of $1.91725 per ton mile, the average revenue per ton mile as computed from Post Office Department, *Cost Ascertainment Report*, 1932, p. 9.

Total Mail Payments	Apportioned Mail Revenues	Excess of Payments over Apportioned Revenues	Excess of Payments per Ton Mile Traffic	Total Mail Payments per Mail Ton Mile
$ 2,608,390	$1,263,868	$ 1,344,522	$ .74	$ 3.96
1,388,940	858,170	530,770	.35	3.10
3,366,325	1,820,770	1,545,555	.78	3.54
1,065,781	274,247	791,534	1.37	7.45
814,650	195,398	619,252	2.76	7.99
981,568	227,202	754,366	1.03	8.28
7,617,264	3,375,787	4,241,477	.85	4.33
1,810,042	461,965	1,348,077	1.20	7.51
539,331	197,235	342,096	1.28	5.24
412,282	23,195	389,087	5.65	34.08
951,613	220,430	731,183	2.18	8.28
163,329	37,777	125,552	5.20	8.29
145,176	21,535	123,641	.33	12.93
708,247	103,616	604,631	5.61	13.10
229,599	31,744	197,855	2.18	13.87
111,610	14,515	97,095	9.75	14.74
934,119	94,428	839,691	1.92	18.97
1,796,536	179,619	1,616,917	2.85	19.18
211,147	13,956	197,191	1.72	28.23
125,905	8,338	117,567	3.70	28.95
298,489	19,132	279,357	1.30	29.91
4,724,157	524,660	4,199,497	2.13	17.26
883,718	89,052	794,666	1.72	19.03
207,218	20,814	186,404	1.09	19.09
142,584	10,330	132,254	1.43	26.46
621,322	32,177	589,145	1.47	37.02
371,815	17,180	354,635	6.68	41.49
$19,938,123	$6,016,263[d]	$13,921,860	$1.22	$ 6.36

[b] The statistics as reported in the *Air Commerce Bulletin* were adjusted to conform to the air mail routes as they have been laid out by the Post Office Department.

[c] This total differs from that used elsewhere in this chapter because passengers carried by mail carriers on non-mail routes are omitted.

[d] This total differs slightly from the mail revenues as estimated by the Post Office Department because of the method of apportioning the revenue among routes.

is apportioned between the two classes of traffic on a weight basis, $7,543,415 may be assigned to mail traffic and $10,211,672 to passenger traffic.[45] On this basis, the federal government appears to have spent a little more than eleven cents on the average five-cent air mail letter during the fiscal year 1932, losing six cents a letter, and to have added almost 12 cents per passenger-mile to the fares paid by the passengers transported by air mail carriers.

The various routes differ greatly in the extent to which they are self-supporting. In the table on pages 742 and 743 the excess of air mail payments over air mail revenues has been allocated to the various routes on the basis of the ton miles of mail and passenger traffic over each route.[46] The table shows that during the fiscal year 1932, the federal contribution in the form of excess payments varied from $0.33 per ton-mile, to $9.75 per ton-mile of traffic aided.[47] The range from $0.78 to $6.68

[45] The excess of payments to carriers over air mail revenues was apportioned between mail and passengers in accordance with weight, and the mail share was increased by $3,833,244, the estimated postal expense in connection with air mail other than payments to carriers. The allocation of loss thus arrived at is at best a first approximation; various refinements would be in order if sufficient information were available.

[46] Postal expenses other than payments to carriers have been disregarded in this table, for two reasons: (1) they are not applicable to passenger traffic; (2) they seem extraordinarily large by comparison with the average expense of handling first-class mail. The longer average haul of air mail may account for the heavy postal expense, but if this is the case, it simply means that first-class mail which would have been carried at a large loss because of the distance it travels has been transferred to air mail. If this is correct much of the loss would have been incurred in any case, and it would hardly be appropriate to allocate it to air mail.

[47] The computations assume that all of the traffic carried over the route by the mail carrier was aided. In the case of the $0.33 per ton-mile route, most of the passengers were carried on schedules on which no mail was carried. It can hardly be doubted, however, that mail payments were an aid in carrying on passenger service over the route.

was more representative of the results achieved on routes over which passengers were carried throughout the year, and over which passengers were carried only in air mail airplanes. Stated differently, the contribution on such routes varied from 8 to 67 cents per passenger mile. The average contribution was about 12 cents per passenger mile.

Total payments per mail ton mile are also shown in the table for comparative purposes. These payments varied from \$3.10 per ton mile to \$41.49 per ton mile. The average postal revenue from air mail amounted to \$1.92 per ton mile.[48]

The history of appropriations for the work of the Aeronautics Branch and the airway service of the Weather Bureau is summarized in the following table:

APPROPRIATIONS FOR THE AERONAUTICS BRANCH AND AIRWAY
WEATHER SERVICE[a]

Fiscal Year	Aircraft in Commerce	Air Navigation Facilities	Airway Weather Service
1927	\$ 250,000	\$ 300,000	\$ 75,000
1928	700,000	3,091,500	120,000
1929	859,500	4,659,850	243,500
1930	958,000	5,458,620	710,080
1931	1,260,830	7,944,000	1,272,660
1932	1,369,660	8,992,600	1,709,340
1933	1,000,000	7,553,500	1,465,440
Total	\$6,397,990	\$38,000,070	\$5,596,020

[a] Assistant Secretary of Commerce for Aeronautics, *Annual Report*, 1932, p. 21; *Aviation*, March 1932, Vol. 31, p. 110; Treasury Department, *Digest of Appropriations*, 1933, p. 184.

Appropriations authorized under the title "Aircraft in Commerce" are devoted to the general administrative, promotional, and regulatory activities of the Aeronautics

[48] Computed from information received from the Post Office Department.

Branch. A portion of these appropriations is applicable to air transport; the remainder is expended in the regulation of aircraft manufacturing, in the regulation of miscellaneous civil flying, and in other activities designed to aid civil aviation generally. The appropriations authorized under the title "Air Navigation Facilities" are expended in the construction, operation, and maintenance of civil airways. Airways are provided with emergency landing fields, beacon lights, radio beacons, and radio weather broadcasts. Special weather service along the airways is provided by the Weather Bureau in co-operation with the Aeronautics Branch; the appropriations used by the Weather Bureau for this purpose are shown in the table.

The airway system provided by these expenditures has not been equalled outside the United States, either in quality or extent.

At the close of the fiscal year 1932 there were in operation and under construction or installation 19,500 miles of lighted airways, 69 radio communication stations, 94 radio range beacons, 118 radio marker beacons, and 233 teletypewriter stations on a leased wire system comprising some 13,000 miles of circuits. The total personnel of the airways division was 2,102, of whom 897 were part-time employees serving as attendants or caretakers at intermediate fields and beacon lights.[49]

The cost of airway construction is relatively small compared to the cost of operation and maintenance. Construction expenditures of the Aeronautics Branch totalled $9,501,290 during the fiscal years 1927-1932.[50] This amounted to 31.26 per cent of the appropriations for aids to air navigation during the same years. Construc-

---

[49] Assistant Secretary of Commerce for Aeronautics, *Annual Report*, 1932, p. 7.

[50] Information received from the Department of Commerce.

tion expenditures amounted to $1,596,650 during the fiscal year 1932, compared with a total appropriation for aids to air navigation of $8,992,600.

Expenditures on airways have been of primary benefit to the mail carriers. The non-mail carriers have received less benefit because they have flown little at night and have been slow to adopt the aircraft radio equipment necessary for use of the radio beacons and weather broadcasts. Miscellaneous civil flying has received a measure of benefit from the airways. Military aviation has benefited greatly, since the airways facilitate the movement of aircraft between military airports. The airways also add to the effective strength of the military air force by increasing its mobility.

The investment in airports in the United States probably amounted to about $135,000,000 at the end of 1931. Commercial and municipal airports were almost equally responsible for the total.[51] Most of the airports used by air transport companies, however, are municipally owned. In many cases municipalities have given airlines the right to use airports free of charge for a term of years as an inducement to the establishment of the service. In other cases, airlines make contributions in the form of hangar rentals and landing fees.[52] So little is known concerning the financial results of municipal airport operation that the extent to which air transport is actually aided is most uncertain.

VII. REASONS FOR FEDERAL AID TO AIR TRANSPORT

Three types of reasons account for the aid lavished upon civil aviation in the United States: military, eco-

[51] *Air Commerce Bulletin*, Feb. 2, 1932, Vol. 2, p. 379.
[52] See *Aeronautics Bulletin*, No. 17, July 1, 1932, pp. 26-27.

nomic, and political. Military, as well as economic, reasons had much to do with the establishment of the Aeronautics Branch of the Department of Commerce. Economic reasons in the form of a desire to expedite the mails were probably the primary consideration in the case of the Post Office Department up to 1929, but air mail policies have been frequently defended by reference to military considerations. Political reasons only can account for the establishment of certain mail routes in sparsely settled regions.

The airplane is unique among vehicles in that it is a weapon as well as a means of transportation, a fact which has led to activities designed to foster aviation in almost all countries. The natural sequel of such aid has been an attempt to include civil aviation within the scope of disarmament programs.[53] This attempt has been strenuously resisted by the United States and Germany, with the result that the stringent restrictions upon civil aviation proposed by France and other countries have been whittled down to the following proposed clause of the draft convention:

The High Contracting Parties undertake not to subsidize, directly or indirectly, air lines principally established for military purposes instead of being established for economic, administrative, or social purposes.[54]

In the case of the United States, this clause merely expresses national policies of long standing which found expression in the Report of the President's Aircraft Board in 1925.[55] Notwithstanding this fact, federal sup-

---

[53] See Kenneth W. Colegrove, *International Control of Aviation*, pp. 134-41.

[54] League of Nations Secretariat, Information Section, *Disarmament-Preparations for the General Conference*, February, 1932, p. 98.

[55] P. 6.

port for civil aviation is constantly being sought on the basis of its military value. The proponents of this view seem not to realize that they are running counter to our traditional policy of a clear separation of the civil and military budgets. Moreover, by resting their case on the military value of civil aviation, they place their industry in danger of a sudden withdrawal of support if the United States enters into the prospective disarmament commitments referred to above, and they also increase the danger of more drastic international control of aviation.

Civil aviation appears to need little aid for military reasons in the United States, even aside from such considerations of national policy. It seems clear that the United States would lead in civil aviation even if all federal support were withdrawn.[56] The non-subsidized passenger air lines without mail contracts were responsible for more passenger miles of actual traffic in 1931 than the combined total for Germany, France, and Great Britain, notwithstanding the competition received from the mail carriers.[57] Miscellaneous civil flying receives only a negligible amount of indirect aid, yet the United States has for many years been outstanding in this field.

These facts might not disprove the military need for aid to civil aviation if our military air forces were greatly restricted and civil aviation were our principal military reliance; but the situation is otherwise. During 1930 and 1931 our military aviation establishments were the most expensive in the world; on the basis of personnel and equipment, the United States was rated third among air powers, which were listed in the following order of strength: France, Great Britain (including India),

[56] Other than purchases of military airplanes.
[57] Computed from *Aviation*, March 1932, Vol. 31, p. 137; and *Air Commerce Bulletin*, May 2, 1932, Vol. 3, pp. 532-35.

United States, Italy, Russia, and Japan.[58] Each of the other five of these leading air powers adjoins one or more of the others, whereas the United States is separated from the others by some thousands of miles.[59] This fact greatly increases the adequacy of our air forces. In summary, there appears to be no present justification for basing aid to civil aviation upon military considerations.[60]

Economic reasons appear to offer sounder ground for aid to air transport. The industry offers a service which has appealed to the imagination of men of all ages. The service has come into existence only through a difficult period of technical development, a period which is far from completed. Meanwhile, traffic is low because of the barriers of cost and fear. Federal support of a distinctly new service does not seem inappropriate under the circumstances, but it should be clearly understood that the aid is not to be permanent.

Air transport has so far shown little tendency toward self-support. Possibly the present non-mail air lines are not as great a source of loss to their owners as were the earlier non-mail air lines. The far larger part of the industry, the mail carriers, were as a class less self-supporting in 1932 than in any previous year, if mail traffic only is considered. Even if the passenger traffic of the mail carriers is given due weight, the total traffic of these carriers appears not to have been self-supporting by more than one-third during the fiscal year 1932.[61]

[58] *Aviation*, March 1932, Vol. 31, p. 134.

[59] Aside from the proximity of Siberia and Alaska, a consideration which will not be relevant until both localities become much more adapted to the operation of air forces than at present.

[60] The military value of our system of airways is so direct that a portion of their cost might well be allocated to the military budget.

[61] Postal patrons paid a little more than $6,000,000 and passengers perhaps $5,000,000 during the fiscal year 1932. The cost of operation

The lack of progress towards self-support can only be explained by recourse to federal policies. The table below sets forth the growth in air mail route mileage and miles of service.[62] The early routes were in most cases those on which the heaviest traffic might be expected; the expansion of route mileage has extended the service to areas where the traffic density is very low. The light traffic routes have been a drain to the service, and have prevented the real improvement achieved on the better routes from becoming manifest.

Fiscal Year	Length of Air Mail Routes	Miles of Service Flown
1926	3,597	396,345
1927	5,551	2,805,781
1928	10,932	5,585,224
1929	14,406	10,212,511
1930	14,907	14,939,468
1931	23,488	21,381,852
1932	26,745	32,202,170

To some extent the Post Office Department appears to have been over-optimistic concerning the prospects of certain routes, but a reading of recent air mail and appropriation hearings will indicate the large part taken by politics in the establishment of some of these routes.

---

of air mail airlines has not been released by the Post Office Department, but the revenues of the carriers were probably little if any in excess of their cost of operation. The revenues of the carriers may be estimated at $25,000,000. Additional postal expense in connection with air mail was estimated by the Post Office Department at nearly $4,000,000, to which may be added at least $5,000,000 of airway expense applicable to air mail carriers. Costs which may be estimated at $34,000,000 were thus offset by revenues from consumers of perhaps $11,000,000. The basic data for these estimates are supplied in the last section.

[62] *Annual Report of the Post Office Department*, 1932, p. 118.

Consider, for example, the Atlanta-Los Angeles route. The excess of mail payments over apportioned mail revenue on this route during the fiscal year 1932 amounted to $1,616,917.[63] The average load of ail mail was 80 pounds,[64] and the average load of passengers was 2.1 passengers.[65] The federal aid on this route in the form of mail payments amounted to 28 cents per passenger mile.[66] The Salt Lake City-Great Falls, Montana, route is a more glaring case; aid on this route amounted to 67 cents per passenger mile, but the total mail payments on the route were less than $400,000. The thin traffic routes cost almost as much for airway aids as do the heavy traffic routes; if the cost of aids to air navigation were allocated to the various routes, the disparity in economic merit would only be accentuated.

The immediate elimination of all parts of air mail routes on which mail cannot be carried for ten dollars a ton mile, or half a cent a pound mile, may well be considered by Congress. The elimination of these routes would permit the reduction of the air mail appropriation by at least one-quarter, and would also permit a very substantial reduction in the appropriation for airway aids. A precise estimate of the savings cannot be made with the information now available, because many high cost routes have their heavy traffic sections, while many low cost routes have weak extensions.[67] It seems entirely

[63] From a table in the last section.

[64] Computed from information supplied by the Superintendent of Air Mail Service.

[65] Computed from *Air Commerce Bulletin*, Mar. 1, 1932, Vol. 3, p. 409, and Sept. 1, 1932, Vol. 4, p. 117. All off-line extensions except the one operated by Western Air Express were included.

[66] From a table in the last section.

[67] For example, the Bay City-Chicago route includes Detroit-Chicago, while the Chicago-San Francisco route includes an extension from Omaha to Watertown, S.D.

probable that the apparently drastic curtailment just suggested could be made without losing more than 10 per cent of the air mail traffic. During the fiscal year 1932 the mail traffic of the routes costing more than ten dollars per air mail ton mile aggregated 354,483 ton miles, or 11.30 per cent of the total mail ton mileage, but cost $7,199,767, or 36.11 per cent of the total mail payments.[68] The loss of passenger traffic from such a curtailment of mail payments would probably be greater, but it is likely that the parts of routes responsible for most of the passenger traffic could be retained. In any case, mail payments up to five times the postal revenue from air mail[69] should be a sufficient amount of federal aid to carriers which in many cases compete with non-subsidized air passenger carriers.

VIII. EXTENT AND CHARACTER OF EXISTING REGULATION

Air transport receives a measure of regulation from two federal agencies—the Department of Commerce and the Post Office Department. Certain state regulatory bodies are also beginning to exert influence.

Broad powers designed to promote safety in air commerce were conferred upon the Department of Commerce by the Air Commerce Act of 1926.[70] Jurisdiction over aircraft and airmen engaged in interstate commerce

[68] Computed from a table in the last section. The better parts of these routes would be retained. Some traffic originating on the eliminated routes would be lost to the retained routes, but, on the other hand, some traffic could be re-routed and thus retained at considerably less than its present cost.

[69] The suggested limit of $10 per ton mile is more than five times the average ton-mile revenue during the fiscal year 1932. The average revenue per ton mile is doubtless higher under the present postage rates. If the present postage rates are retained, a limit of possibly $15 per ton mile might be more appropriate.

[70] 44 Stat. L., 568.

was assumed almost at once; regulation in these fields has become progressively more complex and more stringent.[71] Jurisdiction over interstate scheduled passenger air transport services was assumed in 1930. No such service may now be placed in operation without first securing a certificate of authority from the Secretary of Commerce. Existing services are required to adhere to high standards of operation, set forth in detailed regulations.[72]

The Department of Commerce concerns itself little with regulations of an economic nature; its powers are severely limited in this respect. Possibly the Department might find some justification for an examination of the financial ability of certificate seekers, since financial strength is intimately associated with safety of operation in most transport fields, but so far the Department has taken no steps in this direction. Stringent safety regulations doubtless restrict airline competition to some extent, particularly competition from small, newly organized companies, but the Department is specifically forbidden to establish airline monopolies.[73]

Regulation by the Post Office Department applies only to air mail carriers, but is quite comprehensive within that field. The air mail carriers in many respects are in the position of participating in a regulated industry. Their air mail route certificates represent a monopolistic right to carry mail over their respective routes until April 5, 1936.[74] This right is sufficient to assure a com-

[71] For the current regulations applicable to aircraft and airmen, see *Aeronautics Bulletins* 7 and 7-A through 7-H.

[72] *Air Commerce Bulletin*, Sept. 15, 1931, Vol. 3, pp. 131-36.

[73] 44 Stat. L., 568, at p. 571.

[74] All certificates expire on this date according to information received from the Superintendent of Air Mail Service.

plete monopoly of air transport in most cases, since only exceptional routes offer possibilities attractive enough to lead a non-mail carrier to compete for passenger and other traffic. The Postmaster General has the right to extend and consolidate air mail routes. He may require mail and passenger service in such amounts as he may see fit, and he may require the employment of satisfactory equipment and personnel. He has prescribed a system of uniform accounts for the use of air mail carriers.[75] Finally, the Postmaster General determines the rate of compensation for the transportation of air mail subject to the limits of the appropriations provided by Congress.[76]

The present location of the powers just noted may well be challenged. The powers are clearly analogous to those commonly exercised by regulatory commissions. Such quasi-legislative and judicial powers are seldom conferred on single individuals, since by definition they involve the making of decisions rather than the performance of work, and decisions involving property rights are best made with some consultation and exchange of ideas among equals. It may also be noted that the Postmaster General is in the position of sitting as judge in cases to which his department is a party. Procedural safeguards have been almost wholly lacking, and the utmost secrecy has been maintained concerning the financial position of the carriers. It is not strange under the circumstances that the transfer of regulatory authority from the Postmaster General to the Interstate Com-

[75] *Uniform System of Accounts for Carriers by Air*, Post Office Department, July 1, 1930.

[76] For the statutory and contractual expressions of the Postmaster General's authority, see 44 Stat. L., 259-60, and 72 Cong. 1 sess., S. doc. 70, pp. 19-22 (a typical air mail route certificate).

merce Commission is being suggested with increasing frequency.[77]

Regulation of all air transport by the Interstate Commerce Commission has often been suggested in the past, but no action has yet been taken. The cost characteristics of air transport indicate that duplication of service over the same route is wasteful and likely to lead to uneconomic competition. The Interstate Commerce Commission should therefore be granted authority to issue certificates of convenience and necessity, with the expectation that duplicate services will seldom be authorized. Existing carriers capable of meeting adequate standards should be permitted to continue, but the consolidation of carriers serving the same route might well be encouraged.

The present non-mail carriers may be considered typical of air transport in its unregulated state. Previous sections of this chapter have indicated the instability of these carriers as a group, their relative lack of reliability, and their unfavorable accident record. The Department of Commerce has done its work well; but it seems unlikely that any amount of policing will insure safety from carriers which as a class are unseasoned and financially insecure. Some form of economic regulation is necessary to prevent such carriers from coming into existence.

Commission regulation of air transport by the states has so far been confined to the activities of eleven regulatory bodies. The public utility commissions of Arizona, Colorado, Illinois, Maryland, Nevada, New Mexico, North Dakota, Pennsylvania, Tennessee, and Wyoming, and the Board of Aeronautics of West Virginia have as-

[77] For example, by a former Second Assistant Postmaster General, now an officer of the largest air mail carrier. 72 Cong. 1 sess., *Air Mail*, Hearings on H. R. 8390 and 9841 before House Committee on Post Offices and Post Roads, 1932, pp. 67, 69, 72.

sumed jurisdiction over scheduled air transport.[78] In view of the intrenched position of the Department of Commerce in safety regulation and the predominantly interstate character of air transport, regulatory activities by the states seem unlikely to become important in this field.

IX. CONCLUSIONS

The conclusions supported by the information in this chapter may be summarized as follows:

1. Air transport is now the least important of the forms of organized transportation available to the American public, but is growing rapidly in importance and in this country has already far surpassed the development abroad.

2. Study of factors in which the industry must compete with other forms of transportation indicates that it will be a serious competitor of surface transportation only for passengers. Speeds of 150 miles per hour, a degree of safety approaching that of passenger automobile transportation, and passenger fares of five cents a mile all appear likely to become typical on major air routes during the next few years.

3. Air transport passenger traffic is now in excess of one per cent of Pullman passenger traffic. Growth to a level of more than 10 per cent in ten years appears possible. Some traffic is likely to be drawn from passenger automobiles because of the speed advantage.

4. Air mail pound miles amounted to 4 per cent of first-class mail pound miles during the fiscal year 1932.

[78] Fred B. Fagg, Jr., and Abraham Fishman, "Certificates of Convenience for Air Transport," *Journal of Air Law*, Vol. 3, pp. 226-50, at p. 240.

Lower postage rates appear necessary to develop this class of traffic; it is not believed that this change would increase the loss on air mail service. First-class mail is so minor a source of income to other forms of transportation that the diversion of traffic would not be important.

5. Federal aids to air transport amounted to $26,774,027 during the fiscal year 1932. Contributions of passengers and postal patrons did not exceed $15,000,000. Much of the aid took the form of mail payments and airway aids on routes of extremely light traffic density. It is believed that the aid dispensed on these routes could be eliminated without a substantial loss of traffic.

6. Air transport companies comprise two groups: mail carriers and non-mail carriers. Both groups carry passengers. The mail carriers operate over a unified system of routes totaling about 26,000 miles; the non-mail carriers operate over about 6,000 miles of disconnected route.

7. The mail carriers receive a large measure of regulation from the Postmaster General, who supervises service, requires uniform accounts, and determines the compensation for the transportation of mail. These powers are exercised under air mail route certificates which expire in 1936.

8. The non-mail carriers are regulated as to safety by the Department of Commerce, but are subject to no regulation of an economic nature. Of 77 non-mail airlines started during the period 1925-32, only 17 were in existence as such an January 1, 1933. The service offered is distinctly less reliable than that offered by the regulated mail carriers. Despite the more frequent cancellation of schedules, the passenger fatality risk on non-mail lines

was three times as great as that on mail lines during the only period for which information is available.

9. Air transportation is an industry of decreasing unit cost with increasing size, principally because of high overhead expense and light traffic. Competition within the industry should accordingly be limited to service over alternative routes between large centers. The competition of surface transportation seems adequate to promote efficiency. Commission regulation appears to be prerequisite to the granting of monopolistic certificates of convenience and necessity for particular routes.

The following recommendations are suggested for consideration:

1. The payment of more than half a cent per pound mile for transporting mail over any air mail route or part thereof should be prohibited. Air mail carriers should be permitted to withdraw from service on routes where such rates prove not to be compensatory. The savings resulting should be impounded and returned to the federal treasury.

2. Expenditures in aid to air navigation should be reduced on routes on which air mail service is eliminated.

3. At some time prior to the expiration of air mail route certificates in 1936, provision should be made for the transfer of regulatory authority from the Postmaster General to the Interstate Commerce Commission. This change should be made to remove air mail service from the political sphere as far as possible and to provide for the orderly liquidation of the present subsidy policy.

4. General jurisdiction over air transport should be conferred upon the Interstate Commerce Commission, in order to prevent the establishment of new airlines incapable of meeting reasonable financial standards and in

order to prevent unwise competition among airlines. Existing airlines capable of meeting reasonable standards should be permitted to continue. This change should be made as soon as possible, in the interests of safety.

5. The present jurisdiction of the Department of Commerce over matters connected with safety should not be disturbed; the preceding recommendation should not be interpreted as a reflection upon the existing administration of the Department.

6. Air transport should eventually be placed upon a completely self-supporting basis. It would then be desirable to allocate a share of the cost of airways to the companies using them.

PART VIII

STABILIZATION OF THE RAILROAD INDUSTRY

INTRODUCTORY STATEMENT

We turn in this division of our study to an analysis of the problems involved in restoring the railroad industry to a stable and prosperous condition. The reorientation in regulation that is required in connection with the entire transportation system of the country is, however, reserved for consideration in Part IX. Here we shall confine our attention to the problem of railroad stabilization, to the end that this basic industry may contribute toward the resumption of general prosperity.

The preceding analysis has shown that the present condition of the railway is the result of two factors: First, the increasing competition of other transportation agencies, particularly the highway, and, second, the depression, which has affected the railroads in common with all other industries and at the same time intensified competition. Of the two factors, the depression is of primary significance so far as the ability of the roads to meet fixed charges and earn a modest return upon stock investment is concerned. An increase in traffic of moderate proportions would enable those roads whose capital structure is sound and whose general position is favorable to meet fixed charges and to make progress in restoring their credit position and in rehabilitating the condition of their physical properties. The railroads cannot, however, maintain a passive attitude in connection with the general problem of recovery. They must participate actively in the readjustment processes upon which general prosperity depends.

In the following chapters we shall consider the problem of readjusting rates and costs and the possible economies that might be obtained by means of terminal unification and through general consolidation of railway companies. Attention will also be given to the relation of transportation to constructive planning of city development.

CHAPTER XXXII

THE READJUSTMENT OF RATES AND COSTS

The railroads have been looked upon during this depression as a favored industry. This is the only industry in which an effort has been made to maintain financial solvency through the process of raising rates. It was hoped that the downward movement of prices and of business might be arrested if railroad rates and earnings could be maintained. The anticipated result was not, however, attained and, as we have seen, the railroads have been forced by sheer pressure of circumstances to reduce to some extent individual rates both on freight and passenger traffic.

The disparity between the price of railway transportation service and the prices of commodities generally may be summarily indicated. The average freight revenues per ton mile decreased from 1.094 cents in 1928 to 1.062 at the end of 1931, or a decline of 2.9 per cent. During the same period the wholesale commodity price index declined by 24.5 per cent. The commodity price level for the year 1932 showed a decline of 33 per cent from 1928. While data are not as yet available for the average freight revenue per ton mile for the year 1932, it is known that the decline has been only moderate. Between 1913 and 1931 freight rates increased 45 per cent, while the wholesale price level in 1931 was only 5 per cent above the pre war figure.

When one considers the trend of prices in certain particular industries the nature of the problem becomes even clearer. Freight rates now absorb a substantially larger proportion of the value of many leading commodities, particularly in the case of agricultural products and certain raw materials where the price declines have been most pronounced. The burden of freight rates on farm produce, measured by the ratio of rate per ton to value, more than doubled from 1928 to 1932.[1]

There can be no doubt that high freight rates now serve as a deterrent to business recovery. The uneven character of price declines has, however, resulted in great variations in the weight of the transportation burden. Accordingly, the argument for a simple horizontal rate reduction is not strong at this juncture. What is needed is a downward readjustment of railroad rates, with attention given to the conditions prevailing in different regions, and particularly with reference to different types of traffic. The suggestion that the reduction of rates should proceed along experimental lines is, however, not to be interpreted as indicating that the need for substantial reductions is not an urgent one. A considerable reduction in rates is clearly essential to the readjustment of production costs to purchasing capacity, and hence to the resumption of business activity.

A reduction in railroad rates would doubtless mean, immediately speaking, an increase in railroad operating deficits. While in individual items of traffic lower rates might stimulate the volume of traffic sufficiently to offset the reduction in charges, such a result could not be expected for traffic as a whole—at least until general business recovery occurs. In any event, the financial con-

---

[1] Average freight revenue per ton on agricultural and animal products in 1928 was $6.83; for the first six months of 1932, the figure was $7.20. The Bureau of Labor Statistics index number of farm produce prices fell from 105.9 in 1928 to 49.2 in the first half of 1932. The ratio of freight rate per ton to value thus increased 2.3 times from 1928 to the first half of 1932.

dition of the railroads is such that reductions in the expenses of operation are essential if the railroad industry is to be placed upon a solid foundation. At the same time that rates are being adjusted downward, it is therefore necessary to cut costs.

We have indicated in Chapter VIII the nature of the drain imposed upon railroad systems by obsolete, and obsolescent, branch lines and in Chapter XXIX we have suggested the possibility of saving expenses by a more extensive utilization of trucks and buses on branches of light traffic density. In the same chapter we also pointed out that very substantial economies may be realized in terminal areas through the co-ordination of rail and highway transport facilities. We have also indicated that certain lines possess unbalanced capital structures which must be reorganized as a preliminary to the restoration of sound financial conditions.

Another possible means of reducing operating expenses is to effect savings in wages and in the costs of materials. It is assumed by many that the only practical means of reducing the cost of railroad operation further is to reduce wages. Inasmuch as the wage bill represents approximately 60 per cent of the entire cost of railway operations, they urge that here and here alone lies the possibility of large economies. Our analysis of the wage situation in the railroad industry indicates that the wage rates for most classes of workers for which comparable wage data are available increased by about 90 per cent between 1915 and 1929. A considerable part of this rise came in the pre-war and federal control periods, the increases after 1923 accounting for but a small portion of the total advance. After the 10 per cent cut negotiated in 1932, the average rates for railroad employees were approximately 70 per cent above the 1915 level. The reported rates for other organized labor show a slower rise from 1915 to 1920 but a much more rapid advance thereafter, and in 1929 stood 150 per cent above the 1915 level. Since 1929 *actual* reductions in general trade union rates have apparently been at least 25 per cent, leaving the level around 90 per cent above that of 1915.[2]

During this same period the cost of living for the United States as a whole rose from an index of 105.1 in 1915 to 170.8 in 1929, and fell thereafter to 135.7 in June 1932. In terms of real wages, in other words, railroad wage rates in 1932 were approximately 30 per cent higher than they had been in 1915.

It seems not unreasonable that full time employees in the higher paid wage groups should contribute something toward the establishment of financial stability in the industry upon which they are dependent; and the same observation is applicable to the salaried groups. But for reasons set forth in the introductory chapter it should be the policy to maintain wages as high as is economically possible; and there is much to be said for leveling up wages in competing lines of transportation rather than forcing railway wages down to the plane of the lowest. It should be borne in mind, moreover, that even if there were a further wage reduction of 10 per cent, the net saving of $150,000,000 would not be sufficient to cover even the deficit in fixed charges that accrued in 1932.

In any event there is no justification for a program which would require those who are employed in the railway services to make the primary contribution to the re-

[2] See pp. 199-202 for supporting data. For wages on boat lines see p. 461; on trucks see pp. 522-23.

habilitation of railroad finances. The price of steel rails, which has declined much less than the prices of other commodities, should also be reduced. The railway equipment industry has just as much stake in the restoration of a sound railroad financial situation as have other interested groups. Moreover, it is of the utmost importance not only in the interest of stabilizing the railroad situation but with a view to giving this country the kind of transportation service which it requires that the efficiency of railroad operation be increased.

We shall consider first the possibilities of effecting economies by individual roads acting independently. Many who charge the existing railroads with gross inefficiency, and point to the great economies that are possible, fail to differentiate between economies that might be possible under a consolidated system which would eliminate competitive wastes and those which might be accomplished by independent roads. Competitive companies can hardly be expected to ignore competitive requirements. In the following analysis we shall endeavor to distinguish between the economies that are possible for individual roads and those which are contingent upon co-operation or unification. The latter type of economies will be considered in later chapters.

It is contended by many that the quasi-monopolistic position of the railroads has tended to make railroad managers content with what they have and slow to act with reference to new possibilities. This point of view is well expressed in the following statement made to the National Transportation Committee by one who has devoted a life-time to the study of railroad transportation:[3]

[3] Dr. Eugene Davenport, Dean and Professor Emeritus, the University of Illinois.

I have known railroad service from the outside for over half a century and its most pronounced feature, next to safety of operation and special equipment of the de luxe trains, has been its indifference to changing conditions and the growing necessities of a rapidly advancing civilization. The result is that with thousands of country and small town people the flying machine is actually a more vivid reality than are the railroads.

It is not difficult to cite instances of this apparent indifference to the public need as well as to changing conditions. For example, I knew personally, some forty years ago, one Emory Cobb of Kankakee, Illinois. As a young man he was associated with Ezra Cornell in the promotion of the telegraph and the effort to induce the railroads to run their trains by telegraph. They considered the proposition absurd and would not even permit the company to erect poles on the railroad right of way. This he told me with vast satisfaction after the wire had, reluctantly at first, but of necessity at last, been adopted as the only possible way to handle the increased traffic.

It was only recently that the roads were able to boast that they were moving heavy freight at the rate of twenty miles a day. Back in the days when it moved only ten miles a day—ox-cart speed—the demand arose for faster movement, especially of the lighter and more valuable stuff. The railroads refused to give a better service and the express companies were organized. So the railroads lost an opportunity and a source of revenue that has supported the express companies rather handsomely for a service that the railroads could have rendered cheaper.

Again, the public desired to sleep while it was spending the night upon the train and asked for service. It was not granted by the railroads and the Pullman and the Wagner companies were organized to furnish it. And for many years the roads actually paid the sleeping car companies for the privilege of hauling their cars and passengers.

Still again: When Mr. Armour desired to ship refrigerated meats he urged the roads leading out of Chicago to build and operate refrigerator cars. They would not even consider it. (See *The Packers, the Private Car Lines and the People*, by J. Ogden

Armour, pp. 22 and 23.) So again the parties interested in developing transportation were obliged to provide their own equipment and take over this branch of the transportation problem. They have done the same in other interests, such as fruit.

To mention one more instance: The railroads, even the small branch lines, permitted the electric interurban to parallel their tracks and take away from them not only their local business but the direct contacts with the people of their own territory. The roads had the initial advantage, having already the right of way and the track upkeep, all of which was in most cases idle from 90 to 99 per cent of the time with plenty of opportunity to run "scooters" which would have put the interurbans out of business before they were fairly started.

I once called a conference between the farmers of Illinois and the railroads that served the state. There was a fine attendance on both sides. One of the questions put up by the farmers was: "Why does a bull always weigh 2000 pounds when he is shipped whether he is six years, six months, or six weeks old?" After a bit of "stalling" the answer was: "Well, we don't want the business anyhow and receive it only as a matter of accommodation." Could any reason have been weaker? Besides, James J. Hill was at that time shipping bulls of any age *free* if billed to the territory served by his line, and good business it was as events proved.

By these short-sighted policies long continued the railroads have reduced themselves to agencies for maintaining tracks, locomotives, and the most ordinary freight cars and day coaches, handling the grosser freight and keeping up terminals, while private companies have skimmed the cream off the transportation business.

Before they can get out of the rut that they have dug for themselves the railroads will have to win back the real *regard* of the Public and it will be a sorry day for all of us if they do not succeed. We need a universal conviction that the railroads are the foundation of the national problem of transportation and that they will take care of it. But if this *feeling* of confidence is to become a reality the roads will have to institute a radical change of policy regarding the public they serve.

While remarkable progress, as we show in Chapter VI, has been made in railroad operating efficiency since 1922, railroad managements have nevertheless not been perhaps as alert as they might have been with reference to new developments in the transportation field. They failed to realize the potentialities of highway transportation. The short-haul freight and passenger traffic and the less-than-carload services were regarded by railroads as unprofitable and no serious attempt was made to arrest diversion to the highways. But now that these classes of traffic are going or have gone to the highways the railroads are deeply concerned.

In the matter of operating efficiency there is wide variation on different roads. The railway journals, the proceedings of the professional railroad societies, and the utterances of experienced officials speaking for individual railroads, afford innumerable specific instances both of inefficient practices and of progress made by certain roads that reveal the backwardness of others. The extent of variations in operating efficiency between different roads is illustrated in the following table where the results attained in 1928 by 142 Class I railroads in gross ton miles per train hour, car miles per car day, and pounds of coal consumed per 1000 gross ton miles are compared.[4]

In the interpretation of the variations in efficiency shown in the table it must be remembered that it is extremely difficult to eliminate the disturbing effects of differences in the conditions under which the various companies operate. With respect to gross ton miles per train

[4] Data embrace 142 companies whose reports are available in *Comparative Statement of Operating Averages*, 1925-29, Bureau of Statistics, Interstate Commerce Commission.

hour, for instance, we find that the companies producing over 30,000 gross ton miles are mostly roads with
heavy coal or ore traffic—like the Pittsburgh and Lake

Efficiency Grouping	Number of Roads	As a Percentage of Total
Gross ton miles per train hour:		
Under 5,000	4	2.82
5,001–10,000	18	12.68
10,001–15,000	28	19.72
15,001–20,000	32	22.53
20,001–25,000	31	21.83
25,001–30,000	18	12.68
30,001–35,000	4	2.82
35,001–40,000	3	2.11
40,001–45,000	3	2.11
45,001 and over	1	.70
Car miles per car day		
Under 10.0	11	7.75
10.1–20.0	25	17.61
20.1–30.0	50	35.21
30.1–40.0	35	24.65
40.1–50.0	13	9.15
50.1–60.0	5	3.52
60.1 and over	3	2.11
Pounds of coal consumed per 1,000 gross ton miles		
Under 90	4	2.82
91–110	29	20.42
111–130	33	23.24
131–150	34	23.95
151–170	12	8.45
171–190	7	4.93
191–210	6	4.23
211–230	3	2.11
231–250	1	.70
251–270	4	2.82
271–290	3	2.11
291–310	3	2.11
311 and over	3	2.11

Erie, Chesapeake and Ohio, Norfolk and Western, Virginian, and Duluth, Mesaba, and Northern. Likewise,
we find that roads making extensive use of oil are almost

invariably making good showing with respect to fuel consumption.[5]

Under these circumstances, it is impossible to draw precise conclusions as to managerial efficiency. Yet there is a presumption that at least some of the showings are attributable to differences in management. It is true that roads showing excellent results with regard to gross ton miles per train hour are mostly roads with heavy coal or ore traffic; but it is also true that many of the roads with equally heavy coal or ore traffic are making very poor showings. In fact, one of the roads in the lowest class shown in the table above has traffic in mine products to the extent of 81.4 per cent of its total traffic. When, therefore, eleven companies can maintain an average of 30,000 gross ton miles per train hour, it is hardly probable that companies now under 5,000 gross ton miles cannot do better.

In the field of passenger service numerous improvements in service have been suggested. Passenger service is the channel through which railroads come into contact with the public, and accordingly the public attitude as to railroad transportation generally is largely determined by the character of such service. On long distance "crack" trains there is little ground for criticism, but anyone familiar with local service, particularly on branch lines, cannot fail to be impressed with the fact that passenger accommodations are little if any better, and that

[5] One difficulty here is in adopting a common unit for comparison between oil and coal consumption. See L. F. Wilson, "Comparing Unit Fuel Consumptions," *Railway Age*, July 14, 1928. The choice between oil and coal lies within managerial discretion, but if the present management has a large surplus of serviceable coal-burning locomotives, it may be cheaper to continue to use them than to make expensive changes to oil burners, even though the showing with respect to fuel consumption remains poor.

train schedules are less satisfactory than they were a generation ago. As a result vast numbers of people nowadays never think of traveling by train, but instead automatically go by private car or bus. Some of this attitude is merely the reflection of a motor-minded age; but much of it is directly attributable to high rates and inferior railroad service.

While it may be argued that declining traffic makes deterioration of service inevitable the fact remains that aggressive efforts have in most cases not been made to prevent the diversion of traffic. For example, high speed combination passenger freight train service, now advocated by some leading railroad men as an aid in recovering both passenger and fast freight traffic, might well have been developed earlier. Similarly, the use of motor vehicles to supplement railroad service and the running of motor car trains at frequent intervals are being somewhat belatedly experimented with. Other aspects of the passenger problem, neglected until recently, are differentiated rate structures and popular price excursions.

The Baltimore and Ohio recently inaugurated a night day-coach service between Washington and New York at 30 per cent reduced fares, that is, at 2.5 cents per mile. The number of passengers increased 150 per cent in five months. The transcontinental carriers inaugurated a $40 day-coach fare between Chicago and California. These carriers believe that this new fare has justified itself by preventing further diversion to highways. The Chicago and North Western in November 1932 began to experiment with reduced passenger rates. A reduction from 3.6 cents to 2 cents a mile resulted in a loss of revenue. When the rates were reduced to 1.5 cents there was still a loss as compared with the regular rate, but it was smaller than at the 2 cent rate. A cut to 1 cent a mile resulted in increasing traffic by more than 500 per cent, yielding an increase in revenues as compared with the rate of 3.6 cents. The experiment was tried in three different districts and the results were uniformly the same.

While this development is still in the experimental stage, it appears not unlikely that it points the way to an opportunity for increased usefulness of the railways to the traveling public and increased revenues for the carriers themselves. The experiences of the roads in handling commutation traffic over a long period of years shows that passengers can be carried profitably for 1.1 cents a mile if the trains are full. Passenger traffic which the railroads have lost to private automobiles and buses is gone forever if the railroads can offer services only at 3.6 cents, or for that matter 2.6 cents, a mile. But if they can carry passengers at one cent a mile, or perhaps at 1.5 cents a mile, it would appear impossible for buses to compete with them since volume of business for buses means almost proportionately increased expenses. Moreover, for runs of more than a few hours the railroads have the advantage in speed, in comfort, and in safety.

Likewise with reference to the private passenger automobile: while it appears unlikely that any rate policy will enable the railroads to recover that part of the traffic which represents vacation and other recreational travel, the bulk of the traffic which has forsaken the railroads and taken to the highways is probably available for the railroads whenever they can offer transportation at a figure below the direct cost of gasoline and oil involved in running an automobile—say 1.5 cents per passenger mile.

In other words, given the existing investment in railway right of way, equipment, and terminals, it seems almost certain that railway transportation of passengers, in reasonably full train loads, is basically cheaper than highway transportation and that a rate level can be found which, coupled with inexpensive improvements in quality of service[6] would make the use of the railways once more a standard method of personal transportation.[7] If these devices show results now they would presumptively have shown results earlier, preventing in some measure the persistent decline of the passenger business.

Having called attention to the possibility of improvements in efficiency both in freight and in passenger business, it is only fair to point out that many improvements theoretically possible are frequently not immediately practicable. If it were feasible for any railroad to scrap all of its present plant and equipment and make replacements with 1933 models there is not the slightest doubt that operating costs could be greatly reduced. But a railroad, like every other business enterprise, is concerned with a financial problem. Even when the raising of capital is not difficult there is always a question as to the best time in which to scrap old equipment or properties and

[6] Such as fine mesh screens in day coaches, free reclining chairs such as have been in use on certain Western roads for many years, and added attention to cleanliness of cars, convenience of schedules, and similar details of service.

[7] The loss of revenue on very long distance travel which roads have so far been able to retain could largely be obviated by the retention of somewhat higher fares on tickets good in sleeping cars, and by the institution of some differentiation of fares between first and second class coaches. It is to be noted, however, that in European countries, where several classes of service are maintained, very little revenue is obtained from higher class transportation. Excess fares on the fastest and most convenient trains have been more successful as revenue producers both in Europe and in America.

replace them with new. There were submitted to the National Transportation Committee a wide variety of suggestions for increasing efficiency—by an earlier replacement of old locomotives with new and improved equipment, by better purchasing methods, by the abandonment of individual company shops, by the modification of certain practices, etc.; but the financial aspects of the problem were usually not carefully considered. Some of the suggestions may be immediately feasible, while others are not.

In concluding this discussion of the problem of railroad management attention may be called to the fact that the railroad managers have been confronted with certain very time consuming problems which have militated against concentrated attention upon the business of transportation. Reference is here made to the problems connected with the system of legislation and commission regulation, to financial issues incident to acquisitions and potential mergers or consolidations, and to the adjustment of labor problems. So important have such problems become that in the selection of railroad officials nowadays emphasis is commonly placed rather more upon legal training and diplomatic qualities than upon railroad operating ability.

Looking forward, the prospect for significant increases in railway efficiency, accomplished by individual roads operating under competitive conditions, does not appear promising. Between 1923 and 1930 it was possible to accomplish results of great importance, thanks to the prosperous condition of the country as a whole and to the comparative ease with which new capital could be raised. During the next few years it is improbable—assuming no basic changes in railroad organization—that the necessary capital can be obtained to effect significant operating improvements—and in any event the most obvious types of improvement have already been effected. The economies of the near future will depend primarily upon the extent to which the wastes which are incident to the duplication of services and costs under a competitive system can be eliminated.

CHAPTER XXXIII

THE PROBLEM OF TERMINAL UNIFICATION

Public interest in the consolidation of railroads may be said to date from the experience with unified operation obtained during the period of federal control. Its interest in the railroad terminal problem, on the other hand, antedates the war experience, though receiving positive stimulus during the congestion of terminal facilities which occurred at that time. The present chapter examines the difficulties which terminals present and considers possible lines of betterment. In so doing it continues the analysis of means of securing a greater degree of transportation efficiency through the development of a more fully co-ordinated and unified system of transportation.

The word "terminal" is used in a broad sense to embrace all facilities directly or indirectly called into use in the loading and unloading of cars and the making up and breaking down of trains. It includes not only tracks, stations, and freight houses, but also industrial sidings, storage facilities, and whatever else contributes to the performance of the tasks mentioned. Ownership need not necessarily rest with the railroads; facilities furnished and owned by the large shipper or receiver of freight, and expenditures (such as those for highway improvement incident to terminal development) borne from the public purse, all enter into the picture. So likewise "terminal operations" embrace activities of carriers, of shippers, and of a public that may be affected by the manner of terminal operation and the location of terminal facilities. The problem is distinctly a many-sided one.

Terminals fall into two classes, namely, freight and passenger. The freight terminal problem is of greater concern and is considered in this chapter more fully than the passenger terminal problem. Special attention is also given to the significance of the produce terminal.

I. THE PLACE OF THE FREIGHT TERMINAL IN RAILWAY OPERATIONS

Freight terminals do not permit of ready classification. In size they range from a single loop dropped off a main line to give service to a small community, to the gigantic networks of tracks found at such traffic centers and gateways as Chicago, Indianapolis, and St. Louis. Classified on the basis of location, there are terminals at the termini of railroads, at ocean ports, at intermediate points, and at points of junction with other carriers. This classification is not entirely satisfactory, however. Thus the port terminal may handle a large volume of domestic traffic; and intermediate terminals, where the carriers re-make their trains, may originate and receive much traffic on their own account. Nearly all terminals are, then, of a mixed character.

To many, a railway terminal suggests a maze of tracks, laid down according to no discernible pattern and apparently used with no particular show of system. It is hard to appreciate how much effort has gone into their development or to what extent close supervision goes into their daily use. The essential parts of a freight terminal are tracks or "yards" devoted to the receiving, classifying, storing, and repairing of cars, as well as delivery or "team" tracks for the loading and unloading of carload shipments, scale tracks for the weighing of shipments, icing tracks, departure tracks, interchange tracks with other roads, etc., with, of course, the attendant structures. In the case of port terminals, piers, and pier stations, lighters and car floats are included. Spurs and sidings reach out to the industries along the carrier's lines. As terminals grow in size the tendency is to multiply the number of distinct units rather than to expand existing units. The object here is, of course, to avoid unnecessary switching.

Seldom does our industrial system show itself in a more complicated form; for here we see a myriad of movements, each of which must take place as quickly as possible in order that the yard may be kept clear for other trains soon to follow, that equipment may be promptly released for other uses, and that shipper and consignee may not be kept waiting for commodities essential to the continuous operation of their businesses. Particularly complicated is the handling of less-than-carload freight, both because it represents small units, each requiring separate billing, weighing, checking, etc., and because it usually has to pass through the freight house in being loaded onto or unloaded from the cars. Carload shipments, on the other hand, require the "spotting" of cars, either on team tracks or on the shipper's own industrial track.

Terminals exert a controlling influence over the character and cost of transportation service. They have contributed on many occasions to seriously delayed and irregular transportation service. A large number of the delinquencies charged against the railroads in the last two decades or so have really had their origin in faulty terminal situations. The congestion, particularly at the Eastern port terminals, during the recent war will long be remembered. Here equipment, badly needed in other parts of the country, was piled up and rendered practically useless. What is not so obvious is that, even under the best of conditions, terminals constantly put a brake on the rapidity with which traffic moves and cause irregularities which shippers or receivers of freight find it difficult to contend with. As Mr. Loree has well expressed it, "the large terminal stations and the large terminal yards are the graveyard of cars."[1] His calculations indicate that considerably more than two-thirds of the 14.9 days involved in a typical completed car movement is spent in terminals. If such items as surplus cars, Sunday and holiday delays, and delays due to repairs be eliminated from the calculations, 86 per cent of the time is chargeable to terminal operations and only 14 per cent to the line haul. There has been improvement in recent years, but this has been general and it is doubtful whether the proportions indicated have undergone much change. More expeditious and regular movement of freight is, therefore, conditioned very largely by the adequacy of terminal facilities and the effectiveness shown in their use.

Terminal costs form a large part of the aggregate cost of furnishing transportation service. The lay public thinks of railroads too exclusively in terms of road mileage. Terminals involve extremely large investments of capital. Unfortunately, no figures are available showing the aggregate investment in terminal property, but one railroad authority has said that "the terminals alone represent a greater amount of money than all the remainder of the properties of the roads."[2] This same authority es-

[2] J. A. Droege, *Freight Terminals and Trains*, (2d ed.), 1925, p. 8.
[1] L. F. Loree, *Railroad Freight Transportation*, p. 34.

timated in 1912 that the New York freight terminals for a new four-track trunk line to extend from Chicago to New York would cost anywhere from $125,000,000 to $150,000,000 (if on the Jersey water front, $75,000,000), or the equivalent of from $75,000 to $150,000 per mile of line for the tidewater terminal alone. These figures would be very much higher to-day.

Some conception of the extent and multiplicity of terminal operations is obtained from a comparison of the mileage made in a year by road locomotives and yard switching locomotives. In 1925, the mileage made in yard switching was, in the case of the ten largest Eastern roads, 60 per cent of that made in road movements, ranging from 44 per cent in the case of the Erie to 87 per cent in the case of the Michigan Central. Of the single item "transportation" in the operating expense accounts, considerably more than a third is attributable to yard operations. These are but rough measurements, but they serve to indicate the extent to which terminal operations enter into the determination of transportation costs and suggest that there may be inefficient practices here that will bear looking into.

Terminal costs behave differently from line-haul costs. Line-haul costs are, roughly speaking, proportionate to distance; terminal costs are practically the same whatever distance shipments are sent.[3] Their effects on rate construction are, therefore, divergent. Furthermore, terminal operations pass out of the "increasing returns" stage much sooner than line-haul operations. The matter is simply one of capacity. There is an elasticity of

[3] We refer here, of course, to costs incurred at a particular terminal. With increased distance the necessity of passage through intermediate yards or of interchange with other carriers presumably increases.

capacity in the case of road mileage that enables increases in traffic to be handled with increased effectiveness and, therefore, at lower costs; whereas in the case of terminals, owing to the multiplicity of operations, the point is much sooner reached where increases in traffic to be handled pile up costs at a disproportionate rate.

The terminal is a competitive device of major importance. It is difficult for laymen to appreciate how all-important it is to carriers to have terminal facilities as good as those which their competitors enjoy. The explanation rests in the controlling influence which terminal facilities exert over the securing of the line haul. Nearness to the wholesale center of a city and to the chief industrial districts and direct connection with as many large industrial establishments as possible are of decisive importance in the securing of business. It is small wonder that carriers will undergo enormous terminal expense in order to attract business away from their competitors. Nor is it surprising that, with rates minutely regulated as they are at present, carriers will "absorb" terminal costs of one kind or another in order to attract business from rival carriers. In some cases actual losses are known to be taken on terminal operations in order to secure business. The terminal, then, is one of the last strongholds of carrier competition. However, much of the competition originating at terminals has brought about such questionable practices and so much waste in duplication that on the whole no resultant advantage accrues to any one railroad—and only harm to the entire industry. When terminal cities reach a certain point in growth and importance, the value of the competitive feature—considering the vast outlays of money involved —becomes an illusion.

1. *Problems of the individual terminal*. The discussion divides at this point into two major parts, one relating to aspects of the individual terminals of a carrier, considered apart from the terminals of other carriers, and the other relating to the functioning of the terminals of various railroads in their necessary relations with one another.

Many terminals are poorly adapted to present needs. The reasons are largely historical, reflecting enormous growths of traffic in the past, lack of planning, the large increase in normal times in urban land values, the complexity of urban building and street developments and the lack of available land. Droege, speaking particularly of the individual terminal, says:

> Most of our larger freight terminals are examples of evolution from smaller to large yards. Like Topsy, they "jus' growed." Additional tracks were hung on wherever there happened to be a vacant piece of land and where the least grading was required. In many cases it was necessary to get any additional track facilities that could be had at any place available, to avoid congestion or blockade on the line. In other cases it was due to lack of foresight. The bill has been paid many times over.[4]

He also refers to the "shortsightedness of years ago, in not providing for necessary expansion where it was most needed and before industrial development and increased property values rendered it almost prohibitive." To this general cause of weakness in the terminal situation he adds such special ones as "the paramount desire of running a line to a large city and the failure to provide sufficient funds to carry the line well into the terminal city," and, in the matter of design, the effect of the pay-

---

[4] *Freight Terminals and Trains*, p. 9.

ment for the use of other carriers' cars on a mileage basis (changed to a per diem basis in 1902), which resulted in the yards being operated "in an expensive and awkward manner," because the "tracks were built for storage purposes rather than for switching."

There is much reason to believe that a considerable part of our terminal problems in normal times can be solved by a moving from crowded in-town centers to the open spaces on the outskirts of cities. Here land can be had of sufficient area to permit a comprehensive design with adequate provision for the future. Such a moving out would not be feasible if it were not for the availability of the modern motor truck and the possibility of making greater use of belt lines, especially the inner belt lines, which will make for a facilitated transfer of cars from road to road and district to district.[5]

"The possibilities for savings in yard operation are practically limitless." This editorial utterance of the *Railway Age*[6] suggests lines of inquiry into operating practices which, as in the case of terminal design, might easily lead us far afield. Perhaps a single example of what improved methods can accomplish will suffice to demonstrate the need for new ideas and energetic study of terminal practices. The example used relates to the manner of making up trains in terminals, giving rise to the so-called "main-tracker" freight train. The process is well described in a report of the Interstate Commerce Commission:

The importance of preclassifying freight trains has been repeatedly called to the attention of the carriers. One of the important features of operating efficiency is to move traffic in solid

[5] See Chapter XXIX.
[6] "Panaceas for Yard Ailments," Mar. 19, 1927, p. 925.

trains, kept together for the longest possible distances. Under this practice freight is assembled in trainload lots at or near the originating point. These trains are then dispatched through to destination, or, where that is not possible, to break-up points near destination.

This practice not only promotes expeditious movement but minimizes switching in transit and at intermediate terminals, with resultant savings to the carriers. We have also urged the carriers to deliver cars to their connections in blocks so that pre-classification may be worked out easily and with less switching. Many carriers have adopted our suggestions along this line, with savings which amply demonstrate the soundness of the practice.[7]

This single improvement is working large changes in carriers' outlook on their terminal problem. It has, in fact, made necessary a re-planning of many terminal operations, some intermediate terminals losing in importance and a greater burden being thrown on others.

There is so much repetition in terminal operations that standards of good performance readily suggest themselves. These might take the form of number of cars handled in a period of time, as suggested by Droege, or the number of "yardings"[8] per car handled, or the daily percentage of cars moved of total to be moved, as suggested by Charles E. Lee, or they might take more minute forms: percentage of cars or contents damaged, number of "rides" per yard brakeman per hour or day, number of tons of less-than-carload freight handled per gang per day, and so on. These are mentioned here merely to emphasize the possibilities of doing with greater

[7] *Annual Report*, December 1, 1925, p. 55. For a lucid description of this type of operation, see H. R. Fertig, "System Classification Plan Improves Yard Efficiency," *Railway Age*, Feb. 19, 1927, pp. 515-22.

[8] Defined as "any halt in movement in which the car yarded is set out and its movement interrupted."

efficiency the multitude of tasks which, day in and day out, go to make up the round of terminal operations.

2. *Securing greater unity of terminal operations.* So much, then, by way of brief analysis of the problems of the individual terminal. Let us now consider the more deeply seated and stubborn problems presented by the two basic facts that, to perform a completed service, carriers must interchange traffic, and that, in a particular locality, carriers are almost certain to be unequally provided with terminal facilities.

For the most part, extreme individualism has characterized the development of American railroad terminals. As just indicated, there is constant need for transfer of shipments from the lines and yards of one carrier to those of another. Carriers' terminals, therefore, should be designed in such a way as to facilitate interchange in order that extensive switching and related operations may not be necessary. But, if individual terminals have represented constant compromise with the most efficient design, there literally has been no designing of the terminals of various carriers in many localities for effective joint use.[9] The greatest number of freight terminals, including most of the important ones, reflect extreme individualism in their design and lack of co-ordination in their daily use.

The outstanding example is, of course, New York City and vicinity, where each carrier has acquired land and erected facilities for its exclusive use. The effect is duplicated facilities; in many instances the holding of land

---

[9] It should be especially noted that the terminals, either of an individual road or of groups of roads, do not permit of treatment solely on the basis of conditions in a single locality. Defects in a terminal at one point are reflected backward and forward in the operation of all related terminals.

beyond reasonable requirements in order to prevent its acquisition by rival carriers; and confusion, delay, and extra costs for the shipper, who must make use of a number of freight houses or piers when concentration would serve his needs better and relieve congestion of the city's streets. Duplicate lighterage and car ferrying facilities add to costs. This service is similar in character to the car switching which takes place in other terminals in transferring freight between the lines or yards of individual carriers.[10]

Excessive individualism in the design or operation of terminals adds cost and detracts from quality of service. As is seen in the case of New York, it causes extra car handlings and often unduly long car movements within terminals; it adds confusion, necessitates complicated accounting and record-taking, often results in unnecessary empty car movements, and in general injects elements of constraint into a situation where the maximum of speed and fluidity is to be desired.

The reasons for the highly individualistic character of our terminals have been suggested by what has gone before. There is principally the historical fact that carriers reached a particular city at different times, with the result that some secured the most advantageous terminal sites, while others, coming later, were required to build in less desirable locations or go without. It is also true that some carriers have shown greater foresight and skill in developing their terminal facilities than others. Back

[10] The development of "inland," "off-rail" freight stations for shippers' convenience and of store-door delivery has afforded some relief in New York, as has the somewhat recent construction of a belt line by the Port of New York Authority. The new union off-rail station is designed to give further relief, but is not a permanent solution.

of situations created in this way is the obvious fact that differential advantages in terminal location, secured as a result of early building into a city or of foresight, would not be shared with other carriers, where the latter were competitive, except on onerous terms.

Varying degrees of joint use of terminals are found in different centers. In some cases carriers lacking terminal facilities at a certain point will turn over their traffic to another carrier, "absorbing" the latter's switching charges in the rate.[11] Such joint use may not go far toward a unification of terminal operations; it may be merely a partial correction of an irksome situation. Carriers in any way competitive with the grantor company may use its facilities, if at all, only on onerous terms. In other cases, a separate terminal company may be found. It may be controlled by and be used primarily in the interest of one company, as the Baltimore and Ohio Chicago Terminal Railroad Company, which, however, grants the use of its facilities to, and does switching for, other carriers. Or it may be controlled by a group of railroads in their joint interest. A random example is the Atlantic and East Coast Terminal Company at Jacksonville, Florida.[12]

Belt lines and other terminal facilities, such as warehouses, elevators, piers, etc., are in a relatively few cases furnished by some public authority, as in New Orleans and San Francisco.

The situations at Chicago and St. Louis require special mention. In the former, "the largest and most important

[11] Sometimes, on non-competitive traffic, the switching charge is included in the rate the shipper pays.

[12] Owned jointly by the Atlantic Coast Line Railroad and the Florida East Coast Railway.

cross-roads and nerve center of the world's greatest system of transportation, land or water,"[13] there is said to be "the greatest common use of trackage and terminal facilities in America. . . . Not only is there more actual co-operation, but it is co-operation between greater units."[14] In other words, the Chicago terminal presumably has reached—we do not know just when—that point in size and maturity where carriers are willing to combine to prevent or minimize losses. The principal methods used are "reciprocal switching," the so-called belt and switching lines, and numerous joint facility agreements.[15]

There are eight belt or switching lines, all but one of which are owned in varying combinations by all but three of the twenty-odd trunk line railroads entering the district. These lines facilitate a more rapid and direct movement of freight between points in the district on different carriers' lines. They also facilitate much purely local switching. Some of the belt lines serve the downtown district, making possible a reduction in the number of separate lines required to furnish service to that congested area. Others are outer belt lines, such as the Elgin, Joliet, and Eastern, the Indiana Harbor Belt, and the Chicago and Western Indiana Railroad, which serve to divert traffic from the busy in-city terminals.[16]

[13] Introduction to recent report, *The Freight Traffic of the Chicago Terminal District*, rendered by the Committee on Co-ordination of Chicago Terminals, 1927, p. 171.

[14] The same, p. 17.

[15] There are also certain joint clearing facilities for "trap" and transfer cars.

[16] The actual count made in the detailed study indicated above showed that only an eighth of the total traffic in the district represented by-pass traffic, whereas it had been the common belief that approximately half the traffic was of that character.

So much for what the railroads in Chicago do in common. A somewhat different aspect is placed on the situation by the statement in the report[17] that "so great is the service of the individual railroads to industries *on their own lines,* that something like half of all the terminal services rendered by railroads in the Chicago Metropolitan area is taken care of wholly on their own lines." This can mean only that in many instances more than one carriers' lines reach a single industry's yards. In very large part, then, the Chicago terminal facilities are still competitive in character, bearing witness to the course pursued in the original laying down of the facilities and to present attitudes in favor of a continuance of competition.[18]

At St. Louis, though the Terminal Railroad Association has long since unified the passenger terminal facilities, there is still much "going it alone" in the handling of freight traffic. The interchange and team yards, less-than-carload freight houses, and other facilities provided by the Association (in addition to those of the individual carriers) are, to be sure, used to great advantage. Nevertheless, both the Chicago and the St. Louis situations reflect merely a partial compromise with extreme individualism.

As has been stated, most terminal layouts and methods employed in their operation are the outgrowth of attempts on the part of a multiple system of railroads to build up competitive machines, now so powerful and

---

[17] P. 17. Italics ours.

[18] Professor Dixon stated in 1922 that in some cases as many as 19 different railroads were serving one plant or district, and that owing to duplication 70 per cent of the train track capacity in the Chicago terminals was unused. *Railroads and Government,* pp. 138, 348.

unwieldy that they have at last become veritable Frankensteins as far as terminal operation is concerned.

The complete unification of terminals in many cities is needed. Probably the most advanced view yet taken by a person of responsibility and judgment is that of Mr. E. E. Clark, expressed when he was a member of the Interstate Commerce Commission:

> I would provide, if I had my way, and the direction of it, in every large commercial center for a terminal association or corporation which would be a separate entity. I would make the terminal agency of all the roads that reach the place, operated as nearly as could be figured out at cost. Then the railroads serving that place would turn over the traffic destined to the place to this terminal agency, and it would be delivered where the consignee wanted it delivered on any of the tracks; there would not be any question about closed or open terminals; there would be one terminal for all.[19]

The Commission itself said, in the *New York Harbor* case:[20]

> It is necessary that the great terminals of the port of New York be made practically one, and that the separate interests of the individual carriers, so long an insuperable obstacle to any constructive plan of terminal development, be subordinated to the public interest.

Conditions that prevailed during the war, when faltering private operation was followed by government operation, made painfully clear the need and advantages of co-operative action.[21] Since the return of the railroads

---

[19] Quoted in *Chicago Junction* case, I.C.C. Finance Docket 1165, p. 17 (1922).

[20] 47 I.C.C. 643, 733 (1917).

[21] Under federal control much was done in the way of the unification of terminal operations, thereby avoiding much wasteful switching and reducing the expense of car checking and other related operations.

to their owners, however, there has been a distinct falling off in interest on the part of the railroads in such far-reaching changes as complete unification would require. The reasons can be discerned with little difficulty.

A completely unified set of major terminals owned by the carriers jointly, by a separate corporation, or publicly, would present certain advantages. Rebuilding along new physical, economic, and corporate lines would assure the planning of facilities for the maximum of effective use. Competitive advantages held by some carriers and used to draw traffic from other carriers would be nullified. The joint backing of many railroads, or the assured business which such an enterprise would command, would make the financing of improvements a less costly process than if carriers individually undertook such improvements as necessity dictated. Capital could be raised at extremely low interest rates, an item of considerable importance where the capital requirements are so large. So complete a revision of terminals would afford opportunity for large improvements in the planning of cities.[22]

What improvement may be expected from a more co-operative use of individual carriers' terminal facilities? In answering this question one must consider the basis on which carriers co-operate at present and for changes which future developments may bring about.

Under a system of complete unification, all carriers would have equal access to the services and facilities available. Payment would be proportioned to the use made. No distinction between strong and weak roads, competitive and non-competitive ones, could be drawn. Where, however, the question is one of effecting a more

[22] See Chapter XXXIV.

co-operative use of individual carriers' facilities, such distinctions continue to be of importance. Whether, then, the "opening up" of the terminals of one carrier to use by other carriers promises much, depends on what voluntary action and what compulsion can accomplish.

There is no reason to believe, nor in fact any right to expect, that individual carriers will voluntarily sacrifice any resultant economic advantage they may now possess in the matter of terminals in order that other carriers, and presumably some public interest, may be served. To be sure, we have a statement from the late Julius Kruttschnitt, a prominent railroad president, which might seem to afford encouragement. He said:

There, of course, existed, up to a few years ago, the old theory among owners of railroads that when they had, by prudence and foresight, acquired certain positions of advantage, the matter was settled; that those positions belonged to them; but I think railroad managers and owners have advanced with the times; that their views have changed materially; that now public opinion rules that these facilities must be used in common.[23]

With this statement may be compared one of E. G. Buckland, vice-president of the New York, New Haven and Hartford Railroad, in the course of the hearing some years ago on the New York Central's application to be allowed use of the Hell Gate route:

When it comes to giving our terminals, which we have constructed at a great expense, to a competitor who has taken our traffic, or traffic which would otherwise come to us . . . so long as we have private operation and competition, the only terms on which a competitor can use our terminals is by paying us the

[23] Senate Hearings on Extension of Tenure of Government Control of Railroads, 1919, p. 588.

net revenue which we would have earned on that particular freight.[24]

A similar attitude, easily understood, is found in the much mooted York switching case, before the Commission and the courts a few years ago.

Voluntary action at present will accomplish little in those instances where carriers are competitive. And these are the most common cases.[25] Where the situation is non-competitive, payment for such shared use would not be difficult to determine and might not be unduly onerous, as witness the many joint facility agreements— literally thousands—that exist to-day. But where the grantor is in direct competition with the potential grantee, the payment required would be such as practically to nullify any advantage the latter might find in the arrangement, as witness the statement of the New Haven Railroad official quoted above.[26]

The shipping public, as well as the carriers, has responsibilities in connection with terminal betterment. The foregoing discussion has purposely been in terms of what the railroads should do, with only incidental

[24] *Traffic World,* Oct. 18, 1924, p. 848.

[25] The relationships of railroads are non-competitive only where, at a given gateway or at any alternative gateway, traffic must be turned over to a single carrier. Such cases are rare. Commonly there are a number of carriers at important traffic interchange points and alliances are built up between groups of carriers which throw traffic to one another to their mutual advantage. Carriers outside such arrangements would be regarded as competitive, and could hardly gain access to coveted terminal facilities. However, in other cases, delivering carriers of great strength may divide their traffic up among connecting roads at a given gateway, thus fostering competition between the latter. In such instances there would be less objection to the opening up of terminal facilities.

[26] For discussion of the problem of compulsory unification, see Chapter XXIX.

reference to the things which might be done to advantage by the public or by regulatory agencies. In keeping with a broad conception of what a terminal embraces, we may also add that cities should not overreach in their demand for the improvement of local conditions and that the shipping public also has an obligation in the use of terminals. We have previously referred to the various privileges (reconsignment and diversion of shipments, milling in transit, etc.) which shippers are accustomed to expect. For the most part these were granted in the first place by the carriers themselves in their competition with one another. They have become very costly, in many cases unremunerative at the special rates charged, and add to the complexity of terminal operations. Such special privileges should clearly be limited to those for which shippers are willing to make adequate payment. There are also delays which come from the failure of shippers to load and unload promptly. Instances have been not uncommon in which freight cars have been regularly used for storage purposes; this being cheaper than the provision of storage space elsewhere. Demurrage rules suffice to correct most of these abuses, but there always are some consignees who will pay demurrage rather than give up cars promptly. Special effort should be made to reduce the number of consignees who contribute to poor terminal operation in this manner, although it is doubtful whether much can be done unless carriers act jointly and with the backing of the Commission. Fortunately, there has been improvement in this respect of late. Needless to say, prompt release of equipment, prompt loading and unloading, and the reduction of the special privileges to the necessary minimum required by commercial conditions will do much to make terminal operations simpler, more expeditious, and less costly.

II. PRODUCE TERMINALS

In recent years produce terminals have become important in the larger cities. Previous to 1920 such facilities were generally unsatisfactory from the standpoint of location, equipment, and operation. During the past decade there has been a substantial improvement in the physical facilities for this type of business. The following extracts from the report of the Committee on Yards and Terminals, of the American Railway Engineering Association summarizes this subject so comprehensively that it is worthy of quotation.[27]

The object of produce terminals is to expedite, concentrate and segregate the delivery of perishable farm products, such as fruits, vegetables, and in some cases, butter, eggs, and poultry. The design of these facilities varies widely from that of freight houses and team yards handling non-perishable freight.

Business of this character is seasonal for various commodities and for the same commodity from different producing sections. It is highly desirable that the time involved in making deliveries be reduced to the absolute minimum and that the commodities be removed from buildings or cars as soon as possible. Most produce terminals have rigid rules setting forth definite periods for the display, sale, and removal of commodities from auction and sales buildings, which benefit all concerned. They promise early delivery to retail stores, enabling a jobber to purchase with the assurance that prices will not be lowered a few hours after he makes his purchase; they release the facilities for the next day's business and reduce the amount of produce that may be spoiled by waiting too long for a favorable price.

For these reasons, produce terminals must be considerably

[27] "Produce Terminals Expedite the Handling of Perishables," *Railway Age*, Oct. 22, 1932, p. 565.

larger than similar facilities for handling non-perishable freight. Obviously, traffic during peak periods must be handled without delay, and each day's traffic must be handled during a relatively short portion of the day.

From the standpoint of general economy, union terminals are favored, since they serve the entire trade of a community and can be served by all railroads, directly if practicable, or under equitable switching arrangements. This conclusion may be modified, however, in very large metropolitan areas, such as New York and Chicago.

Where two or more terminals are located in a city of average size, it is usually found that one terminal does practically all of the business. In the limited time allowed between the opening of the auction or private sales buildings to the jobbers and the closing times for sales, the jobbers naturally wish to inspect and compare the quality and price of all produce reaching the market. From a railroad standpoint, joint operation is usually cheaper and the first investment considerably less, as the joint terminal can take care of the various peaks of commodities which are shipped from different regions as already mentioned. For example, the peak of far western produce traffic is in the late summer and early fall, while that from the southern territory is heaviest during the spring and early summer.

This quotation covers most of the basic principles which should be given consideration in the planning of a terminal. Special attention should be called to the recommendation for joint ownership or operation of a terminal from the standpoint of original investment and the subsequent cost of operation to the railroad and the dealers who are using the terminal facilities.

The real impetus to modern terminal construction was the movement of the South Water market in Chicago at the time that the original market was taken over by the city. This forced concerted action by all of the dealers at one time. As a result a large part of the trade moved to the new market, which was located outside the downtown area but at a point which was central to all of the outlying sections of the city. In connection with this development, the railroads jointly arranged for the use of a new yard facility at a point which was about one mile distant from the market itself. This was equipped with house and auction facilities, had ample team track space, and permitted direct delivery of produce trains by most of the carriers to a nearby yard.

The Chicago development resulted in improved terminals in many cities. These have been generally of two types. Where there has been only one terminal in a city, it has proved successful and satisfactory to all concerned. In other instances, however, duplicate facilities have been constructed for various reasons. As is stated in the Committee's report, in such cases on terminal usually handles most of the business, although the presence of the second terminal greatly adds to its complexity and expense.

Among the developments which can be classed as reasonably satisfactory are those at Boston, Pittsburgh, Cleveland, Providence, and other points where only a single terminal has been constructed. But there are a number of cities in which the terminal situation has not been handled satisfactorily, largely because of the refusal or inability of the railroads involved to combine in a central facility. As a result duplicate terminals have been constructed and are being operated. At Philadelphia the construction of the new Pennsylvania passenger station forced the abandonment of the old and inadequate produce terminal. Repeated efforts on the part of the produce trade failed to effect a joint development of new facilities because of the refusal of the carriers to co-operate.

It was found that in November, 1926, the Baltimore and Ohio Railroad Company and the Reading Company jointly opened a produce terminal costing approximately $3,100,000 and that in July, 1927, the Pennsylvania Railroad Company opened a competitive produce terminal costing about $6,500,000. These two produce terminal facilities were then being used to less than half of their capacity, and it appeared that either of them would have been adequate alone to serve the needs of the business at Philadelphia.[28]

A similar situation developed at Detroit which is briefly summarized in the same report as follows:

> Some three or four years ago during a produce terminal war between the carriers at Detroit, Mich., the Michigan Central built a large produce terminal at Detroit, for the purpose of inducing commission merchants to locate in that building. The results were disappointing for the reason that the Detroit Union Produce Terminal, which was built by the Pennsylvania, the Wabash and the Pere Marquette Railroad Companies, has had the bulk of the produce trade.

In the case of the Detroit terminals, one of the results has been the shifting of dealers from terminal to terminal, with its disturbing effect on the industry as a whole.

The removal of the wholesale market in Washington, D.C., to permit the construction of new government buildings forced consideration of a new location to which the trade could move as a unit. Despite long consideration, the plan for a single terminal was dropped and the trade was divided into two sections. One group is now located close to the Pennsylvania produce yards, and the other several miles distant in close proximity to the Baltimore and Ohio yards. The result has been

---

[28] Interstate Commerce Commission, *Duplication of Produce Terminals*, Ex Parte No. 109, pp. 324, 336.

a definite disruption in the trade, requiring the adjustment of many trade relationships.

The situation at New York is somewhat different as the bulk of the tonnage from the Southern states has been handled by the Pennsylvania, that from the West by the Erie, that from the North and West by the New York Central, that from Maine by the New Haven, and that from Long Island by the Long Island in Brooklyn. The volume of traffic is relatively large and several of the terminals are devoted to handling special commodities such as potatoes.

The Erie and Pennsylvania railroads, which are the principal carriers of fruits and vegetables to New York, maintain separate terminals in that city, the aggregate annual rental for which at the present time amounts to $440,000 or over $4.00 per car handled. This cost does not include charges for maintenance or interest on an investment in structures and equipment, which investment exceeds $2,000,000. The Pennsylvania Railroad traffic reaches a peak in the early summer and the traffic of the Erie reaches a peak in the fall, so that the combined traffic could be handled by a union terminal of considerably less capacity than the aggregate of the individual terminals.

Probably the most flagrant case of duplication of facilities is that at Buffalo, which is outlined quite fully in the report of the Interstate Commerce Commission just cited.[29] The facilities at Buffalo were inadequate and there was consideration of the possibility of the construction of a new joint produce terminal which would be served by all railroads:

Following requests in 1928 and 1929 which did not produce

[29] The same, p. 325.

results, the Produce Exchange at Buffalo advised that a union terminal should be constructed with equal access to all railroads, and pursuant to this suggestion the interested carriers held meetings for the purpose of considering the matter. The Pennsylvania recommended a union terminal of the character suggested, and thereafter appears to have remained neutral in the controversy between other known carriers.

Following this failure to reach an agreement, the Erie and Nickel Plate interests financed the development of the Niagara Frontier Food Terminal, with total expenditures estimated at $6,711,534.61. The New York Central reconstructed its Elk Street Market at a total expenditure estimated to be $2,732,147.82. Buffalo now has two terminals, constructed at a total expenditure of over nine million dollars, with facilities greatly in excess of any immediate need. As a part of the project it was necessary to purchase the existing property of many of the dealers, and this is now closed and producing no earnings on the investment.

The situation in the markets outlined above has been given in detail as it indicates the wasteful and unnecessary expenditures which have been made by the railroads during the past five years at points where competitive conditions were acute. Investment in duplicate facilities will be claimed as a basis for freight rates on fruits and vegetables, although the only reason for such duplicate facilities is the unwillingness of the carriers involved to co-operate with each other in joint facilities.

Not only are the original investments excessive, but the maintenance of the duplicate facilities by the railroads and the increased expenses of the trade will continue as long as the duplicate facilities are in use. In each case cited, efforts have been made to consolidate operations in one terminal open to all roads, but they have not been successful because of the refusal of one or more roads to participate. The primary motive for the refusal appears to have been to force the shippers to route produce over the lines of the carrier which controlled the terminal.

III. PASSENGER TERMINALS

Passenger terminals often represent investments beyond absolutely essential requirements. The principal question to be faced, aside from the matter of design and the general scale of expenditures, is that of securing the co-operative use of facilities. This problem is less difficult than the corresponding problem in the case of freight terminals, for carriers appear more willing to enter into co-operative arrangements.

That they are able to reconcile their differences here when individualism is rampant in the use of freight terminals is but evidence of the relative unprofitableness of passenger operations. Railroads will willingly combine to reduce direct losses, but prefer to go their separate ways when their individual profits are jeopardized.[30] In some cases, however, carriers have found it difficult to reconcile their differences, as witness the long controversy in Los Angeles,[31] and the friction between carriers in Cleveland.[32] The Pennsylvania's refusal to allow the Baltimore and Ohio to continue to use its New York terminals is another illustration, though here the question of adequacy was of some importance.

[30] The Chicago Union Passenger Station (costing 75 millions) and the St. Paul Union Depot, are examples.

[31] See *Los Angeles Passenger Terminal Cases*, 100 I.C.C. 421 (1925).

[32] See 70 I.C.C. 342, and 70 I.C.C. 659 (1922). Also R. M. Lovett, "A Non-Union Union Station," *New Republic*, June 27, 1922, pp. 119-22.

At the present time the city of Philadelphia offers an excellent example of what seems to point toward a wasteful duplication; although it is understood that a joint committee of the two railroads involved are now trying to reach an agreement. The Pennsylvania Railroad is completing a large station in West Philadelphia, the inner and outer facilities of which are ample to take over the needs of the Baltimore and Ohio Railroad which has had under consideration the construction of a similar layout located nearby. There seems to be no good reason why the latter railroad should not run its trains through the new Pennsylvania station to the mutual financial advantage of both roads and at the same time eliminate an enormous outlay of money.

Some union terminals, such as the one at Washington, D.C., are operated by terminal companies owned by the railroads served by them; others are controlled and operated by one or more of the roads using them. In the cases of Washington and Philadelphia, the municipality pays for part of the cost of new terminal improvements; the city pays for those features pertaining to municipal betterments, such as new streets, and for changes in sewers, water lines, and general utilities; while the railroad pays for those features that are primarily railroad in character. The layouts in Washington and Philadelphia are excellent examples of structures built to fit into a comprehensive city plan.

The cost of operation of passenger stations is a large item in the total cost of passenger service. Terminal unification is the major force that can bring the costs into proper line. It will eliminate the wastes due to duplication of stations and terminal facilities of railroads entering the same city. It will also permit, in most cases, a re-arrangement of present passenger and train facilities to allow a much more economical operation. Economies can also be effected by building less ornate stations and elaborate layouts, except where such projects are warranted by their effect on the value of nearby railroad real estate. The valuable air rights and increase of real estate value in connection with Pennsylvania Railroad improvements in Philadelphia and the Grand Central Terminal in New York justify a large proportion of the attendant expenditures.

In a number of cities there are union bus terminals into and out of which are operated groups of bus lines. Since many of the lines operating through a city are highly competitive, often being participants in rate wars, universal terminals are somewhat out of the question. When, and if, the bus business becomes stabilized, universal terminals would permit the elimination of much waste. Bus terminals often serve as points of interchange routes for passengers. Usually the buses are serviced at garages located some distance from the passenger terminals.

IV. CONCLUSIONS

Since the cost of terminal handling amounts to a large part of the total cost of railroad transportation, it is obvious that any substantial improvements at the terminals will result in enormous savings. It is not too much to say that, if terminal facilities were unified along lines that are demonstrably feasible, annual savings in transportation costs running into scores of millions of dollars are possible. At the same time, as we shall see in the following chapter, railroad terminal reorganization is a prerequisite to the proper development of large metropolitan areas.

There are three general ways of bringing about improvements in railroad terminals, the last two being each a step in advance of the preceding one.

1. The first calls for more intensive and efficient motorization of terminal areas as indicated in Chapter XXIX. It consists mainly of developing a high degree of rail and truck co-ordination. Certain relatively minor changes in the present layout of freight houses and their facilities would be involved and certain facilities would be added.

2. The second way is an extension of the first, and includes consolidation and equal interchange of facilities and services of various railroads entering the same terminal center, thus involving complete terminal unification. Besides union freight terminals the program recognizes the use of the highway and city street as an important part of the terminal set-up. The construction of a simple system of rail belt lines would probably be included. In some cities it would be necessary only to build connecting links in existing belt lines. Construction of universal off-rail freight stations at strategic points, and changes in certain freight stations from a "will call" basis to one more suitable for pick-up and delivery service might be included. The elimination of duplicate stations and other facilities in some of the present terminal centers, together with a consolidation of lighterage and car-float services and pier stations (in the case of port cities like New York) would constitute part of the program under this second method.

3. The third way is an extension of the second whereby an ideal layout would be created. It calls for a complete re-arrangement and re-design of a large part of the present layout, involving (in some cases) a reloca-

tion of rail heads. In the case of some cities an elaborate system of rail belt lines, involving subways, tunnels,
and bridges, would be built. Under this plan terminal
unification, general consolidation of services, and truck
co-ordination would be developed to the maximum. In
the case of most large ports and terminals the expense
attached to this method of improvement precludes its
consideration at this time, but it may constitute the basis
for a comprehensive plan of future development.

It is realized that each terminal city has its own special problem to solve. Geographical layout and general
topography vary widely and expansions and plans for
improvement must be adapted to the needs of each case.
However, in general, the proper solution will involve
a high degree of railway terminal unification and extensive co-ordination with trucks and with port and waterway facilities.

CHAPTER XXXIV

TRANSPORTATION AND CITY PLANNING

The need for unification or close co-ordination of railroad terminal facilities, as demonstrated in the previous chapter is only a part of a larger terminal problem. Other methods of transport have equally difficult terminal problems and all of them have a bearing on the railroad situation in our great cities. This relationship vitally affects the city-dweller in the cost of living and in the efficiency and amenities of urban life.

Transportation facilities and commodity interchange have been principal causes for the very existence of cities and towns. Without relying too far on a strictly economic interpretation of history in terms of trade routes and commerce, it is obvious that points of interchange between carriers, such as harbors, heads of navigation on important rivers, railway junctions, and places where highway travel is interrupted, have been the locations where urban developments typically have started and thrived.

Similarly an examination of the growth of cities shows that both the direction and the speed of development have been largely controlled by the transportation facilities provided within the area at any particular time. American cities have a common characteristic in the similarity of the form of their development—following the transportation lines and producing a finger-like plan often compared to an octopus.[1]

A living octopus presumably is not forced to conscious effort to make his arteries, veins, and nerves function

[1] See Arthur C. Comey, *Regional Planning Theory*, 1923.

without conflict. Our cities, however, are forced to attempt the co-ordination of different methods of transport within the urban area or to suffer various forms of
strangulation and paralysis.

Each system of transportation has been developed
with little or no regard for all other systems and in many
cases with large amounts of duplication in both terminals
and line facilities within the same field. Competition
rather than co-ordination has been the primary motive.
Interference and lack of co-ordination handicap the efficiency of each method and the resulting confusion constitutes a waste and loss for both the carriers and the
public.

Except in a few unusual cases[2] the street systems of
our towns have borne little if any relation to harbors or
wharves, railroad locations have done violence to the
street systems, and the last agency to arrive on the scene
—air transport—has had to be satisfied with terminals
located without adequate rail or highway connections.

The conflicts and confusion resulting from lack of co-
ordination among transport methods has become so great
and so wasteful that one by one towns, cities, and regions
have turned to planning commissions and planning
studies for an answer to their problems.

The experience of the last few decades in city and regional planning is suggestive of larger possibilities in the
development of a co-ordinated national transportation
plan as well as in the solution of terminal transfer problems. City planning deals with a living organism of related activities in which there is a delicate balance between different functions—all of which must be cared

[2] The 1811 Plan of New York provided frequent cross-town streets
connecting the wharves on the East and North Rivers.

for if a healthy body is to result. The arteries, breathing spots, and main centers of activity must be carefully correlated. The "City Effective" is one goal of city planning. It is primarily preventive medicine applied to the urban organism.

From another point of view, the city plan is a great composition or painting, illustrating existing and proposed uses of land and composed so that the indications of different uses by different colors form a unified and harmonious whole. This conception of city planning as a great design has given rise to the term "City Beautiful."

The first requirement of city planning is a clear understanding and statement of the situation in any given city. Upon the basis of such a statement specific preventive measures, remedies, and cures may be worked out. Then, there must be a measure of control over such factors in city growth as zoning, highway layout, and public expenditures for improvements; finally public support is necessary if specific projects and phases of the plan are actually to be put into effect.

To construct and formulate a city plan, it has been found useful to develop systems of various elements and then to work these systems together into a composite pattern. Thus we have park systems and highway systems—each presumably highly developed and efficiently organized for its primary purpose. We are now concerned with:

1. The co-ordination of transport facilities to form a single co-ordinated system serving the city or region and
2. The relation of the transportation system to other aspects of city development which are caused or effected by transportation decisions.

Each transport method in our cities has its own problems and special problems in relation to other methods. Each one of these problems must be viewed not only from the transportation angle, but also from the standpoint of its effect on the use and development of adjoining lands. What part does each method or agency play in the whole city plan?

I. THE PRESENT CHAOTIC SITUATION

1. *The railroad terminals.* The railroad system in urban and terminal areas is usually a series of highly developed, but competing units. As was shown in the preceding chapter we have separate lines and terminals with overlaps and duplication of services as well as frequent conflicts. Under a competitive system the most heroic efforts have been necessary to secure the minimum of co-ordination in the form of belt lines, common user spurs, and occasional union passenger stations, produce markets, or inland freight terminals. A *system* implies the integration of the many elements—the organization of all facilities to a single end. The city dweller in general—the manufacturer, shipper, taxpayer, and passenger—regards the railroad as one agency, not as a series of disconnected and separate companies.

The lack of a single integrated railroad layout in most urban areas involves enormous waste in use of ground space with high taxes, in duplication of buildings, rails, and countless other improvements. There are wastes such as those created by the necessity for grade separations to care for the interweaving of competitive or conflicting railroad lines. In brief, there has been a mad scramble to get favored locations for in-town terminals which has inevitably resulted in scrambled lines to reach those points.

The union passenger station has proved its value and yet in the average American city it is still the exception rather than the rule.[3] Almost every comprehensive city plan prepared by competent professional advisers has included proposals for consolidation of railway passenger stations. Among the more noteworthy of these proposals, those in the 1908 Chicago Plan[4] or the 1925 Cincinnati Plan[5] or in the 1930 Rochester, N. Y. Plan may be cited as examples. Completed or authorized projects for union passenger stations exemplifying the value and efficiency of such joint endeavors are too numerous for detailed mention but the work at Washington, D.C., Cleveland, Cincinnati, Buffalo, Omaha, and Tulsa shows the trend. Indianapolis claims the first union station in the United States. The recent decision of the Supreme Court on the Los Angeles Terminal case is indicative of the future. There is small excuse for the duplication of passenger service with expensive trackage over expensive rights-of-way into the center of our large cities when all the traffic could be handled over a smaller number of tracks and in much less space by joint use of such facilities.[6]

Similarly with freight terminals. In a few notable instances, joint terminals have been arranged and in a

[3] "Of the 68 cities of the U.S. with a population of 100,000 or over (1920 census) there are only 18 that have what may be called bona fide union stations." W. H. Hudson in *Proceedings of the National Conference on City Planning*, 1926, p. 145.

[4] The Union Station on Canal Street is now in use, an Illinois Central Terminal is covered by ordinance, and the Chicago River straightening has prepared the way for a solution of the South Side Terminal problem in general accordance with the plans originally advocated by Mr. F. A. Delano and later incorporated in the Chicago Plan. See *Chicago Railway Terminals*, 1906.

[5] The $55,000,000 project now under construction is all in accordance with the Official Plan of Cincinnati.

[6] See discussion of same subject in Chapter XXXV.

few other cases union produce markets have been created —but over against the successful accomplishment of a union produce market in Chicago must be placed the failures in Washington and Philadelphia where competing produce markets largely sponsored by competitive railroads have been misplaced and now cause confusion and loss to both railroads and city.

Separate development of competing railroads has left the problem of interchange in many cities unsolved and often not even faced. The belt line, common clearing yard, and joint car float system, are devices to meet this need which could be developed further to great advantage, as was shown in the preceding chapter.

These terminal and interchange facilities no longer need be located close to the business district. As was shown in the chapter on "Co-ordination of Rail and Motor Transport," the truck and new methods for transfer of goods between truck and railroad car, have made possible the use of cheaper land in the suburbs for large scale union terminal arrangements. These outer terminals may be supplemented by inland terminals served by motor.

Relocations of terminals requiring large areas further from the center of the city—retreating along the main line—is no new suggestion in railroad history and is a natural accompaniment of improved and speedier transportation of people and goods by other transport methods. With the replacement of the horse-car by the rapid transit railway, the location of a passenger station many times further from the business district is still the same time-distance from the office or store. The change from horse-drawn dray to the motor truck with an interchangeable body makes a similar removal of freight stations possible without increasing the time from rail-road car to store door.

The withdrawal of terminals back on the railroad line has many precedents, among which may be cited the Boston and Lowell Railroad from Haymarket Square in Boston and the Pennsylvania from Broad Street in Philadelphia. The New York Central retreated its passenger terminal in the seventies from 4th Avenue and 26th Street in New York and went out into the country to 42nd Street. By the Act of February 28, 1903 the Pennsylvania Railroad gave up its passenger terminal in "down-town" Washington to combine with other railroads in the new Union Station. More recently removal of freight terminals has been accomplished or agreed upon in Louisville, Madison, and Asheville.[7]

Such withdrawals would place the large areas needed for railroad purposes on cheaper land and free the present locations for new and more lucrative development. They involve difficulties in adjustment of established street, rapid transit, and similar services to the new locations and in the case of industries with spur tracks a radical readjustment of shipping methods. Relocation also means outlay for construction on the new site. In spite of these difficulties, the long range plan for relocation seems certain to prevail. If that is the eventual plan, steps taken now may be related to that aim and fitted to that pattern.

Immediate consolidations and joint use of tracks possible under partial unification of competing lines or under complete unification within terminal areas might well produce substantial economies pending the time when funds may be available for more thorough read-

[7] Hubbard and Hubbard, *Our Cities Today and Tomorrow*, p. 234.

justments. Through terminal companies owned jointly by groups of railroads, passenger stations, belt lines, spur tracks, inland freight terminal, and produce markets are now operated. To this list of activities more might be added, such as joint car float stations, tugs and lighters, joint clearing yards, etc.

The organization of the railroad terminals as a single system is necessary to secure the efficiency and economy of transportation which the railroads can supply.[8] The terminals are the knots in the transport system. We must untangle the knots.

2. *Railroads and other transport methods.* Not only must the railroads be treated as a unified system in terminal areas, but that system must be co-ordinated with other transport methods, such as highway, water, rapid transit, and air. In the urban terminal areas each of these methods is or could be supplementary to others. To secure the health of the "octopus" the veins and nerves must be co-ordinated with the arteries and not be in competition with them.

Highway and railroad inevitably cross and recross with consequent problems of grade crossing eliminations and expensive investments in bridges, tunnels, and elevated structures. Locations of railroads in the streets as in Syracuse, or on a Chinese Wall as in Philadelphia, create additional problems not only of interference between different transportation methods but in the life of the community. The use of parts of Maryland and

---

[8] "Unified management and operation also is, I believe, essential to a successful solution of the steam railroad problem, for without it jealousies, non-progressiveness, financial impotence, and a natural devotion to the interests of the stockholder rather than the public will continue to spell inefficiency." Col. W. J. Wilgus, "Transportation—the New York Region," *Regional Survey of New York and its Environs,* 1925, Vol. 4, p. 162.

Virginia Avenues in Washington, for instance, interferes with traffic lines to the highway bridge over the Potomac, with the development of Southwest Washington for residence, and with the proper setting of government buildings in the central composition of the city.[9] These "interferences" are important not only because of the actual inconveniences which they put upon the public but also, and perhaps to greater degree, because of their psychological effect upon large numbers of people. Just the phrase—"Chinese Wall"—is indicative of the psychological aspect of the problem.

The development of a supplementary relationship between rail and highway carriers, with resultant avoidance of the necessity for rail heads in the center of many urban areas, may reduce the number of rail lines which conflict with the streets. If superfluous railheads can be withdrawn there will be fewer grade crossings to be eliminated.

Enormous outlays for grade crossing eliminations have been made in recent years with consequent burdens on both railroads and taxpayers. Some of the larger programs have been carefully integrated with city plans, as in the case of the $25,000,000 Dayton project toward which an $8,000,000 bond issue was voted in 1926, the Cincinnati project previously referred to, and the $5,000,000 bond issue approved in 1924 for Louisville.[10] The division of costs between the railroads and the public for grade crossing eliminations varies from city to city and from state to state according to local

[9] See *Annual Report of National Capital Park and Planning Commission*, 1931, pp. 22-24.

[10] For brief review of grade separation projects in accordance with city plans see Hubbard and Hubbard, *Our Cities Today and Tomorrow*, pp. 338-40.

circumstances. The cost of grade separations is so great that the railroads should be taking more active interest in city plans which determine the number and locations of necessary underpasses and overpasses. The development of major street plans by planning commissions for cities, counties, and regions foreshadows the future highway arrangement and its conflicts with the railroad lines. By attention to these plans and concentration on the through routes, there are possibilities of very considerable ultimate savings to both railroads and municipalities.

Costs of new highway facilities in built-up areas are so nearly prohibitive that opportunities to use abandoned railway locations for express highways warrant serious consideration, particularly when grade separation structures can be utilized. Conversion of unnecessary railroad locations to highway use with trucking facilities might care for the lighter class of industries which formerly felt themselves dependent on spur tracks along such lines. The effect on values of property adjoining railroad rights of way converted to highway use may also justify considerable municipal outlays for such streets. The experience gained from Park Avenue, New York, and the new Pennsylvania Avenue in Philadelphia indicates the enormous possibilities in such developments, for these projects have both been handled with careful attention to the interrelation between transport facilities and uses of adjoining lands.

The removal of freight terminals from the center of urban areas to less congested sites and the gradual development of store door delivery will shift the emphasis in street and highway construction from the radial lines to the circumferential routes around and across the built-up area. Because of the natural relation between highway facilities and growth of the normal city, the radials of most American towns are usually well located for their purpose. The cross-connections, diagonals, and circumferential routes have received insufficient attention.[11]

Shifting of the railroad freight terminals would release property in congested areas and simultaneously prove a boon to highway travel in the stimulation of action to fill the long felt need for cross-town through streets. Here again, we find a need for close attention on the part of terminal authorities or railroad companies to the city planning proposals for new major highways so that new yards and terminals may be conveniently served and at the same time not themselves interfere with the orderly arrangement of major thoroughfares.

3. *Railroads and rapid transit.* Numerous suggestions and a few examples have been worked out for the use of railroad rights of way in urban areas for rapid transit. Some of these cases like that of the Illinois Central in Chicago, or the New Haven, New York Central, and Long Island out of New York,[12] have involved railroad operation of a rapid transit suburban service as a modern development of the commuter's train. In other cases use of abandoned branch lines for rapid transit has been arranged with local transit companies as along the Ashmont-Milton line south of Boston.

If passenger services are combined in union stations, parts of the abandoned rights of way with investments in grade separations may be useful for rapid transit.

[11] See recommendations of Committee on City Planning and Zoning, National Conference on Street and Highway Safety, Dec. 9, 1924, p. 12.

[12] An ambitious scheme for consolidating all railroad and rapid transit lines in metropolitan Boston has recently been presented in a bill now pending before the Massachusetts General Court.

Similarly, unnecessary branch railroad lines or parallel lines in urban centers may prove far more economical and otherwise preferable to subway or elevated construction for transit service[13]

The cumbersome methods of passenger transfer between local transportation methods and the railroads, together with the formalities of railroad embarkation of passengers, impede the development of the commuter or suburban traffic on the railroads in many cities.

The ordinary passenger in metropolitan areas has to use one or more methods of transport between train and destination. Whether his route involves bus and ferry, as in the New York Baltimore and Ohio service, or subway and taxi as in the more common case, each change or delay along the route is an added obstacle to the efficient organization of the journey. To minimize these obstacles both the physical arrangement and the operating control of all the transport agencies involved must be highly co-ordinated.

4. *Railroads and waterways.* For various rather uncertain reasons water-borne traffic has the right of way at a drawbridge regardless of the relative costs, convenience, or number of people involved. The railroads in most instances have to bear the full cost of both construction and operation of the drawbridge. This is the most obvious conflict between the railroads and shipping interests in urban areas.

Conflicts of this sort have been faced at the North Station in Boston and along the Chicago River. The great project for the relocation of the Chicago River

[13] "Railroad commuter traffic, up to 1924, had been doubling every nine years and total railroad traffic every 13 years." *Regional Survey of N.Y. and Its Environs*, Vol. 3, p. 84.

south of Twelfth Street in Chicago has finally been accomplished after almost 30 years of agitation and illustrates the many kinds of advantages that may accrue from a well planned project.

Transfer of goods from rail to ship and *vice versa* is the expensive item in port operation. Lighterage, trucks, and similar devices all involve handling goods several times. The marginal railroad is limited in its utility when the pier and slip arrangement of docks is adopted. The experience of many ports, such as Antwerp and New Orleans, with a marginal railroad along a quay deserve more attention in this country.

5. *Railroads and airports.* The possibilities of rail-air transfer have hardly been touched in the recent phenomenal development of air lines. Locations of airports near or on railroad lines is admitted as desirable for convenient service of an airport or of aircraft factories. Occasional efforts have been made to simplify or encourage transfer of passengers or goods between the two methods, but this opportunity has hardly been examined in the large metropolitan areas.

There have been a number of proposals for the construction of airports over terminal yards and passenger stations in close association with post offices, but such use of valuable air rights on a large scale seems unlikely to be economically justified. A more logical development would appear to be the construction of railroad stations adjoining or near the airports when railroad locations are convenient.

II. THE PLACE OF RAILROADS IN THE CITY PLAN

In our country the railroads have played a major part in determining the pattern of city growth. The distribution of land uses and the appearance of the city show the importance of railroad activities.

The location of passenger stations, for instance, has had a marked influence on the character and location of business districts—a waning influence since other methods of transportation have come into the field—but still one of the controlling factors. Because of its importance it is natural that the entrance to the city should have been treated as a special feature in the city plan and often made a part of the civic center or central composition. The Washington Union Station and the new Cleveland Terminal are perhaps the best examples of this tendency, while the approaches to the new Pennsylvania Station in Philadelphia illustrate the value placed on an appropriate setting and its relation to other elements of the city plan.

The location of freight terminals has been an equally effective influence in the location of industries. The freight line, and particularly the belt line, has been the natural location for industrial growth, but in almost every city there is much more so-called industrial frontage than is ever likely to be utilized for industrial purposes. The railroads have cast a blight on these areas for residential use and in many cases through subsidiary or related companies the railroads are now "loaded up" with this kind of property holding.

A consistent movement of large industries to decentralize or rather recentralize outside the densely built up sections of metropolitan centers, in order to secure better labor conditions, lower taxes, or other advantages has been encouraged by the availability of large tracts of relatively low values and near the place of residence of employees. This movement has been hailed by city planners not only because of its social significance but also because it provides suitable use of otherwise blighted areas on the outskirts and makes possible a more economical and efficient use of abandoned areas in the older parts of the city.[14]

Industrial districts and freight yards are necessarily extensive and therefore constitute blockades and interferences with the normal city growth. Their proper location or relocation in the city and regional plan is therefore a major item in the development of better conditions in our cities. Whichever movement comes first—the change in the railroads or in industries—a large amount of inconvenience is sure to result for the other. Perhaps the "withdrawal" of rail heads may prove an added stimulus to industrial "recentralization."

The zoning plans of most cities—and over 1200 communities are zoned in this country—usually set aside industrial areas along the railroads. Such zoning is obviously to the advantage of the railroads. Zoning plans are, however, subject to change and there is constant need for stabilizing influences to preserve the plan. The railroads have paid too little attention to zoning plans in metropolitan areas where by their support and interest zoning might be promoted and upheld.[15]

The location of freight lines in relation to the service of industries involves numerous complications. To avoid grade crossings of streets and highways the tracks must ordinarily be either elevated or depressed. The elevated

[14] The railroads might well follow this trend in their own activities, relocate offices not necessarily in close contact with the public in attractive neighborhoods on the outskirts instead of on expensive in-town property. Accounting, claims, tariff printing and similar activities could be better conducted and at less overhead cost for rents, etc.

[15] See C. F. Loweth, Chief Engineer, C. M. & St. P. Ry., *Proceedings of National Conference on City Planning*, 1926, pp. 138-39.

line presents complications for construction of spur tracks to serve manufacturing plants but is advantageous for bottom dumping cars. The depressed line has special advantages in the creation of possible air rights such as those along Park Avenue in New York and as are utilized for post offices in New York and Chicago. The increased use of air rights over railroad lines appears to be a possible source of much additional railroad revenue, but to secure the benefits great outlays for electrification or smoke control[16] are a prerequisite.

Electrification is an important item to the city planner because of its effects in permitting the greater use of air rights, elimination of noise and smoke in residential areas, and its possibilities of increased rapidity of pick-up and changes in switching costs in relation to railroad services. These same advantages may, of course, come through future development of the Diesel engines or turbo-generator engines.

These few items illustrating the relationship of railroad problems to uses of adjoining lands and general city development would not be truly indicative of the problems involved without some mention of the effect of railroad activities on apparently unrelated projects. The union station in Washington, for instance, made possible the restoration of the original L'Enfant plan for the Mall Avenue connecting the Capitol and the Washington Monument. The new Pennsylvania Station in Philadelphia, as previously noted, is intimately connected with the Schuylkill River improvement. Waterfront parks in several cities are said to owe their existence in part at least to the desire of railroads to see areas which might be served by rival water carriers removed

[16] Steam engines are used in Chicago by supply of ventilating ducts.

from competition with sites near or adjacent to their tracks.

Railroads are therefore potent factors in the development and growth of urban life. To play their full part they must be more efficiently organized in themselves, co-ordinated with other transport methods, and their facilities arranged to promote the orderly and efficient use of land and the social well-being of the community. On the other hand railroads should take, for their own benefit, a much more active part in city and regional planning which eventually directly or indirectly will affect the railroad situation. Other public utilities such as the telephone companies, have already seen this need and have undertaken long range studies both of their own and in co-operation with official and unofficial planning agencies. The planning point of view involving a comprehensive analysis of future distribution of land use and services should be recognized and fostered by the railroads.

III. STREETS AND HIGHWAYS AS TRANSPORTATION LINES IN THE CITY PLAN

Since this statement is intended to deal with all avenues of communication in the broadest sense—streets and highways—furnishing the access to every individual lot—are perhaps the most important subjects for consideration. Before starting a brief discussion of these points, however, it is well to note that streets in the city are far more than means of access or movement; they provide light and air, the location for water and sewer services, and countless other purposes, which are outside the scope of our inquiry.

Many people think that the street layout is the city plan. Certainly it is a major element, but from what has already been said here the reader will realize that all kinds of land use—parks, commercial areas, airports, railroads and reservoirs—are all parts of the city plan. The streets, like the railroads, are an element in the larger composition.

Problems of street efficiency are similar to those on the railroads. The system is incomplete. To make the roads and avenues of urban areas serve as a transportation system, the first requirement is a unification of the street arrangement through the preparation, adoption, and execution of a major street plan which will differentiate between the kinds of streets and tie the loose ends together in a pattern. Most major street plans, by which are meant the chief arteries of communication generally adopted by American cities, emphasize the inadequacy of by-passes, circumferential and diagonal routes, or other means of supplying needed connections to fill in the gaps. The provision for interchanges among suburban sections is as incomplete in many highway plans as are the corresponding facilities among competing railroads. This situation frequently represents the last vestige of the original small town roads radiating from the center of our older communities or feeding old toll bridges. Now, however, the street system must be unified as must the railroad system.

Besides the inadequacies and gaps in right-of-way, traffic delays and blockades often interfere with the efficient use of the street system. Three kinds of attacks on this problem are now being tried which among them bid fair greatly to increase the efficiency of street transportation.

The "freeway" is an adaptation of the parkway idea to serve all kinds of traffic.[17] With a right of way along

[17] For example, the Wayne County super-highways out of Detroit.

which abutters have no rights of access, turning and stopping is reduced to a minimum. If frontage is permitted a "three barrelled" road with an expressway in the center and access roads on each side may accomplish the same purposes.[18] With grade separations and few entrances, speeds can be maintained.

Grade separation is an expensive matter but already on parkways and such lines as U. S. Route No. 1 in New Jersey, great efforts and much money have been expended with remarkable results. The intersections of roads, like the railroad terminals, are the knots in the system and to untie the knots progressive steps of rotary traffic and grade separation must be resorted to.

Still another method of reducing traffic delays which is advocated by many planners is greater differentiation of highway use with standardization of sizes and weights of vehicles. Differentiation of main thoroughfares from ordinary streets and from parkways is already common, and further classification by restrictive rules applying to the weight or width of vehicles, or to speeds, should further increase efficiency of highway use. Restrictions limiting left hand turns and crossings aid in relieving congestion.

Streets are legally areas dedicated to movement, but many a traffic tie-up is due to use of street area for storage, that is, parking, or for loading and unloading of trucks. The problem has become so acute in some congested areas that parking is altogether prohibited, as in the Chicago Loop. The solution of the problem lies in the definite adoption of consistently more and more stringent regulations to make possible the commercial

[18] See Gilmore D. Clarke, "Modern Motor Arteries," *Proceedings of National Conference on City Planning*, 1930, pp. 61-75.

supply of storage space off the street.[19] Ultimately we may come to the "self-contained" block as advocated by Dr. Miller McClintock of the Erskine Bureau of Traffic Research at Harvard University,[20] which proposes that each city block should provide parking space for all vehicles doing business on that block without encroaching on street area.

A limited application of this principle has already been placed in the zoning regulations of Denver, which requires provision inside lot lines in business districts for suitable areas to be used for off-street loading and unloading of trucks.

The cost of the highway system may well be reduced in many cities by recognition of the different purposes served by different streets and the more careful classification of uses and construction requirements. The major street plan should assist in the classification of streets and make possible large economies in construction of grade separations at points of conflict with rail and water lines.

The street system, like the railroads, has its conflicts with other transport methods. The use of the streets for mass transport on street cars and buses has brought special difficulties and confusion. The place of the electric railway or street car in the city plan is not yet determined but there are many obvious changes that must be expected in the present set-up in most cities. The elevated railway which was once hailed as the final and complete answer to the problem is now cursed for obstruction of

[19] Competition between free parking space in the streets and garages paying taxes and investment costs naturally operates to prevent private investment in off-street parking facilities.

[20] See *Proceedings of National Conference on City Planning*, 1930, pp. 42-52; also *Parking and Garage Problem, Washington, D.C.*, 1930.

light and air and because of its noise. The advantages of the bus in increased mobility and rapidity of pick-up are partly offset by the number of units necessary to carry the load. The taxicab has further confused the situation with cheap rates competing directly with the bus and street car. The present chaotic conditions in this field clearly demonstrate the necessity of a single regulatory agency to secure transit service for the public.

Streets must give access to the waterfront, but opinions differ as to how that access can best be provided. Each port and pier is a separate problem. The marginal street parallel with the waterfront and serving a quay or slips is the most obvious method which has general endorsement.

Airports necessarily interfere with the street system, and, therefore, must be carefully located, in relation to both through traffic routes and business centers.

Freight and mail tubes of small bore for relief of congestion on the streets and for speedier movement have been tried in Chicago and Boston and were projected on an extensive scale by the Port Authority of New York. The economic justification for such developments is now questioned, but the value of such facilities cannot be judged solely by the present paying traffic.

The street system is perhaps the most important single factor in the city plan, for it not only provides the chief method of transport within the city but also determines by the spacing of streets the sizes of blocks and lots, and the suitability of lots for different uses. The location of a street parallel with a railroad line, for instance, may serve as an interceptor for many vehicular traffic lines and divert them to a single grade separation. The distance between such a street and the railroad tracks will also determine the arrangement or size of industrial plants along the railroad and that distance will facilitate or complicate grade separations of rail and highway.

The efficiency of the street system is also a major factor in determining land values. The highly organized vehicular traffic system, including parkways, boulevards, freeways, and other categories for street or park travel, provides accessibility combined with amenity. The huge success of such projects as the Bronx Parkway in Westchester County New York, and the Mt. Vernon Memorial Highway south of Washington, D.C., show how practical requirements for traffic and beautiful surroundings can be combined to everyone's advantage.

IV. WATERFRONTS AND PORTS

The ports and waterfronts of the United States have long histories of private ownership, with consequent spurts and delays in their accommodation to new conditions and new needs. Many railroads have actively participated in port development through ownership of property and construction of piers and other facilities.

In this field again there has been little co-ordination except under compulsion, government aid, or public ownership. A few notable examples of co-ordinated factory, rail, and water terminals under private management, like the Bush development in Brooklyn, may be cited, and others have been partially successful under public control. A most ambitious combination of rail, air, and water facilities is proposed at Hog Island by the city of Philadelphia.[21]

The desirability of public ownership of waterfronts is now generally recognized not only as a means of securing capital for needed improvements but also to assure

[21] See *Regional Plan of the Philadelphia Tri-state District*, 1932, pp. 204-07, 232-33.

flexibility in meeting future requirements which often seem to require changes on considerable stretches of harbor frontage.

V. AIRPORTS

Airports are the last terminal facility to be adjusted to the city plan.[22] They should be as close as possible to the business district in terms of time, because long traffic delays on the ground cut into the gains of speed in the air. Few cities can provide close-in airport sites because of the special area requirements of an air field. It is not just a field that is needed, but a very large field of slight slope with long runways in the directions of the prevailing winds and control of factory chimneys, wires, and building heights for considerable distances outside the limits of the field. Such extensive areas are not often available close to business districts unless they may be reclaimed from the sea or from some marsh or riverbed.

Airways have not yet become the problem which many anticipated with the development of aviation, but already the air beacons have been located on the principal routes. What the effect of air routes will be on the use of lands beneath them is not yet evident. At all costs, the air-billboard must be prevented.

VI. CONCLUSION

The efficiency and adaptation of various transport methods to changing needs in urban areas requires not only the unification of facilities within each separate transport method, but also the co-ordination of all methods in a unified transportation plan. Not only must railroad terminals be consolidated but all terminals must be co-ordinated.

[22] See *Airports*, Harvard City Planning Studies, 1930, Harvard University Press.

Railroads, highways, rapid transit, ports, and airports in urban areas are all working parts of a vital organism. By working through a city plan, each transportation agency can fit its program and function into a larger composition. Co-ordination of transport facilities in urban areas is a logical first step toward a national transportation plan.

CHAPTER XXXV

METHODS OF EFFECTING TERMINAL UNIFICATION

The co-ordination of *all* transport methods in terminal areas is essential to the healthy growth and existence of the whole community. How may such co-ordination be secured? We have seen in the preceding chapter the need and advantages both to the public and the carriers of unification of terminals in accordance with a comprehensive city or regional plan. In fact, city planning has often been a synonym for co-ordination of land uses and services. Planning shows the possibilities but does not necessarily involve organization of the accomplishment. What methods have been tried and what new methods are open to us?

Varying degrees of co-ordination have been obtained and are now being obtained through three principal methods—voluntary joint agreements, public regulatory action, and outright public ownership. This is the day of co-operation instead of cut-throat competition.

I. VOLUNTARY CONSOLIDATION

Organization by voluntary agreement among carriers for joint use of facilities is no new development in the transportation field. There are literally hundreds of agreements involving every terminal facility from an industrial spur track to a whole system of clearing yards.[1] The different forms for joint action may be considered in order of their completeness—from the railroad ter-

[1] For brief summary of conditions along these lines in 50 cities and ports in the United States and Canada, see *Report of Terminal Commission*, Massachusetts Senate, 401, Apr. 1, 1916.

834

minal facility owned by the various railroads which jointly use it, through the facility used on a rental basis, to the ownership of subsidiary services by principal carriers and the inclusive terminal company operating many varieties of transport facility under unified control. As was shown in Chapter XXXIII there has been considerable co-ordination of terminal facilities in various metropolitan centers. In some cases there is joint ownership, but a more common plan is for one carrier to grant the use of its facilities to another on some agreed basis. The examples cited there show also the fundamental weakness of this method—that wherever one or more railroads in a given terminal area hold a dominating position, it is next to impossible to secure voluntary agreements which will permit competing lines to use the facilities of the dominant carrier, except upon terms which offset any likely financial advantages.

Railroad control of subsidiary terminal facilities for other transport methods is another common form of voluntary consolidation. The railroads, as the most wealthy and in many respects the strongest transportation agency, have reached into other fields, controlling bus lines, constructing grain elevators, operating trucking services, and building piers for ocean-going vessels. Naturally in such cases there is a high degree of co-ordination between the facilities under single control—but again we find lack of co-ordination between competing lines or a tendency to utilize subsidiary facilities in an uneconomical manner in the interest of the owner railroad. It is said, for instance, that because of railroad ownership of pier facilities in Boston Harbor and the switching or transfer charges between railroads, a cargo destined for points on more than one road runs the risk of delays and costs which militate against the use of the port even though Boston is nearer Liverpool than is New York.[2] It is not difficult to understand, therefore, why there should be a strong movement for consolidation of facilities in Boston.

The terminal company is perhaps the best example of the organization of many facilities in close co-ordination on a voluntary basis. The Bush Terminal in Brooklyn, with piers, factories, warehouses, and its own railroad, as well as its own residential district for employees, shows what can be done. The Canton Company in Baltimore also operates docks, warehouses, and railroad facilities, as does the Galveston Wharf Company with 30 blocks of waterfront in Galveston, Texas. There are a few other successful examples of unified control of terminal facilities in restricted areas in this country.

The significance of these examples lies in their rarity. Whether the difficulties lie in lack of capital or lack of vision, the success of the trials already made indicates the desirability of extension of the principles involved to whole terminal districts.

It has sometimes been said that the anti-trust laws have been an important factor in preventing the joint development of terminals. Obviously, the removal of legal restraint could have done little where, as we have just seen, the will to act together was generally lacking. The anti-trust laws, however, did tend to check carriers from uniting in providing terminal facilities, exclusion from which would have worked serious hardship to other carriers.[3] It is also a fact that the Interstate Commerce Act (until its amendment in 1920) and the many de-

[2] See *Port of Boston*, New England Development Association, 1931.
[3] See the *Terminal Railroad Association of St. Louis* case, a suit instituted in 1905 and finally decided in 1917, which established the

cisions under it presupposed an individualistic control of terminals. The only instances in which a carrier was required to open its terminals to other carriers arose when a carrier which had voluntarily opened its terminals to some carriers refused to open them to others. Even in such cases the Commission required the opening of terminals to applicant carriers only if convinced that the public would thereby be afforded needed relief.

The possible deterrent effect of the anti-trust laws upon terminal cooperation has been wholly voided by the Transportation Act of 1920. The way is now clear for any amount of joint action legitimately required for the furnishing of adequate terminal facilities.

II. PUBLIC CONTROLS

To promote or compel just such joint arrangements as these, various public agencies have been created by local, state, and federal authority with general and special powers. These controls may be grouped for convenience of discussion according to the degree of their authority.

Planning controls have been set up in almost all of the metropolitan areas of the United States under planning commissions which are preferably outside the regular administrative and legislative machinery of the local government. To be effective, these commissions must have mandatory powers to secure information and to prepare and constantly revise a comprehensive plan. Planning is a continuing function because the city plan like the city itself is never finished and constantly chang-

---

right of carriers to join in the furnishing of terminal facilities, provided all carriers are admitted on equitable terms and operations are strictly of a terminal character.

ing conditions require changing plans. To prevent too
great fluidity with consequent losses from lack of stabilization some planning commissions have additional powers to check public improvements which conflict with the
requirements of the plan. This check may take the form
of compulsory reference of projects to the commission
for advice before final action by the legislative or administrative authority or it may go further and require
a two-thirds or three-fourths vote of the legislative body
to secure approval of a project against the recommendation of the planning commission.[3] Most city planning
acts follow the model prepared by the United States
Department of Commerce in requiring the approval of
the planning commission for the opening of new streets
or for plats and subdivisions of property.

Through these powers over public improvements,
streets, subdivisions, and zoning, planning commissions
have played a large part in securing closer co-ordination
of transportation facilities in urban areas. Their advice
has been so generally well considered that their influence has far outreached their formal powers. With the
more active interest and support of the carriers, the planning commission can even further promote the efficiency
and co-ordination of transportation in terminal areas.

Terminal commissions or port commissions of various
names have been created from time to time for many of
the larger terminal areas in this country. These commissions have been fact-finding bodies, advisers on legislation, in charge of construction of public works, or engaged in the actual operation of terminal facilities of

[3] See *Official Plan of Cincinnati and Standard City Planning Enabling
Act*, U. S. Department of Commerce.

various kinds. Our larger cities have had experience with a long series of such commissions. Most of these commissions have been handicapped by restriction of their field to special aspects of the larger terminal problem— as, for instance, to rapid transit, or public piers, or electrification of railroads, etc.

The development of ports after investigations has been stimulated by such boards as the Port of Seattle Commission and the Port Development Commission of Baltimore, Board of Harbor Commissioners of Wilmington, the Port District Commission of Portland, Oregon, and the Board of Commissioners of the Port of New Orleans. This list is a random selection of names from a long array of such organizations and shows the customary adoption of this kind of governmental action for port development.

The most comprehensive governmental organization in this field is the interstate board known as the Port of New York Authority, which has successfully constructed numerous and enormous aids to the integration of transport facilities about New York Harbor as "self-liquidating" projects. With the prestige of its past accomplishments and its position as a creature of the states of New York and New Jersey, it has been able to find capital for projects like the George Washington Bridge and the Inland Freight Terminal when such projects would have been practically beyond the reach of ordinary private organizations. Although its powers are very broad, the success of its past ventures has rested on its powers of persuasion and its comprehensive plans. Compulsion is not its method and projects are delayed or abandoned if agreement cannot be reached. The existence of the

power to take over ownership may make actual possession unnecessary. Much may be accomplished through
persuasion, backed by well-digested plans, and with the
threat of condemnation lurking in the background.

Aids and subsidies from governmental sources provide another kind of control. These aids may take the
form of a loan from the Reconstruction Finance Corporation or a city appropriation for a grade separation
structure. The public purse has had to "sweeten the pot"
frequently in order to secure the co-operation of privately controlled public utilities. It will again. The point is
to secure with each payment, the control that the public
pays for.

The large number of sources of subsidy and the overlapping jurisdictions of numerous governmental agencies
on terminal areas (particularly ports) makes it next to
impossible to exercise the control which the public aids
fully warrant.

Unfortunately, it is the rule rather than the exception
for different government agencies to go their separate
ways in bureaucratic splendor. There are consequent
overlaps in investigations, construction of facilities, and
operation of services. In the federal government, for
instance, there are more than a half-dozen departments
and bureaus involved in the terminal problems of urban
areas with little or no co-ordination among their activities. The interstate carriers are, of course, under the
regulation of the Interstate Commerce Commission
while shipping subsidies and control come under the
Shipping Board. Control of pierhead and bulkhead lines,
and maintenance of channels, come under the Chief of
Engineers of the War Department, while the Light-
house Service is in the Department of Commerce. Federal

highway aids come through the Bureau of Public Roads in the Department of Agriculture, and general aid to all kinds of "self-liquidating" projects has more recently been forthcoming from the Reconstruction Finance Corporation. To that list must be added the corresponding state and local authorities on each subject, with a result which makes one wonder how this extraordinary governmental machinery functions at all.

It is to the great credit of the government officials— large and small—that existing machinery works as well as it does, and it is no criticism of them to point out the need of co-ordination among these regulatory and service agencies of the government along with the co-ordination of the transportation facilities in terminal areas. With co-ordination based upon an agreed program or plan, the aids and subsidies granted from public funds can become a strong lever towards accomplishment of unified organization of transport facilities in terminal areas.[4]

The Interstate Commerce Commission has specific powers in terminal areas to promote co-ordination and joint use of facilities. But direct compulsion by this public authority can accomplish very little under the present form of the Transportation Act of 1920. The authority is given the Commission by Section 3 of the act to require one railroad to permit the use of its terminals by another, on terms, where the carriers are unable to agree, to be fixed by the Commission. The right thereby established is, however, a limited one, for any order of the

[4] An example of the possibilities, using a governmental ownership or subsidy as a basis, is seen in the Los Angeles Harbor situation (150 I.C.C. 649) where city and railroads entered into agreements organizing the Los Angeles Harbor Belt Line Railroad, for joint operation of facilities in the port area.

Commission must avoid "substantially impairing the ability of a carrier owning or entitled to the enjoyment of terminal facilities to handle its own business," and terms fixed by the Commission are "to be ascertained on the principle controlling compensation in condemnation proceedings."

In other words, if one carrier aspires to the use of another carrier's facilities it must pay pretty much the latter's price, presumably to be redetermined at intervals so as to enable the grantor to share in any advantages which the grantee may try to reap by using the facilities with increasing effectiveness. Under these conditions, the grantor could absorb all—or nearly all—of the advantages which such an arrangement might promise. There is also considerable doubt whether the courts will sustain the constitutionality of this provision. As yet there has been no testing of the issue.[5]

Compulsory unification of terminal facilities will inevitably result in loss of favored positions for some interests to the gain of others. It is probably true, however, that compulsion over a wide field, instead of in strictly local areas, would balance out many inequalities. Among constitutional lawyers opinions as to the constitutionality of compulsory unification of all railroads or of terminal facilities vary radically. In the long run, however, it is safe to assume that where a great public advantage is at stake, the Constitution will either be amended or interpreted to secure those advantages for the people.

III. PUBLIC OWNERSHIP

Public ownership of streets and highways is taken for granted. The days of the toll road are limited if not past.

---

[5] For a discussion of the legal aspects of the terminal problem, see Vanderblue and Burgess, *Railroads: Rates-Service-Management*, Chap. XVIII (1923).

Since Lindbergh's flight to Paris, city after city all over the United States has gone into the business of building, owning, and operating airports. In recent years, since the private automobile began to cut seriously into the street car business, public ownership or substantial subsidies to transit lines has become more and more common. From time immemorial navigable streams and waterways have been public property and a public responsibility. The public ownership of waterfront property to secure its efficient use and adaptability to changing requirements has been a basic policy of almost every port commission. Even in the railroad field, public ownership has been tried in such cases as the San Francisco Belt line which is state owned, and the New Orleans Public Belt Railroad owned by the city.

The history of transportation developments seems to have almost an evolutionary trend towards public ownership. The earliest method—the navigable stream—has been public property since feudal times. The next method of transport, over the road, has passed through stages of toll road and private way to the practically complete ownership of the highway system by the public. Many believe that public ownership of railways is an absolute essential to effective co-ordination.

If it be assumed, for the sake of argument only, that some kind of public ownership is inevitable, there are still various degrees of control to be considered. Ownership might be restricted to just the right of way with private equipment and a private operating company— or public ownership might go to the other extreme of control of all transport lines and equipment. Then there is the question of how public ownership to any given degree will be organized for administration of the property. These questions are outside the field of this chapter, which is now concerned only with the point that through public ownership it is obviously possible to secure co-ordination of transport facilities within the limits of practical administrative organization.

IV. CONCLUSIONS

The methods of securing co-ordination in terminal areas outlined in the previous pages show the need and advantages of closer organization of transport facilities. Voluntary agreements have accomplished much but in the difficult cases are either too slow or too complicated to meet the need. Public controls have so far proved insufficient to force action in these difficult cases. Public ownership, however inevitable it may be in the long run, is not entirely acceptable either to the public or the carriers as an immediate step.

The best opportunity for immediate progress, therefore, seems to lie in simplifying the procedure for private consolidation, tightening the controls to balance the monopolistic trend, and in providing for public ownership in cases where agreements are delayed or impossible.

In these circumstances, it is necessary to increase and concentrate the public controls and as a first step it is suggested that the Transportation Act be amended to place power in the Interstate Commerce Commission upon showing of public advantage to compel consolidation of all or specifically designated facilities within terminal areas in accordance with the planning requirements of regional or city planning commissions.

This power is now implied in the Transportation Act of 1920 but is ineffective because of the requirements concerning compensation under condemnation procedure for facilities consolidated against the will of the owners.

To simplify that procedure it is now further suggested that acts be passed by the appropriate state legislatures to authorize the organization of terminal districts about principal railroad and shipping terminals, with a terminal commission or port authority having power to acquire by purchase or condemnation terminal facilities within the district, to issue bonds covered by the credit of the terminal district, and to operate its facilities either directly through an operating company, or by agreement with the railroads serving the district.

Many of the existing terminal commissions or port authorities already have specified terminal districts within which they now operate and some of them already have powers not very different from those suggested in the proposed acts. In some instances it may, of course, be desirable to give these powers to an existing board with other duties; or in other cases to utilize an existing tax district such as a county, or metropolitan district as the terminal area.

CHAPTER XXXVI

CONSOLIDATION AND EFFICIENCY

We turn now from the analysis of the problems of terminal unification to a discussion of the movement for the general consolidation of railroad systems. Three principal types of railway consolidation are now under consideration. The first involves the amalgamation of independent railroad lines and systems into some 18 or 20 larger systems which would remain more or less competitive. This is the plan which was contemplated by the Transportation Act of 1920 and toward which we have been working for a dozen years. The second plan involves the consolidation of roads on a regional basis into a number of large systems. The essential differences between this plan and the preceding one are that there would be a much smaller number of systems and that competition between systems would be virtually eliminated. The regional consolidation plan is exemplified in the British and French systems. The third type of consolidation involves a complete unification of all railroad properties under a single control, as is the case in Germany, Russia, and Japan. Such a system need not necessarily involve government ownership and operation; it might be conducted by privately owned corporations, subject to governmental regulation.

I. ECONOMIC ASPECTS OF CONSOLIDATION

In the following pages we shall discuss the advantages and disadvantages of consolidation in general and the degree to which they inhere in different types of consolidation. We shall confine our attention to the economic aspects of the problem and shall be satisfied if our analysis helps to clarify the fundamental issues involved. We shall begin with a statement of the various wastes inherent in the present plan of operation by 155 Class I railroads and more than seven hundred other railroad companies, and of the economies that might result from some form of consolidation.

1. *Duplicate lines and services.* The elimination of unnecessary lines is one of the most obvious economies that might be realized by consolidation. In the early days numerous railroad lines were built which were unnecessary from the transportation point of view but were useful tools in the hands of financiers. There are many other lines the construction of which was justifiable as parts of a competitive transportation system but which would never have been built under a unified plan of national transportation development. After consolidation, many of these lines would in due course be scrapped since it would no longer be important that traffic be directed over particular routes.

The elimination of duplicate services also presents important possibilities. In certain regions many trains now necessary if standards of competing service are to be maintained, might be discontinued. Similarly, it might be possible to operate a number of parallel single track lines as a double track system, as was done during the period of federal control on about 100 miles of Norfolk and Western and Virginian tracks, and to use certain roads for low grade traffic and others for fast freight and passenger service. In England since consolidation has taken place it has been found advantageous to divert slower types of traffic to roundabout routes, keeping the more direct lines free of congestion for the movement of fast trains.

2. *Utilization of equipment.* There are numerous ways in which the consolidation of systems would make for a more effective utilization of equipment. The elimination of unnecessary roads and duplicate train services would reduce the amount of equipment needed, because the necessary equipment could be used more effectively. A greater concentration of traffic would make possible, on the average, greater train loads. Important economies could also be realized in connection with the consolidation of repair shops.

One of the most important economies in the utilization of equipment would be the great decrease of empty car mileage that would result. As is shown in Chapter VI, the desire of every road to return "foreign" cars as quickly as possible in order to avoid the payment of per diem charges results in hurrying cars home either empty or loaded only to partial capacity. Not infrequently empty cars are found moving in opposite directions on the same line at the same time—all trying to escape the per diem charge. Cars of other roads are also commonly used with little consideration of the need for repairs. This results in their wearing out prematurely and creates difficulties on roads with heavy grades requiring the highest standard of brake maintenance.[1]

3. *Roundabout movements and cross-hauling.* Under a competitive system every road endeavors to obtain as much traffic as possible even though it involves the diversion of traffic from shorter or more direct routes. Sometimes the distance that the traffic moves is only 10 or 20 per cent greater than the minimum necessary haul;

[1] See *Investigation of Power Brakes and Appliances for Operating Power Brake Systems*, 91 I.C.C. 481, 517 (1924).

while in other cases the distance is more than double. Innumerable instances of cross-hauling and circuitous routing might be cited. To mention a few extreme cases much traffic moves from Chicago to Los Angeles by way of the Great Northern and Northern Pacific, and thence down the coast. In *Wasteful Service by Tap Lines*,[2] the Interstate Commerce Commission found that certain carriers controlled by lumber companies sent their shipments by long roundabout routes in order to obtain a greater proportion of the joint through rate; in one instance shipments were sent 76 miles and brought back practically to the starting point, when a switching movement of one mile would have advanced the shipments just as far toward their destination. In *Routing of Transcontinental Grain and Grain Products*,[3] the Commission pointed out the waste involved in the practice of hauling grain east for hundreds of miles to the market and back again on its way to the coast at the same rate that would apply for the direct haul.[4]

4. *Competition for traffic.* Very important economies would also result from the elimination of competitive services and practices. Reconsignment and diversion privileges and milling in transit are examples of economically useful practices which are likely to be overdone, because inadequately paid for, when roads are competing vigorously for all potential traffic. The cost of maintaining traffic departments would be greatly reduced, as would the number of ticket offices and freight

[2] 89 I.C.C. 327 (1924).
[3] 73 I.C.C. 116 (1922).
[4] In 1918 Commissioner Clyde B. Aitchison prepared an extensive report for the Director General of Railroads on the subject, *Cross-hauling and Unnecessary Transportation.*

and passenger agencies. A gain of no little general importance would be the elimination of the modern substitutes for rebates and discriminations which industrial traffic managers are able to procure by playing off one road against another.

Competitive efforts to secure traffic also absorb an enormous amount of the energy of the higher officials of railway systems. Attempts to control the routing of through traffic lead to otherwise unproductive investment in the securities of connecting carriers, resulting in large expenditures both of money and of effort in ways which add nothing to the effectiveness of operation or the adequacy of service rendered to the public by the railways as a whole.

5. Miscellaneous economies. Numerous minor economies, of real importance in the aggregate, may be briefly mentioned. Among these are the development of better purchasing policies and the unified control of purchases; more accurate budgeting of railroad expenditures generally; reduction of stocks of miscellaneous materials and supplies; the elimination of inter-company accounting in connection with per diem charges, the allocation of through rates, the division of joint damage claims, and the division of joint facility rents—not to mention the accounts connected with intercorporate financial control.

6. *Capital costs.* The consolidation of railroad systems might also make possible very substantial reductions in capital costs. The economies in this connection would be twofold. First, the amount of capital required to perform a given volume of railroad service would be less than under the existing system; and, second, the improved credit position resulting from the greater stability of railroad investment would make it possible to borrow

capital at lower rates. As a corollary the process of eliminating obsolescent lines would be simplified, as would also the problem of financial reorganization of the industry generally.

7. *Regulation.* Finally, the problem of railroad regulation would be greatly reduced in complexity. Many, if not most, of the issues which arise between the railroads on the one side and Congress and the Interstate Commerce Commission on the other are incidents of the system of competing lines. We may merely cite the control of capital issues by a multitude of roads; the keeping of separate accounts for each individual carrier; the supervision of acquisitions; and the division of joint through rates. The readjustment of the complex rate structure along constructive lines would also be greatly simplified.

Thus far we have been considering only the possible *advantages* which various students of the problem assign to railroad consolidation. Attention must now be directed to the possible *disadvantages.* The following shortcomings of consolidation are most commonly cited. The first is that we would lose the stimulus which comes from competition, particularly as it relates to pace-setting in the adoption of new equipment and operating methods, and to furnishing new and better types of service. The second disadvantage is that inherent in sheer bigness. The inefficiency of existing railroad companies, it is often urged, is attributable in no small measure to their very magnitude. If the size were multiplied, would not the managerial task become so difficult as virtually to nullify the obvious advantages of consolidation? Finally, it is urged that political interference in the control of railroads would present an insuperable barrier to efficiency.

II. ADVANTAGES AND DISADVANTAGES OF
PROPOSED PLANS

The various advantages suggested above, and also the disadvantages, will differ somewhat in importance, depending upon whether consolidation proceeds along one or another of the lines indicated at the beginning of the chapter. We must therefore now seek to relate these various advantages and disadvantages more particularly to the several forms of consolidation.

1. *Consolidation into competitive systems.* The plan to consolidate existing railroads into competitive systems, some 18 or 20 in number, is regarded as having one primary advantage. It was argued strongly by its original sponsors that such a plan would retain the primary advantages of competition, particularly in connection with service. In suggesting the roads which might be consolidated into particular systems, the Interstate Commerce Commission gave special attention to the preservation of competition. For example, the eastern consolidations, which involve four systems between the Atlantic seaboard and Chicago—the New York Central, the Pennsylvania, the Baltimore and Ohio, and the Chesapeake and Ohio—embodied as a fundamental idea the maintenance of effective competition in service among these roads. Consolidation along these lines would undoubtedly preserve a considerable measure of competition, whereas either regional consolidation or a unified system for the entire country would seek to eliminate the competitive feature.

The retention of the feature of competition among consolidated systems, however, naturally limits the extent to which transportation economies may be effected. Competition in service implies the continuation of many competitive practices which are responsible for the wastes inherent in the present system. For example, it would still be necessary for these competing lines or systems to maintain competitive advertising and competitive traffic agencies, and to run an unnecessary number of trains between competitive centers. Such consolidation would not solve the empty-car evil resulting from per diem charges for foreign cars, nor would it eliminate the losses incident to circuitous routing.

It is true that some economies of importance would be realizable. It would appear, indeed, that along most of the lines suggested above, the wastes involved in the present system, with its thousand individual roads, would be reduced to some extent, though in varying degrees in different systems and in connection with particular elements of cost. For example, intercompany accounting would be greatly reduced in volume, the elimination of unprofitable branch lines would be made easier, and a greater mileage would be brought under efficient management.

The principal purpose in making provision for this form of consolidation by the Transportation Act of 1920, however, was not to effect a maximum of transportation economies. The major objective was to facilitate the working of the rule of rate making, under which the roads as a whole were to be afforded a fair return upon their investment. The consolidation provision was relied upon to eliminate the problem presented by the large number of weak roads. Statements by the sponsors of the act of 1920 and debates before Congress leave no doubt on this score. The economies that might be realized were regarded as incidental to the solution problem presented by the existence of weak and strong roads.

2. *Consolidation by regions.* Regional consolidation loses the advantage of competition in service, but goes considerably further in the direction of effecting economies in transportation. If the country were divided into, say, four to six major districts, within each of which there was a single operating system, the amount of circuitous routing, empty-car mileage, inter-company accounting, and duplication of facilities would be greatly lessened. The financial risks, and hence the cost of capital, would also be reduced. Moreover, regional consolidations would facilitate terminal unification, whereas amalgamation into competing systems would not.

While regional consolidation would eliminate the wastes incident to competition for traffic—and the possible stimulating advantages thereof as well—there would still remain competition between certain market areas. For example, the Eastern roads would doubtless endeavor to divert traffic originating in the Ohio Valley and Great Lakes region to the Eastern seaboard and thence by water to the Pacific coast, whereas it would be to the interest of the Western roads to send this traffic over the mountains to the Pacific coast region. The disturbing effects of market competition upon the general rate structure would thus persist. In fact, it is not improbable that regional consolidation would intensify what is known as market competition with its disruptive effects.

Attention should also be called to the fact that great difficulties would be encountered in delimiting the regions. Should New England constitute a region by itself, or should it be a part of a larger region extending from New England to the Middle West? New England industrial and commercial groups are even now sharply divided on this question. In view of the fact that existing commercial connections have been developed largely without reference to regional considerations, divergencies of interests of this sort would be found in nearly every part of the country.

The problem of effecting regional consolidations is also complicated by the fact that in many cases existing railroad systems traverse more than one of the regions which would presumably be established, while their financial inter-connections are even more extensive. In fact, so difficult are the problems presented by these ramifications that in the view of many students, regional consolidation is impracticable. Regional consolidation also has another possible disadvantage in that it tends to promote industrial, social, and political regionalism in a country which aspires to national unity.

3. *Complete consolidation.* Absolute consolidation of all existing roads into a single transportation company presents certain obvious advantages over, and at the same time raises certain issues not present in, the other forms of consolidation. It would make possible—theoretically at least—the realization of all the economies outlined in the general discussion above. Of particular importance would be the elimination of duplicate facilities and services, the automatic solution of the problem of terminal unification, the simplification of the problem of regulation, and the increased financial stability and accompanying lower costs of capital which would be involved. Similarly, it would facilitate a solution of the problem of articulating the railroads more effectively with other forms of transportation and relating all transportation more intelligently to the problem of city and national planning.

The problems of a particular character which would arise in connection with a unified system relate, on the one hand, to the magnitude of the enterprise, and on the other, to the dangers of political control. A $25,000,000,000 enterprise whose operations extend to nearly every community throughout a continental country certainly challenges thoughtful consideration. In the view of many such a gigantic corporation would inevitably fail because of the remoteness of its officials from the people they must serve, and also because of the inability of any single board of directors or president to direct intelligently the operations of so vast an organization.

Others believe that the managerial difficulties are much less serious than would on first thought appear to be the case. It is pointed out that many of the problems which now prove so difficult and so time-consuming to railroad managers would be eliminated under a unified system—such as those incident to merger negotiations and to legislative and Commission regulation. Indeed, it is urged by some that the management of a single railroad company for the country as a whole, freed from the multitude of special problems that grow out of the system of independent competing companies, would readily attain a higher degree of operating efficiency than is to be found in many of our existing single companies.

It is also pointed out that for operating purposes such a company would have regional divisions similar to the divisions of our larger railroad system. By this means it is believed that the necessary close touch with local requirements might be maintained. At the same time, some of the advantages of competition would be retained—not competition between roads in the matter of rates and services, but competition between divisions in the setting of standards of performance. At any rate, the experience of some of our larger railroad companies appears to point to possibilities in this direction. The general efficiency maintained by the American Telephone and Telegraph Company, which operates throughout the country, is held to be indicative of possibilities in the railroad field.

The possible political impediments to the efficient management of a unified system cannot be ignored. It should be borne in mind, however, that the system here under consideration does not necessarily involve government ownership or operation. Government representation on the board of directors would perhaps be justified by the large public interest involved, but a government guarantee of the earnings of such a corporation would not necessarily be required. However, the fixing of rates with a view to maintaining the financial stability of so great a national enterprise would inevitably be regarded as essential. Neither the officials nor other employees in the industry need be under the civil service.

The financial and legal problems involved in effecting consolidation along any of the foregoing lines present great obstacles to its accomplishment. In fact, so great are the practical difficulties that some observers, impatient for results, urge that the only solution of the railroad problem is to accept government ownership and "be done with it." We are not here interested in attempting to indicate the financial issues that would have to be surmounted in bringing about either regional or national consolidation, nor are we concerned with the legal questions which are involved. These are problems which would obviously have to be given detailed consideration before any feasible plan might be adopted.

It may be pointed out, however, that it is clear that

little or no progress has been or is likely to be made along the lines of voluntary consolidation. The consolidation provisions of the Transportation Act have now been in force for over a decade, yet the results accomplished up to the present are negligible. While some progress seems likely in the Eastern district, we can expect, under the present provision for voluntary consolidation, only such consolidations as are in the interest of the carriers involved. The strenuous objection voiced by the Great Northern to amalgamation with the Milwaukee and the scramble of the New York Central and the Baltimore and Ohio for control of the Philadelphia and Reading, exemplify the desire to amalgamate with profitable properties and the unwillingness to consolidate with weak roads.

If our railroads are to be consolidated, compulsion is plainly necessary. Whether such compulsion is possible under the power of eminent domain vested in the government, is a constitutional question which would have to be decided by the courts.

PART IX

REORIENTATION IN TRANSPORTATION REGULATION

CHAPTER XXXVII

DEVELOPMENT OF THE PRESENT SYSTEM OF REGULATION

Modern transportation is characterized by extreme complexity. Involved in the situation of today is the age-old problem of adjustment of the relations of government to carriers. That problem, never simple, has become more complex within recent years because of the increased activity of government in creating and improving facilities for transportation by land, water, and air and the concomitant and consequent increase in the numbers and types of carriers.

A new type of carrier has appeared: the commercial airplane, dependent upon landing facilities generally provided by government and dependent for its air operations upon facilities generally provided and maintained by government. An old type has reappeared: the common carrier for hire on the public highway. On the public highway, also, are carriers operating under contract and vehicles operated solely for the use and convenience of their owners; the one competing with the common carrier, the other substituting self-service for the service of the common carrier. On the inland waterways, improved and maintained at government expense, are barges owned and operated by government and private barges operated with the aid of facilities provided and maintained by government. On the coastal waters, connected by a canal constructed and operated by government, are carriers whose operations are conducted under the fostering care of government.

All of these agencies of transportation have one characteristic in common: their capital is in movable form. If the results of their operations prove unprofitable, with certain formalities, they can shift to other scenes, or in the last extremity they can liquidate. This the railroad, with its permanent way and structures, can not do. Nor can the pipe line, another competitor in the transportation field.

The problem has been further complicated by the persistence of two inconsistent policies of government; promotion of competition among carriers and different types of carriers, and strict regulation of the railroad as the only one that, through a long period of years, has been able to survive the stress of competition.

There is the related problem of adjustment of the relations of government to a variety of interests among the several types of carriers and within the organization of individual carriers of the same type: interests of proprietors and of preferred creditors, interests of employees, including those in the management and those in the various classes of labor; and interests of shippers and of passengers. Finally, there is the interest of the all-inclusive groups of taxpayers and of consumers, whose welfare it is the government's duty to conserve. There is also the problem of adjusting the relations between the national government and the several state governments in the matter of transportation, involving questions of fiscal policy, highway administration, and police power.

I. THE RAILROADS

There has always been a railroad problem. The advent of the railroad itself created a whole series of problems necessitating readjustments in a wide variety of human relationships. Landowners, waterways, turnpikes, stage lines, and innkeepers were all affected by its introduction. The opposition of these and other vested interests as well as the inert force of indifference and skepticism had to be overcome before railroads could be chartered, financed, and built. Railroad development gave rise to new problems at every stage; problems of engineering, of technology, of management, and of personnel, as well as problems of routes, rates, and service. The matter of public relationship has involved such dissimilar features as uninterrupted transportation through cities and across state boundaries; differences in gauge of track and in equipment; postal service; military use; safety; grants of subsidies and special privileges; receivership; consolidation and other intercorporate relationships; railroad participation in politics and political interference with the railroads. Railroads have in turn enjoyed exemptions from taxation, indulged in the practice of evasion, and suffered from inequitable exactions. From time to time they have brought their relationships with rival agencies of transportation into an approximation of stable equilibrium, sometimes by questionable means. This has been disturbed both by action of government and by the introduction of new facilities and new forms of competition. Now there are rivals in the air, on the water, and on the highway; competition is more complex than before, and the forces behind it are more potent. Out of the perennial railroad problem has emerged a transportation problem, with its challenge to the political and economic leadership of today.

Railroad regulation is as old as the railroad. It began with the earliest English charters. The first American railroads were projected in states along the Atlantic seaboard in which a measure of economic stability had been attained. Conditions in those states were roughly comparable to English conditions, and English experience was relied upon as a safe guide to American legislators as well as to those who were directly interested in the ownership and management of American railroads. English railroad charters, in turn, had been based upon turnpike charters, which were restrictive in nature.

American charters of the early period do not call for mention here except to give point to the statement that in its first stage of development, the American railroad was the subject of regulation in a variety of ways. All early charters contained provisions to govern the taking over of private property; many of them specified maximum rates and fares—often at rates too high to be effective; some provided residence qualifications for directors; others provided that the voting power of shares owned by a single person should be progressively reduced as the number of his shares increased. In some of these instruments, the right of state purchase was reserved; in others the right of the legislature was reserved to reduce rates in case the yield on investment should exceed a fixed percentage. Annual reports were generally required, whether to the shareholders, the legislature, or both. Provisions for the safety of life and property were not uncommon.

By charter and by general legislation, both New York and Pennsylvania imposed restrictions upon their railroads in the interest of state-owned waterways. By early general laws New York and the New England states imposed the requirement of probable "public use" before a company could be incorporated to undertake a project.

As the railroad was extended westward, charters generally became less restrictive and liberal provisions increased in number and variety. When, therefore, in response to a changed public sentiment after the Civil War, the states of the Middle West took action to curb railroad abuses—chiefly unjust discrimination in rates—they were more or less consciously trying to remedy a situation brought about by their own generosity in a period in which unrestrained competition had been regarded as a safeguard. The action taken was the enactment of restrictive legislation, which because of its volume and complexity called for administrative tribunals or commissions for its enforcement.

Railroad supervision by state commission was of early origin. There had been sundry commissions of a supervisory character in the older states from an early date, but they were specifically limited in power and in function. Rhode Island in 1839 created the first commission to exercise more than routine supervision. Other states created offices for the collection of railroad statistics for public use. Massachusetts, in 1869, was the last New England state to set up a supervisory commission; that body, under wise leadership, became the model for states willing to rely upon purely advisory powers and confident as to the efficacy of the corrective influence of an informed public opinion. In some of the less settled states, where the absence of elementary restrictions had invited abuse, where public opinion as to the distinction between abuse and legitimate railroad practice was more or less confused, and where absentee-ownership was the rule, a commission of wide powers was demanded.

All states but one now have regulatory commissions. The movement for the regulatory commission, as distinguished from the advisory type, began with the adoption of the Illinois Constitution of 1870, under which a railroad and warehouse commission was established and vested with power to fix maximum charges for service. Similar commissions were set up in most of the other states in the Middle West and South, and also in California. In 1877 the United States Supreme Court sustained the authority of state legislatures to fix railroad charges; and in the absence of federal legislation it was assumed that this decision served to put interstate rates under the control of the state commissions, but this was denied by the Court in 1886. In their zeal for regulation some states, notably Wisconsin, over-reached themselves and brought about a reaction in the direction of a more liberal railroad policy. Generally, however, the states have preferred to follow the model of Illinois, rather than that of Massachusetts, in their legislation and in the type of commission adopted. To-day Delaware alone is without a regulatory commission.

Similarly, the scope of state commissions has been extended. Illinois and Minnesota began with "railroad and warehouse commissions," and as early as 1879 California adopted a policy of commission control of "railroad or other transportation companies," but the needs of most states were initially thought to be satisfactorily served by simple "railroad commissions." Now, however, the representative state commission is a "public service commission," whatever its official name, with jurisdiction that includes a wide variety of utilities conducted in the public interest. Their major interest is no longer railroad regulation.

It was not until 1887 that agreement could be reached in Congress upon a measure that purported to "regulate commerce," but was in effect little more than a declaration of intention to enter the field of railroad regulation. This act contained few new features. It restated the common law rule that the charges made for a public carrier's service must be reasonable in themselves and impartial as between persons, places, and kinds of traffic. It created the Interstate Commerce Commission as an agency of enforcement, but it did not authorize the Commission to fix rates. Instead, it required the railroads to print their rates, fares, and tariffs, and to make them available to the public and to the Commission; and it provided an open and orderly procedure for changes therein. In its specification of powers to be exercised by the Commission, it generally followed the Illinois model, except as to the matter of prescribing maximum rate schedules. It required railroads to submit detailed annual reports to the Commission, but it withheld from the Commission authority to inspect or to audit their accounts.

One of the most noteworthy features of the act was its prohibition of agreements among carriers designed to restrict competition, reflecting the belief, common to legislators and the public, in the efficacy of competition as a universal remedy for transportation troubles. This put an end to the practice of "pooling"; but it was not designed to affect agreements harmless in themselves and in the public interest. Such agreements, however, were put under a ban in 1897 by a Supreme Court decision declaring that concerted maintenance of rates, admittedly reasonable, was forbidden by the Sherman Anti-Trust Act; a measure which up to that time had been regarded as in no way applicable to railroad corporations or to their proper interrelationships.

Until 1906 the Interstate Commerce Commission was

a body of restricted authority. Its statutory powers were extremely limited, and the law itself was defective, inviting judicial disapproval. It had no power to enforce its decisions. Much of the authority which had been ostensibly granted to it was whittled away by successive court decisions, some of which, at least, reflected a spirit of hostility on the part of the federal judiciary. Even its power of investigation was held up by litigation until 1896. Year after year this situation was brought before Congress, but remedial legislation was slow in coming.

By the Hepburn amendment of 1906, the Commission's jurisdiction was extended and its authority was increased and better defined. Sleeping-car companies, private car lines, industrial railroads, and terminal and switching facilities, as well as pipe lines for commodities other than gas and water, were put under its control. The Commission was now empowered, upon complaint, to prescribe maximum rates; it was also authorized to prescribe and to inspect accounts and to require needed information from the carriers. Its decisions were made binding upon the carriers, subject to appeal to the courts.

Further increase in scope and power came through the Mann-Elkins Act of 1910. Telegraph, telephone, and cable companies—with which this study is not concerned—were brought within the Commission's jurisdiction. The Commission was authorized, upon its own initiative, to fix maximum rates; also to suspend proposed increases in rates until their reasonableness could be proven by the carrier. Its power to put an end to discrimination between places (the long-and-short-haul problem) was reaffirmed.

Water competition was a persistent factor in the long-and-short-haul problem, creating special conditions calling for through rates by rail lower than the normal rates charged to intermediate rail points unaffected by such competition. On the inland waterways the effect of this competition tended to decline, in part because of natural causes and in part because of the practice of the railroads of cutting rates temporarily and restoring them after the competing water carrier had been eliminated. This practice the act of 1910 attempted to restrain by endowing the Commission with discretionary authority over proposed restorations of rates, subject to the requirement that the reasons for an increase must be based on considerations unrelated to water competition.

Transcontinental rates had always been affected by potential intercoastal water competition, and in the Panama Canal Act of 1912, effective 1914, Congress imposed restrictions upon railroad use of the canal sufficient to insure the continuance of such competition. It went further and, by a provision in no way related to the major purpose of the act, directed the Interstate Commerce Commission to restrain railroad operation or control of competitive water carriers elsewhere than through the canal, meaning on the Great Lakes, inland rivers, coastal waters, and the high seas. It also authorized the Commission to require practicable physical connections between rail and water carriers, to determine through routes and maximum joint rates, and to take related steps, specified in the law, to prevent exclusive arrangements as to facilities or traffic.

By the Clayton Antitrust Act of 1914, effective 1921, the Commission was made responsible for the enforcement of provisions forbidding any corporation under its jurisdiction to acquire control over competitors or to participate in major construction or maintenance contracts affected by adverse interest. By a series of acts, beginning as early as 1893, its authority was extended into the field of management in the interest of safety of passengers and of employees.

In the Transportation Act of 1920, there is evidence of a changing legislative attitude toward competition, but by no means a complete reversal of policy. "Pooling" may now be permitted, but subject to the approval of the Interstate Commerce Commission and only when it will not unduly restrain competition. Construction of extensions and of branch lines may be undertaken only after the issuance of certificates of public convenience and necessity by the Commission. Consolidation and combination of railroads is now to be encouraged, but only in accordance with a "plan" of the Commission in which competition "shall be preserved as fully as possible." The Commission, however, may prescribe minimum rates and thus restrain destructive competition among carriers and, to some extent, between different types of carriers.

Other provisions of the act added to the powers of the Commission. It now has authority to supervise the issuance of new securities (except short-term notes); to require the joint use of terminal facilities; to compel carriers to provide safe and adequate facilities; to control abandonments of line; and even to require the extension of lines.

One of the most significant provisions in the act is that in which a "Rule of Rate Making" is prescribed for the Commission's use. Under this rule the Commission is not to lessen its efforts to protect the public interest in the matter of rates, but its action to that end must be taken after due consideration is given to the continuing transportation needs of the country and to the need of the carriers as a whole (or in separate rate groups) for operating revenues sufficient under proper management to yield a fair rate of return upon the value of the property used in transportation. The fostering care of the Commission, henceforth, must be extended to the protection of railroad credit.

Federal control has generally superseded state control of railroads. As early as 1911 a decision of the Supreme Court established the paramount right of the national government to control safety devices on railroad equipment whether used in intrastate or interstate service. This was reaffirmed in 1915.

In another decision the Court in 1914 affirmed the right of the Interstate Commerce Commission to change intrastate rates and fares inconsistent with those which it had prescribed for interstate traffic. By the Transportation Act of 1920 the Commission was granted power over intrastate rates which are discriminatory against persons or places and also over intrastate rates which are discriminatory against interstate and foreign commerce as a whole. The former provision was a reiteration in statutory form of the declaration of the Court; the latter granted a new power designed to facilitate the Commission in its application of the new rule of rate making so as to produce the fair rate of return essential to the preservation of an adequate system of transportation. In the exercise of these powers co-operation with the states concerned is indicated but not required.

Another section of the Transportation Act gave the Interstate Commerce Commission authority over the issuance of new securities by railroad corporations; a field which had hitherto been left to the states. Here, as in the matter of rates, a measure of co-operation with the state authorities is provided for, but exclusive control is vested in the Commission.

The authority of the states and of the state commissions over railroads has thus been reduced to a minimum, the precise extent of which is yet to be determined. The states still retain their police power under the Constitution, but their "strong" regulatory bodies have been weakened as a necessary step toward the realization of the objective of the Act of 1920,—a comprehensive system of transportation developed along national lines.

II. COASTAL AND INLAND SHIPPING

Water carriers have been subject to some federal regulation from the beginning. One of the compelling reasons for the adoption of the Constitution was the acknowledged need for uniform control of navigation and shipping. The primary need, however, was for fiscal control, and in the body of navigation laws enacted from 1789 on, the major objective was control of vessels engaged in foreign commerce. Yet the interests of coastwise navigation were not neglected. One of the earliest acts of the First Congress included a provision to govern the documentation of vessels in the "coasting trade." Such vessels were required to be registered or enrolled, to establish the fact of American ownership, and their movements were controlled through a system of permits.

No special organization was set up in the Treasury Department for the enforcement of the navigation laws until 1884, when a Bureau of Navigation was created. This Bureau in 1886 extended into the coastwise field the services of the shipping commissioners in matters concerned with the relations of seamen to the masters or owners of vessels. Beginning in 1910 it became responsible for the regulation of radio communications on merchant vessels. From time to time it has had imposed upon it certain duties of a marine police nature, designed to promote good order and safety. In the performance of these duties it has the active co-operation of the Coast Guard, the federal marine police service, whose history, under a variety of names, goes back almost to the creation of the Treasury Department.

Another Treasury organization, the Steamboat-Inspection Service, developed out of a series of safety laws, the first of which was enacted in 1838 for the protection of passengers on vessels propelled by steam power. This act provided for periodical examinations of hulls and boilers by inspectors at the various ports, and it required masters or owners of such vessels to equip them with lifeboats, signal lights, and other safety devices.

Regional supervising inspectors were authorized in 1852 by an act which also established a license system for the control of engineers and pilots on steam vessels, and imposed additional requirements for safety equipment. This act also provided for licenses to control the handling of certain dangerous or inflammable articles. In 1855 the number of passengers and the accommodations therefor on steam vessels were brought under control.

A Supervising Inspector General was appointed as chief of the Service under authority of an act of 1871, which for the first time made provision for the safeguarding of crews as well as passengers. Subsequent legislation has promoted the development of the Service without basic change of function.

Both the Bureau of Navigation and the Steamboat-Inspection Service were transferred to the Department of Commerce and Labor in 1903, and in 1913 to the new Department of Commerce. In 1932 the two services were consolidated.

Since 1916 the Shipping Board has had nominal authority over interstate water rates. Its jurisdiction includes common carriers on the high seas or the Great Lakes operating on regular routes from port to port; it does not include carriers on inland rivers. In general it has regulatory, investigatory, and quasi-judicial authority similar to that of the Interstate Commerce Commission, except in matters of safety and corporate finance. Its authority, however, does not extend to intrastate commerce.

It may modify or cancel agreements relating to rates, fares, and practices which it finds to be unjustly discriminatory or unfair, and all water carriers under its jurisdiction are required to file all such agreements for its approval. It may inquire into unfair practices and require the filing of periodical or special reports. It has power to prescribe maximum rates.

Carriers are required to file with the Board and keep open to public inspection, their maximum rates, fares, and charges, which may not be increased except with the Board's approval and after public notice of ten days, or less, as the Board may determine. A competitive rate, reduced below a fair and remunerative basis, may be increased only upon the Board's finding, after a hearing, that the proposed change has other basis than the elimination of the competition which occasioned the reduction.

Maximum rates are of no significance in intercoastal business. They are invariably above the actual rates, over which the Shipping Board has no semblance of control. If it was the intent of Congress to put the Board in a position of authority over rates, the legislation enacted to that end has been ineffective.

III. MOTOR VEHICLES

Common carrier motor vehicles engaged in intrastate commerce are generally subject to state regulation. As the commercial use of the motor carrier developed, the public interest became involved, and the logical legislative reaction was the enactment of measures placing the new type of common carrier under the jurisdiction of public service commissions. The movement began in Pennsylvania in 1910. All states except Delaware now regulate common carriers of passengers and four-fifths of them regulate common carriers of property.

The nature and extent of the regulatory requirements vary as among the different states, but the tendency is toward uniformity along the following lines: (1) Permits or certificates of public convenience and necessity; (2) rate regulation; (3) reports; less commonly, (4) control of accounts; and still less commonly, (5) control over security issues. The discretionary power vested in the regulatory authorities naturally differs, particularly in the matter of granting certificates, and there are also marked differences in the effectiveness of the enforcement of regulatory provisions.

Motor vehicles are subject to state laws governing the use of the public highway. Such laws go back to antiquity. As developed to meet the need of modern conditions, they are concerned with the rule of the road and other matters involved in public safety, including liability for damage or injury, the types, equipment, dimensions, and load limits of vehicles; the qualifications and working hours of operators; and the conditions of operation, including speed, signals, interference with the normal flow of traffic, etc.

In the absence of federal legislation the states may exercise a measure of police control over interstate motor carriers, requiring them to register and to conform to reasonable rules and regulations, and they may exclude from the highways those who fail to do so. Their authority to impose a tax upon such carriers is, however, absolute.

Private motor carriers operating intrastate under contracts with shippers are subject to state regulation. Here is a carrier that makes use of the public highway for the conduct of a private business as distinguished from the non-gainful use of all. It competes with the established common carrier, the rates of which are regulated by the state, or at least subject to such regulation, but it may not be converted into a common carrier by legislative fiat. Attempts to this end have been disapproved by the Supreme Court, which has also ruled against control through the withholding of certificates of convenience and necessity.

It is yet to be determined by that Court "whether the operation of trucks for the transportation of freight under private contracts, carried into effect by the use of the public highway, is a business impressed with a public interest,"[1] but the case from which this quotation is taken has clarified to a considerable extent the question of the status of the contract carrier.

This case was concerned with a Texas statute,[2] which, among other things, (1) Requires that before engaging in business a private contract carrier must obtain a permit upon considerations relating to the effect of its competition upon existing common carriers adequately serving the same territory, and (2) authorizes and directs the Railroad Commission to prescribe minimum rates of such

---

[1] *Stephenson* v. *Binford*, No. 326—October term, 1932, at p. 9.
[2] General Laws, 1931, c. 277.

contract carriers, "which shall not be less than the rates prescribed for common carriers for substantially the same service." Both of these provisions were sustained by the Court in the *Stephenson* case, the importance of which justifies quotation in some detail:

. . . during recent years the unregulated use of the highways of the state by a vast and constantly growing number of private contract carriers has had the effect of greatly decreasing the freight which would be carried by railroads within the state, and, in consequence, adding to the burden upon the highways. Certainly, the removal or amelioration of that burden, with its resulting injury to the highways, interference with their primary use, danger and inconvenience, is a legitimate subject for the exercise of the legislative power. . . .

. . . it is to be observed that the requirement is not that the private contract carrier shall obtain a certificate of public convenience and necessity, but that he shall obtain a permit, the issue of which is made dependent upon the condition that the efficiency of common carrier service then adequately serving the same territory shall not be impaired. Does the required relation here exist between the condition imposed and the end sought? We think it does. . . . Debatable questions of this character are not for the courts, but for the legislature, which is entitled to form its own judgment. (*Sproles* v. *Binford*, 286 U.S. 374, 388-389.) Leaving out of consideration common carriers by trucks, impairment of the railway freight service, in the very nature of things, must result, to some degree, in adding to the burden imposed upon the highways. Or stated conversely, any diversion of traffic from the highways to the railroads must correspondingly relieve the former, and, therefore, contribute directly to their conservation. There is thus a substantial relation between the means here adopted and the end sought. This is made plain by the *Sproles* case, *supra* (p. 394):

"The state has a vital interest in the appropriate utilization of the railroads which serve its people, as well as in the maintenance of its highways as safe and convenient facilities. The state provides its highways and pays for their upkeep. Its people make railroad transportation possible by the payment of transportation charges. It cannot be said that the state is powerless to protect its highways from being subjected to excessive burdens when other means of transportation are available. The use of highways for truck transportation has its manifest convenience, and we perceive no constitutional ground for denying to the state the right to foster a fair distribution of traffic to the end that all necessary facilities should be maintained and that the public should not be inconvenienced by inordinate uses of its highways for purposes of gain. This is not a case of a denial of the use of the highways to one class of citizens as opposed to another, or of limitations having no appropriate relation to highway protection."

What has just been said applies in the main to the other challenged provision authorizing the commission to prescribe minimum rates not less than those prescribed for common carriers for substantially the same service. This provision, by precluding the contract carriers from rendering service at rates under those charged by the railroad carriers, has a definite tendency to relieve the highways by diverting traffic from them to the railroads. The authority is limited to the fixing of minimum rates. The contract carrier may not charge less than the rates so fixed, but is left free to charge as much more as he sees fit and can obtain. . . .

Here the circumstance which justifies what otherwise might be an unconstitutional interference with the freedom of private contract calls for a service, the performance of which contemplates the use of facilities belonging to the state; and it would be strange doctrine which, while recognizing the power of the state to regulate the use itself, would deny its power to regulate the contract so far as it contemplates the use. . . .

We need not consider whether the act in some other aspect would be good or bad. It is enough to support its validity that, plainly, one of its aims is to conserve the highways.

There is no federal control of interstate commercial transportation by motor vehicles. Under a decision of the Supreme Court, made in 1925,[3] a state is without authority to withhold a permit for the operation of a pub-

[3] *Buck* v. *Kuykendall*, 267 U.S. 307.

lic motor vehicle over its roads in interstate commerce where such permit is designed to restrict competition. Therefore, if there is to be control of the rates, service, and practices of such interstate carriers it can come only through action by Congress. The need for such action has been repeatedly asserted by the National Association of Railroad and Utilities Commissioners, and recently (1932) affirmed by the Interstate Commerce Commission.[4]

IV. AIR TRANSPORT

Commercial aircraft are subject to safety regulation by both state and federal authority. The examination and registration of air pilots was first required by Oregon in 1921, and many other states have since enacted laws to that effect. The machines themselves are also subject to state licensing. A number of states exercise a measure of control over scheduled air transportation within their respective jurisdictions. This is generally done through the public service commissions.

National regulation was first provided for by the Air Commerce Act of 1926, authorizing the Secretary of Commerce to test and license all commercial aircrafts operated over state lines; to make periodical examinations of airmen serving in connection with a licensed craft; to require inspections; to establish traffic rules for air navigation; and to suspend, revoke, or renew licenses at his discretion. This authority is exercised through the Aeronautics Branch of the Department of Commerce.

Carriers of air mail are subject to regulation by the Post Office Department through its control of mail contracts. The regulatory authority has to do with the allocation, extension, and consolidation of routes, the nature

[4] *Co-ordination of Motor Transportation*, 182 I.C.C. 263.

of the equipment, and the personnel; also the nature of the service, and the accounts to be kept. It is made effective by virtue of the power granted to the Postmaster General to fix the financial terms of the contracts; and since these contracts produce the largest item of operating revenues the Postmaster General is the dominant factor in the air transportation situation.[5]

The evolution of the regulation of transportation in the United States indicates that the principle of protecting the public interest, whatever the form of transportation, has been accepted by both state and national authority. We find, however, the widest diversity in practice, the regulation of railroads extending to financial policies and practices, rates, service, and safety; while in the case of other forms of transportation it is confined in the main to police and protective functions. There has been as yet no agreement upon common objectives, and, as we shall see in the following chapter, we have nothing which resembles a national transportation policy.

[5] Compare above, pp. 753-57.

CHAPTER XXXVIII

THE NEED FOR A NEW TRANSPORTATION POLICY

That the United States has no unified national transportation policy is clearly evident from the analysis which we have made of the several forms of transportation in this country. Instead of being welded into a co-ordinated system our various transport agencies are working more or less at cross purposes. Instead of a unified program of regulation designed to promote a common objective, we have a series of unrelated and often antagonistic policies carried out by a variety of government agencies. In this concluding chapter we shall endeavor to outline what is required if our transportation system as a whole is to serve in the most effective possible manner our national transportation needs.

As was indicated in the introductory chapter, the ultimate goal of all transportation policy should be to insure that the people obtain the service they require in the cheapest and most efficient manner. In pursuit of this objective there should be no predisposition in favor of any particular type of transportation agency. It is immaterial whether all traffic moves by one form of transportation or another; whether certain types of traffic are carried exclusively by some particular agency; or whether all forms of transportation are used as parts of a co-ordinated or integrated system. The primary requirement is that traffic actually move by the particular transportation agency or agencies which can carry it, all elements of cost considered, in the most economical and serviceable way. Such a principle might mean that all low-grade traffic in certain areas would move by water; that all passenger traffic for certain distances would move by bus and for other distances by air; that all long distance high grade freight traffic would move by rail; and that all within-city traffic would move by truck—or it might mean none of these things. The answer to the question in each case should depend solely upon the test of efficiency.

In the analysis which follows we shall seek to answer three main questions: (1) What general principles of regulation and government support are necessary in order to promote the most efficient possible transportation system? (2) What conditions are responsible for the failure of existing regulation to attain this objective? (3) What reorientation in our system of regulation is necessary if we are to obtain the desired results in the future?

The various forms of transportation must be placed upon the basis of economic parity. This, in a sentence, is the answer to the first question. To establish economic parity it is necessary, first, to treat all transportation agencies exactly alike in the matter of government aid, legal rights, and taxation. When this is done traffic will automatically move over that agency which can render service at lowest cost; but if any particular type of transportation agency is given special advantages, traffic may be diverted to the less economical type of carrier. Moreover, when any form of transportation is subsidized by the government, either directly or indirectly, we are not likely to know thereafter whether traffic is in fact actually moving by the cheapest method of transport. This is because some of the costs are buried in the general accounts of the government, and it is only when they are painstakingly extricated therefrom and converted to ton-mile rates for the routes in question that anyone knows what the total cost really is.

Regulation should be solely in the public interest; it should not seek to favor or retard one form of transportation as against another. It should have as its primary objective the establishment of rates which are not unnecessarily high and do not discriminate unfairly between persons, places, and commodities. This general principle of regulation is applicable to every form of transportation—although in the nature of the case the problems arising in connection with their enforcement present greater difficulties with some types of transportation than with others. For example, as we have seen in previous chapters, the problem of regulating the general level of railroad rates presents special difficulties, as does also that of regulating rates at all in the field of highway transportation, where common carriers, contract carriers, and private carriers operate side by side. But whatever the special difficulties with any particular form of transportation the goal remains the same, namely, to protect the public interest.

Our present system does not place transportation agencies on a plane of economic equality. Our analyses have shown that pipe lines obtain no subsidies or free services from the government; and that they pay their proportionate share of property and income taxation. The railroads, taken as a whole, have received, in the form of early land grants and other financial aids, a subsidy equivalent to approximately 4 per cent of the book value of their properties, though many individual roads received no grants of any kind. In return for land grants, railroads are bound by agreement to carry mail and military supplies and troops at low rates. Railroad taxation, both property and income, is levied in accordance with general taxation principles. In the case of inland canals and canalized rivers, all the capital costs and maintenance charges are borne by the government, and in some cases the government itself operates barges on a basis which is not self-sustaining. Boat companies pay personal property and income taxes; but the water highway is untaxed. Some of the intercoastal shipping carriers are given government aid in the form of mail subsidies and favorable terms in connection with the purchase of ships.

Until recently the users of the highways did not contribute, through license fees and gasoline taxes, sufficient revenues to cover capital costs and maintenance outlays on the highways; but for the country as a whole, with the situation varying widely in different states, these user contributions now approximately cover the current annual cost of state and county highways (not including city street divisions of such highways). Thus far state and local governments, except in particular instances, have not received from license fees and gasoline taxes anything for the general support of government, such as is furnished by the railroads and pipe lines. Other taxes on automobiles are levied in accordance with general principles of personal property taxation. Air transport receives heavy mail subsidies and also large municipal aids in connection with airports. The airplane companies pay personal property and income taxes, but little or no real estate taxes.

Similar variations exist with respect to regulation. Pipe-line rates and standards of service are subject to regulation by the Interstate Commerce Commission, but few regulations have been laid down. The railroads are regulated both by federal and state governments in a wide variety of ways. Inland waterway carriers, apart from certain safety requirements, are subject to no control, while regulation of intercoastal carriers is limited to the filing of ineffective maximum rates. Truck and bus companies and also private passenger vehicles are subject to numerous regulations made by state and local governments with reference to physical specifications, speed, and safety, but there is no regulation pertaining to rates and service. The regulation of airplanes is confined virtually to considerations of safety.

The explanation of these wide variations in government policy is two-fold: first, the various agencies came into existence at different periods of time and under dissimilar conditions of public favor; and, second, the regulatory agencies are divergent in character and lodged in different divisions of the government.

We passed through an early period, 1820-50, when canals, highways, and railways were looked upon with substantially equal favor by fostering state governments. Then the railways, from 1850 to 1870, were the particular objects of government largess. Beginning in the nineties, construction of waterways by the federal government became the favored policy, this development being attributable primarily to a natural hostility to railroad corporations grown rich and powerful and over-conscious of their power. The same conditions were of course responsible for the development of regulation designed on the one hand to restrain the monopolistic tendencies of the railroads and on the other to make them contribute more fully from their wealth of resources to the support of government.

The motor vehicle and the improved highway opened up for the rank and file of people new and fascinating possibilities of movement. In the nascent state of this great development it was but natural to assume that governments should do everything possible to facilitate "the march of progress" by giving financial aid on the one hand and by granting freedom from hampering restrictions on the other. It was the railway story over again, only more so in that the highways were constructed by state and local governments. In view of the glamour that has always attached to flying and the great publicity that has accompanied every exploit incident to its development, it was inevitable, once the possibility of the airplane was demonstrated, that every encouragement should be given to air transport.

Our various agencies of regulation are unco-ordinated and often conflicting in purpose. The scattering of regulatory agencies among many departments of government, as was indicated in the introductory chapter, is simply in keeping with the unsystematic and planless character of development which is found in all large-scale organization, and particularly in government organization. The location of a new type of activity or regulatory body may depend upon technical or political considerations, or upon the influence of a particularly powerful government official.

For example, waterway development was lodged in the War Department because, until after 1825, the only facilities for training engineers in this country were those provided at West Point, and also because the services of the Army Engineers have always been available, in peace times, without extra cost to the government. By a natural process the Army engineers came to play a primary rôle in passing upon the *economic* feasibility of waterway projects—though the West Point curriculum even to this day includes no courses in economics. The Bureau of Public Roads, established in 1893, was placed in the Department of Agriculture presumably because the roads of that day were of primary interest only to farmers. The regulation of aeronautics was lodged with the Department of Commerce chiefly because of the rapidly growing importance of that department at the particular time when air transport became significant. The Interstate Commerce Commission was set up as an independent agency because of the special character and magnitude of the problem involved; the Shipping Board because of an emergency situation of great complexity.

Once organized, either separately or in connection with a given department, the regulatory or promotional activities are governed in part by Congressional acts and in part by policies formulated within the interested bureau or department. The character of Congressional legislation is moreover greatly influenced by the policies and requests of the various regulatory or promotional agencies. This is particularly the case with the promotional phases of the problem.

Under a system that developed in this haphazard fashion it was inevitable that regulatory and promotional agencies should have varied and conflicting objectives. The very system itself, moreover, militates against thinking in terms of *transportation*, as distinguished from some particular form of transportation. The only instance in which congressional legislation has clearly had in mind more than one form of transportation is in connection with rail and water transportation. Congress declared in the Transportation Act of 1920 that its policy was "to foster and preserve in full vigor both rail and water transportation." But this meant, or at least it has been interpreted to mean, that regulation and subsidies should be utilized to promote the movement of goods by water. Instead of establishing economic parity this policy destroys it.

The primary explanation of policies such as this is the persistent fear of railroad monopoly. The unfair competitive practices and the "public be damned" attitude of prominent railroad corporations in former days have left an almost indelible impression upon the minds and attitudes of the majority of the American people. Though our regulatory powers have long since removed the menace of monopoly, and although new forms of transportation, notably the pipe line and the motor vehicle, have become effective competitors, the spectre of railroad monopoly still persists.

Since our capacity to protect the public interest through regulation of large transportation companies has been demonstrated in practice, it is no longer necessary to subsidize competing forms of transportation for regulatory purposes. Every form of transportation should stand on its own feet, with competition in a free field deciding the issue of survival. This means that such transportation agencies as may be constructed and maintained by the government should be subjected to the test of self-liquidating capacity.

A properly integrated national transportation system is dependent upon unified regulation. In recent years there has been no little discussion of the need of coordination or unification in the entire field of transportation. It has been commonly assumed in this connection that *every* form of transportation has its proper place in the system, and that all forms should thus be encouraged. There is, however, no means by which the government can automatically determine the proper economic sphere of each agency; hence the tendency is to help those that cannot take care of themselves.

Efficient co-ordination and the movement of traffic by the cheapest possible agency, or combination of agencies, cannot possibly be realized under an unco-ordinated regulatory system such as we now possess. Not until we establish a unified system of regulation which will place all transportation agencies upon a basis of economic parity will a unification of transportation that means anything from an economic standpoint be possible.

Co-ordination would also be facilitated if the present system of conducting transportation by specialized agencies were abandoned. Indeed, one of the surest means of promoting real integration, of getting traffic routed in the most economical way, is by developing *transportation* companies as distinguished from railroad, or highway, or waterway, or airplane companies. In principle there can be no objection to boat or truck companies' engaging in the railroad business, or vice versa—so long as public control is adequate to prevent abuse.

As the largest factor in the transportation situation, the railroad company is perhaps ideally designed to serve as the nucleus of a comprehensive agency of transportation. Indeed, the early railroads were conceived as something more than roads of rails; their primary business was transportation. This basic idea was expressed in the titles named in some of the early chapters, as, for example, "The New Jersey Railroad and Transportation Company" (1832). Some railways have interests in airplane companies; and others operate motor vehicles, usually through subsidiary or affiliated corporations. They are forbidden, however, by the Panama Canal Act of 1912 to engage in water transportation on that canal "or elsewhere," if the water route and the railway are competitive.

The fear which some express that if railroad companies were permitted to engage in other forms of transportation they would proceed at once to throttle competition, regardless of transportation economies, seems unwarranted. A railroad company, converted to a transportation company, would still be interested in maximum profits. If it proved cheaper to send certain commodities, or for that matter all traffic, by truck, or bus, or airplane, or boat, as the case might be, such companies would be shortsighted indeed if they failed to use the alternative agencies.

Federal control is essential to a comprehensive system of transportation. If transportation is to develop in a comprehensive way along national lines regulation by the federal government must be extended to all agencies operating interstate: carriers by water, carriers by air, and carriers on the highway, as well as rail carriers and pipe lines. Unless the national authority is paramount, as it now is in the case of the railroads, our regulatory machinery will be inadequate to meet the nation's requirements.

This does not imply the negation of state regulation under the police power. State authority has a proper place in any scheme of regulation. The state commissions are informed as to regional and local conditions, and their co-operation will continue to be helpful in any national system of control. They have a jurisdiction of their own, particularly with reference to policing functions, which it is not practicable for the national authority to assume.

Federal regulation should be centralized under the Interstate Commerce Commission. Regulation to be comprehensive must be centralized; and this means control exercised, in so far as may be practicable, through a single governmental body. For various reasons the Interstate Commerce Commission would seem to be the logical agency for the purpose in hand.

The Commission already has wide authority over railroads and pipe lines, and a measure of authority over the inter-relationships of rail and water carriers. When the Commission was created Congress did not follow state precedents in the choice of a name, despite the fact that, with the sole exception of joint rail and water lines engaged in continuous shipments, the jurisdiction of the Commission was originally confined to railroads. Constitutional considerations doubtless had something to do with the choice, but in any event the name chosen was one of broad implication, indicating that the Commission was to be concerned not merely with railroads as such but with the railroad as an instrumentality of commerce. Consistent with this principle was the succession of acts extending its power in matters pertaining to safety and widening its jurisdiction to include pipe lines, communication companies, express companies, special equipment lines, and terminal and other facilities related to railroad operation and service.

The Interstate Commerce Commission is clearly the logical federal agency to exercise control over interstate rates and service. With a single exception it is the only federal body that has authority over rates. The exception is the United States Shipping Board, which is primarily concerned with the foreign field. In the matter of interstate and intercoastal rates, the authority of this Board is limited to the point of ineffectiveness by virtue of the fact that only maximum tariffs need be filed. The burden of duties in connection therewith is slight. This being the case, the Shipping Board would lose nothing through the transfer of its nominal duties with reference to rates to the Interstate Commerce Commission. Nor would there be any injustice to the water carriers in a system which would co-ordinate their rates with rail rates under the common authority of the Commission. On its record the Commission cannot be charged with favoritism toward the railroads or hostility toward other types of carriers. Nor can it be accused of immoderate use of the authority which has been conferred upon it.

The Commission is competent to meet greater responsibilities. It is a mature organization of 45 years' experience, and, however opposed and criticized it may have been, its position is established. Not a few of the criticisms against it are in effect criticisms of the lawmaking branch of the government, which has often been slow to act upon corrective suggestions repeatedly made by the Commission. This is true particularly of recommendations relating to reorganization of the Commission's structure and procedure and designed to facilitate and to expedite the performance of its work.

Within recent years the burden of work imposed upon the Commission has been excessive, largely because the depression came at a time when the Commission was still concerned with a number of temporary undertakings, notably the valuation of railroad property and the formulation of consolidation plans as required by the legislation of 1920, and the investigations necessitated by the ill-considered Hoch-Smith Resolution. The Commission's task will be simplified if some form of consolidation is eventually adopted. The unification of the entire system of regulation would of itself simplify the work of the Commission.

The amount of detailed regulation of railway operations may also be reduced. There is a degree of detail beyond which regulation may not go without imposing excessive demands and handicaps upon management and depriving the public of the advantages which it is the purpose of regulation to promote. The point at which a balance may be struck between public regulation and managerial initiative is not to be arrived at easily. It cannot be determined at all without a spirit of co-operation —which is inconsistent with the punitive spirit sometimes manifest in the attitude of the public and sometimes dominant in the minds of those who are charged with the shaping or execution of public policy, and inconsistent as well with the baronial spirit sometimes disclosed by railroad spokesmen.

Existing regulations affecting management, particularly those relating to technical questions, might well be re-examined to determine whether they serve the purpose for which they were imposed; whether the need for them has passed; whether they are too weak and should be strengthened; whether they are too stringent and should be lessened; whether they are too detailed or too general; finally, whether a lessening of control by federal authority would tend to stimulate the regulatory activities of 48 state authorities.

Making the Commission the central agency of regulation does not imply shifting to it all functions pertaining to transportation now performed by other departments of government. For example, the exercise of marine police functions by the Commission is not essential to a comprehensive system of regulation. There is nothing to gain by disturbing the arrangement by which such matters are handled by the Coast Guard and the Bureau of Navigation and Steamboat-Inspection, both of which are equally concerned with domestic and with foreign commerce. Some of the services of the latter Bureau are analogous to the safety service of the Commission, but they are technologically dissimilar. The same is true of the administration of air-transport safety legislation by the Department of Commerce. Similarly, the authority of the Department of Agriculture to prevent inhumane transportation of livestock on rail or water carriers need not be disturbed.

The policy of the Commission has developed in the direction of a truer perspective. At the outset it seems consciously to have leaned toward the side of the shipper, who at that time was assumed to be ill-prepared to match strength against the railroad. The shipper is in no such helpless position today, and the record of shippers as a whole is not free from instances of abuse.[1] The original attitude of the Commission was that it could not properly concern itself with the effect upon railroad revenues of its action on rate matters; and this attitude it seems to have maintained until 1914, when in the *Five Per Cent* case[2] it gave its approval, not without dissent, to an increase in rates on the ground that an advance was justified by the need of the carriers for adequate revenue, and hence in the public interest. The principle involved in this departure from precedent was legislatively confirmed in the Transportation Act of 1920, in the provision of the rule of rate making, which in effect directs the

---

[1] Witness: *Reciprocity in Purchasing and Routing*, 188 I.C.C. 417.
[2] 31 I.C.C. 351.

Commission to have a care as to the financial results of its decisions. This means not that the shipper is to receive less consideration but the railroads more. To serve the public interest is the only proper objective of regulation; that interest is best served when the relation of carrier to shipper, as well as that of carrier to carrier, is maintained on an equitable basis.

We are not concerned here to suggest the detailed provisions which might appropriately be incorporated in a new transportation act. We are interested only in calling attention to the primary essentials of a satisfactory national transportation system. We confine our analysis therefore to a discussion of fundamental policies with respect to transportation and to the plan of regulation that is required if these policies are to be carried into effect. If the regulation of transportation is concentrated in a single agency, substantial economies in government regulation may be realized. If the Interstate Commerce Commission is reorganized in such a way as to permit the delegation of routine administrative tasks and to enable the Commissioners to plan constructively in national terms, the whole transportation system may be placed upon a new plane.

SELECT BIBLIOGRAPHY

AIR TRANSPORT

1. Books, Pamphlets, and Documents

Kennedy, Thomas Hart, *An Introduction to the Economics of Air Transportation*. Macmillan, 1924.

Pynchon and Co., *The Aviation Industry*, New York, 1929.

Rohlfing, Charles C., *National Regulation of Aeronautics*, University of Pennsylvania Press.

Security Owners' Association, Inc., *A Study of Transportation by Airways as Related to Competition with Rail Carriers in Continental United States*, New York, 1932.

U. S. 72 Cong. 1 sess., *Investigation of the U. S. Postal Air Mail Service*. Prepared for Committee on Post Offices and Post Roads, 1933.

2. Periodical Publications

Air Commerce Bulletin (bimonthly), Department of Commerce.

Aviation (monthly), McGraw-Hill, New York.

Official Aviation Guide (monthly), The Official Aviation Guide Co., Inc., Chicago.

U. S. National Advisory Committee for Aeronautics, *Bibliography of Aeronautics*, 1906—(annual since 1922), G.P.O.

————, *Annual Reports*.

U. S. Postmaster General, *Annual Reports*.

HIGHWAY TRANSPORT

1. Books, Pamphlets, Articles, and Documents

Agg, T. R., *American Rural Highways*, McGraw-Hill, 1920.

————, and Brindley, John E., *Highway Administration and Finance*. McGraw-Hill, 1927.

American Bankers' Association, *Automotive Transportation and the Railroads*, N.A.C.C., 1927.

"The Automobile, Its Province and Problems," *Annals of Am. Acad. of Pol. and Soc. Science*, November, 1924.

American Electric Railway Association, *The Urban Transportation Problem*, New York, 1932.

Bateman, J. H., *Highway Engineering*, Wiley, 1928.

Blanchard, A. H., and Morrison, R. L., *Elements of Highway Engineering*, New York, 1928.

Bratschi, Robert, *Railway and Motor Transport*, International Transport Workers' Federation, Amsterdam, 1930.

Brousseau, A. J., *Highway Finance*, Address Delivered at the Annual Meeting of the International Chamber of Commerce, Amsterdam, July, 1929.

————, *Motor Transportation*, N.A.C.C., 1929.

Chamber of Commerce of the United States of America, *Referendum No. 61 on the Report of the Special Committee on City Passenger Transportation*, Washington, 1932.

Chatburn, George R., *Highways and Highway Transportation*, Crowell, 1923.

General Motors Corporation, *National Motor Truck Analysis*, Detroit, 1930.

Great Britain, Ministry of Transport, *Report of the Conference on Rail and Road Transport*, London, 1932.

Grupp, G. W., *Economics of Motor Transportation*, Appleton, 1924.

International Road Congress, *Proceedings of the Sixth Congress*, Washington, 1930.

Joint Committee of Railroads and Highway Users, *Regulation and Taxation of Highway Transportation*, New York, 1933.

Lilienthal, D. E., and Rosenbaum, I. S., *Motor Carrier Regulations by Certificates of Necessity and Convenience*, N.A.C.C., 1926.

Meighan, John M., *Motor Bus Laws and Regulations*, National Association of Motor Bus Operators (mimeographed), Washington, 1932.

Mississippi Valley Railroads' Research Committee, *The Validity of State Statutes Regulating the Operation of Motor Vehicles*, Louisville, 1932.

National Association of Motor Bus Operators, *The Motor Bus Tax Burden*, Washington, 1930.

National Association of Railroad and Utilities Commissioners, *Report of Committee on Motor Vehicle Transportation*, Hot Springs, Ark., 1932.

———— (Same title), Richmond, Va., 1931.

National Automobile Chamber of Commerce, Motor Truck Committee, *Regulation of the Contract Motor Carrier under the Constitution*, New York, 1931.

National Industrial Conference Board, *The Taxation of Motor Vehicle Transportation*, 1932.

Sandage, C. H. and Nelson, R. W., *Motor Vehicle Taxation for Highway Purposes*, Iowa Studies in Business, State University of Iowa, 1932.

"The Traffic Census and its Use in Deciding Road Width," *Public Roads*, July, 1921.

Trumbower, H. R., *Economics of Highway Transportation*, N.A.C.C., 1926.

U. S. Bureau of Foreign and Domestic Commerce, *Motor Freight Transportation*, Domestic Commerce Series No. 66, 1932.

U. S. Bureau of Public Roads, Reports of Surveys of Transportation on State Highway systems: *Ohio*, 1927; *Vermont*, 1927; *New Hampshire*, 1927; *Pennsylvania*, 1928; *Eleven Western States*, 1930.

United States Chamber of Commerce, *Highway Finance Report*, Washington, 1932.

U. S. 69 Cong. 1 sess., *Interstate Commerce by Motor Buses Operating or to Operate as Common Carriers of Passengers for Hire over Routes, Part or Whole of Which are through Interstate Tunnel now being Constructed under Hudson River between New York, N.Y., and Jersey City, N.J., and over Interstate Bridge now being Constructed across Delaware River between Philadelphia, Pa., and Camden, N.J.*, Hearings on S. 3894, before Committee on Interstate Commerce, 1926.

U. S. 69 Cong. 1 sess., *Interstate Commerce by Motor Vehicles Operating as Common Carriers on the Public Highways*, Hearings on S. 1734 before Committee on Interstate Commerce, 1926.

U. S. 71 Cong. 1 sess., *Regulation of Motor Carrier Transportation*, Hearings on S. 2793 before Committee on Interstate Commerce, 1932.

"Urban Aspects of Highway Finance," *Public Roads*, January, 1926.

2. *Periodical Publications*

American Association of State Highway Officials, annual reports, Washington.

American Highways (quarterly), Amer. Assoc. of State Highway Officials, Washington.

Automotive Industries (weekly), W. Chilton Class Journal Co., Philadelphia.

Bus Facts of 1932 (annual), National Association of Motor Operators, Washington.

Bus Transportation (monthly), McGraw-Hill.

Facts and Figures of the Automobile Industry (annual), National Automobile Chamber of Commerce, 1932.

Good Roads (weekly), Burton Pub. Co., 53 W. Jackson Blvd., Chicago.

Highway Education Board, *Highways Handbook*, Washington, 1929 (latest published).

Highway Tax Costs (annual), National Automobile Chamber of Commerce.

National Research Council, Highway Research Board, annual *Proceedings*, Washington.

Power Wagon (monthly), Power Wagon Pub. Co., Chicago.

Public Roads (monthly), U. S. Bureau of Public Roads, Washington.

Western Truck Owner (monthly), Keystone, Los Angeles.

Public Roads (monthly), Bureau of Public Roads of the U. S. Department of Agriculture, 1932.

PIPE LINES

Federal Trade Commission, *Pipe Line Transportation of Petroleum*, 1916.

————, *Petroleum Industry—Prices, Profits and Competition*, 1928.

———, *Petroleum Industry in California, Parts I and II,* 1922.

———, *Report on Pipe-Line Transportation of Petroleum,* 1916.

Fraser, C. E., and Doriot, G., *Analyzing our Industries,* chapter on Petroleum, McGraw-Hill, 1932.

Lamp, Irwin, "The Pipe Line Era," *Pipe Line News,* June, 1932.

Pogue, Joseph E., "Economics of Pipe Line Transportation in the Petroleum Industry," reprinted serially in *Pipe Line News,* 1932.

U. S. 72 Cong. 2 sess., *Oil Pipe Line Industry,* Report from House Committee on Interstate and Foreign Commerce (in press), 1933.

U. S. Interstate Commerce Commission, *Selected Items from the Annual Reports of Pipe Line Companies* (mimeographed).

RAILROADS

1. Books, Pamphlets, Articles, and Documents

American Short Line Railroad Association, *Special Report of the Executive Board to the Members,* relating to danger of government having to take possession of some of the railroads, Washington, 1932.

Acworth, W. M., *Historical Sketch of State Railway Ownership,* J. Murray, London, 1920.

Aitchison, C. B., *A Century of Transportation Problems,* G.P.O., 1926.

———, *Interstate Commerce Acts Annotated,* 5 volumes, 1930.

Bogen, Jules I., *Analysis of Railroad Securities,* Ronald Press, 1928.

Bonbright, J. C., *Railroad Capitalization,* Columbia University Press, 1920.

Buck, S. J., *The Granger Movement,* Harvard University, 1913.

Bureau of Railway Economics, *Capital Expenditures and Purchases in the Railway Industry,* Miscellaneous Series No. 48, Washington, 1929.

———, *Government Ownership of Railways,* A List of Publications 1917-29, Bulletin No. 49, Supplement to Bulletin No. 62, Old Series, Revised 1917, 1929.

———, *Railroad Consolidation*, A List of References, Special Series No. 52, 1930.

———, *The Railways and Economic Progress*, Miscellaneous Series No. 50, 1929.

Chamber of Commerce of the United States of America, *Referendum No. 62 on the Report of the Special Committee on Railroads*, Washington, 1932.

Cunningham, William J., *American Railroads: Government Control and Reconstruction Policies*, Shaw, 1922.

Daniels, Winthrop M., *American Railroads: Four Phases of their History*, Princeton University Press, 1932.

Dixon, Frank Haigh, *Railroads and Government*, Scribner's, 1922.

———, and Parmelee, J. H., *War Administration of the Railways in the United States and Great Britain*, Oxford University Press, 1919.

Dudley, A. S., *The Economics of Railroad Valuation*, J. J. Collins & Sons, Chicago, 1928.

Duncan, Kenneth, *Equipment Obligations*, Appleton, New York, 1924.

Dunn, S. O., *Regulation of Railways*, Appleton, 1919.

Ellingwood, A. R. and Coombs, Whitney, *The Government and Railroad Transportation*, Ginn & Co., 1930.

Ely, Owen, *Railway Rates and Cost of Service*, Houghton Mifflin, 1924.

Frederick, J. H., *Federal Regulation of Railway Securities under the Transportation Act of 1920*, Westbrook Publishing Co., Philadelphia, 1927.

———, Herring, J. M. and Hypps, F. T., *Regulation of Railroad Finance*, Simmons-Boardman, New York, 1930.

Grodinsky, Julius, *Federal Regulation of Railway Security Issues*, Univ. of Penn., 1925.

———, *Railroad Consolidation*, Univ. of Penn., 1930.

———, and Johnson, Emory R., *Railroad Consolidation*, Appleton, 1930.

Herring, James M., *The Problem of Weak Railroads*, University of Pennsylvania Press, 1929.

Hines, Walker D., *War History of American Railroads*, Yale University Press, 1928.

Hinshaw, David, and Albig, W. E., *Stop, Look and Listen: Railroad Transportation in the United States*, Doubleday, 1932.

Huang, Hsien-Ju, *State Taxation of Railways in the United States*, Columbia University Press, 1928.

Hypps, Frank T., *Federal Regulation of Railroad Construction and Abandonment under the Transportation Act of 1920* (thesis), Univ. of Penn., 1929.

Interstate Commerce Commission (compiler), *The Interstate Commerce Act, as amended*, 1929.

———, *Railways in the United States in 1902; A Twenty-two Year Review of Railway Operations; A Forty-Year Review of Changes in Freight Tariffs; A Fifteen-Year Review of Federal Railway Regulation; A Twelve-Year Review of State Railway Taxation*, Washington, 1903.

Jackman, William T., *Economics of Transportation*, A. W. Shaw, 1926.

Johnson, Emory R. and Van Metre, Thurman W., *Principles of Railroad Transportation*, Appleton, 1923.

Joint Commission of Agricultural Inquiry, *Transportation* (Vol. III of the Commission Report), 1921.

Jones, Eliot, *Principles of Railway Transportation*, Macmillan, 1924.

Locklin, David P., *Regulation of Security Issues by the Interstate Commerce Commission*, University of Illinois Studies in the Social Sciences, 1927.

———, *Railroad Regulation since 1920*, McGraw-Hill, 1928.

Loree, L. F., *The Railroads, Their Relation to the Causes and Cure of the Commercial Depression* (before Senate Committee on Finance), New York, 1933.

———, *Railroad Freight Transportation*, Appleton, 1922.

———, *Save the Railroads, a Proposed Revision of the Interstate Commerce Law*, privately printed, New York, 1932.

Lust, Herbert C., *Consolidated Digest of Decisions under the Interstate Commerce Act*. H. C. Lust Co., Fowler, Ind., 1925.

MacVeagh, Rogers, *The Transportation Act of 1920.* Holt, 1923.

Miller, S. L., *Railway Transportation, Principles and Point of View,* Shaw, 1924.

National Industrial Conference Board, *The Consolidation of Railroads in the United States.* The Board, New York, 1923.

New England Railroad Committee, *Report to the Governors of the New England States,* 1931.

Oldham, John E., *A Plan for Railroad Consolidation,* Cosmos Press, Cambridge, 1921. (Also published by the Investment Bankers' Association of America.)

Partington, J. E., *Railroad Purchasing and the Business Cycle,* Brookings Institution, 1929.

Presentation in behalf of the Chesapeake and Ohio Railway Company Shop Craft Employees, before the Federal Arbitration Board. Richmond, 1928.

Railroad Wage Commission, *Report to the Director General of Railroads,* U. S. Railroad Administration, 1918.

Railway Business Association, *Trends in the Passenger Service and Traffic of the Class I Steam Railways of the United States,* 1920-32, Chicago, 1932.

Railway Security Owners' Association, *A Study of the Highway Situation as Related to Motor Truck Competition with Rail Carriers in Eastern United States,* 1932.

Ripley, W. Z., *Railroads, Finance and Organization,* Longmans, Green & Co., 1915.

——, *Railroads, Rates and Regulation,* Longmans, Green & Co., 1912.

Robins, E. C., *The Railway Conductors,* Columbia Univ. Press, 1914.

Sharfman, I. L. *The American Railroad Problem,* Century, 1921.

——, *The Interstate Commerce Commission,* Commonwealth Fund, New York, 1931. 4 Vols. (Volumes III and IV not yet published.)

Splawn, Walter M. W., *Consolidation of Railroads,* Macmillan, 1925.

————, *Government Ownership and Operation of Railroads*, Macmillan, 1928.

U. S. 67 Cong. 1 sess., *Bills to Amend the Transportation Act of 1920*, Hearings before the Committee on Interstate Commerce on S. 1150 and S. 2510, 1922.

U. S. 69 Cong. 1 sess., *Railroad Legislation*, Hearings on H.R. 6359 before Committee on Interstate and Foreign Commerce, 1926.

U. S. 71 Cong. 2 sess., *To Suspend Railroad Consolidation*, Hearings on S. J. Res. 161 (a joint resolution to suspend the authority of the I.C.C. to approve consolidations or unification of railway properties) before Committee on Interstate Commerce, 1930.

U. S. 68 Cong. 1 (2) sess., *Consolidation of Railway Properties*, Hearings on S. 2224 before Committee on Interstate Commerce, 1925.

U. S. 69 Cong. 1 sess., *Railroad Consolidation*, Hearings on H.R. 11212 before Committee on Interstate and Foreign Commerce, 1926.

U. S. 69 Cong. 2 sess., *Unification of Carriers Engaged in Interstate Commerce*, Hearings on S. 4892 before the Committee on Interstate Commerce, 1927.

U. S. 70 Cong. 1 sess., *Consolidation of Railway Properties*, Hearings on S. 1175 before Committee on Interstate Commerce, 1928.

U. S. 70 Cong. 1 sess., *Railroad Consolidation*, Hearings on H.R. 5641 before Committee on Interstate and Foreign Commerce, 1928.

U. S. 71 Cong. 2 sess., *Long and Short Haul*, Hearings on S. 563 before Subcommittee of the Committee on Interstate Commerce, 1930.

U. S. 71 Cong. 2 sess., *Railroad Legislation*, Hearings on H.R. 9084 before a Subcommittee of the Committee on Interstate and Foreign Commerce, 1930.

U. S. 71 Cong. 3 sess., *Regulation of Stock Ownership in Railroads*, Hearings on H.R. 2789 before Committee on Interstate and Foreign Commerce, 1931.

U. S. 71 Cong. 3 sess., *Preliminary Report of Study of Rail-*

road Consolidations and Unifications, submitted to Committee on Interstate Commerce, S. Res. 290, 1931.

U. S. 72 Cong. 1 sess., *Control of Common Carriers by Railroads,* Hearings on H.R. 1387 before Committee on Interstate and Foreign Commerce, 1932.

U. S. 72 Cong. 1 sess., *Railroad Legislation,* Hearings on H.R. 7116 and 7117 before Committee on Interstate and Foreign Commerce, 1932.

U. S. 72 Cong. 1 sess., *Railroads—Recapture and Valuation,* Hearings on H.R. 1386 before Committee on Interstate and Foreign Commerce, 1932.

U. S. 72 Cong. 1 sess., *Regulation of Railroad Holding Companies,* Hearings on H.R. 9059 before Committee on Interstate and Foreign Commerce, 1932.

Vanderblue, H. B., and Burgess, K. F., *Railroads: Rates—Service—Management,* Macmillan, 1923.

Wagner, W. H., *The Hoch-Smith Resolution; the Contentions as to its Interpretation and Application,* Traffic Pub. Co., New York, 1929.

Ward, F. B., *The United States Railroad Labor Board and Railway Labor Disputes* (thesis), University of Pennsylvania, 1929.

Woo, V. W., *Efficiency in Railroad Management; a Study of the Requirements of Section 15-a of the Transportation Act of 1920,* University of Pennsylvania Press, 1926.

Wood, L. A., *Union-Management Co-operation on the Railroads,* Yale University Press, 1931.

2. *Periodical Publications*

Bureau of Railway Economics, *Statistics of Railways of Class I, United States,* Statistical Summary No. 14 (1920-31), Washington.

———, *A Review of Railway Operations in 1931,* Special Series No. 58 (annual, 1932 in press).

Emergency Boards Appointed by the President of the United States, under Section 10 of the Railway Act, *Annual Reports,* 1927-32.

Journal of Land and Public Utility Economics (monthly), Chicago.

National Association of Railroad and Utilities Commissioners, *Proceedings* (annual).

Railway Age (weekly), New York.

Traffic World (monthly), Chicago.

U. S. Director General of Railroads, *Annual Reports*, 1918-19.

U. S. Board of Mediation, *Annual Reports*, 1927-32.

U. S. Railroad Labor Board, *Annual Reports*, 1920-26.

U. S. Interstate Commerce Commission, *Annual Report.*

———, *Operating Revenues and Operating Expenses by Class of Service, Class I Steam Railways in the United States* (annual).

———, *Comparative Statement of Operating Averages, Class I Steam Railways in the United States* (annual).

———, *Statistics of Railways in the United States* (annual).

———, *Wage Statistics* (annual).

———, *Fuel for Locomotives, Class I Steam Railways* (monthly).

———, *Freight and Passenger Operating Statistics of Class I Steam Railways* (monthly).

———, *Freight Commodity Statistics, Class I Steam Railways in the United States* (annual).

———, *Graphical Supplement to Monthly Reports.*

———, *Operating Revenues and Operating Expenses, Class I Steam Railways* (monthly).

———, *Operating Revenues and Operating Expenses of Large Steam Roads—Selected Items for Roads with Annual Operating Revenues above $25,000,000* (monthly).

———, *Operating Statistics of Large Steam Roads—Selected Items for Roads with Annual Operating Revenues above $25,000,000*

———, *Revenue Traffic Statistics of Class I Steam Railways* (monthly).

———, *Selected Income and Balance-Sheet Items of Class I Steam Railways* (monthly).

———, *Summary of Accidents Reported by Steam Railways* (monthly).

———, *Wage Statistics, Class I Steam Railways* (monthly).

3. *Important Decisions of the Interstate Commerce Commission*

A. General rate and revenue cases:

Revenues in Western District, 113 I.C.C. 3 (1926).
Western Trunk-line Class Rates, 164 I.C.C. 1 (1930)
Eastern Class Rate Investigation, 164 I.C.C. 314 (1930).
Southern Class Rate Investigation, 100 I.C.C. 513 (1925).
Consolidated Southwestern Cases, 123 I.C.C. 203 (1927).
Rate Structure Investigation:

   a. *Grain and Grain Products within Western District for Export,* 164 I.C.C. 619 (1930).
   b. *Livestock—Western District Rates,* 176 I.C.C. 1 (1931).
   c. *Cotton,* 165 I.C.C. 595 (1930).
   d. *Petroleum and Petroleum Products,* 171 I.C.C. 286 (1931).
   e. *Rates on Refined Petroleum Products from, to and between Points in the Southwest,* 171 I.C.C. 381 (1931).
   f. *Fifteen Per Cent Case,* 178 I.C.C. 539 (1931) and 179 I.C.C. 215, (1931).

B. Consolidation of Railroads:

Compare 63 I.C.C. 455 (1921), 159 I.C.C. 522 (1929), 183 I.C.C. 663 (1932), and 185 I.C.C. 403 (1932).

C. Valuation:

Excess Income of St. Louis and O'Fallon Railway Company, 124 I.C.C. 3 (1927). (Decision in this case was overruled by the Supreme Court in *St. Louis and O'Fallon Railway Company and Manufacturers' Railway Company* v. *United States of America and Interstate Commerce Commission,* 279 U.S. 461.)
Excess Income of Richmond, Fredericksburg and Potomac Railroad Company, 170 I.C.C. 451 (1931).

D. Highway Transport:

Motor Bus and Motor Truck Operation, 140 I.C.C. 685.
Co-ordination of Motor Transportation, 182 I.C.C. 263 (1932).

E. Labor Relations:
  Report of an investigation completed in 1932, under the
  title of *Six Hour Day Investigation,* has been presented to
  Congress but not yet published.

WATER TRANSPORT

1. Books Pamphlets, and Documents

Bureau of Railway Economics, *Comparison of Transportation
  Costs by Rail and via Barge Canal,* Washington, 1925.
———, *An Economic Survey of Inland Waterway Transpor-
  tation in the United States,* Washington, 1930.
———, *Transportation Costs on the New York State Barge
  Canal,* Washington, 1926.
Engineering, Operating and Traffic Committee on New York
  Harbor, *Associated Report,* New York, 1926.
Joint Board of Engineers appointed by the Governments of the
  United States and Canada. *Report on the Improvement of
  the St. Lawrence River between Lake Ontario and Mon-
  treal* (mimeographed), 1927.
Kidd, Howard C., *Regulation of Intercoastal Commerce,* Uni-
  versity of Pittsburgh Bulletin, Vol. 28, No. 21, June 15,
  1932.
Moulton, H. G., *Waterways versus Railways,* Houghton
  Mifflin, 1926.
———, Morgan, C. L., and Lee, A. L., *The St. Lawrence
  Navigation and Power Project,* Brookings Institution,
  1929.
St. Lawrence Commission [United States], *Report and Recom-
  mendations to President Calvin Coolidge by Secretary
  Herbert Hoover, Chairman.* December 27, 1926.
Security Owners' Association, Inc., *A Study of Transportation
  by Waterways as Related to Competition with Rail Car-
  riers in Continental United States,* New York, 1932.
Switzer, J. E., "The Completed Ohio River Project," *Proc.
  Indiana Acad. of Sci.,* Vol. 41, 1931, p. 346.
U. S. Army Corps of Engineers, *Transportation on the Ohio
  River System (Interim Report),* 1927.
———, and Bureau of Operations U. S. Shipping Board,
  Transportation in the Mississippi and Ohio Valleys, 1929.

U. S. Bureau of Foreign and Domestic Commerce, *Great-Lakes-to-Ocean Waterways*, 1927.

————, *Inland Water Transportation in the United States*, 1923.

U. S. Bureau of the Census, *Transportation by Water, 1906*, 1908.

————, *Transportation by Water, 1916*, 1920.

U. S. 62 Cong. 2 sess., *Final Report of the National Waterways Commission*, S. doc. 469, 1912.

U. S. 71 Cong. 2 sess., *Report from the Chief of Engineers of the War Department on a Partial Survey of Mississippi River*, H.R. doc. 290, 1930.

U. S. 72 Cong. 2 sess., *Great Lakes-St. Lawrence Deep Waterway Treaty*, Report submitted by Committee on Foreign Relations, Sen. Exec. Report No. 1, 1933.

U. S. 72 Cong. 2 sess., *Regulation of Intercoastal Water Carriers*. Hearings on S. 4491 before House Committee on U. S. Merchant Marine, Radio and Fisheries, 1933.

U. S. 72 Cong. 2 sess., *St. Lawrence Waterway*, Hearings on S. Res. 278 before a Subcommittee of the Committee on Foreign Relations, 1932.

U. S. Inland Waterways Commission, *Preliminary Report*, S. doc. 325, 1908.

U. S. 67 Cong. 2 sess., *Report of the International Joint Commission Concerning the Improvement of the St. Lawrence River between Montreal and Lake Ontario for Navigation and Power*. S. doc. 114, 1921.

2. Periodical Publications

U. S. Army Chief of Engineers, *Annual Reports*.

U. S. Inland Waterways Corporation, *Annual Reports*.

GENERAL AND MISCELLANEOUS

American Federation of Labor, *Proceedings of Annual Conventions*, Washington.

American Labor Year Book, Rand School Press, New York, 1932.

Bonbright, J. C., and Means, G. C., *The Holding Company, its Public Significance and its Regulation*, McGraw-Hill, 1932.

Chamber of Commerce of the United States, Special Committee on Competing Forms of Transportation, *Report*, Washington, 1933.

Daggett, Stuart, *Principles of Inland Transportation*, Harpers, 1928.

Haines, H. S., *Efficient Railway Operation*, Macmillan, 1919.

Johnson, Emory R., Huebner, G. E., and Wilson, G. L., *Principles of Transportation*, Appleton, 1928.

National Bureau of Economic Research, Inc., *Recent Economic Changes*, Vol. I, Chap. IV (Transportation), McGraw-Hill, 1929.

Royal Commission to Inquire into Railways and Transportation in Canada, *Report*, F. A. Acland, Ottawa, 1932.

Meyer, B. H., *History of Transportation in the United States before 1890*, Carnegie Institution of Washington, 1917.

National Tax Association, *Proceedings of Annual Conventions*.

U. S. 72 Cong. 2 sess., *Government Competition with Private Enterprise*, Report of the Special Committee Appointed to Investigate Government Competition with Private Enterprise (Shannon Committee), H. R. 1985, 1933.

Willey, Malcolm M., and Rice, Stuart A., *Communication Agencies and Social Life*, Recent Social Trends Monographs (President's Research Committee on Social Trends), McGraw-Hill, 1933.

INDEX

PUBLICATIONS OF THE BROOKINGS INSTITUTION*

INSTITUTE OF ECONOMICS SERIES

* The parentheses indicate that the volume itself does not carry the number since it was given subsequent to publication.

LIST OF PUBLICATIONS

LIST OF PUBLICATIONS

44. JAPAN: AN ECONOMIC AND FINANCIAL APPRAISAL.
    By Harold G. Moulton with the collaboration of Junichi Ko. 645 pp. 1931. $4.

45. CREDIT POLICIES OF THE FEDERAL RESERVE SYSTEM.
    By Charles O. Hardy. 374 pp. 1932. $2.50.

46. WAR DEBTS AND WORLD PROSPERITY.
    By Harold G. Moulton and Leo Pasvolsky. 498 pp. 1932. $3.

47. ADVERTISING ALLOWANCES: A PHASE OF THE PRICE-MAKING PROCESS.
    By Leverett S. Lyon. 125 pp. 1932. $1.

48. TEN YEARS OF FEDERAL INTERMEDIATE CREDITS.
    By Frieda Baird and Claude L. Benner. (In press.)

49. SILVER: AN ANALYSIS OF FACTORS AFFECTING ITS PRICE.
    By Y. S. Leong. (In press.)

50. THE AMERICAN FEDERATION OF LABOR: HISTORY AND OUTLOOK.
    By Lewis L. Lorwin. (In press.)

INSTITUTE FOR GOVERNMENT RESEARCH SERIES

Studies in Administration

(1.) THE SYSTEM OF FINANCIAL ADMINISTRATION OF GREAT BRITAIN.
    By W. F. Willoughby, W. W. Willoughby, and S. M. Lindsay. 362 pp. 1917. $3.

(2.) THE BUDGET: A TRANSLATION.
    By René Stourm. 619 pp. 1917. $4.

(3.) THE PROBLEM OF A NATIONAL BUDGET.
    By W. F. Willoughby. 220 pp. 1918. Out of print.

(4.) THE MOVEMENT FOR BUDGETARY REFORM IN THE STATES.
    By W. F. Willoughby. 254 pp. 1918. $3.

(5.) THE CANADIAN BUDGETARY SYSTEM.
    By H. C. Villard and W. W. Willoughby. 379 pp. 1918. $3.

LIST OF PUBLICATIONS

Principles of Administration

(6.) Principles of Judicial Administration.
By W. F. Willoughby. 662 pp. 1929. $5.

Service Monographs of the United States Government

1. Geological Survey. 163 pp. 1918. Out of print.
2. Reclamation Service. 177 pp. 1919. Out of print.
3. Bureau of Mines. 162 pp. 1922. $1.
4. Alaskan Engineering Commission. 124 pp. 1922. $1.
5. Tariff Commission. 71 pp. 1922. $1.
6. Federal Board for Vocational Education. 74 pp. 1922. $1.
7. Federal Trade Commission. 80 pp. 1922. $1.
8. Steamboat-Inspection Service. 130 pp. 1922. $1.
9. Weather Bureau. 87 pp. 1922. $1.
10. Public Health Service. 298 pp. 1923. $2.
11. National Park Service. 172 pp. 1922. $1.
12. Employees' Compensation Commission. 86 pp. 1922. $1.
13. General Land Office. 224 pp. 1923. $1.50.
14. Bureau of Education. 157 pp. 1923. $1.
15. Bureau of Navigation. 124 pp. 1923. $1.
16. Coast and Geodetic Survey. 107 pp. 1923. $1.
17. Federal Power Commission. 126 pp. 1923. $1.
18. Interstate Commerce Commission. 169 pp. 1923. Out of print.
19. Railroad Labor Board. 83 pp. 1923. $1.
20. Division of Conciliation. 37 pp. 1923. $1.
21. Children's Bureau. 83 pp. 1925. $1.
22. Women's Bureau. 31 pp. 1923. $1.
23. Office of the Supervising Architect. 138 pp. 1923. $1.
24. Bureau of Pensions. 111 pp. 1923. $1.
25. Bureau of Internal Revenue. 270 pp. 1923. $1.50.
26. Bureau of Public Roads. 123 pp. 1923. $1.
27. Office of the Chief of Engineers. 166 pp. 1923. $1.
28. United States Employment Service. 130 pp. 1923. $1.
29. Bureau of Foreign and Domestic Commerce. 180 pp. 1924. $1.
30. Bureau of Immigration. 247 pp. 1924. $1.50.
31. Patent Office. 127 pp. 1924. Out of print.

LIST OF PUBLICATIONS

MISCELLANEOUS SERIES

PORTO RICO AND ITS PROBLEMS.
  By Victor S. Clark and Associates. 707 pp. 1930. $5.
STEPHEN J. FIELD: CRAFTSMAN OF THE LAW.
  By Carl Brent Swisher. 473 pp. 1930. $4.
THE SPIRIT OF '76 AND OTHER ESSAYS.
  By Carl Becker, J. M. Clark, and William E. Dodd. 135 pp.
  1927. $1.50.
ESSAYS ON RESEARCH IN THE SOCIAL SCIENCES.
  By W. F. G. Swann and others. 194 pp. 1931. $2.
THE SOCIETY OF NATIONS: ITS ORGANIZATION AND CONSTI-
  TUTIONAL DEVELOPMENT.
  By Felix Morley. 678 pp. 1932. $3.50.
THE AMERICAN TRANSPORTATION PROBLEM.
  By Harold G. Moulton and Associates. 895 pp. $3.

PAMPHLETS

No. 1. RECENT GROWTH OF THE ELECTRIC LIGHT AND
  POWER INDUSTRY.
  By Charles O. Hardy. 53 pp. 1929. 50 cents.
No. 2. FIRST MORTGAGES IN URBAN REAL ESTATE FI-
  NANCE.
  By John H. Gray and George W. Terborgh. 69 pp. 1929.
  50 cents.
No. 3. THE ABSORPTION OF THE UNEMPLOYED BY AMERI-
  CAN INDUSTRY.
  By Isador Lubin. 36 pp. 1929. 50 cents.
No. 4. SOME TRENDS IN THE MARKETING OF CANNED
  FOODS.
  By Leverett S. Lyon. 57 pp. 1929. 50 cents.
No. 5. THE FECUNDITY OF NATIVE AND FOREIGN-BORN
  WOMEN IN NEW ENGLAND.
  By Joseph J. Spengler. 63 pp. 1930. 50 cents.
No. 6. SOURCES OF COAL AND TYPES OF STOKERS AND
  BURNERS USED BY ELECTRIC PUBLIC UTILITY POWER
  PLANTS.
  By William H. Young. 83 pp. 1930. 50 cents.
No. 7. FEDERAL SERVICES TO MUNICIPAL GOVERNMENTS.
  By Paul V. Betters. 100 pp. 1931. 50 cents.

LIST OF PUBLICATIONS